THE OXFORD HANDBOOK OF

U.S. JUDICIAL BEHAVIOR

THE OXFORD HANDBOOKS OF

AMERICAN POLITICS

General Editor: George C. Edwards III

The Oxford Handbooks of American Politics is a set of reference books offering authoritative and engaging critical overviews of the state of scholarship on American politics.

Each volume focuses on a particular aspect of the field. The project is under the General Editorship of George C. Edwards III, and distinguished specialists in their respective fields edit each volume. The *Handbooks* aim not just to report on the discipline, but also to shape it as scholars critically assess the current state of scholarship on a topic and propose directions in which it needs to move. The series is an indispensable reference for anyone working in American politics.

THE OXFORD HANDBOOK OF

U.S. JUDICIAL BEHAVIOR

Edited by

LEE EPSTEIN

and

STEFANIE A. LINDQUIST

OXFORD
UNIVERSITY PRESS

OXFORD
UNIVERSITY PRESS

Great Clarendon Street, Oxford, OX2 6DP,
United Kingdom

Oxford University Press is a department of the University of Oxford.
It furthers the University's objective of excellence in research, scholarship,
and education by publishing worldwide. Oxford is a registered trade mark of
Oxford University Press in the UK and in certain other countries

First Edition published in 2017

Published in the United States of America by Oxford University Press
198 Madison Avenue, New York, NY 10016, United States of America

British Library Cataloguing in Publication Data
Data available

Library of Congress Control Number: 2016961438

ISBN 978–0–19–957989–1

In Memory of the Incomparable Harold J. Spaeth

In Memory of Scholar, Mentor and Friend Don Songer

Preface

Some Thoughts on the Future of the Study of Judicial Behavior

With its origins in the works of C. Herman Pritchett in the 1940s and Walter F. Murphy, Glendon Schubert, Harold J. Spaeth, and S. Sidney Ulmer (among others) in the 1950s and 1960s, the study of judicial behavior is now an established field in political science and, increasingly in law, history, sociology, psychology, and economics. Written by leading scholars, the chapters in this volume show off the interdisciplinary nature of the factors and institutional dynamic(s) that shape the choices judges make. We hope they offer useful roadmaps to those who are new to the field, and that they provide veteran scholars with ideas for fruitful directions for future research. So too, although the chapters focus exclusively on state and federal American courts, they illuminate theories and perspectives on judicial behavior and provide insights that might assist or inspire comparative research outside the United States. In short, we hope that these chapters push along study in this area by illustrating where we have been and where our scholarly travels might take us.

We have divided the Handbook into five parts. Part 1 focuses on the critical issue of staffing the courts. In her chapter on federal judicial appointments in the lower federal courts, Nancy Scherer explores the changing dynamics and forces that have affected the nomination and confirmation process over time. Chapter 2 shifts to the U.S. Supreme Court. Christine Nemacheck explains the strategies that presidents have used to secure their preferred appointments—including how they anticipate and manage the preferences of senators who must confirm the presidents' choices. James Gibson and Michael Nelson move us from the federal bench to state judges, many of whom must be elected and re-elected to retain their jobs. Gibson and Nelson describe and explain how institutional, electoral, and behavioral factors in the context of judicial elections affect the nature of decisions those state court judges make.

Once appointed or elected, judges must make decisions about when to step down (unless, of course, they are forced to do so because of an electoral defeat, impeachment, illness, or death). In his comprehensive chapter on the factors that affect federal judges' decisions to depart or retire from the bench, Albert Yoon reviews the literature and presents data demonstrating the effect of personal and institutional factors on federal judges' decisions to leave active status. Judges are not the only court personnel who influence legal outcomes; judges' law clerks also have the potential to shape judicial decisions through the process of advising their judges. Artemus Ward's essay reviews the key decision-making stages in which clerks participate, concluding ultimately that while clerks exercise some influence, it is more modest than we might think.

Part 2 includes four chapters that address the process of appellate review, with emphasis on access to courts and oral argument. Christina Boyd's chapter on access to trial courts highlights the complex dynamics associated with case filings, settlements, and plea bargains—and the influence of parties and lawyers on these key stages in the litigation process. Losers in the trial courts may appeal to an appellate court, though such an appeal does not guarantee that the higher court will grant full review of the lower court judgment. Donald Songer and Susan Haire's chapter on access to intermediate appellate courts explores the calculations made by litigants in deciding whether to appeal, as well as the influence of jurisdictional constraints and other factors on the likelihood and scope of appellate review. Next, Ryan Owens and Joe Sieja take up the process of case selection in the U.S. Supreme Court, focusing on four possible explanations of why the justices grant or deny review. Timothy Johnson explores procedures that govern the litigation process, from trial to appellate review, with a particular focus on variations in procedures across appellate courts. He also explores how oral arguments have the potential to affect case outcomes in the U.S. Supreme Court. Finally, Pam Corley's chapter on opinion writing in the U.S. Supreme Court highlights how bargaining between the justices over opinion content—in combination with the options available to the justices in concurring, dissenting, or joining the majority—ultimately affects the nature of legal rules and holdings.

Chapters in Part 3 take up the core question: How do judges make decisions and what influences their votes? The first two chapters focus on the influence of law and precedent on the outcome of cases. For the sake of efficiency and predictability lower courts are expected to follow the legal principles and interpretations articulated by courts higher in the appellate hierarchy. Thomas Hansford's chapter explores the influence of top-down *stare decisis*, as well as the potential for bottom-up influences on judicial policy-making. David Klein also stresses the influence of law and legal doctrine on court decision-making—an area that has been particularly challenging for social scientists who seek to distinguish between the effects of legalistic versus more political factors. Professor Klein suggests a new strategy for meeting that challenge. Judges may also be strategic as they shape judicial policy in anticipation of reactions from political actors who have the potential to constrain the courts through budgetary and other oversight processes. Chad Westerland's chapter reviews the literature on the U.S. system of separated powers, with emphasis on how it may create an institutional context that causes judges to act strategically under particular circumstances. Tom Clark's chapter is related. He explores both normative and empirical theories of judicial review in U.S. courts, noting the implications for non-U.S. courts as judicial review has become prevalent in many other countries.

Part 3 also includes chapters that consider how judges' personal and policy preferences, along with their background experiences and characteristics, influence the way they resolve the cases brought before them. As Tracey George and Taylor Weaver explain, judges bring their own personal and background attributes to the bench; in fact, they are often selected on the basis of those background characteristics. George and Weaver assess theories that seek to explain judicial decisions on the basis of judges' attributes and experiences. Judges' ideological attitudes are among those key characteristics. In their chapter on partisanship and decision-making, Jeffrey Segal and Justine D'Elia-Kueper consider how partisanship—either as a proxy for ideology or as a group affiliation—influences judicial decision-making, and whether the Supreme Court's decisions reflect party polarization. Lee Epstein and Jack Knight conclude this section with a chapter exploring the economic analysis of judicial behavior that posits judges as rational actors motivated by preferences for multiple goals, including leisure time and policy outcomes. Epstein and Knight apply this approach to help explain judicial behavior in a number of different contexts.

Part 4 shifts our attention to external forces and parties that operate to shape the context in which judges reach their decisions, as well as the effect of their decisions. Although we often think about judges' decisions as having an impact on the public by shaping the rule of law, Lawrence Baum points out that judges are influenced by their audiences, including the elites with whom Supreme Court justices, in particular, interact in Washington D.C. Interest groups, so influential in legislative and executive decision-making, also play a vital role in the litigation process, as Jared Perkins and Paul Collins' chapter reminds us. They explain how interest groups, as parties or amicus curiae, can influence case outcomes. Thomas Keck's chapter explores how the courts interact with another key institutional partner: the legislature. Professor Keck demonstrates that although several theories provide leverage on understanding the relationship between U.S. courts and legislatures, an "interbranch" perspective may be the most promising for future scholarship. Similarly, the executive branch has a significant stake in judges' decisions, with its own administrative agencies and lawyers frequent participants in litigation. Jeffrey Yates and Scott Boddery explain how court decisions have shaped the power of the president; and how the president, in turn, has altered court outcomes through appointments and legal arguments made by the Solicitor General. The general public also constitutes a key constituency. Americans' reactions to court decisions can determine the likelihood of compliance and, ultimately, the strength of the rule of law. Rorie Solberg's chapter explains, first, how the media presents court decisions to the public and second, how media coverage may affect the courts' institutional legitimacy. As for public opinion more generally, Joseph Ura and Alison Higgins analyze the reciprocal relationship between court decisions and public opinion, with each influencing the other in the formation of public policy.

Part 4 concludes with Matthew Hall's discussion of judicial impact. As institutions that lack the power of the purse (appropriation) or the sword (enforcement authority), U.S. courts are formally weak institutions relative to the legislature and executive. Hall addresses the conceptual ambiguity associated with the term "impact," and identifies conditions under which the relevant actors will follow and enforce judicial policies.

This book concludes with three chapters in Part 5 that address methodological issues and approaches in the study of judicial behavior in U.S. courts. Eileen Braman does double duty, exploring both various theoretical approaches from social psychology and behavioral economics and experiments that scholars have used to assess them. Daniel Ho and Michael Morse revisit how we calculate the justices' ideal points. They argue for the inclusion of more nuanced jurisprudential data that recent advancements in the automation of data collection will allow us to collect. Finally, Sarah Benesh reflects upon the influence and impact of Harold J. Spaeth et al.'s widely used U.S. Supreme Court Database; she also offers insights on how scholars can most effectively deploy it to study the justices' decisions.

As you can probably tell by now, all our authors offer exciting opportunities for research in their particular bailiwick. Again, whether you are new to the field or a veteran court scholar, we urge you to consider their ideas; pursuing any one of them could lead to important breakthroughs.

Here we want to conclude by emphasizing a few broader avenues for future research—some on theory and others on design, data, and methods. Beginning with theory, we have two suggestions. The first centers on the way that scholars have long framed their studies of judicial behavior: as a veritable competition between "law versus politics" or among the "attitudinal model" versus the "legal model" versus "strategic accounts."

Although we too have run these races in our work (e.g., George and Epstein 1992; Hettinger, Lindquist, and Martinek 2004), we now think they are unproductive (live and learn!) and should be abandoned. We suggest supplanting the competing model/division approach with a more encompassing and realistic judicial utility function. Baum (1997, 2006), Epstein and Knight (2013), and Epstein, Landes, and Posner (2013) all gesture in this direction. In different ways, they contend that we should take seriously not only the the political scientists' emphasis on ideology and the law community's interest in legalism but also the importance of personal motivations for judicial choice—including job satisfaction, external satisfactions, leisure, income, and promotion, among others.

Actually, we're now to the point where we no longer "should" but must attend to personal motivations. That's because a growing body of empirical evidence demonstrates their importance. Take external satisfactions. Scholars have long posited that judges, no less than academics, care about maximizing their "reputation, prestige, power, influence, and celebrity" (e.g., Drahzoal 1998; Miceli and Cosgel 1994; Shapiro and Levy 1994). This desire could be related to policy goals. But the pursuit of external satisfactions also takes more direct forms such as when judges (and indeed most humans) engage in "reputation-seeking behavior" (Levy 2005). Garoupa and Ginsburg (2015), for example, find that the increasingly global implications of many court cases have paved the way for a competition of sorts among judges and their "teams" for worldwide influence on law. Advancing in this game seems to require competitor-judges to hone their reputations by hobnobbing at conferences, teaching abroad, and considering developments elsewhere (see also Breyer 2015). Likewise, in explaining Benjamin Cardozo's fame, Posner (1990: 132) shows that the judge/justice "cultivated the good opinion of academics" by regularly citing to their work in his opinions. Cardozo was also far more likely than his colleagues to cite to the opinions of other judges thus fostering their good will as well. Finally, Baum (2006) and Davis (2011) offer some evidence of Supreme Court justices adjusting their behavior to conform to the preferences of "reputation creators" and "esteem grantors" (Schauer 2000: 629).

Collapsing the various distinctions we have long made (e.g., law versus politics) and simultaneously expanding the set of relevant preferences will help us account for these and the many judicial choices that we simply ignore because they are neither about law nor politics—whether the tendency of busy trial court judges to apply access doctrines more strictly than judges with lower workloads; or the inclination of judges with some potential for promotion (the "auditioners") to impose harsher sentences on criminal defendants, all else equal. Proceeding in this way will also allow us to adapt (or weight) preferences depending on the institutional context in which the judge works. Epstein, Landes, and Posner (2013: 103), for example, offer a simpler utility function for Supreme Court justices than for all other federal judges because the justices can't be promoted to a higher court and have such a large staff (relative to their workload) that "leisure activities and nonjudicial work activities are not significantly constrained by [their] judicial duties."

Note that our suggestion of reconceptualizing judicial preferences does not require a change in a key assumption in many studies: that judges are rational actors (meaning they make decisions consistent with their goals and interests). We believe this is a reasonable assumption, and one that gets us pretty far in developing explanations of judicial behavior. But it's hardly infallible, as Epstein and Knight note in their chapter. The problem is that scores of studies tell us that that in many situations, people—judges not excepted—have difficulty suppressing or converting their intuitions, prejudices, sympathies, and the like into rational decisions (see generally Thaler 2015; Kahneman 2011; on judges, see, e.g., Guthrie et al. 2007; Wistrich et al. 2015).

Which brings us to a second suggestion: We need to take seriously these studies and assess the extent to which non-rational factors alter what we would expect to see if we assume that judges act rationally. Again, Epstein and Knight say as much in their chapter; and we take note of some limited moves in this direction (see, e.g., Owens 2010)—but not nearly enough. We strongly advocate more studies along these lines, whether observational or experimental.

These are some theoretical suggestions. On the design and empirical ends, we think it obvious that we should continue to expand the targets of inquiry. Even today U.S. Supreme Court justices and federal appellate court judges receive the lions' share of attention. We should set our sights on trial court judges (state and federal) and also, despite the Handbook's focus on the United States, on judges abroad for many reasons, including the illumination of the behavior of U.S. judges.

Following from our theoretical suggestion about rethinking judicial preferences, we also want to encourage readers to expand the set of judicial choices. Back in the 1960s when the systematic study of judicial behavior exploded (see e.g., Schubert 1965; Spaeth 1963; Ulmer 1962), scholars focused on the judges' votes or the dispositions of cases. That emphasis continues today, and with good reason: dispositions and votes matter a lot. But because other aspects of judicial behavior matter too our focus should be far broader. To provide just one example: What with many courts/governments (here and abroad) making judicial decisions available online (coupled with advances in the systematic analysis of text), opportunities now abound for the rigorous study of judicial opinions. Work has already begun (e.g., Black et al. 2016; Corley and Wedeking 2014); and more sophisticated efforts will soon follow as scholars move away from canned one-size-fits-all software and libraries to tools more tailored to our needs.

As we develop new research questions and construct new sources of data to answer them, we must be mindful of the way we design our work and conduct our analysis. Many studies of judicial behavior seek to establish causal relationships, for example, war triggers justices to favor the government in cases of rights and liberties, fear of losing a judicial election causes judges to impose harsher sentences on criminal defendants, concerns about enforcement lead judges to write vague opinions, and on and on. Attention to how to make and test causal claims have become obsessions among political scientists and economists but not so much among scholars of judicial behavior. For example, we can identify only a few studies (e.g., Epstein et al. 2005; Boyd et al. 2010; Black and Owens 2012) that make explicit use of the potential outcomes framework (which emphasizes the counterfactual nature of casual inference; see, e.g., Rubin 1974; Ho and Rubin 2011)—despite its domination in "statistical thinking about causality" over the last two decades or so (Keele 2015: 314).

We could point to other related gaps (e.g., inattentiveness to identification strategies). But rather than belabor the point (or sound like the causal inference cops now terrorizing political science), we'll conclude with the good news: We should embrace, not evade, the challenge of designing studies for credible causal inference; and we should take up, not dismiss, the equally demanding challenges our authors present. As their chapters reveal, meeting them in the past has led to enormous progress; no doubt we'll say the same about the current crop in the next edition of the Handbook.

References

Baum, L. 1997. *The Puzzle of Judicial Behavior*. Ann Arbor, MI: University of Michigan Press.

Baum, L. 2006. *Judges and their Audiences: A Perspective on Judicial Behavior*. Princeton, NJ: Princeton University Press.

Black, R. C., and Owens, R. J. 2012. *The Solicitor General and the United States Supreme Court*. Cambridge: Cambridge University Press.

Black, R. C., Owens, R. J., Wedeking, J., and Wohlfarth, P. C. 2016. *U.S. Supreme Court Opinions and their Audiences*. Cambridge: Cambridge University Press.

Corley, P. C., and Wedeking, J. 2014. "The (Dis)Advantage of Certainty: The Importance of Certainty in Language." *Law & Society Review* 48: 35–62.

Davis, R. 2011. *Justices and Journalists: The U.S. Supreme Court and the Media*. Cambridge: Cambridge University Press.

Drahozal, C. R. 1998. "Judicial Incentives and the Appeals Process." *SMU Law Review* 51: 469–503.

Epstein, L., and Knight, J. 2013. "Reconsidering Judicial Preferences." *Annual Review of Political Science* 16: 19.1–19.21.

Epstein, L., Landes, W. M., and Posner, R. A. 2013. *The Behavior of Federal Judges: A Theoretical and Empirical Study of Rational Choice*. Cambridge, MA: Harvard University Press.

Garoupa, N., and Ginsberg, T. 2015. *Judicial Reputation: A Comparative Theory*. Chicago, IL: University of Chicago Press.

George, T. E., and Epstein, L. 1992. "On the Nature of Supreme Court Decision Making." *American Political Science Review* 86: 323–37.

Guthrie, C., Rachlinkski, J. J., and Wistrich, A. J. 2007. "Blinking on the Bench: How Judges Decide Cases." *Cornell Law Review* 93: 1–43.

Hettinger, V. A., Lindquist, S. A., and Martinek, W. L. 2004. "Comparing Attitudinal and Strategic Accounts of Dissenting Behavior on the U.S. Courts of Appeals." *American Journal of Political Science* 48: 123–37.

Ho, D. E., and Rubin, D. B. 2011. "Credible Causal Inference for Empirical Legal Studies." *Annual Review of Law & Social Science* 7: 17–40.

Kahneman, D. 2011. *Thinking, Fast and Slow*. New York, NY: Farra, Straus and Giroux.

Keele, L. 2015. "The Statistics of Causal Inference: A View from Political Methodology." *Political Analysis* 23: 313–35.

Miceli, T. J., and Cosgel, M. M. 1994. "Reputation and Judicial Decision-Making." Journal of Law, Economics & Organization 23: 31–51.

Murphy, W. F., and Tanenhaus, J. 1972. *The Study of Public Law*. New York, NY: Random House.

Owens, R. J. 2010. "The Separation of Powers, Judicial Independence, and Strategic Agenda Setting." *American Journal of Political Science* 54: 412–27.

Posner, R. A. 1990. *Cardozo: A Study in Reputation*. Chicago, IL: University of Chicago Press.

Pritchett, C. H. 1948. *The Roosevelt Court*. New York, NY: Macmillan.

Pritchett, C. H. 1941. "Divisions of Opinion among Justices of the U.S. Supreme Court, 1939–1941." *American Political Science Review* 35: 890–8.

Rubin, D. B. 1974. "Estimating Causal Effects of Treatments in Randomized and Nonrandomized Studies." *Journal of Educational Psychology* 6: 688–701.

Shapiro, S. A., and Levy, R. E. 1994. "Judicial Incentives and Indeterminacy in Substantive Review of Administrative Decisions." *Duke Law Journal* 44: 1051–80.

Spaeth, H. J. 1963. "An Analysis of Judicial Attitudes in the Labor Relations Decisions of the Warren Court." *Journal of Politics* 25: 290–311.

Thaler, R. H. 2015. *Misbehaving: The Making of Behavior Economics*. New York, NY: Norton.

Ulmer, S. S. 1962. "The Political Party Variable in the Michigan Supreme Court." *Journal of Public Law* 11: 352–62.

Wistrich, A. J., Rachlinski, J. J., and Gutherie, C. 2015. "Heart versus Head: Do Judges Follow the Law or Follow their Feelings?" *Texas Law Review* 93: 855–923.

Acknowledgments

This project would not have been possible without the cooperation of our outstanding contributors, whose patience and hard work we greatly appreciate. Several other individuals also made this volume possible. First, we thank our Graduate Assistant Thomas K. Valentine, who served as the Technical and Project Editor for this volume and remained dedicated to ensuring that the authors were supported through the drafting process and that the administrative tasks associated with an edited volume were completed. We are grateful for his persistence and dedication to detail. We also thank Olivia Wells, Assistant Commissioning Editor for Oxford University Press, for her great care and helpfulness in completing this volume. Finally, we note, with sadness, that one of our contributors, Professor Donald Songer, passed away before the volume went to press. Don was a wonderful colleague and mentor and a creative scholar in the field of Law and Courts and we are so pleased that his work is included here (co-authored with Susan Haire).

Contents

PART III JUDICIAL DECISION-MAKING AND OPINION CONTENT

PART IV JUDGES AND THEIR PUBLICS

List of Figures

List of Tables

List of Abbreviations

ABA	American Bar Association
ACA	Patient Protection and Affordable Care Act
ACLU	American Civil Liberties Union
ACS	American Constitution Society
ADA	Americans for Democratic Action
ADR	Alternative Dispute Resolution
AEDPA	Antiterrorism and Effective Death Penalty Act
CFR	call for a response
CVSG	call for the views of the Solicitor General
CRT	Cognitive Reflection Test
FDR	Franklin Delano Roosevelt
FELA	Federal Employee Liability Act
FICA	Federal Insurance Contributions Act
FJC	Federal Judicial Center
FMLA	Family Medical Leave Act
FRAP	Federal Rules of Appellate Procedure
FTC	Federal Trade Commission
GSS	General Social Survey
GVR	grant, vacate, and remand
IAT	Implicit Associations Test
IRT	item response theoretic
JCS	Judicial Common Space
LDF	Legal Defense Fund
MCMC	Markov Chain Monte Carlo
MQ	Martin-Quinn
NAACP	National Association for the Advancement of Colored People
NOW	National Organization for Women
NRA	National Rifle Association

NSF	National Science Foundation
OSG	Office of the Solicitor General
PAIJD	party-adjusted judicial ideology
PLRA	Prison Litigation Reform Act
QPC	*question prioritaire de constitutionnalité*
SG	Solicitor General
SOP	separation of powers
SSA	Social Security Act
SCDB	Supreme Court Judicial Database
WL	Westlaw

List of Contributors

Lawrence Baum is Professor of Political Science at Ohio State University.

Sara C. Benesh is Associate Professor of Political Science at the University of Wisconsin, Milwaukee.

Scott Boddery is Visiting Assistant Professor of Political Science at Davidson College.

Christina L. Boyd is Associate Professor of Political Science at the University of Georgia.

Eileen Braman is Associate Professor of Political Science at Indiana University, Bloomington.

Tom Clark is the Asa Griggs Candler Professor of Political Science at Emory University.

Paul M. Collins, Jr. is Professor of Political Science at the University of Massachusetts, Amherst.

Pamela C. Corley is Associate Professor of Political Science at Southern Methodist University.

Justine D'Elia-Kueper is a Ph.D. candidate, Political Science at Stony Brook University.

Lee Epstein is the Ethan A. H. Shepley Distinguished University Professor at Washington University in St. Louis.

Tracey E. George is the Charles B. Cox III and Lucy D. Cox Family Chair in Law and Liberty at Vanderbilt University.

James L. Gibson is the Sidney W. Souers Professor of Government at Washington University in St. Louis.

Susan B. Haire is Professor of Political Science at the University of Georgia.

Matthew E. K. Hall is Associate Professor of Political Science at the University of Notre Dame.

Thomas G. Hansford is Associate Professor of Political Science at the University of California, Merced.

Alison Higgins Merrill is a Ph.D. candidate, Political Science at Texas A&M University.

Daniel E. Ho is the William Benjamin Scott and Luna M. Scott Professor of Law at Stanford Law School.

Timothy R. Johnson is the Morse Alumni Distinguished Professor of Political Science and Law at the University of Minnesota.

Thomas M. Keck is Professor of Political Science at Syracuse University, Maxwell School of Citizenship and Public Affairs.

David Klein is Professor of Political Science at Eastern Michigan University.

Jack Knight is the Frederic Cleaveland Professor of Law and Political Science at Duke University.

Stephanie A. Lindquist is Deputy Provost and Vice President for Academic Affairs, and Foundation Professor of Law and Politics at Arizona State University.

Michael Morse is a Ph.D. candidate, Government at Harvard University.

Michael J. Nelson is Assistant Professor of Political Science at the Pennsylvania State University.

Christine L. Nemacheck is Associate Professor of Government at the College of William & Mary.

Ryan J. Owens is Professor of Political Science at the University of Wisconsin, Madison.

Jared Perkins is a Ph.D. candidate, Political Science at the University of North Texas.

Nancy Scherer is Associate Professor of Political Science at Wellesley College.

Jeffrey A. Segal is SUNY Distinguished Professor at Stony Brook University.

James Sieja is Visiting Assisting Professor of Government at Skidmore College.

Rorie Solberg is Associate Professor of Political Science at Oregon State University.

Donald R. Songer is Professor of Political Science at the University of South Carolina.

Joseph Daniel Ura is Associate Professor at Texas A&M University.

Artemus Ward is Professor of Political Science at Northern Illinois University.

Taylor Grace Weaver is a 2014 J.D. Graduate of Vanderbilt University.

Chad L. Westerland is Associate Professor of Political Science at the University of Arizona.

Jeffrey L. Yates is Professor of Political Science at Binghamton University.

Albert Yoon is Professor and Chair in Law and Economics at the University of Toronto.

PART I

STAFFING THE COURT

CHAPTER 1

APPOINTING FEDERAL JUDGES

NANCY SCHERER

The Lower Court Appointment Process

Although the Constitution did not create the lower federal courts—i.e., the U.S. Courts of Appeals and the U.S. District Courts—it is clear the Framers contemplated that such courts would exist. Article I, Section 8, expressly accords Congress the power to create "inferior courts." Article III further states:

> The judicial power of the United States shall be vested in one Supreme Court, and in such inferior courts as the Congress may from time to time ordain and establish. The judges, both of the supreme and inferior courts, shall hold their offices during good behavior, and shall, at stated times, receive for their services, a compensation, which shall not be diminished during their continuance in office.

Not surprisingly, one of the first pieces of business taken up by the First Congress was the creation of the lower federal courts through the Judiciary Act of 1789.

As Article III indicates, these lower court judges were to enjoy life tenure ("shall hold office during good behavior"), just as Supreme Court justices do. However, what was less clear in the Constitution was the manner in which these judges should be chosen. The best we can glean from the Constitution is a clause in Article II that vests in the president the power to make high-level appointments, with the "advice and consent of the Senate." The 1789 Act did little to clarify this point. Instead, George Washington and the First Congress merely followed the procedures laid out in the Constitution for the appointment of Supreme Court justices. It is the interaction of the elected branches with lower court nominations/confirmations that is the subject of this chapter.

For most of our nation's history, judicial politics scholars almost exclusively focused their attention on understanding the interaction of politics and the Supreme Court of the United States, including appointments to the Court. Significantly less attention has been devoted to understanding the political significance of appointments to the lower federal courts notwithstanding the fact that each president makes *hundreds* of lower court appointments each term, and that the lower federal courts decide *thousands* of cases daily.

Because lower court appointments are regional in nature, each judgeship attached to a particular state, they differ in some important respects from the Supreme Court norms in that home state senators wield more power over the fates of the nominations attached to their states (Steigerwalt 2010). After the president nominates someone, likely in conference with the home state senators,[1] the Senate officially begins its vetting process.

There are several paths to confirmation that a nomination may take (Steigerwalt 2010). At several stages in the process the nomination could be stalled by Senators and ultimately blocked from confirmation (Scherer 2005; Bell 2002a). As detailed below, these tactics are largely driven by interest groups, who do most of the vetting of the nominees on behalf of the senators, signaling their objections to a specific nomination (Aron interview 2002).[2] Though once a process that spanned, from nomination to confirmation, just a matter of weeks, in the last few decades the lower federal court appointment process has grown increasingly divisive and lengthy. There are a host of indicators that point to an increase in the politicization of the lower court appointment process over the past few decades. For example, as set forth in Figure 1.1, the percentage of lower court

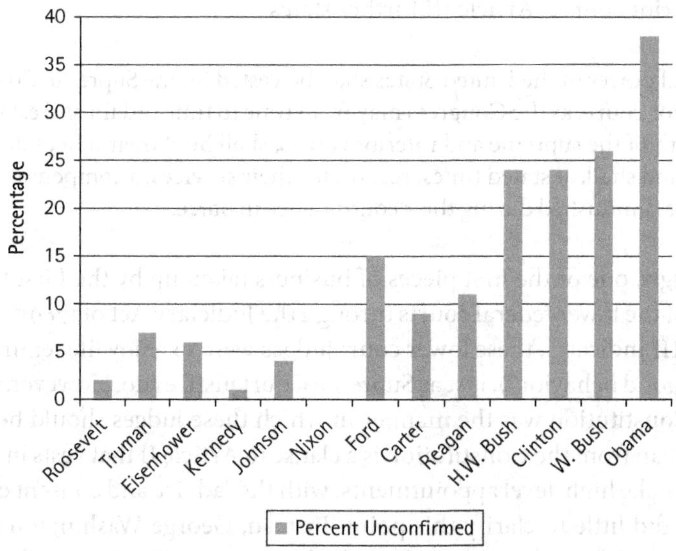

FIGURE 1.1 Percentage of lower court nominations not confirmed by the Senate 1933–2012

Source: Adapted from Scherer, *Scoring Points* (2005) and *The New York Times*, November 15, 2003, at A10. George W. Bush and Obama data obtained through Thomas.org.

Note: The figure for the Ford administration should be seen as an outlier. This is because of the unusual circumstances that put him into office. Twelve of Ford's nineteen months in office were in a presidential election year, when traditionally fewer lower court nominees are confirmed.

nominations *not* confirmed by the Senate has increased dramatically since the Franklin Delano Roosevelt administration, and reached a high water mark of 38 percent in the Obama administration.

Similarly, the average number of days from nomination to confirmation, as well as the median number of days, for lower court judgeships has steadily increased since the Reagan administration. As set forth in Figure 1.2A, the median number of days for an appellate nominee to be confirmed during the Reagan administration was forty-five days; by the G. W. Bush and Obama administrations, that number rose to 216 and 229, respectively. The average number of days for confirmation was highest during the G. W. Bush administration at 350 days.

As seen in Figure 1.2B, the average and median number of days for U.S. District Court judges to be confirmed mimics the pattern seen with courts of appeals nominations. During the Reagan administration it took the median district court nomination merely forty-one days to be confirmed, but 215 days during the Obama administration.

In conjunction with this increased politicization of the lower court appointment process, political scientists have turned their attention to the politics of judicial appointments to the lower courts. Though scholarship on the Supreme Court dominates the field of public law, in the last twenty years, a substantial literature has developed about the presidential appointment process, including the lower federal court appointment process. Books on the issue include Goldman's (1997) historical study of judicial selection from FDR through Reagan; Bell's (2002a) historical analysis of the Senate confirmation process, including lower court judges; Scherer's (2005) book on why there is

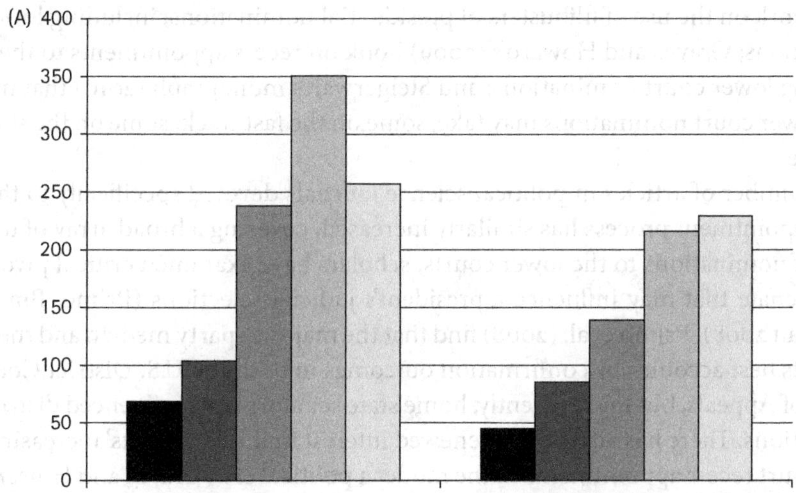

FIGURE 1.2A Average and median number of days from nomination to confirmation on the federal courts of appeals, 1981–January 13, 2013

Source: Brookings Institution, Weaver (2012).

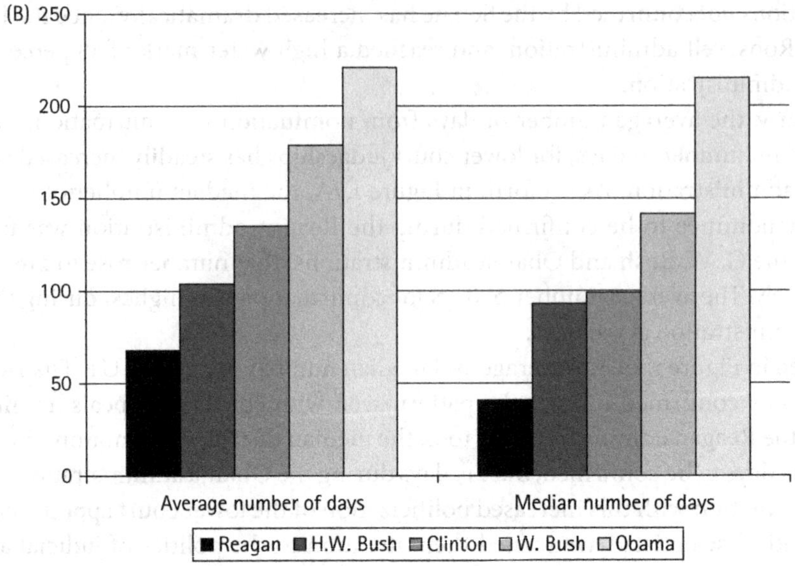

FIGURE 1.2B Average and median number of days from nomination to confirmation on the U.S. district courts, 1981–January 13, 2013

Source: Weaver (2012).

increased politicization of the lower court appointment process; Epstein and Segal's (2006) book focusing on the role of merit and ideology on judicial confirmations, including the lower federal courts; Wawro and Schickler's (2007) historical and theoretical work on the use of filibusters of presidential nominations, including lower court nominations; Graves and Howard's (2009) book on recess appointments to the courts, including lower court nominations; and Steigerwalt's monograph (2010) that maps the paths lower court nominations may take, some on the fast track, some on the slow track to failure.

The number of articles in political science journals devoted specifically to the lower court appointment process has similarly increased, covering a broad array of topics. In terms of nominations to the lower courts, scholars have examined critical pivot points in the Senate that may influence a president's judicial selections (Primo, Binder, and Maltzman 2008). Primo et al. (2008) find that the majority party median and the filibuster pivots best account for confirmation outcomes in both the U.S. District Courts and Courts of Appeals, but more recently, home state senators have influenced district court nominations. There has also been a renewed interest in the presidents' increasing use of lower court recess appointments in the modern political era (Graves and Howard 2010) Graves and Howard studied all recess appointments made from the beginning of the Republic to 2004; they concluded that presidents in the modern political era use recess appointment sparingly and strategically. Much attention has also been paid to the lower court confirmation process in the Senate, since the percentage of nominations unconfirmed, and the span of a confirmation proceeding, has grown substantially.

Because it is rare for senators to win a floor fight to defeat a nominee at roll call,[3] they instead engage in activities intended to delay confirmation of a controversial nomination, and hopefully make the nominee withdraw. Troubled lower court nominations are more often "killed" at the pre-floor stage of the confirmation process through a variety of procedural tactics including secret holds, filibusters, and delay of votes (Steigerwalt 2010). Scholars thus argue that the focus of research on lower federal court confirmations should be on the *process* rather than the *votes*.[4] This corpus of research has sought to identify the forces that impact confirmation *timing*; it presumes that the longer it takes to confirm a lower court nomination, the more "troubled" the nomination. Shipan and Shannon (2003: 656) make the most compelling case as to why delaying a nomination is an important end in and of itself, apart from the ultimate confirmation outcome. They argue that, even if a nomination is ultimately confirmed, delay by the Senate may weaken a president's standing with his constituents and thus hinder the president's ability to enact his policy agenda regarding other matters. Moreover, the longer a nomination is delayed, the more likely the nominee will never be confirmed.

Accordingly, scholars started to turn their attention to the factors driving delay in the lower court confirmation process (Bell 2002; Binder and Maltzman 2002; Martinek, Kemper, and Van Winkle 2002). Although all of these duration studies used similar methodological techniques, hazard-based duration models, their models focused on different possible causes for delay. Bell found that having a "patron" on the Judiciary Committee shortened a nominee's confirmation time. Binder and Maltzman's model demonstrated that the nomination's ideological distance from the median senator increases the number of days a nomination will languish before confirmation, if such confirmation happens at all. Martinek et al. established that, under divided government, a nomination will wait longer to be confirmed. One notable variable missing from all of these studies is interest group opposition. Scherer, Bartels, and Steigerwalt (2008) did a similar examination of confirmation durations, but accounted for the impact of opposition from activists.[5] Holmes (2007) also looked at outside influences on judicial confirmations, and found that the more outside written submissions presented to the Senate Judiciary Committee for consideration, the more likely the nomination will fail; this is true regardless if the submissions are favorable or unfavorable.

Since the filibuster became a common procedural tactic for senators to indefinitely delay confirmation of lower court judges, particularly during the Clinton, G. W. Bush, and Obama presidencies (Steigerwalt 2010), scholars began consider the impact of this Senate procedural tactic on lower court confirmations, and the possibility of doing away with filibustering judicial nominations all together, known as the "nuclear" option (Klotz 2004; McGuiness and Rappaport 2005).[6]

In sum, we have a litany of books and articles about different aspects of the lower court appointment process in the modern political era, from nomination to confirmation to appointment. What all of the articles have in common is a focus on the effects of increased politicization of the lower court appointment process. Yet, as an initial matter, the fundamental question that must be addressed here is: *why* did the lower court appointment process become so politically contentious in the first place, particularly given the low visibility of these offices?[7] The answer lies in the conjunction of historical changes to two U.S. political institutions: the party system and the U.S. courts (Songer 1991).

Transformation of the Old Mass Party System

Prior to 1968, under the old mass party system, parties were loosely connected systems of local party organizations, established to solve the collective action problem that politicians faced in terms of mobilizing voters (Aldrich 1995; Mayhew 1974). There was one critical aspect of the old party system that shaped judicial appointment politics. Because the activists who ran the local party organizations were predominantly interested in obtaining material incentives from politicians—i.e., jobs and contracts in return for helping the candidate get elected—the activists working within the party system were seen as largely non-ideological in nature (Conway and Feigert 1968). Party activists "engage in a conflict without principles, a struggle between the ins and outs which never become fanatical and creates no deep cleavage in the country" (Duverger 1964: 418). Characterized by a pragmatism that made them willing to compromise and strike deals in order to deliver the jobs and contracts they desired for their supporters, these old-line party activists came to be known as "professionals"(Wilson 1962). Second, as little more than a loosely connected group of local organizations, regional conflicts abounded between politicians in Washington, each representing different factions (Aldrich 1995). It was the job of the national organization to find ways to hold together these various factions (Aldrich 1995).

In the 1960s, the old mass party system crumbled (Aldrich 1995). In place of the professionals came ideologically driven political activists known as "amateurs" (Wilson 1962) or "purists" (Wildavsky 1965); these activists were characterized by their unwillingness to compromise on ideological causes (Wildavsky 1965).[8] "Purists consider the stock-in-trade of the politician—compromise and bargaining, conciliating the opposition, bending a little to capture support—to be hypocritical; they prefer a style that relies on the announcement of principles and on moral crusades" (Wildavsky 1965). During the 1960s, purists came to fill the ranks of both the Democratic (liberal purists) and Republican (conservative purists) Parties (Polsby and Wildavsky 1971). Although activists in the parties had become more unified, mass voters were becoming less enchanted with the two major parties. In short, fewer Americans began identifying themselves as a Democrat or a Republican (Rosenstone and Hansen 1996). This meant that the two major political parties were less capable of mobilizing voters on behalf of political candidates—the very reason they were originally conceived in the early nineteenth century (Aldrich 1995). Picking up much of the slack in national elections were interest groups (Frymer and Yoon 2002; Gibson, Frendreis, and Vertz 1987; Grossman and

Dominguez 2009). Determined to exercise influence over the outcomes of important federal elections, interest groups began spending millions of dollars on campaign advertising aimed at mobilizing voters to support their favored candidates (Frymer and Yoon 2002). Interest groups also began to contribute volunteers and money to their preferred candidates (Gibson, Frendreis, and Vertz, 1987).

By the 1970s, the old mass party system had transformed into the modern party system. According to John Zaller, political parties cater to interest groups because "the public isn't watching, and the interest groups are watching" (quoted in Griffiths 2012). What does party politics have to do with federal court appointments? Under both the old and modern party systems, party activists closely monitored the selection of lower court judges. But, while local party activists under the old party system viewed lower court judgeships as jobs to be distributed to friends and campaign contributors, in the modern political era, party and issue activists view judicial appointments as having crucial policy consequences. Why did lower federal court judgeships begin to figure into the policy goals of the new breed of political activists? The reason turns on the second historic event in American politics to occur during the 1950s–60s period: the transformation of the federal judiciary.

Transformation of the Federal Judiciary

At the same time that the political parties were undergoing seismic changes, federal courts were undergoing major changes as well; they began, once again to engage in social policy-making, only this time it was liberal social policy.[9] As Epp (1998) explains, rights-oriented litigation by interest groups did not begin in the 1960s, it began earlier in the twentieth century; however, there is little doubt that liberal interest groups *intensified* their litigation strategy in the 1960s–70s. Under the leadership of Chief Justice Earl Warren, however, liberal interest groups like the NAACP and the ACLU sensed that the Court was now sympathetic to the claims of liberal activists for broader constitutional protections for individuals, particularly minorities denied civil rights and liberties in Southern states (Epp 1998). These groups correctly gauged the Court's trajectory, as justices during the Warren Court era (Silverstein 1994) significantly expanded civil rights and civil liberties in accordance with their personal social policy preferences (Segal and Spaeth 1993).[10]

The Warren Court also made it much easier for aggrieved parties to bring lawsuits in federal court (Silverstein 1994). By the end of the 1960s, Congress amended the Federal Rules of Civil Procedure, making it easier to bring class action suits.[11] This included rules on standing so as to afford the federal courts the opportunity to hear the substantive claims of aggrieved groups.

This transformation prompted noted scholar Alexander Bickel to observe that "all too many federal judges have been induced to view themselves as holding roving commissions as problem solvers, and as charged with a duty to act when majoritarian institutions do not (Bickel 1970, at 134)." To this day, conservative activists see this litigation strategy as a means to bypass conservative state legislatures (Pilon interview 2002).

Whether a favorable court order standing alone—without some extra-judicial assistance in implementation—can ever deliver the policy results sought by the claimants has been the subject of much scholarly debate (see, e.g., Horowitz 1977; Rosenberg 1991; Scheingold 1974). Nevertheless, what is important is that, during this period, liberal activists came to share a deep-rooted belief in the efficacy of the federal courts to achieve social change. And they continue to cling to this belief even today. As Nan Aron, president of the Alliance for Justice, a liberal interest group that monitors the U.S. judicial appointments, reaffirms:

> The way our democracy works is that poor people, people of color, disenfranchised people, [and] women have very little recourse to the Executive Branch. They don't make contributions to Democratic or Republican presidential campaigns. They tend not to know people in power. And, therefore, [they] have very little access to the executives ... of the world. They have almost no access to members of Congress because they clearly don't contribute to congressional or senate races. The only recourse they have is to the judiciary. It's the only branch of government that will hear ... cases brought by people without power ... This is the only branch whereby a disenfranchised person or group has any ability to have redress for grievances.
>
> (Aron interview 2002)

In sum, the rights revolution of the 1950s–70s encompassed three broad areas of constitutional rights: race, crime, and women's rights. After *Roe v. Wade*,[12] counter-activists began to use the courts to undermine the rights accorded women in *Roe* (Epstein 1985). Thus, conservatives, too, turned to the Court to create social policy. At first, they were met with a liberal majority, but eventually the Court had a majority of justices willing to make conservative social policy.[13] Critically, the Court makes social policy in the very same issues with which the Democratic and Republican Parties' new issue-oriented activists, who had emerged in the 1960s, were concerned.

Activists Begin to Want the "Right" Kind of Judges Appointed

Given these institutional changes to the U.S. political system, critical new demands for certain kinds of judicial appointments were made. Under the earlier regime, party activists demanded only that the president and senators seat campaign contributors and friends on the lower federal courts (i.e., patronage), producing nominations that lacked much party polarization; newly emerging policy-oriented activists had different priorities. Though they understand why a politician may want to reward a big contributor to his or her previous election campaign, the new breed of activists, on both the left and right, do not believe patronage concerns should detract from the main goal of appointing judges who can be depended on to further the president's policy agenda. What that means is that only patrons who are known to share the activists' commitment to certain policy outcomes are now acceptable to serve on the federal courts (Aron 2002). What we now see are party-polarized nominations who in turn engage in party-polarized voting on the bench.

In her 2005 book, *Scoring Points*, Scherer looks at the judicial decision-making behavior of judges from three distinct time periods in order to establish whether party transformation is, as her theory posits, at the heart of modern-day appointment politics. The hypothesis is that, in earlier periods in history there will be less ideological voting (because judgeships were based on patronage, not ideology) than there is today, when interest groups demand ideologically pure appointments. The three periods are The Old Party System (judges appointed 1921–44), the Party System in Transition (judges appointed 1945–67) and the Modern Party System (1968–2000). She theorized that, in the two early periods, there would be no significant difference between Republican- and Democratic-appointed judges (even though Democrats and Republicans in Washington sharply disagreed on these issues) and in the modern era, there would be a significant difference in the voting patterns of Democratic and Republican-appointed judges, mimicking the party positions of the elected branches.

Set forth in Table 1.1 are the differences between Democratic and Republican-appointed judges in each of the three periods; the numbers are predictions of the likelihood of a liberal vote. And, in order to rule out the fact that Southern Democrats shifted

Table 1.1 Comparison of judicial voting by party of appointing president: Greater likelihood of Republican-appointed judge casting a conservative vote compared to Democratic-appointed judge, U.S. Courts of Appeals

	Old Party system	Party in transition		Modern party system	
	Labor cases	Race discrimination cases		Race discrimination cases	Abortion cases
	Judicial appointees from:	Judicial appointees from:		Judicial appointees from:	Judicial appointees from:
	1920–44	1953–63	1964–74	1977–2000	1977–2000
All circuits	.07	–.05	.17**	.27**	.44**
Non-Southern circuits	.05	–.04	.16*	.26**	.45**
Southern circuits	.12	–.06	.18*	.27**	.42**

Note: *** p ≤ .001; ** p ≤ .01; * p ≤ .10 (all two-tailed test).

to the Republican Party beginning in the 1960s, which is an alternative hypothesis as to why Democrats became more liberal during this period of transition—in other words, as Southerners left the Party, Democrats became more liberal—and could also explain why there is more party-polarized voting in the modern political era, Table 1.1 shows that the results remain the same with and without Southern Democrats in the Democratic and Republican Parties.[14]

Activists, both on the left and right, discourage patronage nominations. As one liberal activist, Nan Aron, stated, "If the [Clinton] administration nominates candidates who lack a sensitivity and commitment to constitutional principles, we will work hard to make our voice heard" (Aron, quoted in Klaidman 1993). A conservative activist would go further than Aron; he would eliminate patronage completely from the judicial selection process (Jipping 2002). His idea to ensure ideological purists are nominated is to bar home state senators and local party leaders from suggesting names to the president for vacancies on the courts. Jipping believes it detracts from the main focus, the judicial philosophy of the nominee (Jipping interview 2002).

As the activists emphasize, what they want is for the president to nominate (or not nominate), and for the Senate to confirm (or not confirm), federal court judges who will be sympathetic to their political causes. Indeed, these activists are so convinced that their desired policy outcomes are dependent on litigation outcomes that, today, seating judges who are sympathetic to their causes, in effect, has become a policy goal unto itself—almost as important as achieving the underlying substantive policy goals at issue. For example, liberal activists spend almost as much time fighting the appointment of pro-life judges as they do fighting pro-life legislation. And, though their desire to secure sympathetic judges originally focused solely on Supreme Court nominations (Silverstein 1994), for a number of reasons, activists began to shift their focus to lower federal court appointments as well.

With regard to the lower courts, most of their attention focuses on the appellate courts; however, activists make clear they monitor judges at all levels of the federal judiciary (e.g., Aron, Gandy, Cavendish, and Jipping interviews 2002). Accordingly, activists monitor all of a president's judicial nominations at all levels of the federal judiciary. Due to the sheer volume of district court appointees every year and the limited resources activists have to monitor these nominations, it makes sense that district court nominations get less attention than courts of appeals nominations.

Activists Shift their Attention from the Supreme Court to the Lower Federal Courts

Why do activists focus so much attention on lower federal court appointments, when the general public has little interest in their decisions? First, activists realize that there are so few opportunities to affect Supreme Court appointments in the modern political era. Justices are simply serving longer terms than was historically true, affording presidents fewer opportunities to make appointments to the High Court. In contrast, a president names hundreds of judges to the lower federal courts in each four-year term.

Second, with the Rehnquist and Roberts Courts hearing about half the number of cases that the Burger Court did, activists began to recognize that, as a practical matter, the lower federal courts today serve as the final arbiter in over 99 percent of all federal court litigation; in other words, important policy is being made every day in the lower federal courts (Raddazzo and Waterman 2014). According to Elizabeth Cavendish, former Legal Director of NARAL Pro-Choice America (NARAL), today, it is the *lower* federal courts where important legal issues in the pro-choice/pro-life debate are being decided: "There's a real recognition that lower court judges hold vast power over women's reproductive lives and right now the composition of the Supreme Court is stable, and so there isn't an immediate threat to overturn *Roe*" (Cavendish 2002).

Ralph Neas, the director of People for the American Way, believes that certain circuits, specifically the Fourth and the Fifth Circuits, generally considered the more conservative circuits, require special attention because the judges there are setting bad precedents for millions who live within those jurisdictions (Neas interview 2002).

Third, in an apparent attempt to reduce uncertainty about the way Supreme Court nominees are likely to vote once they secure their seats, presidents have increasingly turned to the courts of appeals in searching for Supreme Court candidates.[15] Indeed, eight of the nine current justices were elevated from the federal appellate courts. As Kim Gandy, former president of the National Organization for Women (NOW) aptly notes, the courts of appeals are now the "farm team" for the Supreme Court (Gandy interview 2002). And so, for these litigation- and conservative-oriented liberal interest groups, having the "right" kind of judges seated on the appellate courts ensures the "right" kind of judges on the Supreme Court.

Fourth, Ronald Reagan began a trend of nominating relatively young men and women to seats on the lower federal courts. While less than 3 percent of Eisenhower, Kennedy, Johnson, and Carter appellate judges appointed were under age forty, 10 percent of Reagan's court of appeals appointments were in their thirties (Schwartz 1988: 60). A judicial appointment was once "meant to cap your career" (Gandy interview 2002). Appointing people so young to the federal bench also raises the stakes of these nominations when senators know that many of these nominees will serve for another thirty-plus years.

The Emergence of Elite Mobilization Strategies

In the face of these new policy demands from key political activists, politicians adapted their nomination/confirmation strategies, from patronage to policy, so as to conform to the changing demands of political activists. Herein lies the core problem with today's lower court appointment process: the system turns on satisfying competing policy demands that center on the most divisive issues of the day such as race, crime, abortion, and homosexual rights. With the Senate so highly polarized today, compromise on these hot-button issues is difficult in the legislature. The courts seem more attractive to settle these divisive policy areas. To satisfy the demands of one party's activists, by definition, means that the other party's activists cannot be satisfied. Indeed, they become extremely *dissatisfied* with appointment outcomes that only lead to more contentiousness in the process. And, yet, politicians continue to accede to these demands even though lower federal court cases are not salient issues with their constituents. Why not simply ignore these demands and continue with the old patronage system? The simple answer: re-election concerns.

Judicial scholars have previously suggested that there is an electoral component to the Supreme Court selection process. For example, Perry (1991) argues that Supreme Court nominations are often made to generate support among the mass electorate—e.g., Reagan's appointment of Sandra Day O'Connor to shore up support among women voters. However, this conventional explanation is problematic even for the Supreme Court, and certainly when we talk about lower court nominations. Consider public opinion polls, which demonstrate that the mass electorate knows virtually nothing about the Supreme Court, let alone the lower federal courts. For example, an oft-cited poll conducted by *The Washington Post* found that more people could identify Judge Wapner, former host of the television program *The People's Court*, than could identify Chief Justice of the United States, William H. Rehnquist (Caldeira 1991). Why, then, would elected officials invest so much political capital in the lower court appointment process if their constituents are not paying attention?[16]

There is, in fact, an electoral strategy at play in the lower federal court appointment process, but one much different from that suggested by Perry. Rather than using lower federal court judgeships to curry favor with the mass electorate, Scherer (2005) argued that these nominations are used by the Democratic and Republican Parties to curry favor with only an elite constituency within each party; specifically, conservative activists affiliated with the Republican Party and liberal activists affiliated with the Democratic Party. This includes both party activists and interest group activists (sometimes called "issue activists"). As stated above, *these* constituents actually care about the composition of the federal bench, and *these* constituents are the key to politicians' re-election prospects.

Activists are central to re-election efforts because they are responsible for mobilizing the party's base to get out and vote on election day (Katz and Eldersveld 1961; Sorauf 1967; Sorauf and Beck 1988). "Under the old party system, political activists would be willing to mobilize voters provided the candidate delivered the promised jobs and contracts—i.e., a patronage-based system" (Aldrich 1995). Today, politicians look to those who are "well-positioned in social networks, people who are influential in politics, and people who are *likely* to participate" (Rosenstone and Hansen 1993: 6–7): In sum, for winning candidates to the Senate or Presidency, lower federal court judgeships were once used as plum jobs that they could bestow upon the activists who helped them get elected (e.g., Baum 1990; Carp and Stidham 1998; Chase 1972; Evans 1948; Goldman 1997, 1967). Dating back as far back as the Andrew Jackson presidency (Bell 2002b), lower court judgeships were nothing more than "rewards for political service" (Howard 1981). Under the modern party system, however, patronage appointments no longer satisfy political activists; rather, they want all appointments used to further policy goals. If a patronage appointment is to be made, the person must be in line with the Party's base. It has thus become incumbent upon politicians to develop new nomination and confirmation strategies to satisfy the activists' policy-oriented demands—leading to a judicial appointment process based much more on ideological considerations and much less on patronage considerations.

The Methods Used to Satisfy Activists' Demands

Though their efforts to shape the federal judiciary go largely unnoticed by the American public, politicians are nevertheless still engaging in electoral politics through a variety of judicial nomination/confirmation strategies, all designed to satisfy activists' policy demands. Collectively, these new nomination/confirmation strategies are known as "elite mobilization" strategies (Scherer 2005) because they are specifically intended to satisfy key elites affiliated with the two major political parties. Briefly, the new policy-oriented appointment strategies are: (1) presidents choosing judges pursuant to ideological litmus tests; (2) presidents choosing judges pursuant to diversity criteria; and (3) senators engaging in "obstructionist" confirmation tactics against nominees found ideologically objectionable. As previously stated, all of these strategies are ultimately designed to satisfy the policy demands of party elites and activists so that they will aid in mobilizing the mass electorate come election day.[17]

What do all of these strategies have in common? They all involve strategic actions of politicians in choosing (in the case of the president) or confirming (in the cases of sitting senators) on federal court judgeships. By definition, elite mobilization requires politicians to take a *public* stand regarding lower federal court appointments.[18] Politicians let their targeted elite constituents know exactly where they stand on a particular judicial nominee or on the direction of the federal courts as a whole. Politicians thereby send important cues to these elite constituents, telling them that they are directly responding to their demands regarding the composition of the lower federal courts. In this sense, elite mobilization efforts resemble "position taking"—one of the three classic forms of congressional activity identified by Mayhew in his seminal book *Congress: The Electoral Connection* (1974), though the audience to whom the position statements are directed is somewhat different than that envisioned by Mayhew. In the case of judgeships, politicians speak to an elite audience, rather than a mass audience.

To the extent such elite mobilization cues are successful, the political activists at whom the tactics are aimed can then be counted on to mobilize the mass electorate on the candidate's behalf come the next election (in the case of grass-roots activists), or to donate money to a candidate (in the case of grass-top elites). To the extent such elite mobilization cues are not forthcoming, or convey the wrong message, activists and elites may then choose to mobilize the mass electorate *against* a particular candidate, or alternatively, but an equally effective tactic, *not* mobilize potential voters at all (Gandy interview 2002).

Empirical Testing of the Elite Mobilization Theory

Elite Mobilization Strategy One: Ideological Litmus Tests

Starting with the first strategy, ideological litmus tests, and the first hypothesis is that presidents in the modern political era are more likely to appoint lower court judges who share their party's ideological positions than judges who do not. The data consists of all non-consensual courts of appeals cases 1994–2001 in three legal, but partisan policy issues. The three types of cases chosen to analyze were: search and seizure decisions, pitting tough law-and-order Republicans against more civil-liberties-oriented Democrats; [19] race discrimination cases, pitting civil-rights proponents from the Democratic Party against color-blind-society advocates in the Republican Party;[20] and federalism cases, pitting states'-rights-oriented Republicans against federal-government-oriented Democrats.[21] If partisan voting patterns are detected in these three types of cases, then there is support for the first elite mobilization strategy.[22]

Table 1.2A displays the probabilities that judges appointed by modern Republican presidents vote more conservatively than judges appointed by Democrats, consistent with the theory. Table 1.2B shows the probabilities of a conservative vote by Republican versus Democratic judges, and the appointees of Nixon, Reagan, G. H. W. Bush, and G. W. Bush are, indeed significantly more conservative than appointees of Carter and Clinton. This pattern repeats itself with the race discrimination cases (Tables 1.3A–1.3B) and the states' rights cases (Tables 1.4A–1.4B). The judges voting patterns mirror that of the presidents who appointed them. Just as Clinton shifted the Democratic Party to the center on the crime issue, his appointees voted in a more conservative direction than the Carter appointees. And, just as Nixon was more towards the center of the ideological spectrum than either Reagan, G. H. W. Bush or G. W. Bush, so too did Nixon's judges exhibit less conservative voting than the other Republican presidents' judges.

Elite Mobilization Strategy Two: Diversify the Federal Bench

The hypothesis behind the second elite mobilization strategy, diversifying the bench, is that Democratic presidents will appoint more people of color and women to the federal

Table 1.2A Logit cofficients for the probability of a vote by Court of Appeals judge against a criminal defendant, non-consensual search and seizure cases, January 1, 1994 to December 31, 2001

	B	Robust SE	Δ *Probability*
Constant	−.45*	.20	NA
Appointing president			
Clinton	Baseline	NA	.00
G. H. W. Bush	.74***	.18	.18
Reagan	.79***	.15	.19
Carter	.64***	.18	−.13
Nixon	.73**	.28	.18
(Vote against criminal defendant coded 1; vote for criminal defendant coded 0.)			

Notes: *** p ≤ .001; ** p ≤ .01; * p ≤ .10 (all two-tailed test).

Change in probability is measured at the distance from a probability of 0.5, assuming the presence of that variable.

N = 1,469

Likelihood ratio test (14df) = 162.59***

% correctly predicted = 63.785

% observed in null model = 50.30

Proportional reduction in error = 27.12

Throughout this chapter, non-consensual cases shall be defined as all appellate cases with a dissent plus all unanimous appellate cases that reverse a district court decision.

This represents the change in likelihood of a vote against a criminal defendant from a starting place of .50 probability.

courts than Republican presidents, and that the number of diversity appointments will be significant rather than mere tokenism. The underlying theory is based on the fact that most minority- and women's-based interest groups lean Democratic; they are part of the Democratic Party's base. As such these groups are critical to mobilizing their constituencies on election day. Thus, currying favor with minority and female activists by significantly increasing diversity on the bench has more benefits for Democrats than it does Republicans.

Looking at Figures 1.3A and 1.3B, the evidence is consistent with this hypothesis. Democratic presidents are appointing significant numbers of minority and female judges, much more than Republican presidents. Beginning with Carter, with each Democratic administration we see a focus on raising the levels of diversity on the federal bench across racial, ethnic, and gender lines.

It should be noted that both Presidents G. H. W. Bush and G. W. Bush appointed fair percentages of women to the bench. And, President G. W. Bush appointed more

Table 1.2B Comparison of voting across presidential cohorts: Probability that a judge will vote to uphold a search or seizure, non-consensual search and seizure cases, U.S. Courts of Appeals, January 1, 1994–December 31, 2001

	Clinton judge	G. H. W. Bush judge	Reagan judge	Carter judge	Nixon judge
Clinton judge compared to:		–.18**	–.19**	+.13*	–.18*
G. H. W. Bush judge compared with:	+.18***		–.01	–.32**	.00
Reagan judge compared with:	+.19	+.01		+.33***	.01
Carter judge compared with:	–.13**	–.32***	–.33***		–.32***
Nixon judge compared with:	+.18***	.00	–.01	+.32***	–

Notes: *** p ≤ .001; ** p ≤ .01; * p ≤ .10 (all two-tailed test).

Table 1.3A Logit cofficients for the probability of a vote by Court of Appeals judge against a civil rights plaintiff, non-consensual cases, January 1, 1994–December 31, 2001

	B	Robust SE	Δ *Probability*
Constant	–1.29***	.19	NA
Appointing president			
Clinton	Baseline	NA	.00
G. H. W. Bush	1.29***	.21	.28
Reagan	1.26	.19	.28
Carter	.16	.22	.04
Nixon	.92**	.32	.21

(Vote against criminal defendant coded 1; vote for criminal defendant coded 0.)

Notes: *** p ≤ .001; ** p ≤ .01; * p ≤ .10 (all two-tailed test).

N = 1,408

Likelihood ratio test (13 df) = 193.46***

% correctly predicted = 67.75

% observed in null model = 65.28

Proportional reduction in error = 7.11

This represents the change in likelihood of a vote against a criminal defendant from a starting place of .50 probability.

Table 1.3B Comparison of voting across presidential cohorts, probability that a judge will vote for a minority in a race discrimination case, non-consensual race discrimination cases, U.S. Courts of Appeals, January 1, 1994–December 31, 2001

	Clinton judge	G. H. W. Bush judge	Reagan judge	Carter judge	Nixon judge
Clinton judge compared with:	–	–.28***	–.28***	–.04	–.21**
G. H. W. Bush judge compared with:			+.01	+.25***	+.10
Reagan judge compared with:				+.25***	+.08*
Carter judge compared with:					–.18*
Nixon judge compared with:					

Notes: *** p ≤ .001; ** p ≤ .01; * p ≤ .10 (all two-tailed test).

Table 1.4A Logit cofficients for the probability of a vote by Court of Appeals judge against the federal government, non-consensual states' rights cases, January 1, 1994–December 31, 2001

	B	Robust SE	Δ *Probability*
Constant	–.56*	.29	NA
Appointing president			
Clinton	Baseline	NA	.00
G. H. W. Bush	1.21***	.34	.27
Reagan	.90**	.31	.21
Carter	–.29	.37	–.07
Nixon	.67	.65	.16
(Vote against federal government coded 1; vote for federal government coded 0.)			

Notes: *** p ≤ .001; ** p ≤ .01; * p ≤ .10 (all two-tailed test).

N = 337

Likelihood ratio test (9 df) = 31.26***

% correctly predicted = 64.99

% observed in null model = 50.10

Proportional reduction in error = 29.77

This represents the change in likelihood of a vote against a criminal defendant from a starting place of .50 probability.

Table 1.4B Comparison of voting across presidential cohorts: Probability that a judge will vote against the federal government, non-consensual state's rights cases, U.S. Courts of Appeals, January 1, 1994–December 31, 2001

	Clinton judge	G. H. W. Bush judge	Reagan judge	Carter judge	Nixon judge
Clinton judge compared with:		.27**	.21**	+.07	−.16
G. H. W. Bush judge compared with:			+.06	+.32**	+.13
Reagan judge compared with:				+.26**	+.06
Carter judge compared with:					−.18*
Nixon judge compared with					

Notes: *** p <.001; ** p < .01; * p < .10 (all two-tailed test).

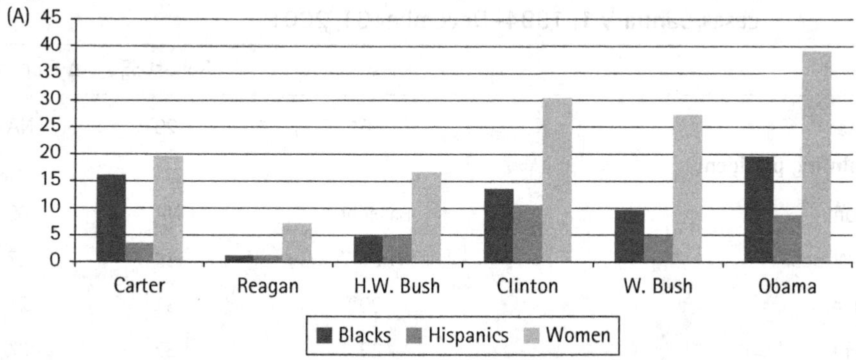

FIGURE 1.3A Minorities and women on the courts of appeals, percentage of total judges appointed by president, January 1977–May 2014

Source: Author.

Hispanics than his predecessor, President Clinton, but not as many as his successor, President Obama, would. Obama would be the first president to appoint more minorities and women to the federal bench than white men. It may be that women and Hispanics fare better under Republican administrations than African Americans do is because most African Americans affiliate with the Democratic Party, and Republicans have yet to make inroads with this voting bloc. Moreover, this being the case, there is presumably a smaller pool of black conservative attorneys than female

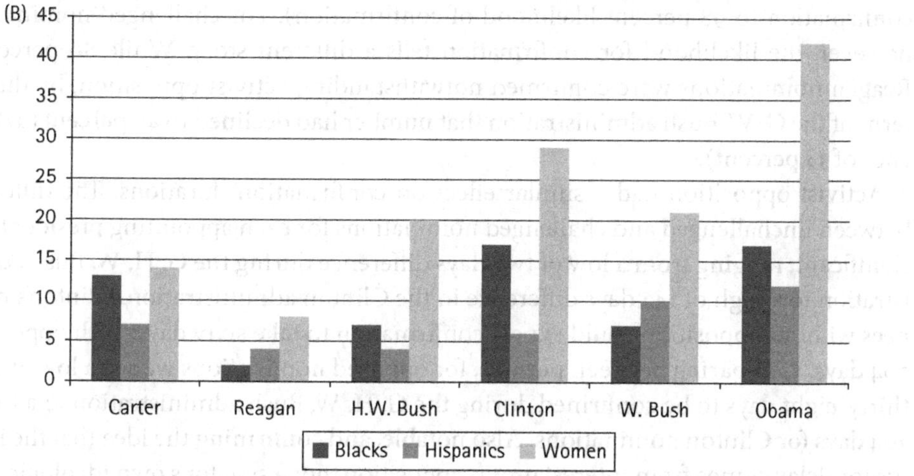

FIGURE 1.3B Minority and female appointees to the U.S. district courts, January 1977–May 2014

Source: Author.

or Hispanic attorneys, from which potential nominations for the federal bench are chosen.

Elite Mobilization Strategy Three: Delay, Delay, Delay

As discussed above, the focus of the lower court appointment process has been on the extraordinary delay nominations suffer at the hands of interest groups (Scherer, Bartels, and Steigerwalt 2008). These scholars examined confirmation delay, but unlike previous studies, accounted for the impact of opposition from activists and interest groups. Their hypotheses was that interest group opposition to a nomination would significantly affect both the likelihood of confirmation and the duration of confirmation notwithstanding the nominee's ideological distance from the Senate. Looking at post-1985 data, about the time interest groups started formally objecting to lower court nominations (Scherer 2005), they found that activist opposition does, in fact, significantly drive both the likelihood of confirmation and the number of days from nomination to confirmation. Also, interest group opposition has a large effect on confirmation and delay, particularly in the G. W. Bush and Clinton administrations. Set forth in Table 1.3A are the predicted probabilities for confirmation and the elapsed number of days from nomination to confirmation for nominations made in the period 1985–2004, with and without interest group opposition. The models also controlled for all of the variables that past studies found to be statistically significant predictors of lower court confirmation durations.

This model predicted fairly stable rates of confirmation for unchallenged nominees in the four presidential administrations (ranging from an 88 percent chance of confirmation to 98 percent likelihood of confirmation). For challenged nominations, however, the likelihood for confirmation tells a different story. While 80 percent of Reagan nominations were confirmed notwithstanding activist opposition, by the first term of the G. W. Bush administration that number had declined to 46 percent (a difference of 34 percent).

Activist opposition had a similar effect on confirmation durations. The difference between unchallenged and challenged nominations for each appointing president were significant, ranging from a low of two days difference during the G. H. W. Bush administration to a high of 142 days difference in the Clinton administration. Clinton's nominees without opposition could expect confirmation to take sixty days; with opposition, 204 days. Comparing between periods, for opposed nominations we see a low of about thirty-eight days to be confirmed during the G. H. W. Bush administration to a high of 204 days for Clinton nominations. Also notable, and confirming the idea that the impetus for delay comes from interest group opposition, not a senator's own ideological distance from a nominee, Table 1.5 also shows that it takes less time for an ideologically distant nominee without interest group opposition to be confirmed than it does for an ideologically closer nominee with interest group opposition to be confirmed. This suggests that senators do not engage in an independent analysis of a nominee's ideology, instead relying on sympathetic interest groups' analyses of the nominee. If the interest group does not object then the senator does not object.

Table 1.5 Predicted probabilities on confirmation outcomes and predicted median durations until confirmation, nominations to the U.S. Courts of Appeals, 1985–2004

	Likelihood of confirmation		Median duration until confirmation	
	With interest group opposition	Without interest group opposition	With interest group opposition	Without interest group opposition
G. W. Bush nominations	.46	.96***	152.22 days	88.35 days**
Clinton nominations	.76	.88	204.39 days	60.49 days****
G. H. W. Bush nominations	.66	.96**	36.72 days	34.15 days
Reagan nominations	.80	.98*	79.05 days	32.87 days****

Note: All probabilities and median durations assume all other variables set at their means. Tests of significance are two-tailed tests.

Statistical difference between opposed and unopposed: *p ≤ .10; ** p ≤ .05; *** p ≤ .01; **** p ≤ .001 (two-tailed tests).

This is solid evidence consistent with the hypothesis that interest groups are influencing senators to delay, delay, delay, doing whatever possible to see that their objectionable nominee does not get confirmed.

Conclusion

The lower court appointment process has dramatically changed over time. The transformation of the appointment process is the result of two important developments in American politics that began to take shape in the 1950s and 60s. First, there was an historic transformation of the mass party system that had existed since the Jacksonian era. Second, political activists (party activists, affiliated interest groups, and public interest law firms) increasingly began to turn to litigation in the federal courts, rather than lobbying in federal and state legislatures, to achieve policy goals. Working in tandem, these changes would forever raise the stakes of lower federal court appointments leading to drastic changes in presidents' appointment strategies. Presidents and senators would cease using lower federal court judgeships predominantly for *patronage* purposes and instead, in accordance with the demands of political activists, would come to view federal judgeships as a means to satisfy the activists' *policy* demands.

Beginning with the establishment of lower court judicial watchdogs, the interest groups discussed above which monitor the lower court appointment process very carefully, in the late 1980s and early 1990s, the lower court confirmation process went from one that took mere weeks to complete to one in which confirmation delays drag on for hundreds of days (sometimes stretching over multiple congressional sessions if the president chooses to re-nominate the candidate). We have also seen evidence of senators catering to interest groups. While once the use of a filibuster to block a lower court nomination was rare, during the G. W. Bush administration, and then again during the Obama administration, it became one of the most-used weapons in the Senate's arsenal to block lower court nominations. Only the implementation of the "nuclear" option would bring these wars to a temporary truce. And, so, we are left with a confirmation process that has been captured by party and outside activists who want only to seat judges likely to agree with their respective visions of justice, for example, judges who they can count on to decide cases in their favor.

Because presidents and senators are so dependent upon political activists to mobilize the electorate at-large to turn out at the polls, politicians are now forced to pursue nomination/confirmation strategies that satisfy first and foremost the policy demands of these influential players within their respective parties and only then may they consider patronage. Simply stated, it is the politicians' pursuit of these policy-oriented strategies in the selection and confirmation of lower federal court judges, which touch on the most divisive partisan issues of the modern political era, that has led to the heightened politicization of the lower federal court appointment process. It also explains why elected representatives and candidates expend such an inordinate amount of political capital deciding who shall sit on the lower federal courts when the issue has no salience with the American electorate.

Notes

1. The president, particularly with district court judges, consults with home state senators because, if such senators do not approve of the favored nominee of the president, they may file a blue piece of paper expressing to the Judiciary Committee Chair their lack of support for the nomination (2005). This "blue slip" stops the nomination in its tracks (Steigerwalt 2010).
2. The one exception may be the use of a parliamentary procedure known as a "hold." According to Steigerwalt (2010), a strategic hold "many times capture judicial nominations by coincidence; in a number of instances, the strategic hold was applied to whoever happened to be on the floor at that time" (p. 87). In other words, a nomination is held up by a senator as a strategic ploy concerning another political fight then being waged between that senator and another political actor (e.g., the president or a member of the opposite party).
3. The last time this happened was 1999, during the Clinton administration, when Ronnie White, nominated to a seat on the Eastern District of Missouri was defeated by a floor vote. Though it looked like he had the necessary votes to break a filibuster (sixty votes) with some bi-partisan support, at the eleventh hour, the Republicans switched sides, claiming White was soft on crime (Scherer 2005); the vote thus went strictly along party lines and the Democrats now lacked the votes to break the filibuster. In 2014, fifteen years after his original defeat, Obama nominated White to a seat on the same court, and this time he was confirmed (Raasch 2014).
4. Scholars have also started to broaden the scope of study on the Supreme Court confirmation process beyond mere roll-call voting analyses. Shipan and Shannon (2003), looking at Supreme Court nominations from 1866–1994, found that nominations made during divided government, nominations for Chief Justice, "critical" nominations (those which would tip the ideological balance of the Court) and nominations made at the end of congressional sessions face longer confirmation periods; older nominees and nominees who currently serve in the Senate face shorter confirmation periods.
5. This study will be discussed in detail in the section "Transformation of the Old Party System."
6. In 2013, with the Democrats in control of the Senate, Senate Majority Leader, Harry Reed (D-NV), invoked a procedural tactic whereby only fifty votes were needed (rather than the sixty needed for a filibuster) to end filibusters, in most cases, of judicial nomination and other Executive appointments. Voting along party lines, the motion passed. This cleared the way for three Obama nominations that had been filibustered to be immediately confirmed to the U.S. Court of Appeals for the D.C. Circuit with a simple majority vote (Kane 2013), available at: https://www.washingtonpost.com/politics/senate-poised-to-limit-filibusters-in-party-line-vote-that-would-alter-centuries-of-precedent/2013/11/21/d065cfe8-52b6-11e3-9fe0-fd2ca728e67c_story.html. When Republicans took control of the Senate in 2006, they kept the nuclear option in place (Ferrechio 2015).
7. Throughout this chapter, I use the term "modern political era" to mean the period 1968–2000. As explained, I focus on this period because it is when we begin to see the use of the first "elite mobilization" strategies, and it is these strategies that have led to increased politicization of the lower court appointment process.

8. Some have suggested that, in the modern political era, ideologically motivated local party leaders have developed quite sophisticated and professional organizations (Gibson, Frendreis, and Vertz 1989). Thus, the terms "amateur" and "professional" are somewhat misnomers.
9. During the period known as the Lochner era, roughly 1905–37, the Court was controlled by jurists who believed that the government should not interfere with the economy. Thus, they struck down almost every state and federal statute in which the government attempted to regulate working conditions for the protection of laborers (e.g., *Lochner v. N.Y.*, 198 U.S. 45 (1905); *Adkins v. Children's Hospital*, 261 U.S. 525 (1923); *Hammer v. Dagenhart*, 247 U.S. 251 (1918)). Regarding state statutes, the Court created the Substantive Due Process doctrine, which took the word "liberty" used in the text of the Fourteenth Amendment (states shall not deny "life, liberty, or property without due process of law") out of context; it had previously been interpreted as strictly a trial procedures clause with no substantive rights attached to it (Slaughterhouse Cases, 16 Wall 36 (1873) and imbue it with a new conservative substantive meaning. The Court held in *Lochner* that the liberty protected in the Fourteenth Amendment included a freedom to contract, and that state laws regulating the relationship between employer and employee violated their freedom to contract. (*Lochner v. N.Y.*, 198 U.S. 45(1905)).
10. See e.g., *Brown v. Board of Education (Brown II)*, 349 U.S. 294 (1955) (school desegregation); *Florida ex.rel. Hawkins v. Board of Control of Florida*, 350 U.S. 413 (1956) (school desegregation); *Aaron v. Cooper*, 358 U.S. 5 (1958) (school desegregation); *Garner v. Louisiana*, 368 U.S. 157 (1961) (desegregation of restaurant facility); *Turner v. City of Memphis*, 369 U.S. 350 (1962) (desegregation of restaurant facility); *Griffin v. Maryland*, 378 U.S. 379 (1964) (desegregation of amusement park); *Heart of Atlanta Motel v. U.S.*, 379 U.S. 241 (1964) (upholding constitutionality of Civil Rights Act of 1964).
11. Class Action | Wex Legal Dictionary / Encyclopedia, Class Actions, available at: https://www.law.cornell.edu/wex/class_action.
12. 410 U.S. 113 (1973).
13. e.g., *U.S. v. Lopez*, 514 U.S. 549 (narrowing scope of federal power under Commerce Clause); *District of Columbia v. Heller*, 554 U.S. 570 (2008) (finding a constitutional right for individuals to bear arms under the Second Amendment); *Shelby County v. Holder*, 570 U.S. __ (2013) dismantling the Voting Rights act of 1965).
14. For details of this analysis, see Scherer (2005), Chapter 2.
15. Associate Justice Elena Kagan is the one exception to this rule. Her employment background is grounded in academia (former dean of the Harvard Law School) and public service (former Solicitor General) (https://www.oyez.org/justices/elena_kagan).
16. At the behest of activists, senators expend political capital on lower court nominations in several ways, all of which will anger the president and the senators in the president's party: issuing a negative blue slip, harsh questioning at the Judiciary Committee confirmation hearing, voting "no" at the Committee hearing, delaying the scheduling of a floor vote, voting "no" on the floor of the Senate chamber, filibustering a nomination (though that is more difficult to do under today's rules that limit the number of judges that may be filibustered by the opposition party). All of these tactics are discussed later and constitute mobilization strategies by senators to please interest groups.
17. There are two ways these elites help with mass mobilization efforts: large donations which can then be used for "get out the vote" efforts, or (2) large grass roots organizations which have large constituencies and are already organized and willing to engage in "get out the vote" efforts (Skinner 2007).

18. It is clear that "holds" on judicial nominations are not considered elite mobilization strategies because they are not done at the behest of interest groups and they almost always have nothing to do with the nominee's ideological suitability for the bench. The hold is really about a political fight outside the realm of the judiciary.
19. Scherer (2005: 50–3, 58–60).
20. Scherer (2005: 53–5, 60–1).
21. Scherer (2005: 55–7, 61–2).
22. Because the Democratic Party shifted to the right on their long-standing support of criminal rights, particularly between the Carter and Clinton administrations, Scherer looked beyond mere party affiliation of the appellate judges. Instead, she coded them according to the appointing president. Therefore, we should anticipate that the judges appointed by Clinton are more conservative than those by Carter on the crime policy cases. However, both sets of Democrats should be to the left of Republican presidential appointees.

References

Aldrich, J. H. 1995. *Why Parties? The Origin and Transformation of Party Politics in America*. Chicago, IL: University of Chicago Press.

Aron, N. 2002. Face-to face interview with Amy Steigerwalt and Nancy Scherer. Tape recorded, July 9, Washington, DC.

Baum, L. 1990. *American Courts: Process and Policy*. Boston, MA: Houghton Mifflin.

Bell, L. C. 2002a. *Warring Factions: Interest Groups, Money, and the New Politics of Senate Confirmation*. Columbus, OH: Ohio State University Press.

Bell, L. C. 2002b. "Senatorial Discourtesy: The Senate's Use of Delay to Shape the Federal Judiciary." *Political Research Quarterly* 55: 589–608.

Bickel, A. M. 1970. *The Supreme Court and the Idea of Progress*. New York, NY: Harper and Row.

Binder, S., and Maltzman, F. 2002. "Senatorial Delay in Confirming Federal Judges, 1947–1998." *American Journal of Political Science* 46 (January): 190–9.

Caldeira, G. A. 1991. "Courts and Public Opinion." In *The American Courts*, edited by J. B. Gates and C. A. Johnson. Washington, DC: Congressional Quarterly Press, 303–34.

Carp, R. A., and Stidham, R. 1998. *The Federal Courts*, 3rd ed. Washington, DC: Congressional Quarterly Press.

Cavendish, E. 2002. Face-to-face interview with Nancy Scherer. Taped recorded July 10. Washington, DC.

Chase, H. 1972. *Federal Judges: The Appointment Process*. Minneapolis, MN: University of Minnesota Press.

Conway, M. M., and Feigert, F. B. 1968. "Motivation and Incentive System and the Political Party Organization." *American Political Science Review* 62: 1159–73.

Duvager, M. 1964. *Political Parties*. New York, NY: Wiley Press.

Epps, C. R. 1998. *The Rights Revolution*. Chicago, IL: University of Chicago Press.

Epstein, L. 1985. *Conservatives in Court*. Knoxville, TN: University of Tennessee Press.

Epstein, L., and Segal, J. 2006. *Advise and Consent*. New York, NY: Oxford University Press.

Evans, E. A. 1948. "Political Influences in the Selection of Federal Judges." *Wisconsin Law Review*: 330–51.

Ferrechio, S. 2015. "Republicans Stop Worrying, Learn to Love Nuclear Option." *Washington Examiner*. Available at: http://www.washingtonexaminer.com/republicans-stop-worrying-learn-to-love-nuclear-option/article/2563402.

Frymer, P., and Yoon, A. 2002. "Political Parties, Representation, and Federal Safeguards." *Northwestern University Law Review* 96: 977–1026.

Gandy, K. 2002. Interview with the author. Tape recording, July 11. Washington, DC.

Gibson, J. L., Frendeis, J. P., and Vertz, L. L. 1987. "Party Dynamics in the 1980s: Change in County Party Organizational Strength, 1980–1984," *American Journal of Political Science* 33: 67–90.

Goldman, S. 1997. *Picking Federal Judges: Lower Court Selection from Roosevelt through Reagan*. New Haven, CT: Yale University Press.

Goldman, S. 1966. "Voting Behavior on the United States Courts of Appeals, 1961–1964." *American Political Science Review* 60: 374–83.

Graves, S. E., and Howard, R. M. 2009. *Justice Takes a Recess: Judicial Appointments from George Washing to George W. Bush*. Lanham, MD: Lexington Books. Lexington Books.

Graves, S. E., and Howard, R. M. 2010. "Ignoring Advice and Consent? Uses of Judicial Recess Appointments." *Political Research Quarterly* 63(3): 640–53.

Griffiths, B. 2012. "UCLA Prof: Interests Groups, Activists Are Running Politics." *The Daily Iowan* (Sept. 25).

Grossmann, M., and Dominguez, C. B. K. 2009. "Party Coalitions and Interest Group Networks." *American Politics Quarterly* 37: 767–800.

Holmes, L. M. 2007. "Outsider Participation and Influence in Judicial Confirmation Hearings, 1979–2004." *The American Review of Politics* 28: 205–27.

Horowitz, D. L. 1977. *The Courts and Social Policy*. Washington, DC: Brookings Institution Press.

Jipping, T. 2002. Face-to-face interview with Amy Steigerwalt and Nancy Scherer. Tape recorded, June 6, Washington, DC.

Katz, D., and Eldersveld, S. J. 1961. "The Impact of Local Party Activities upon the Electorate." *Public Opinion Quarterly* 25: 1–24.

Klotz, R. 2004. "The Nuclear Option for Stopping Filibustering." *PS: Political Science and Politics*. October: 843–6.

Martinek, W. L., Kemper, M., and Van Winkel, S. R. 2002. "To Advise and Consent: The Senate and Lower Federal Court Nominations, 1977–1998." *Journal of Politics* 64: 337–61.

Mayhew, D. 1974. *Congress: The Electoral Connection*. New Haven, CT: Yale University Press.

McGuinness, J. O., and Rappaport, M. B. 2005. "The Judicial Filibuster, the Median Senator, and the Countermajoritarian Difficulty." *Supreme Court Review* 2005: 257–305.

Neas, R. 2002. Face-to-Face interview with Amy Steigerwalt. Tape recorded, August 6, Washington, DC.

Perry, B. A. 1991. *A Representative Supreme Court? The Impact of Race, Religion, and Gender on Appointments*. New York, NY: Greenwood.

Polsby, N. W., and Wildasky, A. 1971. *Presidential Elections: Strategies of American Electoral Politics*. New York: Scribners.

Primo, D., Binder, S., and Maltzman, F. 2008. "Who Consents? Competing Pivots in Federal Judicial Selection." *American Journal of Political Science* 52 (July): 471–89.

Raasch, C. 2014. "Senate Confirms St. Louis' Ronnie White as Federal Judge: *St. Louis Post Dispatch*. Available at: http://www.stltoday.com/news/local/govt-and-politics/senate-confirms-st-louis-ronnie-white-as-federal-judge/article_c758368a-534d-59e1-8ad6-5367e272c5e6.html.

Randazzo, K. A., and Waterman, R. W. 2014. *Checking the Courts: Law, Ideology, and Contingent Discretion*. Albany, NY: State University of New York Press.

Rosenberg, G. N. 1991. *The Hollow Hope: Can Courts Bring about Social Change?* Chicago, IL: University of Chicago Press.

Rosenstone, S. J., and Hansen, J. M. 1993. *Mobilization, Participation, and Democracy in America*. New York, NY: Macmillan.

Rosenstone, S. J., and Hansen, J. M. 1996. *Mobilization, Participation, and Democracy in America*. Chicago, IL: University of Chicago Press.

Scheingold, S. A. 1974. *The Politics of Rights: Lawyers, Public Policy, and Political Change*. New Haven, CT: Yale University Press.

Scherer, N. 2005. *Scoring Points: Politicians, Activists, and the Lower Federal Court Appointment Process*. Palo Alto, CA: Stanford University Press.

Scherer, N., Bartels, B., and Steigerwalt, A. 2008. "Sounding the Fire Alarm: The Role of Interest. Groups in the Lower Federal Court Confirmation." *Journal of Politics* 70: 1026–39.

Schwartz, H. 1988. *Packing the Courts: The Conservative Campaign to Rewrite the Constitution*. New York, NY: Charles Scribners Sons.

Segal, J. A., and Spaeth, H. J. 1993. *The Attitudinal Model*. New York, NY: Cambridge University Press.

Shipan, C. R., and Shannon, M. L. 2003. "Delaying Justice(s): A Duration Analysis of Supreme Court Confirmations." *American Journal of Political Science* 47: 654–68.

Silverstein, M. 1994. *Judicious Choices: The New Politics of Supreme Court Confirmations*. New York, NY: W. W. Norton.

Songer, D. R. 1991. "The Circuit Court of Appeals." In *The American Courts: A Critical Assessment*, edited by J. B. Gates and C. A. Johnson. Washington, DC: Congressional Quarterly Press.

Sorauf, F. J. 1967. "Political Parties and Political Analysis." In *The American Party System: Stages of Political Development*, edited by W. N. Chambers and W. D. Burnham. New York, NY: Oxford University Press.

Sorauf, F. J. and Baeck, P. A. 1988. *Party Politics in America*, 6th ed. Boston, MA: Scott Foresman Press.

Steigerwalt, A. 2010. *Battle over the Bench: Senators, Interest Groups, and Lower Court Confirmations*. Charlottesville, VA: University of Virginia Press.

Wawro, G. J. and Schickler, E. 2007. *Filibuster: Obstruction and Lawmaking in the Senate*. Princeton, NJ: Princeton University Press.

Wildavsky, A. 1965. "The Goldwater Phenomenon: Purists, Politicians and the Two-Party System." *Review of Politics* 27: 386–413.

Wilson, J. Q. 1962. *The Amateur Democrat*. Chicago, IL: University of Chicago Press.

Woodford Howard, J. Jr., Courts of Appeals in the Federal Judicial System (Princeton University Press, 1981)

CHAPTER 2

APPOINTING SUPREME COURT JUSTICES

CHRISTINE L. NEMACHECK

IN the eight years since President George W. Bush appointed Third Circuit Court of Appeals Judge Samuel Alito to the U.S. Supreme Court, filling the seat left vacant by Justice Sandra Day O'Connor's retirement, the Court's decisions have changed significantly. In areas such as affirmative action, abortion, or campaign finance reform, the Court's rulings are likely quite different than they would have been had Justice O'Connor, long the Court's swing vote, remained on the bench. One can also reasonably argue that, not only would the language of many rulings have been different if Justice O'Connor had participated in the cases, but that several 5–4 rulings would likely have been resolved for the opposite party. Indeed, Justice O'Connor's own criticism of the Court's controversial 2010 ruling in *Citizens United v. Federal Election Commission,* invalidating much of the Court's decision in *McConnell v. Federal Election Commission* rendered just seven years earlier, provides evidence of the impact that can result from even a single appointment to the U.S. Supreme Court. Referring to the 2010 decision, Justice O'Connor said, "Gosh, I step away for a couple of years and there's no telling what's going to happen" (Liptak 2010).

To put it succinctly, appointments to the U.S. Supreme Court matter. They matter to the president, whose name will forever be associated with his Court appointments, and who hopes to influence the kinds of decisions the Court makes for years after leaving office. They matter for senators who want to influence the Court's composition and, by extension, the policy that results from its decisions. And, of course, appointments matter to the public whose lives and expectations will be shaped by the institution's rulings.

Given its institutional importance, it should be no surprise that staffing the Court has piqued the interest of the popular media and scholars alike. From early historical accounts of individual appointments or those of a particular president, to more recent theoretical and empirical analyses of the nomination and confirmation process, we have learned a great deal about the process of appointing justices to the U.S. Supreme Court, the actors involved, and the institutional and political constraints on the appointment process.

This chapter discusses the relevant literature on the Supreme Court appointment process, assesses the current state of that literature, and suggests some promising directions for future research. The first section addresses some early efforts to understand Supreme Court appointments by several leaders in the field of judicial politics. That work provided the foundation for more recent inquiries into the process. This more recent literature is divided into the two stages of the appointment process: the selection stage and the confirmation stage. The chapter concludes by discussing some developing questions that may provide interesting avenues for future research.

A Political Court, the Political Environment, and Appointments

Prior to C. Herman Pritchett's work developing a positive theory of Supreme Court decision-making, political scientists largely neglected the politics of the Supreme Court justice appointment process. Indeed, prior to the legal realism movement, there was little reason to critically examine the appointment process since the Court's decisions were largely understood as determined by the logical, mechanical application of legal precedent.[1] Under such circumstances, the identity of individuals seated on the Court made little difference as long as they possessed the necessary qualifications and capability to apply legal precedent.

Pritchett's analysis of justices' votes during the 1939 and 1940 Court terms signaled a major development in the political science literature, and judicial politics more specifically. Pritchett embraced legal realism by evaluating how President Roosevelt's appointees voted compared to other sitting justices, not only in terms of the direction of their votes, but also in terms of agreement or disagreement with other Court members. In doing so, he explicitly recognized the importance of judicial attitudes as an explanatory variable. According to Pritchett, "it is the private attitudes of the majority of the Court which become public law" (Pritchett 1941: 890). And for Pritchett, this conclusion was not only evident based on his analysis of the justices' votes, it was also normatively desirable that the "political philosophies of the justices and their personal judgments as to the role of law and the Constitution in relation to economic and social development" should influence Supreme Court decisions (Pritchett 1946: 499).

Though the debate between legal realists and legal formalists continues in the academy, there is little if any doubt among political actors and the American public that judges' and justices' votes are an expression of their political philosophies and personal judgments regarding the role of the law in American society. The natural extension of that view is that appointments to the federal courts, and to the Supreme Court in particular, are indeed political.

With the publication of his 1964 book, *A Supreme Court Justice Is Appointed*, David Danelski provided the basis for much of the early work on appointments to the Supreme Court. Danelski sought to explain why President Warren G. Harding chose Pierce Butler for appointment to the Court in 1922. By analyzing Butler's nomination, Danelski began to build a framework to examine nominations to the Court more generally (1964). Danelski's transactional theory helped explain Butler's appointment, as well as factors that presidents more generally might consider in making appointments to the High Court. According to Danelski, a nominee's qualifications and personality are integral to the president's choice, but other political actors can also influence the president's decision by shaping how the president views the nominee. In other words, while a candidate's specific characteristics helps to explain their appointment, factors external to the candidate also play a role in that process.

Following Danelski's work, Joel Grossman evaluated the influence of the American Bar Association (ABA), whose ratings of judicial quality have the potential to influence the context in which presidents make appointment decisions (1965). Like his predecessors, Grossman's approach recognized that judicial candidates' backgrounds affected the decisions they reached on the courts. Important for Grossman's argument is the understanding that the courts and judges are political institutions and actors, respectively. Indeed, in one review of Grossman's work, the reviewer took pains to note that while Grossman's work "comes from a political scientist (and from the preface one assumes a 'judicial behaviourist')," it is likely to appeal to all lawyers with an interest in securing better judges (Weir 1967: 243).

Robert Scigliano's 1971 work examining presidential control over the appointment process focused more explicitly on the way institutions shape the appointment process. Scigliano's overarching interest in *The Supreme Court and the Presidency* was the potential for the executive and judiciary to work together to check Congress. His focus on the president's authority in making appointments and the degree to which judicial nominees represented their appointing presidents' views from the bench led Scigliano to distinguish between the selection and the confirmation stages of the process. This is an important distinction on which later work would build; the appointing president has the greatest potential for unfettered authority at the selection stage (the time up until a formal appointment is sent to the Senate), but in making decisions at the selection stage, he must be cognizant of the constraints he faces at the confirmation stage (Moraski and Shipan 1999; Nemacheck 2007).

Scigliano asserted presidents' control over the selection stage has two bases: knowledge and power. Presidents often had personal knowledge of their nominees prior to appointment and that, of course, led to greater confidence in the person's likely behavior as a justice compared to a candidate a president did not know. In particular, Scigliano's treatment of political actors' attempts to influence appointments laid the groundwork for future, systematic analyses of nomination dynamics. While he recognized the importance of considering attributes of those nominated, Scigliano also incorporated into his analyses the political conditions in which the nominations took place. He considered the Senate's partisan composition and the possible exercise of senatorial courtesy by a senator from a nominee's home state, as well as the time in the president's term at which the nominations arose (1971).

An important question underlying Scigliano's research was whether presidential success in securing Senate confirmation resulted from Senate deference to the president's authority to appoint Supreme Court justices, or from presidential anticipation of the Senate's likelihood to confirm a nominee and choosing accordingly (1971). Later inquiry into the relative power of the president and Senate in the appointment process used various terms, but essentially framed the question as one of presidential domination or presidential anticipation (Chang 2001; Hammond and Hill 1993; Krehbiel 2007). The bulk of the evidence points toward the latter.

Approximately 80 percent of the time, the Senate votes to confirm presidents' nominees to the Court. Based on a theory of presidential anticipation, that success rate is evidence that presidents correctly gauge senators' concerns about nominee ideology or method of constitutional interpretation, along with the potential for those senators to block the nomination, and choose nominees they expect will be confirmed within those constraints (Moraski and Shipan 1999; Nemacheck 2007; Shipan, Allen, and Bargen 2014). But, what explains the 20 percent of nominations that fail in the Senate? This question has animated a number of studies.

Some scholars have examined the appointment process by focusing on unsuccessful nominations (Massaro 1990; Whittington 2007), while others have analyzed the variation in the amount of time it takes the Senate to confirm Supreme Court nominees (Shipan and Shannon 2003). In examining failed nominations, scholars have generally found that "mistakes" presidents make at the selection stage are typically the key to understanding why the Senate refuses to confirm a nominee. If presidents fail to effectively manage what Massaro refers to as the "pre-nomination stage," which might include consulting with members of Congress on the appointment, their nominees are likely to experience difficulty at the confirmation stage (1990).

Whittingon (2007) emphasizes the importance of selection deliberations in examining the relative power of the Senate and the executive in making Supreme Court appointments. If theories of presidential anticipation are correct, and Whittington believes they are, it is important for voters to consider future federal court appointments when casting a presidential election ballot. But, voters should also keep those considerations in mind when voting for their senators. Whittington recognizes that presidents have an advantage over senators in making appointments since senators can only vote to accept or reject candidates, they do not hold the positive power to choose candidates. But, he argues that presidents should anticipate the confirmation process at the selection stage, particularly when the opposite party controls the Senate (2007). Furthermore, analyzing the length of time required for the Senate to act on a nominee, Shipan and Shannon (2003) find that as the ideological distance between the president and the Senate increases, the Senate is increasingly likely to delay voting on the candidate. Thus, under relatively more difficult confirmation settings, strategic presidents should consider that distance when choosing the nominee.

Following Danelski and Grossman, scholars began to analyze more explicitly the factors affecting the relative constraints under which presidents made their nominations. For example, Harold Chase examined factors shaping the confirmation environment and asserted that neither presidents nor senators operate in a vacuum in the judicial appointments process (1972). He identified four contextual elements that would influence the president's choice of a nominee and his discretion in making that nomination. These elements included the balance of power in the Senate, the Senate's support for the president, the public's support for the president, and the attributes of the seat left vacant on the Court.

Although many of the factors shaping the confirmation environment are outside of the president's control, that is not true of all of them. For scholars asserting presidents' ability to improve their nominees' likelihood of confirmation, it was important they consider those variables over which presidents could exercise control. In examining appointments of federal appellate judges, including Supreme Court justices, John Schmidhauser (1979) understood presidential evaluation of nominees' ideological preferences to be primary. In addition, Schmidhauser stressed the importance of appointees' background characteristics, which presidents do control. These include ethnicity, sex, religious affiliation, educational background, prior judicial experience, and paternal occupation. Furthermore, although he emphasized the president's "domination" of the Supreme Court appointment process, Schmidhauser recognized the institutional constraints bearing on the decision, particularly the need for Senate confirmation. Additionally, Schmidhauser examined the role of interest groups in pressuring the president and, in a departure from Grossman's focus on the ABA's role in judicial selection, Schmidhauser analyzed the potential for the group to conflate competence and ideology in conducting its evaluation of a nominee's qualifications for the Court (1979).

In much of the theory-driven empirical studies of the appointment process, judicial politics scholars remained focused on the Senate's confirmation decision. Much of the more recent work seeks to explain the confirmation votes and influence of particular senators and committee chairs. For example, they asked whether members cast their votes according to their own ideological distance from the candidates. Or, did they instead tow the party line regardless of that distance (Segal 1987; Cameron, Cover, and Segal 1990; Segal, Cameron, and Cover 1992)? Given the rise of interest groups, particularly single interest groups, scholars have sought to understand sources of interest group influence (Caldeira and Wright 1998; Segal, Cameron, and Cover 1992). Because these questions are inherently inter-institutional in nature, much of the research has depended on some means of measuring characteristics like ideology across institutions. Thus, several scholars have devoted significant time and attention to finding a means by which to compare the ideological positions of presidents, senators, and justices (Bailey and Chang 2001; Martin and Quinn 2002; Bailey 2007). As a result, we know quite a lot about why senators vote as they do and how characteristics of the candidate, the members' constituents, and interest groups affect senators' confirmation votes. It is to that literature that I now turn.

The Confirmation Stage

Because the Constitution requires the president to appoint justices with the Senate's advice and consent, much of the work on the confirmation stage seeks to explain senators' votes on Supreme Court nominees (Segal 1987; Cameron, Cover, and Segal 1990 and Segal, Cameron, and Cover 1992; Ruckman 1993; Overby, Henschen, Walsh, and Strauss 1992; Guliuzza, Reagan, and Barrett 1994; Moraski and Shipan 1999; Shipan and Shannon 2003; Johnson and Roberts 2004; Shipan 2008). In his initial analysis of Senate confirmation votes, Jeffrey Segal found that partisan and institutional factors significantly affect members' votes (1987). And, in their 1990 and 1992 analyses, Segal, Cameron, and Cover, developed a spatial model of Senate confirmation votes finding that, along with candidates' qualifications, senators' votes were largely a product of their own ideological distance from the nominee.

One factor that is universally thought to be an important, if not *the* most important factor in the appointment process, is the nominee's ideology. There is widespread agreement that justices of the U.S. Supreme Court have discretion in making decisions on the Court; they are not solely constrained by the letter of the law or Court precedent (Spaeth and Segal 1999; Segal and Spaeth 2002; Maltzman, Spriggs, and Wahlbeck 2000; Epstein and Segal 2005; Collins 2008; Bailey and Maltzman 2011; Collins and Ringhand 2013). Even beyond their final votes, the way justices articulate legal rules and the language they use has important consequences for the rule of law (Epstein and Kobylka 1992; Wahlbeck 1997). This has been clear to presidents since the very first appointments to the Supreme Court when George Washington chose six justices who shared his views on the importance of a stronger national government to the U.S. Supreme Court; all were Federalists.

Given the widely asserted prominence of ideology, it is not surprising that scholars have examined its importance relative to, and controlling for, other variables in the appointment process. In order to examine the importance of ideology in the appointment process empirically, however, scholars needed some way to measure a judicial candidate's ideology. This was a difficult proposition, not least because most ideological measures were based in whole or in part on representatives' voting records. Given that Supreme Court nominees came from different walks of life, it was no easy task to develop a single ideological measure across which candidates and those responsible for their appointment, could be compared.

One of the earliest attempts to measure justices' ideology was to analyze pre-confirmation newspaper reports on the candidate's ideological positions between the date the nomination was announced and the date of confirmation (Segal and Cover 1989). These Segal-Cover scores were then compared to scores of senators' relative liberalism or conservatism (through the use of Americans for Democratic Action (ADA) scores), to test the premise that senators were more likely to vote for candidates with whom they were ideologically proximate. Segal and his coauthors utilized these scores in their 1990 and 1992 analyses of judicial confirmation discussed above; that work went a long way toward advancing our knowledge of important factors in the confirmation process.

While the Segal-Cover measure of judicial ideology was a significant advancement, the measure's inherent limitation is its stasis. The newspaper accounts of a justice's ideology prior to confirmation provide an ideological measure apart from a justice's voting record, but it is a static measure and thus assumes that ideology is stable over time (1989). Aimed at addressing some of the limitations of the Segal-Cover measures, Andrew Martin and Kevin Quinn developed a dynamic ideological measure based on the justices' votes (2002). Because they are dynamic, the Martin-Quinn scores allow for across-time comparisons and they are good ideological indicators across issue areas.

Although Martin-Quinn scores provide a better measure of justices' ideology over time, comparing justice ideology with that of senators and presidents still posed a significant hurdle to empirical, cross-institutional studies. Developing a cross-institutional ideological measure would allow for the systematic, empirical analysis of whether ideology plays the role in appointment politics that it has long been asserted to play. Michael Bailey and Kelly Chang (2001) addressed the need for a cross-institutional ideological measure using a bridging technique.

Baily and Chang's measure utilizes indicators of congressional members' ideology developed by Keith Poole and Howard Rosenthal (1991, 1997). Poole and Rosenthal developed what they call "Common Space Scores" for members of Congress and presidents. These scores are derived from a spatial model in which members' preferences on policy alternatives are maximized at particular "ideal points" (see Poole and Rosenthal 1991, 1997). To allow for the ideological comparison across all three branches, Bailey and Chang used a bridging technique in which they examined Supreme Court cases on which presidents and members of Congress took public positions (2001). In further work on cross-institutional ideological measures, Bailey used a Bayesian Markov Chain Monte Carlo approach to measuring ideal points that allows for ideological comparisons across institutions and across time (Bailey 2007).

In other work measuring the effects of ideology inter-temporally and across institutions, Epstein, Lindstädt, Segal, and Westerland (2006) rescaled Segal-Cover scores using Martin-Quinn scores (2002) for justice ideology and Poole and Rosenthal's scores, for members' ideology (1991, 1997). The results of the 2006 analysis largely mirror Segal et al.'s earlier findings; ideology and merit, or the nominee's perceived qualifications for office based on newspaper editorials, are significant factors in senators' confirmation votes, though there is a heightened role for ideology in more recent confirmation votes (Epstein et al. 2006).

Scholars and close observers of judicial confirmation politics almost universally assert that Robert Bork's confirmation hearings signaled a significant change in the substance and tenor of the confirmation process. It became more politicized, more focused on nominees' ideological positions and less concerned with a nominee's qualifications (Epstein, Lindstädt, Segal, and Westerland 2006). Members of both political parties have become critical of the substance and focus of confirmation hearings. Amid that criticism, some scholars, and even a current Supreme Court justice prior to her appointment, have questioned their utility and have called for reform (Carter 1994; Davis 2005; Eisgruber 2007; Kagan 1995; Yalof 2008).

Some critics deride the politicized nature of the process and the nominees' refusal to answer questions. When Supreme Court Associate Justice Elena Kagan was a professor of law at the University of Chicago, she contended that since Bork's defeat, confirmation hearings have been a "vapid and hollow charade in which repetition of platitudes has replaced discussion of viewpoints and personal anecdotes have supplanted legal analysis" (Kagan 1995). That said, others defend the process and argue that confirmation hearings allow for a national debate on important constitutional issues and thus have the potential to enhance the Court's legitimacy (Comiskey 2004; Collins and Ringhand 2013a; Collins and Ringhand 2013b).

In their examination of Supreme Court confirmation hearings, Collins and Ringhand argue that by focusing on the questions nominees refuse to answer, such as those pertaining to abortion and affirmative action, these earlier analyses miss the important role the hearings play in providing democratic legitimacy to the Court's important constitutional decisions. For example, the authors contend that it is valuable for a Chief Justice nominee like John Roberts to say that cases such as *Brown v. Board of Education* (1954) and *Roe v. Wade* (1973) are settled law and "entitled to respect out of principles of *stare decisis*" (2013a). According to this understanding of confirmation hearings, Robert Bork failed to be confirmed because he refused to support precedent such as *Roe* and explicitly criticized the Court's reasoning in the case.

As mentioned above, many point to the Bork confirmation hearings as a tipping point in the politicization of the appointment process, and particularly the confirmation environment. And, the popular press has given substantial attention to interest groups' lobbying tactics during and since Judge Bork's confirmation hearings. But, interest group activism in the judicial appointment process is hardly new. Groups have attempted to affect judicial staffing at least since the 1880s. For example, the National Grange and the Anti-Monopoly League lobbied against former Senator Stanley Matthews' appointment to the Court, first by President Hayes and then by President Garfield (Maltese 1995).

Interest group activity became even more prominent after the Seventeenth Amendment, by which voters began electing their U.S. senators directly, was ratified in 1913. In the wake of ratification, senators had to appeal directly to their constituents. Senators' need to connect with those constituents created an avenue for interest group influence and, at least arguably, left them more susceptible to interest group influence (Bell 2002). A change in the Senate rules also influenced interest groups' involvement in confirmation debate. Prior to 1929, the Senate considered Supreme Court nominations in near total secrecy, but a rules change that year moved debate on nominations to the floor and provided an opportunity for interest groups to assert their influence (Maltese 1995).

The literature on interest group involvement is largely in agreement that interest groups are active in Supreme Court confirmation politics and that they can have a significant effect on senators votes (Caldeira and Wright 1998; Segal, Cameron, and Cover

1992). Interest groups provide senators with information about the nominees as well as their constituents' views and the importance of the appointment to their constituents. And, in attempting to influence the confirmation vote, they do, as we would expect, target those members with the institutional clout to affect the outcome (1998). Although some lament the amount of interest group lobbying in the confirmation process, others have argued that groups' involvement has made the process more transparent and democratic (Silverstein 1994). Regardless of which position one espouses, it seems clear that groups' lobbying and influence is here to stay.

The Selection Stage

As mentioned above, much, though not all, of the scholarly investigation into the selection stage has built on the work of scholars studying confirmation politics. As it became clear that nominee-specific and institutional factors had an important bearing on the likely confirmation of the president's nominee, some scholars turned their attention to analyzing how and why the president and his advisors chose particular nominees. Given that the Senate has voted to confirm just over 80 percent of all Supreme Court nominees, it is critical to understand the process prior to the president's announcement of a nominee.

The selection stage of the Supreme Court appointment process has received less attention than the confirmation stage, but the literature devoted to presidents' considerations in making appointments to the Supreme Court has grown significantly over the last fifteen years. That said, Henry Abraham's seminal work on judicial appointments, *Justices, Presidents, and Senators,* first appeared in 1974 and is now in its fifth edition. Although Abraham did not restrict his discussion to the selection stage, his political history of Supreme Court appointments since Washington's first six nominations includes extensive coverage of each president's Supreme Court appointees from Washington to George W. Bush. Although his approach is historical and focused on individual appointments to the Court, Abraham does assert that presidents' considerations can be generalized into four broad categories: the candidate's objective merit, the president's interest in balancing representation or representativeness on the Court, the president's personal friendship with the candidate, and the candidate's political and ideological compatibility with the appointing president (Abraham 2007).

Abraham's categorizations have motivated much of the literature on the selection stage since it was first published in 1974. The first characteristic Abraham asserts as prominent in the nomination process is the candidate's objective merit. Although the Constitution does not set any particular requirements for service on the Supreme Court, the framers understood that the structural requirements they established (presidential nomination and Senate confirmation) would result in the most qualified candidates being appointed. Scholars studying the selection of Supreme Court justices uniformly agree that merit is an important factor in the nomination process (Scigliano

1971; Massaro 1990; Perry 1991; Yalof 1999; Abraham 2007; Nemacheck 2007; Baum 2012; O'Brien 2014).

Service as a federal judge, particularly on the federal appeals courts, can be an especially good indicator of a nominee's qualifications. Since the mid-1980s, experience as a federal court of appeals judge has become the norm among Supreme Court nominees and it is sometimes suggested that such service has become a "requirement" for the appointment. In fact, when scholars examine the qualifications of candidates seriously considered for an appointment, it is evident that presidents are increasingly less likely to even consider candidates who lack experience on the federal courts of appeals (Nemacheck 2007).

In addition to merit, Abraham also asserted that presidents consider balancing representation when choosing nominees for the Supreme Court. A number of scholars have addressed the role representational concerns can play in presidents' deliberations (Scigliano 1971; Schmidhauser 1979; Baum 1981; Perry 1991; Sheldon and Maule 1997; O'Brien 2014). There are several reasons presidents might be concerned about the representative nature of their appointments. They might wish to curry favor with particular religious, ethnic, or racial groups. For example, in an attempt to limit the gender gap between male and female voters in 1980, particularly female Republicans, Ronald Reagan promised that he would appoint the first female justice to the Supreme Court. When Potter Stewart announced his retirement from the Court in 1981, the year following Reagan's election, the President sought counsel as to whether his campaign promise bound him to make such an appointment during his first opportunity to do so, or whether he could wait for another vacancy to fulfill that promise (Nemacheck 2007). Though there was debate on the question in the administration, one aide urged the president to appoint a woman to the then-open seat, arguing that it was "imperative that you *appoint a woman to the Supreme Court* ... It means you will live up to a commitment you made and have that behind you" (Nofziger 1981, emphasis in the original). Though he did not know it at the time, had President Reagan not chosen a woman to fill that first vacancy, he would not have had another opportunity to make good on his campaign promise until after the 1984 presidential election.

More recently Hispanic groups lobbied George W. Bush to identify an Hispanic nominee and he seriously considered appointing the first Hispanic justice to the Supreme Court. Given the importance of the Latino vote, this is not surprising. And, of course, Barack Obama, who received the overwhelming majority of the Latino vote in 2008 (67 percent) and 2012 (71 percent) (Lopez 2008: i; Lopez and Taylor 2012: 4), appointed Latina Sonia Sotomayor to fill the seat left vacant by Justice David Souter's retirement in 2009.

Another reason presidents might consider representational factors in making appointments to the Supreme Court is to shore up the institution's legitimacy with the American public (Boyd, Epstein, and Martin 2010). A "representative" Court might achieve that legitimacy through simple descriptive representation, that is a Court that demographically resembles the American public, or the president's goal may be to achieve substantive representation, whereby a female justice might be particularly concerned with women's issues and rule differently on such issues as workplace discrimination than would a male justice, or a black justice might take a different perspective than a white justice on an issue like capital punishment, where there is ample evidence that black defendants are more likely to be sentenced to death than are their white counterparts (Pitkin 1967). A significant literature has developed as to whether substantive representation occurs (see Boyd, Epstein and Martin 2010), but regardless of the degree to which substantive representation actually occurs, presidents certainly might consider descriptive representation when choosing nominees.

For the most part, empirical analyses have not lent support to the idea that presidents choose nominees to enhance descriptive representation on the Supreme Court. In fact, Perry concludes that rather than making it more likely that a president would choose a candidate who would have made the Court more representative, based on characteristics like religion, race, and gender, these were more likely to be seen as potential obstacles to Supreme Court appointment (1991). And, many scholars have concluded that while factors such as religious representation may have historically been important, that is no longer the case (Perry 1991; Ruckman 1993; Watson and Stookey 1995; Sheldon and Maule 1997; Epstein and Segal 2005; Nemacheck 2007; Baum 2012; O'Brien 2014). However, while representational factors may not significantly affect presidents' deliberations on a nominee under most circumstances, they might reasonably play a more important role when a president is faced with filling a vacancy for a specific "seat" on the Court (e.g., a historically Catholic, Jewish, or black seat).[2]

Given the presence of women and minorities on the Supreme Court today, we might expect that such factors will matter less in future appointments. For example, Justice Ginsburg certainly lamented that another female justice was not appointed to replace Justice O'Connor upon her retirement, but now that there are three female justices on the Court, the notion of a woman's "seat" seems fairly antiquated. And, for the first time in the Court's history, there are no Protestants on the bench. Instead, prior to Justice Scalia's death, the 2015 Court was composed of six Catholic and three Jewish justices. It is reasonable to assume, however, that unless another African-American justice is appointed before Justice Clarence Thomas (who was appointed to fill the seat left vacant by Justice Thurgood Marshall's retirement) steps down, the appointing president would feel significant pressure to appoint an African-American justice to replace him.

Given the modest demographic diversity on the Court, one interesting question is whether there might begin to be some demand for experiential diversity on the Court. When Justice Elena Kagan was appointed to the Court in 2010, she became the first justice without any federal judicial experience since Justice O'Connor was appointed in 1981.[3] The fact that most Supreme Court nominees now come from the federal courts of appeals has not escaped either scholarly or popular media interest (Epstein, Knight, and Martin 2003; Bratton and Spill 2004; Epstein, Martin, Quinn, and Segal 2009; Liptak 2009; Barton 2012). While the selection literature assesses such experience as an important indicator of future behavior as a Supreme Court justice (Yalof 1999; Abraham 2007; Nemacheck 2007), the potential effects of having so many life-long federal judges on the Supreme Court, as opposed to justices who have experience on the state courts or in elected office, has generated debate (see Epstein et al. 2009).

Another characteristic scholars have found common among Supreme Court nominees is a close personal or professional relationship with the president (Scigliano 1971; Perry 1991; Sheldon and Maule 1997; Abraham 2007; Baum 2012; O'Brien 2012). Presidents do not necessarily appoint friends or colleagues due solely to cronyism or as a reward for dedicated service. In appointing friends to the High Court, presidents choose candidates they understand well and those whose future behavior they can confidently predict (Watson and Stookey 1995).

While personal or professional relationships with the president are plainly relevant, those relationships do not provide a clear advantage to particular candidates. During the modern era, approximately one-third of all individuals who make it onto presidents' short lists for appointment to the Court could be categorized as having a personal or professional relationship with the appointing president. And, nearly the same percentage of candidates actually chosen could be so categorized (Nemacheck 2007).

There are a few possible explanations for this phenomenon. It may be that a friendship with the president improves one's odds of being considered for appointment, a prospect that often leads to a fair bit of publicity for the candidate, but does not go so far as to yield the nomination itself. Another possibility is that concerns over accusations of cronyism makes the stakes too high to risk nominating a friend for this plum position. For example, Lyndon Johnson failed in his attempt to elevate his close friend, Justice Abe Fortas, to become chief justice. Johnson perhaps sealed his Fortas's fate when he chose another close friend, Homer Thornberry, to fill the associate justice seat that would be left vacant by Fortas's elevation to chief. Such cronyism would be particularly dangerous when the president faces a Senate controlled by the opposite party.

Finally, most scholars agree that ideological agreement between the president and the nominee is critical to the president's choice of a nominee (Chase 1972; Perry 1991; Watson and Stookey 1995; Abraham 2007; Nemacheck 2007; Baum 2012; O'Brien 2014). In fact, most scholars would contend that ideology is *the* most important factor in presidents' selection decisions (Pritchett 1948; Schubert 1965; Rohde and Spaeth 1976; Schmidhauser 1979; Massaro 1990; Segal and Spaeth 2002; Nemacheck 2007; Baum 2012; O'Brien 2014). And, of course, much of the research on the confirmation stage also asserts that candidate ideology itself and/or the candidate's ideological distance from the voting senator is essential (Segal, Cameron, and Cover 1992; Epstein and Segal 2005; Massaro 1990; Ruckman 1993; Cameron, Cover, and Segal 1990; Segal and Cover 1989; Watson and Stookey 1995). Presidents recognize the importance of Supreme Court appointments and their potential to have lasting effects on public policy long after the president leaves office.

Presidents average about two Supreme Court appointments in each of their four-year terms, though some have had the opportunity to appoint far more (e.g., Roosevelt's nine appointments is second only to George Washington's ten), while several presidents did not have the opportunity to appoint even a single justice during their time in office

(William H. Harrison, Zachary Taylor, Andrew Johnson, and Jimmy Carter). Sometimes even a single appointment can have significant consequences for the Court's rulings, such as when Justice Alito replaced Justice O'Connor who was frequently the swing vote in closely decided cases. Given that the Supreme Court decided nearly one-fifth of its cases by a 5–4 margin over the last couple decades, a single appointment had the potential to change the outcome in these cases (Epstein, Segal, Spaeth, and Walker 2012).

Because presidents clearly value the opportunity to make appointments to the Court, a reasonable question for scholars studying Supreme Court appointments is whether presidents have been successful in making those appointments. Although there are many ways to define success in this context, here I refer to presidents' ability to accurately gauge candidates' preferences and get his like-minded nominee confirmed. Indeed, in his seminal work on Supreme Court decision-making, Herman Pritchett's analysis implicitly acknowledged President Franklin Roosevelt's success in appointing like-minded candidates to the Court. By examining votes in non-unanimous cases, Pritchett found that Roosevelt's appointees tended to vote as a bloc and the preferences these votes revealed were largely in line with Roosevelt's (Pritchett 1948).

Scholars have taken different approaches in evaluating presidential success in making appointments to the Court, but there is a large degree of consensus that presidents, particularly those who expend significant time and resources attempting to determine candidates' ideological preferences, choose Supreme Court nominees with whom they are ideologically compatible (Scigliano 1971; Segal, Timpone, and Howard 2000; Epstein and Segal 2005; Szmer and Songer 2005; Eisgruber 2007; Nemacheck 2007). Stories of presidents' disappointments in their nominees' voting behavior are not uncommon, and at least partly because they are so colorful, they tend to be repeated frequently. For example, President Eisenhower's response to a question about mistakes he made while in office is frequently cited in these discussions: "Yes, two, and they are both sitting on the Supreme Court" (Baum 1998: 45). President Theodore Roosevelt's angry reaction to his appointee Oliver Wendell Holmes's vote in a trust-busting case is less often cited but colorfully in line with what one might expect of Roosevelt: "I could carve out of a banana a judge with more backbone than that" (Purdum 2005).

At least one study focusing on whether a president's Court nominees consistently voted in a unified bloc found that presidents' appointees votes often cancelled each other out (Lindquist, Yalof, and Clark 2000). For example, President George H. W. Bush may have accurately gauged Clarence Thomas's preferences, but was not as successful when he chose David Souter. Because Thomas's and Souter's votes were often at odds, the net influence on legal policy was zero. However, in several cases in which presidents were likely disappointed with decisions made by "their" justices, the presidents had lost Senate confirmation battles and were consciously choosing candidates who, while not as ideologically proximate as the president might have hoped, were more likely to garner Senate confirmation (Nemacheck 2007). For example, President Reagan nominated Anthony Kennedy to the Court after the Senate rejected his first candidate, Judge Robert

Bork, and his second choice, Judge Douglas Ginsburg, withdrew his nomination after the press revealed he had smoked marijuana.

In other cases, justices who were once quite ideologically compatible with the president might drift left or right during their two to three decades of service on the Court (Epstein, Martin, Quinn, and Segal 2007; Owens and Wedeking 2012; Epstein, Landes, and Posner 2013). Justice Blackmun is often held up as a prime example of ideological drift for his evolution on issues like the death penalty. For example, in 1972 Blackmun dissented from the Court's opinion striking down state death penalty statutes,[4] but in a 1994 dissent he stated his opposition to the death penalty altogether writing that he would "no longer tinker with the machinery of death."[5]

Future Directions

The growing literature on Supreme Court appointments provides a fuller understanding of the factors important in selection and confirmation, and perhaps most importantly, the explicit connection between the two stages (Scigliano 1971; Chase 1972; Schmidhauser 1979; Massaro 1990; Moraski and Shipan 1999; Nemacheck 2007). Focusing on either stage without regard to the other misunderstands the broader process. The argument that the very high rate at which the Senate confirms Supreme Court nominations evinces congressional deference to the president's constitutional appointment power misses entirely the important foundation on which administrations build during the selection stage. Due to the Senate's constitutional prerogative to advise the president and potentially consent to a nominee, presidents have an incentive to consult with members of Congress as they choose their nominees. Presidents are wise to anticipate senators' reactions to a nominee, to involve key members in discussion, and to choose candidates they believe the Senate will confirm, especially when they are less certain about the confirmation environment.

One interesting direction for future research concerns the ways candidates might try to position themselves for appointment to the Court. Given the prominence of federal court judges among those considered for the Court, scholars have begun to examine whether courts of appeals judges, aware that they may be under consideration for appointment to the Court, modify their behavior (i.e. campaign) to improve their chances of being selected (Black and Owens 2016). That work, in turn, informs research on presidents' ability to accurately gauge candidates' ideology when considering them for appointment to the Court. Campaigning federal court judges could make it more difficult for presidents to choose candidates whose sincere preferences align with the presidents' and continue to do so throughout their tenure on the Court (Epstein, Martin, Quinn, and Segal 2007; Owens and Wedeking 2012).

Notes

1. This is a gross simplification, but for the purposes of this discussion the rather crude delineation of legal formalism and legal realism is sufficient. For much more in-depth analyses of the debate between formalism and realism, see Dworkin (1977) and Posner (2008).
2. When examining representational effects in appointment to such seats, the evidence still fails to indicate a statistically significant role for a candidate's race, sex, or religion in the appointment process. However, this may well be an artifact of the small number of these seats over the Court's history (Nemacheck 2007, 2008).
3. Although Harriet Miers, who also lacked federal judicial experience, or any judicial experience for that matter, was nominated by President George W. Bush in 2005, her nomination was widely criticized and she withdrew from consideration prior to a vote on her candidacy. The criticism of Miers was largely levied at Bush for having chosen someone whom his base found lacking in conservative bona fides. Of course, experience on the federal courts of appeals would likely have led to fewer concerns both over her qualifications and her ideological preferences.
4. *Furman v. Georgia,* 408 U.S. 438 (1972) (Blackmun, J., dissenting).
5. *Callins v. Collins,* 510 U.S. 1141, 1145 (1994) (Blackmun, J., dissenting).

References

Abraham, H. J. 2007. *Justices, Presidents, and Senators: A History of the U.S. Supreme Court Appointments from Washington to Bush II.* Lanham, MD: Rowman and Littlefield.

Bailey, M. A. 2007. "Comparable Preference Estimates across Time and Institutions for the Courts, Congress, and Presidency." *American Journal of Political Science* 51(3): 433–48.

Bailey, M. A., and Change, K. 2001. "Comparing Presidents, Senators, and Justices: Institutional Preference Estimation." *Journal of Law, Economics & Organization* 17(October): 192–210.

Bailey, M. A., and Maltzman, F. 2011. *The Constrained Court: Law, Politics, and the Decisions Justices Make.* Princeton, NJ: Princeton University Press.

Barton, B. H. 2012. "An Empirical Study of Supreme Court Justice Pre-Appointment Experience." *Florida Law Review* 64: 1137–87.

Baum, L. 1998. *The Supreme Court,* 6th ed. Washington, DC: CQ Press.

Baum, L. 2012. *The Supreme Court,* 11th ed. Washington, DC: CQ Press.

Bell, L. C. 2002. *Warring Factions: Interest Groups, Money, and the New Politics of Senate Confirmation.* Columbus, OH: Ohio State University Press.

Black, R. C., and Owens, R. J. 2016. "Courting the President: How Circuit Court Judges Alter Their Behavior for Promotion to the Supreme Court." *American Journal of Political Science* 60(1): 30–43.

Boyd, C. L., Epstein, L., and Martin, A. D. 2010. "Untangling the Causal Effects of Sex on Judging." *American Journal of Political Science* 54(2): 389–411.

Bratton, K. A., and Spill, R. L. 2004. "Moving up the Judicial Ladder," *American Politics Research* 32: 198–218.

Caldeira, G. A., and Wright, J. R. 1998. "Lobbying for Justice: Organized Interests, Supreme Court Nominations, and the United States Senate." *American Journal of Political Science* 42(2): 499–523.

Cameron, C. M., Cover, A. D., and Segal, J. A. 1990. "Senate Voting on Supreme Court Nominees: A Neoinstitutional Model." *American Political Science Review* 84(2): 525–34.

Carter, S. L. 1994. *The Confirmation Mess*. New York: Basic Books.

Chang, K. H. 2001. "The President versus the Senate: Appointments in the American System of Separated Powers and the Federal Reserve." *Journal of Law, Economics & Organization* 17(2): 319–55.

Chase, H. W. 1972. *Federal Judges*. Minneapolis, MN: University of Minnesota Press.

Collins, P. M., Jr. 2008. *Friends of the Supreme Court: Interest Groups and Judicial Decision Making*. New York, NY: Oxford University Press.

Collins, P. M., Jr., and Ringhand, L. A. 2013a. *Supreme Court Confirmation Hearings and Constitutional Change*. New York, NY: Cambridge University Press.

Collins P. M., Jr., and Ringhand, L. A. 2013b. "Functioning Just Fine: The Unappreciated Value of the Supreme Court Confirmation Process." *Drake Law Review* 61(4): 1025–48.

Comiskey, M. 2004. *Seeking Justices: The Judging of Supreme Court Nominees*. Lawrence, KS: University of Kansas Press.

Danelski, D. J. 1964. *A Supreme Court Justice Is Appointed*. New York, NY: Random House.

Davis, R. 2005. *Electing Justice: Fixing the Supreme Court Nomination Process*. New York, NY: Oxford University Press.

Dworking, R. 1977. *Taking Rights Seriously*. Cambridge, MA: Harvard University Press.

Eisgruber, C. L. 2007. *The Next Justice: Repairing the Supreme Court Appointment Process*. Princeton, NJ: Princeton University Press.

Epstein, L., Knight, J., and Martin, A. D. 2003. "The Norm of Prior Judicial Experience and Its Consequences for Career Diversity on the U.S. Supreme Court." *California Law Review* 91(4): 903–66.

Epstein, L., and Kobylka, J. F. 1992. *The Supreme Court and Legal Change: Abortion and the Death Penalty*. Chapel Hill, NC: University of North Carolina Press.

Epstein, L., Landes, W. M., and Posner, R. A. 2013. *The Behavior of Federal Judges: A Theoretical and Empirical Study of Rational Choice*. Cambridge, MA: Harvard University Press.

Epstein, L., Lindstädt, R., Segal, J. A., and Westerland, C. 2006. "The Changing Dynamics of Senate Voting on Supreme Court Nominees." *Journal of Politics* 68(2): 296–307.

Epstein, L., Martin, A. D., Quinn, K. M., and Segal, J. A. 2007. "Ideological Drift among Supreme Court Justices: Who, When, and How Important?" *Northwestern Law Review* 101(4): 1483–542.

Epstein, L., Martin, A. D., and Quinn, K. M., Segal, J. A. 2009. "Circuit Effects: How the Norm of Federal Judicial Experiences Biases the Supreme Court." *University of Pennsylvania Law Review* 157: 833–80.

Epstein, L., and Segal, J. A. 2005. *Advice and Consent: The Politics of Judicial Appointments*. New York, NY: Oxford University Press.

Epstein, L., Segal, J. A., Spaeth, H. J., and Walker, T. G. 2012. *The Supreme Court Compendium*, 5th ed. Washington, DC: CQ Press.

Grossman, J. B. 1965. *Lawyers and Judges: The ABA and the Politics of Judicial Selection*. New York, NY: John Wiley and Sons.

Guliuzza, F. III, Reagan, D. J., and Barrett, D. M. 1994. "The Senate Judiciary Committee and Supreme Court Nominees: Measuring the Dynamics of Confirmation Criteria." *Journal of Politics* 56(3): 773–87.

Hammond, T. H., and Hill, J. S. 1993. "Deference or Preference? Explaining Senate Confirmation of Presidential Nominees to Administrative Agencies." *Journal of Theoretical Politics* 5(1): 23–59.

Johnson, T. R., and Roberts, J. M. 2004. "Presidential Capital and the Supreme Court Confirmation Process." *Journal of Politics* 66(3): 663–83.

Kagan, E. 1995. "Confirmation Messes Old and New," Review of Steven L. Carter's *The Confirmation Mess* (1994), *The University of Chicago Law Review* 62(2): 919–42.

Krehbiel, K. 2007. "Supreme Court Appointments as a Move-the-Median Game." *American Journal of Political Science* 51(2): 231–40.

Lindquist, S. A., Yalof, D. A., Clark, J. A. 2000. "The Impact of Presidential Appointments to the U.S. Supreme Court: Cohesive and Divisive Voting within Presidential Blocs." *Political Research Quarterly* 53(4): 795–814.

Liptak, A. 2009. "Roberts Sets off Debate on Judicial Experience." *The New York Times* February 16.

Liptak, A. 2010. "Former Justice O'Connor Sees Ill in Election Finance Ruling." *The New York Times* January 26.

Lopez, M. H. 2008. "The Hispanic Vote in the 2008 Election." *Pew Research Hispanic Trends Project*, November 5. Available at: http://www.pewhispanic.org/2008/11/05/the-hispanic-vote-in-the-2008-election/.

Lopez, M. H., and Taylor, P. 2012. "Latino Voters in the 2012 Election: Obama 71%; Romney 27%." *Pew Research Hispanic Trends Project*, November 7. Available at: http://www.pewhispanic.org/2012/11/07/latino-voters-in-the-2012-election/.

Maltese, J. A. 1995. *The Selling of Supreme Court Nominees.* Baltimore, MD: Johns Hopkins University Press.

Maltzman, F., Spriggs, J. F., II, and Wahlbeck, P. J. 2000. *Crafting Law on the Supreme Court: The Collegial Game.* New York, NY: Cambridge University Press.

Martin, A. D., and Quinn, K. P. 2002. "Dynamic Ideal Point Estimation via Markov Chain Monte Carlo for the U.S. Supreme Court, 1953–1999." *Political Analysis* 10(2): 134–53.

Massaro, J. 1990. *Supremely Political: The Role of Ideology and Presidential Management in Unsuccessful Supreme Court Nominations.* Albany, NY: State University of New York Press.

Moraski, B. J., and Shipan, C. R. 1999. "The Politics of Supreme Court Nominations: A Theory of Institutional Constraints and Choices." *American Journal of Political Science* 43(October): 1069–95.

Nemacheck, C. L. 2007. *Strategic Selection: Presidential Nomination of Supreme Court Justices from Herbert Hoover through George W. Bush.* Charlottesville, VA: University of Virginia Press.

Nemacheck, C. L. 2008. "Have Faith in Your Nominee? The Role of Candidate Religious Beliefs in Supreme Court Selection Politics." Symposium on Judicial Selection. *Drake Law Review* 56: 705–28.

Nofziger, L. 1981. Memorandum to the President, 22 June. Ronald Reagan Presidential Library, Simi Valley, CA.

O'Brien, D. M. 2014. *Storm Center: The Supreme Court in American Politics*, 10th ed. New York: W. W. Norton and Company.

Overby, L. M., Henschen, B. M., Walsh, M. H., and Strauss, J. 1992. "Courting Constituents? An Analysis of the Senate Vote on Justice Clarence Thomas." *American Political Science Review* 86(December): 997–1002.

Owens, R. J., and Wedeking, J. 2012. "Predicting Drift on Politically Insulated Institutions: A Study of Ideological Drift on the United States Supreme Court." *Journal of Politics* 74(2): 487–500.

Perry, B. A. 1991. *A "Representative" Supreme Court? The Impact of Race, Religion, and Gender on Appointments.* Westport, CT: Greenwood.

Pitkin, H. F. 1967. *The Concept of Representation.* Berkeley, CA: University of California Press.

Poole, K., and Rosenthal, H. 1991. "Patterns of Congressional Voting." *American Political Science Review* 35(February): 228–78.

Poole, K., and Rosenthal, H. 1997. *Congress: A Political-Economic History of Roll Call Voting.* Oxford: Oxford University Press.

Posner, R. A. 2008. *How Judges Think.* Cambridge, MA: Harvard University Press.

Pritchett, C. H. 1941. "Division of Opinion among Justices of the U.S. Supreme Court, 1939–1941." *American Political Science Review* 35(5): 890–8.

Pritchett, C. H. 1946. "Politics and Value Systems: The Supreme Court, 1945–1946." *Journal of Politics* 8(4): 499–515.

Pritchett, C. H. 1948. *The Roosevelt Court: A Study in Judicial Politics and Values.* New York, NY: Macmillan.

Purdum, T. S. 2005. "Presidents, Picking Justices, Can Have Backfires." *The New York Times* July 5.

Rohde, D. W., and Spaeth, H. J. 1976. *Supreme Court Decision Making.* San Francisco, CA: Freeman.

Ruckman, P. S., Jr. 1993. "The Supreme Court, Critical Nominations, and the Senate Confirmation Process." *Journal of Politics* 55(August): 793–805.

Schmidhauser, J. R. 1979. *Judges and Justices: The Federal Appellate Judiciary.* Boston, MA: Little, Brown and Company.

Schubert, G. 1965. *The Judicial Mind.* New York, NY: Free Press.

Scigliano, R. 1971. *The Supreme Court and the Presidency.* New York, NY: Free Press.

Segal, J. 1987. "Senate Confirmation of Supreme Court Justices." *Journal of Politics* 49(4): 998–1015.

Segal, J. A., Cameron, C. M., and Cover, A. D. 1992. "A Spatial Model of Roll Call Voting: Senators, Constituents, Presidents, and Interest Groups in Supreme Court Confirmation." *American Journal of Political Science* 36(1): 96–121.

Segal, J. A., and Cover, A. D. 1989. "Ideological Values and the Votes of U.S. Supreme Court Justices." *American Political Science Review* 83(2): 557–65.

Segal, J. A., and Spaeth, H. J. 2002. *The Supreme Court and the Attitudinal Model Revisited.* New York, NY: Cambridge University Press.

Segal, J. A., Timpone, H. J., and Howard, R. M. 2000. "Buyer Beware? Presidential Success through Supreme Court Appointments." *Political Research Quarterly* 53(3): 557–95.

Sheldon, C. H., and Maule, L. S. 1997. *Choosing Justice: The Recruitment of State and Federal Judges.* Pullman, WA: Washington State University Press.

Shipan, C. R. 2008. "Partisanship, Ideology, and Senate Voting on Supreme Court Nominees." *Journal of Empirical Legal Studies* 5(1): 55–76.

Shipan, C. R., Allen, B. T., and Bargen, A. 2014. "Choosing When to Choose: Explaining the Duration of Presidential Supreme Court Nomination Decisions." *Congress and the Presidency* 41(1): 1–24.

Shipan, C. R., and Shannon, M. L. 2003. "Delaying Justice(s): A Duration Analysis of Supreme Court Confirmations." *American Journal of Political Science* 47(October): 654–68.

Silverstein, M. 1994. *Judicious Choices: The New Politics of Supreme Court Confirmations.* New York, NY: W.W. Norton & Company.

Spaeth, H. J, and Segal, J. A. 1999. *Majority Rule or Minority Will: Adherence to Precedent on the U.S. Supreme Court.* New York, NY: Cambridge University Press.

Szmer, J., and Songer, D. R. 2005. "The Effects of Information on the Accuracy of Presidential Assessment of Supreme Court Nominee Preferences." *Political Research Quarterly* 58(1): 151–60.

Wahlbeck, P. J. 1997. "The Life of the Law: Judicial Politics and Legal Change." *Journal of Politics* 59(3): 778–802.

Watson, G., and Stookey, J. A. 1995. *Shaping America: The Politics of Supreme Court Appointments.* New York, NY: HarperCollins College Publishers.

Weir, J. T. 1967. "Review of *Lawyers and Judges.*" *The University of Toronto Law Journal* 17(1): 243–6.

Whittington, K. E. 2007. "Presidents, Senates, and Failed Supreme Court Nominations." *The Supreme Court Review* 10: 401–38.

Yalof, D. A. 1999. *Pursuit of Justices: Presidential Politics and the Selection of Supreme Court Nominees.* Chicago, IL: University of Chicago Press.

Yalof, D. A. 2008. "Confirmation Obfuscation: Supreme Court Confirmation Politics in a Conservative Era." *Law, Politics, and Society* 44: 141–71.

CHAPTER 3

JUDICIAL ELECTIONS

Judges and their "New-Style" Constituencies

JAMES L. GIBSON AND MICHAEL J. NELSON

THE American people love elections. Although perhaps there is a natural tendency for citizens in all democracies to believe in some form of the consent of the governed, as expressed through elections, the Americans are unusual in the degree to which they rely on elections to select an astonishing variety of public officials (Ellis 2012; Kritzer 2015). This penchant for elections extends not just to the executive and legislative branches of government, but to the judiciary as well. Today, approximately 90 percent of American judges must face the electorate in one fashion or another. Perhaps democrats worldwide favor elections, but, with only a handful of exceptions, the Americans are exceptional in holding judges accountable to the people for their actions.[1]

For most of American history, the processes of electing judges have not been interesting to scholars; the elections had few attributes of bona fide contests. Campaigning was tepid, at best, competition was often non-existent, and voter interest was practically nil. Gibson and his colleagues (2011: 545) described these elections as "decent, docile, and dirt cheap, even if drab and dull." Scholars studying elections all but ignored judicial elections.[2]

In the last few decades, however, the landscape of judicial elections has changed dramatically, with Schotland (1998: 150) now characterizing these elections as "nastier, noisier, and costlier." The descriptor "new-style" has firmly entered the lexicon among those studying judicial elections (Hojnacki and Baum 1992; Gibson 2008). Some date the onset of "new-style" elections with the decision by California voters to remove Justice Rose Bird and two of her colleagues from office via a 1986 retention election in California (e.g., Canes-Wrone, Clark, and Kelly 2014); others (e.g., Bonica and Woodruff 2012) emphasize the Supreme Court's 2002 ruling in *Republican Party of Minnesota v. White* as the starting point for this sea change in judicial elections.[3] Whatever the exact date of origin, some of the most interesting elections in the United States today pit candidates seeking judgeships against each other.

These "new-style" elections have indisputably changed the way the state courts function. In the past, judges thought little about how their judging would affect their chances of being retained or promoted, and state judgeships attracted lawyers seemingly more interested in law than in politics. In the past few decades, all that has changed (see, e.g., Hall 1987). The rules for how judicial elections are contested have changed. The political importance and salience of the state high courts has vastly increased, and other state political actors (e.g., governors and legislators) now feel more threatened by the rulings of state courts because their rulings increasingly constrain the actions of state government. Moreover, interest groups now devote a great deal more attention and effort to influencing who serves on these courts, and the mass media provides greater coverage of the rulings of these courts. To at least some degree, state courts have become nationalized, especially given the nationalization of law and processes of diffusion of legal innovations across state borders. As a result, the judges sitting on the state benches have found it necessary to think about their "constituents" in ways not true of the past. A new era in the politics of state judiciaries has unquestionably emerged.

This new era has ignited great interest among scholars in the methods by which state judges are selected and retained. No question, however, is more interesting and important than that of how state judges relate to a variety of "new-style" constituencies, many of which (e.g., interest groups) have heretofore been irrelevant.

Our purpose in this chapter is to assess what the growing body of research has discovered about how the state courts influence and are influenced by the emergence of these new constituencies. Most obviously, the role of the electorate in the selection and retention of state judges has become dramatically more influential of late. So too have interest groups, political parties, campaign contributors, and the mass media become more relevant, often in conjunction with judicial campaigns. But state courts have also become considerably more intertwined with other institutions of state government, as separation-of-powers issues become more politically relevant. Perhaps never have we witnessed the sort of inter-branch conflict that has become commonplace in many states. In the past, state courts were independent because they were able to act with few constraints from their constituents. Today, state courts are entangled with a largely new constellation of institutions and actors. Ours is not a comprehensive review of all aspects of judicial elections.[4] Instead, we focus on these new interconnections and constraints associated with the new-style constituencies.

The Electorate and Public Opinion

The most "new-style" attribute of state judicial elections is that they have come to resemble true elections. As Bonneau and Hall (2009) have so amply demonstrated, judicial elections today attract large percentages of voters, who seem as well informed as possible given institutional constraints, who are often presented with policy-relevant campaigns, and whose actions affect the behaviors of judges. Much of this research focuses on state high courts.[5,6] Hall (1987, 1992) was the first to systematically investigate the responsiveness of state supreme court justices to public opinion, studying state judicial decision-making in capital punishment cases. In an early study, Hall (1987) interviewed justices of the Louisiana Supreme Court and analyzed their votes, finding empirical evidence that justices who perceive their views to be incongruent with the public's or who find themselves in the minority on salient issues may suppress their dissent in order to avoid providing an eventual challenger a potent campaign issue. Hall (1992), studying death-penalty decisions in four state supreme courts, found that "constituency influence in state supreme courts is enhanced by competitive electoral conditions and experience with electoral politics" (p. 427, see also Hall 1995; Brace and Hall 1990, 1997).

Brace and Boyea (2008) contributed to this literature as well, finding that public opinion and judicial voting patterns on death-penalty cases co-varied. In particular, they find that elected, but not appointed, judges are directly affected by constituency opinion. While some studies (e.g., Bruhl and Leib 2012; Shepherd 2009) suggest that partisan elections seem to produce the highest levels of judicial responsiveness, the most thorough treatment of this issue comes in a series of studies by Canes-Wrone, Clark, and their colleagues. Canes-Wrone, Clark, and Kelly (2014) have investigated the effects of selection/retention systems in the most detail, focusing in particular on non-partisan selection methods and death-penalty decisions by state supreme courts. Following up on the finding that non-partisan and retention elections seem to be connected to heightened judicial responsiveness on setting public policy on abortion rights (Caldarone, Canes-Wrone, and Clark 2009; Canes-Wrone, Clark, and Park 2012), Canes-Wrone, Clark, and Kelly conclude that the information deficit created by non-partisan elections heightens the effects of highly salient death-penalty decisions, and consequently that, in this policy domain, non-partisan selection/retention systems maximize responsiveness to public opinion. Thus, perhaps not unconditionally, the elective state judiciaries seem, to at least some degree, to represent the preferences of their constituents.

In addition to this work on the decision-making of state supreme courts, research on the responsiveness of state trial courts has generated some provocative and controversial findings. In a paper published in 2004, Huber and Gordon continued a line of inquiry focusing on the responsiveness of trial judges to their constituents' preferences.[7] They discovered that the sentences of Pennsylvania trial judges—who are subject to retention elections after an initial partisan election—became more severe as the retention elections approached. Indeed, they claimed that the electoral dynamic "added" approximately two thousand additional years of prison time for the guilty defendants.[8]

This finding has been partially reproduced with Kansas judges (Gordon and Huber 2007). Kansas allows its counties to decide how to select and retain their judges. In counties using partisan elections, this election-cycle effect was present; in counties using retention elections, it was not observed. In an analysis of Washington state trial judges, Berdejó and Yuchtman (2013) report a finding similar to Pennsylvania: the judges—selected and retained via non-partisan elections—seemed to alter their sentences for the most serious crimes as the election season approached.[9] Following up on the research of Kuklinski and Stanga (1979), Nelson (2014) discovered that Colorado judges became more responsive to their constituents' preferences on the legalization of marijuana after a referendum made those preferences clear.

This variation is not unique to elected judges in the states; career concerns similarly affect federal judges. Black and Owens (2016) find that, during periods of a Supreme Court vacancy, individuals likely to be nominated to fill the vacancy are more likely to vote in accordance with presidential preferences. Similarly, Epstein, Landes, and Posner (2013) demonstrate that U.S. Courts of Appeals judges with viable chances to be nominated to the Supreme Court vote more punitively in death-penalty cases. District court judges seeking to become appeals court judges may exhibit similar behavior. Furthermore, Epstein, Landes, and Posner (2013) find that harsh sentencers are more likely to be promoted. Thus, it seems apparent that variation in sentencing that corresponds with career concerns is not an issue specific to judicial elections; rather, career concerns affect judges of all stripes, irrespective of the method of selection/retention.

Beyond their specific empirical findings of changes in sentencing, most of these authors seem to assume a decision-making process of which they disapprove. The logic goes as follows. (1) The American people favor their judges imposing punitive sentences.[10] (2) Judges believe that sentences should be less severe. (3) But the fear of being turned out of office causes judges to alter their behavior during the period when they under greatest scrutiny—as the election approaches. (4) To please the voters, judges penalize those convicted of crimes.

Most authors assume (or imply)[11] that a shift toward harsher sentencing decisions made in proximity to an election are "improper," and, conversely, that decisions made outside the electoral period, however defined, are "proper". Of course, "proper" and "improper" are normative judgments and are not empirical findings. All the data show is that the behavior differs at different points in time.

Are there legitimate reasons why a judge might vary her or his sentences over time and across cases? For example, should judges use individual defendants (e.g., Martha Stewart) to make an example so as to try to deter others who might commit the same crime (e.g., inside traders) in the future? Should judges ignore public opinion completely, as in maintaining the same rates of incarceration for draft evaders when a war is popular as compared to when it is wildly unpopular (e.g., Cook 1977; Kritzer 1979)? Is it appropriate for judges who ride circuits to take into account variability in the degree of affront a particular crime might represent to local community values (e.g., drugs, pornography)[12] when issuing a sentence (Gibson 1980)? When public opinion changes over time (e.g., family law and the rights of gays), should judges evoke doctrines of equity to change their decisions to recognize changing social values and mores (Jacob 1988)? For that matter, should defendants who plead guilty get lighter sentences than defendants who plead innocent but who are convicted at trial, even though the conviction is on the very same charge? Should judges seek guidance from the preferences of voters in a marijuana referendum when considering how severely to sentence those convicted of marijuana crimes (Kuklinski and Stanga 1979; Nelson 2014)? It is actually not at all difficult to continue to imagine circumstances when (a) deviation from equal treatment is acceptable if not desirable,[13] and (b) the exercise of judicial discretion appropriately takes into account the general preferences of the constituents.

At least some of the critics' concerns about variation in sentences across a judge's electoral cycle have to do with worries about equal treatment and justice. These worries, in turn, are grounded in larger normative understandings of justice and the rule of law. Is a just decision one that treats equally situated defendants equally, or is a just decision one that takes into account a variety of defendant-specific circumstances? In thinking about the rule of law, this debate is typically framed as one between "particularism" and "universalism" (e.g., Gibson 2007). Many critics seem to ignore the justice associated with particularism, claiming instead that equal treatment is the only appropriate criterion.

Variation in the law should not be surprising. After all, in a federal system like the United States, there exists no guarantee that the law will be the same, or even will be enforced the same,[14] across jurisdictions. For example, in some states, citizens have ready access to class-action lawsuits, while in other states, practically no reasonable access exists. The existence of a well-established federal system in the United States renders many equal protection claims impotent from a legal point of view (and perhaps from a normative one as well).

Aside from cross-jurisdiction variability in the law, a more serious question these studies raise has to do with within-jurisdiction variability. To our knowledge, being sentenced by a "hanging judge" instead of a "bleeding heart judge" is not grounds for an equal protection claim in any jurisdiction (absent any abuse of discretion on the judge's part). Despite the fact that we know that Democratic and Republican judges differ markedly in their decisions (Epstein, Landes, and Posner 2013), Democratic defendants have no equal protection right to be tried before a Democratic judge. Women have no right to be tried or sentenced by female judges. Even the concept of a jury of one's peers refers to the outputs of the mechanisms by which juries in the aggregate are selected, not the individual jury one draws in one's own case. Getting strictly equal sentences is not a defendants' right recognized in any legal jurisdiction in the United States.

Having discussed why judges' sentences may vary across cases and over time, let us return to the specific findings of Gordon and Huber on the electoral cycle. In doing so, we will navigate a different route on both the Gordon and Huber and Berdejó and Yuchtman findings.

For simplicity, let us assume two periods of decision-making—a period under external scrutiny (the election period) and a period not under external scrutiny (the non-election period).[15] Assume that prosecutors are motivated by producing as high a "conviction rate" as possible, defense attorneys (and defendants) primarily want the lightest possible sentence, and judges shoot for a record of not ever being overturned on appeal. All of these motivations fuel the plea bargaining process.

Plea bargaining is a messy process. Crimes typically are associated with a "going rate," around which increments and decrements are sought. An important goal of the process is conflict minimization and maintenance of the relationships among the repeat players—the courtroom workgroup. Under these circumstances, the average sentence for a second conviction on burglary might be a very far cry indeed from the maximum sentence for the crime provided by the state legislature.

Assume these authors are correct about temporal variability in sentencing. Could it not be that the sentences issued under periods without scrutiny are sentences that primarily serve the interests of the courtroom workgroup, and that those sentences are "too low" (whatever that means)? When under scrutiny, the actors in the workgroup are compelled to consider societal interests more strongly, and therefore cannot "give away the store" just to secure a guilty plea from a defendant. To treat sentences in the non-electoral period as somehow more "correct" does not at all fit with the reality of plea bargaining in American criminal courts. If the workgroup is simply negotiating self-serving sentences in the non-election period, then the scrutiny that comes during the electoral period may actually be desirable from the point of view of the public good. Regardless, future work is essential to determine conclusively whether the more punitive sentences issued near election time result from a judge "overpunishing" to burnish her credentials to her constituents or from a judge "underpunishing" during the rest of the electoral cycle in order to further the interests of the courtroom work group.

The most general conclusion to emerge from research on constituency influence on courts is that the nature of the selection/retention mechanisms influences the degree of judicial responsiveness to public preferences. Whether this is desirable or undesirable, this chapter cannot judge.

Legislatures, Governors, and Bureaucrats

Though the majority of state supreme court judges keep their seat on the bench through elections, most state supreme court judges reach the bench *through appointment* (Reddick, Nelson, and Caufield 2009).[16] All judges, regardless of how they are selected and retained, have an interest in ensuring compliance with their decision, and the state legislature, the governor, and the state bureaucracy are key implementing populations for many judicial opinions.[17] Thus, though only a minority of state supreme court judges owe their continued service on the bench to the governor or the legislature, all judges have an interest in considering the reactions of other branches of government in order to ensure acceptance and eventual implementation of their decisions.[18]

As discussed above, the use of judicial elections as a retention mechanism affects judicial decision-making by increasing the effect of public opinion in a judge's decision-making calculus. Judges who face reappointment feel a similar pressure, though reappointment creates a linkage between judges and the other branches of state government, and not necessarily to the mass public. To this end, Shepherd (2009) finds that judges who face reappointment by the legislature or the governor, rather than to voters, are more likely to vote in favor of governmental litigants when they come before the Court.

Importantly, this effect increases as a judge's reappointment date approaches and dissipates in a judge's last term before mandatory retirement, providing particularly stark evidence that this effect is driven by their desire to decide cases in a way that maximizes their chance at reappointment.[19]

Perhaps the most direct conflict between the decisions of state supreme courts and the other branches of government comes when the judiciary exercises its power of judicial review over laws duly enacted by the legislature and governor. Support for the claim that appointed judges are more likely to defer to state legislatures comes from Shugerman's (2010, 2012) careful analysis of the adoption of judicial elections in the United States. Briefly, Shugerman shows that, in the mid-1800s, state legislatures were recklessly overspending their states' funds. At this point in time, legislatures also appointed and reappointed judges, and, because they relied on the legislature for their continued tenure on the bench, judges were reluctant to use their power of judicial review to curb this legislative overspending. To remedy this problem, states adopted judicial elections as institutions of judicial selection and retention, thereby increasing judges' independence from the legislative branch of government and emboldening them to check the legislative branch. In response to this increased independence, Shugerman shows, the use of judicial review by state supreme courts increased markedly.

The most comprehensive study of judicial review in state supreme courts comes from Langer's (2002) examination of judicial behavior in four issue areas: election law, workers' compensation, unemployment compensation, and welfare legislation. Langer's results indicate that, conditional on the salience of the issue area, judicial retention institutions affect both judges' decision to docket a case and their eventual vote on the merits. In particular, Langer finds that judges who face reappointment are less likely to docket cases in highly salient issue areas (which, in Langer's study, are election law and workers' compensation cases), but the effects of judicial selection methods are unclear for less salient issues. Likewise, Langer finds that, when elected and appointed judges behave differently, as they often do in salient issue areas, judges who face re-election are more likely than judges who face reappointment to vote to find a law unconstitutional.

Other work has corroborated this finding. Graves and Teske (2003), studying judicial review of administrative regulations, present similar findings: judges who face reappointment are less likely to overturn state regulatory actions than judges who face uncontestable retention elections. Likewise, Lindquist (2013) finds that judges who face nonpartisan or partisan elections are more likely to invalidate legislative enactments than judges who rely upon retention or reappointment to keep their jobs.

As this short review demonstrates, this area is ripe for future investigation. Much has been made of the effects of prior experiences of U.S. Supreme Court judges, particularly their professional background and prior occupational experience (Epstein, Martin, Quinn, and Segal 2009), yet we know little about how state judges' prior political experience affects both their ability to obtain a seat on a state supreme court and their eventual behavior once they reach the bench. Likewise, our understanding of the strategic environment at the state level is incomplete. Clark (2011), for example, shows that legislative threats against the U.S. Supreme Court make it less likely to exercise its power of judicial review. Though state judges are increasingly threatened with impeachment for unpopular decisions (Raftery 2011), we know little about how the decisions of state supreme courts are affected by these threats. It seems clear, however, that abolishing judicial elections would not necessarily increase judicial independence.

Interest Groups as Constituents

Perhaps one of the biggest changes in judicial elections over the past two decades has been the explosion of participation by interest groups in these elections. Whereas interest group involvement in judicial campaigns in the mid-1900s was mainly limited to unions and trial attorney groups, interest groups across the spectrum of American politics have now become key players in judicial campaigns (Shugerman 2012). In recent times, interest group participation in state supreme court elections has become commonplace, with these groups' efforts becoming both "more visible and very likely more influential" (Goldberg 2007: 91).

Before the 1980s, interest groups, particularly those affiliated with business, had devoted their energies on campaigns to change state methods of judicial selection and retention; but, as the twentieth century drew to a close, "businesses returned to trying to win judicial elections outright, and they did so by ... pouring money into key races" (Shugerman 2012: 241). Although left-leaning groups have remained active in judicial campaigns (Hojnacki and Baum 1992), attention has largely shifted toward a focus on the actions of right-leaning groups. This shift happened, in large part, because key Republican Party strategists began to devote their energies toward building Republican majorities on state supreme courts. Karl Rove, for example, harnessed unpopular anti-business and pro-plaintiff rulings by state high courts to engineer successful judicial campaigns in key southern states, like Alabama and Texas, that flipped the high courts in these two states from Democratic to Republican control (Shugerman 2012).

Legally, the landscape of judicial elections has been altered by changes in election law brought about by the U.S. Supreme Court. Most notably, in 2002, the U.S. Supreme Court ruled in *Republican Party of Minnesota v. White*—a case concerning the constitutionality of the American Bar Association's code of judicial ethics, adopted in various forms by many states, including Minnesota, that judicial candidates cannot be prohibited from providing voters with information on their issue positions, even when those issue positions were likely to come before the Court. Various interest groups and scholars (e.g., American Bar Association Commission on the 21st Century Judiciary 2003; Caufield 2005, 2007) have argued that the *White* decision had injurious effects on the judiciary. While the data necessary to test this assertion directly do not exist, Bonneau, Hall, and Streb (2011) examine changes in judicial elections pre- and post-*White* on a variety of metrics, such as incumbent vote shares, the costs of campaigns, and voter participation. Their analysis reveals no significant changes in state supreme court or intermediate appellate court races on any of these measures before and after *White*.

Moreover, Gibson (2012) reports that large proportions of voters want to know the policy positions of candidates for judicial office. If more information on candidates' policy positions assists voters as they make their decisions at the polls as much as research on vote choice (e.g. Delli Carpini and Keeter 2004) generally has shown, then liberalized speech codes, like those allowed by *White*, may aid voters seeking to make informed choices on election day. Perhaps as significant, policy talk is quite unlikely to have any legitimacy-threatening consequences for the state courts (Gibson 2012).

We note, however, that Bonneau, Hall, and Streb's (2011) analysis only examines aggregate changes in elections before and after 2002, the year that the U.S. Supreme Court decided *White*. Not all states had adopted the portion of the canon of ethics in question when the Court decided *White*, so not every state was directly affected by the *White* ruling (Caufield 2007). Studies that have examined the effects of the presence or absence of particular canons of ethics have found that the presence of these canons do shape judicial races. Peters (2009) finds that the presence of ethical prohibitions on candidate actions tends to make individuals less likely to challenge incumbents and that a prohibition on the ability of candidates to make pledges or promises to voters reduces incumbent vote shares. Likewise, Hall and Bonneau (2013) find that restrictive speech codes tend to make voters less likely to participate in judicial election: perhaps, again, because voters want to know the policy positions of judicial candidates in order to make reasonable decisions about for whom to vote. Bonica and Woodruff (2012), also examining the effects of *White*, find that the decision made it more difficult for ideologically extreme candidates to hide their true policy preferences from constituents. In short, the extant literature strongly suggests that reducing restrictions on candidate speech serves to assist voters, embolden challengers, and improve the quality of judicial elections.

These legal developments have been brought about by interest groups' attempts to shape the rules by which elections are fought. For instance, Jim Bopp, representing The Family Trust Foundation, has been at the forefront of efforts to allow judges to state their policy preferences during campaigns. The Family Trust Foundation sued to overturn Canon 5B(1)(c) of Kentucky's Code of Judicial Conduct after failing in its effort to survey all candidates for judicial office in Kentucky in 2004 on a variety of contentious legal issues. The foundation succeeded in getting the Canon declared to be in violation of the First Amendment to the U.S. Constitution (*Family Trust Foundation of Kentucky v. Wolnitzek*, 345 F. Supp. 2d 672 (E.D. Ky. 2004)).[20] Bopp then successfully argued *Republican Party of Minnesota v. White* before the U.S. Supreme Court. Thus, interest groups are supporting candidates in elections, but they are also actively seeking to shape electoral rules.

Research on judicial elections is clear that the costs of campaigns have dramatically increased over the past two decades. Bonneau and Hall (2009) report, for example, that the average cost of a partisan judicial election more than doubled, accounting for inflation, between 1990 and 2004; the average campaign cost \$404,937 in 1990 and \$1,097,978 in 2004. The trend is the same, though moderated, in nonpartisan elections, with the average 1990 race costing \$303,464 and the average 2004 race costing \$452,575 (p. 52). Importantly, not all spending in judicial campaigns comes directly through the candidates; interest groups often make substantial independent expenditures, and these independent expenditures are increasing.[21] Kritzer (2015) notes that approximately 30 percent of campaign expenditures in state supreme court campaigns in 2009–10 were independent expenditures not funneled through candidates' official campaigns.

How do increasingly expensive judicial campaigns effect judicial politics? One vitally important, but extraordinarily difficult to answer, question involves the extent to which judges' decisions are affected by campaign contributions. The issue is a tricky one for scholars, as it is difficult to ferret out a causal effect of receiving a campaign contribution on a judge's vote from the fact that savvy donors may choose to give funds to judges who are already predisposed to support the donor's position. Some studies have found a correlation between decisions and dollars. Across a range of cases, Shepard and Kang (2011) find a positive relationship between campaign contributions from business groups and elected judges' votes for businesses, although, as we have noted, the specific causal structure of this relationship is highly ambiguous. The clearest evidence on this point comes from Hazelton, Montgomery, and Nyhan (2014), who rely on North Carolina's implementation of a voluntary public financing system to compare judges funded by campaign contributions to those who took public financing and were thus not tied to individual donors. They find some suggestive evidence that public financing makes elected judges less responsive to donors' desires. Whether this finding is generalizable to all state courts is at present unclear, especially in light of the widespread lack of enthusiasm in the states for public financing of judicial campaigns.

Moreover, contributions from these groups (as well as from individual donors) have played an important mobilizing role. Bonneau and Hall (2009) write that "money is a necessary condition for educating and mobilizing voters and for publicizing the candidacies of challengers" (p. 133). To this end, Bonneau and Hall (2009) report that, as more money is spent in a judicial election, citizen participation in these contests increases, as measured by the rate of ballot roll-off.

Of course, aside from any mobilizing effect it might have, campaign funds are primarily useful when they are spent, and a primary expenditure of modern state supreme court campaigns is television advertising; Kritzer (2015) notes that, until recently, television advertising constituted about 50 percent of the total amount of money raised by campaigns until the 2011–12 election cycle, when (due to independent expenditures by interest groups), the total amount of money spent on campaign advertising was more than the total amount of money contributed to candidate campaigns. In this cycle, outside groups, including political parties, sponsored 60 percent of the cost of television advertising. Television advertising in judicial campaigns has exploded since the year 2000, with over sixty thousand television advertisements aired during the 2011–12 election cycle (Kritzer 2015). Still, as Hall (2014) notes, television advertising—let alone attack advertising—is absent in a large proportion of contested state supreme court elections.

Importantly, these television advertisements play a significant important role in shaping citizen participation in state supreme court elections. In their analysis of state supreme court elections held between 2002 and 2006, Hall and Bonneau (2013) find that campaign advertisements tend to mobilize voters, making them more likely to participate in judicial elections. Likewise, examining the electoral fates of candidates, Hall (2014) finds that attack advertising does not reduce incumbent vote shares in partisan elections, but that incumbent vote shares are reduced in the presence of attack advertising if their party affiliation is not listed on the ballot. This is another piece of empirical evidence that nonpartisan election formats impede the electoral process. As Hall aptly put it (2014): "Nonpartisan elections are influenced to a greater extent by hard-fought campaigns not because judicial elections are intrinsically different but because nonpartisan elections alter some of the most fundamental rules governing the conduct of these races" (p. 6).

Aside from their consequences for who participates in judicial elections, judicial elections have vital effects on the esteem in which the public holds the courts. Gibson (2012) shows in Kentucky and Gibson et al. (2011) show in Pennsylvania that judicial elections seem to have legitimacy-boosting effects on the courts' constituents. That is, from before the election to after it, citizens in these states increased the legitimacy they accorded their state high court. This is most likely due to the fact that most Americans want some degree of direct accountability from their judges. When they are reminded that their judges are elected, as they are during the election season, their regard for the institution increases.[22]

It is certainly true that some campaign activities can "cross the line," having detrimental effects on judicial legitimacy (Gibson 2012). This happens when courts and judges are portrayed as ordinary politicians, as in the legislators and legislatures that attract the disdain of their constituents (e.g., Hibbing and Theiss-Morse 1995). Indeed, Gibson and Caldeira (2009) have shown that the campaigns for and against the confirmation of Samuel Alito to a seat on the U.S. Supreme Court harmed the institutional legitimacy of the Court. Certain campaign activities—especially campaign contributions that imply that candidates are being "bought" by interest groups—are thought despicable by the American people, and these campaign activities harm *both* judicial and legislative institutions (Gibson 2012).[23]

However, the crucial finding of the Kentucky and Pennsylvania research is that the *net effect* of judicial elections is positive. That is, the positive lift to judicial legitimacy that comes from electing judges outweighs the negative knock from churlish campaign activities. When the good of elections (from the viewpoint of enhancing judicial legitimacy) is balanced against the bad, the result is still positive. It is unclear whether every type of system for selecting and retaining judges has this effect—we would be surprised if retention elections, in which voters do not have the opportunity to select among candidates, have this legitimacy-reinforcing effect. And, of course, the type of election structures some aspects of campaigning, meaning that the quantity of detrimental campaign activity may vary by method of selection (although Kentucky uses nonpartisan elections, and the Pennsylvania election studied by Gibson et al. was a partisan one). If there a difference across selection systems, it most likely has to do with the degree of experience citizens have accumulated with politicized campaigns (Gibson 2009).

Information and Judicial Accountability

Emerging from the research on these constituencies—particularly with respect to interest groups and the mass public—is a clear concern with political communication. Constituents must rely upon elite competition (i.e., elections) to learn about the behavior of their judges. When elites are not in competitive mode, information is difficult to come by. This information deficit can be overcome when cases become salient (e.g., Cann and Wilhelm 2011), but salient cases are uncommon, unrepresentative, and perhaps not even especially important. Nelson concludes from his study of Colorado judges' responses to a marijuana referendum (2014: 140): "These results suggest that access to information is a crucial precursor to judges' abilities to respond to public opinion. If one wishes one's judges to be more responsive to public opinion, these results would suggest that one seek to develop new ways for judges to learn about public preferences." At present, citizens' ability to monitor the behavior of their judges is not great, although it seems to be increasing as a result of scholarly studies and greater willingness of state administrative agencies to make performance data available.

It may also be that different methods of selection and retention stimulate different information streams that affect the criteria upon which voters make their decisions about who should serve as judges. Indeed, as Bonneau and Hall (2009) have argued, partisan elections are more likely to generate competition, that competition is enhanced by candidate and interest group spending, and, consequently, that partisan elections provide the greatest amount of information to voters and consequently may be the most rational form of election.[24]

At the very least, voters want to know the party associations of candidates for judicial office (e.g., Iyengar 2002; Klein and Baum 2001), and in the absence of that information, they seek other rational ways of making their decision on which candidate to support. This opens the door to influence from interest groups (e.g., Baum 2003), but also to a heightened effect of a small number of highly salient decisions (typically in criminal justice, as in the claim that "the judge let the rapist go free due to legal technicalities").

Indeed, while Cann and Wilhelm (2011) emphasize case salience as a key mechanism of judicial accountability, they also found that the method of judicial retention strongly affected the strength of the electoral connection between state supreme court judges' voting behavior and the general preferences of their constituents. Judges who must face contestable elections are more responsive to public opinion in their states. Similarly, Bonica and Woodruff (2012) find that partisan selection systems are more likely to select judges who are ideologically congruent with the other political actors in the state. Judges elected by nonpartisan elections are decidedly less representative than those selected by partisan systems.

These studies are consistent with the view that, when deprived of partisan labels, voters are less able to match their policy and ideological preferences to the list of candidates for judgeships (Canes-Wrone and Shotts 2007), which may increase the influence of interest groups (e.g., Baum 2003). To this end, the impact of *Republican Party of Minnesota v. White* (2002) (and the accompanying changes in state judicial speech codes) seems to be significant. Regardless of whether *White* caused an increase in campaign dynamics, the post-*White* era is indisputably one where television advertising—a medium in which voters have access to high-quality information about candidate's positions—has increased. Indeed, with campaign advertising becoming more common, judicial races becoming salient enough to garner significant media coverage, and candidates becoming more likely to share their policy views openly to voters, the inescapable conclusion seems to be that "new-style" judicial elections have done much to ameliorate the information deficit in state judicial elections.

The Importance of Judicial Legitimacy

As we have just noted, the net effect of electing judges seems to be positive from the standpoint of the legitimacy of state courts. However, the evidence of this effect is limited to studies of only two states (although we recognize that Gibson (2012) replicated some but not all of his findings using nationally representative survey data). It is therefore useful to consider broader (but perhaps less valid) evidence of the legitimacy of state high courts, and to speculate a bit about the consequences of that legitimacy.

In 2001, the group Justice at Stake Campaign conducted a national survey on public attitudes toward the state and local courts (for earlier analyses of these data, see Cann and Yates 2008). One of the questions they asked their respondents is: "How much trust and confidence do you have in courts and judges in your state?" Responses were collected on a four-point scale that varied from "nothing at all" to "a great deal." The data reveal that most Americans think quite highly of their state courts, with 25 percent asserting a great deal of trust and confidence and another 53 percent expressing some confidence, for a total of 78 percent asserting at least some confidence in the institutions.

All fifty states are included in the Justice at Stake data set, although many states are represented by a tiny number of respondents. The average number of interviews per state is 19.3 (with a standard deviation of 18.1), with the number ranging from 1 to 84. A total of sixteen states had fewer than 10 respondents in the sample. Of the states with 10 or more respondents, the average percentage of citizens expressing at least some confidence in their state judiciary is 78.4. Figure 3.1 reports the distribution across these states.

The first conclusion from this Figure is that *not* a great deal of variability in court confidence exists across the states. Moreover, in every state, a majority of the respondents express confidence in their state courts, and in most states the majority is a quite sizable one. Although this survey question is not a very good indicator of the legitimacy of the state courts in the United States (it is probably a better indicator of performance

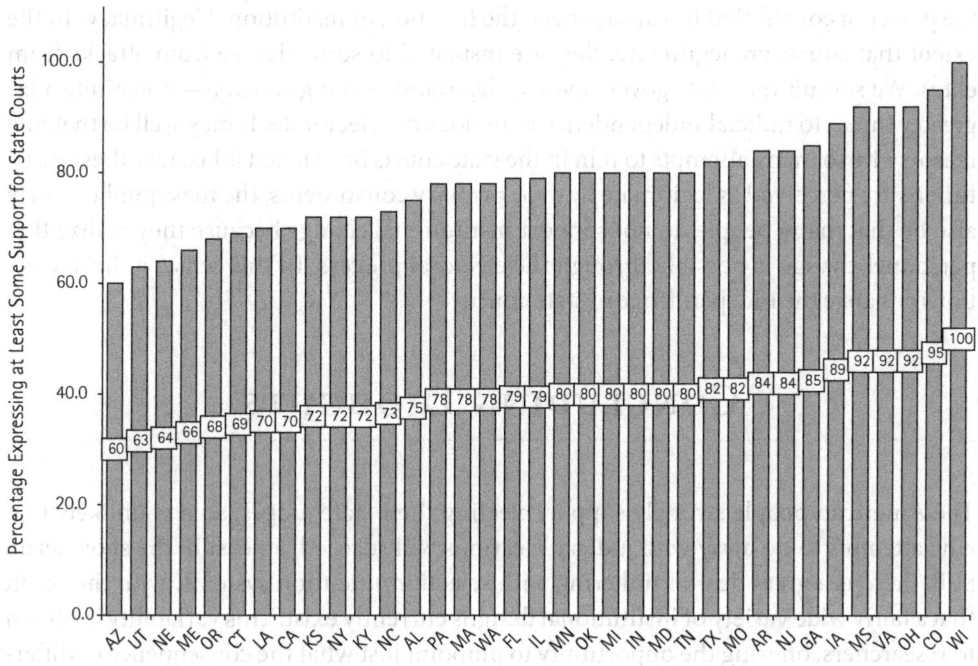

FIGURE 3.1 Confidence in state courts, by state

Source: Justice at Stake Campaign Survey, 2001.

satisfaction), it does at least suggest that these courts enjoy considerable support from their constituents (see also Benesh 2006).

This survey evidence may go some distance toward explaining how the state courts are able to fend off attacks on their basic structure and functions. These days, state legislatures are awash with proposed legislation attacking the state courts, ranging from bills that would prohibit the courts from citing foreign precedents to efforts to alter the fundamental structure of the judiciary (just as is also true of the U.S. Congress and the federal judiciary—see Clark 2011). Although research on this point is scant (but see Leonard 2014), it seems that many of these institutional attacks fail (just as FDR's attack on the U.S. Supreme Court in 1936–7 failed; see Caldeira 1987). It may well be that the legitimacy these courts derive from judicial elections actually strengthens the institutions, making them more resilient to the most powerful constraints on judicial independence, the state governments—a point which Shugerman (2012) notes was the reason that states started adopting judicial elections in the first place. It is useful to explore the logic of these relationships just a bit further.

There can be no doubt that judicial elections have made state judges more accountable for their decisions, and this fact is decried by many legal interest groups. But just as judicial elections were implemented in the nineteenth century as a means of *enhancing* judicial independence (e.g., Shugerman 2010, 2012), that may still be the role that these elections play today.[25] The support of their constituents—the mass public—enhances the power of courts; that has always been the function of institutional legitimacy. To the extent that courts are legitimate, they are insulated to some degree from attacks from elites. We submit that state governments—legislatures and governors—constitute a far greater threat to judicial independence than does the electorate. It may well be that one reason why so many attempts to rein in the state courts have failed is because these institutions are perceived as legitimate by their primary constituents, the mass public. It may also be that many people do not support institutional change because they realize that personnel change is possible through the electoral process. In this sense, judicial elections enhance the independence of state courts.

Concluding Thoughts

The American people strongly support electing their state judges, so it is unlikely that elite attempts to do away with judicial elections will succeed, at least in the short term. Still, there is a great deal of tinkering with selection/retention systems, with the result that a fairly wide variety of institutional designs currently exist. This variability is a boon to researchers, offering the opportunity to pinpoint just what the consequence of different selection/retention systems are. This research is just beginning, but it is beginning in earnest (as documented by the recent publication of three major books on state judicial elections: Bonneau and Cann 2015; Hall 2014; and Kritzer 2015).

Our most minimalist conclusion from the current research is that judicial independence in these courts has been significantly constrained. Much of the scholarship focuses on the role of the electorate, but substantial constraints from the other institutions of state governments exist, and the mass media and interest groups scrutinize state courts far more than in the past. The important issue no longer seems to be "whether state courts should be independent," but is instead "to whom should these courts be accountable." These "new-style constituencies" are undoubtedly changing the ways state courts function, although not always in entirely predictable ways. Whether these changes are desirable or not reflects observers' ideological positions, especially the relative weight they assign to the two halves of the democratic equation: majority rule and minority rights.

The larger question raised by all of this research is a normative one: to what extent are judicial elections "good" or "bad"? There are clear costs and benefits to any institutional design, and judicial elections are no exception. The simplistic dismissal of judicial elections because they seem to determine outcomes in some types of cases, without consideration of the benefits of such elections, is just as inappropriate as touting the legitimacy-enhancing power of elections without considering whether some litigant classes bear significant costs. Clearly, every selection/retention system generates benefits for some and costs for others. Research indicates that judicial elections provide some real benefits, including increased legitimacy of the state judicial branch and increased information about that branch of government among the public. On the other hand, the burgeoning literature on the effects of campaign contributions and spending on judicial decision-making and the survey evidence indicating that judicial campaign conduct can be harmful to courts suggests that judicial elections can impose real costs on litigants in some types of lawsuits. As with any normative question, individuals will choose to weigh the costs and benefits, and normative judgments about the wisdom of institutional design hinge on the weight to which individuals ascribe these costs and benefits. In the end, whether one prefers or opposes judicial elections ought to be determined by the *net* benefits or costs of such systems, instead of considering the costs or benefits in isolation from one another.

Notes

1. Bolivia became the first country in the modern era to popularly elect their national-level judges in 2011, though the French also elected their judges from 1790–9 and several Latin American countries used popular elections in the 1820s (Driscoll and Nelson 2013, 2015). The Japanese use uncontestable retention elections to retain their Supreme Court, and a handful of other local jurisdictions use elections to elect local judges (Driscoll and Nelson 2012).
2. The works of Dubois (e.g., 1980) and Watson and Downing (e.g., 1969) are notable exceptions.
3. Schotland (2011: 119) argues that "new-style" legal elections actually began in Los Angeles in 1978 when deputy district attorneys organized to try to defeat an incumbent trial court judge.
4. See Bonneau (2012) for a concise and insightful overview of recent empirical findings. For a masterful documentation of how judicial elections have changed in the U.S. over the last several decades, see Kritzer (2015).
5. For studies of elections to lower state courts, see Nelson (2011) and Streb and Frederick (2009).
6. States vary in the terminology they use to describe their high courts. The New York Supreme Court, for example, is a trial (rather than appellate) court. We use the terms "state supreme court" and "state court of last resort" interchangeably in this chapter to refer to the court in each state with the final say over state constitutional law.
7. Research on this specific question dates at least as far back as Kuklinski and Stanga (1977) and Gibson (1980).
8. Studying analogous behavior in civil cases, Tabarrok and Helland (1999) demonstrate that elected judges redistribute dollars to their constituents by ruling against out-of-state defendants in tort suits brought by in-state plaintiffs.
9. They also found that the judges did not alter their sentencing behavior for the more numerous less-serious crimes.
10. Because they do not have direct measures of constituents' preferences, these authors must assume that public preferences for punitiveness are uniform in all judicial districts. Nelson (2014), using votes on an initiative to legalize marijuana, shows that, at least in Colorado, an assumption of cross-district uniformity is not valid.

11. There is still some use of the term "pandering" to refer to representative linkages (e.g., Canes-Wrone, Clark, and Kelly 2014: 25), although the usage of the term seems to be on the decline. Huber and Gordon (2004: 248) use the term "whims of public opinion."
12. Obviously, any "community standards" criterion for pornography explicitly admits of cross-community variation in the severity of the offense, as determined by local public opinion.
13. Berdejó and Yuchtman (2013) summarize their findings as indicating that: "essentially the same defendant (based on observable characteristics), having committed the same crime, facing the same judge, with his case ending in the same sentencing guidelines cell, receives a significantly longer prison sentence if he is sentenced at the end of the judge's political cycle rather than the beginning" (pp. 749–50). Of course, without changing their empirical evidence, their summary could be modified to say "… receives a significantly shorter prison sentence if he is sentenced during a period in which the judge's constituents have little or no information about the judge's sentencing behavior."
14. The amount of discretion granted to judges in deciding what sentence to impose pales in comparison to the unfettered statutory discretion given to prosecutors when it comes to the decision to charge or not charge for a criminal offense. Dyke (2007) found that district attorneys prosecute more cases during their election years. Nelson's (2014) analysis of prosecutorial dismissal decisions suggests the same finding.
15. What we mean by "external" is that in the period not under scrutiny, the courtroom workgroup (the prosecutor, the defense attorney, and the judge) is able to implement its preferences without the constraint of any external visibility or review.
16. This occurs because vacancies in elective states often, due to retirement, resignation, or death, happen in the middle of a term; states typically fill these vacancies through some sort of legislative or gubernatorial appointment (Holmes and Emrey 2006).
17. State courts often face vocal threats of noncompliance from other branches of government and legislative threats of impeachment in response to unpopular decisions. For example, in March 2014, "a constitutional crisis appeared to be brewing" when Oklahoma governor Mary Fallin, in response to a stay of execution issued by the Oklahoma Supreme Court, instructed that the execution would proceed as scheduled, and state legislators threatened all of the Oklahoma justices who stayed the execution with impeachment (Eckholm 2014). The justices reversed their decision, and the execution proceeded as planned. The Iowa justices faced similar threats (Schotland 2011; Buller 2012). Leonard (2015) finds that court-curbing legislation is most likely to be introduced in states where judges face neither reappointment nor retention.
18. Savchak and Barghothi (2007) demonstrate that judges are more influenced by prospective, rather than retrospective concerns; they respond more heavily to the preferences of their retaining population than their appointing population.
19. There is some debate on this point, however. Johnson (2014), examining judicial deference to administrative agencies, finds that appointed courts are no more or less likely to find in favor of administrative agencies after taking into account the level of control the governor holds over administrative agencies in a state.
20. For a discussion of campaign speeches by candidates for judicial office, see Bopp and Woudenberg (2007).
21. The U.S. Supreme Court dealt with the responsibilities of sitting judges hearing cases involving individuals who made independent expenditures on their behalf in a 2009 case: *Caperton v. A.T. Massey Coal*, holding that judges must recuse themselves when there

is "a risk of actual bias" which may occur when a judge has a "direct, personal, substantial pecuniary interest." The contribution that caused so much consternation was an independent expenditure: one by an individual acting in his private capacity (though that individual was the CEO of Massey Coal). Gibson and Caldeira (2012) have shown that this sort of independent expenditure can weaken perceptions of impartiality and the recourse—recusal—can restore some faith in the judiciary, but it cannot completely ameliorate the harm done by the presence of a conflict of interest (see also Gibson and Caldeira 2013).

22. Gibson (2009) reports an important amendment to this general conclusion. He found that policy talk had a delegitimizing influence in states in which judges are not subject to elections. Gibson speculates that (2009: 1299): "Politicized judicial campaigns may provide a 'shock' to an electorate, but that shock may not have enduring consequences as citizens alter their expectations of proper behavior for candidates." As citizens acquire experience with politicized campaigns, they come to see them as normal and therefore not objectionable.
23. Gibson (2009) shows that the effects of campaign activities on citizen assessments of political institutions do not vary across courts and legislatures.
24. Of course, parties play a larger role in partisan elections than simply providing a ballot cue: they help with candidate recruitment, often provide financial resources, and help candidates with their campaign organizations (Nelson, Caufield, and Martin 2013).
25. Driscoll and Nelson (2013), comparing the political and historical circumstances surrounding the adoption of judicial elections in both the United States and Bolivia find strikingly similar circumstances. Importantly, in both cases, judicial elections were adopted as methods of judicial selection primarily to increase the institutional power of the judiciary vis-à-vis other branches of government. Those pushing for the adoption of judicial elections in Bolivia argued that adopting elections would increase public esteem for the judiciary.

References

American Bar Association Commission on the 21st Century Judiciary. 2003. *Justice in Jeopardy*. Chicago, IL: American Bar Association.

Baum, L. 2003. "Judicial Elections and Judicial Independence: The Voter's Perspective." *Ohio State Law Journal* 64(1): 13–41.

Benesh, S. C. 2006. "Understanding Public Confidence in American Courts." *The Journal of Politics* 68(3): 697–707.

Berdejó, C., and Yuchtman, N. 2013. "Crime, Punishment, and Politics: An Analysis of Political Cycles in Criminal Sentencing." *The Review of Economics and Statistics* 95(3): 741–56.

Black, R. C., and Owens, R. J. 2016. "Courting the President: How Circuit Court Judges Alter Their Behavior for Promotion to the Supreme Court." *American Journal of Political Science* 60(1): 30–43.

Bonica, A., and Woodruff, M. J. 2012. "State Supreme Court Ideology and 'New Style' Judicial Campaigns." Working Paper.

Bonneau, C. W. 2012. "A Survey of Empirical Evidence Concerning Judicial Elections." *The Federalist Society*. Available at: http://www.fed-soc.org/library/doclib/20120719_Bonneau2012WP.pdf.

Bonneau, C. W., and Cann, D. M. 2015. *Voters' Verdicts: Citizens, Campaigns, and Institutions in State Supreme Court Elections*. Charlottesville, VA: University of Virginia Press.

Bonneau, C. W., and Hall, M. G. 2009. *In Defense of Judicial Elections*. New York, NY: Routledge.

Bonneau, C. W., Hall, M. G., and Streb, M. J. 2011. "White Noise: The Unrealized Effects of *Republican Party of Minnesota v. White* on Judicial Elections." *Justice System Journal* 32(3): 247–68.

Bopp, J., Jr., and Woudenberg, A. Y. 2007. "An Announce Clause by Any Other Name: The Unconstitutionality of Disciplining Judges Who Fail to Disqualify Themselves for Exercising Their Freedom to Speak." *Drake Law Review* 55(3): 723–61.

Brace, P., and Boyea, B. D. 2008. "State Public Opinion, the Death Penalty, and the Practice of Electing Judges." *American Journal of Political Science* 52(2): 360–72.

Brace, P., and Hall, M. G. 1990. "Neo-Institutionalism and Dissent in State Supreme Courts." *Journal of Politics* 52(1): 54–70.

Brace, P., and Hall, M. G. 1997. "The Interplay of Preferences, Case Facts, Context, and Rules in the Politics of Judicial Choice." *Journal of Politics* 59(4):1206–31.

Bruhl, A. P., and Leib, E. J. 2012. "Elected Judges and Statutory Interpretation." *The University of Chicago Law Review* 79(4):1215–83.

Buller, T. J. 2012. "Framing the Debate: Understanding Iowa's 2010 Judicial-Retention Election through a Content Analysis of Letters to the Editor." *Iowa Law Review* 97(5):1745–86.

Caldarone, R. P., Canes-Wrone, B., and Clark, T. S. 2009. "Partisan Labels and Democratic Accountability: An Analysis of State Supreme Court Abortion Decisions," *The Journal of Politics* 71(2): 560–73.

Caldeira, G. 1987. "Public Opinion and the American Supreme Court: FDR's Court-Packing Plan." *American Political Science Review* 81(4):1139–53.

Canes-Wrone, B., and Shotts, K. W. 2007. "When Do Elections Induce Ideological Rigidity?" *American Political Science Review* 101(2): 273–88.

Canes-Wrone, B., Clark, T. S., and Kelly, J. P. 2014. "Judicial Selection and Death Penalty Decisions." *American Political Science Review* 108(1): 23–39.

Canes-Wrone, B., Clark, T. S., and Park, J. 2012. "Judicial Independence and Retention Elections" *Journal of Law, Economics & Organization* 28(2): 211–34.

Cann, D., and Wilhelm, T. 2011. "Case Visibility and the Electoral Connection in State Supreme Courts." *American Politics Research* 39(3): 557–81.

Cann, D., and Yates, J. 2008. "Homegrown Institutional Legitimacy: Assessing Citizens' Diffuse Support for State Courts." *American Politics Research* 36(2):297–329.

Caufield, R. P. 2005. "In the Wake of White: How States are Responding to *Republican Party of Minnesota v. White* and How Judicial Elections Are Changing," *Akron Law Review* 38(3): 625–47.

Caufield, R. P. 2007. "The Changing Tone of Judicial Election Campaigns as a Result of *White*." In *Running for Judge: The Rising Political, Financial, and Legal Stakes of Judicial Elections*, edited by Matt Streb. New York, NY: New York University Press, 34–58.

Clark, T. S. 2011. *The Limits of Judicial Independence*. New York, NY: Cambridge University Press.

Cook, B. B. 1977. "Public Opinion and Federal Judicial Policy." *American Journal of Political Science* 21(3): 567–600.

Delli Carpini, M. X., and Keeter, S. 1996. *What Americans Know about Politics and Why It Matters*. New Haven, CT: Yale University Press.

Driscoll, A., and Nelson, M. J. 2012. "The 2011 Judicial Elections in Bolivia." *Electoral Studies* 31(3): 628–39.

Driscoll, A., and Nelson, M. J. 2013. "The Political Origins of Judicial Elections: Evidence from the United States and Bolivia." *Judicature* 96(4): 151–60.

Driscoll, A., and Nelson, M. J. 2015. "Judicial Selection and the Democratization of Justice: Lessons from the Bolivian Judicial Elections." *Journal of Law and Courts* 3(1): 115–48.

Dubois, P. L. 1980. *From Ballot to Bench: Judicial Elections and the Quest for Accountability*. Austin, TX: University of Texas Press.

Dyke, A. 2007. "Electoral Cycles in the Administration of Criminal Justice." *Public Choice* 133(3–4): 417–37.

Eckholm, E. 2014. "One Execution Botched, Oklahoma Delays the Next." *The New York Times* April 29: A1.

Ellis, M. J. 2012. "The Origins of the Elected Prosecutor." *The Yale Law Journal* 121(6):1528–69.

Epstein, L., Landes, W. M., and Posner, R. A. 2013. *The Behavior of Federal Judges: A Theoretical and Empirical Study of Rational Choice*. Cambridge, MA: Harvard University Press.

Epstein, L., Martin, A. D., Quinn, K. M., and Segal, J. A. 2009. "Circuit Effects: How the Norm of Federal Judicial Experience Biases the U.S. Supreme Court." *University of Pennsylvania Law Review* 157(3): 101–46.

Gibson, J. L. 1980. "Environmental Constraints on the Behavior of Judges: A Representational Model of Judicial Decision Making." *Law & Society Review* 14(2): 343–70.

Gibson, J. L. 2007. "Changes in American Veneration for the Rule of Law." *DePaul Law Review* 56(2): 593–614.

Gibson, J. L. 2008. "Challenges to the Impartiality of State Supreme Courts: Legitimacy Theory and 'New-Style' Judicial Campaigns." *American Political Science Review* 102(1): 59–75.

Gibson, J. L. 2009. "'New-Style' Judicial Campaigns and the Legitimacy of State High Courts." *The Journal of Politics* 71(4): 1285–304.

Gibson, J. L. 2012. *Electing Judges: The Surprising Effects of Campaigning on Judicial Legitimacy*. Chicago, IL: University of Chicago Press.

Gibson, J. L., and Caldeira, G. A. 2009. *Citizens, Courts, and Confirmations: Positivity Theory and the Judgments of the American People*. Princeton, NJ: Princeton University Press.

Gibson, J. L., and Caldeira, G. A. 2012. "Campaign Support, Conflicts of Interest, and Judicial Impartiality: Can the Legitimacy of Courts Be Rescued by Recusals?" *The Journal of Politics* 74(1): 18–34.

Gibson, J. L., and Caldeira, G. A. 2013. "Judicial Impartiality, Campaign Contributions, and Recusals: Results from a National Survey." *Journal of Empirical Legal Studies* 10(1): 76–103.

Gibson, J. L., Gottfried, J. A., Delli Carpini, M. X., and Jamieson, K. H. 2011. "The Effects of Judicial Campaign Activity on the Legitimacy of Courts: A Survey-based Experiment." *Political Research Quarterly* 64(3): 545–58.

Goldberg, D. 2007. "Interest Group Participation in Judicial Elections." In *Running for Judge: The Rising Political, Financial, and Legal Stakes of Judicial Elections*, edited by Matt Streb. New York, NY: New York University Press, 73–95.

Gordon, S. C., and Huber, G. A. 2007. "The Effect of Electoral Competitiveness on Incumbent Behavior." *Quarterly Journal of Political Science* 2(2): 107–38.

Graves, S., and Teske, P. 2003. "State Supreme Courts and Judicial Review of Regulation." *Albany Law Review* 66(3): 857–65.

Hall, M. G. 1987. "Constituent Influence in State Supreme Courts: Conceptual Notes and a Case Study." *The Journal of Politics* 49(4): 1117–24.

Hall, M. G. 1992. "Electoral Politics and Strategic Voting in State Supreme Courts." *The Journal of Politics* 54(2): 427–46.

Hall, M. G. 1995. "Justices as Representatives: Elections and Judicial Politics in the American States." *American Politics Quarterly* 23(4): 485–503.

Hall, M. G. 2014. *Attacking Judges: How Campaign Advertising Influences State Supreme Court Elections*. Stanford, CA: Stanford University Press.

Hall, M. G., and Bonneau, C. W. 2013. "Attack Advertising, the *White* Decision, and Voter Participation in State Supreme Court Elections." *Political Research Quarterly* 66(1): 115–26.

Hazelton, M. L.W., Montgomery, J. M., and Nyhan, B. 2014. "Does Public Financing Affect Judicial Behavior? Evidence from the North Carolina Supreme Court." Working Paper.

Hibbing, J. R., and Theiss-Morse, E. 1995. *Congress as Public Enemy: Public Attitudes toward American Political Institutions*. Cambridge: Cambridge University Press.

Hojnacki, M., and Baum, L. 1992. "New Style Judicial Campaigns and the Voters: Economic Issues and Union Members in Ohio." *Political Research Quarterly* 45(4): 921–48.

Holmes, L. M., and Emrey, J. A. 2006. "Court Diversification: Staffing the State Courts of Last Resort through Interim Appointments." *Justice System Journal* 27(1): 1–13.

Huber, G. A., and Gordon, S. C. 2004. "Accountability and Coercion: Is Justice Blind When It Runs for Office?" *American Journal of Political Science* 48(2): 247–63.

Iyengar, S. 2002. "The Effects of Media-Based Campaigns on Candidate and Voter Behavior: Implications for Judicial Elections." *Indiana Law Review* 35(3): 691–99.

Jacob, H. 1988. *Silent Revolution: The Transformation of Divorce Law in the United States*. Chicago, IL: The University of Chicago Press.

Johnson, G. 2014. "Judicial Deference and Executive Control over Administrative Agencies." *State Politics and Policy Quarterly* 14(2): 142–64.

Klein, D., and Baum, L. 2001. "Ballot Information and Voting Decisions in Judicial Elections." *Political Research Quarterly* 54(4): 709–28.

Kritzer, H. M. 1979. "Federal Judges and Their Political Environments: The Influence of Public Opinion." *American Journal of Political Science* 23(1): 194–207.

Kritzer, H. M. 2015. *Justices on the Ballot: Continuity and Change in State Supreme Court Elections*. New York, NY: Cambridge University Press.

Kuklinski, J. H., and Stanga, J. E. 1979. "Political Participation and Government Responsiveness: The Behavior of California Superior Courts." *American Political Science Review* 73(4): 1090–9.

Langer, L. 2002. *Judicial Review in State Supreme Courts: A Comparative Study*. Albany, NY: State University of New York Press.

Leonard, M. 2015. "State Legislatures, State High Courts, and Judicial Independence: An Examination of Court-Curbing Legislation in the States." *Justice System Journal* 37(1): 1–13.

Lindquist, S. 2013. "Judicial Activism in State Supreme Courts: Institutional Design and Judicial Behavior." Working Paper.

Nelson, M. J. 2011. "Uncontested and Unaccountable? Rates of Contestation in Trial Court Elections." *Judicature* 94(5): 208–17.

Nelson, M. J. 2014. "Representative Justice? Retention Elections, Prosecutors, and Public Opinion." *Journal of Law and Courts* 2(1): 117–52.

Nelson, M. J., Caufield, R. P., and Martin, A. D. 2013. "OH, MI: On Empirical Examinations of Judicial Elections." *State Politics and Policy Quarterly* 13(4): 495–511.

Peters, C. S. 2009. "Canons of Ethics and Accountability in State Supreme Court Elections." *State Politics & Policy Quarterly* 9(1): 24–55.

Raftery, B. 2011. "2011 Year in Review: Record Number of Impeachment Attempts against Judges for their Decisions." *Gavel to Gavel*. 27 December. Available at: http://gaveltogavel.us/2011/12/27/2011-year-in-review-record-number-of-impeachment-attempts-against-judges-for-their-decisions/.

Reddick, M., Nelson, M. J., and Caufield, R. P. 2009. "Racial and Gender Diversity on State Courts." *The Judge's Journal* 48: 28–32.

Savchak, E. C., and Barghothi, A. J. 2007. "The Influence of Appointment and Retention Constituencies: Testing Strategies of Judicial Decisionmaking." *State Politics & Policy Quarterly* 7 (4): 394–415.

Schotland, R. A. 1998. "Comment." *Law and Contemporary Problems* 61(3): 149–55.

Schotland, R. A. 2011. "Iowa's 2010 Judicial Election: Appropriate Accountability or Rampant Passion?" *Court Review* 46(4): 118–28.

Shepherd, J. M. 2009. "Are Appointed Judges Strategic Too?" *Duke Law Journal* 58(7): 1589–626.

Shepard, J. M., and Kang, M. S. 2011. "The Partisan Price of Justice: An Empirical Analysis of Campaign Contributions and Judicial Decisions." *New York University Law Review* 86(1): 69–130.

Shugerman, J. H. 2010. "Economic Crisis and the Rise of Judicial Elections and Judicial Review." *Harvard Law Review* 123(5): 1061–150.

Shugerman, J. H. 2012. *The People's Courts: Pursuing Judicial Independence in America*. Cambridge, MA: Harvard University Press.

Streb, M. J., and Frederick, B. 2009. "Conditions for Competition in Low-Information Elections: The Case of Intermediate Appellate Courts." *Political Research Quarterly* 62(3): 523–37.

Tabarrok, A., and Helland, E. 1999. Court Politics: The Political Economy of Tort Awards. *Journal of Law and Economics* XLII(1): 157–88.

Watson, R. A., and Downing, R. G. 1969. *The Politics of the Bench and Bar: Judicial Selection under the Missouri Non-Partisan Court Plan*. Hoboken, NJ: John Wiley and Sons.

CHAPTER 4

FEDERAL JUDICIAL TENURE

ALBERT YOON

INTRODUCTION

A common sentiment shared by lawyers, journalists, legal scholars, and much of the public is that federal judges are politically motivated. While judges are required by Article VI of the U.S. Constitution to uphold both the Constitution and federal law, they nevertheless have different conceptions of the law that map onto traditional conceptions of liberal, moderate, and conservative.

If judges are indeed politically motivated, it logically follows that they would prefer that their successor share a similar conception of the law. Toward that end, Democratic-appointed judges are more inclined to create a judicial vacancy when a Democratic president is in office, and Republican-appointed judges will create the vacancy during a Republican presidency. In short, politics influence judicial tenure.

A competing explanation for judicial tenure focuses on the work challenges that federal judges face. Chief Justice Rehnquist (2002) and, more recently, Chief Justice Roberts (2006) have warned of the burgeoning caseload, the rise in judicial vacancies, and declining real salaries that are threats to the future quality of the federal judiciary. At the same time, contrary to claims by Chief Justice Rehnquist, federal judges in the preceding half-century had been serving slightly longer, not shorter, tenures (Yoon 2003).

This chapter is intended to summarize the existing literature on federal judicial tenure, and to evaluate the relative importance of political, demographic, and economic factors. Early scholarship in this area was primarily descriptive (Goldman 1997; Fairman 1938; Danelski 1965; Schmidhauser 1962), but in recent years has become more theoretically motivated (Bailey and Yoon 2011) and empirically (Choi, Gulati, and Posner 2013; Hansford, Savchak, and Songer 2010; Yoon 2005, 2006; Baker 2000; Spriggs and Wahlbeck 1995).

It turns out that the story about federal judicial tenure is largely a story about pensions. Judges have an attractive pension if they reach the requisite chronological age and years of service, and the overwhelming percentage of judges have responded by attaining this benchmark. At the same time, nearly half of all judges act end active service—and thereby allowing the president and Senate to appoint a successor—the very year that they qualify for their pension. Political motivations do appear to play a role once judges vest in their pension, but this effect is relatively small.

In addition to reviewing the literature, this chapter also presents recent statistics on judicial tenure, to include judicial appointments through 2013, using data from the Federal Judicial Center (FJC), a division of the Administrative Office of the U.S. Courts. The FJC provides information on all Article III judges since the judiciary's inception, including biography, employment, and judicial service.

The chapter proceeds as follows: the first section explores the entering characteristics of judges appointed to the federal bench. The second section briefly describes the distinction between different types of judicial tenure, namely active service and senior status. The third section describes the creation of judicial pensions, its relation to senior status, and the evolving rules for qualification. The fourth section discusses empirical evidence on judicial tenure, both from existing scholarship and more recent data. The fifth section discusses other factors that may influence judicial tenure, particularly from the perspective of selection onto the judiciary. The concluding section briefly discusses the policy implications of the increased presence of senior federal judges on federal appointments and the performance of federal courts.

Entering Characteristics of the Federal Bench

Article II, section 2 of the U.S. Constitution provides that the president and Senate jointly determine, amongst other appointments, federal judges. Article III, section 1 succinctly states that, upon confirmation to the bench, that judges "shall hold their offices during good behavior."

Tables 4.1A and 4.1B provide summary statistics for Article III district and circuit judges, beginning with President Truman, whom the Senate confirmed to the bench. The number of appointments vary by president, but follow a general secular grown, reflecting that the number of authorized judgeships have increased.

A couple of notable patterns: The fraction of female judges has increased over time. President Truman appointed one woman during his tenure (Burnita Matthews—District Court of Columbia); President Eisenhower appointed none. Since this time, both Democratic and Republican presidents have appointed more women, with Democratic presidents in greater numbers. Similarly, the presence of non-white judges has increased, from zero during the Truman and Eisenhower administrations to over a third of President Obama's administration (thus far).

By contrast, the average age at commission has declined, albeit modestly, from the Truman to Obama administrations. This figure is more significant, given that life expectancy has increased during this time, from 47 years old for someone born in 1900 (corresponding to the birth year based on the average commission age during the Truman

Table 4.1A Summary statistics when federal judges join the bench, U.S. District Court

Nominating president	Number of appointments	Age at commission	Female	Non-White	Attended Yale, Harvard, or Stanford Law School	Job prior to joining bench		
						Judge	Private practice	Prosecutor
Truman	88	52.36	0.01	0.00	0.09	0.19	0.19	0.22
Eisenhower	103	53.36	0.00	0.00	0.12	0.24	0.29	0.17
JFK	85	53.28	0.01	0.01	0.16	0.36	0.21	0.12
LBJ	115	51.96	0.02	0.06	0.13	0.33	0.22	0.22
Nixon	152	50.13	0.00	0.05	0.12	0.30	0.30	0.17
Ford	42	50.78	0.02	0.10	0.17	0.36	0.21	0.14
Carter	193	50.53	0.14	0.22	0.12	0.40	0.29	0.07
Reagan	246	49.98	0.05	0.07	0.11	0.31	0.30	0.16
Bush, G. H.	137	49.05	0.20	0.10	0.08	0.38	0.34	0.14
Clinton	286	50.64	0.28	0.23	0.17	0.38	0.29	0.11
Bush, G. W.	258	50.87	0.21	0.19	0.08	0.35	0.28	0.21
Obama	214	51.80	0.42	0.37	0.20	0.32	0.31	0.18

Table 4.1B Summary statistics when federal judges join the bench, U.S. Court of Appeals

Nominating president	Number of appointments	Age at commission	Female	Non-White	Attended Yale, Harvard, or Stanford Law School	Job prior to joining bench: Judge	Job prior to joining bench: Private practice	Job prior to joining bench: Prosecutor
Truman	27	50.00	0.00	0.04	0.11	0.30	0.19	0.22
Eisenhower	43	52.81	0.00	0.00	0.21	0.30	0.35	0.16
JFK	24	49.01	0.00	0.00	0.13	0.13	0.17	0.29
LBJ	42	49.72	0.02	0.05	0.26	0.17	0.26	0.12
Nixon	52	50.85	0.00	0.04	0.29	0.17	0.38	0.15
Ford	7	50.15	0.00	0.00	0.00	0.00	0.29	0.29
Carter	55	50.33	0.20	0.22	0.31	0.31	0.40	0.02
Reagan	82	47.89	0.07	0.02	0.21	0.28	0.29	0.10
Bush, G. H.	39	46.75	0.18	0.08	0.26	0.15	0.36	0.10
Clinton	65	49.79	0.29	0.25	0.28	0.29	0.28	0.14
Bush, G. W.	60	48.19	0.28	0.13	0.20	0.37	0.23	0.13
Obama	49	48.92	0.39	0.35	0.34	0.26	0.22	0.26

administration) to 70 for someone born in 1960 (birth year for average Obama appointee) (CDC 2010).[1]

Other characteristics indicate the absence of any clear trend, suggesting that preferences vary across presidents. For example, approximately one-third of district judges were, immediately prior to joining the federal bench, state judges. For those appointed to the court of appeals, the fraction varies: George W. Bush drew heavily from the state judiciary, while his father (George H. W. Bush) did not. Similarly, the affinity of presidents to appoint graduates of Yale, Harvard, or Stanford law school (as a proxy for the most elite law schools), varies across presidents, although all presidents drew more heavily from these three schools for appointments to the court of appeals than for the district court.

While outside this scope of this chapter, we briefly note the considerable scholarship—primarily from political science—debating the factors that influence the appointments process. Political scientists have analyzed the judicial appointments process, paying particular attention to who the president appoints, and why (Abraham 1999; Moraski and Shipan 1999; Krehbiel 2007). The intuition justifying this focus is that judicial appointments represents the key—and perhaps best—opportunity for the president (and Senate) to influence the judiciary. While the president and Congress can respond legislatively to particular judicial opinions (Eskridge 1991), the appointments process provides a potentially more lasting influence. On the U.S. Supreme Court, the president and Senate will deliberate most of those appointments with the potential to shift the Court's ideological balance (Segal, Cameron, and Cover 1990; Segal, Cameron, and Cover 1992). Scholars examining appointments to the U.S. District and Circuit Courts have similarly found that differences in political ideology between the Senate and president influence the confirmation process (Martinek, Kemper, and Van Winkle 2002).

Judicial States of the World

Once confirmed to the bench, judges serve in one of three states. The first state is active status, which is akin to working full-time. Active judges hear a full docket, and are responsible for participating fully in court governance, including any administrative responsibilities. As active judges, they are entitled to lifetime, non-diminishing compensation, and receive any salary raises bestowed by Congress. With few exceptions—most notably royalties from writing books—they are prohibited from earning outside income. And, in accordance with Article III, section 2, judges have the freedom to remain on the federal bench for as long as they like.

Judges on active status occupy one of a limited number of authorized judgeships until they decide to create a vacancy. They can do this in one of two ways. Perhaps the most direct route is to simply resign. Resignation, the second state, is where judges leave the bench entirely. By retiring, judges enable the president and Senate to select their successor. Resigned judges no longer hear cases or write opinions, nor participate in any other judicial administrative matters. Retirement also liberates judges by allowing them to return to private practice or to otherwise earn non-judicial income. Also, by resigning, judges no longer maintain the chambers, clerks, or any other administrative support that their retired counterparts in private practice or academia may enjoy.

Senior status, representing a hybrid between active status and resignation, is the third state. Like active judges, senior judges continue to earn their salary as well as receive any raises by Congress. The also continue to use their chambers, hire law clerks, and receive administrative support, although they no longer participate in court governance. Senior status allows judges greater control over their docket: they can elect to hear less than a full caseload and request inclusion or exclusion from certain types of cases. Moreover, senior judges, like active judges, are restricted from earning outside income. Senior judges are similar to resigned judges in that they may enjoy beneficial tax treatment of any judicial income they earn, such as exemption from federal (FICA) and Medicare taxes (Block 2007). Table 4.2 summarizes the similarities and differences across these states.[2]

Scholars have debated the merits of senior status. Stras and Scott (2007) questioned the constitutional basis for senior judges, suggesting that it represents a separate constitutional office that requires a second confirmation process. Others (Fletcher 2007) describe it as "an elegant response to a real problem," that being active judges who elect to retain active status thereby prevent the president and Congress from appointing their successors, a view shared by others who view that lifetime tenure is adequate to provide the necessary incentives for judges to vacate their seat (Choi, Gulati, and Posner 2011). Others have taken a more critical view of lifetime tenure, generally, arguing that it compels judges to remain on the bench long after they should have left (Garrow 2000). Much of the early work on judicial tenure was descriptive in nature (Van Tassel),

Table 4.2 Comparison across different judicial states

	Active status	Senior status	Resignation
1. Lifetime non-diminishing compensation (if applicable)	Y	Y	Y
2. Subsequent Congressional increases in compensation	N	Y	N
3. Exemption from federal taxes on annual compensation (if applicable)	N	Y	Y
4. Creation of judicial vacancy	N	Y	Y
5. Freedom to earn non-judicial income	N	N	Y
6. Judicial chambers, clerks, administrative support	Y	Y	N
7. Discretion regarding caseload a) number; b) type; c) calendar	N	Y	NA
8. Participation in court governance, en banc decisions	Y	N	N

focusing on fascinating but relatively uncommon reasons (e.g., judicial misconduct) why judges left the federal bench.

These three states, conceptually distinct, become blurred in practice. Some judges experience all three states, progressing from active to senior status to ultimately resignation. Other judges skip senior status, and resign right after their time on active status. To understand the choices—and incentives—that underlie these decisions warrants a succinct but separate discussion about judicial pensions.

Judicial Pensions

Since 1919, senior status has been inextricably linked to judicial pensions. While pensions have long been of interest to economists for their effect on the labor market (e.g., Even and Macpherson 1996; Anderson, Gustmand, and Steinmeier 1999; Ashelter and Card 2002; Chan and Stevens 2003), it has gone relatively unexplored in the legal profession, in part because pensions are less prevalent than in other professions. The judiciary is one area where pensions do exist, and in recent years have drawn the attention of scholars (Baker 2000; Yoon 2005).

A judge is eligible to take senior status upon qualifying for her judicial pension. Reaching this point is a function of a judge's chronological age and years of active service. Congress has modified the requirements for pension qualification over time to better address judges who joined the bench at a younger age and judges who have or develop disabilities while on the bench.

A brief history: Article III, section 1 guarantees judges a non-diminishing annual salary, but only for as long as they remain on the bench. As written, this requirement creates an incentive for some older judges to remain on the bench for financial reasons, to the potential detriment of the federal judiciary. Prior to 1869, judges lost their judicial salary once they left the court, for any reason.

In 1869 Congress passed legislation that permitted Article III judges, upon reaching seventy years of age and completing ten years of judicial service, to continue drawing their existing salary after leaving the bench. The rule was categorical, however: to draw their pension, judges had to retire. Thus, judges during this time who preferred to remain on the bench after vesting in their pension remained on active status.

In 1919, Congress passed legislation that allowed judges an option of exiting more gradually from the bench. This option was tied to the existing pension eligibility requirements; the different now was that judges who had qualified for their pension now could choose between active status, senior status, and resignation (or retirement).[3] As stated above, by opting for senior status, judges could exercise greater control over their docket (including a reduced caseload), while remaining eligible for salary raises by Congress. If pension-eligible judges opted to retire or resign, their salary would remain the same in nominal terms for the rest of their lives.

In subsequent years, Congress made only minor changes to pension eligibility (and thereby, senior status). In 1939, Congress enacted legislation that allowed judges with certified disabilities to work a lighter caseload, and to take senior status earlier.[4] The law addressed instances where disabled judges remained on the bench until they qualified for the standard pension (Burbank, Plager, and Ablavsky 2012). In 1954, it relaxed the eligibility requirements for judges appointed at a younger age, allowing them to vest upon reaching sixty-five years of age and fifteen years of judicial service. In 1989, they created the Rule of 80, which filled intervening years between sixty-five and seventy years. Judges who met the minimum age of sixty-five and minimum service of ten years, provided their combined age and years of service equaled eighty, were eligible for a pension.

A defining feature of the judicial pension is its categorical, all-or-nothing design. Judges either fully vest or not at all. By contrast, other branches of government, as with the president and Congress, provide pensions after shorter eligibility requirements as well as partial vesting.

Most recently, amidst concerns that some senior judges were performing little work on the court while continuing to receive salary increases (Burbank, Plager, and Ablavsky 2012), Congress enacted the Ethics Reform Act of 1989, which set conditions for senior judges to receive subsequent raises: a minimum 25 percent caseload; "substantial" judicial duties outside the courtroom; some combination thereof; or "substantial" administrative duties. While this legislation provides a floor for judicial service, recent scholarship suggest that senior judges vary dramatically in their workload: senior judges at the 25th percentile reduced their workload by two-thirds, while those at the 75th percentile dropped only one-quarter (Choi, Gulati, and Posner 2011). Table 4.3 provides a summary of the major legislative changes regarding judicial pensions and senior status.

Table 4.3 Legislation for pension qualification and senior status

	Statute	Minimum requirements: Age (years)		Minimum requirements: Service (years)
Pre-1869	–	No pension plans		
1869–1953	Jidiciary Act of 1869, ch.22, §5, 16 Stat. 44, 45	70		10
1919	Act of Feb. 25, 1919, ch. 29, §6, 40. Stat. 1156, 1157–8	Created senior status for judges who vested in their position		
1939	Act of Aug. 5, 1939, ch. 433, 53 stat. 1204	Reduced pension eligiblity requirements for judges with certified disablity		
1954–83	Act of Feb. 10, 1954, Pub. L. No. 294, §4, 68 Stat. 8, 12–13	65 70	or	15 10
1984–present	Bankruptcy Amendments and Federal Judgeship Act of 1984, Pub. L. No. 98-353, tit. II, §204, 98 Stat. 333, 350	*Rule of 80* 1. Judge's age and years of service ≥80 2. Judge ≥65 at time of vacancy 3. Judge serves ≥10 years at time of vacancy		

Empirical Evidence Regarding Judicial Tenure

Federal judicial tenure has two defining moments: when a judge ends active status, thereby allowing the president and Congress to appoint her successor; and when a judge retires or resigns from the court altogether. Conceptually distinct, these moments blur for many judges. Some judges end active status by taking senior status, and then later retire or resign. Others end active status by simply resigning or retiring. We examine each of these in turn.

Ending Active Status

As a first take, we look at the summary statistics, provided in Tables 4.4A and 4.4B, for when judges end active status. We note that the data are partially censored: judges who were appointed by recent presidents are more likely to still be serving on active status. For example, Judge Manuel Real (Central District—California), appointed by President Johnson, remains on active service. All of President Obama's district court appointees remain on active service. Accordingly, these latter figures may not accurately predict the numbers when all the judges complete active status.

Taking this into account, a couple of clear patterns emerge. The average age at which district and circuit judges end active status has generally declined, which reflects the changing rules for pension qualification from seventy years (and ten years of service) to sixty-five years (and fifteen years of service), and now the Rule of 80. Also, the vast majority of judges remain on active status until they qualify for the pension (although this pattern does not hold true for George W. Bush appointees, for whom a modest majority have qualified for the pension when they ended active status).

The tenure patterns, however, diverge. District judges, on average, serve approximately fifteen years on active status, converging towards the minimum required years for those who turn sixty-five years old. By comparison, circuit judges for each nominating president, serve on active status for longer, even though the pension requirements are exactly the same. This longer duration reflects that circuit judges are more likely than district judges to remain on active status, even after they qualify for their pension.

District and circuit judges diverge in their transition from active status. The majority of district judges transitioned from active status to senior status. The coupling of years of active service with taking senior status is consistent with surveys of senior district judges, two-thirds of whom perceived a norm of assuming senior status as soon as they became eligible (Yoon 2005). The majority of circuit judges also transition from active status to senior status, albeit remaining additional years on active status before doing so.

Table 4.4A **Active service on federal judiciary, 1945–2014, U.S. District Court**

Nominating president	Number of appointments	Number of appointments who ended active status	Age when ended active status	Years of active service	Ended active status during president of *different* party than appointing president	Qualified for pension when ended active status	How ended active status	
							Senior status	Resignation/ Retirement
Truman	88	88	69.26	16.90	0.50	0.75	0.63	0.38
Eisenhower	103	103	67.82	14.46	0.28	0.79	0.72	0.28
JFK	85	85	68.79	15.50	0.61	0.89	0.81	0.19
LBJ	115	114	67.72	15.66	0.75	0.84	0.82	0.18
Nixon	152	152	65.33	15.18	0.20	0.78	0.75	0.25
Ford	42	41	65.31	14.55	0.32	0.78	0.73	0.27
Carter	193	190	66.50	15.90	0.54	0.89	0.84	0.16
Reagan	246	221	66.65	15.74	0.60	0.92	0.89	0.11
Bush, G. H.	137	106	66.26	15.51	0.43	0.88	0.85	0.15
Clinton	286	171	66.88	13.67	0.26	0.87	0.82	0.18
Bush, G. W.	258	24	62.04	7.65	0.75	0.50	0.46	0.54
Obama	214	–	–	–	–	–	–	–

Table 4.4B Active service on federal judiciary, 1945–2014, U.S. Circuit Court

Nominating president	Number of appointments	Number of appointments who ended active status	Age when ended active status	Years of active service	Ended active status during president of *different* party than appointing president	Qualified for pension when ended active status	How ended active status: Senior status	How ended active status: Resignation/ Retirement
Truman	27	27	68.76	18.76	0.52	0.78	0.67	0.33
Eisenhower	43	43	70.85	18.04	0.30	0.95	0.86	0.14
JFK	24	24	70.11	21.09	0.67	0.92	0.83	0.17
LBJ	42	42	67.17	17.46	0.67	0.76	0.69	0.31
Nixon	52	51	67.73	16.55	0.14	0.84	0.67	0.33
Ford	7	7	69.49	19.33	0.43	1.00	0.86	0.14
Carter	55	53	69.82	19.29	0.45	0.96	0.85	0.15
Reagan	82	67	66.23	17.05	0.58	0.88	0.87	0.13
Bush, G. H.	39	30	65.82	19.13	0.57	0.93	0.83	0.17
Clinton	65	24	68.31	16.69	0.25	0.88	0.71	0.29
Bush, G. W.	60	8	60.93	11.04	0.50	0.63	0.50	0.50
Obama	49	1	65.00	18.54	0.00	1.00	1.00	0.00

This result is also consistent with the surveys of senior circuit judges, only a third of who perceive this same norm (Yoon 2005).

Much of the existing scholarly discussion about judicial tenure has centered on political motivations for departure. At the U.S. Supreme Court, where the stakes are higher, some argue that political factors influence when justices depart (King 1987; Hagle 1993; Stolzenberg and Lindgren 2010), while others that politics do not play a systematic effect (Squire 1988; Brenner 1999; Zorn and Van Winkle 2000). More recently, Bailey and Yoon (2011) find that while there are certainly anecdotal accounts for politically motivated retirement from the Court (Ward 2003; Toobin 2007; Toobin 2010), justices' departures do not appear to be politically motivated.

Scholars are divided in their analysis of the lower federal courts. Barrow and Zuk (1990) find a small but statistically significant political effect for district judges, while Spriggs and Whalbeck (1995) find a similar effect for circuit judges. Nixon and Haskin (2000) argue that political effects are modest, and are most likely to emerge during presidential election years. More recently, Hansford, Savchak, and Songer (2010) finds a political effect that emerges once judges have vested in their pension.

The summary statistics are consistent with the view that political factors do not systematically influence when judges transition from active status. For both district and circuit judges, over half (54 percent at each level) the judges ended active status during a presidency whose party differed from the president who appointed them to the bench. Judges varied by administration, with Nixon appointees the most likely, and LBJ the least likely to time their departure to ensure their successor would be from the same political party as the party who appointed them.

To say that many judges do not appear to be acting strategically when ending active status, however, is not the same as saying that judges do not have preferences over their successor. The complexity arises because judges have competing concerns. Bailey and Yoon (2011) note that the federal judiciary presents institutional, personal, and structural constraints that undermine judges in the aggregate from exercising their political preferences. Judges may not have the luxury of ending active status during what they perceive as a favorable president and Senate. Even if the political environment is favorable, financial and professional factors militate against ending active status. Judges have a strong financial incentive to remain on active status until they vest in their pension. To leave before they vest—absent a certified disability—would require them to leave the bench altogether. They also have professional reasons to remain on active status, including prestige and the opportunity to influence their fellow judges through en banc and other administrative mechanisms.

These factors help explain why departures do not appear to follow a clearly defined political pattern. For example, George W. Bush, purported to have made ideological appointments to the bench, nevertheless had the highest percentage (as of 2014) of judges ending active status during a presidency of a different party. This is an artifact, at least in part, of a Democratic president (Obama) in office since 2008.

Summary statistics, while informative, are limited in identifying the influence of chronological age, pension, politics, as well as other factors (e.g., gender, ethnicity) when taken together. To examine these factors more rigorously, we construct a discrete duration ("hazard") model that takes into account these factors, and others (e.g., time trends, differences across courts). This approach is similar to Yoon (2005) and Yoon (2006), which we believe effectively captures the question of interest, namely when do active judges decide to end active status, thereby freeing their seat for their successor.

Towards that end, we construct a probit model that captures the probability of a judge ending active status in any given year:

$$P(Y_1 = 1 | x_i) = F[X(i,a,c,t) * \beta]$$

where $y_i = 1$ is the probability that judge *i*, aged *a* and serving on court *c*, vacates her seat before the start of the next calendar year, conditional on having remained on active status the prior year. The term, *X(i, a, c, t)*, represents a set of observed characteristics of judge *i* on court *c*, β is the coefficient vector, and Φ is the cumulative distribution function of the standard normal distribution. More simply stated, the model looks to explain what factors influence judges' decision to end active status.

Table 4.5 reports the results across different model specifications. Columns (1) and (2) report a simple model that regresses pension factors on whether the judge ends active status during the given year. Column (1) looks at whether the judge had qualified for her pension, whether in the current year or prior. Column (2) is more restrictive, looking at whether the judge had qualified for her pension in the current year. Judges are much more likely to end active status when they have qualified for their pension, and particularly when they have qualified in the same year. Interpreting the coefficients as marginal effects, judges (district and circuit) were 27 percent more likely to end active status after qualifying for their pension (Column (1)), and 43 percent more likely to leave in the same year they qualified for their pension (Column (2)).

When taking into account demographic and political factors (Columns (3) and (4)), female judges were roughly 1 percent less likely than male judges to end active status in any given period, controlling for these factors. Similarly, judges were 0.4 percent less likely to retire when the current president was from a different party than the president who appointed them. These effects, while of statistical significance, are small and are not of obvious substantive significance.

In this full model, the point estimates for the pension effects –qualified in or before the current year; qualified in the current year—are nearly identical. Judges were 27 percent more likely to qualify for their pension before ending active status pension (Column (3)) and 42 percent more likely to qualify for their pension and leave the same year (Column (4)).

We also run the full model separately for district and circuit courts, finding stronger pension effects amongst district judges. These judges were 31 percent more likely to end active status after vesting in their pension (Column (5)) than those who did not vest; and 46 percent more likely to end active status the very year they vested than other years (Column (6)). Circuit judges were 17 percent (Column (7)) and 30 percent (Column (8)) more likely to end active status, respectively. These results are consistent with what we

Table 4.5 Factors influencing end of active status on federal judiciary, 1945–2014

	U.S. District and Circuit Court				U.S. District Court		U.S. Circuit Court	
	(1)	(2)	(3)	(4)	(5)	(6)	(7)	(8)
Qualified for pension in or before current year	1.847*** (51.18)		1.835*** (50.82)	1.788*** (46.36)	1.916*** (45.30)	1.895*** (42.05)	1.639*** (24.90)	1.515*** (19.44)
Qualified for pension in current year		1.808*** (46.95)	−0.237*** (−4.13)	−0.333*** (−9.55)	M.208** (−3.24)	M.330*** (−8.48)	M.323** (−2.65)	M.373*** (−4.86)
Female			0.0582 (1.02)	0.208*** (6.70)	0.0122 (0.19)	0.174*** (5.00)	0.191 (1.64)	0.315*** (4.56)
Non-White			−0.0189 (−0.57)	0.0701*** (4.20)	−0.00104 (−0.03)	0.0618** (3.25)	−0.0630 (−0.94)	0.102** (2.83)
Appointed by Democratic president			−0.113*** (−3.99)	−0.105*** (−4.27)	−0.121*** (−3.58)	M.105*** (−3.67)	−0.0867 (−1.59)	−0.102* (−2.07)
Current president different party than appointing president	40,503		−0.0346 (−0.75)	−0.0573** (−2.59)	−0.0685 (−1.16)	M.0768** (−2.81)	0.0202 (0.28)	−0.0313 (−0.81)
Attended Yale, Harvard, Stanford Law School		40503	0.0137 (0.38)	−0.00343 (−0.19)	−0.0150 (−0.37)	−0.00678 (−0.34)	0.0790 (0.99)	−0.000769 (−0.02)
Prior job as judge			−0.0349 (−0.73)	−0.0290 (−1.32)	−0.0605 (−1.07)	−0.0157 (−0.64)	0.0189 (0.20)	−0.0830 (−1.63)
Prior job as prosecutor								
N			40,503	40,503	29,968	29,968	10,318	10,318

Notes: Dependent variable is whether the judge ended active status, either by taking senior status or leaving the bench altogether in a given year, and is reported as probit coefficients. Standard errors in parentheses. Year dummies included for individual court and year. Clustering by individual judge. The number of district and circuit observations run separately are fewer than the number collectively because in 1946 and 1975, no circuit judges left active status (217 observations) and accordingly drop from the regression. Single, double, and triple asterisks indicate statistical significance at the 5 percent, 1 percent, and 0.1 percent levels, respectively.

observe in the summary statistics (Tables 4.4A and 4.4B), which show that circuit judges are more likely to remain on active status even after vesting in their pension.

These regressions are consistent with the interpretation that pensions are the driving explanation behind federal judicial tenure, at least with respect to duration of active status. Although not reported, we run additional specifications isolating the other demographic and political factors. The point estimates are consistently small compared with the pension variables and highly sensitive to model specification. Statistical significance also is sensitive to the specification. The pension variables, by comparison, remain constant in their point estimates and are statistically significant across an array of model specifications.

The histogram in Figure 4.1 succinctly captures the influence of pensions. Looking at the same period as in the tables and regressions—judges appointed on or after 1945—of the 1,691 federal judges who ended active status, 85 percent (1,444) qualified for their pension. Nearly half (47 percent) ended active status the same year they vested.[5] Of the 247 judges who ended active status prior to qualifying for their pension, 60 percent (151) died that same year, suggesting that their departure from the court was involuntary due to health reasons. Thus, this leaves only ninety-six (6 percent) of all federal judges during this period who left the court prior to vesting in their pension. These results are consistent with existing work (Hansford, Savchak, and Songer 2010; Yoon 2006; Baker 2000) showing that pensions provide a strong incentive for judges to remain on active status.

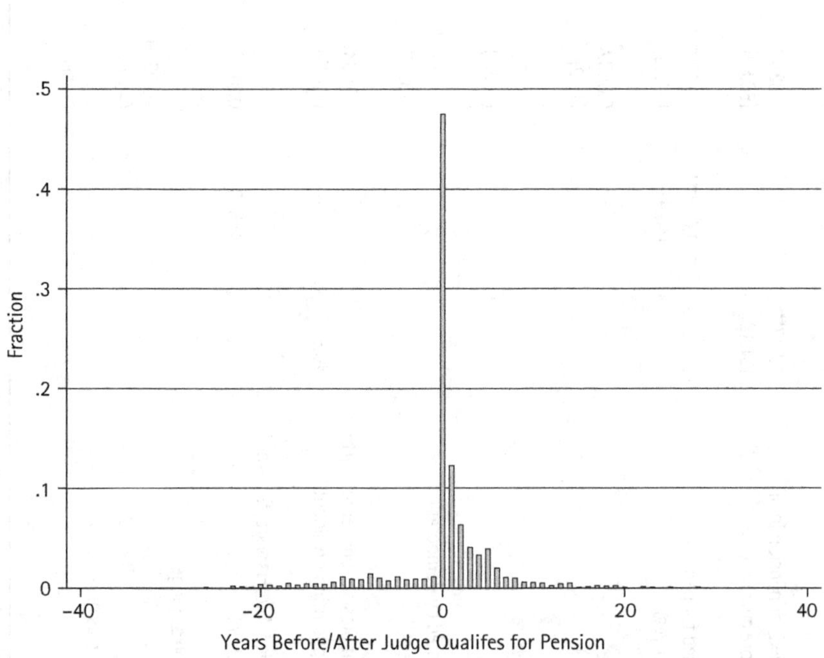

FIGURE 4.1 When federal judges end active status relative to pension qualification, 1945–2014

Source: Author.

Given the strong influence of pensions, one can argue that the political factors influencing ending active status is more nuanced. Some scholars (Hansford, Savchak, and Songer 2010) argue that these political factors become relevant only after judges have vested in their pension. In effect, judges care about political considerations, but only after addressing financial ones. Table 4.6 reports the same model specifications as in Table 4.5, but limiting observations to the period *after* judges have vested in their pension.

Table 4.6 When federal judges end active status after vesting in their pension, judges appointed 1945–2014

	USDC and USCA		USDC	USCA
	(1)	(2)	(3)	(4)
Qualified for pension in current year	0.598*** (13.92)	0.590*** (13.72)	0.567*** (10.88)	0.618*** (7.51)
Female		M.162* (−2.00)	−0.0466 (−0.44)	−0.379** (−2.76)
Non-White		0.0261 (0.29)	−0.0633 (−0.58)	0.172 (1.12)
Appointed by Democratic president		M.135** (−3.07)	M.115* (−2.15)	−0.190* (−2.38)
Current president different party than appointing president pointing President		−0.216*** (−5.34)	−0.264*** (−5.21)	−0.131 (−1.82)
Attended Yale, Harvard, Stanford Law School		0.0110 (0.18)	−0.0318 (−0.39)	0.0624 (0.67)
Prior job as judge		0.0580 (1.15)	0.00239 (0.04)	0.142 (1.35)
Prior job as prosecutor		−0.0176 (−0.30)	−0.0512 (−0.72)	0.0221 (0.19)
N	6,092	6,092	3,982	2,059

Notes: Dependent variable is whether the judge ended active status, either by taking senior status or leaving the bench altogether in a given year, and is reported as probit coefficients. Standard errors in parentheses. Year dummies included for individual court and year. Clustering by individual judge. The number of district and circuit observations run separately are fewer than the number collectively because in 1946, 1950, and 1975 no circuit judges left active status (51 observations) and accordingly drop from the regression. Single, double, and triple asterisks indicate statistical significance at the 5 percent, 1 percent, and 0.1 percent levels, respectively.

In the post-pension-vesting period, however, political factors do appear to have a greater influence on when judges end active status. Judges collectively are 6 percent less likely to end active status when the sitting president is of a different political party than the president who appointed them. Of the two types of judges, district judges are 9 percent less likely to end active status during this political climate, compared with circuit judges being 3 percent less likely (although for circuit judges this effect is not statistically significant). These results are consistent with Hansford, Savchak, and Songer (2010) and others (Spriggs and Wahlbeck 1995; Barrow and Zuk 1990) who find a political effect for judicial turnover.

Even in this specification, however, pensions remain the dominant factor. In fact the motivation to end active status the year they vest appear stronger than any political consideration: across all specifications, judges are 16 percent to 19 percent more likely to leave in the year that they vest in their pension, than any subsequent year. Even in the limited time frame when judges have vested in their pension but are free to remain on active service, they are most likely to leave the first year of eligibility. Accordingly, the story behind active status judicial tenure is that judges are strongly motivated to vest in their pension, and strongly motivated to transition away from active service once they do.

The above analysis excludes analysis of U.S. Supreme Court justices. Yoon (2006), looking at all levels of Article III judges, finds that justices, unlike district and circuit judges, are not motivated by pension eligibility. One explanation is that being a justice on senior status represents a more dramatic departure, since they are no longer involved with cases before the Court and are limited to hearing cases at the lower courts.

Leaving the Bench Altogether

Examining years of active status tells much, but not all, of the story behind judicial tenure. As discussed in the third section of this chapter, once judges decide to end active status, those who vest in their pension (representing the vast majority of judges) have the choice between senior status and completely leaving the court—or *termination*, using the parlance of the Federal Judicial Center.

Tables 4.7A and 4.B provide summary statistics that isolates the period after active status for the same cohort of judges as in Table 4.4A and 4.4B. The tables look at the subset of appointed judges who have ended their active status and have left the court altogether. This data is more heavily censored than for ending active service, because many judges who have ended active status remain on the bench on senior status, and therefore have not completely left the court. For example, two Kennedy appointments—Edward McManus, ND-Ia; William Nealon, MD-Pa—continue to hear cases as senior judges.

A few notable patterns emerge. First, those who transitioned from active to senior status remained on the bench remained on average an additional 7.7 years. District judges remained slightly longer (7.8 years) compared with circuit judges (7.4 years). Judges who remained on senior status did so for largely non-monetary reasons. While senior judges

Table 4.7A Summary statistics when federal judges completely depart the court, U.S. District Court

		Judges who took senior status			Judges who switched from active status to leaving court altogether		Judges who died	
Nominating president	Number of appoint-ments	N	Age when created judicial vacancy	Age when left bench altogether	N	Age when left bench altogether	N	Age when died
Truman	88	55	71.19	81.80	33	66.02	88	76.48
Eisenhower	103	74	69.59	83.40	29	63.32	103	78.72
JFK	85	67	69.51	82.68	16	66.16	83	80.86
LBJ	115	88	68.99	82.67	21	62.00	105	81.22
Nixon	152	87	68.08	81.31	38	57.81	115	77.81
Ford	42	22	68.09	82.54	11	57.89	28	76.44
Carter	193	88	68.09	77.49	30	58.99	97	77.26
Reagan	246	72	68.39	76.03	24	59.01	67	75.34
Bush, G. H.	137	17	68.63	72.01	16	58.25	13	71.32
Clinton	286	20	68.14	71.21	31	62.39	19	67.65
Bush, G. W.	258	1	69.00	69.00	13	55.15	5	60.78
Obama	214	–	–	–	–	–	–	–

Table 4.7B Summary statistics when federal judges completely depart the court, U.S. Circuit Court

Nominating president	Number of appoint-ments	Judges who took senior status			Judges who switched from active status to leaving court altogether		Judges who died	
		N	Age when created judicial vacancy	Age when left bench altogether	N	Age when left bench altogether	N	Age when died
Truman	27	18	70.70	81.10	9	64.88	27	76.06
Eisenhower	43	37	70.29	84.17	6	74.32	43	82.80
JFK	24	20	71.25	80.06	4	64.40	24	78.82
LBJ	42	26	68.81	83.29	13	63.70	38	78.84
Nixon	52	27	69.44	83.88	17	65.59	41	81.13
Ford	7	5	70.44	83.95	1	66.24	6	81.00
Carter	55	25	70.23	80.23	8	70.23	26	80.39
Reagan	82	20	67.75	77.50	9	59.24	23	75.15
Bush, G. H.	39	3	63.31	72.37	5	59.54	4	71.95
Clinton	65	2	69.89	71.19	7	65.95	4	67.26
Bush, G. W.	60				4	55.6	1	49.41
Obama	49							

are eligible for pay increases, pension-eligible judges receive their existing salary for life, irrespective of any work obligations, and with tax advantages. In effect, these judges are working for consumptive reasons. Yoon (2005) reports survey results of senior judges in support of this view, with one judge responding, "Judging is what I do; it is what I am," (p. 495) and another stating, "I will die while on senior status—if still competent" (p. 527).

Judges who transitioned from active status to senior status directly represent a much smaller fraction of departed judges. They were much younger on average, a perhaps unsurprising result, given that 60 percent (208 out of 349) died the same year they completely left the court. This finding supports the view that the decision to depart the court directly from active status is largely an involuntary decision. These numbers are buttressed by the reasons provided by the judges themselves for leaving the court. Of the 787 judges who transitioned from active to senior status during this period, 678 (86 percent) ultimately left due to death. Of the 349 judges who left the court, 208 (60 percent) reported death as the reason. Collectively, 78 percent (886) of departing judges during this period staying until death.

Richard Posner (1993: 40) wrote that "the conditions of judicial employment enable and induce judges to vote their personal convictions and policy preferences—or in a word their values." The same can be said for federal judges with respect to their tenure on the bench. They decide the terms on which they serve, and ultimately leave (Yoon 2003). These findings support the view that judges take serious the notion of lifetime tenure. Most judges qualify for the pension, meaning a minimum of age sixty-five. While a sizable fraction of them transition to senior status shortly after vesting in their pension, most remain until they die or are physically incapable of doing so.

Other Considerations Influencing Judicial Tenure

Any discussion of judicial tenure is incomplete without an inquiry into selection into the federal judiciary. Judge Henry Friendly (1973) wrote of the importance of prestige on the federal bench, as a means of attracting highly qualified individuals. At the time, Friendly was concerned about the threatened dilution of prestige due to expansion in the number of federal judges, something that nevertheless occurred. His general point about prestige, however, remains valid. The above analysis observes judicial tenure, conditioned on those who join the bench. Since Friendly's writing, the Chief Justice of the Supreme Court has cautioned of the federal judiciary's inability to attract qualified candidates to the bench (Year-End Report 2006; Year-End Report 2002).

The findings in this chapter support earlier work that contends that judicial tenure have remained constant over time (Yoon 2003). These findings, however, are limited in scope in three significant ways. First, they do not speak to the quality of judging, something of keen interest to judicial behavior. Recent scholarship analyzing judicial opinions offer evidence that judges increasingly rely on clerks to write their opinions (e.g., Rosenthal and Yoon 2011; Choi and Gulati 2005; Mahoney 1988). Judicial scholars are critical of the variation in the quality of judging and the inability of current institutional mechanisms to address these concerns (Choi, Gulati, and Posner 2013; Farber 2005; Choi and Gulati 2004). Other scholars point to the trend towards bureaucratization of the judiciary, including reliance on magistrate judges and law clerks, fewer trials and oral arguments (Newman 1989). Taken together, the "proliferation of staff and subjudges and the delegation of power to them weaken the judge's individual sense of responsibility" (Fiss 1983: 1456).

Second, they do not speak to the factors that influence a lawyer's willingness to be considered for the federal bench. The Federal Judicial Center does not maintain statistics on the universe of individuals who were approached but declined to be nominated. Chief Justices Rehnquist and Roberts have expressed concern that the current condition of the federal judiciary—particularly as it relates to salary—is discouraging prospective nominees (Report on the Federal Judiciary 2002, 2006). Third, and related to the second, they ignore the confirmation experience for judicial nominees, not merely for those who are ultimately confirmed, but for the growing fraction who are nominated but ultimately denied confirmation.

While a discussion of the quality of adjudication is beyond this chapter's scope, we briefly examine the second and third factors, both of which can affect the composition of the federal judiciary, and thereby the tenure for those who join the bench.

Salary

Article III, Section 1 of the U.S. Constitution prohibits the nominal diminution of judicial salaries, but does not require Congress to provide raises or even ensure that salaries keep pace with inflation. Figure 4.2 reports judicial salaries in constant dollars since 1945. The trends reflect that Congress intermittently adjusts salaries; in the intervening periods, salaries remain constant in nominal but decline in real terms. Since their high in 1969, salaries for all Article III judges have declined, most markedly for Supreme Court justices.[6]

The decline in real dollars actually understates the potential financial loss for many judges. In 1970, at the time of the peak in (real) judicial salaries, judges earned salaries comparable to partners at most large law firms. Since that time, however, the disparity has dramatically increased (Forr 2010). In 2014, partners at law firms ranked in the Top 100 in *American Lawyer* earned average profits of $1.47 million (*American Lawyer* 2014). Accordingly, judicial salaries are declining by both absolute (constant dollars) and relative measures. This trend has generated concern from the

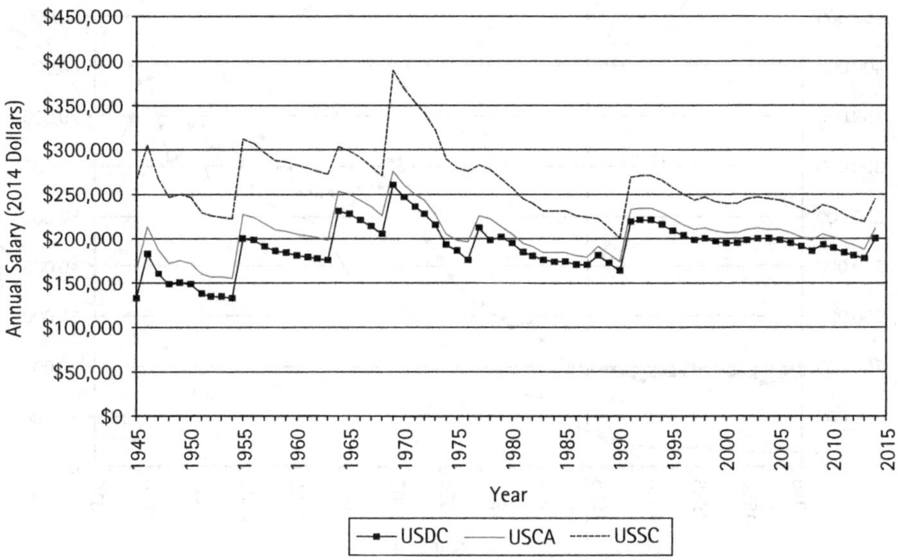

FIGURE 4.2 Federal judicial salaries, inflation adjusted, 2014 dollars

Source: Author.

legal academy, the American Bar Association, as well as members of the corporate bar (Baker 2008).

Most of the studies on judicial compensation have focused on state courts. In their study of state court judges, Choi, Gulati, and Posner (2009) challenge the view that judges collectively are underpaid. Their analysis of high state courts finds scant support that raising salaries would improve judicial performance. On federal judicial compensation, Baker (2008) concludes that judicial salaries have little or no effect on how federal circuit judges perform on the bench, with respect to voting, citation of cases, time to disposition, or their perceived prominence (based on citations) by their fellow judges. Their study examines performance on the bench, and does not speak to the effect of salary on selection to the bench. Anderson and Helland (2012) find a small but significant effect of salary on tenure of state judges, as well as on the observable characteristics of incoming judges.

Caseload

During this same period, the number of cases federal judges adjudicate annually has steadily increased at both the district and circuit level. Figure 4.3 reports the aggregate number of cases terminated at each level. While district courts adjudicate more cases than appellate courts, the rate of increase during this period has been higher for circuit courts, particularly since 1980. District courts over this seventy-year period experienced a four-fold increase in cases, while cases increased in circuit courts by a factor of twenty.

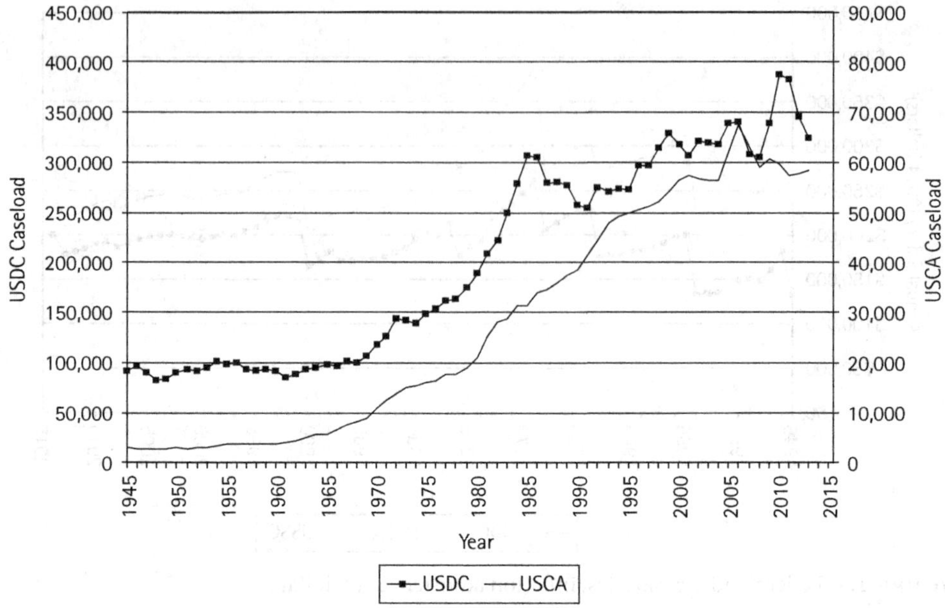

FIGURE 4.3 Federal judicial caseload, terminated by year-end

Source: Author.

Previous examinations of judicial caseload attempted to construct average caseload per lawyers (Yoon 2005), but such calculations are elusive because the federal bench consists of both active and senior judges, and the Administrative Office of the U.S. Courts does not report caseloads by individual judges. Other scholars looking at caseload have observed that the type of cases affect judges' willingness to stay on the bench, such as federal sentencing guidelines (Boylan 2004).

Number of Judges

As illustrated by Figure 4.4, the number of authorized judgeships over this same period has increased for both district and circuit courts, with the rate of increase higher for district (3.5) than for circuit (2.8) over this period. Reading Figures 4.2 through 4.4 together, it appears that judges are being asked to adjudicate more cases at the same or declining pay.

The Confirmation Process

One remaining factor that may influence judicial tenure is the confirmation process. The advise and consent process was never meant as a *pro forma* process, but the

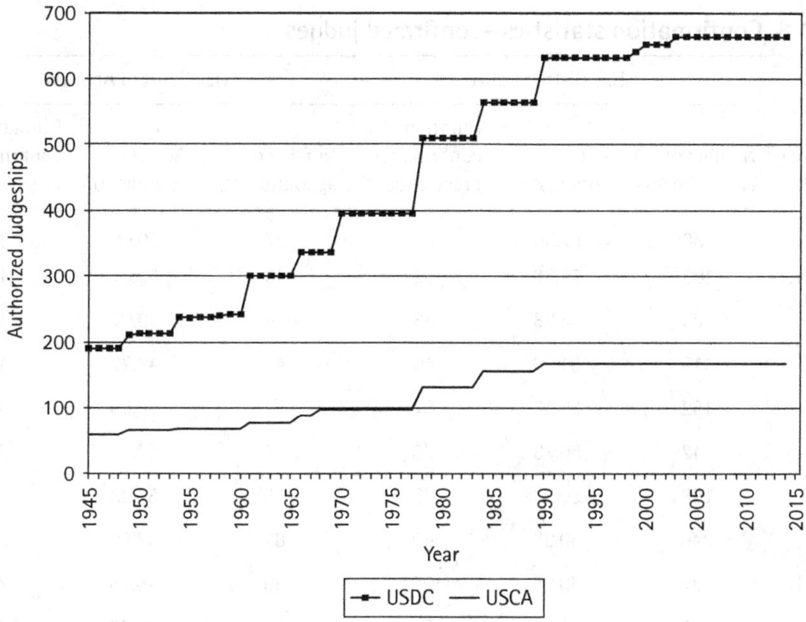

FIGURE 4.4 Number of authorized federal judges

Source: Author.

confirmation process is notable for its increased partisanship, not just at the Supreme Court (Tribe 1985), but at all levels of the judiciary (Carter 1993).

The confirmation statistics, reported in Table 4.8, quantify the extent to which the confirmation process has become more partisan, and therefore more protracted. The number of days from nomination to confirmation has steadily increased over time. From Truman through Ford, the duration for judges ultimately confirmed was shorter than two months on average. The confirmation period began to lengthen under Carter for his appellate appointments. The confirmation duration declined during the Reagan administration, a mild surprise given that during this period, he nominated Robert Bork to the Supreme Court, one of the most acrimonious confirmation hearings for the Court (Bronner 1989).

Since Reagan, the number of days for confirmation has monotonically increased for both district and circuit judges. Appointees under Bush (G. H. W.) waited roughly three months to become confirmed to the district court, and two and half months for the court of appeals. Most recently, Obama nominees have waited nearly twice as long: six months for the district court, and five months for the court of appeals. The explanation for these increased delays cannot be readily explained by divided government: for example, Carter enjoyed a Democratic-controlled Senate, as does Obama. The reasons can be traced to more subtle political factors like the filibuster and the blue slip, which allows a Senator to place a hold on a judicial nominee (Binder 2007).

Table 4.8 Confirmation statistics—confirmed judges

	U.S. District Court			U.S. Court of Appeals		
Nominating president	Number of appointments	Age at commission	Duration of confirmation process (days)	Number of appointments	Age at commission	Duration of confirmation process (days)
Truman	88	52.36	47	27	50.00	38
Eisenhower	103	53.36	52	43	52.81	47
JFK	85	53.28	38	24	49.01	41
LBJ	115	51.96	40	42	49.72	45
Nixon	152	50.13	57	52	50.85	41
Ford	42	50.78	36	7	50.15	70
Carter	193	50.53	72	55	50.33	62
Reagan	246	49.98	60	82	47.89	55
Bush, G. H.	137	49.05	105	39	46.75	77
Clinton	286	50.64	122	65	49.79	142
Bush, G. W.	258	50.87	147	60	48.19	153
Obama	214	51.80	171	49	48.92	156

The true duration of the confirmation process is, of course, actually longer, since presidents nominate individuals who on average wait longer only to have the Senate decline to confirm them (Rutkus 2003). For example, Ronald Reagan over two terms submitted 337 district nominees, 292 of whom were confirmed; and 101 circuit nominees, eighty-three of whom were confirmed (Rutkus 2004). More recently, President Obama in his first term nominated 173 to the district court, only 143 of whom were confirmed; and forty-two individuals to the circuit court, only thirty of whom were confirmed (McMillion 2013). The confirmation process requires nominees to provide considerable disclosure and preparation, and the uncertainty over outcome—up or down—only adds to the demands.

These factors, taken together, may influence the selection of judges into the profession. The attractiveness of a federal judgeship may also depend on the professional alternatives that prospective nominees have. The opportunity cost for someone in a major urban area may differ from someone in a less populated area. Similarly, the federal bench may appear more attractive to older members of the bar than younger members, because the latter will have to work more years forgoing higher earnings. Based on observable characteristics (Tables 4.1A and 4.1B), the trend in current federal judicial appointments appear consistent with historical norms (e.g., prior job, type of schooling), but these are blunt measures and may not capture underlying changes in the composition of those who ultimately join the bench. These issues of selection into the profession have been relatively unexplored for the aforementioned reasons, but warrant a closer examination.

Conclusion

This chapter explores the factors the influence judicial tenure on federal courts. Judicial tenure deconstructs into three stages: active service, senior status, and retirement. Active judges who have vested in their pension (currently determined by the Rule of 80) can choose whether to remain on active status, transition to senior status, or retire. The data presented herein supports the general findings in the literature that pensions strongly influence when judges end their active tenure.

Although it may be true that judges are politically or institutionally motivated—and there are noted examples (Bailey and Yoon 2011; Toobin 2012)—these factors do not meaningfully predict when district and circuit judges end active status. However strong their motivations to facilitate a like-minded president to facilitate their successor, these factors do not predict judicial tenure.

After judges vest in their pension, political considerations appear stronger: judges are less likely to leave when the president is of the same party than the president who appointed them. District, not circuit, judges primarily drive this effect. More significantly, pension considerations still dominate, as nearly half of all judges who vest in their pension end active status the same year that they qualify.

These findings suggest that judges, like most individuals, respond to incentives (Posner 1993). Judges have compelling financial incentives to stay on active status. Once they vest in their pension, judges have strong financial and institutional incentives to take senior status rather than simply retire or resign. Senior status offers superior financial incentives while allowing them to choose their caseload, and while enabling the president and Senate to choose their successors.

One final consideration, unexplored here in this chapter and in the judicial behavior literature generally, is the efficacy of senior judges. Table 4.9 reports the 2014 composition of active and senior judges for district and circuit courts. For both levels, senior judges comprise 40 percent of the total number of judges. As judges live longer and as delays in judicial confirmations continue, the ratio is likely to skew towards more senior judges.

There are two ways to interpret this trend. The first is that senior judges represent a windfall for the federal judiciary. They are, for all intents and purposes, working for free. They could simply resign or retire and not hear any cases at all while essentially earning the same compensation. In this respect senior judges are institutionally loyal contributors to the federal judicial workload.

The second, more critical, interpretation is that senior judges mask the increasing partisanship of the judicial appointments process. The number of authorized judgeships is 663 on the district court and 167 on the circuit court, and much of this gap can be explained by the Senate's reluctance to confirm presidential nominees. Senior judges help to address the labor shortage of active judges, but do little to address the judicial confirmation trends.

Moreover, the trade-off between senior and active judges is unclear. Statistics from the 1990s estimate the recurring operating costs of a single district or circuit judgeship

Table 4.9 2014 Composition of the federal bench

	Total judges on bench	Article	Senior status
U.S. District Court	1067	624	443
U.S. Court of Appeals	279	168	111

to exceed $700,000 (Levin and Kunz 1995). The fixed costs of a judicial chamber are high, and caseload statistics of senior judges suggest that the average judge hears fewer than half the cases of an active judge (Choi, Gulati, and Posner 2013). Finite resources might be better allocated towards filling judicial vacancies. Some scholars have suggested term limits for judges (Calabresi and Lindgren 2006; DiTullio and Schochet 2004). Other countries—e.g., Canada, England, India—all have mandatory retirement for judges. Either path would require a constitutional amendment. A more viable path is for senior judges to modify their norm of remaining on the bench until death. Filling more judicial vacancies might advance that goal.

Notes

1. The average life expectancy for a federal judge have been consistently higher than the general population, as noted by Tables 4.7A and 4.7B.
2. Table 4.2 excludes three other states: retirement, voluntary disability, and involuntary disability. We exclude them because they represent a small number of judges. Retired judges retain some aspects of aspects of judgeships, such as title and limited use of chambers. In 1939, Congress passed legislation that provided for judges with certified disabilities to either continue service or receive continued compensation upon leaving the bench.
3. A judge on active status creates a judicial vacancy whether she takes senior status, resigns, or retires.
4. Pursuant to 28 U.S.C. § 372(a), a judge, irrespective of age, with a certified disability can receive 50 percent of her salary after five years of service, and 100 percent of her salary after ten years.
5. This figure includes eighty-three judges who qualified for senior status due to a certified disability, and accordingly did not have to comply under the standard pension qualification requirements.
6. Choi, Gulati, and Posner (2009) point out, however, that the pay increase in 1969 was aberrational. Excluding this period, salaries have still declined over time, albeit more modestly.

References

American Lawyer, The 2014. "AmLaw 100." Available at: http://www.americanlawyer.com/id=1202489912232/The-2014-Am-Law-100-The-Super-Rich-Get-Richer?slreturn=20140622181950.

Abraham, H. J. 1999. *Justices and Presidents and Senators: A History of the US Supreme Court Appointments from Washington to Clinton*. Lanham, MD: Rowman & Littlefield.

Anderson, J. M., and Helland, E. 2012. "How Much Should Judges Be Paid? An Empirical Study on the Effect of Judicial Pay on the State Bench." *Stanford Law Review*, 64: 1277–342.

Anderson, P. M., Gustman, A. L., and Steinmeier, T. L. 1999. "Trends in Male Labor Force Participation and Retirement: Some Evidence on the Role of Pensions and Social Security in the 1970s and 1980s." *Journal of Labor Economics* 17: 757–83.

Ashenfelter, O., and Card, D. 2002. "Did the Elimination of Mandatory Retirement Affect Faculty Retirement?" *American Economic Review* 92(4): 957–80.

Bailey, M., and Yoon, A. 2011. 'While There's a Breath in My Body: The Systemic Effects of Politically Motivated Retirement from the Supreme Court." *Journal of Theoretical Politics* 23: 293–316.

Baker, K. 2000. "Senior Judges: Valuable Resources, Partisan Strategists, or Self-Interest Maximizers?" *Journal of Law & Politics* 16: 139–60.

Baker, S. 2008. "Should We Pay Federal Circuit Judges More?" *Boston University Law Review*, 88: 63–112.

Barrow, D. J., and Zuk, G. 1990. "An Institutional Analysis of Turnover in the Lower Federal Courts, 1900–1987." *Journal of Politics* 52: 457–76.

Binder, S. 2007. "Where Do Institutions Come from? Exploring the Origins of the Senate Blue Slip," *Studies in American Political Development* 21: 1–15.

Block, F. 2007. "Senior Status: An "Active" Senior Judge Corrects Some Common Misunderstandings." *Cornell Law Review* 92: 533–47.

Boylan, R. T. 2004. "Do the Sentencing Guidelines Influence the Retirement Decisions of Federal Judges?" *Journal of Legal Studies* 33(1): 231–53.

Brenner, S. 1999. "The Myth That Justices Strategically Retire." *Social Science Journal* 36: 431–9.

Bronner, E. 1989. *Battle for Justice: How the Bork Nomination Shook America*. New York, NY: Union Square Press.

Burbank, S. B., Plager, S. J, and Ablavsky, G., 2012. "Leaving the Bench, 1970–2009: The Choices Federal Judges Make, What Influences those Choices, and their Consequences." *University of Pennsylvania Law Review*, 161: 1–102.

Calabresi, S., and Lindgren, J. 2006. "Term Limits for the Supreme Court: Life Tenure Reconsidered." *Harvard Journal of Law and Public Policy* 29: 770–877.

Carter, S. 1993. *The Confirmation Mess: Cleaning Up the Federal Appointments Process*. New York, NY: Basic Books.

Chan, S., and Stevens, A. H. 2003. "Do Changes in Pension Incentives Affect Retirement? A Longitudinal Study of Subjective Retirement Expectations." *Journal of Public Economics* 88(7–8): 1307–33.

Choi, S. J., and Gulati, M. 2004. "Choosing the Next Supreme Court Justice." *University of Southern California Law Review* 78: 23–117.

Choi, S. J., and Gulati, M. 2005. "Which Judges Write their Opinions (and Should We Care)?" *Florida State University Law Review* 32: 1077–122.

Choi, S. J., Gulati, M., and Posner, E. A. 2009. "Are Judges Overpaid? A Skeptical Response to the Judicial Salary Debate," *Journal of Legal Analysis*, 1: 47–117.

Choi, S. J., Gulati, M., and Posner, E. 2013. "The Law and Policy of Judicial Retirement: An Empirical Study." *Journal of Legal Studies* 42: 115–50.

Danelski, D. J. 1965. "A Supreme Court Justice Steps Down." *Yale Law Journal* 54: 411–25.

DiTullio, J., and Schochet, J. 2004. "Saving this Honorable Court: A Proposal to Replace Life Tenure on the Supreme Court with Staggered Nonrenewable Eighteen-Year Terms." *Virginia Law Review* 90: 1094–149.

Eskridge, W. N., Jr. 1991. "Reneging on History? Playing the Court/Congress/President Civil Rights Game." *California Law Review* 79: 613–84.

Even, W. E., and Macpherson, D. A. 1996. "Employer Size and Labor Turnover: The Role of Pensions." *ILR Review* 49(4): 707–28.

Fairman, C. 1938. "The Retirement of Federal Judges." *Harvard Law Review* 51(3): 397–443.

Farber, D. 2005. "Supreme Court Selection and Measures of Past Judicial Performance." *Florida State University Law Review* 32: 1175–96.

Fiss, O. M. 1983. "The Bureaucratization of the Judiciary." *Yale Law Journal* 92: 1442–56.

Fletcher, B. 2007. "A Response to Stras and Scott's 'Are Senior Judges Unconstitutional?'" *Cornell Law Review* 92: 523–32.

Forr, T. 2010. "Comment: Want Less Ideology on the Federal Bench? Pay Judges More." *University of Pennsylvania Law Review* 158: 859–60.

Friendly, H. J. 1973. *Federal Jurisdiction: A General View*. New York, NY: Columbia University Press.

Garrow, D. 2000. "Mental Decrepitude on the U.S. Supreme Court: The Historical Case for a 28th Amendment." *University of Chicago Law Review* 67: 995–1087.

Goldman, S. 1997. *Picking Federal Judges*. New Haven, CT: Yale University Press.

Hagle, T. 1993. "Strategic Retirements: A Political Model of Turnover on the United States Supreme Court." *Political Behavior* 15: 25–48.

Hansford, T. G., Savchak, E. C., and Songer, D. R. 2010. "Politics, Careerism, and the Voluntary Departures of U.S. District Court Judges." *American Politics Research* 38(6): 986–1014.

King, G. 1987. "Presidential Appointments to the Supreme Court: Adding Systematic Explanation to Probabilistic Description." *American Politics Quarterly* 15: 373–86.

Krehbiel, K. 2007. "Supreme Court Appointments as a Move-the-Median Game." *American Journal of Political Science* 51: 231–40.

Levin, A. L., and Kunz, M. E. 1995. "Thinking about Judgeships," *American University Law Review* 44(5): 1627–54.

Mahoney, J. D. 1988. "Foreword: Law Clerks; For Better or For Worse?" *Brooklyn Law Review* 54: 321–39.

Martinek, W. L., Kemper, M., and Van Winkle, S. R. 2002. "To Advise and Consent: The Senate and Lower Federal Court Nominations." *Journal of Politics* 64: 337–61.

McMillion, B. J. 2013. "President Obama's First-Term U.S. Circuit and District Court Nominations: An Analysis and Comparison with Presidents since Reagan." Congressional Research Service, Washington, DC.

Moraski, B., and Shipan, C. 1999. "The Politics of Supreme Court Nominators: A Theory of Institutional Constraints and Choices." *American Journal of Political Science* 43: 1069–95.

Newman, J. O. 1989. "Restructuring Federal Jurisdiction: Proposals to Preserve the Federal Judicial System." *University of Chicago Law Review* 56: 761–6.

Nixon, D. C., and Haskin, J. D. 2000. "Judicial Retirement Strategies: The Judge's Role in Influencing Party Control of the Appellate Courts." *American Politics Quarterly* 28: 458–89.

Posner, R. A. 1993. "What Do Judges and Justices Maximize? (The Same Thing Everybody Else Does)." *Supreme Court Economic Review* 3: 1–41.

Rehnquist, W. 2002. "2002 Year-End Report on the Federal Judiciary," Third Branch. Available at: http://www.supremecourt.gov/publicinfo/year-end/2002year-endreport.aspx.

Roberts, J. G., Jr. 2007. "2006 Year-End Report on the Federal Judiciary," Third Branch, Admin. Office of the U.S. Courts, Washington, DC. Available at: http://www.uscourts.gov/uscourts/news/ttb/archive/2007-01%20Jan.pdf.

Rosenthal, J. S., and Yoon, A. 2011. "Judicial Ghostwriting: Authorship on the U.S. Supreme Court." *Cornell Law Review* 96: 1307–43.

Rutkus, D. S. 2003. "Judicial Nomination Statistics: U.S. District and Circuit Courts, 1977–2002." Congressional Research Service, Washington, DC.

Schmidhauser, J. R. 1962. "When and Why Justices Leave the Court." In *Politics of Age: Proceedings of the University of Michigan Fourteenth Annual Conference on Aging, Ann Arbor, Michigan, June 19–20, 1961*, edited by W. Donahue and C. Tibbitts. Ann Arbor, MI: Division of Gerontology, University of Michigan.

Segal, J. A., Cameron, C., and Cover, A. 1990. "SenateVoting on Supreme Court Nominees: A Neoinstitutional Model." *American Political Science Review* 84: 525–34.

Segal, J. A., Cameron, C., and Cover, A. 1992. "A Spatial Model of Roll Call Voting: Senators, Constituents, Presidents and Interest Groups in Supreme Court Confirmations." *American Journal of Political Science* 36: 96–121.

Spriggs, J. F., III, and Wahlbeck, P. J. 1995. "Calling It Quits: Retirement on the Federal Courts of Appeals, 1893–1991." *Political Research Quarterly* 48: 573–97.

Squire, P. 1988. "Politics and Personal Factors in Retirement from the United States Supreme Court." *Political Behavior* 10: 180–90.

Stolzenberg, R, and Lindgren, J. 2010. "Retirement and Death in Office of US Supreme Court Justices." *Demography* 47: 269–98.

Stras, D., and Scott, R. 2007. "Are 'Senior' Judges Unconstitutional?" *Cornell Law Review* 92(3): 453–522.

Toobin, J. 2007. *The Nine: Inside the Secret World of the Supreme Court*. New York, NY: Anchor Books.

Toobin, J. 2010. "After Stevens: What Will the Supreme Court Be Like without its Liberal Leader." *The New Yorker*, March 22.

Toobin, J. 2012. *The Oath: The Obama White House and the Supreme Court*. New York, NY: Doubleday.

Tribe, L. H. 1985. *God Save this Honorable Court: How the Choice of Justices Shapes our History*. New York, NY: Random House.

Van Tassel, E.F. 1993. "Resignations and Removals: A History of Federal Judicial Service—and Disservice—1789–1992." *University of Pennsylvania Law Review* 142: 333–430.

Ward, A. 2003. *Deciding to Leave: The Politics of Retirement from the United States Supreme Court*. New York, NY: SUNY Press.

Yoon, A. 2003. "Love's Labor's Lost? Judicial Tenure among Federal Court Judges: 1954–2000." *California Law Review* 91(4): 1029–60.

Yoon, A. 2005. "As You Like it: Senior Federal Judges and the Political Economy of Judicial Tenure." *Journal of Empirical Legal Studies* 2: 495–549.

Yoon, A. 2006. "Pensions, Politics, and Judicial Tenure: An Empirical Study of Federal Judges, 1869–2002." *American Law and Economics Review* 8(1): 143–80.

Zorn, C. J. W., and Van Winkle, S. R. 2000. "A Competing Risks Model of Supreme Court Vacancies, 1789–1992." *Political Behavior* 22: 145–66.

CHAPTER 5

LAW CLERKS

ARTEMUS WARD

JUDGES do not work alone. They are assisted by a group of young attorneys who are intimately involved in each step of the judicial decision-making process. From recommending which issues courts will address to drafting the opinions issued under their judges' names to acting as informal ambassadors through the "clerk network" during the coalition formation process, fifty years of research has steadily demonstrated how law clerks have become an increasingly central part of the judicial process (e.g., Newland 1961; Dorsen 1963; Baier 1973; Marvell 1978; Oakley and Thompson 1980; Sheldon 1981, 1988; Perry 1994; Cohen 2002; Peppers 2006; Ward and Weiden 2006; Wasby 2008; Peppers and Ward 2012; Peppers and Cushman 2015). As the clerks have taken on more responsibility over time, critics have suggested and attempted to demonstrate through journalistic and first-person accounts that they wield undue influence over the law (Rehnquist, 1957, 1958; Woodward and Armstrong, 1979; Lazarus, 1998). To be sure, clerks are expected to make recommendations to their judges and otherwise work closely with them to craft the law. Still, regardless of the question of undue influence—which empirical research suggests may be occurring—it is plain that law clerks are firmly entrenched as key participants in the judicial process, both during and after their clerkships.

While there is some literature that addresses the role of clerks and other judicial assistants—either directly or tangentially—on non-U.S. courts such as law clerks at the Supreme Court of Canada (Sossin 1996; Morton and Knopff 2002; Bodwin, Rosenthal, and Yoon 2013; Szmer, Kaheny, and Christensen 2014; Kaheny, Szmer, Hansen, and Scheurer 2015), Referendaires at the European Court of Justice (Kenney 2000), the Secretariat of the Russian Constitutional Court (Epstein, Knight, and Shvetsova 2001), legal assistants at the German Federal Constitutional Court (Wieland 2002), and staff at Brazil's Supreme Federal Court (Szmer, Kaheny, and Christensen 2014), the literature is dominated by studies of American courts generally and the U.S. Supreme Court in particular. This chapter begins by posing the normative question that drives the literature: do clerks have undue influence? It then explores the empirical literature on law clerks, largely in the American context but noting comparative work where appropriate, focusing on the major areas of research—clerk selection, agenda-setting, votes on the merits, opinion writing, coalition formation, and post-clerkship activity. Overall, the research demonstrates that while clerks do influence judges, they have not usurped judicial authority.

At the outset it is important to note that there are two types of clerks in the American context (see Stras 2014; Wasby 2014). The first are "staff attorneys," also known as "court attorneys," "pro se" clerks, "long-term" clerks, or "career" clerks who are the professional, centralized research staff for courts and who routinely serve for multiple years. The second are "in-chambers" clerks, "short-term" clerks, or "elbow" clerks who serve individual judges usually for a single year.[1] There has been some research on staff attorneys including how they are selected, their role in screening petitions, and the question of improper delegation to an unaccountable bureaucratic group (see e.g., Kearney 2014; Peppers, Giles, and Tainer-Parkins 2014). This line of research has found strong correlations between staff attorney recommendations and the judges' decisions on granting discretionary cases, the type of opinion to be issued, and case disposition (Meador 1974; Oakley and Thompson 1980, 1986; Oakley 1991; Stow and Spaeth 1992; Hanson, Flango, and Hansen 2000). Yet little, if any, evidence suggests that staff attorneys wield excessive power, either because they may be internalizing judicial preferences or because the cases themselves may be relatively routine. Further research is necessary to answer the question of staff attorney influence fully.

The second body of research has largely focused on in-chambers clerks because it is thought that they have greater opportunities for influence since they work directly for individual judges and participate in tasks—such as opinion writing—that staff attorneys do not. This literature comprises the vast majority of studies on judicial assistants. Thus, unless otherwise noted, the terms "law clerk" and "clerk" should be understood to mean the short-term, elbow clerk who works directly for an individual judge in chambers and who is involved in every stage of the judicial decision-making process.

Additionally, it should be noted that most of what we know about law clerks comes either from archival materials such as the personal papers of judges or from the judges and clerks themselves through first-person accounts, interviews, and surveys. Perhaps the best sources of information about what clerks do are the original documents produced through the judge–clerk working relationship. What happens to a judge's personal papers, however, is determined by the judge. Some judges have kept every scrap of paper produced in connection with their service on the bench, and made them publicly available at universities or the Library of Congress in Washington, DC. Others have taken the opposite approach and either "scrubbed" their papers of internal communications before making them available or simply destroyed them. The Federal Judicial Center lists the locations of the papers of all federal judges in its online Biographical Directory of Federal Judges.[2] Collins (2013) recently detailed the locations of, literature about, and controversy surrounding the papers of U.S. Supreme Court justices.[3]

First-person accounts have also been informative. Many individual clerks that have published memoirs in law journals, usually on the death of a judge or to commemorate an anniversary (e.g., Sokolow 1995; Small 2007; Wilkinson 2008), and judges themselves have written about the work of clerks (e.g., Rehnquist 1987). Though many are reluctant or refuse, some judges and clerks have agreed to be interviewed and surveyed by journalists, judicial biographers, and scholars who study the clerkship institution (see Ward and Wasby 2010; Armstrong 2014; Epstein 1990). In all, the relative accessibility of judicial papers and the willingness of judges and clerks to discuss the institution has resulted in a great deal of information about the role of law clerks and their effect on the judicial process.

Normative Concerns

Since the early twentieth century, American government and the responsibilities of political elites have grown exponentially (see e.g., Skowronek 1982, 1997, 2008; Schickler 2001; Crowe 2012). To cope with the expansion, political officeholders have been aided by increasing numbers of political advisors. For example, both the president and Congress have ten times as many staffers as they did a century ago and research shows that they have considerable influence with those they serve (see e.g., Fox and Hammond 1977; Patterson 1988, 2000, 2009). The Supreme Court too has been aided by a growing number of staffers with law clerks serving as the chief advisors and assistants to the justices (see e.g., Peppers 2006; Ward and Weiden 2006; Peppers and Ward 2012; Peppers and Cushman 2015). While research on clerks, like other political advisors, demonstrates that they are influential, the question that drives the literature is whether the influence is inappropriate.

But what constitutes undue influence? To be sure, if clerks rather than judges are choosing winners and losers in cases that would certainly constitute an improper abdication of responsibility on the part of the judge. But there is no known example of such a case occurring—though the lengthy, debilitating illnesses of some Supreme Court justices such as Frank Murphy, Charles Whittaker, John Marshall Harlan II, William O. Douglas, and Thurgood Marshall have provided such opportunities and raised suspicion that the clerks, rather than their justices, were making the decisions. Still, the literature contains examples from the papers of the justices of clerks using the tasks they have been delegated with for arguably inappropriate ends such as Supreme Court clerks trading cases randomly assigned to them in the pool, slanting pool memoranda through argumentation, and even omitting key information (Ward and Weiden 2006; Greenhouse 2006). Further research needs to be done to determine when and how clerk influence can be thought of as inappropriate and this is particularly true for non-U.S. courts where empirical research is relatively scarce (e.g., Massing 2002).

One way to think about law clerk influence is by comparing their behavior to other high-level political advisors. Research shows that legislative staffers write speeches, develop policy, conduct research, draft legislation, and communicate and negotiate on behalf of their members (Porter 1975; Fox and Hammond 1977; Salisbury and Shepsle 1981). Executive aides also write speeches and develop policy expertise to advise presidents and governors who in turn delegate to them both routine and policy tasks

(Patterson 1988; Rudalevige 2005). Is a law clerk's role essentially the same as that of a legislative staffer or executive aide? In many ways the answer is yes as clerks play the same kinds of advisory roles to their judges that staffers in the elected branches do. But there are obvious differences such as the drafting of opinions that constitute the law of the land and are binding on lower courts and future cases. Furthermore, most of the advising done for executives and legislators is done informally and orally, unlike the written advising done for judges. This may explain why much of the research on staffers for elected officials is based on interviews (e.g., Whiteman 1995; Romzek and Utter 1997; Ponder 2000). Despite these challenges, future work in this area might employ a comparative framework to assess influence—and whether that influence is perhaps inappropriate—among staffers across institutions and outside the U.S. context.

While the studies discussed in this chapter show that clerks have a great deal of responsibility and influence in the judicial process, it is important to note that there is little evidence to suggest that their influence supersedes that of their judges. For their part, judges know that clerks have the potential to exercise undue influence and have taken steps over time to minimize this from happening. For example, an informal norm of hiring clerks for only a single year developed, the chambers of one Supreme Court justice does an independent review of cert petitions as a check on the cert pool, and former Supreme Court clerks are barred from participating in cases before the justices for two years after they leave the Court. But critics have suggested more radical reforms such as Senate confirmation of law clerks, hiring all law clerks for a particular court into a pool and assigning them randomly to work on individual cases, and having a nonpartisan committee of former clerks, law professors, and attorneys select and assign them to judges (see Liptak 2010; *The New York Times* 2010). Others have called for lessening clerk influence by reducing caseloads, increasing judicial salaries, and hiring more mature, experienced clerks (e.g., Yoon 2014). While there is no shortage of potential fixes, the question remains whether the institution of law clerk is broken. In an attempt to help answer this question, the balance of this chapter reviews the growing number of studies from clerk selection to post-clerkship careers.

Clerk Selection

Legal practitioners, including judges, have always had apprentices. Before the formalization of legal education at the end of the nineteenth century, prospective attorneys learned the law by working with lawyers and judges. Once law school education became the standard path to a career in the law, judges turned to the law schools for apprentices seeking an experiential component to their studies and for assistance in dealing with judicial workloads. Chief Judge Horace Gray of the Massachusetts Supreme Judicial Court is credited with beginning the clerkship institution in the 1870s when he began hiring assistants selected by his half-brother, Harvard Law School Professor John Chipman Gray (Peppers 2006, 2007; Peppers and Ward, 2012). Judge Gray paid these assistants out of his own pocket and continued the practice when he was appointed to the U.S. Supreme Court in 1882.

Not long thereafter, however, Gray's model became formalized. Four years after Gray joined the Court, Congress authorized funds for each Supreme Court justice to hire a "stenographic" clerk and ultimately a "law clerk" in 1919. Over time, Congress extended funding to hire clerks for lower court judges—in 1930 for the courts of appeals and in 1936 for the federal district courts—and increased the number of clerks per judge as workloads grew (Peppers, Giles, and Tainer-Parkins 2008, 2014). Currently, federal judges employ as many as four clerks each, the overall number of federal law clerks totals more than 2,000, the application process has exploded as greater numbers of students seek clerkships at all levels of the judiciary, and there have been numerous calls to reform the application process (see e.g., Wald 1990; Kozinski 1991; Oberdorfer and Levy 1992; Becker, Breyer, and Calabresi 1994; Avery, Jolls, Posner, and Roth 2001, 2007; Priest 2005; Haruvy, Roth, and Unver 2006; Aldisert, Kirkpatrick, and Stevens 2006; Peppers, Giles, and Tainer-Parkins 2008; Nielson 2014).

Law students seek clerkships for a variety of reasons (Wasby 2006). In general, clerks typically desire to obtain an advanced education in the law, in terms of both process and substance. Wasby (2006) found that this was the most common response given by clerks at the federal courts of appeal. Another common response was that a clerkship simply provided the budding attorney with a transitional year of good experience before choosing a more permanent career path. Wasby (2006) also notes that a clerkship is a prestigious form of public service that will serve the clerk well no matter what they choose to do afterwards. Certainly, this is the draw for a U.S. Supreme Court clerkship, which is the next step for federal courts of appeal clerks who want to continue clerking for another year. And the education and prestige of a Supreme Court clerkship translates into nearly any job that a former clerk desires.

How do judges select their clerks? Gray's initial model of hiring promising students from Harvard Law School has remained largely unchanged. Though the list of law schools providing clerks has increased and diversified over time, Harvard and other elite schools such as Yale, Chicago, Columbia, Stanford, Virginia, and Michigan provide a larger share of clerks than other schools, particularly at the U.S. Supreme Court. Prior to joining the Court, clerks spend one year clerking for a judge on the U.S. Courts of Appeals where they gain experience and are recommended by so-called "feeder judges" who routinely place their clerks at the Supreme Court (Ditslear and Baum 2001; Ward and Weiden 2006; Baum and Ditslear 2010; Katz and Stafford 2010; Baum 2014; Kromphardt 2014; Stras 2014; Hess 2015). Feeder judges are the small group of influential federal courts of appeal judges who often have personal relationships with, and are ideologically compatible to, the justices they place their clerks with. Researchers have even made distinctions among feeder judges with "major," "super," or "elite" feeder judges signifying those who place at least one clerk per term on the Supreme Court (Kaye and Gastwirth 2009; Hess 2015). The justices trust feeder judges to help screen prospective clerks and recommend only those who can handle the Supreme Court's workload.

Individual judges choose their own clerks, either with the help of their current clerks, or through delegating the task to screening committees of trusted confidants—generally former clerks. During the early decades of the American clerkship institution, clerks regularly served their judges for multiple years with some making careers of their clerkships—not unlike present-day "staff attorneys" and clerks in many non-U.S. courts such as the European Court of Justice (Kenney 2000). As clerk responsibility and influence grew at the U.S. Supreme Court—the justices adopted the norm of having their clerks serve for a single year, a practice that remains largely in place today.

Research demonstrates that the key factors in clerk selection are the law school the clerk attended, class ranking, work on the law review and writing sample, prior clerkship experience, the clerk's personality (which is particularly important at the interview stage), and recommendations (Wieland 2002; Ward and Weiden 2006; Wasby 2006; Peppers, Giles, and Tainer-Parkins 2008, 2014). Popular and scholarly criticism of the selection process has often focused on the lack of racial and gender diversity in the clerking corps, long the province of privileged white males (Rhinehart 1994; Brown 1996; Mauro 1998a; Agostini and Corrigan 2001; Benson 2007; Kaye and Gastwirth 2009; Mauro 2014; Szmer, Kaheny, and Christensen 2014; Kaheny, Szmer, Hansen, and Scheurer 2015).

In addition to racial and gender diversity, a key empirical question that typically preoccupies those interested in clerk selection is whether there is an ideological element to the process. Do judges select ideologically compatible clerks? Federal judges self-report that ideology plays little if any role in their selection process (Peppers, Giles, and Tainer-Parkins 2008, 2014; Wasby, 2006). Yet studies show that over time the ideological congruence between Supreme Court justices and their clerks has increased leading to a much more polarized clerking corps than was true during the early years of the clerkship institution through most of the twentieth century (Ditslear and Baum 2001; Ward and Weiden 2006; Peppers and Zorn 2008; Nelson, Rishikof, Messinger, and Jo 2009a; Baum and Ditslear 2010; Baum 2014).

The relatively recent development of a largely partisan clerking corps may be the result of at least three developments. First, there has been an explosion of applications. Historically, prospective clerks only applied to one, two, or maybe three justices they might want to work with. And it was not uncommon for the justices or their screening committees to ask which other justices a clerk had applied to. But in recent years, prospective clerks have been applying to all of the justices, both active and retired, in order to increase their chances of securing a job that can lead to great fortune and influence after their clerkships end (Ward and Weiden 2006; Baum 2014). The result is that justices, current clerks, and their screening committees have selected clerks who they think will be compatible, ideologically and otherwise, with their justice. A second factor, related to the first, is that the feeder judge that the clerk works for may not only be an ideological indicator for determining compatibility but may play a role in training the clerk to think and act in partisan ways (Garrow 2006). The final explanation for the increased ideological congruence among judges and their clerks is the relatively recent developments of the rise of the New Right political regime (e.g., Skowronek 1997, 2008;

Clayton and Pickerill 2006), conservative legal mobilization (e.g., Teles 2008; Avery and McLaughlin 2013; Hollis-Brusky 2015), and the resulting increase in mass and elite political polarization in American politics more generally (e.g., McCarty, Poole, and Rosenthal 2006; Fiorina and Abrams 2009; Baum 2014).

A recent study by Kromphardt (2014) suggests that we may need to change the way we think of clerk selection. Instead of focusing on the selection of individual clerks, Kromphardt (2014) argues that judges seek to assemble a group or team of clerks to work in their chambers. Analyzing the ideological characteristics of the teams of clerks selected by U.S. Supreme Court justices from 1969–2007, the study found that justices frequently hire clerks with different preferences from their own and from the other clerks in their chambers (see e.g., Kozinski and Bernstein 1998). These "crosswind" chambers comprise the vast majority of chambers and are generally desirable because they provide judges with more and varied perspectives than do "foxhole" chambers where judges and clerks are like-minded. Kromphardt (2014) finds intriguing differences among the justices with Souter, Blackmun, Burger, and O'Connor most often constructing crosswind chambers while Stewart, Powell, Stevens, and White had the highest percentage of foxhole chambers.

The chief question clerk selection research gives rise to is whether the ideological element in clerk selection translates into a partisan influence over the judicial decision-making process. Do clerks who sought or were selected for their positions for ideological ends behave differently from clerks who sought or were selected for non-ideological reasons? The balance of this chapter is devoted to exploring the role of clerks at each stage of the decisional process. In brief preview, research shows that clerks are not only influential but that their influence is also ideological in nature. Clerks use their positions to advise judges and influence the law in the same way that congressional staffers use their positions to advise members of Congress and influence legislation.

Agenda-Setting

Clerks are essential to the agenda-setting process, particularly where courts have discretionary jurisdiction. Clerks read petitions, briefs, and lower court opinions and draft memos and make recommendations to aid judges in deciding which cases to place on the docket. Research demonstrates that clerks are not only indispensable to the agenda-setting process but can also wield considerable influence at this stage (Perry 1994; Epstein, Knight, and Shvetsova 2001; Wieland 2002; Ward and Weiden 2006; Swanson and Wasby 2008; Avtonomov 2009). Clerks provide both legal analysis that bears on whether a case should or should not be granted—for example, because there is disagreement among lower courts[4]—but also political and strategic analysis of the positions that other judges and political actors outside the courts have taken or are likely to take if a case is granted or denied review (Ward and Weiden 2006).

Petitions for certiorari (known as "cert petitions") are requests from litigants who lost in lower courts asking the Supreme Court to review their cases. Historically, each petition was reviewed by every justice (or a clerk for every justice) separately, leading to inefficiencies in the selection process. Beginning in the 1970s, some justices began pooling their clerks to share in the review of cert petitions and avoid duplication of effort. Known as the "cert pool," it was expanded over time and fewer justices and clerks independently reviewed cases. Eventually, only one justice operated independent of the pool, currently Justice Samuel Alito and his clerks fill this role. Thus, pool clerks write their memos for eight justices of different ideological and jurisprudential persuasions.

Studies by Perry (1994) and Ward and Weiden (2006) based on interviews with justices and clerks and archival analysis of pool memos and internal court documents suggest that the cert pool has two major effects. First, there has been a chilling effect. Pool clerks have often been less candid in their analyses and are reluctant to recommend granting a case for fear of being ostracized if they are wrong. Second, some pool clerks have attempted to slant their memos in a particular ideological direction in an attempt to influence the justices' votes on whether to grant certiorari (Brenner and Palmer 1990; Ward and Weiden 2006). With the justices deciding roughly eighty cases each term in recent years compared with two or three times as many when there were fewer justices and clerks in the pool, critics suggest that the cert pool has contributed to the Court's shrinking docket (see O'Brien 1997: 58). But there is debate in the empirical literature about whether the cert pool is the cause (Cordray and Cordray 2001; Owens and Simon 2012).

Empirical work on agenda-setting shows that both clerks and judges at the U.S. Supreme Court and at state high courts self-report that they have more influence at this stage than at any other (Ward and Weiden 2006; Swanson and Wasby 2008) and that clerk recommendations are highly correlated with the decisions of their judges (Brenner and Palmer 1990; Palmer 2001; Stras 2007). While this may not be too surprising at the U.S. Supreme Court given that the justices receive thousands of petitions each term, the vast majority of which must be necessarily denied given the Court's limited capacity to hear cases, it is nonetheless suggestive of clerk influence. Subsequent work on the U.S. Supreme Court has further demonstrated that when controlling for alternative factors, such as a justice's initial voting inclinations based on their ideology and the information contained in and quality of the cert petition, clerk influence can be the determining factor in "close" cases that are not obvious denials (Black and Boyd 2012) and where pool clerks are ideologically compatible with the justice and write pool memos in ways that provide justices with specific cues and recommendations (Black and Boyd 2012; Black, Boyd, and Bryan 2014; Wallander and Benesh 2014). Many of these cues such as a real conflict in the lower court and the participation and arguments of amici have long been found to be influential in granting cert yet Wallander and Benesh (2014) also found empirical support for Perry's (1994) percolation hypothesis: when clerks highlight the "readiness" of a case to be heard, as measured by the cert pool memo discussing many feeder judges and the reasoning they used in their opinions, the more likely the justices are to grant cert. Future research in this area should be able to test the influence of factors highlighted by clerks independent of outside influences on the justices, such as legal briefs and other information the justices may obtain on their own.

Oral Argument

Once a case is accepted, clerks help their judges prepare for oral argument. The first step is drafting bench memos analyzing the issues in the case, including the introduction of new issues beyond those raised in the briefs; posing potential questions for their judges to ask of the attorneys; and possibly a recommendation for the disposition of the case (Peppers 2006; Ward and Weiden 2006; Wasby 2014; Stras 2014). Historically, early clerks at the U.S. Supreme Court did not draft bench memos and generally did not participate in the oral argument process (Peppers 2012; Peppers and Driver 2012). With the arrival of Earl Warren in 1953, however, he and an increasing number of subsequent justices began the practice of having their clerks prepare bench memos (Peppers 2006; Ward and Weiden 2006; Choper 2012; Smith 2012).

Lower court judges may also have their clerks prepare bench memos. One study found that 88 percent of federal courts of appeals judges have their clerks draft bench memos but only 44 percent have them prepare questions for oral argument (Peppers, Giles, and Tainer-Parkins 2014). Some courts such as the Ninth Circuit and the Minnesota Supreme Court use shared or pooled bench memos (Wasby 2014; Stras 2014).[5] In such instances, a judge may circulate her clerk's bench memo to the other judges on the panel, sometimes without reviewing it first. The clerks for the other judges may prepare response memos which are also circulated. This bench-memo, back-and-forth creates an ongoing written dialogue among the clerks for the judges to consider (Wasby 2014). It remains to be determined how often this happens and the effects it has on both oral argument and the case dispositions.

Research shows that oral argument matters and is part of the decision-making and coalition formation processes as justices engage in a conversation with each other through the questions they pose to the attorneys (Johnson 2001, 2004; Johnson, Black, and Wedeking 2012). Despite its demonstrated importance, there is little empirical work on the role that clerks play in preparing their justices for oral argument. Anecdotal evidence shows that many contemporary justices expend considerable resources by having their clerks draft lengthy bench memos and meeting face to face with them for discussion before oral argument takes place (e.g., Peppers 2006; Ward and Weiden 2006; Ward 2012). The question is whether this pre-oral argument work by the clerks has any effect on the justices.

Johnson, Stras, and Black (2014) compared the questions posed in forty bench memos prepared for Justice Blackmun by his clerks with the actual questions Blackmun asked as determined by both his oral argument notes and oral argument transcripts. The authors found that Blackmun asked more than 40 percent of the questions drafted for him by his clerks with more than half of the questions he asked focusing on policy issues rather than precedent or the views of external actors. Still, there was wide variation in the cases examined where Blackmun might ask all the questions posed for him, some, none, and might add his own questions. While their findings await a more sophisticated analysis that controls for other factors and goes the next step in exploring the extent to which clerk-written questions and bench-memo analyses find their way into judicial opinions, the initial results suggest that clerks can directly influence the actions their justices take at oral argument.

Along these lines, Wasby (2014) reports that in complex cases clerks may have an information advantage over their judges, depending on the judges' level of experience with the issue (Wasby 2008), because the clerks can devote more time to analyzing the issues in a bench memo. This may lead to a framing affect in the way that judges view the case and ultimately how opinions are written. Anecdotal evidence shows that bench memos can provide the initial basis for the draft opinions that clerks write with the clerk who authored a bench memo commonly chosen to be the clerk to draft an opinion (Ward and Weiden 2006; Wasby 2014). Future research in this area can examine the extent to which opinions reflect approaches set out in bench memos as opposed to post-argument conference discussion. Archival evidence suggests that this does occur, particularly on courts with shared bench memos (Wasby 2008, 2014).

Votes on the Merits

At the U.S. Supreme Court, justices meet with their clerks after oral argument and before the justices' private conference to discuss the merits of the cases. As with clerk analysis and recommendations at the agenda-setting stage, clerk-written bench memos, questions, and pre-conference discussions can influence the positions judges take with regard to the merits of a case. Furthermore, even after the conference vote on the merits, clerks can continue to exert influence on the merits. Indeed, the literature on voting fluidity demonstrates that it is not uncommon for judges to change their initial votes and positions from the time of oral argument to the final vote on the merits (e.g., Howard 1968; Maltzman, Spriggs, and Wahlbeck 2000).

Of all the areas where clerks exercise influence, the merits stage is where they self-report that they have the least influence (Ward and Weiden 2006). This finding makes theoretical sense as the merits vote is the most central to the job of judging. It also mitigates normative concerns that clerks are improperly exercising judicial power. Furthermore, this finding is consistent with empirical work that demonstrates that other factors, namely a combination of law, strategy, and ideology, drive judicial votes (Pacelle, Curry, and Marshall 2011; Bailey and Maltzman 2012; Corley, Steigerwalt, and Ward 2013). Yet, anecdotal evidence, such as the case of Justice Lewis Powell's clerks lobbying him throughout the coalition formation process in the gay rights case *Bowers v. Hardwick* (1986), plainly shows that clerks can and do lobby justices, sometimes repeatedly and strenuously, on case outcomes (Murdoch and Price 2001: 271–354).[6] We know from archival documents and interviews that clerks have persuaded judges to change positions (Wasby 2008, 2014). But how influential are clerk recommendations and how often are clerks able to change the minds of their judges?

Systematic research shows that the votes of high court judges at both the state and federal level correlate strongly with their clerks' recommendations, with a higher level of agreement than with the other judges they serve with (Palmer and Benner 1995; Swanson and Wasby 2008). But this may be due to a principle–agent relationship between judge and clerk where the clerk anticipates the judges' preferences. However, it might also mean that clerk recommendations are more persuasive than the arguments of other judges. According to Swanson and Wasby (2008), 10 percent of state high court judges said that they changed their minds on case outcomes because of arguments made by their clerks. The authors concluded that it was the clerks' research rather than their recommendations that affected the judges. In their survey of former U.S. Supreme Court clerks, Ward and Weiden (2006) found similar results for clerks being able to change the minds of the justices. Peppers and Zorn's (2008) multivariate analysis of Supreme Court decisions employed clerk ideology as measured by former clerks' self-reports on survey instruments. They controlled for the justices' policy preferences and found that clerks exerted an independent ideological influence on the justices' votes on the merits. They further estimated the magnitude of the effect to be roughly one-third that of a justice's ideology.

Kromphardt (2015) first replicated the analysis by Peppers and Zorn (2008) and found a similar, if slightly stronger effect. But Kromphardt went further, employing a novel approach to determine clerk influence on merits votes. For each term of the Supreme Court (1985–2001), the author examined the ideological influence of clerks collectively in each chamber relative to the ideology of the justice. Kromphardt operationalized clerk ideology by assigning to each clerk the Judicial Common Space score of the federal court of appeals judge they previously clerked for, allowing for a particular justice's chambers to be categorized as a liberal foxhole (all liberal clerks), conservative foxhole (all conservative clerks), or a crosswinds (mix of liberal and conservative clerks). Lagged JCS scores were used for justice ideology. These measures allowed the author to determine the ideological direction and distance between a chambers clerking corps and their justice. Kromphardt found that while both crosswinds and liberal foxhole chambers had no influence on justices' votes on the merits, conservative foxholes were able to influence both liberal and conservative justices to move in a conservative direction (justices were one-quarter to one-third less likely to cast a liberal vote).

While these studies show clerk influence, they may best be understood as complimentary to the research that show merits votes being influenced by the range of informational sources that justices encounter during the resolution of cases including litigants' briefs (e.g., Corley 2008), amicus briefs (e.g., Collins 2008), and oral argument (Johnson 2001, 2004). Thus, while clerks can influence how judges vote on the outcomes of cases, clerks have by no means assumed judges' authority to choose winners and losers any more than a persuasive legal brief or oral argument has.

Opinion Writing

Perhaps the most controversial aspect of clerks' duties is their contribution to the opinion-writing process. Over time, clerks have taken on the responsibility of drafting the opinions, orders, memoranda, and even jury instructions delivered under their judges' names. The scope of clerks' duties has grown so much that it is now considered rare for judges to do their own first drafts (Wieland 2002; Peppers 2006; Ward and Weiden 2006). For example, one study found that 97 percent of federal district court judges delegated opinion writing to their clerks (Peppers, Giles, and Tainer-Parkins 2008). Another found that 95 percent of federal appeals court judges also assigned opinion writing to their clerks (Peppers, Giles, and Tainer-Parkins 2014). We know from interviews with specific judges and clerks that some judges draft their own opinions such as Justices William O. Douglas and John Paul Stevens on the U.S. Supreme Court and Judges Richard Posner and Frank Easterbrook on Court of Appeals. Others, such as Justices Thurgood Marshall and Sandra Day O'Connor largely delegated the task to their clerks with relatively little if any oversight (author's interviews; see also Ward and Weiden 2006: ch. 5). Empirical research confirms this with opinions issued by judges who are the least engaged in the opinion-writing process exhibiting the most stylistic variation from one opinion to another (Wahlbeck, Spriggs, and Sigelman 2002; Choi and Gulati 2005; Rosenthal and Yoon 2011; Bodwin, Rosenthal, and Yoon 2013). This variation suggests that multiple authors were significantly involved in the opinion-writing process over time.

Regardless of the level of direction that a judge provides, when writing the initial draft clerks will necessarily make stylistic decisions such as word choice, phrasing, sentence and paragraph construction, and opinion structure. And while clerks can make more substantive choices about which arguments to make and which authorities to cite, their stylistic choices can have lasting effects on legal doctrine (Posner 1995). In their interviews with state high court judges, Swanson and Wasby (2008) found that clerks have more influence over the language of opinions than they do over case outcomes. Consider the emergence of the phrase "exceedingly persuasive justification" in the U.S. Supreme Court's sex discrimination jurisprudence. We can readily trace its origins to Justice Potter Stewart's majority opinion in *Personnel Administrator of Massachusetts v. Feeney* (1979: 273). The phrase matters because it may be either constitute a simple restatement of the intermediate scrutiny test required by the Court's sex discrimination precedent, or it may suggest a new, potentially more difficult standard to meet. Stewart's opinion only used the phrase once, with no citation to precedent. Yet the phrase reappeared in subsequent sex discrimination cases so that when it was used in Justice Ruth Bader Ginsburg's opinion in *United States v. Virginia* (1996) to strike down the male-only admissions policy at Virginia Military Institute (VMI), Justice Antonin Scalia's dissent argued that it was not a simple restatement of intermediate scrutiny but a new standard akin to the much more difficult test of strict scrutiny. Did the phrase originally come from Stewart, the clerk who drafted the opinion, or from somewhere else such as a legal brief? Was the original use of this phrase a seemingly harmless stylistic choice of the Stewart clerk who drafted *Feeney*, or a strategic attempt to raise the level of scrutiny as Scalia later suggested was at work in the VMI case?

This is the crucial question that implicates the role of clerks in the opinion-writing process. It can be argued that judges are ultimately responsible for even the stylistic choices made by their drafting clerks because judges, at least, should review and approve those choices. Nevertheless there are examples of egregious errors made by clerks that somehow find their way into published opinions. Consider the firestorm of media coverage surrounding Scalia's dissent in *EPA v. EME Homer City Generation* (2014). Scalia argued that the Court's decision was inconsistent with a unanimous precedent that Scalia said invalidated EPA efforts to consider costs when setting regulations: "This is not the first time EPA has sought to convert the Clean Air Act into a mandate for cost effective regulation. *Whitman v. American Trucking Assns., Inc.*, 531 U.S. 547 (2001), confronted EPA's contention that it could consider costs in setting [National Ambient Air Quality Standards]." The problem with this assertion was that it was false. The EPA's stance in *Whitman* was the opposite and it was the trucking industry that wanted the EPA to consider cost. The unanimous opinion in *Whitman* ruled for the EPA and, in a further embarrassing twist, was authored by none other than Scalia himself.

How could this mistake happen? Whether Scalia or one of his clerks drafted the dissent, everyone in his chambers missed it. In addition, Justice Clarence Thomas joined the dissent and, as is customary, at least one of his clerks would have been responsible for reading Scalia's draft and providing comments and recommendations about possible changes and whether or not to join it. Indeed, every justice who participated in the case would have received a draft of Scalia's dissent and, like Thomas, would have had one of their clerks review it and make suggestions.

Of course courts can correct errors in opinions when they are found, and Scalia ultimately did so in this instance, but such mistakes do happen each term and have been happening for a long time. For example, in 1952 Yale law professor and former clerk George Braden wrote Justice Sherman Minton about an error he found in Minton's opinion in a recent case: "I object to your statement that in *Northwest Airlines* 'this Court said.' Actually, in *Northwest Airlines* Frankfurter, Douglas, and Murphy 'said'. Perhaps Black said so also, but that is an unanswered question" (Braden 1952). Minton replied, "Thanks for the suggestion about *Northwest Airlines*. Two of us are to blame there. My clerk wanted to insert the *Northwest* quote and I consented without checking the matter you refer to. If the alert reporter of this Court hasn't found it already we will call his attention to it" (Minton 1952). Thus, even with all the checks in place to ensure that draft opinions are carefully scrutinized before being issued, it is plain that clerks can and do use their opinion-drafting authority to shape the law.

Clerk influence may also be seen in the proliferation of separate opinions. A number of scholars have argued that law clerks influence U.S. Supreme Court justices' decisions to issue separate opinions (Best 2002; Ward and Weiden 2006). One recent study of Supreme Court decisions issued since 1954 employed a multivariate analysis with dummy variables for the years before and after the doubling of clerks at the start of the 1970s (Corley, Steigerwalt, and Ward 2013). The authors found, perhaps somewhat paradoxically, that having more clerks was correlated with increases in voting unanimity among the justices but had no discernable effect on the ability of the justices to achieve opinion consensus. Thus, the question of clerk effects on the proliferation of separate opinion writing is still an open one, ripe for further study.

Coalition Formation

Clerks can exert influence over the coalition formation process both before and after the conference vote on the merits. While votes can and do change after opinions are drafted and circulated (e.g., Howard 1968; Maltzman, Spriggs, and Wahlbeck 2000), there are further aspects to the coalition formation process in which clerks are involved. They read draft opinions and memoranda and make recommendations to their judges on how to reply and whether to suggest changes to an opinion, join an opinion, or write separately. On collegial courts, clerks work collectively through an informal "clerk network" to aid their judges in the bargaining and accommodation process (Ward and Weiden 2006). This is most pronounced in high courts such as the U.S. Supreme Court where clerks and judges work closely together in a single building. Harvard law professor Martha Minow, who clerked for Justice Thurgood Marshall during the 1980 term, explained, "It's almost an ambassadorial role, trying to pick up information behind the scenes" (Mauro 1998b).

On the U.S. Supreme Court, the clerk network emerged after the Supreme Court building was completed in 1935. At first, only Chief Justice Charles Evans Hughes and Justice Owen Roberts regularly worked in their chambers, while their colleagues preferred to continue doing their work at home (Hutchinson and Garrow 2002). With Hugo Black's appointment in 1937, new justices chose to work primarily at the Court. By 1941, every member of the Court was regularly using his High Court chambers except for Chief Justice Harlan Fiske Stone. The Court was fully occupied by all the justices and their staffs beginning in 1946 when Chief Justice Fred Vinson was appointed.

The result was that instead of working in the homes of their justices, geographically isolated from one another, every clerk worked in the same building, on the same floor, and in offices next to each other. The importance of this new working environment cannot be overstated. Clerks from different chambers saw each other on a daily basis: on the way to work, in the Court's parking garage, during lunch, and after work. Clerks began regularly lunching together and their discussions frequently involved the cases they were working on. When the Court established a separate dining room for the clerks, which is still in use today, they saw even more of each other. For their part, the justices realized that they could benefit from gaining information through the clerk network about their colleagues' positions, and formally establishing a clerk's dining room was a way to foster it.

Clerks became an important resource to their justices as the least obtrusive means of obtaining details about what was happening in the other chambers. Because clerks were already commenting on the memoranda and opinions from the other chambers, and making recommendations on whether or not to issue separate opinions, both clerks and justices recognized the benefits of obtaining further information. For example, 1957 Harlan clerk Norman Dorsen wrote his justice: "The Court is still 5–4 on *Nilva*, although rumor has it that Justice Burton himself is wavering. Justice Frankfurter, it is said, is willing to consider amending Rule 42(b), but until it is amended would affirm. The clerks are about 18–0 for reversal, including both the Burton clerks" (Dorsen 1957).

There has yet to be any systematic research on how clerks influence coalition formation. Thus we know little about how often and to what extent bargaining and negotiation occur in the clerk network, or about the relationship between the clerk network and the judge or justice network. There may be differences across judges and courts in how the clerk network operates, if it operates at all—particularly given that the chambers of U.S. Courts of Appeals judges, for example, are dispersed and some judges have adopted the rule that their clerks cannot discuss pending appeals outside of individual chambers (see Peppers, Giles, and Tainer-Parkins 2014).

Indeed, it may be that separate clerk and judge networks may not be the correct way to conceptualize coalition formation. Perhaps a more appropriate conception is to think of courts as small-group environments where all the judges and clerks work together to decide cases. In such a "judge–clerk network," as Swanson and Wasby (2008: 43) suggest, "there is no judge–judge or judge–clerk interaction in isolation; rather, judges and clerks are all extensively interacting with other judges and clerks. Hence, one might more appropriately speak of the judge–clerk relationship network ... Thus, judge–judge interaction and judge–clerk interaction are integrally interrelated even if scholars study them separately" (see generally Cohen 2002). Indeed, one might even add secretaries, now increasingly referred to as judicial assistants, into such analyses (Wasby 2005, 2014).

Post-Clerkship Career Paths and Influence

Very few law clerks are fired by their judges and when they are it is generally for poor work performance or personality conflicts, rather than for violating the rule of confidentiality (Hutchinson and Garrow 2002; Peppers 2006; Murphy 2012; Peppers, Giles, and Tainer-Parkins 2014). The vast majority of former law clerks leave their positions in good standing and are highly sought after by prospective employers. Most choose to work in private practice, while some choose government or academic positions, and a few select public interest work (Wasby 2006; Nelson, Rishikof, Messinger, and Jo 2009b; Ward, Dwyer, and Gill 2014). Those who choose to sign with major law firms secure signing bonuses and command salaries that exceed the salaries of the judges they clerked for. Former law clerks have gone on to influential positions in business and government including the federal bench and the U.S. Supreme Court. Research on what clerks do after leaving their clerkships shows that they continue to influence, or at least seek to influence, their judges in varying ways—both professionally through the jobs they take and personally through correspondence, get-togethers, and clerk reunions (Ward 2012). At the same time, judges influence the career choices of clerks through advice and recommendations (Ward 2012). In short, the relationship between clerk and judge does not end when the clerk leaves the clerkship.

McGuire (1993) detailed how former law clerks, along with alumni of the Office of the Solicitor General, law firm partners, and public interest lawyers, comprise the Supreme Court bar: the Washington legal elites who act as gatekeepers and help shape the decisions of the justices. Subsequent research and commentary has illuminated how former clerks comprise a specialized group of attorneys who are hired by a small group of firms that focus on U.S. Supreme Court practice (Roberts 2005; Swanson 2007; Lazarus 2008; Nelson, Rishikof, Messinger, and Jo 2009a, 2009b; Ward, Dwyer, and Gill 2014). It has become increasingly common for the justices to find themselves reading legal briefs authored by their former clerks and asking questions of them at oral argument.

O'Connor and Hermann (1995) found that more than half of all former U.S. Supreme Court clerks have participated as counsel or amicus at least one time before the Court and are twice as likely to participate as are non-clerks with comparable educational backgrounds. Former clerks of Justices Blackmun, Brennan, Harlan II, and Stevens generally had average or higher than average participation rates as attorneys before the Court. On the other hand, former clerks for Justices Clark, Douglas, O'Connor, Rehnquist, Warren, and White generally participated at lower rates than the average former clerk. An updated study would likely find higher rates of participation across the board given the creation of specialized Supreme Court practices and former clerks now flocking to them. It is not that clerks for particular justices are in demand but rather that any former clerk is prized by such firms. Indeed, so prized are former clerks that some firms are now encouraging their associates to temporarily leave their jobs to clerk for federal judges (Mauro 2015).

Nelson, Rishikof, Messinger, and Jo (2009a) argued that an institutional change in post-clerkship career paths occurred around 1990 with efforts by the conservative legal movement to gain legitimacy by populating institutions previously dominated by legal liberals. Ward, Dwyer, and Gill (2014) agree in part but argue that the change was broader and peg its inception at 1986: the first year that law firms began offering signing bonuses to former Supreme Court law clerks. Prior to 1986, clerks made employment decisions relatively free from monetary incentives and naturally sorted themselves into various jobs. After 1986, this Natural Sorting Regime was fundamentally transformed into a new era with clerks becoming "bonus babies": as sought after by major law firms as amateur athletes are by professional sporting teams. The change to the present Bonus Baby Regime for post-clerkship career paths has resulted in both in increase in private practice employment as well as growing partisanship in career choices (Ward, Dwyer, and Gill 2014). Research has demonstrated that the ideological polarization found among the clerking corps carries over into their job choices. Clerks for liberal justices are more likely to take on positions in government, academia, and public interest work, while clerks who worked for conservative justices show a higher propensity to take positions in private practice (Nelson, Rishikof, Messinger, and Jo 2009a, 2009b; Ward, Dwyer, and Gill 2014). Yet that difference has become far less pronounced in the past decade as huge signing bonuses—as high as $330,000 for Supreme Court clerks in 2014—have made private practice positions too lucrative to pass up for the vast majority of clerks. Still, most clerks leave their first jobs in private practice either for a position at another firm, a government job, or an academic post (Ward, Dwyer, and Gill 2014). And the positions they do take in firms adhere to ideological or partisan divisions with clerks for liberal justices being concentrated in one set of firms while clerks for conservative justices largely work for a different group of firms (Ward, Dwyer, and Gill 2014).

There is also evidence that the job choices of clerks also vary by the justices they clerk for. Ward, Dwyer, and Gill (2014) examined clerks from the Bonus Baby Regime, the Rehnquist and Roberts Courts, and found that while private practice has become an increasingly common job choice for every recent justices' clerks, they found that there were significant differences among the other job categories. Thus, the authors conclude that some justices might promote certain types of post-clerkship employment while at the same time discouraging others, for example government service as opposed to public interest law.

Nearly all former clerks continue to have subsequent contact with their judges in the years following their clerkships but that contact is necessarily minimal given that judges generally have busy schedules (Wasby 2006; Ward 2012). While a small number of former clerks sit on clerk selection committees and write the occasional letter of recommendation for clerkship applicants, the vast majority of clerks have only sporadic contact that includes postcards, holiday cards, marriage and birth announcements, and notifications of new jobs or awards received. But, beyond participating in cases before their judges, there are three other types of contact that illustrate how clerks seek to continue to have influence with their judge after their clerkship ends: correspondence about on the ongoing work of their judge and the court they serve on, sending law review articles and other publication to their judge, and forwarding news stories about issues that have been, are, or may be coming before their judge (Ward 2012).

Consider 1975 Rehnquist clerk William S. Eggeling's 1983 letter to Rehnquist, commenting on the opinion of Justices Stevens and Powell in *EEOC v. Wyoming* (1983): "JPS's concurrence was extraordinarily depressing, indicating a simplistic view of the Constitution which seems difficult to square with any meaningful concept of a federal republic. I was glad to see that LFP felt it appropriate to challenge the entirely vapid arguments advanced by JPS for overruling *National League of Cities*" (Eggeling 1983). In another instance, Rehnquist wrote Eggeling: "I enclose a copy of an extremely obscure opinion which we handed down today, *Railroad Retirement Bd. v. Fritz*, in which I think we have gained considerable ground in the year-long fight over the Equal Protection Clause application that went on during the Term you were here in *Massachusetts v. Murgia*. It was a negotiated opinion, as you might imagine, but I think we have finally buried most of the 'fair and substantial relationship to a legitimate state' language from some of the earlier cases" (Rehnquist 1980).

Similarly, Craig M. Bradley, who clerked for Rehnquist in 1975, wrote his former boss in 1994: "I enclose a copy of my latest article, as well as a letter to your colleagues. I really believe that you are on the verge of a major clarification of Fourth Amendment law, if only the Court will acknowledge that the search warrant requirement has been abandoned for outdoor searches" (Bradley 1994). Gary Born, who clerked for Rehnquist in 1982, wrote him in 1996: "I am enclosing the third edition of my book on *International Civil Litigation in the United States Courts* … Although the book is designed for practitioners and law schools, I hope that you will also find it of value in the international cases that come before the Court" (Born 1996).

As these examples and the studies of clerks' post-clerkship practices demonstrate, research in this area is important because it shows that clerks not only influence their judges while they work for them but also seek to do so after they leave, albeit through different means. Thus, the effect of law clerks on the work of the judges continues long after the clerks end their official time in a judge's chambers. But many questions remain. How often does each type of post-clerkship interaction take place? Are some clerks more prone, and some judges more receptive, to it than others? How effective is it? The post-clerkship relationship between judge and clerk is an area ripe for future study.

Conclusion

As this review of the literature demonstrates, those who engage in normative arguments about law clerk influence have a considerable and growing amount of empirical work to draw on. For reformers, however, who argue that clerks have undue influence, the evidence is not determinative—at least not yet. Despite continued calls for reform, research shows that while law clerk influence is considerable it has yet to show that clerks are inappropriately wielding influence and that judges are merely reviewing and approving clerk decisions. Instead, research suggests that, at a minimum, judges rely heavily on their clerks as sounding boards and advisers and at most that clerks are sometimes able to change the minds of their judges. Undue influence or not, it is plain that clerks are an important part of the judicial decision-making process—a part that must be considered in future analyses of judicial decision-making. And future research will go a long way to determining whether reforms are warranted and if so what ought to be done.

Notes

1. Although clerks for U.S. District Court judges often serve for two years, clerks for U.S. Courts of Appeal judges and U.S. Supreme Court justices rarely do so.
2. http://www.fjc.gov/history/home.nsf/page/judges.html.

3. For the U.S. Supreme Court, see also: http://www.scotusblog.com/2013/08/accessing-the-papers-of-supreme-court-justices-online-other-resources/.
4. The Court's internal rules state that lower-court disagreement (so-called circuit splits) will ordinarily make a case worthy of review.
5. Wasby (2014) reports that only a few U.S. Courts of Appeals use shared bench memos and several Ninth Circuit judges opt out of the practice.
6. For similar stories, see Woodward and Armstrong's (1979: 3–4) discussion of *O'Connor v. Donaldson* (1975) and Lazarus' (1998: 119) telling of *Patterson v. McLean Credit Union* (1989).

References

Agostini, R. M., and Corrigan, B. P. 2001. "Do as We Say or Do as We Do?: How the Supreme Court Law Clerk Controversy Reveals a Lack of Accountability at the High Court." *Hofstra Labor and Employment Law Journal* 18: 625–58.

Aldisert, R. J., Kirkpatrick, R. C., and Stevens, J. R., III. 2006. "Rat Race: Insider Advice on Landing Judicial Clerkships." *Penn State Law Review* 110: 835–52.

Armstrong, S. 2014. "Supreme Court Clerks as Judicial Actors and as Sources." *Marquette Law Review* 98: 387–439.

Avery, C., Jolls, C., Posner, R. A., and Roth, A. E. 2001. "The Market for Federal Judicial Law Clerks." *University of Chicago Law Review* 68: 793–902.

Avery, C., Jolls, C., Posner, R. A., and Roth, A. E. 2007. "The New Market for Federal Judicial Law Clerks." *University of Chicago Law Review* 74: 447–86.

Avery, M., and McLaughlin, D. 2013. *The Federalist Society: How Conservatives Took the Law Back from Liberals*. Nashville, TN: Vanderbilt University Press.

Avtonomov, A. S. 2009. "The Secretariat of the Constitutional Court in Russia: The Filter to Sift our Frivolous Complaints or Brake on Constitutional Justice." [in Russian] *Journal of Constitutional Justice* 5: 26–30.

Baier, P. R. 1973. "The Law Clerks: Profile of an Institution." *Vanderbilt Law Review* 26: 1125–77.

Bailey, M. A., and Maltzman, F. 2012. *The Constrained Court: Law, Politics, and the Decisions Justices Make*. Princeton, NJ: Princeton University Press.

Baum, L. 2014. "Hiring Supreme Court Law Clerks: Probing the Ideological Linkage between Judges and Justices." *Marquette Law Review* 98: 333–60.

Baum, L., and Ditslear, C. 2010. "Supreme Court Clerkships and 'Feeder' Judges." *Justice System Journal* 31: 26–48.

Becker, E. R., Breyer, S. G., and Calabresi, G. 1994. "The Federal Judicial Law Clerk Hiring Problem and the Modest March 1 Solution." *Yale Law Journal* 104: 207–25.

Benson, C. R. 2007. "A Renewed Call for Diversity among Supreme Court Clerks: How a Diverse Body of Clerks Can Aid the High Court as an Institution." *Harvard BlackLetter Law Journal* 23: 23–54.

Best, B. J. 2002. *Law Clerks, Support Personnel, and the Decline of Consensual Norms on the United States Supreme Court, 1935–1995*. New York, NY: LFB Scholarly Publishing.

Black, R. C., and Boyd, C. L. 2012. "The Role of Law Clerks in the U.S. Supreme Court's Agenda-Setting Process." *American Politics Research* 40: 147–73.

Black, R. C., Boyd, C. L., and Bryan, A. C. 2014. "Revisiting the Influence of Law Clerks on the U.S. Supreme Court's Agenda-Setting Process." *Marquette Law Review* 98: 75–109.

Bodwin, K., Rosenthal, J. S., and Yoon, A. H. 2013. "Opinion Writing and Authorship on the Supreme Court of Canada." *University of Toronto Law Journal* 63: 159–92.

Born, G. 1996. Letter to William H. Rehnquist, May 22. Rehnquist Papers Box 145, Hoover Institution, Stanford University, Stanford, CA.

Bradley, C. M. 1994. Letter to William H. Rehnquist, August 23. Rehnquist Papers Box 144, Hoover Institution, Stanford University, Stanford, CA.

Brenner, S., and Palmer, J. 1990. "The Law Clerks' Recommendations and Chief Justice Vinson's Vote on Certiorari." *American Politics Research* 18(1): 68–80.

Brown, M. R. 1996. "Gender Discrimination in the Supreme Court's Clerkship Selection Process." *Oregon Law Review* 75: 359–88.

Choi, S. J., and Gulati, G. M. 2005. "Which Judges Write their Opinions (and Should We Care)?" *Florida State University Law Review* 32: 1077–122.

Choper, J. H. 2012. "Clerking for Chief Justice Earl Warren," in *In Chambers: Stories of Supreme Court Law Clerks and Their Justices*, edited by T. C. Peppers and A. Ward. Charlottesville, VA: University of Virginia Press, 263–83.

Clayton, C. W., and Pickerill, J. M. 2006. "The Politics of Criminal Justice: How the New Right Regime Shaped the Rehnquist Court's Criminal Justice Jurisprudence." *Georgetown Law Journal* 95(5): 1385–425.

Cohen, J. M. 2002. *Inside Appellate Courts: the Impact of Court Organization on Judicial Decision Making in the United States Courts of Appeals*. Ann Arbor, MI: University of Michigan Press.

Collins, P. 2008. *Friends of the Supreme Court: Interest Groups and Judicial Decision Making*. New York, NY: Oxford University Press.

Collins, R. 2013. "Accessing the Papers of Supreme Court Justices: Online & Other Resources." *SCOTUSblog*. August 22. Available at: http://www.scotusblog.com/2013/08/accessing-the-papers-of-supreme-court-justices-online-other-resources/.

Cordray, M. M., and Cordray, R. 2001. "The Supreme Court's Plenary Docket." *Washington & Lee Law Review* 58: 737–94.

Corley, P. C. 2008. "The Supreme Court and Opinion Content: The Influence of Parties' Briefs." *Political Research Quarterly* 61: 468–78.

Corley, P. C., Steigerwalt, A., and Ward, A. 2013. *The Puzzle of Unanimity: Consensus on the United States Supreme Court*. Stanford, CA: Stanford University Press.

Crowe, J. 2012. *Building the Judiciary: Law, Courts, and the Politics of Institutional Development*. Princeton, NJ: Princeton University Press.

Ditslear, C., and Baum, L. 2001. "Selection of Law Clerks and Polarization in the U.S. Supreme Court." *Journal of Politics* 63: 869–85.

Dorsen, N. 1957. Letter to John Marshall Harlan, II, February 9. Harlan Papers Box 553, Mudd Manuscript Library, Princeton University, Princeton, NJ.

Dorsen, N. 1963. "Law Clerks in Appellate Courts in the United States." *Modern Law Review* 26: 265–71.

EEOC v. Wyoming, 460 U.S. 226 (1983).

Eggeling, W. S. 1983. Letter to William H. Rehnquist, April 13. Rehnquist Papers Box 113, Hoover Institution, Stanford University, Stanford, CA.

EPA v. EME Homer City Generation, 572 U.S. __ (2014).

Epstein, L., Knight, J., and Shvetsova, O. 2001. "The Role of Constitutional Courts in the Establishment and Maintenance of Democratic Systems of Government." *Law & Society Review* 35: 117–64.

Epstein, L. 1990. "Interviewing U.S. Supreme Court Justices and Interest Group Attorneys." *Judicature* 73: 196–8.

Fiorina, M. P., and Abrams, S. J. 2009. *Disconnect: The Breakdown of Representation in American Politics*. Norman, OK: University of Oklahoma Press.

Fox, H. W., Jr., and Hammond, S. W. 1977. *Congressional Staffs: The Invisible Force in American Lawmaking*. New York, NY: Free Press.

Garrow, D. J. 2006. "Acolytes in Arms." *Green Bag* 9(4): 411–21.

Greenhouse, L. 2006. "How Not to Be Chief Justice: The Apprenticeship of William H. Rehnquist." *University of Pennsylvania Law Review* 154: 1365–72.

Hanson, R. A., Flango, C. R., and Hansen, R. M. 2000. *The Work of Appellate Court Legal Staff*. Williamsburg, VA: National Center for State Courts.

Haruvy, E., Roth, A. E., and Unver, M. U. 2006. "The Dynamics of Law Clerk Matching: An Experimental and Computational Investigation of Proposals for Reform of the Market." *Journal of Economic Dynamics & Control* 30: 457–86.

Hess, A. G. 2015. "The Collapse of the House That Ruth Built: The Impact of the Feeder System on Female Judges and Federal Judiciary, 1970–2014." *Journal of Gender, Social Policy & the Law* 24(1): 62–106.

Hollis-Brusky, A. 2015. *Ideas with Consequences: The Federalist Society and the Conservative Counter-revolution*. New York, NY: Oxford University Press.

Howard, J. W., Jr. 1968. "On the Fluidity of Judicial Choice." *American Political Science Review* 62: 43–56.

Hutchinson, D. J., and Garrow, D. J., eds. 2002. *The Forgotten Memoir of John Knox: A Year in the Life of a Supreme Court Clerk in FDR's Washington*. Chicago, IL: University of Chicago Press.

Johnson, T. R. 2001. "Information, Oral Arguments, and Supreme Court Decision Making." *American Politics Research* 29: 331–51.

Johnson, T. R. 2004. *Oral Arguments and Decision Making on the United States Supreme Court*. Albany, NY: SUNY Press.

Johnson, T. R., Black, R. C., and Wedeking, J. 2012. *Oral Arguments and Coalition Formation on the U.S. Supreme Court: A Deliberate Dialogue*. Ann Arbor, MI: University of Michigan Press.

Johnson, T. R., Stras, D. R., and Black, R. C. 2014. "Advice from the Bench (Memo): Clerks Influence on Supreme Court Oral Arguments." *Marquette Law Review* 98: 21–42.

Kaheny, E. B., Szmer, J. J., Hansen, M. A., and Scheurer, K. F. 2015. "High Court Recruitment of Female Clerks: A Comparative Analysis of the U.S. Supreme Court and the Supreme Court of Canada." *Justice System Journal* 36: 355–77.

Katz, D. M., and Stafford, D. K. 2010. "Hustle and Flow: A Social Network Analysis of the American Federal Judiciary." *Ohio State Law Journal* 71: 457–509.

Kaye, D. H., and Gastwirth, J. L. 2009. "Where Have All the Women Gone? The Gender Gap in Supreme Court Clerkships." *Jurimetrics Journal* 49: 411–37.

Kearney, J. D. 2014. "A Truth about Career Law Clerks." *Marquette Law Review* 98: 13–19.

Kenney, S. J. 2000. "Beyond Principals and Agents: Seeing Courts as Organizations by Comparing Referendaires at the European Court of Justice and Law Clerks at the U.S. Supreme Court." *Comparative Political Studies* 33: 593–625.

Kozinski, A. 1991. "Confessions of a Bad Apple." *Yale Law Journal* 100: 1707–30.

Kozinski, A., and Bernstein, F. 1998. "Clerkship Politics." *Green Bag* 2: 57–64.

Kromphardt, C. D. 2014. "Fielding an Excellent Team: Law Clerk Selection and Chambers Structure of the U.S. Supreme Court." *Marquette Law Review* 98(1): 289–311.

Kromphardt, C. D. 2015. "US Supreme Court Law Clerks as Information Sources." *Journal of Law and Courts* 3: 277–304.

Lazarus, E. 1998. *Closed Chambers: The First Eyewitness Account of the Epic Struggles inside the Supreme Court*. New York, NY: Times Books.

Lazarus, R. J. 2008. "Advocacy Matters before and within the Supreme Court: Transforming the Court by Transforming the Bar." *Georgetown Law Journal* 96: 1487–564.

Liptak, A. 2010. "A Sign of the Court's Polarization: Choice of Clerks." *New York Times*, September 6. Available at:http://www.nytimes.com/2010/09/07/us/politics/07clerks.html

Maltzman, F., Spriggs, J. F., II., and Wahlbeck, P. J. 2000. *Crafting Law on the Supreme Court: The Collegial Game*. New York, NY: Cambridge University Press.

Marvell, T. B. 1978. *Appellate Courts and Lawyers: Information Gathering in the Adversary System*. Westport, CT: Greenwood Press.

Massinig, O. 2002. "The Legal Assistants at the German Federal Constitutional Court: A 'Black Box' of Research? A Comment." In *Constitutional Courts in Comparison: The U.S. Supreme Court and the German Federal Constitutional Court* edited by R. Rogowski and T. Gawron, New York, NY: Berghahn Books, 209–16.

Mauro, T. 1998a. "Corps of Clerks Lacking in Diversity." *USA Today*. June 5.

Mauro, T. 1998b. "For Lawyers, Clerkship Is Ultimate Job." *USA Today*. June 5.

Mauro, T. 2014. "Diversity and Supreme Court Law Clerks." *Marquette Law Review* 98: 361–66.

Mauro, T. 2015. "When Associates Leave their Jobs to Clerk at the Supreme Court." *National Law Journal*. April 17.

McCarty, N., Poole, K. T., and Rosenthal, H. 2006. *Polarized America: The Dance of Ideology and Unequal Riches*. Cambridge, MA: MIT Press.

McGuire, K. T. 1993. *The Supreme Court Bar: Legal Elites in the Washington Community*. Charlottesville, VA: University Press of Virginia.

Meador, D. J. 1974. *Appellate Courts: Staff and Process in the Crisis of Volume*. St. Paul, MN: West.

Minton, S. 1952. Letter to George Braden, February 9. Braden Papers Box 2, Truman Library, Independence, MO.

Morton, F. L., and Knopff, R. 2002. "The Role of Clerks in the Supreme Court of Canada." In *Law, Politics, and the Judicial Process in Canada*, edited by F.L. Morton, 3rd ed. Calgary: University of Calgary Press, 555–9.

Murdoch, J., and Price, D. 2001. *Courting Justice: Gay Men and Lesbians v. the Supreme Court*. New York, NY: Basic Books.

Murphy, B. A. 2012. "Fifty-Two Weeks of Boot Camp," in *In Chambers: Stories of Supreme Court Law Clerks and Their Justices*, edited by T. C. Peppers and A. Ward. Charlottesville, VA: University of Virginia Press, 179–97.

Nelson, W. E., Rishikof, H., Messinger, I. S., and Jo, M. 2009a. "The Liberal Tradition of the Supreme Court Clerkship: Its Rise, Fall, and Reincarnation?" *Vanderbilt Law Review* 62: 1749–814.

Nelson, W. E., Rishikof, H., Messinger, I. S., and Jo, M. 2009b. "The Supreme Court Clerkship and the Polarization of the Court." *Green Bag* 13: 59–71.

New York Times, The 2010. "Politically Charged Clerks." September 21. Available at: http://www.nytimes.com/2010/09/22/opinion/22wed3.html.

Newland, C. A. 1961. "Personal Assistants to Supreme Court Justices: The Law Clerks." *Oregon Law Review* 40: 299–317.

Nielson, A. L. 2014. "The Future of Federal Law Clerk Hiring." *Marquette Law Review* 98: 181–226.

O'Brien, D. M. 1997. "Join-3 Votes, the Rule of Four, the Cert. Pool, and the Supreme Court's Shrinking Plenary Docket." *Journal of Law & Politics* 13: 1779–808.

O'Connor, K., and Hermann, J. R. 1995. "The Clerk Connection: Appearances before the Supreme Court by Former Law Clerks." *Judicature* 78: 247–9.

Oakley, J. B. 1991. "The Screening of Appeals: The Ninth Circuit's Experience in the Eighties and Innovations for the Nineties." *Brigham Young University Law Review* 1991: 859–922.

Oakley, J. B., and Thompson, R. S. 1980. *Law Clerks and the Judicial Process: Perceptions of the Qualities and Functions of Law Clerks in American Courts*. Berkeley, CA: University of California Press.

Oberdorfer, L. F., and Levy, M. N. 1992. "On Clerkship Selection: A Reply to the Bad Apple." *Yale Law Journal* 101: 1097–108.

Owens, R. J., and Simon, D. A. 2012. "Explaining the Supreme Court's Shrinking Docket." *William & Mary Law Review* 53: 1219–85.

Pacelle, R. L., Jr., Curry, B. W., and Marshall, B. W. 2011. *Decision Making by the Modern Supreme Court*. New York, NY: Cambridge University Press.

Palmer, B. 2001. "The 'Bermuda Triangle?' The Cert Pool and its Influence over the Supreme Court's Agenda." *Constitutional Commentary* 18: 105–20.

Palmer, J., and Brenner, S. 1995. "The Law Clerks' Recommendations and the Conference Vote on-the-Merits on the U.S. Supreme Court." *Justice System Journal* 18: 185–97.

Patterson, B. H. 2000. *The White House Staff: Inside the West Wing and Beyond*. Washington, DC: Brookings Institution Press.

Patterson, B. H., Jr. 2009. *To Serve the President: Continuity and Innovation in the White House Staff*. Washington, DC: Brookings Institution Press.

Peppers, T. C. 2006. *Courtiers of the Marble Palace: The Rise and Influence of the Supreme Court Law Clerk*. Stanford, CA: Stanford University Press.

Peppers, T. C. 2007. "Birth of an Institution: Horace Gray and the Lost Law Clerks." *Journal of Supreme Court History* 32(3): 229–48.

Peppers, T. C. 2012. "Isaiah and his Young Disciples: Justice Louis Brandeis and his Law Clerks," in *In Chambers: Stories of Supreme Court Law Clerks and Their Justices*, edited by T. C. Peppers and A. Ward. Charlottesville: University of Virginia Press, 67–87.

Peppers, T. C., and Cushman, C., eds. 2015. *Of Courtiers and Kings: More Stories of Supreme Court Law Clerks and their Justices*. Charlottesville, VA: University of Virginia Press.

Peppers, T. C., and Driver, B. S. 2012. "Half Clerk, Half Son: Justice Felix Frankfurter and his Law Clerks," in *In Chambers: Stories of Supreme Court Law Clerks and Their Justices*, edited by T. C. Peppers and A. Ward. Charlottesville, VA: University of Virginia Press, 141–60.

Peppers, T. C., Giles, M. W., and Tainer-Parkins, B. 2008. "Inside Judicial Chambers: How Federal District Court Judges Select and Use their Law Clerks," *Albany Law Review* 71: 353–70.

Peppers, T. C., Giles, M. W., and Tainer-Parkins, B. 2014. "Surgeons or Scribes? The Role of United States Court of Appeals Law Clerks in 'Appellate Triage.'" *Marquette Law Review* 98: 313–32.

Peppers, T. C., and Ward, A., eds. 2012. *In Chambers: Stories of Supreme Court Law Clerks and their Justices*. Charlottesville, VA: University of Virginia Press.

Peppers, T. C., and Zorn, C. 2008. "Law Clerk Influence on Supreme Court Decision Making: An Empirical Analysis." *DePaul University Law Review* 58(1): 51–77.

Perry, H. W., Jr. 1994. *Deciding to Decide: Agenda Setting in the United States Supreme Court*. Cambridge, MA: Harvard University Press.

Ponder, D. E. 2000. *Good Advice: Information and Policy Making in the White House*. College Station, TX: Texas A&M Press.

Porter, H. O. 1975. "Legislative Information Needs and Staff Resources in the American States," in *Legislative Staffing: A Comparative Perspective*, edited by J. J. Heaphey and A. P. Balutis. New York, NY: Halstead, 39–59.

Posner, R. A. 1995. "Judges' Writing Styles (and Do They Matter?)" *University of Chicago Law Review* 62: 1421–51.

Priest, G. L. 2005. "Reexamining the Market for Judicial Clerks and Other Assortative Matching Markets." *Yale Journal on Regulation* 22: 123–204.

Rehnquist, W. H. 1957. "Who Writes Decisions of the Supreme Court?" *U.S. News and World Report*. December 13.

Rehnquist, W. H. 1958. "Another View: Clerks Might 'Influence' Some Actions." *U.S. News and World Report*. February 21.

Rehnquist, W. H. 1980. Letter to William S. Eggeling, December 9. Rehnquist Papers Box 113, Hoover Institution, Stanford University, Stanford, CA.

Rehnquist, W. H. 1987. *The Supreme Court: How It Was, How It Is*. New York, NY: William Morrow.

Rhinehart, L. K. 1994. "Is There Gender Bias in the Judicial Law Clerk Selection Process." *Georgetown Law Journal* 83: 575–603.

Roberts, J. G., Jr. 2005. "Advocacy and the Re-emergence of a Supreme Court Bar." *Journal of Supreme Court History* 30: 68–81.

Romzek, B. S., and Utter, J. A. 1997. "Congressional Legislative Staff: Political Professionals or Clerk?" *American Journal of Political Science* 41: 1251–79.

Rosenthal, J. S., and Yoon, A. H. 2011. "Judicial Ghostwriting: Authorship on the Supreme Court." *Cornell Law Review* 96: 1307–43.

Rudalevige, A. 2005. "The Structure of Leadership: Presidents, Hierarchies, and Information Flow." *Presidential Studies Quarterly* 35: 333–60.

Salisbury, R. H., and Shepsle, K. A. 1981. "Congressional Staff Turnover and the Ties-That-Bind." *American Political Science Review* 75: 381–96.

Schickler, E. 2001. *Disjointed Pluralism: Institutional Innovation and the Development of the U.S. Congress*. Princeton, NJ: Princeton University Press.

Sheldon, C. H. 1981. "Law Clerking with a State Supreme Court: Views from the Perspective of the Personal Assistants to the Judges." *Justice System Journal* 6: 346–71.

Skowronek, S. 1982. *Building a New American State: The Expansion of National Administrative Capacities, 1877–1920*. New York, NY: Cambridge University Press.

Sheldon, C. H. 1988. "The Evolution of Law Clerking with the Washington Supreme Court: From 'Elbow Clerks' to 'Puisne Judges.'" *Gonzaga Law Review* 24: 45–84.

Skowronek, S. 1997. *The Politics Presidents Make: Leadership from John Adams to Bill Clinton*. Cambridge, MA: Harvard University Press.

Skowronek, S. 2008. *Presidential Leadership in Political Time: Reprise and Reappraisal*. Lawrence: KS: University Press of Kansas.

Small, M. L. 2007. "William O. Douglas Remembered: A Collective Memory by WOD's Law Clerks." *Journal of Supreme Court History* 32(3): 297–334.

Smith, C. A. 2012. "Strained Relations: Justice Charles Evan Whittaker and his Law Clerks," in *In Chambers: Stories of Supreme Court Law Clerks and Their Justices*, edited by T. C. Peppers and A. Ward. Charlottesville, VA: University of Virginia Press, 243–60.

Sokolow, D. S. 1995. "A Tribute to the Honorable Thomas Gibbs Gee: The Best Boss a Guy (or Gall) Ever Had." *Texas Law Review* 73: 471–6.

Sossin, L. M. 1996. "The Sounds of Silence: Law Clerks, Policy Making, and the Supreme Court of Canada." *University of British Columbia Law Review* 30: 279–308.

Stow, M. L., and Spaeth, H. J. 1992. "Centralized Research Staff: Is There a Monster in the Judicial Closet?" *Judicature* 75: 216–21.

Stras, D. R. 2007. "The Supreme Court's Gatekeepers: The Role of Law Clerks in the Certiorari Process." *Texas Law Review* 85: 947–97.

Stras, D. R. 2014. "Secret Agents: Using Law Clerks Effectively." *Marquette Law Review* 98: 151–80.

Swanson, J. W. 2007. "Experience Matters: The Rise of a Supreme Court Bar and its Effect on Certiorari." *Journal of Appellate Practice & Process* 9: 175–204.

Swanson, R. A., and Wasby, S. L. 2008. "Good Stewards: Law Clerk Influence in State High Courts." *Justice System Journal* 29: 24–46.

Szmer, J. J., Kaheny, E. B., and Christensen, R. K. 2014. "Taking a Dip in the Supreme Court Clerk Pool: Gender-Based Discrepancies in Clerk Selection." *Marquette Law Review* 98: 261–87.

Teles, S. M. 2008. *The Rise of the Conservative Legal Movement: The Battle for Control of the Law*. Princeton, NJ: Princeton University Press.

Thompson, R. S., and Oakley, J. B. 1986. "From Information to Opinion in Appellate Courts: How Funny Things Happen on the Way through the Forum." *Arizona State Law Journal* 1986: 1–79.

Wahlbeck, P. J., Spriggs, J. F., II., and Sigelman, L. 2002. "Ghostwriters on the Court? A Stylistic Analysis of U.S. Supreme Court Opinion Drafts." *American Politics Research* 30: 166–92.

Wald, P. M. 1990. "Selecting Law Clerks." *Michigan Law Review* 89: 152–63.

Wallander, Z., and Benesh, S. C. 2014. "Law Clerks as Advisors: A Look at the Blackmun Papers." *Marquette Law Review* 98: 43–73.

Ward, A. 2012. "Making Work for Idle Hands: William H. Rehnquist and his Clerks," in *In Chambers: Stories of Supreme Court Law Clerks and Their Justices*, edited by T. C. Peppers and A. Ward. Charlottesville, VA: University of Virginia Press, 350–90.

Ward, A., Dwyer, C., and Gill, K. 2014. "Bonus Babies Escape Golden Handcuffs: How Money and Politics Has Transformed the Career Paths of Supreme Court Law Clerks." *Marquette Law Review* 98: 227–60.

Ward, A., and Wasby, S. L. 2010. "'Get a Life!': On Interviewing Law Clerks." *Justice System Journal* 31: 125–43.

Ward, A., and Weiden, D. L. 2006. *Sorcerers' Apprentices: 100 Years of Law Clerks at the United States Supreme Court*. New York, NY: New York University Press.

Wasby, S. L. 2005. "A Judicial Secretary's Many Roles: Working with an Appellate Judge and Clerks." *Journal of Appellate Practice and Process* 7: 151–66.

Wasby, S. L. 2006. "Why Clerk? What Did I Get Out of It?" *Journal of Legal Education* 56(3): 411–29.

Wasby, S. L. 2008. "Clerking for an Appellate Judge: A Close Look," *Seton Hall Circuit Review* 5: 19–97.

Wasby, S. L. 2014. "The World of Law Clerks: Tasks, Utilization, Reliance, and Influence." *Marquette Law Review* 98: 111–30.

Whiteman, D. 1995. *Communication in Congress: Members, Staff, and the Search for Information*. Lawrence, KS: University of Kansas Press.

Wieland, J.. 2002. "The Role of the Legal Assistants at the German Federal Constitutional Court." In *Constitutional Courts in Comparison: The U.S. Supreme Court and the*

German Federal Constitutional Court, edited by R. Rogowski and T. Gawron. New York, NY: Berghahn Books, 197–208.
Wilkinson, J. H., III. 2008. "Lewis F. Powell, Jr.—A Personal View." *Washington and Lee Law Review* 65(1): 3–8.
Woodward, B., and Armstong, S. 1979. *The Brethren: Inside the Supreme Court*. New York, NY: Simon & Schuster.
Yoon, A. 2014. "Law Clerks and the Institutional Design of the Federal Judiciary." *Marquette Law Review* 98: 131–49.

Other Readings

Rust v. Sullivan, 500 U.S. 173 (1991).
Segal, J. A., and Spaeth, H. J. 2002. *The Supreme Court and the Attitudinal Model Revisited*. New York, NY: Cambridge University Press.

Cases Cited

Bowers v. Hardwick, 478 U.S. 186 (1986).
Bray v. Alexandria Clinic, 506 U.S. 263 (1993).
Massachusetts v. Murgia, 427 U.S. 307 (1976).
National League of Cities v. Usery, 426 U.S. 833 (1976).
Nilva v. United States, 352 U.S. 385 (1957).
O'Connor v. Donaldson, 422 U.S. 563 (1975).
Patterson v. McLean Credit Union, 491 U.S. 164 (1989).
Personnel Administrator of Massachusetts v. Feeney, 442 U.S. 256 (1979).
Railroad Retirement Bd. v. Fritz, 449 U.S. 166 (1980).
United States v. Virginia, 518 U.S. 515 (1996).

PART II

THE LITIGATION PROCESS AND APPELLATE REVIEW

CHAPTER 6

GATEKEEPING AND FILTERING IN TRIAL COURTS

CHRISTINA L. BOYD

WHILE not always the most popular courts of study, state and federal trial courts play a highly important role in the judicial system in the United States. Ninety-four federal trial courts (called district courts) geographically distributed across the country adjudicate over 350,000 cases per year (Administrative Office of the U.S. Courts 2013b). The hundreds of state trial courts of general and limited jurisdiction adjudicate upwards of 30,000,000 criminal and civil cases each year (Court Statistics Project 2010). By contrast, the U.S. Supreme Court hears fewer than one hundred cases per year and the U.S. Courts of Appeals terminate fewer than 60,000 cases per year. It is thus no surprise that Henry Abraham famously referred to federal district judges as "the workhorses of the federal judiciary" (Lyles 1995: 11), something he could have said just as easily about state trial judges. A similar point was made by Kenneth Dolbeare (1967: 3) when he noted that "for most practical purposes, the local trial court is *both* the Supreme Court and the state's court of last resort."

In addition to serving as the entry point for millions of cases, trial courts can also play an important policy-making role. These courts regularly make critical decisions in cases involving salient issues like abortion, voting rights, desegregation, religious liberty, and affirmative action (Lyles 1995), all of which, arguably, place them squarely at the center of local and national policy and political battles. This is particularly true when district courts are tasked with making decisions in cases of first impression—i.e., those without relevant precedent binding the outcome—but can hold for other trial court decisions as well. Trial courts can also bring otherwise overlooked issues to the public's attention. As Mather (1995) noted, media attention and public opinion resulting from trial level actions can raise the salience of issues and give the impression that the trial ruling or decision is very important.

Rather than always following the traditional definition of judicial policy-making through things like crafting new rules, standards, and binding precedents, trial courts often occupy this role through the subtle, cumulative impact of their decisions on communities (Mather 1995). This often comes through the numerous decisions that trial judges make throughout the life of cases (from filing to termination), the choices that litigants make in deciding to file their case, crafting their lawsuits, and negotiating with each other, and the interaction that judges and litigants have with one another throughout this frequently lengthy process. It is not a coincidence that these same factors that can lead to cumulative trial court policy-making are also at the heart of why trial courts are important gatekeeping and filtering institutions in the judiciary. The decisions that trial judges and case participants make throughout their trial court cases (and prior to their filings) affect what cases and claims remain within and progress through the judicial hierarchy.

In what follows, this chapter discusses the gatekeeping and filtering that takes places in trial courts. The chapter proceeds by first examining the selection of disputes and charges that takes place by parties, prosecutors, and other lawyers prior to a case being filed in a trial court. Next, the chapter details the uniquely important decision-making of parties and lawyers within trial courts. Finally, the chapter tackles the roles and decisions of and constraints on trial court judges.[1]

(Pre) Trial Court Filtering

As a rich literature details, cases are "selected into" trial courts. That is, those cases that enter the trial courts and judiciary are, generally speaking, not a random sample of all incidents, crimes, or grievances. For civil disputes, Miller and Sarat (1980–1) populated the pyramid of grievances, claims, and disputes that exist across different issue areas, with only a subset of those disputes turning into filed civil cases in trial courts. Potential litigants often choose not to communicate their grievance to the other party (especially in certain civil rights grievances), and, even when they do, conflict may not arise or the case may informally reach a compromise outcome before the necessity of filing a civil case in the trial court arises.

When it comes to the decision of whether to file a civil lawsuit in a trial court, Sloan and Hsieh (1995) found empirical evidence that, at least for medical malpractice claims following an adverse birth, injured parties will choose to file when the expected value of doing so exceeds zero. As discussed in further detail later in the chapter, this is very similar to the calculations that many litigants make after filing a trial court case—from deciding whether to settle or proceed to trial to deciding whether to appeal or not. The filtering of potential cases into trial courts follows a similar pattern in the criminal context, albeit with different actors involved in the decision-making roles. Acting on behalf of the State, prosecutors decide whether to file criminal charges and what charges to bring. These prosecutorial decisions are driven by numerous factors such as the nature of the offense, availability and strength of evidence, politics and policy goals, the defendant's prior record, and limited resources (O'Neill 2004; Mather 1979).

Only when prosecutors or prospective plaintiffs choose to file their case in the court system do the trial courts begin their role in the system. For both criminal counts and civil claims, this filtering of cases into the trial courts is filled with strategic, non-random behavior that is itself important to understand and study as forms of gatekeeping and filtering.[2] As the above discussion reveals, prior to filing, the adversaries have likely already begun negotiating or posturing with one another over the underlying dispute and thus do not enter the trial court system unfettered by the previous interactions by the parties.

Parties (and their Lawyers) in Trial Courts

More so than in any other court setting, the parties and their attorneys help shape the playing field for trial court litigation and prosecutions. Their decisions hold great potential to affect whether and where cases are filed, whether they settle, are dismissed through a non-trial adjudication, or go to trial, and, following the outcome, whether there is an appeal. Importantly and uniquely to the trial court setting, while justice "is sometimes sought by courtroom proceedings, but it is more often pursued in offices and corridors" (Jacob 1972: 164). Indeed, in both the civil and criminal realms in state and federal courts, cases rarely reach trial (Galanter 2004). Rather, settlement (civil) and plea bargaining (criminal) dominate as termination methods today. Both case resolutions involve case parties opting out of the legal system via compromise after first choosing, at least nominally, to resolve their dispute within the legal system.

While the literatures examining settlement and plea bargaining have evolved in very different ways across academic communities, the occurrence of both, along with the resulting models of litigant compromise and settlement behavior, share more similarities than differences. These compromise outcomes, and the litigant calculations that lead to them, are always important to discuss. However, given this chapter's focus on the gatekeeping role of trial courts, it is all the more necessary to account for these prevailing trial court termination methods. Of similar importance, the same types of calculations that affect litigant decisions to settle or plea bargain also affect the decision of the losing parties to appeal their outcomes to the supervising appellate courts.

Civil Cases

Settlements are the most frequent termination method in filed civil cases. While this number varies greatly by a case's issue area, it can be as high as 85 or 90 percent (Eisenberg and Lanvers 2009). The settlement of civil cases is argued to produce "greater disputant satisfaction with the decision" and to permit "compromise positions that are unattainable through adjudication" (Galanter 1985). By choosing to settle a case, litigants are able to control their case's outcome and avoid the uncertainty and risk that comes from continuing a case toward trial and potential appeal. While settlements are very common, many cases conclude as a result of adversarial proceedings such as trials or summary judgment. The prevalence of settlement begs the question: with such clear benefits for all parties involved, why do only some cases settle while others continue on to contentious terminations via trials and non-trial judge-based decision-making?

A vast body of scholarship has developed on this very topic. Chief among this work are Priest and Klein's (1984) and Bebchuk's (1984) seminal articles. Priest and Klein (1984) theorized that civil litigants determine whether to settle or pursue litigation toward trial depending on the expected costs of favorable or adverse trial decisions, the information that the parties hold about their potential for success if the case goes to trial, and the direct costs of litigation and settlement. As a result of this selection, the cases remaining unsettled are likely to be close disputes, where both the defendant and the plaintiff reasonably believe that their chances of success at trial are good. The empirical implication of this "divergent expectations theory" and the selection of settling cases that takes place is that the likelihood of plaintiff success in those cases proceeding to trial should tend toward 50 percent.[3]

By contrast, Bebchuk (1984) offered an asymmetric information theory of litigation in which one party holds a monopoly on the case's likely outcome should it reach trial. This vast inequality of trial outcome information has enormous implications for the types of cases that will settle, with the informed party incentivized to settle only those cases in which his expected liabilities at trial are particularly high relative to his opponent. In a severe case of information asymmetry held by the defendant, Bebchuk predicted that plaintiff success rates for the very small and non-random set of cases advancing to trial will approach zero.

While Priest and Klein (1984) and Bebchuk (1984) vary in their predictions of when disputes will advance toward trial, both agree that strategic litigant decision-making because of the threat of court-adjudicated outcomes is at the heart of this litigation-settlement decision. To quote the famous line from Priest and Klein (1984), "disputes selected for litigation (as opposed to settlement) will constitute neither a random nor a representative sample of the set of all disputes." Rather, as Lawrence Baum argued, the cases advancing to trial "tend to involve conditions that make negotiated settlements difficult or unattractive to achieve" (Baum 2013: 213).

While the thirty years of formal and empirical literature stemming from Priest and Klein (1984) and Bebchuk (1984) is too expansive to cover here, this resulting work has led to major advancements (and continued debate) regarding our understanding of the choices that civil litigants make regarding settlement. Of particular note, Waldfogel (1998) provided empirical evidence that unifies the two models' expectations. His work indicates that settlements and pretrial adjudications like involuntary dismissal and summary judgment are largely due to asymmetric information (per Bebchuk). However, Waldfogel (1998) also indicated that for cases terminating later in litigation, when information asymmetries have been greatly reduced by discovery and other case proceedings, trial outcomes follow along the lines outlined in Priest and Klein and tend toward a 50 percent plaintiff win rate.

The push toward civil settlements in trial courts is often described as "bargaining in the shadow of the law" (Mnookin and Kornhauser 1979). The mere filing of the case raises the stakes in the negotiation of the dispute's resolution, sending the signal that the plaintiff is serious about the claim (Baum 2013). That filing may be enough for some defendants to approach the bargaining table in earnest, leading to a number of civil cases settling very quickly after filing. For other cases, however, compromise is not so quickly reached. To reflect these distinct stages of settlement, Spier (1992) modeled civil litigation bargaining in which a "U-shaped" pattern of settlement emerges: while many cases will settle very soon after filing, others will not settle until the threat of a looming trial nears—i.e., the "deadline effect." Between the two time periods, cases develop through things like motions practice and discovery, all of which, as Waldfogel (1998) argued, unveil greater detail about the case and reduce information asymmetries.

Scholars have unveiled a number of other interesting findings regarding settlement timing and litigant behavior in civil litigation. For example, Kessler (1996) found that case complexity influences the timing of settlements, with more serious motor vehicle claims taking longer to settle than less serious ones. Boyd and Hoffman (2013) provided evidence that just as the filing of a civil case can almost immediately propel certain cases toward settlement, so too can the filing of a dispositive motion. In other words, the threat that the judge could grant a motion to dismiss or a motion for summary judgment can be enough to encourage serious settlement efforts.

The litigant calculations that are made regarding settlement and litigation during a civil case are very similar to those made about the decision to appeal following the trial court disposition. Once again acting in the shadow of courts, litigants deciding whether to appeal their adverse trial court outcome evaluate their likelihood of success on appeal and what will be gained from an appellate victory against the costs of pursuing the case further (Priest and Klein 1984; Songer, Cameron, and Segal 1995). Just as with the settlement decision, this appeal decision leads to case filtering into the judicial hierarchy that is decidedly non-random in nature. For federal courts, Eisenberg (2004) reported that fewer than 20 percent of trial court cases are appealed.

Without question, the selection of trial court disputes for litigation or settlement or, later, appeal, can be greatly affected by attorneys. For example, Johnston and Waldfogel (2002) revealed that the repeat interaction of opposing attorneys corresponds to swifter litigation compromises and fewer trials. Kritzer (1990) found that both plaintiffs and defendants in civil cases are more likely to view their litigation as a success, even in the case of settlement, when their lawyer engaged in strategic bargaining.

But not all civil cases, or their filing parties, are created equally. Rather, as Epstein, Landes, and Posner (2013) noted, "many cases are filed by pro se or emotional litigants and by litigants represented by inept or inexperienced lawyers" (p. 232). Most of these cases, as the authors argue, will be dismissed or abandoned rather than selected for litigation or settlement.

Attorney compensation structure is also important. For the contingency fee attorney engaging in litigation and possible settlement negotiation, there is an important need to manage a client's interests and expectations with an attorney's short- and long-term reputation and goals (Kritzer 1998). Despite these competing considerations, Hellend and Tabarrok's (2003) analysis of medical malpractice cases revealed, compared to hourly attorneys, contingency-fee attorneys file fewer low-quality lawsuits and help yield faster settlement times.[4]

Criminal Cases

Just like settlements in civil cases, plea bargaining is also the predominate way that criminal cases in trial courts terminate. While there is some variance across state and federal courts, as many as 90 to 95 percent of criminal trial court cases each year are resolved through plea bargains (Administrative Office of the U.S. Courts 2013a). As a reflection of this, Justice Kennedy's majority opinion in 2012's *Lafler v. Cooper* argued that "criminal justice today is for the most part a system of pleas, not a system of trials." Simply put, because of the way the criminal court system is designed and the time and money that it takes to advance most cases to trial, judges and counsel for both sides are incentivized to encourage plea bargains (Blumberg 1967).

As with civil cases and settlements, the defendant's decision to accept a plea bargain in a criminal case is theorized to be a strategic one, informed by the defendant's knowledge, information, and preferences along with those of his adversary, the prosecutor. After assuming that the prosecution and defendant maximize their utilities, Landes (1971) famously argued that the decision whether to plea bargain or go to trial is dependent on "the probability of conviction by trial, the severity of the crime, the availability and productivity of the prosecutor's and defendant's resources, trial versus settlement costs, and attitudes toward risk" (p. 61). In other words, the decision to accept a plea is made very much within the ominous "shadow of the trial" (Bushway and Redlich 2012) and, at least in some cases, does not begin in earnest until after a trial date has been set (Mather 1979).

Ultimately, a plea bargain can be reached only when the parties' expectations converge. Elder (1989) provided empirical evidence to support this, finding that as the parties' have increased agreement about the outcome at trial (via the evidence in the case), plea bargains are more likely. Many pleas are entered with "a tacit understanding of the likely sentence or with an informal indication by the judge as to the probable sentence" (Mather 1979: 55). For the most serious criminal cases, reaching a plea bargain can be very difficult, with the process involving "proposals and counterproposals in which the terms of the final agreement are clearly specified" (Mather 1979: 93). And, even after the bargaining is complete, the defense counsel must get the defendant to sign off on the plea agreement. With divergent estimations between the defense and prosecution, bargaining failure does occur, thereby leading cases toward trial. After all, rational defendants are only expected to accept plea deals when doing so will produce more of a benefit for them than going to trial would (Bushway and Redlich 2012).

Prosecutors are quintessential repeat players in their local trial courts, with some even arguing that it is the prosecutor, rather than the judge or defense attorney, who is key to administering criminal justice (Jacob 1972). "The prosecutor's power stems in large part from her role as gatekeeper in the criminal justice system. Juries convict, judges sentence, and wardens incarcerate, but it is the prosecutor who at the outset of a criminal case selects those individuals who will enter the system" (Gordon and Huber 2002: 349). Following Galanter's (1974) logic, prosecutors will primarily favor long-term goals, policy, reputation, and voters' preferences[5] rather than single, one-shot victories in cases. This is likely to affect decisions that prosecutors make prior to filing (e.g., whether to decline prosecution and what charges to bring) and will also invariably influence post-filing bargaining over whether to offer a plea bargain, the terms of plea deal, the strategy to pursue at trial, and the severity of the sentence to recommend to the judge (Mather 1979; Gordon and Huber 2002).

While criminal defense lawyers are also often repeat players in their local trial courts (Blumberg 1967), their associated list of strengths emerging from that is likely to be far less lengthy, with issues like low pay, high caseloads, lack of ability to filter cases in the way that prosecutors do, and limited control over clientele having the greatest negative effect. Stuntz (1997) detailed the assembly-line nature of most criminal defense work, noting that "the law operates from the premise that effective representation [by defense attorneys] can be minimal" (p. 20). Blumberg (1967) further described criminal defense attorneys as "double agents" where they are first placed in a difficult position to get their client to trust them and then convince him to plea out.

Critics of plea-bargaining dominance in the criminal court system exist on both sides and continues to rage today, with some concerned about the leniency that it promotes in criminal outcomes, "allowing guilty defendants to obtain unwarranted reductions in charges and/or sentences by threatening an overworked system with requiring a time-consuming and pointless trial" (Kritzer 1990: 16). Others worry about the potentially coercive nature of the system, with the vast inequalities that many defendants face when forced to decide whether to accept a plea deal (Bibas 2004). This argument generally rests on the strength and repeat-player status of the prosecutor, often bolstered by the judge's incentives to encourage pleas (Alschuler 1968), combined with limited bargaining power for many defendants oppressed by poverty and focused on short-term goals of getting out of jail as quickly and cheaply as is possible (Bowers 2008).

Trial Court Judges as Gatekeepers

While judges serving on appellate courts receive a great deal of attention in political science scholarship, most judicial decision-making takes place in trial courts. Indeed, for most litigants involved in legal disputes, trial judges are the only judicial actors they will ever encounter. The decisions that these important trial judges make throughout a case have important gatekeeping implications, influencing how a case develops, whether it settles or not, the degree of satisfaction that the parties and lawyers have with the outcome, whether it will be appealed, and, if appealed, whether it will be reversed.

The job of judging varies greatly depending on a judge's position in the judicial hierarchy, with this being particularly true when comparing trial court judges to those serving on multi-member appellate courts. Unlike appellate court judges, trial judges' workloads are dominated by the complexities and multi-staged proceedings inherent in trial court litigation (Boyd and Hoffman 2013; Kim et al. 2009). This litigation process means that trial judges have numerous decision-making opportunities in each case over which they preside, with the potential to be a mediator and settlement encourager, a fact-finder, a law-applier, and a law-creator with enormous discretion in how a case develops and is resolved. This level of judging is also likely to present unique pressures on and considerations for trial court judges that simply do not exist for appellate court judges, including, as discussed in detail above, the predominance of settlement and the particularly important role of attorneys. Other unique pressures for trial judges are the real possibility for judicial elevation and the credible risk of decision appeal and reversal from judicial superiors.

Trial Judge Decision-Making

How do trial court judges make decisions? Are they ideologically driven decision-makers? Or, instead, do other considerations such as the law and precedent, their place in the judicial hierarchy, or their other characteristics dominate their behavior? Trial court scholars have pondered these questions for many years, but to date, they remain far from being resolved.

There is little debate regarding the significant role that law and precedent have in trial courts, particularly compared to appellate courts. From their time as law students and practicing lawyers to their time within the judicial profession, judges are indoctrinated on the merits of judicial restraint and following precedent. The nature of trial court cases further reinforces this, with a great many cases being weak, routine, or ordinary in nature, thereby making legalistic, non-discretionary judicial decision-making viable (Epstein, Landes, and Posner 2013). However, various duties within the job of a trial judge have no clear legal answer and, therefore, provide room for the trial judge to exercise considerable discretion (Levin 2008). This discretion can exist in numerous judicial decisions throughout a case (e.g., how to rule on dispositive motions, whether to actively encourage settlement, and whether to write opinions) and opens the door for trial judges to make decisions based on things other than the law—whether those other things be ideological preferences, personal background characteristics, experience, or hierarchical constraints.

Turning first to ideological preferences, the theoretical and empirical findings for trial court judges is unquestionably mixed. Lyles (1995) argued that we have every reason to believe that trial judges will behave in a political way. "The frequency and salience of district court policymaking, their gatekeeping role in the federal judiciary, the characteristics and attitudes of the individual judges appointed to these courts, as well as the dynamics of the appointment process itself, suggest a political nature and function" (Lyles 1995: 2). District judges themselves also often seem to believe that their preferences enter into their decision-making. When asked whether their "personal attitudes and values affect their discretionary judgments," 58 percent of the district judges responded "often" or "sometimes"; when asked the same question about other district judges' judgments, however, that number skyrocketed to 75 percent (Lyles 1995: 25).

Empirical work supports the role of ideology. Rowland, Carp, and Stidham (1984) found that federal trial court judges appointed by Democratic presidents are often more likely to support criminal defendants than those judges appointed by Republican presidents. Relatedly, Schanzenbach and Tiller (2006) found evidence that federal district courts with higher percentages of Republican-appointed judges impose longer sentences for criminal sentences, with Epstein, Landes, and Posner (2013) confirming a modest sentencing-partisanship effect for data coded at the individual district judge level. Work by Rowland and Carp (1996) extended these findings to include differences among judges in civil rights, civil liberties, economics, and labor-related cases, with Democrat-appointed trial judges ruling more liberally in each area. Rowland and Todd (1991) also indicated that federal trial judges can use procedural rulings, such as those regarding whether a plaintiff has standing, to exert their policy preferences.

These findings stand in sharp contrast to scholarship indicating that ideology and partisanship is generally not a strong predictor of trial judge decision-making. Zorn and Bowie (2010) found that judicial preferences and ideology predict conservative voting in the federal appellate courts, but when it comes to district judges, "ideological and policy-related influences ... are but two of several competing considerations, and in many instances not the most important ones" (p. 1213). This mirrors an earlier finding by Ashenfelter, Eisenberg, and Schwab (1995), who noted that "the political aspects of that [judicial] selection process may not filter down to the mass of litigation" (p. 281). Similarly, Keele et al.'s (2009) study of federal U.S. Forest Service litigation revealed that for district judges, there was no evidence of ideological decisions in either published or unpublished opinions. Other notable work failing to find evidence that federal district judges systematically decide cases based on ideological or partisan considerations includes Howard (2002) (taxpayer suits against the IRS), Walker (1972) (civil liberty decisions), Yarnold (1997) (religious freedoms cases), Baum (1980) (patent cases), King (1998) (fair housing cases), and Perino (2006) (securities fraud actions).[6]

Bridging the gap in this area is Gibson (1978), who provided support for ideological decision-making among certain trial judges. In this groundbreaking study, Gibson found that state trial court judges in Iowa make sentencing decisions according to their personal role orientations, meaning that these trial judges hold individual beliefs about what factors "can properly be allowed to influence their behavior" (p. 917). Based on this, Gibson's theory is that the effect of judicial ideology for trial judges is conditional on the judge's role orientation—i.e., a trial judge's "attitudes are related to behavior only insofar as the judge's role orientation allows it." And this is exactly what Gibson's study found: attitudes are good predictors of trial judge sentencing behavior when the judge has a "broad" role orientation that permits attitudes to affect his decisions.

Beyond ideology and attitudes, scholars have found that other trial judge characteristics can be, at times, meaningful predictors of their behavior. For example, Giles and Walker (1975) found that Southern federal district judges' degree of connection to their community affected the way that they made decisions in school desegregation cases following *Brown v. Board of Education*. Their results indicate that these federal district judges were more vigilant in enforcing desegregation in remote, rural areas where the enforcing judge had little-to-no community linkage to the school. In a similar way, Baum (2006) argued that state trial judges can be influenced by those working in local government with them: "Judges who serve a city or county are likely to have personal ties with other local officials through schooling, politics, and community activities. They often work in close proximity to people in the other branches and interact with them outside of work" (p. 170). Other studies of trial judge behavior have found some evidence that these judges' decisions are, at least in certain circumstances, also affected by the judge's sex (Steffensmeier and Herbert 1999; Walker and Barrow 1985) and race (Sisk, Heise, and Morriss 1998), among other factors.

Trial Judges, the Hierarchy, and the Public

Many argue that trial judges are uniquely constrained by non-personal considerations such as their institutional position at the bottom of the judicial hierarchy. When a trial court case is proceeding, the judge and the parties cannot predict with certainty whether the dispute will ultimately end up before the appellate courts. While such an appeal is not assured, losing parties generally have a right to appeal. This looming possibility of review, and with it, reversal, means that appellate courts are an ever-present influence in case dispositions. Indeed, trial court judges are controlled and sanctioned by their supervising judges through reversals, since such an outcome overturns a district judge's decision, holds the potential to add additional work to the judge, and can affect a trial judge's reputation (Hettinger, Lindquist, and Martinek 2006; Scott 2006).

Institutional constraints on trial judging may help explain why many scholars, as detailed above, have struggled to find consistent evidence of ideological decision-making among trial judges. Rather than acting as unconstrained pursuers of their personal preferences, the hierarchical system in which they serve demands responsiveness to superiors. Baum (1997) suggested:

> Lower-court judges want judicial doctrine to match their policy preferences as closely as possible. But judges cannot simply set doctrine at their ideal points. Rather, because of the threat of reversal by the reviewing court, they must balance their preferences against the preferences of that court: they sometimes take positions that diverge from their own preferences in order to avoid reversal that would move policy even further from those preferences. This, of course, is a form of strategic voting. (p. 115)

A number of recent studies have found empirical evidence of this hierarchical influence on trial judge behavior. Studying cases from 1925 to 1996, Randazzo (2008) found that district court judges anticipate the preferences of their courts of appeals superiors in civil liberties and economics cases but not in criminal cases. In securities fraud action cases, Perino (2006) found that district judges moderate their behavior in anticipation of an ideologically dissimilar circuit court. Epstein, Landes, and Posner (2013) provided evidence that federal district judges are less likely to sentence defendants below the sentencing guidelines range when they sit in a Republican-judge-dominated circuit. Choi, Gulati, and Posner (2012) revealed strategic publication rates (fewer published opinions) as district judges' ideologies move farther way from those of their reviewing circuit. Baum (1980) found that "courts of appeals exert real influence over the decisions" of their district court subordinates in patent cases, a result that is not dependent on the judges' ideologies and that indicates a "degree of hierarchical control in the judicial system" (p. 223). Finally, studies from Schanzenbach and Tiller (2006) and Buchman (2007) indicated that trial court judges strategically use deferential standards of review to help protect their sentencing and evidential decisions from reversal.

Interestingly, scholarship indicates that district judges are not just influenced by the judicial hierarchy, but that they also are influential themselves, especially when they play the role of gatekeeper. First, research indicates that a number of actions taken by trial judges greatly decrease the likelihood of the case being appealed. Encouraging settlement is certainly one such action, a topic discussed in greater detail later in this chapter. In non-settling cases, rational litigants will undoubtedly assess their chances of success on appeal (Posner 1985). However, if the trial judge's decision was guided by consideration of preferences of judges on the appeals court, this should affect the litigants' calculations and, correspondingly, decrease the chance of appeals. Scholarship also tells us that unpublished district court decisions are less likely to be appealed than those that are published (Siegelman and Donohue 1990). Similarly, when litigant satisfaction with the process in their trial court case is high, despite their loss, they may also be less likely to appeal (Barclay 1999).

Second, in cases that are appealed, trial judges may influence not only the outcome of the case (i.e., the likelihood of reversal) and the substantive legal standard that is applied by the appeals court but also the content of the law that results. On this latter point, recent research by Corley, Collins, and Calvin (2011) found that the U.S. Supreme Court's opinions regularly repeat the exact language present in the lower court judges' opinions from the case.

Finally, trial courts are well positioned to influence the decisions of their judicial superiors through the implementation of remand orders. When appellate courts remand decisions to the trial courts, the remand decrees regularly require the trial court to implement the higher court decision, a scenario famously played out in the federal courts in the context of local school district desegregation. As in *Brown v. Board of Education*, remands for trial court implementation place trial judges in an important policy-making role while simultaneously granting these judges considerable discretion.[7] That discretion is not without its own constraints—remanded trial court decisions can be re-appealed—but, as Murphy (1959) argued, trial courts on remand are well positioned to construe or criticize appellate court precedent in their preferred way. At its extreme, this can even lead to trial judges evading the remanding decision altogether. The result of this is that remanding courts like the U.S. Supreme Court must take into consideration the anticipated reaction of the lower court judges when returning cases (Rosenberg 1991).

In addition to (or perhaps instead of) considerations about appellate review, some trial judges may be influenced by public opinion. This is especially true in areas of salience to voters for the many state judges who are elected.[8] Many U.S. states select or retain their trial judges through some form of election, and this selection mechanism is likely to affect decision-making. Kuklinski and Stanga (1979) found that California trial court judges alter their sentencing behavior for marijuana-related crimes based on their county's level of support for a state initiative proposing to decriminalize personal marijuana use. Similarly, Huber and Gordon (2004) found that the criminal sentencing behavior of elected Pennsylvania trial court judges is very much affected by election proximity and voters' desires to see punitive justice on the bench. As predicted by their theory, Huber and Gordon's analysis finds a unilateral convergence toward punitive sentencing the closer the judge gets to reelection.

Trial Judges as Settlement Judges?

When ruling on potentially case-ending motions or presiding over a bench trial, trial judges serve in publicly salient posts. Even with jury trials, trial judges have a great deal of responsibility and visibility, including managing jury selection, ruling on important dispositive and evidentiary motions during, before, and after trial, and crafting jury instructions. Beyond these salient duties, trial judges can also serve as case managers and facilitators of settlements and plea bargains. Indeed, given the ongoing pressures related to rising caseloads, understaffing, budget cuts, and lingering judicial vacancies, many argue that trial judges are increasingly in these roles (Resnik 1982; Kritzer 1986; Baum 2013). "There is more to "it" than trials. Judicial actions can play an important role in the processing of civil cases, even in the vast majority of cases that never come to trial" (Kritzer 1986: 165). Given the above-noted dominance of these compromise outcomes in trial courts today, this role thus places these judges in the middle of many decisions to filter cases out of the court system.

What can and do trial judges do to facilitate these compromises? As the above litigant discussion notes, there are many cases that settle or plea out almost immediately upon filing. These cases need no assistance from a judge; the mere filing raises the negotiation stakes and propels the parties to the bargaining table. However, in many other cases, the settlement negotiations are often "encouraged, brokered, or actively mediated by the judge" (Galanter 1985). Within a case's proceedings, judges can "meet with parties in chambers to encourage settlement of disputes and to supervise case preparation" (Resnik 1982). And, indeed, Federal Rule of Civil Procedure Rule 16 lists "facilitating settlement" as one of the express purposes of a case's pretrial conference (Provine 1986).

In the criminal trial court context, Mather (1979) described how judges and attorneys develop informal norms as to their interactions, behavior, information sharing, and strategies. One such common norm among many trial judges is their willingness to "chamberize" (Mather 1979), where the attorneys and the judge meet to discuss the possibility of a plea bargain, with the judge often weighing in on what sentence he would likely impose. This judicial participation is undoubtedly critical in many cases in reducing information uncertainty that exists between the prosecution and defense, thereby further increasing the odds of a bargain being struck and the defendant agreeing to the deal. As one California prosecutor put it, with judicial involvement in bargaining, "you get more guilty pleas [than if the judge were not involved]" (McCoy 1993: 150).

Trial judges also often take two common institutionalized steps to encourage civil case compromise: referring the case to a type of Alternative Dispute Resolution (ADR), such as mediation, and requiring the parties to participate in a settlement conference. The occurrence of ADR or settlement conferences forces parties to formally come together and attempt to settle. Generally with the help of a neutral evaluator, parties are often able to better understand their chances of success and the expectations of their opponent. Since initiating settlement talks can be perceived as a sign of case weakness (Provine 1986), the judge's role in facilitating settlement discussions serves not only to breathe realism into the case but to also alleviate the pressure from the attorneys to force the issue themselves. Spurr (1997) found empirical evidence that this judicial strategy is successful, with personal injury litigation cases settling more quickly when they have been referred to a settlement specialist during litigation.

Ultimately, how actively a trial judge manages his cases and affirmatively presses the parties to settle when they may not otherwise do so is often at his discretion. As such, as with much about judging, the identity of a trial judge and specific trial court on which he sits can affect the type of case manager that a trial judge becomes and how this affects processing of cases. Boyd (2013) found that female federal trial judges, predicted by theory to be more collaborative and compromise-seeking case managers, have their cases settle more often and more quickly than their male counterparts' cases. Kritzer (1990) argued that there is more judge-centeredness in civil justice in federal courts than in state courts, while Plapinger and Stienstra (1996) documented how, even among federal trial courts, there are vast differences as to how much pressure is placed on the judges to actively encourage settlement.

It is worth noting settlement and plea bargains dominate case outcomes in trial courts not only because judges promote settlement and because litigants are often incentivized to pursue compromise outcomes. Indeed, other institutional and political factors influence judicial system efficiency via legislation like the Civil Justice Reform Act (1990) and criminal laws that permit harsher penalties for those advancing their cases toward trial, the growth district level mandated ADR, and the increased reliance on magistrate judges and other non-permanent judges are all geared toward encouraging compromise solutions in federal case filings.

Conclusion

Without question, trial courts and their actors play critical gatekeeping and filtering roles within the judicial hierarchy. As the trial court literature discussed above reveals, the decisions made by litigants and judges in the millions of criminal and civil trial court cases in the United States each year affect things like what cases get filed in trial courts, how cases develop, what cases settle and when, whether losing litigants will appeal, and, if they do, how the appellate courts will respond. Each of these, in turn, acts to shape the contents of the judicial hierarchy, while also presenting the actors involved opportunities to strategically manipulate their outcomes. What results, of course, is a set of disputes advancing through the appellate courts that is very much a non-random representation of disputes and filed trial court cases.

While undeniably important, studying trial courts presents a unique set of challenges to scholars. The heavy involvement of the parties, attorneys, and judges throughout the life of trial court cases and the very real potential for opting out of the system through compromise presents empirical and theoretical complications. When it comes to trial court judges, the construct of the single-judge environment is also difficult to properly capture: "In a collegial court situation, a group of judges responds to exactly the same cases after examining identical briefs and considering the same oral arguments. When disagreement occurs it is relatively easy to measure the differences among the jurists. Students of the trial courts are not afforded this convenience. Each district judge individually hears cases arising out of his or her own judicial district ... We simply can never know how the judges would have ruled had they traded dockets" (Walker and Barrow 1985).

Probably more than anything, the absence of large scale, reliable data on trial courts has impeded systematic research in this area. Unlike with appellate court research, many trial court studies cannot be properly designed using only those data drawn from published, publicly available trial court opinions (something Siegelman and Donohue (1990) refer to as "studying the iceberg from its tip"). Rather, we must also rely on sources such as unpublished and oral decisions from the trial judges, courtroom and deposition transcripts, docket sheets, complaints, and motions (Kim et al. 2009). With electronic docketing an increasing commonplace in trial courts, the sources of these data for recent years are more easily accessible than in the past.

Nonetheless, trial court data collection hurdles are still numerous. For example, great variation exists among state trial courts regarding the electronic availability of case documents and docketed information. At the present time, privacy concerns for trial judges and case participants have caused the federal judiciary to refuse to release the complete data (containing judge, case, and party identifiers) that they collect on every filed criminal and civil case. This therefore makes it very difficult to use these data for projects necessitating any judge-specific or litigant-specific variables. To further complicate data matters, in 2011, the Administrative Office of the U.S. Courts announced that, to save storage costs, they would begin destroying all case files from 1970 to 1995 that either did not have a trial or were not deemed to be "historically significant" (Administrative Office of the U.S. Courts 2011).

Moving beyond data and research design challenges, it is interesting to note how the study of civil and criminal trial court decisions and trends have generally developed separately from one another. While this makes sense in many respects, there may well be areas where better understanding their influences on each other could be informative on the courts and the gatekeeping that takes place within them. For example, it may be worth further examining whether the long-term but still growing dominance of plea bargaining in federal criminal case dispositions has influenced the well-documented gradual growth in settlement frequency in federally filed civil cases. The influence that these two important activities have *on each other* is not well known or understood, but the reasons to expect a connection between plea-bargaining trends and settlement trends are plentiful. One possibility is that the involvement of the same district court judges, magistrate judges, staff, clerks, and other personnel for both criminal and civil cases makes the cross-implementation of bargain-seeking solutions more seamless. In addition, both criminal and civil cases give rise to pressures on the overall trial court system, including caseload and vacancy pressures on judges, the scarce availability of other limited court resources, the overall push for efficiency, etc. If this latter possibility is supported by the data, it could well provide evidence that high levels of plea bargaining and civil settlements were caused by similar factors rather than the former causing a growth in the latter.

Notes

1. The study of trial courts is inherently interdisciplinary, finding its home in fields such as political science, law and society, law and economics, and criminology, just to name a few. While space constraints within this chapter make it impossible to fully review all of the pertinent work from each of these disciplines, the hope is that the literature cited herein reflects the breadth and diversity of scholarship on the subject.
2. While scholars have frequently referred to trial judges and their courts as gatekeepers (see, e.g., Lyles 1995), I am not the first to also suggest that other actors within trial courts, like lawyers, play an important filtering and gatekeeping role. For example, Kritzer (1997) argued that "Lawyers ... are gatekeepers who control the flow of civil cases into the courts" (p. 22), and Gershman (1992) averred that "the prosecutor functions almost literally as a gatekeeper of justice with the obligation to prevent an injustice" (p. 521).
3. The basic rationale for the Priest and Klein's 50 percent hypothesis is that both the plaintiff and the defendant are involved in selecting cases that move toward trial--with the plaintiff only selecting those where he estimates that the defendant's liability is in a range that favors the plaintiff and the only defendant selecting those where he estimates his liability to be outside of that range. The resulting intersecting set of close disputes should thus lead to a probability of victory at trial of about 0.5.
4. There is almost certainly a selection effect built into these results. All other things equal, while attorneys paid hourly fees can pursue less meritorious claims should their clients wish

them to, contingency fee attorneys must carefully consider their likelihood of success (and getting paid) when deciding to accept representation and whether to pursue rapid settlement for a particularly case.

5. This is particularly true for elected state prosecutors (Cole, Smith, and DeJong 2015).
6. A further review of empirical political science work examining trial court ideology through the 1990s can be found at Pinello (1999).
7. In 1954's *Brown v. Board of Education*, the Supreme Court famously announced that "segregation is a denial of the equal protection of the laws." Following additional arguments the next year, the Court announced the remedy (*Brown II*): federal district courts should "take such proceedings and enter such orders and decrees" "to admit to public schools on a racially nondiscriminatory basis with all deliberate speed the parties to these cases." As history has revealed, the high degree of discretion in this remand order led to very uneven implementation of the *Brown* decision across the country.
8. While the connection between elected state trial judges and public opinion is clear, there are also a number of empirical findings that suggest that non-elected trial judges are also responsive to public opinion at times. For example, Rosenberg (1991) and Giles and Walker (1975) found that federal trial court judges were affected by local public opinion in their school desegregation rulings.

References

Administrative Office of the U.S. Courts. 2011. "The Third Branch: Making Room, Saving History." Available at: http://www.uscourts.gov/News/TheThirdBranch/11-05-01/Making_Room_Saving_History.aspx.

Administrative Office of the U.S. Courts. 2013a. "How Federal Courts Work: Criminal Cases." Available at: http://www.uscourts.gov/FederalCourts/UnderstandingtheFederalCourts/HowCourtsWork/CriminalCases.aspx.

Administrative Office of the U.S. Courts. 2013b. "Judicial Business of the United States Courts." Available at: http://www.uscourts.gov/Statistics/JudicialBusiness/2013.aspx.

Alschuler, A. W. 1968. "The Prosecutor's Role in Plea Bargaining." *University of Chicago Law Review* 36(1): 50–112.

Ashenfelter, O., Eisenberg, T., and Schwab, S. J. 1995. "Politics and the Judiciary: The Influence of Judicial Background on Case Outcomes." *Journal of Legal Studies* 24: 257–81.

Barclay, S. 1999. *An Appealing Act: Why People Appeal in Civil Cases*. Evanston, IL: Northwestern University Press.

Baum, L. 1980. "Responses of Federal District Judges to Court of Appeals Policies: An Exploration." *Western Political Quarterly* 33: 217–24.

Baum, L. 1997. *The Puzzle of Judicial Behavior*. Ann Arbor, MI: University of Michigan Press.

Baum, L. 2006. *Judges and their Audiences: A Perspective on Judicial Behavior*. Princeton, NJ: Princeton University Press.

Baum, L. 2013. *American Courts: Process and Policy*, 7th ed. Boston, MA: Wadsworth, Cengage Learning.

Bebchuk, L. A. 1984. "Litigation and Settlement under Imperfect Information." *RAND Journal of Economics* 15(3): 404–15.

Bibas, S. 2004. "The Feeney Amendment and the Continuing Rise of Prosecutorial Power to Plea Bargain." *Journal of Criminal Law and Criminology* 94: 295–309.

Blumberg, A. 1967. "The Practice of Law as a Confidence Game: Organizational Cooptation of a Profession." *Law & Society Review* 1: 15–39.

Bowers, J. 2008. "Punishing the Innocent." *University of Pennsylvania Law Review* 156: 1117–79.

Boyd, C. L. 2013. "She'll Settle It?" *Journal of Law and Courts* 1(2): 193–219.

Boyd, C. L., and Hoffman, D. A. 2013. "Litigating toward Settlement." *Journal of Law, Economics & Organization* 29: 898–929.

Buchman, J. 2007. "The Effects of Ideology on Federal Trial Judges' Decisions to Admit Scientific Expert Testimony." *American Politics Research* 35(5): 671–93.

Bushway, S. D., and Redlich, A. D. 2012. "Is Plea Bargaining in the 'Shadow of the Trial' a Mirage?" *Journal of Quantitative Criminology* 28(3): 437–54.

Choi, S. J., Gulati, M., and Posner, E. A. 2012. "What Do Federal District Judges Want? An Analysis of Publications, Citations, and Reversals." *Journal of Law, Economics & Organization* 28(3): 518–49.

Cole, G. F., Smith, C. E., and DeJong, C. 2015. *Criminal Justice in America*, 8th ed. Boston, MA: Cengage Learning.

Corley, P. C., Collins, P. M., and Calvin, B. 2011. "Lower Court Influence on U.S. Supreme Court Opinion Content." *Journal of Politics* 73(1): 31–44.

Court Statistics Project. 2010. "State Court Caseload Statistics." Available at: http://www.courtstatistics.org/Other-Pages/stateCourtCaseloadStatistics.aspx.

Dolbeare, K. M. 1967. *Trial Courts in Urban Politics: State Court Policy Impact and Functions in a Local Political System*. New York, NY: Wiley and Sons.

Eisenberg, T. 2004. "Appeal Rates and Outcomes in Tried and Nontried Cases: Further Exploration of Anti-Plaintiff Appellate Outcomes." *Journal of Empirical Legal Studies* 1: 659–88.

Eisenberg, T., and Lanvers, C. 2009. "What Is the Settlement Rate and Why Should We Care?" *Journal of Empirical Legal Studies* 6: 111–46.

Elder, H. W. 1989. "Trials and Settlements in the Criminal Courts: An Empirical Analysis of Dispositions and Sentencing." *Journal of Legal Studies* 18: 191–208.

Epstein, L., Landes, W. M., and Posner, R. A. 2013. *The Behavior of Federal Judges: A Theoretical and Empirical Study of Rational Choice*. Cambridge, MA: Harvard University Press.

Galanter, M. 1974. "Why the 'Haves' Come out ahead: Speculation on the Limits of Legal Changes." *Law & Society Review* 9(1): 95–160.

Galanter, M. 1985. "'... A Settlement Judge, not a Trial Judge:' Judicial Mediation in the United States." *Law & Society Review* 12: 1–18.

Galanter, M. 2004. "The Vanishing Trial: An Examination of Trials and Related Matters in Federal and State Courts." *Journal of Empirical Legal Studies* 1(3): 459–570.

Gershman, B. L. 1992. "A Moral Standard for the Prosecutor's Exercise of the Charging Discretion." *Fordham Urban Law Journal* 20: 513–30.

Gibson, J. L. 1978. "Judges' Role Orientations, Attitudes, and Decisions: An Interactive Model." *American Political Science Review* 72: 911–24.

Giles, M. W., and Walker, T. G. 1975. "Judicial Policy-Making and Southern School Segregation." *Journal of Politics* 37: 917–36.

Gordon, S. C., and Huber, G. A. 2002. "Citizen Oversight and the Electoral Incentives of Criminal Prosecutors." *American Journal of Political Science* 46(2): 334–51.

Hellend, E., and Tabarrok, A. T. 2003. *Judge and Jury: American Tort Law on Trial*. Oakland, CA: The Independent Institute.

Hettinger, V. A., Lindquist, S. A., and Martinek, W. L. 2006. *Judging on a Collegial Court: Influences on Appellate Decision Making*. Charlottesville, VA: University of Virginia Press.

Howard, R. M. 2002. "Litigation, Courts, and Bureaucratic Policy: Equity, Efficiency, and the Internal Revenue Service." *American Politics Research* 30(6): 583–607.

Huber, G. A., and Gordon, S. C. 2004. "Accountability and Coercion: Is Justice Blind When It Runs for Office?" *American Journal of Political Science* 48: 247–63.

Jacob, H. 1972. *Justice in America: Courts, Lawyers, and the Judicial Process*, 2nd ed. Boston, MA: Little, Brown, and Company.

Johnston, J. S., and Waldfogel, J. 2002. "Does Repeat Play Elicit Cooperation? Evidence from Federal Civil Litigation." *Journal of Legal Studies* 31: 39–60.

Keele, D. M., Malmsheimer, R. W., Floyd, D. W., and Zhang, L. 2009. "An Analysis of Ideological Effects in Published versus Unpublished Judicial Opinions." *Journal of Empirical Legal Studies* 6(1): 213–39.

Kessler, D. 1996. "Institutional Causes of Delay in the Settlement of Legal Disputes." *Journal of Law, Economics & Organization* 12: 432–60.

Kim, P. T., Schlanger, M., Boyd, C. L., and Martin, A. D. 2009. "How Should We Study District Judge Decision-Making?" *Washington University Journal of Law & Policy* 29: 83–112.

King, K. L. 1998. "Does the Law Matter? Federal District Court Decision-Making in Fair Housing Cases, 1968–89." *Social Science Research* 27(4): 388–409.

Kritzer, H. M. 1986. "Adjudication to Settlement: Shading in the Gray." *Judicature* 70: 161–5.

Kritzer, H. M. 1990. *The Justice Broker: Lawyers and Ordinary Litigation*. New York, NY: Oxford University Press.

Kritzer, H. M. 1997. "Contingency Fee Lawyers as Gatekeepers in the Civil Justice System." *Judicature* 81: 22–9.

Kritzer, H. M. 1998. "Contingent-Fee Lawyers and their Clients: Settlement Expectations, Settlement Realities, and Issues of Control in the Lawyer-Client Relationship." *Law & Social Inquiry* 23: 795–822.

Kuklinski, J. H., and Stanga, J. E. 1979. "Political Participation and Government Responsiveness: The Behavior of the California Superior Courts." *American Political Science Review* 73: 1090–9.

Landes, W. M. 1971. "An Economic Analysis of the Courts." *Journal of Law and Economics* 14: 61–107.

Levin, H. Y. 2008. "Making the Law: Unpublication in the District Courts." *Villanova Law Review* 53: 973–1002.

Lyles, K. L. 1995. *The Gatekeepers: Federal District Courts in the Political Process*. Westport, CT: Praeger Publishers.

Mather, L. M. 1979. *Plea-Bargaining or Trial: The Process of Criminal-Case Disposition*. Lexington, MA: Lexington Books (D. C. Heath & Co.).

Mather, L. 1995. "The Fired Football Coach (or, How Trial Courts Make Policy)," in *Contemplating Courts*, edited by L. Epstein. Washington, DC: CQ Press, 170–202.

McCoy, C. 1993. *Politics and Plea Bargaining: Victims' Rights in California*. Philadelphia, PA: University of Pennsylvania Press.

Miller, R. E., and Sarat, A. 1980–81. "Grievances, Claims, and Disputes: Assessing the Adversary Culture." *Law & Society Review* 15: 525–66.

Mnookin, R. H., and Lewis, K. 1979. "Bargaining in the Shadow of the Law: The Case of Divorce." *Yale Law Journal* 88(5): 950–97.

Murphy, W. F. 1959. "Lower Court Checks on Supreme Court Power." *American Political Science Review* 53: 1017–31.

O'Neill, M. E. 2004. "Understanding Federal Prosecutorial Declinations: An Empirical Analysis of Predictive Factors." *American Criminal Law Review* 41: 1439–98.

Perino, M. A. 2006. "Law, Ideology, and Strategy in Judicial Decision Making: Evidence from Securities Fraud Actions." *Journal of Empirical Legal Studies* 3(3): 497–524.

Pinello, D. R. 1999. "Linking Party to Judicial Ideology in American Courts: A Meta-analysis." *Justice System Journal* 20(3): 219–54.

Plapinger, E., and Stienstra, D. 1996. *ADR and Settlement in the Federal District Courts: A Sourcebook for Judges and Lawyers*. Washington, DC: CPR Institute for Dispute Resolution.

Posner, R. A. 1985. *The Federal Courts*. Cambridge, MA: Harvard University Press.

Priest, G. L., and Klein, B. 1984. "The Selection of Disputes for Litigation." *Journal of Legal Studies* 13: 1–55.

Provine, D. M. 1986. *Settlement Strategies for Federal District Judges*. Rockville, MD: National Institute of Justice.

Randazzo, K. A. 2008. "Strategic Anticipation and the Hierarchy of Justice in the U.S. District Courts." *American Politics Research* 36(5): 669–93.

Resnik, J. 1982. "Managerial Judges." *Harvard Law Review* 96(2): 374–448.

Rosenberg, G. N. 1991. *The Hollow Hope: Can Courts Bring about Social Change?* Chicago, IL: University of Chicago Press.

Rowland, C.K., and Carp, R. A. 1996. *Politics and Judgment in Federal District Courts*. Lawrence, KS: University Press of Kansas.

Rowland, C. K., Carp, R. A., and Stidham, R. A. 1984. "Judges' Policy Choices and the Value Basis of Judicial Appointments: A Comparison of Support for Criminal Defendants among Nixon, Johnson, and Kennedy Appointees to the Federal District Courts." *Journal of Politics* 46(3): 886–902.

Rowland, C. K., and Todd, B. 1991. "Where You Stand Depends on Who Sits: Platform Promises and Judicial Gatekeeping in the Federal District Courts." *Journal of Politics* 53: 175–85.

Schanzenbach, M. M., and Emerson, H. T. 2006. "Strategic Judging under the U.S. Sentencing Guidelines." *Journal of Law, Economics & Organization* 23: 24–56.

Scott, K. M. 2006. "Understanding Judicial Hierarchy: Reversals and the Behavior of Intermediate Appellate Judges." *Law & Society Review* 40: 163–92.

Siegelman, P., and Donohue, J. J., III. 1990. "Studying the Iceberg from its Tip: A Comparison of Published and Unpublished Employment Discrimination Cases." *Law & Society Review* 24: 1133–70.

Sisk, G. C., Heise, M., and Morriss, A. P. 1998. "Charting the Influences on the Judicial Mind: An Empirical Study of Judicial Reasoning." *New York Law Review* 73: 1377–500.

Sloan, F. A., and Hsieh, C. R. 1995. "Injury, Liability, and the Decision to File a Medical Malpractice Claim." *Law & Society Review* 29(3): 413–36.

Songer, D. R., Cameron, C. M., and Segal, J. A. 1995. "An Empirical Test of the Rational-Actor Theory of Litigation." *Journal of Politics* 57(4): 1119–29.

Spier, K. E. 1992. "The Dynamics of Pretrial Negotiation." *The Review of Economic Studies* 59(1): 93–108.

Spurr, S. J. 1997. "The Duration of Litigation." *Law and Policy* 19: 285–316.

Steffensmeier, D., and Herbert, C. 1999. "Women and Men Policymakers: Does the Judge's Gender Affect the Sentencing of Criminal Defendants?" *Social Forces* 77: 1163–96.

Stuntz, W. J. 1997. "The Uneasy Relationship between Criminal Procedure and Criminal Justice." *Yale Law Journal* 107: 1–76.

Waldfogel, J. 1998. "Reconciling Asymmetric Information and Divergent Expectations Theories of Litigation." *Journal of Law and Economics* 41(2): 451–76.

Walker, T. G. 1972. "Note Concerning Partisan Influences on Trial-Judge Decision Making." *Law & Society Review* 6: 645–50.

Walker, T. G., and Barrow, D. J. 1985 "The Diversification of the Federal Bench: Policy and Process Ramifications." *Journal of Politics* 47(2): 596–617.

Yarnold, B. M. 1997. "Factors Related to Outcomes in Religious Freedoms Cases, Federal District Courts: 1970–1990." *Justice System Journal* 19(2): 181–91.

Zorn, C., and Bowie, J. B. 2010. "Ideological Influences on Decision Making in the Federal Judicial Hierarchy: An Empirical Assessment." *Journal of Politics* 72(4): 1212–21.

Cases Cited

Brown v. Board of Education, 347 U.S. 483 (1954).
Brown v. Board of Education (Brown II), 349 U.S. 294 (1955).
Klayman v. Obama, 13–0851 (D.D.C. 2013).
Lafler v. Cooper, 566 U.S. __, 10–209 (2012).

CHAPTER 7

ACCESS TO INTERMEDIATE APPELLATE COURTS

DONALD R. SONGER AND SUSAN B. HAIRE

Introduction

The rule of law presents an empty promise without access to courts that can enforce it. This is true both at the trial and appellate levels. In most court systems in the United States, trial court decisions are first reviewed for defects by intermediate appellate courts. And, with relatively few cases heard by the U.S. Supreme Court or state courts of last resort with discretionary dockets, intermediate appellate courts also play an important policy-making role in the judicial hierarchy.

Yet even in light of the importance of access to these courts, rarely do their decisions to consider or dismiss an appeal capture the attention of scholars or those in the media. Ask yourself, when was the last time you turned on your favorite television evening news show, and the commentator began the broadcast by saying something like, "Today in Atlanta, the U.S. Court of Appeal for the Eleventh Circuit dismissed the appeal of an indigent state prisoner for failure to state a substantial federal question." Not only would it be astounding if any network news show featured such an event as its lead story, it would be quite rare for you to find even a two-column-inch story about such an event on page 17 of any newspaper in the country. We argue in this essay that such decisions are important and examine this infrequently studied topic, with particular attention to the U.S. Courts of Appeals.

Although the public is largely unaware of these courts, the U.S. Courts of Appeals figure prominently in judicial policy-making—a point emphasized by J. Woodford Howard over three decades ago. As one of the first political scientists to study these courts, Howard argued that, "even passing familiarity with federal circuit courts ... suggests that they are important power centers in the American polity. As courts of last resort in the vast majority of federal cases ... they shoulder heavy responsibilities in enforcing national law, declaring federal rights, and holding bureaucrats to account"

(1981: xvii). In the years since the landmark study by Howard, the substantive responsibilities of the courts of appeals have grown and their role as the court of last resort has expanded exponentially. In recent years, fewer than three-tenths of 1 percent of appeals court decisions are reviewed by the Supreme Court.

Although the jurisdiction of these courts is largely mandatory, cases heard by three-judge panels on the U.S. Courts of Appeals, particularly those that result in a "published" opinion, are not representative of all disputes filed in federal district court. In some federal circuits, over half of appeals filed are terminated for procedural reasons. For example, the appellate court may not have jurisdiction or a litigant lacks standing to appeal. Of those appeals that are heard on the "merits," only a minority will be closely scrutinized during oral argument. We argue here that understanding access to these courts therefore requires a perspective that takes into account this winnowing process.

Our essay begins with a consideration of the barriers to access created by the formal organization and jurisdictional rules established by Congress for the federal courts. While some procedural obstacles are straightforward in their application, others require judicial interpretation. As discussed further below, research finds that judges' policy goals may affect decision-making on these threshold issues. Because access to these courts is an option pursued by some litigants and not others, we then turn to a discussion of the decision to appeal. And, because filing an appeal does not guarantee full consideration of the issues raised by an appellant, we also examine how circuit rules and norms shape screening procedures that result in only a minority of cases being closely scrutinized by an appellate panel. Finally, we consider how this winnowing process that characterizes access to these courts potentially allows stronger, more experienced parties and their counsel to prevail in shaping the court's issue agenda and policy outcome. In the final section, we conclude with a brief discussion of promising lines of inquiry on the topic of access to appellate courts in the United States.

The Structure of Courts in the United States

The structure of the federal court system is not specified in the Constitution. Instead, that document confines itself to the general proposition that there will be a single Supreme Court and "such inferior courts as Congress may from time to time establish."[1] Instead of creating a single national appellate court below the Supreme Court, Congress decided to establish a system of geographically delineated regions called "circuits" in which a court of appeal sits to hear appeals from trial (district) courts in the same region. Thus, the U.S. Courts of Appeals are currently divided into twelve geographically defined circuits.[2] From time to time throughout history, Congress has altered the organization of the circuits and may increase (or decrease) the number of judgeships assigned to each. As its name suggests, the Court of Appeals for the District of Columbia hears appeals that originate in the nation's capital, either in the District Court of the District of Columbia or from many federal administrative agencies with offices located in the capital. The remaining eleven numbered circuits hear appeals contained within their geographic regions that follow state boundaries, typically three to nine states plus districts in various U.S. territories (e.g., Guam, Puerto Rico). In some cases the decision of a three-judge panel may be reviewed en banc by (usually) all of the active judges for that circuit. A litigant who loses in a federal court of appeals may file a petition for a writ of certiorari, asking the Supreme Court to review the case.

Another important characteristic of the U.S. judicial system is the existence of a "dual" court system consisting of both state and federal courts. Most state court systems are structured like the federal system (trial courts, intermediate appellate courts, and a court of last resort), but some are not. Forty of the fifty states have intermediate appellate courts. In most of these states, the intermediate court is a "single" court; however, about one-third follow the federal model and have separate intermediate appellate courts with regional coverage. In a few states, there are separate intermediate courts for criminal and civil appeals.[3]

Although the U.S. Supreme Court has declined to hold that constitutional due process includes a right of appeal, the federal court system and forty-seven states provide for appeals as of right in civil and criminal cases (Robertson 2012).[4] In 2010, 75 percent of the judicial caseload in state intermediate appellate courts involved appeals of right (LaFountain et al. 2012). As we discuss below, however, mandatory jurisdiction does not guarantee that a litigant's claims will be fully addressed by an intermediate appellate court.

Jurisdiction as a Constraint on Access

The most basic constraint on access to intermediate appellate courts is subject matter jurisdiction. Rules of jurisdiction are generally established by state and federal constitutions and statutes.[5] In contrast to the police powers exercised by state courts, federal courts are courts of limited jurisdiction. They can hear cases involving the interpretation or application of the U.S. Constitution, statutes passed by Congress (or the regulations of federal agencies created by statute), federal treaties, and executive agreements between the president and other heads of state. In addition to cases that implicate federal law, U.S. courts may also resolve cases that involve state law where the U.S. government is a party, or where the court has diversity jurisdiction.[6] In addition to hearing appeals from federal district courts, judges on the U.S. Courts of Appeals (excluding the federal circuit) review decisions by administrative agencies and the Tax Court.

While the exercise of jurisdiction described in the previous paragraph appears on the surface to be straightforward and clear, a few complications in practice should be noted. First, in the increasingly inter-dependent society of the twenty-first century, facts and circumstances that give rise to a lawsuit may simultaneously implicate both state and federal civil law. For example, an allegation of gender discrimination in employment matters generally would raise a question under Title 7 of the federal Civil Rights Act, but the same allegation might also lead to a lawsuit under state tort law. In such cases plaintiffs may bring a suit in either state or federal court in which both the state and the federal question will be settled. If a single action violates both state and federal criminal law, however, the two levels of government, as distinct sovereigns, may prosecute the defendant in both state and federal courts.

A further complication results from diversity of citizenship cases. Relief for claims brought under state law are typically obtained in a state court that applies state law to the issues before it. However, if the plaintiff and defendant are citizens of different states, either party may pursue the case in federal court.[7] In other areas, litigants may also have a choice of forum. For example, federal tax litigants can pursue disputes against the government in multiple forums and select those arenas that will be more receptive to their claim (Howard 2007).

A third complication is that states generally have exclusive jurisdiction to prosecute violations of their state's criminal laws. Most state criminal prosecutions are not reviewable in any federal court.[8] However, the provision in the Constitution preserving habeas corpus allows federal courts to review state criminal proceedings. If a state criminal defendant who exhausted all state appeals and, while confined to a state prison, alleges that the conviction was illegal because a federally protected right (e.g., the right to counsel) was violated, the prisoner may file a petition for a writ of habeas corpus from a federal district court. While such a petition is classified as an original civil action in federal court, it amounts to allowing a federal district court to review state court rulings in criminal cases. The district court decision to grant or deny the habeas petition is then reviewable in the U.S. Courts of Appeals. During the 1990s the number of habeas corpus petitions filed in federal district courts equaled or slightly exceeded ten thousand cases. This volume translates into about 4 percent of the entire federal district court civil caseload (Hanson and Daley 1995). Since these decisions are potentially appealable to the U.S. Courts of Appeals, habeas corpus relief has always provided a forum for federal circuit courts to review state criminal court proceedings.

In 1996, however, access to federal courts to review state court criminal convictions was severely limited by the Antiterrorism and Effective Death Penalty Act (AEDPA). Among other provisions, the law limits both the procedural and substantive scope of the writ. Procedurally, it bans successive petitions by the same person, requiring defendants to consolidate all claims into one appeal. Substantively, it narrows the grounds on which successful habeas claims can be made, allowing claims only to succeed when the convictions were contrary to "clearly established federal law" or an "unreasonable determination of the facts in light of the evidence" (28 U.S.C. § 2254). As interpreted by the U.S. Supreme Court, the Act placed a significant restriction on federal courts' power to grant habeas writs to state prisoners (Shargel and Fernich 2002). In the same year (i.e., 1996), Congress placed further limits on prisoners' access to the federal courts when it passed the Prison Litigation Reform Act (PLRA).

Other rules governing access to intermediate courts are constantly subject to modification by legislators.[9] For example, fourteen measures to curb diversity jurisdiction passed the House of Representatives between 1875 and 2004 (Curry 2007). While most believe that the original provision was intended to protect commercial interests from being sued by plaintiffs in states hostile to those interests, since the nineteenth century congressional modifications to diversity jurisdiction have largely been in response to judicial workload concerns and center on restricting federal court access by raising the amount in controversy (Curry 2007). In addition to promoting judicial efficiency, Congress has passed measures that restrict or expand access to the federal courts for reasons of political control (Gillman 2002; Smith 2006; Chutkow 2008). For example, in 1875, a Republican-led Congress was pursuing a policy agenda focused on economic nationalism. As part of this agenda, a lame-duck session of Congress passed a removal statute that facilitated moving civil litigation involving national commercial interests out of state courts and into the federal court system made up of appointees who shared their views (Gillman 2002). As long as Republicans occupied either one house of Congress or the presidency, the removal statute could not be changed (Gillman 2002). More recently, members of Congress interested in greater protection for the environment successfully pushed for changes to federal court jurisdiction to include citizen suit provisions that permit individuals to use the courts to enforce environmental regulations (Smith 2006).

Threshold Issues and Judicial Decision-Making

In addition to the constraints created by legislative enactment of jurisdictional statutes, other threshold issues may prevent judges from considering the merits of a litigant's claim. The most prominent constraint is the requirement that a concrete controversy exist between parties with real, conflicting interests that may be remedied through court order. Further, the courts can only entertain cases brought by litigants with proper standing, requiring that the plaintiff must have suffered a direct and significant injury in fact. Third, courts will not hear cases that have become moot because the original controversy—through intervening factors or the passage of time—no longer exists (e.g., a suit for divorce becomes moot if the defendant spouse dies). In some cases, litigants must exhaust administrative remedies before pursuing a claim in the judiciary. Courts also may decline to hear an appeal if a litigant has not complied with other procedural requirements, including those associated with the timeliness of a filing. Taken together, these threshold issues allow courts to dispose of a case without considering the substantive legal merits of the claim.

Recent Supreme Court decisions illustrate how judges themselves can modify rules relating to access. For example, the Supreme Court expanded access in two challenges to executive power during the Bush administration, holding that federal courts had habeas corpus jurisdiction over detainees at Guantanamo Bay.[10] In another decision that had the effect of restricting access to the legal system, the Supreme Court held that a group of women comprised of potentially 1.5 million plaintiffs was too large to certify as a class in an employment discrimination claim filed against Wal-Mart.[11] In these examples, support for access was strongest among liberal justices whereas conservatives adopted positions that limited access.

Because these procedures promote judicial discretion (i.e., whether to address the merits of an appeal), scholars argue that they allow for judicial policy-making opportunities in courts with mandatory jurisdiction (Kaheny 2011; Braselton 2014). Several studies have examined the relationship between judicial ideology and decision-making on threshold issues in the federal circuit courts (Pierce 1999; Staudt 2004; Cross 2007; Fix and Randazzo 2010; Kaheny 2010, 2011; Braselton 2014). When addressing threshold issues that relate to standing, mootness, timeliness, or the statement of a proper claim, courts of appeals judges are more likely to address the merits of the claim when the substantive ideological outcome of a pro-access vote was consistent with their ideological preferences (Kaheny 2010: 150). The same study, however, did not find a relationship between judicial policy preferences and voting on other procedural issues that relate to proper forum (Kaheny 2010). Judges are also sensitive to the preferences of Congress and the executive branch when dealing with threshold issues (Braselton 2014). On questions of national security, one study found that federal judges use threshold questions to avoid resolving challenges to executive branch actions (Fix and Randazzo 2010).

Access and Litigant Decisions to Appeal

Assuming that a court has jurisdiction, access to that court is primarily driven by the decision of a litigant to pursue a case. In the federal system, Federal Rules of Appellate Procedure (FRAP) and each circuit's internal operating procedures lay out the steps and requirements for dissatisfied litigants seeking to overturn or modify the decision of an administrative agency or federal district court. Once the lower court enters a judgment, the losing party can initiate the process by filing a notice of appeal that includes the payment of docketing fees, unless the appellant is granted permission to proceed *in forma pauperis*. Transcript requests associated with the preparation of the record represent an additional cost for litigants. Given the legal and court costs involved, it is not surprising that only a minority of cases are appealed. In a study of federal court filings from 1988 to 2000, 10.9 percent of all criminal and civil cases filed in federal district court were appealed; the appeal rate was much higher—about 40 percent—for cases that were tried (Eisenberg 2004). By comparison, in an analysis of state court civil trials in torts and contracts from 2005 to 2010, 12 percent of losing litigants appealed to an intermediate appellate court (Cohen 2013).

When evaluating whether to pursue a case, including an appeal, parties engage in a decision-making calculus that is believed to take into account who is likely to win and lose (Priest and Klein 1984). If litigants are rational, they will settle simpler cases where both sides anticipate a clear winner (and loser). The remaining cases that are tried in court are typically less predictable. After a trial court has decided, the losing litigant, if rational, will make a decision to appeal based on her assessment that the lower court has committed reversible error. One study of criminal cases appealed to the U.S. Supreme Court provides support for the contention that litigants consider the odds of winning when deciding to appeal (Songer, Cameron, and Segal 1995).

In a system where rationality is assumed to guide litigant decisions, all (and only) cases with reversible error will be appealed. However, contrary to the study noted above, empirical research suggests that is not the case: bad case selection decisions are likely to be made when the stakes are high, costs are low, and there is a misunderstanding of the law (Eisenberg 2004). One study estimates an appeal rate of 20 percent in cases in which the trial court was correct; litigants are estimated to appeal only half of the cases in which the trial court erred (Eisenberg 2004). What accounts for a litigant irrationally appealing a case that will be lost at the appellate level? (This form of irrationality would include decisions to appeal "correct" trial court decisions or choosing not to appeal "incorrect" decisions). Research by behavioral economists suggests a confirmatory bias may lead litigants and counsel to make inaccurate predictions about the likelihood of success when such predictions support their own stake in the litigation (Loewenstein et al. 1993). Furthermore, according to "prospect theory,"[12] decisions to appeal are also potentially subject to a framing effect, such that litigant decisions to appeal will differ depending on whether the potential outcome is viewed by the litigant as a "gain" or "loss," with those perceiving losses more likely to pursue an appeal (Rachlinski 1996). This framing effect may also explain defendants' higher appeal rate, when compared to plaintiffs. From this account, plaintiffs seeking monetary damages in litigation perceive these options as "gains" and will be more willing to settle a case that they could win on appeal (Rachlinski 1996). On the other side, defendants adopt a risk-seeking strategy because monetary damages are viewed as "losses," leading them to appeal cases where the odds of winning are low (Rachlinski 1996).

The perception of potential gains and losses in appellate litigation may be different depending on whether the litigant is a repeat player or one-shotter (Galanter 1974). From this perspective, institutional litigants who have litigated and anticipate future litigation view the current case in the context of their broader litigation strategy across multiple cases. Therefore, a favorable outcome in a case is framed in terms of whether the decision establishes a favorable precedent for future litigation (Galanter 1974). Decisions to appeal, then, are considered more in terms of the effect the appeal is likely to have on the body of precedent that binds future cases. Studies on the efforts of the NAACP Legal Defense Fund and other organized interests to bring about policy change suggest these groups considered the implications of case selection decisions as part of an overall litigation strategy (Vose 1959; Kobylka 1987). The U.S. government represents a type of repeat player that not only writes many of the rules itself through statutory or regulatory law, but also successfully "plays for the rules" in the court system (Kritzer 2003; Kaheny 2010). Research consistently establishes the care with which case selection decisions by attorneys in the Solicitor General's office result in their correctly identifying winning cases that enhance the credibility of the U.S. government as a litigant before the Supreme

Court (Zorn 2002). The U.S. government's high success rate over time in the U.S. Courts of Appeals suggests reinforcing effects: a "win" generates a favorable precedent that binds future appellate panels in that circuit as well as judges in district courts and officials in administrative agencies (Songer, Sheehan, and Haire 1999).

Unlike repeat players, so called one-shotters (i.e., those parties who litigate one rather than multiple cases), are willing to forego a potentially favorable rule if it means a better outcome in their own case (Galanter 1974; Albiston 1999). An individual one-shotter's interest in winning the outcome of his or her case, rather than the establishment of a rule, leads to the "paradox of losing by winning" in which dispositions that favor an individual in settlement or trial are legally invisible (Albiston 1999). The absence of favorable individual one-shotter outcomes at the appellate level potentially contributes to a bias in legal doctrine that favors repeat players. For example, in an analysis of judicial interpretations of the Family Medical Leave Act (FMLA) during the early implementation phase of this remedial statute, Albiston concluded that the strategic settlement and rule-making opportunities in litigation contributed to a body of case law at the appellate level that favored employers (1999: 192). Some strategic litigants also avoid or pursue litigation in anticipation of other constraints stemming from their policy or political environment. These include organized interests that must consider how litigation decisions affect their ability to maintain group allegiance and support. For example, for symbolic reasons groups may decide to appeal a trial court loss that they expect to lose again at the appellate stage because their membership expects them to take a stand. Litigants may also take into account potential political backlash associated with positions taken in litigation. In an interview with one of the authors, a U.S. Department of Justice (DOJ) attorney described the following experience that we use here as an illustration. When she approached opposing counsel about a possible settlement, that attorney admitted (in confidence) that he realized that his client (a state agency) would likely lose if the case went to trial but his political superiors had made it clear that, given the political climate in their state, a settlement with the presidential administration would be politically unpopular. If they (the state agency) lost the case, they would appeal and lose again; the alternative, working out an agreement with administration officials from the opposing party, was not an option.

Resources potentially play a role in limiting access to the courts, particularly at the appellate stage where the costs of litigation can be substantial. In criminal cases, provisions for indigent defense have contributed to the establishment of public defender offices that are instrumental from the earliest trial stages through an appeal. The role of litigant wealth may play a larger role in civil cases. Scholarship on access to civil justice finds that it varies by social class with lower-income people less likely to pursue litigation (Sandefur 2008). To the extent that one-shot litigants have limited resources, case selection decisions, including the decision to appeal, may be left to lawyers, some of whom may employ a decision-making calculus that includes whether legal expenses will be covered. A study of the personal injury bar finds that lawyers' case screening decisions are premised on whether the contingent-fee share of the client's anticipated award will be sufficient to cover expenses (Kritzer 2004).

Although most believe that litigants' counsel inform the bulk of case selection decisions by those who pursue their case at the appellate level, court statistics suggest otherwise, with a very large number of litigants who are not represented by counsel. According to figures from the Administrative Office of the U.S. Courts, in fiscal year 2013, 28,800 of the 56,475 appeals commenced were filed by pro se litigants. At least one reason for this increase is the large number of appeals filed by non-prisoner pro se litigants. Of the 28,800 pro se appeals filed in 2013, over a quarter involved non-prisoners. Although the cost of legal representation is an important factor in the decision of civil litigants to argue their own case, scholars speculate that there are other reasons contributing to this rise, including increased literacy and the availability of legal resources on the Internet (van Wormer 2007). Court officials cannot represent these litigants; however, they still must sort out whether there is merit underlying the claims raised in pro se appeals, compounding a judicial efficiency problem generated by the rising caseloads. Screening procedures designed to deal with these appeals, as well as others filed by litigants, varies across the intermediate appellate courts—a point we explore further in later sections of this chapter.

The Caseload Explosion and Access

As the discussion of appeal rates in the previous section indicates, the majority of losing litigants in trial courts do not file an appeal. Nevertheless, the number of appeals handled by intermediate appellate courts is extremely large. For state intermediate appellate courts, the number of incoming appeals between 2001 and 2010 averaged just under 200,000 cases per year (Court Statistics Project 2010). Growth in the caseload of the U.S. Courts of Appeals over the last fifty years has been substantial. From a caseload of fewer than 4,000 cases in 1960, the number of appeals filed in 2006 hit 68,313. In 2007, the number of filings in the U.S. Courts of Appeals dropped about 13 percent with only modest change in annual filings since that time. Over the same period, Congress increased the number of authorized judgeships from sixty-eight in 1960 to 167 at present. Combining these figures, we can compare the average annual filings per active judgeship in 1960 (59) with the figure for 2011 (338). The burden on these appeals courts has increased five-fold over the past fifty years.

Judges themselves have described the severity of the caseload crisis. In their research, one of the authors of this chapter interviewed over sixty current and former judges on the U.S. Courts of Appeals.[13] All of the interviewed judges recognized the problem produced by rapidly increasing appeals and several labeled it "the biggest crisis" confronting the courts during their lifetime. The judges acknowledged that, over the past several decades, every circuit has taken steps to deal with the problem of increasing caseloads. These responses include the use of non-argument (i.e. screening and motions) panels, delegating some responsibilities for screening to staff attorneys and clerks, reducing the proportion of cases orally argued, increasing participation by those judges who sit by designation (federal district court judges and senior status judges), and limiting the number of published opinions (Hooper et al. 2011; Levy 2013). Despite their widespread use, case management methods have drawn opposition, particularly among legal academics. Critics suggest that these techniques correspond to two-tiered access to the circuit courts with "separate and unequal tracks" for litigants who launch appeals in the federal system (Vladeck and Gulati 2005; Levy 2013).

Since these measures are largely designed to reduce the number of cases that are given the "full treatment," we describe here the traditional model that characterizes the processing of appeals in the federal circuit courts that are orally argued—the method used for most appeals in earlier eras, prior to the development of screening and case management techniques. After the case arrived in the office of the clerk of the court, the clerk assigned the case to a randomly selected panel of three judges on active service. The judges then spent several months studying the appellate briefs, transcripts of the record, and other case materials, often with the assistance of a memorandum of law written by one of their clerks, before scheduling an oral hearing in which each side was given time to argue the merits of their case. Shortly after the oral argument, the three-judge panel held a conference in which only the judges participated, made a tentative decision on the merits of the case, and assigned one judge to prepare a draft of the opinion of the court. After review by each judge and agreement reached on a final opinion, the parties were notified of the result and the opinion was published in the *Federal Reporter*.

Today, a relatively small number of appeals are processed under this traditional model. For those appeals that were addressed on the merits in 2013, less than one-fifth received an oral hearing and about 90 percent of the decisions are unpublished. Below, we describe current screening processes documented in other research and relayed in interviews conducted with appeals court judges. At the outset, we note that interviewed judges were in basic agreement that this caseload explosion required extensive screening of cases that permit the court to adopt time-saving methods of resolving their cases. And, judges seemed generally satisfied with the approaches taken by their court. However, when comparing across the circuits, there is no widespread agreement among interviewed judges on the desirability and effectiveness of screening methods.

Screening on the U.S. Courts of Appeals

In his widely read book on appellate courts, First Circuit Judge Frank Coffin offered the following advice to brief writers, "At the threshold, the brief must seek to persuade a seasoned if not cynical cadre of appellate court staff attorneys that the case does indeed deserve oral argument and should not be summarily affirmed or dismissed with a brief opinion" (1994: 108). Although scholars trace the use of staff attorneys to the 1970s, Congress officially authorized the creation of staff attorney offices in 1982 (Levy 2013). Our judge interviews emphasize the important role played by these lawyers. When asked about screening processes, a majority of those judges interviewed described the following process.

First, judges indicated that when a case is initially filed it goes to a senior staff attorney who takes a quick look at the case. If the staff attorney concludes that a case has an arguable issue (i.e., an issue without an obvious answer), it is forwarded to a three-judge panel randomly selected in the clerk's office for further action,[14] typically, an oral argument hearing and full consideration by the panel. However, the importance of a case is not always obvious. In that event, even if the clerk initially scheduled a case for oral argument, the panel may proceed to make a summary, "unsigned" decision.

The remaining cases are divided among the staff attorneys working for the circuit. These attorneys identify the "open and shut" cases (or, as one judge referred to them, the "slam dunks"). These include appeals with procedural defects (e.g., appeal "out of time," a problem of mootness or standing, or a jurisdictional problem). If such a defect does exist, the attorney will propose procedural termination in the form of a summary disposition. In 2013, 35 percent of the appeals were terminated for procedural defects.

In one interview, a judge described how the staff prepares a list of such cases to dismiss to include a memo explaining the rationale for the disposition. These memos are circulated to all judges in the circuit. A single judge can then put the case back in for assignment to a panel. But if there is not an objection to the summary disposition, a staff attorney then prepares a draft of a proposed opinion disposing of the case without argument. Formal approval is routinely given, resulting in the issuance of a formal disposition in a short "unpublished" opinion.

After screening out candidates for procedural termination, staff attorneys in multiple circuits prepare a list of cases that they believe warrant consideration by a panel of judges, but do not require oral argument. In preparing this list, staff attorneys pay particular attention to habeas petitions and *pro se* cases.[15] A 2000 FJC study reported that, with the exception of the Second Circuit, courts rarely allow a *pro se* litigant to argue orally (McKenna et al. 2000). Interviews with judges and court personnel also suggest that they are more likely to include on the non-argument list social security claims and immigration appeals. In 2002, the decision to reduce the backlog of cases in the Bureau of Immigration Appeals contributed to a flood of appeals in the U.S. Courts of Appeals, particularly the Second and Ninth Circuits. Although the numbers have receded somewhat, immigration appeals continue to make up a significant portion of the docket. In response, one circuit created nonargument panels for immigration cases and identified specific staff attorneys (with expertise in this area) to be involved in the screening process (Palmer et al. 2005). Judge interviews also described a process whereby cases identified as candidates for "nonargument" are circulated to all judges in the circuit with a memo recommending the disposition of the case (usually a dismissal or affirmance) with a provision that allows for a single judge to put the case back on the argument calendar.

All interviewed judges held the view that a decision to grant oral argument is the responsibility of three-judge panels. Although a staff attorney may recommend a case for nonargument, the panel may decide otherwise after examining the full case file. FRAP 34 requires the courts to allow oral argument unless the three-judge panel unanimously decides that oral argument is unnecessary for one of the specified reasons

Table 7.1 2013 case management and workload statistics by circuit

Circuit	Appeals filed (actions per panel)	Procedural terminations (actions per panel)	Merits terminations (actions per panel)	% of merits terminations after an oral hearing	Written, signed decisions (per active judge)	% unpublished
All	1,037	361	631	18.3	59	88.2
DC	278	116	128	41.8	20	54
First	788	253	450	26.9	44	65.3
Second	1,153	601	714	27.9	215	88.4
Third	838	260	615	7.7	136	93.8
Fourth	994	223	737	10.9	43	93.9
Fifth	1,316	476	746	16.2	19	91.4
Sixth	934	311	664	16.8	47	90.5
Seventh	816	312	472	35.7	47	66.5
Eighth	774	153	588	16.5	37	76
Ninth	1,320	522	744	20.4	14	91.9
Tenth	518	175	356	24.3	89	81.9
Eleventh	1,564	606	960	10.8	17	94

Note: Data are from the Administrative Office of the U.S. Courts, figures for calendar year ending December 2013; percentage unpublished figures are from Table S-3, for fiscal year ending September 2013.

(e.g., the appeal is frivolous or the dispositive issues have been authoritatively decided). One judge explained that judges on that circuit will always grant oral argument "if we think there is a chance for reversal or if the appellant really needs to be heard ... We want to make sure that the loser feels that he has had a fair shake."

FRAP 34 establishes the default—an oral hearing—with specific exceptions. Within these parameters, circuits have developed internal operating procedures and norms that reflect on differences among the courts of appeals when comparing oral argument rates. As the data in Table 7.1 suggest, the proportion of cases orally argued varies substantially by court. Oral argument was more frequent in the DC and Seventh Circuits. Comments of several interviewed judges from the Seventh Circuit suggest that this reflects a deliberate choice. As Bowie et al. (2014) report, one judge commented, "We have a strong preference for oral argument" and then accurately noted (with considerable pride), "I believe we have the highest rate of oral argument of any circuit."[16]

A recent statistical analysis confirms the process described by judges and other court personnel. The study found that oral argument was substantially more likely when the panel's workload was relatively light, when the case was complex (e.g., multiple issues or cross appeals), when there was a "paid" appeal (rather than a pro se appeal), in politically salient cases (e.g., a case involving a constitutional issue or one in which amici curiae participated) and when local circuit rules were more supportive of granting oral arguments (Bowie et al. 2014). Although oral argument provides an opportunity for judges and counsel to clarify issues, the brief provides the baseline for judges' questions. Given the emphasis on the appellate brief, we consider more closely in the next section how the content of these briefs shape the opportunities for litigants seeking access to the issue agenda in intermediate appellate courts.

Access and Merits Panels: Appellate Briefs and Information

As the sections above suggest, case screening procedures result in a select number of appeals getting the "full treatment," including oral argument. Information provided by litigants and their lawyers, through appellate briefs, may be important in determining the degree to which one's case will be scrutinized by the court. FRAP 28 provides guidance to litigants on the organization of appellate briefs that are expected to identify the issues to be addressed by the court along with the arguments in support of the litigant's position. The submission of briefs is a sequential process that is initiated by the appellant. These briefs address an important informational need for judges and their staff. As noted by one prominent appeals court jurist, a judge has "very little time to spend on each case and ... lacks specialized knowledge of most of the cases that comes before him. The judge so circumstanced is very badly in need of the advocate's help" (Posner 1999: 3). Those briefs that persuade staff attorneys and judges on screening panels that the issues raised merit further consideration are those where the appellants' advocate(s) successfully framed questions for the court.

The importance of counsel in the preparation of an appellate brief has important implications for the screening process. Interviews with judges and studies on case management techniques highlight how pro se appeals are typically given less scrutiny than appeals filed by litigants represented by counsel. Being represented by an attorney does not, however, translate into a litigant's claims being accorded the "full treatment. " For those litigants whose cases were decided with published opinion, access did not always result in their claims being addressed by the court. In one study of the linkages between appellate briefs and issue agendas on the U.S. Courts of Appeals for two circuits, Haire and Moyer (2007) examined the issues identified by brief writers and compared them against those addressed in the court's opinion. They found that courts routinely suppressed issues; however, suppression was more likely when the brief was submitted by an individual appellant or the appellant was represented by a single attorney. Additional studies suggest that legal resources associated with the experience of counsel and the size of the litigation team potentially affect the ability of a litigant to successfully persuade judges of the merits of their claim (Haire, Lindquist, and Hartley 1999; Szmer, Johnson, and Sarver 2007; Sisk and Heise 2015), including whether to adopt the advocate's use of precedent (Moyer, Collins, and Haire 2013).

Discussion

For a variety of reasons, Congress has been unwilling to expand substantially the size of the federal judiciary to keep up with the increase in appellate filings. As a result, case management techniques in the U.S. Courts of Appeals are likely to be a permanent fixture in sorting out issues of litigant access. The utilization of these techniques is not limited to federal intermediate courts. State officials have also developed methods to deal with heavy caseloads in appellate courts (Marvell 1988; Binford et al. 2007). In the mid-1970s, a majority of cases heard in state appellate courts were orally argued; however, by 1984, the proportion of cases with oral argument dropped to 30 percent (Marvell 1988). In a 2005 survey of intermediate appellate court administrators, Binford et al. reported that "nonargument" dispositions were widespread with less than one tenth of cases orally argued in the surveyed courts. Similar to observations made about the federal court system, there is substantial variation in case management methods used across the states (Marvell 1988; Binford et al. 2007). Critics have raised normative arguments about these screening processes––including the question of whether judicial power has been delegated to staff. The empirical question of whether judicial "triage" techniques used to screen appeals contributes to an appellate body that performs poorly in detecting legal error has been evaluated and generally concludes that dispositions during periods of time marked by high caseloads (and responses to them, including the use of staff attorneys) are no worse than the "traditional" model of appellate justice in dealing with claims of legal error (Levy 2013).

Another criticism that has been leveled specifically at the decline in the proportion of orally argued cases is that the court's legitimacy is undermined (Levy 2013). While it is doubtful that the vast majority of the general public is even aware that there has been a decline in the proportion of appeals that receive oral arguments, elites that are attentive to the courts, especially lawyers, may be concerned. What, if any, consequence flow from a potential decline in the legitimacy accorded by elites is a question that awaits future research.

Current research shows that one consequence of the screening processes employed by all circuits is that litigant access is unequal. Not only do different types of litigants have unequal access, but the likelihood of similarly situated litigants filing appeals that receive the "full treatment" varies across the circuits, a situation that has been characterized as the Balkanization of appellate justice (Lindquist 1996; Solimine 2004; Richman and Reynolds 1996; Sisk 1997). In one analysis focused on court-level causes of inequality in judicial treatment, Lindquist (1996) finds that larger circuits have lower rates of oral argument—a finding that continues to be supported as reflected in 2013 figures reported in Table 7.1. The composition of the docket is an important component as well. In those circuits where judges hear a disproportionate number of pro se appeals, oral argument is less likely. Our judge interviews also emphasized the importance of circuit norms surrounding oral argument. In those circuits where judges perceive oral hearings as important either as an aid in the decision-making process or enhancing the legitimacy of the institution, argument rates were higher. But, in spite of the insights generated by this line of research, we are far from a comprehensive understanding of when and why some litigants' cases will receive the full treatment and others will not. Further research that builds on these studies and draws on interdisciplinary perspectives (i.e. organizational sciences and policy innovation) will help to flesh out why courts are more (or less) responsive to litigant appeals than others.

The focus in judicial politics research on published decisions and litigants in those appeals has meant that we know less about the decision-making process when deciding to appeal and what to argue in that appeal (cf. Zorn 2002; Barclay 1999). Consequently, much of what we think we "know" about the role of litigant strength and decision-making on the courts of appeals may not be true at all; it may only reflect the nature of decision-making about a small, non-random proportion of the total decisional output of the courts. To address this issue, additional research is needed to evaluate whether patterns in outcomes of published decisions (who wins/loses) is reflected not only in unpublished decisions but also in screening decisions. A smattering of quantitative data and the results of judge interviews, some of which are excerpted above, suggest that the patterns of wins and losses is almost certainly different in published decisions than in appeals procedurally terminated or decided without oral argument. But, we need more systematic research to better understand why and how the patterns are different. Studies of the U.S. Supreme Court suggest that those who are successful in shaping the Court's agenda may not be similarly successful in winning their case on the merits. But, the figures and studies reviewed above suggest that the opposite is true on the U.S. Courts of Appeals—that those who are successful in shaping the agenda are highly successful on the merits. If so, evaluating these institutional differences associated with different levels of courts in the United States is a project ripe for future study. Such research may also yield new insights on the causal mechanisms that underlie litigant success, including how the quality of appellate advocates may (or may not) affect case selection decisions, the persuasiveness of arguments made to the judges, and the interrelationships between these two. Future scholarship may heed approaches taken in recent research that draw on psychology to advance our understanding of influences associated with persuading a judicial audience (Braman 2009; Corley and Wedeking 2014) and the potential for implicit bias in the court (Guthrie et al. 2007).

More broadly, research on the impact of the political preferences of appeals court judges and the extent to which they engage in strategic calculations currently rest on analyses of decisions that survived litigant case selection decisions and judicial screening processes. At a minimum, large-scale empirical research is needed to determine whether findings are similar in unpublished cases. Given the reduction in the proportion of cases that are decided with published opinion over time, and extensive circuit-level differences in these rates, the failure to include unpublished decisions may have led us to make overbroad conclusions about the significance and causes of attitudinal voting. Similar concerns have led to calls for scholars to revisit existing approaches to the study of judicial preferences that currently overestimate the effect of liberal-conservative policy views in appellate court decision-making (Epstein and Knight 2013). Consistent with recent scholarship that focuses on how judges are motivated to allocate their time (Epstein, Landes, and Posner 2013), we believe that scholarly attention directed at explaining variation in judicial treatment to litigant claims may lead to the development of a "legal attitudinal" model to supplement—or replace—current understandings surrounding the "attitudinal" model.

Notes

1. U.S. Const. art. III, § 1.
2. For this chapter, we do not discuss the Federal Circuit because it is a unique court of appeal, with nationwide jurisdiction in international trade, government contracts, patents, federal personnel, veterans' benefits, among others.
3. Oklahoma and Texas have separate courts of last resort for criminal and civil appeals.
4. The major exception is that, because of the constitutional prohibition of double jeopardy, the government may not appeal a criminal decision that resulted in a "not guilty" verdict for the defendant.
5. Neither Congress nor state legislatures may expand the jurisdiction of federal or state courts beyond the constitutional limits.
6. A federal court's power to hear any case where the amount in controversy exceeds $75,000 and no plaintiff shares a state of citizenship with any defendant. See 28 U.S.C. Sec. 1332(a).

7. Congress has a long history of limiting federal court access in diversity cases (Curry 2007). The Judiciary Act of 1789 set the limit for federal jurisdiction to actions in which the amount in question was at least $500. That limit has been raised over time to the current requirement in which the dollar amount at stake must be at least $75,000.
8. Criminal defendants convicted in state court may appeal their convictions from the highest state court to the U.S. Supreme Court if and only if there is a "federal question"—which usually means only if the defendant alleges that their conviction was invalid because state officials violated one of the defendant's procedural rights protected by the U.S. Constitution.
9. Including state legislatures with respect to access to state intermediate courts.
10. See *Rasul v. Bush*, 542 U.S. 466 (2004); *Boumediene v. Bush*, 553 U.S. 723 (2008).
11. See *Wal-Mart Stores, Inc. v. Dukes* 564 U.S. 338 (2011).
12. Developed by Kahneman and Tversky, prospect theory has its roots in behavioral economics where it has been employed to explain why people are risk-seeking to avoid losses but risk-averse when faced with options that will accumulate gains (Guthrie 2002: 1116).
13. The interviews were conducted between 2002 and 2011. By the terms of the interviews, the judges were told that no comments would be attributed to a judge by name or by any attributes that might permit expert observers to identity the judge. To avoid identification, all judges are referred to using masculine pronouns and are referred to by a letter (e.g., Judge D, Judge NN) which has no relationship to their name.
14. An FJC study found that staff attorneys play a role in screening for jurisdictional defects in a majority of circuits, although screening for argument/nonargument varies by circuit, with staff responsible for initial screening in the 1st, 4th, 6th, 7th, 9th, 11th, and DC circuits. Judges are responsible for initial case screening in the 2nd, 3rd, 5th, 8th, and 10th circuits.
15. Levy (2013) and Hooper et al. (2011) suggest that screening may also take into account Anders brief cases. *Anders v. California* 386 U.S. 738. In an "Anders" case, defendant's counsel states that the defendant has no meritorious claims on appeal. As a result, a litigant may decide to appeal, but access to these courts is likely to be limited as a result of the contrary position of his lawyer.
16. At the time of the interview, this circuit had the highest rate of oral argument; however, we note that data from the Administrative Office of the Courts indicate that distinction more recently belongs to the DC Circuit.

References

Albiston, C. 1999. "The Rule of Law and the Litigation Process: The Paradox of Losing by Winning." *Law & Society Review* 33(4): 869–910.

Barclay, S. 1999. *An Appealing Act: Why People Appeal in Civil Cases.* Evanston, IL: Northwestern University Press.

Binford, W. et al. 2007. "Seeking Best Practices among Intermediate Courts of Appeal: A Nascent Journey." *Journal of Appellate Practice and Process* 9(1): 37–119.

Bowie, J. B., Songer, D. R., and Szmer, J. 2014. *The View from the Bench and Chambers: Examining Judicial Process and Decision Making in the U.S. Courts of Appeals.* Charlottesville, VA: University of Virginia Press.

Braman, E. 2009. *Law, Politics, and Perception: How Policy Preferences Influence Legal Reasoning*. Charlottesville, VA: University of Virginia Press.

Brazelton, S. 2014. "Federal Circuit Courts and the Implications of the Doctrines of Procedure, Jurisdiction, and Justiciability." Unpublished dissertation, Georgia State University.

Chutkow, D. M. 2008. "Jurisdiction Stripping: Litigation, Ideology, and Congressional Control of the Courts." *Journal of Politics* 70(4): 1053–64.

Cohen, T. H. 2013. "Litigating Civil Cases in State Intermediate Appellate Courts: Analyzing Decisions to Appeal Civil Trial Verdicts or Judgments and the Impact of Appellate Litigation on Trial Court Outcomes." Available at SSRN 2283873.

Corley, P. C., and Wedeking, J. 2014. "The (Dis) Advantage of Certainty: The Importance of Certainty in Language." *Law & Society Review* 48(1): 35–62.

Court Statistics Project. 2010. "Examining the Work of State Courts: An Analysis of 2010 State Court Caseloads." National Center for State Courts, Williamsburg, VA.

Cross, F. B. 2007. *Decision Making in the US Courts of Appeals*. Stanford, CA: Stanford University Press.

Curry, B. 2007. "Institutions, Interests, and Judicial Outcomes: The Politics of Federal Diversity Jurisdiction." *Political Research Quarterly* 60(3): 454–67.

Eisenberg, T. 2004. "Appeal Rates and Outcomes in Tried and Nontried Cases: Further Exploration of Anti-plaintiff Appellate Outcomes." *Journal of Empirical Legal Studies* 1(3): 659–88.

Epstein, L., and Knight, J. 2013. "Reconsidering Judicial Preferences." *Political Science* 16(1): 11–31.

Epstein, L., Landes, W. M., and Posner, R. A. 2013. *The Behavior of Federal Judges: A Theoretical and Empirical Study of Rational Choice*. Cambridge, MA: Harvard University Press.

Fix, M. P., and Randazzo, K. A. 2010. "Judicial Deference and National Security: Applications of the Political Question and Act of State Doctrines." *Democracy and Security* 6(1): 1–16.

Galanter, M. 1974. "Why the 'Haves' Come out ahead: Speculations on the Limits of Legal Change." *Law & Society Review* 9(1): 95–160.

Gillman, H. 2002. "How Political Parties Can Use the Courts to Advance their Agendas: Federal Courts in the United States, 1875–1891." *American Political Science Review* 96(3): 511–24.

Guthrie, C. 2002. "Prospect Theory, Risk Preference, and the Law." *Northwestern University Law Review* 97: 1115–63.

Guthrie, C., Rachlinski, J. J., and Wistrich, A. J. 2007. "Blinking on the Bench: How Judges Decide Cases." *Cornell Law Review* 93(1): 1–43.

Haire, S. B., Lindquist, S. A., and Hartley, R. 1999. "Attorney Expertise, Litigant Success, and Judicial Decisionmaking in the US Courts of Appeals." *Law & Society Review* 33(3): 667–85.

Haire, S. B., and Moyer, L. P. 2007. "Advocacy through Briefs in the US Courts of Appeals." *Southern Illinois Law Review* 32: 593–609.

Hanson, R.A., and Daley, H. W. K. 1995. "Federal Habeas Corpus Review: Challenging State Court Criminal Convictions." U.S. Department of Justice, Bureau of Justice Statistics.

Hooper, L., Miletich, D., and Levy, A. 2011. *Case Management Procedures in the Federal Courts of Appeals*, 2nd ed. Washington, DC: Federal Judicial Center.

Woodford, H. J., Jr. 1981. *Courts of Appeals in the Federal Judicial System*. Princeton, NJ: Princeton University Press.

Howard, R. M. 2007. "Controlling Forum Choice and Controlling Policy: Congress, Courts and the IRS." *Policy Studies Journal* 35(1): 109–23.

Kaheny, E. B. 2010. "The Nature of Circuit Court Gatekeeping Decisions." *Law & Society Review* 44(1): 129–56.

Kaheny, E. B. 2011. "Appellate Judges as Gatekeepers? An Investigation of Threshold Decisions in the Federal Courts of Appeals." *Journal of Appellate Practice and Process* 12(2): 255–81.

Kobylka, J. F. 1987. "A Court-created Context for Group Litigation: Libertarian Groups and Obscenity." *Journal of Politics* 49(4): 1061–78.

Kritzer, H. M. 2003. "The Government Gorilla: Why Does Government Come Out Ahead in Appellate Courts?" In *In Litigation: Do the "Haves" Still Come out ahead.* Stanford, CA: Stanford University Press, 342–70.

Kritzer, H. M. 2004. *Risks, Reputations, and Rewards: Contingency Fee Legal Practice in the United States.* Stanford, CA: Stanford University Press.

LaFountain, R., Schauffler, R., Strickland, S., and Holt, K. 2012. "Examining the Work of State Courts: An Analysis of 2010 State Court Caseloads." National Center for State Courts, Williamsburg, VA.

Levy, M. K. 2013. "Judicial Attention as a Scarce Resource: A Preliminary Defense of How Judges Allocate Time across Cases in the Federal Courts of Appeals." *The George Washington Law Review* 81(2): 401–47.

Lindquist, S. A. 1996. "Bureaucratization and Balkanization: The Origins and the Effects of Decision-Making Norms in the Federal Appellate Courts." *University of Richmond Law Review* 41: 659–706.

Loewenstein, G., Issacharoff, S., Camerer, C., and Babcock, L. 1993. "Self-serving Assessments of Fairness and Pretrial Bargaining." *Journal of Legal Studies* 22(1): 135–59.

Marvell, T. B. 1988. "State Appellate Court Responses to Caseload Growth." *Judicature* 72(5): 282–5.

McKenna, J., Hooper, L. L., and Clark, M. 2000. *Case Management Procedures in the Federal Courts of Appeals.* Washington, DC: Federal Judicial Center.

Moyer, L. P., Collins, T. A., and Haire, S. B. 2013. "The Value of Precedent: Appellate Briefs and Judicial Opinions in the US Courts of Appeals." *Justice System Journal* 34(1): 62–84.

Palmer, J. R. B., Yale-Loehr, S. W., and Cronin, E. 2005. "Why Are So Many People Challenging Board of Immigration Appeals Decisions in Federal Court: An Empirical Analysis of the Recent Surge in Petitions for Review." *Georgetown Immigration Law Journal* 20: 1–94.

Pierce, R. J., Jr. 1999. "Is Standing Law or Politics." *North Carolina Law Review* 77(5): 1741–89.

Posner, R. A. 1999. "Convincing A Federal Court of Appeals from the Bench." *Litigation* 25(2): 3–5.

Priest, G. L., and Klein, B. 1984. "The Selection of Disputes for Litigation." *Journal of Legal Studies* XIII: 1–55.

Rachlinski, J. J. 1996. "Gains, Losses, and the Psychology of Litigation." *Southern California Law Review* 70: 113–85.

Richman, W., and Reynolds, W. L. 1996. "Elitism, Expediency, and the New Certiorari: Requiem for the Learned Hand Tradition." *Cornell Law Review* 81: 273–342.

Robertson, C. B. 2012. "The Right to Appeal." *North Carolina Law Review* 91: 1219–81.

Sandefur, R. L. 2008. "Access to Civil Justice and Race, Class, and Gender Inequality." *Annual Review of Sociology* 34: 339–58.

Shargel, G. L., and French, M. 2002. "An AEDPA Primer." Available at: http://fernichlaw.com/do-not-enter-or-modify-or-erase/client-uploads/FINAL_AEDPA_CLE.pdf.

Sisk, G. C. 1997. "The Balkanization of Appellate Justice: The Proliferation of Local Rules in the Federal Circuits." *University of Colorado Law Review* 68: 1–61.

Sisk, G. C., and Heise, M. 2015. "'Too Many Notes'? An Empirical Study of Advocacy in Federal Appeals." *Journal of Empirical Legal Studies* 12(3): 578–600.

Smith, J. L. 2006. "Judicial Procedures as Instruments of Political Control: Congress's Strategic Use of Citizen Suits." *Legislative Studies Quarterly* 31(2): 283–305.

Solimine, M. E. 2004. "Judicial Stratification and the Reputations of the United States Courts of Appeals." *Florida State University Law Review* 32(4): 1331–63.

Songer, D. R., Cameron, C. M., and Segal, J. A. 1995. "An Empirical Test of the Rational–Actor Theory of Litigation." *Journal of Politics* 57(4): 1119–29.

Songer, D. R., Sheehan, R. S., and Haire, S. B. 1999. "Do the 'Haves' Come out ahead over Time? Applying Galanter's Framework to Decisions of the US Courts of Appeals, 1925–1988." *Law & Society Review* 33(4): 811–32.

Staudt, N. C. 2004. "Modeling Standing." *New York University Law Review* 79: 612–84.

Szmer, J., Johnson, S. W., and Sarver, T. A. 2007. "Does the Lawyer Matter? Influencing Outcomes on the Supreme Court of Canada." *Law & Society Review* 41(2): 279–304.

Van Wormer, N. I. 2007. "Help at your Fingertips: A Twenty-First Century Response to the Pro Se Phenomenon." *Vanderbilt Law Review* 60(3): 983–1019.

Vladek, D. C., and Gulati, M. 2005. "Judicial Triage: Reflections on the Debate over Unpublished Opinions." *Washington and Lee Law Review* 62: 1667–708.

Vose, C. E. 1959. *Caucasians Only: The Supreme Court, the NAACP, and the Restrictive Covenant Cases*. Oakland, CA: University of California Press.

Zorn, C. J. W. 2002. "U.S. Government Litigation Strategies in the Federal Appellate Courts." *Political Research Quarterly* 55(1): 145–66.

CHAPTER 8

AGENDA-SETTING ON THE U.S. SUPREME COURT

RYAN J. OWENS AND JAMES SIEJA

How do Supreme Court justices determine which cases the Court will decide? Before 1925, the answer to this question was relatively simple: the Court heard cases Congress required it to hear. Federal jurisdictional statutes declared that when litigants appealed certain types of cases to the Court, the justices had to decide them—and the types of issues that triggered this mandatory review were extensive. The Court, in other words, largely heard cases at the jurisdictional commands of Congress. The Judiciary Act of 1925, however, changed all that by allowing the justices to decide for themselves which cases the Court would hear.[1] And learning the conditions under which justices vote to hear cases has vexed scholars ever since.

Our goal in this chapter is not to answer every question relating to Supreme Court agenda-setting, nor is it to provide a complete roadmap for lawyers seeking to obtain High Court review. Our goal is more modest. We aim to provide a general overview of how the Court sets its agenda. We do so in three parts. Part one explains the basic nuts and bolts of agenda-setting. It focuses on the Court's decision to grant a "writ of certiorari." Part two highlights political science research on the Court's agenda-setting behavior. It explains the factors that increase the probability justices will vote to grant (and deny) review to cases. Finally, part three discusses limitations with existing understanding of the agenda-setting stage and offers suggestions for future research.

The Supreme Court's Agenda-Setting Process

The primary method of obtaining Supreme Court review today is by obtaining a writ of certiorari ("cert") from the Court. The writ of cert, technically, is an order by the Court to a lower court to send up the record of a case so the Court can review the lower court's decision. Unlike, for example, a statutory appeal—an unusual case in which Congress has ordered the Court to hear the dispute—the decision to review a lower court decision is at the discretion of the justices. In what follows, we explain this process more extensively. Readers interested in less common ways to invoke the Court's jurisdiction (such as via statutory appeals or original jurisdiction) should consult Stern, Gressman, Shapiro, and Geller (2002).

The Petition for a Writ of Certiorari

The Court's agenda process begins when a litigant loses in a lower court and files a petition for a "writ of certiorari" (i.e., a "cert petition") asking the Court to review the lower court's decision. The party who petitions the Court is called the petitioner, while the party who opposes review is called the respondent. The petitioner's brief in support of certiorari contains a number of elements, including the Question(s) Presented, the identity of the parties in the case, the legal authorities cited, and an argument for why the Court should hear the case.

The petitioner's brief begins almost immediately by outlining the legal "Questions Presented" to the Court. The Question(s) Presented are supposed to be concise statements that help justices determine what the case is about. They are longer than a single sentence but shorter than a long paragraph. And while they are supposed to be fairly objective statements, the parties often frame them to sound more compelling. For example, one of the Questions Presented in the petitioner's brief in *States of Florida et al. v. United States Department of Health and Human Services et al.* asked:

> Does Congress exceed its enumerated powers and violate basic principles of federalism when it coerces States into accepting onerous conditions that it could not impose directly by threatening to withhold all federal funding under the single largest grant-in-aid program, or does the limitation on Congress's spending power that this Court recognized in *South Dakota v. Dole*, 483 U.S. 203 (1987) no longer apply?

The answer seems obvious.

The brief then discusses the identity of the parties, lists the legal authorities cited in the brief, provides a summary of the dispute, and describes why the Court has jurisdiction to hear the case. It then explains to the Court the constitutional and statutory provisions involved in the case. Next, it includes a Statement of the Case, which is largely a discussion of what happened in the lower courts.

The brief then moves to perhaps the most important section, the "Reasons for Granting the Petition" section. Here, the petitioner seeks to explain why the Court should hear the case. The petitioner's arguments should be different than the arguments made at the merits stage. That is, during the agenda stage, the petitioner should focus on the reasons why the Court should *hear* the case—and not on why they should *win* the case. While some amount of foreshadowing is to be expected, petitioners should spend their time focusing on why the case is important enough to deserve review. This means less emphasis on the outcome of the decision and more emphasis on the importance of the legal question involved, what resolution of that legal question means for the judiciary, and how the Court can help clarify law.

While there are a handful of factors that can enhance the likelihood of Supreme Court review—and we will discuss them more fully later—perhaps the most critical factor the cert petition can emphasize here is the amount of conflict present in the lower courts over how to interpret federal law. When lower courts disagree over the proper interpretation of a federal legal provision, the Supreme Court is expected to decide a case dealing with that issue and clarify the meaning of that law. And this expectation derives, in large part, from Supreme Court Rule 10, which states the Court will be more likely to grant review to a case when:

- "a United States court of appeals has entered a decision in conflict with the decision of another United States court of appeals on the same important matter"
- a United States court of appeals "has decided an important federal question in a way that conflicts with a decision by a state court of last resort"
- "a state court of last resort has decided an important federal question in a way that conflicts with the decision of another state court of last resort or of a United States court of appeals", or
- "a state court or a United States court of appeals has decided an important question of federal law that has not been, but should be, settled by the Supreme Court."

Not surprisingly, then, petitioners often focus on conflict among the lower courts. When there is substantial conflict, they highlight it. When there is minimal conflict, they elevate it.

After the petitioner files its brief requesting a writ of certiorari from the Court, the respondent has thirty days to respond with its own brief in opposition to granting review. The respondent will frame the case for the Court as well, and will emphasize the reasons why the Court should not hear it. Often, this involves downplaying any conflict the petitioner highlighted, showing how the lower court decision was correct, and emphasizing the needless problems or costs that would arise from Supreme Court review.

The Role of Law Clerks during the Agenda Stage

The Court receives thousands of petitions asking the justices to review lower court decisions. During the 2012 term, justices received 7,509 such requests (Roberts 2013: 12). Given the large number of review requests, justices have been forced to rely heavily upon their law clerks. The clerks help justices identify which petitions are "certworthy" (i.e., worthy of potentially being granted review) and which ones are not.

Law clerks in the "cert pool" help justices sift through these petitions. The cert pool consists of the law clerks for all the justices except Justice Alito (more on Alito later in this chapter). The justices combine their clerks into one collective pool. Each clerk in the pool is randomly assigned to analyze and summarize cert petitions as they are filed with the Court. The (non-Alito) clerk who randomly receives the assignment writes a preliminary memorandum (the "pool memo") to all the justices in the cert pool. The pool memo summarizes the proceedings in the lower courts and all legal claims made in the cert briefs. It concludes with a recommendation for how the Court should dispose of the petition (e.g., grant or deny review). After each pool member justice receives the pool memo, she has one of her own clerks quickly review it and provide her with a private (and often candid) recommendation.

The justices did not always use a certiorari pool. Before the early 1970s, each justice had his law clerks review every cert petition filed with the Court. (Some justices, like William Brennan, maintained that they personally read all their cert petitions, though this is highly unusual.) The clerks in each chamber would then recommend to their justices how to vote on a petition. As the number of petitions grew, though, the practice of having every chamber review every cert petition became unruly and inefficient. Clerks spent nearly all their time analyzing cert petitions and very little time helping justices with other, more pressing, tasks.

When Lewis Powell joined the Court in 1972, he persuaded his colleagues to create the cert pool. His pitch was that, having been freed from spending all their time summarizing cert petitions, the clerks would then have the time to draft opinions for justices. Chief Justice Burger and Justices Blackmun, Powell, Rehnquist, White quickly joined together to create the first cert pool. Yet, Justices Brennan, Douglas, Marshall, and Stewart declined to join, primarily because of their fears that the conservative justices would try to manipulate the cert pool as a tool to make conservative legal policy. They worried that the conservative clerks might shade the facts in an effort to get the Court to hear (and reverse) liberal legal policies. Despite these initial fears, the cert pool has operated fairly objectively over time. Consequently, nearly every justice who joined the Court since then has participated in the cert pool (Ward and Weiden 2006).

Only a few justices since then have declined to join the cert pool. During his tenure, Justice Stevens elected not to participate in the pool. More recently, in 2015, Justice Samuel Alito was the only justice known not to participate in the cert pool. The rationale Stevens and Alito offered for not participating in the cert pool is the desire to have at least one independent check on the clerks. They were not concerned about manipulation; rather, they simply wanted to ensure the pool clerks, and thus, the entire Court, did not overlook something important.

The Discuss List

The discuss list is the first point at which a properly filed cert petition might be denied—indeed, the Court rejects most petitions at this stage. After the clerks prepare summaries of the certiorari petitions, the justices must then decide whether even to discuss the case at conference or simply to deny it without discussion. Given the sheer number of petitions before the Court—and the fact that many of the petitions are frivolous—justices cannot discuss each one at conference. So, they have devised a method to narrow down conference discussion to only some of these cases—the discuss list. The discuss list is a list of the petitions the justices believe merit at least a discussion at conference. Petitions that make it on the discuss list are discussed and voted on by the justices at their next conference. Petitions that do not make the discuss list are denied review without a formal, recorded vote.

The discuss list is drafted by the Chief Justice but revised by his colleagues. More specifically, relying on the pool clerk's memo, comments from his own law clerks, and the briefs, the Chief puts together a list of the petitions he thinks deserve consideration and a vote by the Court at its next conference. He then circulates this list to the Associate Justices. Every Associate Justice has a chance to look over the discuss list before the next conference. If any justice believes a petition should be on the discuss list (but currently is not), he or she can add it to the list; the case will then appear on a revised discuss list (with the justice's initials next to it, alerting others to who put the case there). It then receives discussion and a full vote at conference. One justice cannot take another justice's case off the discuss list. A justice who put a case on the list can remove it, but other justices would then be free, themselves, to return it to the list.

The method of using a discuss list has changed over the years. Until 1950, the Court's default position was to discuss every petition unless a justice put that specific petition on a list of petitions *not* to be discussed. This was called the "dead list." Any justice could revive a petition from the dead list. In 1950, however, the Court changed its practice to the one we observe today. It did so because the number of cert requests simply became unmanageable. In short, today every petition is presumed denied and receives no discussion unless a justice wants to discuss it. Prior to 1950, every petition received a discussion (and vote) unless every justice was comfortable placing it on the dead list.

The Conference

On most Fridays (or Thursdays in May and June), the Court holds a conference at which the justices discuss the cert petitions and vote on them. The justice who put the case on the discuss list (usually the Chief) leads off discussion of the petition. After presenting his or her views, the justice then announces their vote on whether to grant or deny review. In order of seniority (note that the Chief Justice is always the most senior justice), the remaining justices state their positions and announce their votes. The Court's Rule of Four, an informal norm that has developed over the years, holds that if at least four justices vote to grant review, the case will proceed to the merits stage.[2] During this conference, the justices are completely secluded. Not even clerks or staff may enter the room. (The junior justice must answer every knock on the door.)

Each justice can cast a number of votes at the cert stage. They can vote to *grant* review to a petition or *deny* review to it. They can also recommend the Court *call for the views of the Solicitor General* (CVSG) to obtain the Solicitor General's advice on whether to grant or deny review to the petition. They can *affirm* or *reverse* the lower court decision via a summary order without formal briefing or oral argument on the merits. They can vote to *hold* the case while the Court decides a related case under consideration. They can vote to *grant, vacate, and remand* (GVR) the case in light of a recently decided Supreme Court decision.[3] If the respondent in the case never filed a brief in opposition to the petitioner's request for a writ of certiorari, the Court can *call for a response* (CFR) from that party. Since the 1970s, justices also have cast *Join-3* votes, which are "soft" votes to grant (O'Brien 1997; Black and Owens 2009a). A Join-3 vote indicates that, conditional on three other justices' "hard" votes to grant, the Join-3 vote is a vote to grant as well. If fewer than three other justices cast a "hard" vote to grant, the Join-3 vote is a vote to deny.

The Court's lack of formal agenda-setting requirements offers justices nearly complete discretion over which cases they will hear. Certiorari votes are entirely discretionary and, unless indicated by a dissent from the denial of cert or divulged by the personal papers of a former justice, remain completely secret. So, just what, then, explains the Court's agenda decisions? Scholars have offered four general theories. We examine those theories now.

Studying Agenda-Setting: Four Approaches

Scholars have offered four broad theories to explain the Court's agenda-setting behavior: cue theory, a theory about the influence of ideology, a theory about the influence of law and institutions, and a theory that sees justices as strategic (or forward-looking) actors. We address each in turn, focusing on their logic and some of their empirical support.

Cue Theory and Certiorari Voting

Tanenhaus et al.'s (1963) "cue theory" represents one of the earliest lines of inquiry into agenda-setting on the Supreme Court. Cue theory assumes that justices have multiple demands on their time. As a result, they cannot spend much time determining the cert-worthiness of every filed petition. To do so would leave them little time for opinion writing and other potentially more important actions. Yet, justices also do not want to hear frivolous cases that will waste their time. So they must find a balance between not wanting to analyze every cert petition but not letting frivolous ones slip through the cracks because of inattentiveness.

Justices, the theory goes, rely on a set of cues to separate the petitions that are "certworthy" from those that are not. More specifically, they use four cues as heuristics to determine whether a case deserves the Court's attention: (1) whether the federal government was a party to a case, (2) whether a judge dissented on the lower court that heard the case, (3) whether the case involved a civil liberties issue, or (4) whether the case involved an economics issue. The presence of any of these cues, the theory held, would drive up the likelihood the justices would review the case. And they did so because these cues were objective indicators of case importance. For busy justices, these cues could separate cases that merited the Court's attention from those that did not.

Scholars have largely moved away from cue theory. A substantial amount of research shows that justices actually invest more time in selecting cases than cue theory suggests. Justices are not so focused on writing opinions or other judicial activities that they ignore the agenda stage. What is more, scholarship also shows that justices have goals over legal policy and other factors. Cue theory ignores these features. Indeed, as we show later, there is a significant amount of forward-looking behavior at the agenda stage, something cue theory neglects. Accordingly, this theory is no longer sound.

Nevertheless, while scholars have turned away from cue theory, one feature traditionally associated with cue theory continues to explain substantial parts of Supreme Court agenda-setting: the presence of the Solicitor General (SG) as petitioner. The SG represents the interests of the U.S. government before the Court. The SG's recommendation significantly influences justices' certiorari votes. As a result, the SG's position is an important predictor of certiorari—it can dramatically increase the chances of review (Black and Owens 2012b; Thompson and Wachtell 2009).

Ideological Influences on Certiorari Voting

Some scholars argue that ideological goals motivate Supreme Court justices to the exclusion of other factors (Segal and Spaeth 2002). Justices who prefer conservative policies will use their powers on the Court to instantiate conservative legal policies. Justices who prefer liberal policies will do the same. What this means generally is that at the agenda stage, justices grant review to cases simply to further liberal or conservative policies. Assuming justices care about setting public policy for the entire country, their goals at the agenda stage would be to grant petitions so as to reverse ideologically distant lower court decisions and affirm those ideologically close to them.

A number of studies suggest justices follow their ideological goals when they set the Court's agenda. For example, Ulmer (1972) examined the private papers of Justice Harold Burton and discovered that justices who voted to grant certiorari also were more likely to support the petitioner at the merits stage. For Ulmer, this indicated the vote to grant cert was a preliminary vote to reverse lower court rulings justices disliked. Ulmer (1973a) showed a positive correlation between justices' conservative votes on the merits and their votes to deny review to cases petitioned by convicts. He suggested an underlying "pro-authority" attitude prompted the justices' behavior at the agenda-setting stage.

Later studies also underscored the importance of justices' ideological goals at the agenda stage. Caldeira and Wright (1988) found that the presence of amicus curiae briefs filed at the agenda stage led the Court to grant review. The number of amicus briefs mattered because they signaled the policy salience of the case. Regardless of whether the briefs were filed in support of or opposition to the certiorari petition, amicus briefs increased the probability the Court granted review because they signaled importance. By bearing the costs to file, groups—even when they advised the Court to deny review—showcased the salience of the case (Collins 2004). And for justices who wanted to effectuate their policy goals, salience was critical. It meant the Court's merits decision would have a broad impact.

Hall (2009) also shows how agenda-setting is often driven by ideological concerns. He took advantage of the random assignment of circuit court judges to three-judge panels to show that partisanship plays a role in the agenda-setting behavior of the High Court. He examined how the conservative Supreme Court treated petitions for review from 1995 to 2004. Hall found the probability of Supreme Court review doubled when a case was appealed from a Democratic-majority panel as opposed to a Republican-majority panel. The probability tripled when an appeal came after an all-Democratic panel heard the case compared to an all-Republican panel (Hall 2009: 214–15). The conservative Supreme Court majority paid attention to the ideological values of the lower court judges.

Recent studies that examine how individual justices vote at the agenda stage confirm the belief that ideology often motivates their behavior. Black and Owens (2012a) argued that, when determining which cases to review, justices rely on both the identity of lower court judges and the ideological disposition of the lower court decision. To pursue this argument, they examined 358 cert petitions between 1986 and 1993. Relying on the digital archives of former Justice Harry A. Blackmun (Epstein et al. 2007), they found that justices were most likely to audit ideologically incongruent circuit court decisions rendered by a panel of ideological foes, and were least likely to audit ideologically congruent circuit court decisions rendered by ideological allies. In other words, the lower court judges' ideological congruence with the justice influenced whether the justice granted review.

Legal and Institutional Influences on Certiorari Voting

Other scholars argue that legal and institutional factors influence certiorari voting. Justices are trained in the law and taught that they must follow it. What is more, external actors (e.g., the political branches, the public, and the bar) expect justices to respect and follow the law. Because justices rely on these actors to sustain the Court's legitimacy, it would be no surprise if they therefore complied with those expectations (Lindquist and Klein 2006). And while there are no legal factors that compel the Court to grant review, the presence of legal conflict exercised by a lower court is, as we stated earlier, a major factor that leads justices to review cases.

Studies show that the Supreme Court is more likely to review a case when the lower courts disagree over the interpretation of law. Perry (1991), for example, gained insight into the Court's agenda-setting behavior through extensive interviews with justices and their clerks. His interviews, if they showed anything, showed how important the resolution of conflict was to justices. And he was not alone in making the argument. Stern, Gressman, Shapiro, and Geller (2002) enjoyed years of Court watching (and clerkships) and made the same point: conflict among the circuits strongly influences whether the Court reviews a case. When multiple lower courts disagree on the proper interpretation of federal law, the Court is expected resolve the conflict by declaring the correct interpretation of the law. Indeed, consider the following quotation from an anonymous justice:

> I would say that [cert votes] are sometimes tentative votes on the merits. Now I would say that there are certain cases that I would vote for, for example, if there was a clear split in circuits, *I would vote for cert. without even looking at the merits.* But there are other cases I would have more of a notion of what the merits were.
>
> (Perry 1991: 269, emphasis added)

Along these lines, Black and Owens (2009a) found that when policy goals and legal considerations collide, legal factors can lead justices to behave in ways that contradict their policy goals. For example, when a justice wants to deny review to a case on policy grounds but there is legal conflict among the circuits over the proper interpretation of the law, the justice will often grant review to clarify the law. The probability a justice casts such a policy-based deny vote decreases from 0.89 in the absence of legal conflict to 0.61 in the presence of strong legal conflict. On the other hand, if legal considerations and policy goals align toward the same end, law frees justices to pursue policy. So, a justice who wants to grant review for policy reasons is even more likely to vote to grant when the lower courts are conflicted over the proper interpretation of federal law. The probability a justice casts a policy-based grant vote more than triples (from 0.17 to 0.56) when there is strong conflict among the lower courts.

A later study by Black and Owens (2011) also provides strong evidence for the influence of legal considerations at the agenda stage. The authors examined the conditions under which justices followed recommendations made by the Solicitor General after the Court called for his views. They found that legal factors (e.g., conflict in the lower courts) present in the case constrain the justices' willingness to agree with the SG's recommendation to grant or deny the petition. Specifically, when the SG makes a recommendation that contravenes legal factors in the case, the justices are roughly 45 percent less likely to follow the SG's recommendation, regardless of the ideological congruence between the justice and the SG. The SG's repeat player status and professional expertise usually make the SG an important influence on the Court. But, a legally inconsistent recommendation can significantly mitigate all of the SG's considerable advantages. Thus, Black and Owens (2011) argue that "there are powerful legal considerations that justices and the SG must follow" at the agenda stage (p. 775; see also Pacelle 2003).

At the same time, institutional norms of respect for Congress as a coordinate branch can lead justices to review cases. Stern and his coauthors argue that when a lower court strikes down a federal law as unconstitutional, the Court is more likely to review the decision (Stern et al. 2002: 244). The following quote by an anonymous justice agrees: "If a single district judge rules that a federal statute is unconstitutional, I think we owe it to Congress to review the case and see if, in fact, the statute they've passed is unconstitutional" (Perry 1991: 269). In other words, respect for Congress as a coordinate branch can lead justices to review cases where lower courts have struck down federal legislation.

Forward-Looking Certiorari Voting

The forward looking theory of agenda-setting posits that justices vote to review cases when they expect their colleagues to support their positions on the merits of those cases. The theory argues that justices are seekers of policy who want to effectuate their policy preferences. The justices are constrained, however, from doing so because of their institutional limitations. That is, they pursue their goals in an interdependent environment in which their decisions are also a function of the preferences of those with whom they must interact, such as their colleagues and—possibly, but less likely—Congress and the president (Owens 2010; Segal 1997; Epstein and Knight 1998).

When justices vote to grant or deny review to cases, they must be forward-looking and predict whether their legal position will win or lose on the merits. They should be wary of putting a case on the Court's docket if they suspect their position will lose on the merits. By taking the case up, deciding it, and setting national precedent, justices on the losing side can take a bad situation and make it worse. What once was perhaps a lower court decision a justice disliked could become binding national precedent if the justice is careless.

The theory of forward-looking agenda-setting got its start (though, slowly) in the late 1950s and remains strong today. Schubert's (1959) specification and elaboration (1962) of the "certiorari game" were among the first studies to argue justices are forward looking at the agenda stage. Schubert created a game-theoretic model to determine probabilistically whether the Court would accept cases arising under the Federal Employee Liability Act (FELA). Because many observers viewed them as highly fact-dependent, the conventional wisdom was that the Court heard FELA cases randomly. Schubert argued that a majority of justices who sought stronger protections for workers—and crafted such law at the merits stage—placed those cases on the Court's docket.

While Schubert's work did not immediately spur new research, the same cannot be said of those who advocated for a strategic approach in the 1990s. Beginning around the time of Perry's (1991) interviews with justices and clerks—where he taught us such terms as aggressive grants and defensive denials[4]—scholars reexamined forward-looking agenda-setting. For example, Caldeira, Wright, and Zorn (1999) found that justices were more likely to vote to grant review to cases as they became similar ideologically to the mean of the Court (see also Boucher and Segal 1995; Caldeira and Wright 1990).

Black and Owens (2009a) found that justices were 75 percent more likely to vote to grant review to petitions when they expected that the policy arising from the Court's merits decision would be an improvement over current law.

Limitations and New Areas for Research

Agenda-setting scholarship has made significant strides—in large part because of the release and digitization of Harry Blackmun's exhaustive files (Epstein et al. 2007). Still, more work remains to be done in this area of scholarship. In this section, we address some of these limitations; we also propose new topics for research.

Circuit Court Splits: Identity and Intentionality

Scholars should direct more attention to circuit splits. As we stated earlier, the Court is much more likely to hear a case when the lower courts disagree over how to interpret a particular federal law. Yet, at least three questions remain unanswered about circuit splits.

First, when there is such a conflict, why does the Court choose to review a case from one circuit but not the other(s)? For example, in a conflict between the Ninth and Seventh Circuits, why would the Court review and reverse the Ninth Circuit rather than review and affirm the Seventh Circuit? Grant, Hendrickson, and Lynch (2012) provide an initial cut at this question. Blending cue theory and an ideological approach to certiorari voting, the authors find that the Court is more likely to grant review to cases in conflicts where the gap between the opposing circuits is wide. Further research in this vein should dig deeper.

Second, do lower court judges strategically induce conflict to heighten the probability of High Court review? We suspect the answer to this question is yes. In fact, one need look no farther than Sixth Circuit Judge Jeffrey Sutton's opinion in *Obergefell v. Hodges*. In that opinion, Sutton held there was no constitutional right to same sex marriage, created a stark conflict with other circuits, and teed up the case for Supreme Court review. If lower court judges can and do intentionally produce conflict to induce upper Court review, that would be an important finding. Strident opinions might increase the perception of a "real" or "square" conflict between the circuits, whereas more conciliatory opinions might indicate that the conflict is not as important to resolve. An important aspect of the agenda-setting process to remember here is that the lower court judges are, in the main, attempting to influence a busy cert pool clerk who will read the petition and lower court record to make a recommendation to the justices. Because many petitions for certiorari allege conflict among circuits, a lower court judge who makes plain the conflict might increase the probability the Court will grant review.

Third, how long must conflict exist before the Court steps in? It is unclear just how much conflict must exist—or how long a conflict must exist—before the Court will step in. Only one post-war justice, Byron White, seemed inclined automatically to hear cases where the lower courts disagreed. White regularly wrote dissents from the denial of certiorari that indicated his passion for the harmonization of federal law. In fact, in one such dissent he argued "there is grave doubt that [the resolution] function is being adequately performed" (quoted in Provine 1980, 39–40). Understanding when the Court will step in and clean up conflicts remains an open topic.

Data Limitations

Perhaps the largest obstacle to studying Supreme Court agenda-setting is a lack of data. The Court's secrecy is stifling.[5] It does not release the votes of justices at the agenda stage. Thus, we only know how justices voted in two instances: when they dissent from the denial of cert and when the justices release their private paper after they leave the Court. No justice has released more recent papers since Harry Blackmun—and his tenure on the Court ended in 1994.[6] What is more, not all justices release their papers. For example, Justice Black directed his papers be destroyed after his death (Ulmer 1973b). Other justices place holds on the release of their papers. Justice Souter's papers will not be released until 2049, fully fifty years after his retirement.

Another limitation is that, even when the justices' files are released, they might be incorrect or incomplete. For example, working with the Burton papers, Palmer and Brenner (1989) ran into incomplete records, confusing notations, and muddled record-keeping. They had to cross-check Burton's docket books with the records of other justices. Maltzman and Wahlbeck (1996) performed a similar analysis. They examined the papers of four justices in the 1967 and 1968 terms and found that there was substantial agreement among the justices' records, though they did discover errors in complex cases and ambiguous cases. The most important innovation in agenda-setting studies has been the digitization of Justice Blackmun's agenda records (Epstein et al. 2007). These records cover the last eight terms (1986–1993) Blackmun sat on the Supreme Court. Black and Owens (2009b) performed an inter-justice cross-check of the Blackmun papers, including the 1971, 1986, and 1990 terms. They found Blackmun's papers were "both accurate and reliable" (2009b: 262). On the whole, then, the most recent data on individual-level certiorari votes, seem largely to be accurate and reliable—if not current.

Clerks, the Discuss List, and State Supreme Courts

Scholars also should consider more fully the role of clerks, the discuss list, and agenda-setting in state supreme courts. The first two topics are crucial to understanding the Supreme Court's behavior. The third topic might offer leverage on the importance of institutional rules.

Despite the fact that law clerks do much of the agenda work, we know little about how, or even if, clerks can influence the justices' agenda votes. Peppers's (2006) otherwise comprehensive study of the relationship between clerks and justices does not devote much analysis to the agenda stage. Some studies focus on the behavior of a single clerk-justice dyad (Brenner 1992–3) or a single justice's interaction with his clerks in multiple terms (Brenner and Palmer 1990). Yet, a further difficulty comes in identifying clerk ideology. Distlear and Baum (2001) present one possible option: assigning to the clerk the ideology of the lower court judge for whom the clerk previously worked. Another option might be to examine which clerks were members of well-known, ideologically based legal groups like the conservative Federalist Society or liberal American Constitution Society. Still, without knowing the clerk's sincere preferences, it is hard to determine whether the clerk actually influences justices. One study finds that clerks can influence justices (Black and Boyd 2012) when the case is of medium certworthiness but more work remains to be done.

Surprisingly, scholars also know little about the first gatekeeping point in the agenda stage—the discuss list. Caldeira and Wright (1990) argue that policy preferences and cues such as amicus briefs drive the placement of cases on the discuss list. They also note that Justice White regularly placed cases with legal conflict on the discuss list. In an unpublished conference paper, Schoen and Wahlbeck (2006) find that forward-looking ideological factors affect the number of cases justices add to the discuss list; specifically, justices who approve of the lower court decisions and are far from the median justice will not add cases to the discuss list (and vice versa). They also find evidence of Justice White's prodigious discuss list additions.

Examining agenda-setting behavior on state supreme courts might provide additional leverage to learn about the U.S. Supreme Court.[7] Due to the variation among state justices, differences in selection methods, and jurisdictional requirements (varying ratios of mandatory to discretionary jurisdictions), comparisons among states might highlight the important factors that induce judges and justices to behave the way they do. Various institutional rules might be more correlated with ideological or strategic behavior. For example, Lindquist and Pybas (1998) determined the New Jersey Supreme Court, which is staffed through executive nomination and has almost complete discretion over the cases it takes, behaved more like the U.S. Supreme Court than like other state supreme courts. Brace and Hall (2001: 410) found ideological measures to have only "very modest explanatory power" for state supreme courts' agenda decisions. These different institutions, and the effect they have on state supreme court agenda-setting, might provide us useful information to learn about the High Court, where there is simply less variation.

Conclusion

Before the Court renders a decision on the merits of a case, the justices must first decide whether to hear that case. And if the numbers tell us anything, it is that Supreme Court review is unlikely. The High Court today hears one tenth of 1 percent of the cases seeking review. The odds, in short, are not good for those seeking review. Yet, there are features that systematically increase the odds the Court grants review to a case. And our goal here was to describe and explain them.

We began this chapter by describing the process through which petitions for certiorari travel. We then discussed the theoretical approaches scholars have used to explain agenda-setting. We presented the empirical results of recent research, which suggest justices employ some combination of law, their ideological predispositions, and forward-looking strategies to decide which cases they will decide.

Despite the well-developed state of knowledge on Supreme Court agenda-setting, there are clear opportunities to explore substantively interesting questions regarding the choice of cases stemming from circuit splits, and how circuit splits arise in the first place. Future research also has the opportunity to explore the significant roles clerks and the discuss list play in the agenda-setting decision, as well as how theories developed for the U.S. Supreme Court apply (or do not apply) to state courts of last resort. We hope that as more scholars examine the agenda-setting stage, we will learn more about it.

Notes

1. Officially, the "Judges' Bill" is the Judiciary Act of 1925 (43 Stat. 936); however, its colloquial name derives from the integral role several of the Supreme Court justices sitting at the time played in drafting the language and urging the passage of the bill. Specifically, Justice Willis Van Devanter, the Court's expert on judicial procedure, argued for the expanded certiorari jurisdiction, and Chief Justice William Howard Taft skillfully exploited the connections he had made as a politician to get the bill passed (Crowe 2007). Even though some mandatory appeals remained after 1925, justices could use artful dodges, like dismissing appeals for want of a federal question, if they did not want to decide the matter. In 1988, Congress eliminated all non-certiorari appeals to the Supreme Court, except those coming from a three-judge district court panel. These cases usually involve issues arising under the Voting Rights Act.
2. The rule of four developed after Congress initially granted the Court some discretionary jurisdiction in the 1891 Courts of Appeals Act (Leiman 1957). By the time it expanded the Court's discretionary jurisdiction in the Judiciary Act of 1925, the rule of four had taken hold on the Court.
3. Typically, when the Court GVR's, it grants review to the case, vacates the lower court decision, and remands to the lower court to reconsider in light of a recently decided case.
4. In his interviews with justices and their clerks, Perry (1991) learned that justices sometimes cast aggressive grant votes, which are votes to take up cases because the justice wants to affirm the lower court and set national precedent. He also learned that justices cast defensive deny votes, which are votes to deny review to cases the justices would otherwise like to review, but refuse to do so for fear of failing to obtain majority support.
5. For some agenda-setting studies, the Court's privacy obstacles are irrelevant. For example, the "agenda change" literature examines changes in the types or numbers of cases the Court

hears (e.g., Caldeira 1981; Pacelle 1991; Owens and Simon 2012). These studies do not require private justice vote information.

6. Chief Justice Rehnquist's papers are released in blocks, covering only the years from which no justices with whom he served remain alive. Most of these files are irrelevant given that Harry Blackmun's papers run through 1994. Rehnquist's files will only contain new information (beyond the Blackmun files) after Justices Stevens, O'Connor, Scalia, Kennedy, Thomas, Souter, Ginsburg, and Breyer pass away.
7. State supreme court agenda studies also have an important history, dating back to Baum's (1976, 1977) individual-level and aggregate-level examinations of California justices.

References

Baum, L. 1976. "Decisions to Grant and Deny Hearings in the California Supreme Court: Patterns in Court and Individual Behavior." *Santa Clara Law Review* 16(4): 713–44.

Baum, L. 1977. "Policy Goals in Judicial Gatekeeping: A Proximity Model of Discretionary Jurisdiction." *American Journal of Political Science* 21(1): 13–35.

Black, R. C., and Boyd, C. L. 2012. "The Role of Law Clerks in the U.S. Supreme Court's Agenda-Setting Process." *American Politics Research* 40(1): 147–73.

Black, R. C., and Owens, R. J. 2009a. "Agenda Setting in the Supreme Court: The Collision of Policy and Jurisprudence." *Journal of Politics* 71(3): 1062–75.

Black, R. C., and Owens, R. J. 2009b. "Analyzing the Reliability of Supreme Court Justices' Agenda-Setting Records." *Justice System Journal* 30(3): 254–64.

Black, R. C., and Owens, R. J. 2011. "Solicitor General Influence and Agenda Setting on the U.S. Supreme Court." *Political Research Quarterly* 64(4): 765–78.

Black, R. C., and Owens, R. J. 2012a. "Consider the Source (and the Message): Supreme Court Justices and Strategic Audits of Lower Court Decisions." *Political Research Quarterly* 65(2): 385–95.

Black, R. C., and Owens, R. J. 2012b. *The Solicitor General and the United States Supreme Court: Executive Influence and Judicial Decisions*. New York: Cambridge University Press.

Boucher, R. L., and Segal, J. A. 1995. "Supreme Court Justices as Strategic Decision Makers: Aggressive Grants and Defensive Denials on the Vinson Court." *Journal of Politics* 57(3): 824–37.

Brace, P., and Hall, M. G. 2001. "Haves versus Have Nots in State Supreme Courts: Allocating Docket Space and Wins in Power Asymmetric Cases." *Law & Society Review* 35(2): 393–417.

Brenner, S. 1992–3. "The Memos of Supreme Court Law Clerk William Rehnquist: Conservative Tracts, or Mirrors of his Justice's Mind?" *Judicature* 76: 77–81.

Brenner, S., and Palmer, J. 1990. "The Law Clerks' Recommendations and Chief Justice Vinson's Vote on Certiorari." *American Politics Quarterly* 18(1): 68–80.

Caldeira, G. A. 1981. "The United States Supreme Court and Criminal Cases, 1935–1976: Alternative Models of Agenda Building." *British Journal of Political Science* 11(4): 449–70.

Caldeira, G. A., and Wright, J. R. 1988. "Organized Interests and Agenda Setting in the U.S. Supreme Court." *American Political Science Review* 82(4): 1109–27.

Caldeira, G. A., and Wright, J. R. 1990. "The Discuss List: Agenda Building in the Supreme Court." *Law & Society Review* 24(3): 807–36.

Caldeira, G. A., Wright, J. R., and Zorn, C. W. 1999. "Sophisticated Voting and Gate-keeping in the Supreme Court." *Journal of Law, Economics, & Organization* 15(3): 549–72.

Collins, P. M., Jr. 2004. "Friends of the Court: Examining the Influence of Amicus Curiae Participation in U.S. Supreme Court Litigation." *Law & Society Review* 38(4): 807–32.
Crowe, J. 2007. "The Forging of Judicial Autonomy: Political Entrepreneurship and the Reforms of William Howard Taft." *Journal of Politics* 69(1): 73–87.
Distlear, C., and Baum, L. 2001. "Selection of Law Clerks and Polarization in the U.S. Supreme Court." *Journal of Politics* 63(3): 869–85.
Epstein, L., and Knight, J. L. 1998. *The Choices Justices Make*. Washington, DC: CQ Press.
Epstein, L., Segal, J. A., and Spaeth, H. J. 2007. The Digitial Archive of the Papers of Justice Harry A. Blackmun, Available at: http://epstein.usc.edu/research/BlackmunArchive.html.
Grant, E., Hendrickson, S. A., and Lynch, M. S. 2012. "The Ideological Divide: Conflict and the Supreme Court's Certiorari Decision." *Cleveland State Law Review* 60(3): 559–83.
Hall, M. 2009. "Experimental Justice: Random Judicial Assignment and the Partisan Process of Supreme Court Review." *American Politics Research* 37(2): 195–226.
Leiman, J. M. 1957. "The Rule of Four." *Columbia Law Review* 57: 975–92.
Lindquist, S. A., and Klein, D. E. 2006. "The Influence of Jurisprudential Considerations on Supreme Court Decisionmaking: A Study of Conflict Cases." *Law & Society Review* 40(1): 135–61.
Lindquist, S. A., and Pybas, K. 1998. "State Supreme Court Decisions to Overrule Precedent, 1965–1996." *Justice System Journal* 20: 17–40.
Maltzman, F., and Wahlbeck, P. J. 1996. "Inside the U.S. Supreme Court: The Reliability of the Justices' Conference Records." *Journal of Politics* 58(2): 528–39.
O'Brien, D. M. 1997. "Join-3 Votes, the Rule of Four, the *Cert.* Pool, and the Supreme Court's Shrinking Plenary Docket." *Journal of Law & Politics* 13: 779–808.
Owens, R. J. 2010. "The Separation of Powers and Supreme Court Agenda Setting." *American Journal of Political Science* 54(2): 412–27.
Owens, R. J., and Simon, D. A. 2012. "Explaining the Supreme Court's Docket Size." *William & Mary Law Review* 53(4): 1219–85.
Pacelle, R. L., Jr. 1991. *The Transformation of the Supreme Court's Agenda: From the New Deal to the Reagan Administration*. Boulder, CO: Westview Press.
Pacelle, R. L., Jr. 2003. *Between Law and Politics: The Solicitor General and the Structuring of Race, Gender, and Reproductive Rights Litigation*. College Station, TX: Texas A&M University Press.
Palmer, J., and Brenner, S. 1989. "Working with Supreme Court Docket Books." *Law Library Journal* 81: 41–6.
Peppers, T. C. 2006. *Courtiers of the Marble Palace: The Rise and Influence of Supreme Court Law Clerks*. Stanford, CA: Stanford University Press.
Perry, H. W., Jr. 1991. *Deciding to Decide: Agenda-setting in the United States Supreme Court*. Cambridge, MA: Harvard University Press.
Provine, D. M. 1980. *Case Selection in the United States Supreme Court*. Chicago, IL: Chicago University Press.
Roberts, J. G. 2013. "2013 Year-End Report on the Federal Judiciary." Available at: http://www.supremecourt.gov/publicinfo/year-end/2013year-endreport.pdf.
Schoen, R., and Wahlbeck, P. J. 2006. "The Discuss List and Agenda-setting on the Supreme Court." Paper presented at the 2006 Annual Meeting of the Southern Political Science Association, Atlanta, GA.
Schubert, G. 1959. *Quantitative Analysis of Judicial Behavior*. Glencoe, IL: Free Press.

Schubert, G. 1962. "Policy without Law: An Extension of the Certiorari Game." *Stanford Law Review* 14: 284–327.

Segal, J. A. 1997. "Separation-of-powers games in the positive theory of congress and courts." *American Political Science Review* 91(1): 28–44.

Segal, J. A., and Spaeth, H. J. 2002. *The Supreme Court and the Attitudinal Model Revisited.* New York, NY: Cambridge University Press.

Stern, R. L., Gressman, E., Shapiro, S. M., and Geller, K. S. 2002. *Supreme Court Practice.* Washington, DC: CQ Press.

Tanenhaus, J., Schick, M., Muraskin, M., and Rosen, D. 1963. "The Supreme Court's Certiorari Jurisdiction: Cue Theory." In *Judicial Decision-Making*, edited by G. Schubert. New York: Free Press, 111–32.

Thompson, D. C., and Wachtell, M. F. 2009. "An Empirical Analysis of Supreme Court Certiorari Petition Procedures: The Call for Response and the Call for the Views of the Solicitor General." *George Mason Law Review* 16(2): 237–302.

Ulmer, S. S. 1972. "The Decision to Grant Certiorari as an Indicator to Decision 'on the Merits.'" *Polity* 4(4): 429–47.

Ulmer, S. S. 1973a. "Supreme Court Justices as Strict and Not-so-strict Constructionists: Some Implications." *Law & Society Review* 8(1): 13–32.

Ulmer, S. S. 1973b. "Bricolage and Assorted Thoughts on Working in the Papers of Supreme Court Justices." *Journal of Politics* 35(2): 286–310.

Ulmer, S. S. 1975. "Voting Blocs and 'Access' to the Supreme Court: 1947–56 Terms." *Jurimetrics Journal* 16: 6–13.

Ward, A., and Weiden, D. L. 2006. *Sorcerers' Apprentices: 100 Years of Law Clerks at the United States Supreme Court.* New York, NY: New York University Press.

Other Readings

Hammond, T. H., Bonneau, C. W., and Sheehan, R. S. 2005. *Strategic Behavior and Policy Choice on the U.S. Supreme Court.* Stanford, CA: Stanford University Press.

Lax, J. R. 2003. "Certiorari and Compliance in the Judicial Hierarchy." *Journal of Theoretical Politics* 15(1): 61–86.

CHAPTER 9

COURTROOM PROCEEDINGS IN U.S. FEDERAL COURTS

TIMOTHY R. JOHNSON

President Barack Obama signed into law the Patient Protection and Affordable Health Care Act on March 23, 2010.[1] Immediately, the State of Florida (along with twelve other states) sued the U.S. Department of Health and Human Services for, inter alia, an "unprecedented encroachment of liberty ... by mandating that all citizens and legal residents of the United States have qualifying healthcare coverage or pay a tax penalty."[2] This suit, filed in the Northern District of Florida, sought declaratory and injunctive relief, and asked the trial court to "protect the individual freedom, public health, and welfare of citizens and residents."[3] On January 31, 2011, Judge Roger Vinson issued an opinion that ultimately found the Affordable Care Act unconstitutional.[4]

On appeal, the Eleventh Circuit upheld Judge Vinson's decision. However, just two short months earlier the Sixth Circuit had ruled in the opposite direction—upholding the controversial health care law. As such, by the end of summer 2011 there was a clear circuit split on the constitutionality of the Affordable Health Care Act.[5] With this circuit split, and given the legal and political salience of the debate surrounding universal health care, it is no wonder that within three months (November 14, 2011) the U.S. Supreme Court granted certiorari to three consolidated cases.[6]

While the foregoing account provides only an abbreviated overview of how the Affordable Care Act found its way to the U.S. Supreme Court, it is the process through which the vast majority of cases make their way through the labyrinth of the federal court system. Scholarly accounts of this process abound (see e.g., Carp et al. 2014; Baum 2008; Tarr 2006). These analyses, largely descriptions contained in judicial process textbooks, focus on the large issues of trials, appeals, decision-making, compliance, and doctrine. They also provide important insights into the least understood branch of the federal government. What they do not provide, however, are insights into what happens within the courtroom during a trial or appellate argument. This chapter seeks to fill this gap to help the court watcher better understand courtroom proceedings.

Specifically, I focus on the courtroom proceedings in the three levels of the U.S. federal judiciary. I begin with an overview of trial court proceedings and consider some of the key cases surrounding rights associated with trials as well as the literature that suggests what transpires during trial can and does affect how cases are decided. I then turn to the proceedings in U.S. circuit courts. After a general overview of these proceedings I consider how several key rules vary across circuits. Finally, I consider the oral arguments in the U.S. Supreme Court. As these proceedings have garnered the most attention from scholars I provide an overview of the arguments and then focus on the extent to which they have any effect on how the nation's highest court decides cases it hears.

Trials in U.S. Federal Courts

Between June 2012 and June 2013, fewer than 3 percent of all criminal cases and only 1.2 percent of all civil cases reached trial.[7] These numbers are commensurate with past years. In short, few cases filed in federal court ever reach the trial stage—rather most cases are dismissed, plea bargained, or settled before the parties involved have a chance to make arguments before a jury of their peers (or before a judge, in the case of a bench trial). Because so few cases reach this point in the process, and because most citizens have little knowledge of what happens at trial—beyond what they see on television dramas—this section focuses on the courtroom proceedings at federal trials. From there it considers some of the major cases that ensure particular rights are guaranteed at trial.

Overview of the Trial Process

Certainly there are differences between criminal and civil trials—the issues vary, the types of evidence vary, and the burden of proof varies. However, the procedures are largely the same in both types of trial. Thus, this overview pertains to both types of cases in federal courts. From there, it parses out with more detail the proceedings of each type of trial.

Trials in federal court are heard by either a jury of citizens selected at random (from across the district within which the case originates) or are overseen by a U.S. District Court judge. However, juries decide the vast majority of trials (juries heard more than 78 percent of cases that reached trial between June 2012 and June 2013). The proceedings pit two attorneys against one another—in criminal trials an Assistant U.S. Attorney argues against defense counsel while in civil trials two private attorneys usually represent their clients.[8] Attorneys have one essential job during trial—they must present the facts of the case in a way that will convince the jury (or judge) to rule in favor of their client. In addition, they must make their case clear to the jury (or judge) in both opening and closing statements. The key is that the presentation of arguments, evidence, and the testimony of witnesses must be done within the bounds of stringent rules and norms of behavior.[9]

Although the attorneys are the focal point of most trials, they are not the only actors who participate in the trial. In fact, nobody would be at trial without the parties—one who has lodged a complaint against the other. More specifically, in criminal trials the government brings charges against the accused, while in a civil trial the plaintiff (the party who brings a lawsuit) makes arguments against a defendant (the party being sued). As will become clear later in this chapter, there are certain rights associated with the interactions between the parties—especially in criminal trials.

Witnesses may be the most important actors in the trial because what they say, and how they say it, can and does affect case outcomes. Note, initially, that witnesses provide facts about a case (eyewitness accounts or expert testimony about evidence for example) to support the arguments made by the attorneys. Witnesses are called to provide testimony and cannot sit in the courtroom prior to being called. Once in the courtroom, they sit on the witness stand (or in the witness box) and answer questions from the attorneys. Questions range from those about evidence admitted into the record, to eyewitness accounts of a crime, to expert testimony about such issues as DNA analysis or environmental impact. The key is that attorneys representing both parties are allowed to question the witness. Thus, while direct questioning is meant to build a case for one side, cross-examination is meant to poke holes in the case made by direct questioning.[10] In criminal trials the standard for the burden of proof (that a crime was committed beyond a reasonable doubt) is on the government. In civil trials, the standard is "preponderance of evidence," which means that whichever side presents more and better evidence should win. Ultimately, while the effects of witness testimony are not fully clear (see e.g. Scheck et al. 2000; Nunez et al. 2012; Smith et al. 2011), attorneys take no chances because they understand that without good and credible witnesses they will not win their case.

As evidence is placed on the record—through witness testimony—the judge plays a key role in the trial proceedings. More specifically, she has five main functions with the trial. First, judges simply preside over the trial and ensure that order is maintained in the courtroom. Second, and related to witnesses, judges determine whether evidence is brought properly before the court or whether it should be excluded.[11] Third, if presiding over a jury trial, judges must provide instructions to the jury about how the law applies and give instructions about the standards it must use when it deliberates about how the facts lead to a particular outcome. Fourth, if it is a bench trial, judges actually determine the veracity of the facts (like a jury would) and then ultimately decide the case. Finally, once a trial is complete the judge must make a decision. In criminal trials the judge sentences a criminal defendant who is found guilty and in civil trials the judge awards damages or decides that there is not enough evidence to do so.

The jury obviously holds a great deal of power in trial court proceedings. While the judge decides on matters of law, the jury decides which side presents the facts in the most believable way and applies the law to the best of its ability once the judge instructs them on how to do so. In short, it is the jury's job to determine which side is telling the truth. That said, data suggest that how attorneys present evidence can and does have an effect on jury decisions—at least in criminal trials (see e.g., Anderson and Heaton 2012; Shinall 2010; Linz et al. 1986). In federal court this is often a tough job for attorneys because, whether arguing in a criminal or civil trial, the jury must reach a unanimous verdict (in contrast this is not always the case in state courts where state legislatures set the standards for whether decisions must be unanimous or decided by majority or super majority).

The interactions between the actors described here make up the trial process. The attorneys put arguments and evidence on the record through opening and closing statements and by drawing out information from witnesses. The judge ensures that the attorneys follow the rules and procedures that govern the trial process. In particular, judges rule on motions, objections, and points of law. Further, judges make rulings about the law, provide the standards the jury must use when deciding the case, and ultimately hands down a decision—whether it is a sentence in a criminal case where the accused is found guilty or an award in a civil case. Finally, the jury makes decisions about facts. That is, it decides which side presented the more credible case within the bounds of the law. As noted above, there is existing evidence that the trial process can and does affect case outcomes but given that these studies are almost exclusively experimental in nature, there is still work to be done in this area.

Reality v. Hollywood in Federal Trials

While the general view of trials, including the actors described above, is often thought of as a Hollywood courtroom scene—impassioned opening and closing statements, dramatic testimony, and fights in the jury room—most trials are actually comprised of mundane proceedings. Indeed, the principal feature of litigation before federal district courts is motion practice, or the process of litigants filing motions and judges ruling on them. Parties file various motions—which are simply requests that a court issue an order—in the hopes of achieving their litigation objectives. These motions range from dispositive motions (e.g., motions for summary judgment), to evidentiary motions (e.g., motions in limine), to case management and procedural motions (e.g., motions to change attorneys or change venue). Attorneys understand that motion practice is the key vehicle to help them win a trial. As such, cases are comprised of a series of interdependent decisions. Litigants, for example, decide which types of motions to file and when to file them, as well as whether to settle a case. Judges' decisions on these motions, moreover, alter the landscape of the case by affecting the final choice that will be presented to a judge or jury. That is to say, rulings on motions establish which of the plaintiffs' claims will be allowed to advance and what evidence will be admitted to substantiate those claims. Keilitz, Hanson, and Daley succinctly describe the impact of motion practice as follows: "The way a judge rules on a motion can have a dramatic effect on the course and outcome of litigation" (1994: 3). In other words, by filing specific types of motions, several motions together, or strategically timing the filing of motions (Herr, Haydock, and Stempel 1998), litigants try to set the agenda of a case.

The institutional setting of trial courts thus highlights the important role litigants play in the judicial process. In appellate courts, litigants' decisions center on whether to appeal and, once having appealed, what types of arguments to put forward. Such decisions can, for example, influence the macro agenda of the Supreme Court (Pacelle 1991) and possibly even affect judges' decisions on the merits. At trial courts, however, the institutional setting of motion practice leads to ongoing interactions between litigants and judges. Thus, litigants' choices of which motions to file can help determine which questions the fact-finder will answer, and judges' rulings on these motions can influence the subsequent choices litigants make. In short, these interactions—the tactics adopted by litigants, as well as judges' responses to them—often structure the course and outcome of trials.

Major Rights Associated with Trials

Understanding the trial process is important but it may be even more important to understand the rights associated with trials. Indeed, the framers intended American trials to be the epitome of justice because under the English system trials were mostly closed proceedings, there were long delays between arrest and trial, and few safeguards existed to protect the rights of the accused. As such, two of the first ten amendments—the Sixth and the Seventh—focused on ensuring the fairness of this process. In this section I consider the two main rights that emanate from these amendments.

The first provision of the Sixth Amendment focuses on the time it takes for a trial to commence; in other words, this amendment guarantees the right to a speedy trial. Prior to the 1960s the notion that trials would not happen quickly was seldom an issue because usually little time elapsed between an arrest and the trial if the accused was indicted (Epstein and Walker 2004: 594). However, as backlogs began to mount, and as caseloads grew on various dockets, the U.S. Supreme Court was asked to interpret the exact meaning of the Speedy Trial Clause. These initial cases were *sui generis*, which means they were being decided without much, if any, case law to help the justices. Initially, *U.S. v. Marion* (1971) made clear that the right to a speedy trial only begins once an indictment has been issued against a criminal defendant. A year later, in *Barker v. Wingo* (1972), the justices indicated trial courts should take a balancing approach to speedy trials and consider what caused the delay, how long was the delay, whether the delay affected the outcome of the trial, and whether the defendant claimed the right to a speedy trial.

In response to these cases Congress passed the Speedy Trial Act of 1974. This law provided for specific time limits for pretrial and trial procedures in all federal courts. Specifically, indictments must be filed within thirty days of an arrest, arraignment must be held within ten days of indictment, and a trial must commence within seventy days of the indictment. In short, there was a one-hundred-day limit between indictment and the initiation of the trial proceedings. Congress provided remedies for violating the law, which include the dismissal of charges.

As indicated above, the heart of the trial is when witnesses testify and are then cross-examined by opposing counsel. The Sixth Amendment focuses on this part of the proceedings as well, as it affords all criminal defendants the right to confront witnesses who may testify against them. In *Pointer v. Texas* (1965) the Court held that defendants have the right to confront witnesses in both federal and state trials. This suggests the right to confront witnesses generally prohibits trials *in absentia*. In short, a trial cannot take place if the defendant is not present. But there are limits to this right. The Court dealt with a specific issue of when this right can be limited in *Illinois v. Allen* (1970). Here, the justices made clear that, if a defendant is so disruptive that the trial cannot proceed, removing the defendant from the courtroom is not violated by removing him from the courtroom.

A controversial question is whether the confrontation clause confers an absolute right on all defendants to face their accusers in open court. The issue is particularly salient because, in the past half-century many states have devised ways to deal with children testifying without being in the presence of the defendant (because it is often too emotional and stressful for them). Some states use closed-circuit television to protect children while others screen child witnesses so they do not have to face the accused during trial. In *Coy v. Iowa* (1988), however, the Court ruled that this type of testimony is only allowed if the case has particular special circumstances. Two years later, in *Maryland v. Craig* (1990), the justices upheld the conviction of an accused child abuser even though the six-year-old witness testified on closed-circuit television. As Justice O'Connor wrote, the "Confrontation clause does not prohibit the use of a procedure that, despite the absence of face-to-face confrontation, ensures the reliability of the evidence by subjecting it to rigorous adversarial testing and thereby preserves the essence of effective confrontation."[12]

There are certainly other rights associated with courtroom proceedings in the United States. For instance, the Court has made clear that, prior to the actual trial, each side must disclose all of its evidence to the other side. In addition, when a jury is chosen for a criminal trial, the prosecution may not discriminate by using all of its preemptory challenges to reject all possible jurors from one race. The point is that, at trial in federal courts (and in state courts for that matter) the U.S. Supreme Court has ensured that those involved in the trial are treated fairly and with due process of law.

U.S. Circuit Courts of Appeals

Just as few cases actually make it to trial in federal courts, even fewer cases are appealed to a circuit court of appeals. This is an interesting fact because these mid-level courts do not have discretion over what cases to hear.[13] Indeed, in both 2012 and June 2013 only a fraction of litigants who lose at trial filed an appeal.[14] An even smaller fraction of these cases—only about 6,900—reached oral argument during this time period. These statistics are consistent with appeals patterns in past years. While many circuits record audio of the courtroom proceedings and two of them record the video (the Second and Ninth Circuits), most citizens have considerably less knowledge of what transpires during these proceedings than they have knowledge about trial proceedings. As such, this section focuses on the rules that dictate these courtroom proceedings in the thirteen federal circuits.

Circuit Courtroom Proceedings and Rules

Oral argument in the U.S. Courts of Appeal is a highly structured discussion between the appellate lawyers and a panel of judges. For reasons of efficiency the full court almost never sits together (en banc) to hear arguments. Rather, a panel of three judges hears the initial arguments.[15] In front of this panel, each side is given a short time to make their case to the judges and the discussion focuses on the legal principles in dispute. Specifically, the arguments focus on whether the trial court acted according to the law or whether it made a mistake in regards to evidence, trial procedure, or rulings of relevant legal issues. Given this focus, the rules dictate that no new facts, witnesses, or arguments may be made to the circuit court. In short, these proceedings differ from trial because they focus only on matters of law, and possibly on matters of mistakes in applying the law, rather than on the factual circumstances of the case.[16]

Federal circuit court rules dictate the general nature and terms of arguments before federal courts of appeals. In fact, this may be somewhat of a misnomer because the rules of courtroom proceedings specify very little—and most of the circuits add their own specific rules. That said, several points are worth noting. First, Rule 34(a)2 specifies oral arguments take place unless the three-judge panel assigned the case unanimously agrees these proceedings are unnecessary.[17] The general rules do not provide a specific time limit for the arguments (34(b)) although most circuits do so. Finally, while these rules do not indicate what the attorneys should provide in terms of arguments they do indicate how the arguments proceed and what not to do during a presentation (34(e)): "The appellant opens and concludes the argument. Counsel must not read at length from briefs, records, or authorities."

Beyond the vague rules specified by the federal guidelines several circuits have added their own local rules. Consider first the time allotted for arguments. The First Circuit "will permit no more than 15 minutes per side for oral argument" (34(c)1). In contrast, the Second and Eleventh Circuits only indicate the clerk will notify the parties of their allotted time. Similarly, DC Circuit rules indicate, "Counsel will be afforded such time for oral arguments as the court may provide" (Local Rule 34(a)). The Third Circuit has an even more interesting rule. Eleven days prior to a panel sitting, the presiding judge notifies the parties as to whether they have been granted the maximum time allowed—twenty minutes—to argue. However, most cases garner only fifteen minutes per side (Circuit Rule 2.1). In the Fourth and Fifth Circuits the normal time allotted is twenty minutes. However, Local Rule 34(d) in the Fourth Circuit decreases the time to fifteen minutes, "In social security disability cases, black lung cases, and labor cases where the primary issue is whether the agency's decision is supported by substantial evidence and in criminal cases where the primary issue involves the application of the sentencing guidelines." The point is that different courts seem to value oral argument differently and some keep the rules vague enough so that counsel have, what the court deems, appropriate time to make their case. In the end, scholars must test the degree to which the variation in time affects the outcome of cases these courts decide.[18]

While time limits dominate the circuit rules covering oral proceedings, the rules also indicate on what types of arguments attorneys should focus. General Rule 34(c) simply indicates the appellant argues first and that counsel must not "read at length from briefs, records, or authorities." Despite this admonition, there is no indication of what can or should be presented to the courts and only Fifth, Sixth, and Seventh Circuits offer any additional guidance. Rule 34.12 in the Fifth Circuit admonishes counsel that the judges will have read the briefs prior to arguments. In addition, it is the only circuit that suggests, "Counsel should be prepared to answer the court's questions." This is an interesting rule given that evidence makes clear that questioning (at least by justices in the Supreme Court) can and does influence case outcomes (Johnson 2004; Black et al. 2012).

The Sixth Circuit is the only other court to provide additional rules for courtroom proceedings. Its Rule (h) (1) makes clear counsel should use their time to clarify the written argument. In addition, the court has its own explicit rules about which authorities counsel may cite during the arguments. Specifically, applicable precedents may not be cited unless they are in the written briefs already.[19] Unlike any of the other courts, however, attorneys can rectify mistakes they may have made when crafting their initial briefs. Indeed, a supplement filing can be made as late as the argument date but the rule states it should be "made sooner." The point is that the Sixth Circuit allows some additional leeway for its arguing counsel, and it would be interesting to determine the extent to which this affects decisions on that court.

One final oddity is worth noting about the rules that cover presentation of arguments, and it emanates from the Seventh Circuit. Of all the circuits only the Seventh allows law students to present oral arguments before the court. These students, as they gain experience in our federal system, may obtain written approval from their client and stand before one of the nation's highest courts. Of course, an attorney must supervise them and the court must be warned, via motion, at least fourteen days in advance of the argument. This motion must include a rationale for why it is appropriate for the student to argue. It is this rule that typifies why the circuits are allowed to control some of their own rules—the concept that they may experiment with their own rules to determine what works and what does not work so well.

Circuit rules about the timing of arguments, and how they should be conducted vary. Rules concerning public access to the audio (or video) of proceedings vary as well. Several circuits now provide online access to the audio of the oral proceedings. These include the First, Third, Fourth, Fifth, Sixth, Seventh, Eight, Ninth, the DC Circuit, and the Federal Circuit. The Second, Tenth, and Eleventh Circuits, however, have different rules. The Second Circuit releases audio upon request and for a fee. In contrast, the Tenth Circuit that has the most stringent policy, indicating that electronic recordings are meant only for use of the court. However, the parties (but not the public) may file a motion to obtain a copy. This motion must include a reason why the recording is needed. It is the Eleventh Circuit that has the most stringent rules. Indeed, its Rule 34(g) indicates the audio is meant for the exclusive use of the court and that it will not be made available to the parties or counsel. Interestingly, counsel may (with advanced approval) hire a qualified court reporter to transcribe the proceedings, but recording the audio is strictly prohibited.

Only two circuits regularly record the video of the oral proceedings. The Second Circuit allows cameras to record all non-criminal cases and the Ninth Circuit regularly uses cameras in almost all cases. These two courts, along with a host of U.S. District Courts will ultimately be the test cases for whether the U.S. Supreme Court will, one day, use cameras as well.

While data are increasingly available in the circuits, they are still not as readily available as is data from U.S. Supreme Court oral arguments. As such, there has been virtually no study of how these proceedings affect the decisions circuit court judges make. Indeed, the vast majority of academic analyses focuses on describing the process (Posner 2013; Cleveland and Wisotsky 2012) or employs a variable that captures whether a case reached oral arguments to help explain other phenomena (Christenson and Szmer 2012). However, with the advent of new technologies to gather data on oral arguments it is clear that analyses can and should be conducted. The reason for this is two-fold. First, what we know about oral arguments comes almost exclusively from one institution—the U.S. Supreme Court. With the variation in rules that exists between circuits it behooves scholars to begin to study these institutions. In addition, most cases do not make it to the Supreme Court and so most law is created at the circuit level. Ultimately this means that the oral arguments in circuits may be more important than the courtroom proceedings I consider in the final section.

Oral Argument Proceedings at the U.S. Supreme Court

The federal government puts on many impressive displays in Washington DC. Every four years the nation celebrates the inauguration of a new president, and hundreds of thousands of people attend various events. Once a year, during a president's term in office, Congress invites him to give an appraisal of the state of the union in front of all senators and representatives, the cabinet, some (or sometimes all) Supreme Court justices, and various other dignitaries. Any day Congress is in session visitors may obtain passes to sit in the Senate or House galleries to watch our legislative process in action. People may also watch extensive coverage of both houses on C-SPAN. What each of these events has in common is that thousands, hundreds of thousands, or even millions of people can and do witness them each year. In other words, to see their elected representatives in action citizens have a relatively easy time watching—sometimes in person, and sometimes through television or Internet outlets.

In contrast, the U.S. Supreme Court is not in the public eye as often as is Congress or the president. In fact, while the Court's proceedings for oral arguments are open to the public, far fewer people see the justices in action than they see members of either of the other branches. Even those who are lucky enough to witness an oral argument usually only glimpse about three minutes of the give-and-take between attorneys and the justices. But if you are willing to stand in line for several hours for most cases it is well worth the wait. Of course in highly salient cases the lines can be extraordinarily long. In fact, the Court anticipates when this may happen. For example, in *Planned Parenthood of Southeastern Pennsylvania v. Casey* (1992) the Court's public information officer, Toni House, sent a memo detailing seating arrangements for the gallery. Among other issues, she noted that only 100 seats were reserved for the public and that the line for those seats officially formed at midnight before the arguments.

The Supreme Court normally hears oral arguments between October and April, scheduling them into two-week sittings during which the Court hears two (although sometimes one or three) arguments per day on Monday, Tuesday, and Wednesday. Generally, the Court allots one hour of argument time for each case, with each party speaking for thirty minutes. Despite the fact that far fewer people see the Court in action than they do Congress or the president, the proceedings are high powered and exciting, and they always start with a bang. At precisely 10 o'clock on argument mornings the justices enter the courtroom through the red velvet curtains behind the bench and the court marshal rises from his or her station to proclaim:

> The Honorable, the Chief Justice and Associate Justices of the Supreme Court of the United States. Oyez! Oyez! Oyez! All persons having business before the Honorable, the Supreme Court of the United States, are admonished to draw near and give their attention, for the Court is now sitting. God save the United States and this Honorable Court!

The pomp and circumstance continues as the Chief Justice bangs his gavel to call the first case to order. Below I explore what happens next.

A Brief Overview of Oral Arguments

As noted above, Supreme Court oral arguments begin with a flourish. After the case is called, the attorney for the petitioner approaches the lectern and begins "Mr. Chief Justice, and may it please the Court."[20] From there the process is relatively straightforward. Indeed, for the past forty years each attorney has been afforded thirty minutes to persuade the justices to rule in a particular way.[21] Mechanically, the attorney stands before the bench to make her argument to the justices. To guarantee attorneys do not go over time, the lectern has two lights. When the white light illuminates the attorney has five minutes left to argue and when the red light turns on, her time is finished.

Despite the seeming simplicity of the proceedings at the Court, the reason the process is only relatively straightforward is that, while the attorneys attempt to forward an argument to persuade the justices, the justices (unlike circuit court judges) often speak more than the advocate. Due to this fact, these proceedings are simply not as structured as are the arguments in the courts of appeals. Consider the 681 cases argued between 1998 and 2007. In these cases the justices asked questions or made comments a total of 87,941 times—an average of more than 129 utterances per case (Black et al. 2012). This average is consistent with Johnson's (2004) finding that the justices collectively ask an average of 133 questions per case—or over two per each minute of oral argument. The point is that the process in the nation's highest court is usually controlled by the justices. However, this was not always how cases were argued.

In the Court's early days great lawyers such as Daniel Webster, John Calhoun, William Pinkney, and Henry Clay often appeared before the justices. In this time period oral arguments were elaborate oratories but, more importantly, they often provided the justices with their only source of information about a case: briefs were rarely if ever submitted and outside parties did not submit amicus curiae (friend of the Court) briefs as they do today. The result was that the justices placed no time limitation on the argument sessions. As such, advocates sometimes spoke for many hours over multiple days. In one case, for instance, Davis (1940) points out that Webster and his rival argued for a full ten days. In stark contrast to contemporary arguments, historians suggest the justices rarely interrupted the advocates with questions or comments (compare Warren 1922 with Black et al. 2009).

Certainly, hearing arguments over many days was possible because the Court heard so few cases in its early days. However, the Court's rising caseload soon made such indulgences impossible. In addition, it seems that, at some point, the justices could no longer handle such long sessions. As one biographer put it, Chief Justice John Marshall complained of boredom (Beveridge 1929) and Justice Joseph Story found the arguments "excessively prolix and tedious" (Hughes 1928). Just as certainly as days-long arguments were possible for the early Court, such a model was untenable as the justices' caseload increased. As a result, in 1849 they instituted Rule 53, which limited each attorney to a two-hour argument (Frankfurter and Landis 1928). The justices simultaneously required the first written arguments, consisting of an abstract of points and authorities (Frankfurter and Landis 1928). Today, and since 1970, the time allotted for these has been limited to thirty minutes per side.

The modern time constraints on oral arguments may be due to the fact that the justices have so much information at their disposal prior to these open court sessions. Indeed, today they possess litigant briefs (Epstein and Kobylka 1992), briefs amicus curiae (Spriggs and Wahlbeck 1997), briefs on certiorari (Caldeira and Wright 1988), the media (Epstein and Knight 1998), and lower court opinions. Further, unlike the Court's early days, when the justices were transfixed by the great orators (or put to sleep from boredom) they largely control the argument sessions today. Another analysis of 347 cases over four recent terms included 43,000 utterances and 1.4 million words spoken by the justices (Black et al. 2011). It seems then, that in modern cases, the justices speak as much or more so than do the attorneys. The question is whether such questioning has some bearing on how the justices decide.

Do the Courtroom Proceedings Affect How Justices Decide?

Evidence accumulated by political scientists and legal scholars over the last two decades establishes that, generally, these the oral proceedings play an integral role in the Court's decision-making process (Johnson 2004; Wrightsman 2008). More specifically, there are myriad ways this one-hour conversation between Court and counsel, as well as between the justices themselves, connects with the outcome of a case. Justices, for example, use these proceedings to gather additional information not contained in the litigants' briefs (Johnson 2004; Wasby, D'Amato, and Metrailer 1976). Such information includes the facts of the case, pertinent precedent, and how Congress or the president might respond if the Court decides in a particular way.

Additionally, there is evidence the quality of arguments forwarded by attorneys during these proceedings affects justices' votes (Johnson, Wahlbeck, and Spriggs 2006). Indeed, even justices predisposed to vote for a particular side (based on their ideological predilections) tend to vote more often for the side that offers better arguments in open court. There is also clear evidence that, during oral arguments, justices foreshadow how they will decide (Shullman 2004; Roberts 2005; Johnson et al. 2009; Black et al. 2013). Such signals emanate from the number of questions justices ask the attorney for each side of the dispute as well as from the emotive tenor of these questions. When justices give one side a harder time (by asking more questions) or when they ask that side questions using less pleasant language, it is more likely to lose the case. Finally, data suggest justices begin their coalition building process while they sit for the arguments (see, e.g., Black et al. 2013; Johnson 2004; Johnson, Spriggs, and Wahlbeck 2007; Wasby, D'Amato, and Metrailer 1976). As such, how they ultimately decide largely begins during these proceedings.

The Justices Concur

Almost universally, past and present Supreme Court justices view the oral arguments as a fundamental part of their decision-making process (this section relies on Johnson 2004). While there is some dissension from this view, Justice Robert Jackson summed up the general sentiment: "I think the justices would answer unanimously that now, as traditionally, they rely heavily on oral presentations … it always is of the highest, and often of controlling, importance" (1951). Justice Lewis F. Powell reaffirmed Jackson's sentiment several decades later: "the fact is, as every judge knows ... the oral argument ... does contribute significantly to the development of precedents" (in Stern, Gressman, and Shapiro 1993: 571). Other justices posit that these proceedings do, at times, have a great effect on their decisions (Hughes 1928; White 1982; Rehnquist 2001).

These accounts resemble Justice John Harlan's experience with oral arguments at the Court. When he kept a diary of his post-argument impressions of a case Harlan found that, "more times than not, the views which I had at the end of the day's session jibed with the final views I formed after the more careful study of the briefs" (1955: 7). Justices from the twentieth century support the conclusions drawn by Justice Harlan. For instance, Justice William Brennan: asserts that, "I have had too many occasions when my judgment of a decision has turned on what happened in oral argument" (in Stern and Gressman 1993: 732). He goes on to suggest that, while not controlling his votes, this process helps form his substantive thoughts about a case: "Often my idea of how a case shapes up is changed by oral argument" (in Stern and Gressman 1993: 732). Former Chief Justice Rehnquist agrees with this assertion and argues that oral advocacy can affect his thoughts about specific cases: "I think that in a significant minority of cases in which I have heard oral argument, I have left the bench feeling different about the case than I did when I came on the bench. The change is seldom a full one-hundred-and-eighty-degree swing" (2001: 243).

Ultimately, the vast majority of evidence suggests justices believe oral arguments are important, but why? Different justices provide different answers to this question. Chief Justice Rehnquist posits that oral arguments allow justices to evaluate counsel's "strong and weak points, and to ask ... some questions [about the case]" (1984: 1025). Similarly, Justice Byron White suggests that during these proceedings the Court treats lawyers as resources (1982: 383). By this, he seems to suggest that counsel come to the Court to provide new or clarifying information, which enables the justices to gain a clearer picture of the case at hand. Indeed, there may be points about which the justices are still unclear after reading the briefs, and this face-to-face exchange can make them clearer. As Chief Justice Rehnquist argues: "One can do his level best to digest from the briefs ... what he believes necessary to decide the case, and still find himself falling short in one aspect or another of either the law or the facts. Oral argument can cure these shortcomings" (2001: 245).

Justice William O. Douglas holds a somewhat different perspective on oral arguments. He argues that these proceedings are meant to teach the justices about the key points of a case: "The purpose of a hearing is that the Court may learn what it does not know ... It is the education of the Justices ... that is the essential function of the appellate lawyer" (in Galloway 1989: 84). Moreover, Justice John Harlan claims oral arguments are the best mechanism for information gathering: "there is no substitute ... for the Socratic method of procedure in getting at the real heart of an issue and in finding out where the truth lies" (1955: 7).

As former Chief Justice Rehnquist wrote: "Oral argument offers a direct interchange of ideas between court and counsel ... Counsel can play a significant role in responding to the concerns of the judges, concerns that counsel won't always be able to anticipate when preparing briefs" (1984: 1021). Thus, for him, oral argument is: "Probably the most important catalyst for generating further thought" (Rehnquist 2001: 241). Rehnquist (1986) best sums up the views in this section: "Justices of the Supreme Court of the United States have almost unanimously agreed that effective oral advocacy is one of the most powerful tools of the professions" (p. 289). Even a principal skeptic such as Justice Scalia changed his view once he joined the Court.

Conclusion

There are many phases to how a case makes it way through the federal court system. While the arguments presented in motions or briefs have an effect on how judges or justices decide, it is clear that the proceedings inside the courtroom at each level also have a clear effect on case outcomes. As such, it is also clear that scholars, students of the judiciary, and court watchers alike should pay attention to the proceedings that take place inside courtrooms despite the fact that they make up only a small portion of the overall judicial process.

Notes

1. This law has become known as Obamacare. While this name was initiated by opponents of the law, and was therefore considered pejorative, both sides of the debate have since adopted it as the name of the law.
2. Complaint filed in U.S. District Court, Northern District of Florida, available at: http://www.healthcarelawsuit.us/webfiles.nsf/WF/MRAY-83TKWB/$file/HealthCareReformLawsuit.pdf. The original case was *Florida ex rel. Bondi v. U.S. Department of Health and Human Services*.
3. Complaint filed in U.S. District Court, Northern District of Florida, available at: http://www.healthcarelawsuit.us/webfiles.nsf/WF/MRAY-83TKWB/$file/HealthCareReformLawsuit.pdf. The original case was *Florida ex rel. Bondi v. U.S. Department of Health and Human Services*.
4. While trial court judges do not often write opinions (a practice reserved for appellate courts in the United States), judge Vinson issued a 78-page opinion explicating the rationale for his decision.
5. Scholars have demonstrated that circuit splits are a key predictor for whether the U.S. Supreme Court will place a case on its docket (Black and Owens 2012; Perry 1991).
6. The Supreme Court often consolidates cases with similar facts or that implicate the same law. More importantly, the Court is likely to consolidate cases where several lower courts have ruled in divergent ways on the same law or issue (see Supreme Court Rule 10). In this instance, there were three cases that dealt with the constitutionality of the Affordable Care Act and that reached different outcomes.
7. The statistics cited here come from statistical tables for the Federal Judiciary, June 2013—the most recent data is available at: http://www.uscourts.gov/Statistics/StatisticalTables

ForTheFederalJudiciary/june-2013.aspx. Specifically, I draw from Tables C-4 and D-4 on the uscourts website.

8. There are several types of attorneys who could represent a criminal defendant. Oftentimes the accused hires a private attorney. However, there are times when a defendant cannot afford an attorney. In these cases a public defender or a court appointed attorney may represent the defendant. Since *Gideon v. Wainwright* (1963) defendants in both state and federal courts are afforded the right to be represented by counsel in criminal trials.
9. Later in this chapter I address the issue of whether or not the trial process affects case outcomes. For now note that rules and norms can and do affect decisions made by political and legal actors (see e.g., Knight 1992; Maltzman, Spriggs, and Wahlbeck 2000; Johnson 2004).
10. Interestingly, there is little research on direct or cross-examination except on questioning of child witnesses or experts. Even these works are only partially illuminating as they are almost exclusively in the experimental setting.
11. There is a long list of cases that cover the admissability of evidence in court. The most important of these cases may be (*Mapp v. Ohio*, 1961), which set the exclusionary rule. This rule suggests that any evidence obtained illegally in a criminal investigation (i.e., in an unconstitutional manner) is not admitted in court.
12. http://www.law.cornell.edu/supct/html/89-478.ZO.html.
13. Rather, as noted above, litigants have the right to one appeal, which means there is no discretion. That said, the statistics indicate that most cases in the circuits are disposed of without oral arguments.
14. The statistics cited here come from statistical tables for the Federal Judiciary, June 2013—the most recent data is available at: http://www.uscourts.gov/Statistics/StatisticalTables ForTheFederalJudiciary/june-2013.aspx. Specifically, I draw from Tables B and B-1 on the uscourts website.
15. Circuit courts can and do sit en banc, but this too is a rare occurrence. En banc opinions tend to carry more weight and are usually decided only after a panel has first heard the case. Once a panel has ruled on an issue and "published" the opinion, no future panel can overrule the previous decision. The panel can, however, suggest that the circuit take up the case en banc to reconsider the first panel's decision.
16. That said, as in the U.S. Supreme Court, the judges can and do raise questions about the specific facts of the case.
17. A case may be denied arguments for one of three reasons: it is frivolous, the issues at stake have already been authoritatively decided, or the briefs adequately present the facts and legal arguments such that the arguments would not add anything to the case.
18. In addition, several of the circuits do not allow counsel to know which judges are on their panel until a short time before the arguments. This is presumably to ensure that counsel do not simply spend their time crafting arguments to a particular judge. However, this is an empirical question that should be tested in the future.
19. Of course, like the justices at the Supreme Court, questions from the bench could implicate precedents that had not been briefs by the litigants (see Johnson 2004).
20. Attorneys may use the hand crank on the side of the podium to raise or lower it to an appropriate height.
21. Of course, some cases garner more time than others, especially when they are present more salient issues to the Court (see e.g. *Bush v. Gore*, the Affordable Care Act cases).

References

Anderson, J. M., and Heaton, P. 2012. "How Much Difference Does the Lawyer Make?" *Yale Law Journal* 122: 154–217.

Baum, L. 2008. *American Courts: Process and Policy*, 6th ed. Independence, KY: Cengage.

Beveridge, A. J. 1929. *The Life of John Marshall*. Boston, MA: Houghton Mifflin.

Black, R. C., Johnson, T. R., and Wedeking, J. 2012. *Oral Arguments and Coalition Formation on the U.S. Supreme Court: A Deliberate Dialogue*. Ann Arbor, MI: University of Michigan Press.

Black, R. C., Sorenson, M. W., and Johnson, T. R. 2013. "Towards an Actor-based Measure of Supreme Court Salience: Information Seeking and Engagement During Oral Arguments." *Political Research Quarterly* 66(4): 804–18.

Black, R. C., Treul, S. A., Johnson, T. R., and Goldman, J. 2011. "Emotions, Oral Arguments, and Supreme Court Decision Making." *Journal of Politics* 73(2): 572–81.

Caldeira, G. A., and Wright, J. R. 1988. "Organized Interests and Agenda Setting in the U.S. Supreme Court." *American Political Science Review* 82: 1109–27.

Carp, R. A., Stidham, R., and Manning, K. L. 2013. *Judicial Process in America*, 9th ed. Thousand Oaks, CA: Sage.

Christensen, R. K., and Szmer, J. 2012. "Examining the Efficiency of the U.S. Courts of Appeals: Pathologies and Prescriptions." *International Review of Law and Economics* 32(1): 30–7.

Cleveland, D. R., and Wisotsky, S. 2012. "Decline of Oral Argument in the Federal Courts of Appeals: A Modest Proposal for Reform." *Journal of Appellate Practice and Process* 13: 119–52.

Davis, J. W. 1940. "The Argument of an Appeal." *American Bar Association Journal*. 26: 895–9.

Epstein, L., and Knight, J. 1998. *The Choices Justices Make*. Washington, DC: Congressional Quarterly Press.

Epstein, L., and Kobylka, J. F. 1992. *The Supreme Court and Legal Change: Abortion and the Death Penalty*. Chapel Hill, NC: University of North Carolina Press.

Epstein, L., and Walker, T. G. 2004. *Constitutional Law for a Changing America: Rights, Liberties, and Justice*. 5th ed. Washington, DC: Congressional Quarterly Press.

Frankfurter, F., and Landis, J. M. 1928. *The Business of the Supreme Court*. New York, NY: Macmillan.

Galloway, R. 1989. "Oral Argument in the Court." *Trial* 25: 78–84.

Harlan, J. 1955. "What Part Does the Oral Argument Play in the Conduct of an Appeal." *Cornell Law Quarterly* 41: 6–11.

Herr, D., Haydock, R., and Stempel, J. 1998. "Strategic Use of Motions." *The Trial Lawyer* 21: 211–18.

Hughes, C. E. 1928. *The Supreme Court of the United States; Its Foundation, Methods, and Achievements: An Interpretation*. New York, NY: Columbia University Press.

Jackson, R. H. 1951. "Advocacy before the Supreme Court: Suggestions for Effective Case Presentation." *American Bar Association Journal* 37: 801–4.

Johnson, T. R. 2004. *Oral Arguments and Decision Making on the United States Supreme Court*. Albany, NY: SUNY Press.

Johnson, T. R., Black, R., and Wedeking, J. 2009. "Pardon the Interruption: An Empirical Analysis of Supreme Court Justices' Behavior during Oral Arguments." *Loyola Law Review* 55(2): 331–51.

Johnson, T. R., Spriggs, J. F., and Wahlbeck, P. J. 2007. "Supreme Court Oral Advocacy: Does It affect the Justices' Decisions?" *Washington University Law Review* 85(3): 457–527.

Johnson, T. R., Wahlbeck, P. J., and Spriggs, J. F. 2006. "The Influence of Oral Argumentation before the U.S. Supreme Court." *American Political Science Review* 100(1): 99–113.

Keilitz, S. L., Hanson, R. A., and Daley, H. W. K. 1994. "Civil Motion Practice: Lessons from Four Courts for Judges and Lawyers." *The Judges' Journal* 33(Fall): 3–8.

Linz, D., Penrod, S., and McDonald, E. 1986. "Attorney Communication and Impression Making in the Courtroom: Views from off the Bench." *Law and Human Behavior* 10(4): 281–302.

Nunez, N., Gray, J., and Beck, J. 2012. "Educative Expert Testimony: A One-Two Punch Can Affect Juror's Decisions." *Journal of Applied Social Psychology* 42: 535–59.

Pacelle, R., Jr. 1991. *The Transformation of the Supreme Court's Agenda: From the New Deal to the Reagan Administration*. Boulder, CO: Westview Press.

Posner, R. A. 2013. "Judicial Opinions and Appellate Advocacy in Federal Courts: One Judge's Views." *Duquesne Law Review* 5: 3–39.

Rehnquist, W. H. 1984. "Oral Advocacy: A Disappearing Art." *Mercer Law Review* 34: 1015–28.

Rehnquist, W. H. 1986. "Oral Advocacy." *South Texas Law Review* 27: 289–303.

Rehnquist, W. H. 2001. *The Supreme Court*. New York, NY: Vintage Books.

Roberts, J. G. 2005. "Testimony before the Senate Judiciary Committee." *New York Times Online*. Available at: http://www.nytimes.com/2005/09/13/politics/politicsspecial1/13text-roberts.html.

Scheck B., Neufeld, P., and Dwyer, J. 2000. *Actual Innocence: When Justice Goes Wrong and How to Make It Right*. New York, NY: Signet Press.

Shinall, J. B. 2010. "Slipping away from Justice: The Effect of Attorney Skill on Trial Outcomes." *Vanderbilt Law Review* 63: 267–306.

Shullman, S. L. 2004. "The Illusion of Devil's Advocacy: How the Justices of the Supreme Court Foreshadow their Decisions during Oral Argument." *Journal of Appellate Practice and Process* 6(2): 271–93.

Smith, L. L., Bull, R., and Holliday, R. 2011. "Understanding Juror Perceptions of Forensic Evidence: Investigating the Impact of Case Context on Perceptions of Forensic Evidence Strength." *Journal of Forensic Sciences* 56: 409–14.

Spriggs, J. F., II. and Wahlbeck, P. J. 1997. "Amicus Curiae and the Role of Information at the Supreme Court." *Political Research Quarterly* 50(2): 365–86.

Stern, R. L., Gressman, E., and Shapiro, S. M. 1993. *Supreme Court Practice: For Practice in the Supreme Court of the United States*. 7th ed. Washington DC: Bureau of National Affairs.

Tarr, A. G. 2006. *Judicial Process and Judicial Policymaking*, 5th ed. Farmington Hills, MI: Cengage.

Warren, C. 1922. *The Supreme Court in United States History*. New York, NY: Little, Brown.

Wasby, S. L., Anthony A. D'Amato, and Metrailer, R. 1976. "The Functions of Oral Argument in the U.S. Supreme Court." *Quarterly Journal of Speech* 62: 410–22.

White, B. 1982. "The Work of the Supreme Court: A Nuts and Bolts Description." *New York State Bar Journal* 54: 346–83.

Wrightsman, L. S. 2008. *Oral Arguments before the Supreme Court: An Empirical Approach*. Oxford: Oxford University Press.

PART III

JUDICIAL DECISION-MAKING AND OPINION CONTENT

CHAPTER 10

OPINION WRITING

PAMELA C. CORLEY

LEGAL scholars and law students study court opinions, analyzing the language in an effort to understand the law. Lawyers study the content of court opinions in order to provide legal advice to their clients because it is the legal rule extracted from the rationale of the decision that provides guidance for the future. Thus, it is important to understand the words used, the reasoning employed, and the tests devised by the court. Court *opinions* matter, not just the vote on the merits, and understanding how the opinion-writing process works is essential to understanding the development of the law. This chapter will review the literature on opinion writing, focusing on the U.S. Supreme Court.

Opinion Assignment

After the justices meet in conference to decide who won the case, the chief justice assigns the opinion if he is in the majority vote coalition. If the chief did not vote in the majority, then the senior associate justice in the majority assigns the opinion. In making opinion assignments, the chief justice is somewhat concerned with distributing the workload evenly to make sure that the justices are assigned an equal number of majority opinions each term (Benesh, Sheehan, and Spaeth 1999; Maltzman, Spriggs, and Wahlbeck 2000). This contributes to the Court working efficiently. Research also suggests that chief justices and senior associate justices assign opinions to themselves and to ideologically similar justices in order to influence the content of decisions (Rohde and Spaeth 1976; Segal and Spaeth 2002).

Chief justices are often strategic in their approach to opinion assignment. For example, anecdotal accounts have suggested that Chief Justice Burger—who would normally have cast his vote first in conference—chose to pass in order to see which way his colleagues were going to vote, and then voted to ensure that he was in the majority vote coalition in order to control the opinion assignment (Woodward and Armstrong 1979). Johnson, Spriggs, and Wahlbeck (2005) provided more systematic evidence on this point. Using the conference notes taken by Justice Lewis Powell during his time on the Court, they demonstrated that both chief justices and senior associate justices are more likely to pass when they are unsure about how the other justices will vote. They also found that justices are more likely to pass when the case is more salient. Recent work by Sill, Ura, and Haynie (2010) demonstrated that Chief Justice Burger assigned opinions to more ideologically extreme justices when he passed in the initial conference vote than when he had not passed.

In closely divided cases, opinions may be assigned to "swing justices"—justices who are perceived to hold moderate positions. The conventional wisdom is that assigning the opinion to the least ideologically extreme justice in the majority coalition allows that justice to control the content of the opinion, which keeps that justice from switching to the minority and potentially transforming the minority into the majority. In contrast, a more ideologically extreme justice may write a majority opinion that could cause a swing justice to change his or her vote because the opinion is written in a way that does not reflect the median justice's policy preferences. In addition, a chief justice may choose to assign an opinion to a moderate member of the majority vote coalition because it could result in an opinion that causes some dissenters to join the majority vote coalition. Scholars have found, however, that this conventional wisdom does not appear to be true. For example, Brenner and Spaeth (1988) found that moderate justices are no more likely to keep the original majority coalition together than ideologically extreme members of the majority coalition and in other work, Brenner, Hagle, and Spaeth (1990) provided evidence that dissenters are not more likely to join a majority opinion written by an ideologically moderate justice than a majority opinion written by a less moderate justice.

Are chief justices more concerned about advancing policy goals or furthering administrative efficiency? Maltzman and Wahlbeck (2004) offer persuasive evidence that chiefs pursue policy goals when they can but that they also take into account other goals, such as making sure the Court runs efficiently. They examined the initial opinion assignment sheets from the papers of Chief Justice Earl Warren, Justice William Brennan, and Justice Thurgood Marshall and used them to determine the assignments made by Chief Justices Warren, Burger, and Rehnquist from 1953 to 1990. Taking into account both ideological factors (e.g., the ideological proximity of the chief justice and the opinion writer) and non-ideological factors (e.g., equity, expertise, efficiency), Maltzman and Wahlbeck found that, all things being equal, chiefs are more likely to assign opinions to ideologically similar justices but that they also pursue other goals. Their empirical results led them to conclude: "Far from single-mindedly seeking ideological gains, the chief justice pursues multiple goals through his power of assignment" (Maltzman and Wahlbeck 2004: 561). Other research suggests that chief justices take into account issue area expertise when assigning the majority opinion (Brenner 1984; Brenner and Spaeth 1986).

Law Clerks

Once the opinion assignment has been determined, the majority opinion writer often instructs his or her law clerk to write the first draft of the opinion. The extent of the instruction given to a clerk depends on the individual justice. Some provide minimal input while others lay out the key arguments and cases in outline form. Justices revise clerk-written drafts—again, more or less depending on both the individual justice's level of engagement in the process and the clerk's skill at opinion writing (Ward and Weiden 2006).

Over time, the justices have relied on their clerks more and more in the opinion-writing process. While they originally were most likely to employ a retention model (in which a justice drafts her own opinion and the clerks edit and add citations and footnotes, they are now more likely to employ a delegation model (in which a clerk drafts the first draft of an opinion and then the justice then revises that draft) (Ward and Weiden 2006). Wahlbeck, Spriggs, and Sigelman (2002) examined the role that clerks play in drafting Supreme Court opinions by analyzing the first drafts of opinions written by Lewis F. Powell Jr. and Thurgood Marshall during the 1985 term of the Court. They asked: "To what extent did Powell and Marshall's opinion drafts bear the distinctive marks of their law clerks?" (Wahlbeck, Spriggs, and Sigelman 2002: 168). Even though Powell delegated opinion writing to his clerks, he was known for being very involved in the process, closely supervising his clerks. On the other hand, once Marshall delegated the opinion writing to one of his clerks, he took a hands-off approach, with sources stating that he barely even edited his clerks' work. Utilizing a stylistic analysis program, they detected the clerks' specific styles in the justices' opinions and the clerks' style was most apparent for Marshall's clerks than for Powell's. Although the authors did not address the question of how much influence clerks have on the substance of Supreme Court opinions, they did find "as a precondition … stylistic traces of the drafting clerks … in Powell's and Marshall's opinions" (Wahlbeck, Spriggs, and Sigelman 2002: 183).

A recent law review article examined the text of majority opinions of all Supreme Court justices, specifically constructing a variability measure (V score) for each justice, which allows the authors to determine and compare each justice's writing style (Rosenthal and Yoon 2011). The authors argued that if the V score is low, it suggests that the justice wrote his own opinions and relied less on law clerks. On the other hand, if the V score is high, it suggests that the justice delegated more opinion writing to his law clerks. The study showed that Justices O'Connor and Kennedy had the highest V scores (3.85 and 3.73 respectively) while surprisingly, Justice Marshall's score was 3.33, which suggests that he did not rely on his clerks as much as it was reported (Rosenthal and Yoon 2011: 1320–1). The study also found that the justices' V scores were low from 1900 to 1950 and, since 1950, the scores have steadily increased, indicating that justices are increasingly relying on their clerks to write opinions (Rosenthal and Yoon 2011: 1337).

Regardless of how much influence the clerks have in opinion writing, when the justice is satisfied with the result, the opinion draft is circulated to the other justices via written memoranda. With the opinion drafted and circulated, the process of forming a coalition behind the opinion begins.

Coalition Formation

After the majority opinion author circulates a draft to the other justices, each justice has the following options: (1) join the opinion, which means he agrees with the majority opinion and does not want the opinion writer to make any changes; (2) ask the opinion writer to revise the opinion; (3) write or join a regular concurrence, which is a concurrence agreeing with the result and the content of the opinion; (4) write or join a special concurrence, which is a concurrence that agrees with the result, but does not agree with the reasoning used by the majority opinion writer; or (5) write or join a dissent, which disagrees with both the result and the reasoning used by the majority opinion writer.

Research provides empirical, systematic evidence that the justices play the "collegial game" in an effort to shape the content of opinions (Maltzman et al. 2000). The authors, relying on the available files of Justice William Brennan during the Burger Court, showed that "justices will try to secure opinions that are as close as possible to their policy positions by basing their decisions in part on the positions and actions of their colleagues" (Maltzman et al. 2000: 17). Specifically, they found that justices are more likely to bargain with the majority opinion author if they are either ideologically distant from the author or the majority opinion coalition, if the majority opinion writer had been extremely uncooperative with a justice in the past, and when the majority conference coalition is smaller. "Although justices are motivated by their policy preferences, they also consider the strategic landscape on the Court when deciding how to respond to drafts of majority opinions" (Maltzman et al. 2000: 83).

They also established that the majority opinion author is more likely to accommodate (as measured by the decision to circulate additional drafts) when he is ideologically farther away from those majority conference coalition justices not having joined the opinion or if the nonjoiners are ideologically heterogeneous. Additionally, the results of their analysis showed that the likelihood of the author circulating an additional draft opinion decreases for larger conference majorities, and, once at least a majority of justices have joined the majority opinion, authors are less likely to accommodate.

According to Black, Johnson, and Wedeking (2012), "coalition formation begins at oral argument" (p. 82). They examined the oral argument notes of Justices Powell and Blackmun, analyzing when they listen to their colleagues during oral arguments. They found that justices are more likely to listen to another justice during oral argument depending on how close that justice is ideologically to them. Justice Blackmun noted comments from justices who were ideologically distant from him whereas Justice Powell noted comments from justices who were ideologically close. Additionally, for both justices, they found that as the number of notes about a colleague during oral argument increased, that colleague was less likely to join the majority opinion draft written by that justice (Black, Johnson, and Wedeking 2012: 80). They argue that Justices Powell and Blackmun are "listening to those who may join a coalition in the hopes of persuading them (Powell) or are likely listening to justices with opposing viewpoints to prepare counterarguments (Blackmun). In sum, these findings are consistent with the argument that coalition formation begins at oral argument" (Black, Johnson, and Wedeking 2012: 81–2).

A justice who agrees with the result of the majority opinion, but is not completely satisfied with the reasoning of the opinion may write or join a concurrence. A concurrence that agrees with both the outcome and the reasoning for that outcome as articulated in the majority opinion is known as a regular concurrence, while a concurrence that agrees with the outcome but not the reasoning for that outcome as articulated in the majority opinion is known as a special concurrence. Concurring opinions are important for many reasons. First, a concurrence can transform a majority opinion into a plurality opinion. A plurality opinion is an opinion in which a majority of the justices agree with the outcome (who won or lost), but a majority of the justices do not agree with the reasoning used to reach that result. Plurality opinions are problematic because they do not provide clear guidance for lower courts and are not necessarily viewed as authoritative precedent (Corley et al. 2010). Second, a concurring opinion may undermine the strength of a majority opinion. In fact, scholars have argued that a unanimous decision accompanied by a concurrence speaks with less authority than a single unanimous opinion (see Ray 1990). However, concurring opinions may be viewed more positively, in that they can enhance the majority opinion. Justice Ruth Bader Ginsburg remarked that "the prospect of a ... separate concurring statement pointing out an opinion's inaccuracies and inadequacies strengthens the test; it heightens the opinion writer's incentive to 'get it right' " (Ginsburg 1990: 139). Additionally, the reasoning used in concurring opinions may become the law. A classic example is Justice Harlan's two-pronged "reasonable expectation of privacy" test in *Katz v. United States* (1967), which became the standard way to analyze whether a search occurred under the Fourth Amendment (although the Court has recently started to rely again on a trespass/property rights theory as well). Finally, since the concurring opinion writer does not have to bargain and accommodate with other justices, writing concurrences may be personally satisfying to a justice and may also be more revealing of that justice's preferred preferences.

Proponents of the attitudinal model explain concurrences primarily as a function of policy preferences (see, e.g., Segal and Spaeth 2002):

> Those who join the majority opinion are ideologically closer to the opinion writer than those who write regular concurrences; regular concurrers, in turn, are ideologically closer to the majority opinion writer than special concurrers; and to complete the picture, special concurrers are ideologically closer to the majority opinion writer than are justices who dissent.
>
> (Segal and Spaeth 2002: 386–87)

On the other hand, proponents of the strategic model understand concurring opinions as part of the majority opinion coalition process. For example, Wahlbeck, Spriggs, and Maltzman (1999) found that justices are less likely to author or join a concurrence if the author has cooperated with them in the past.

Analyzing concurrences aids in understanding the opinion-writing process. For example, Maveety, Turner, and Way (2010) argued that concurrences show that judicial policy goals should be thought of as bifurcated: policy in case outcomes, and policy in doctrinal rules. "Winning *and* speaking are possible at the same time: by filing a concurring opinion" (Maveety, Turner, and Way 2010: 630). They analyzed the Burger and Rehnquist Courts' concurring behavior and showed that the Rehnquist Court justices became a more "choral" Court. Specifically, when comparing the Rehnquist Court justices with the Burger Court justices, the Rehnquist Court justices were more likely to join a concurrence, thus "producing a Court chorus of doctrinal rules for policy development" (Maveety, Turner, and Way 2010: 636).

Way and Turner (2006) analyzed concurrences written by the Court during the 1991 and 2001 terms, coding them according to four categories: ground laying, signaling, preserving, and weakening. They found that several institutional factors, including citations to previous cases and the number of justices joining the concurrence, predict the type of concurrence. Corley (2010) also coded concurrences into different categories in an effort to understand why justices write them and what impact they have on the reach of the majority opinion. She used the following typology: expansive; doctrinal; limiting; reluctant; emphatic; and unnecessary. An expansive concurrence attempts to expand the holding or to add to the reasoning of the majority opinion while a doctrinal concurrence offers a different rationale to support the Court's result. A limiting concurrence attempts to limit the reach of the majority opinion, with the justice writing the concurrence arguing that certain parts of the majority's discussion were unnecessary, or arguing that the Court has gone too far in its reasoning or conclusions. In writing a reluctant concurrence, the opinion writer clearly does not want to join the majority's decision, but makes it clear that he feels compelled to, perhaps because of precedent or because of a desire to produce a majority opinion on an important issue. An emphatic concurrence underscores some aspect of the Court's holding, providing clarification of what the majority opinion means. Finally, an unnecessary concurrence is a concurrence in judgment without opinion.

Corley (2010) found that the factors that influence a justice's decision whether to write or join a concurrence are different depending on the type of concurrence. Specifically, she found that a limiting concurrence is more likely to be written or joined if the justice is a former law professor, if the case is complex, or if the case is legally important. A limiting concurrence is less likely if the case involves a minimum winning coalition, if the justices have a cooperative relationship, if the concurring opinion writer is the chief justice, or if the justice writing the concurrence is new to the Court.

An expansive concurrence is more likely when the justice is a former law professor, or if the case is politically or legally salient. An emphatic concurrence is more likely to be written or joined if the case is complex or if the case is politically salient. An emphatic concurrence is less likely when the justices have a cooperative relationship.

A doctrinal concurrence is more likely if the case is complex and less likely if the case involves a minimum winning coalition, if the justice is the chief justice, or if the justices have a cooperative relationship. A reluctant concurrence is less likely if the justice and the majority opinion writer are ideologically compatible.

Finally, a recent study examined the Roberts Court and found that the more concurrences in a precedent-establishing decision (arguably signaling a weakly reasoned precedent), the more likely the Court is to depart from that decision, suggesting a possible motive for the justices to concur in the judgment (Epstein, Landes, and Liptak 2014).

A justice who disagrees with both the outcome and the reasoning of the majority opinion may write or join a dissenting opinion. The senior justice in the minority may write the main dissent in a case or assign it to another justice in the minority coalition. Similar to concurrences, justices writing dissents may find it more personally satisfying than writing majority opinions since they do not have to worry about compromising the language of the dissent. Justice Kagan explained: "Sometimes I feel that when I sit down at my computer and I'm writing the dissent and you just have this feeling like 'now I'm being myself' in a way that maybe you're not when you're writing for the Court" (Kagan 2012). Justice Scalia seemingly agrees with Justice Kagan, stating:

> To be able to write an opinion solely for oneself, without the need to accommodate, to any degree whatever, the more-or-less differing views of one's colleagues; to address precisely the points of law that one considers important and *no others*; to express precisely the degree of quibble, or foreboding, or disbelief, or indignation that one believes the majority's disposition should engender—that is indeed an unparalleled pleasure.
>
> (Scalia 1994: 42)

While dissents are not precedent and therefore do not have the force of law, a dissent may "appeal ... to the intelligence of a future day, when a later decision may possibly correct the error into which the dissenting judge believes the court to have been betrayed" (Ginsburg 1990: 144, quoting Charles Hughes). Thus, justices who write or join a dissent may hope that their position will ultimately become the law. An example of a dissent becoming law is Justice John Paul Stevens' dissent in *Bowers v. Hardwick* (1986), which was cited by Justice Anthony Kennedy in the majority opinion of *Lawrence v. Texas* (2003).

Research shows that justices are more likely to author or join a dissent the further they are ideologically from the majority opinion author (Wahlbeck, Spriggs, and Maltzman 1999). Additionally, the complexity of a case increases a justice's likelihood of dissenting. Finally, the authors found that justices are less likely to author or join a dissent if the majority opinion author has cooperated with them in the past.

On occasion, a justice will change his mind and switch his initial conference vote during the coalition formation stage. Scholars refer to this as voting fluidity (see Howard

1968; Hagle and Spaeth 1991). Sometimes this occurs because a justice is persuaded by the dissent. Justice Alito explained: "It's not a change of position by the opinion-writing judge, but it's a change of position by others on the Court. When you read the majority opinion and you read the dissent, and you say, 'Well, the dissent actually seems to be correct,' and then a vote can change. That does happen" (Smith 2012).

Other times a justice who is assigned to write the majority opinion changes his vote, although that is more rare. When asked how often this happens, Justice Stevens said: "Not very often, but once in a while it does happen. Once every couple of years at the most" (Garner 2010). Justice Scalia remarked that he has switched his vote: "I have not only done that, I have changed my mind after having been assigned to write the majority opinion. I've written the opinion the other way, it just wouldn't write. There is nothing wrong with that" (Wallace 2012).

Empirical research shows that fluidity is not the norm on the Court. During the 1946–55 period, a justice changed his vote from affirm to reverse (or vice versa) 9 percent of the time (Brenner 1980), during the 1956–67 period, 10 percent of the time (Brenner 1982), and during the 1946–75 period, a justice was likely to switch his or her vote from affirm to reverse or from reverse to affirm 7.3 percent of the time (Dorff and Brenner 1992).

Maltzman and Wahlbeck (1996) found strategic considerations play a role in vote fluidity. Specifically, in an examination of the Burger Court, they found that a justice is more likely to switch if they are ideologically close to the writer of the opposing coalition and ideologically distant from the writer of the original coalition opinion. In fact, the probability of a justice changing his vote in that situation is 0.898. However, the other justices who make up the coalition can also substantively affect the content of the opinion because of the bargaining and accommodation that occurs; thus, Maltzman and Wahlbeck hypothesized and found that the closer justices are to the justices in the opposition coalition, and the farther they are from the justices in their own coalition, the more likely they are to switch (the predicted probability of a vote change is 0.033). Finally, they found that a justice is less likely to switch votes if the initial coalition was a minimum winning one. The authors also found that other considerations, such as complexity, influenced whether a justice switched his vote. If the case was easy, the probability of a vote switch was 0.016 versus 0.020 if the case was hard.

The Content of Opinions

There are different theories regarding which justice is the most influential in shaping the content of Supreme Court opinions. According to the "median justice" theory, the median justice is the most influential because he is necessary to obtain and keep a majority (see Martin, Quinn, and Epstein 2005). According to the "opinion author" theory, the majority opinion writer has the most control over the content of the opinion (see Bonneau et al. 2007). Carruba et al. (2012) developed a model that suggests that opinions are likely to reflect the views of the median justice in the majority coalition.

Regardless of which justice has the most influence, almost all Supreme Court opinions cite previously decided cases. Epstein and Knight (1998) analyzed the number of citations to precedent contained in the opinions in a specific Supreme Court case and subsequent cases that followed that decision. In all but three of the twenty-eight opinions, citations to precedent exceeded those to all other sources combined. Lupu and Fowler (2013) demonstrate how strategic interaction between the justices during the Court's bargaining process affects citations to precedent in the Court's opinion. They found that the majority opinion author relies more heavily on precedent when the Court's decision is accompanied by a concurrence, suggesting that "the possibility of having to contend with concurring opinions creates an incentive for him or her to craft the opinion more thoroughly" (Lupu and Fowler 2013: 170). They also showed that as the variance of the justices' ideologies increases, indicating a period of ideological disagreement, the majority opinion is more "embedded" in past precedent.

Research reveals that the Court's opinions are influenced by the party's briefs on the merits (e.g., Corley 2008), amicus curiae briefs (e.g., Epstein and Kobylka 1992; Spriggs and Wahlbeck 1997), oral arguments (e.g., Johnson 2001; 2004), and lower court opinions (e.g., Corley, Collins, and Calvin 2011). Specifically, Corley compared the litigants' briefs with the majority opinions of the Court utilizing plagiarism detection software and found that the percentage of the Court's majority opinions coming from each party's brief is driven by the quality of the brief, the ideological compatibility of the brief's argument with the Court, and the political salience of the case.

With regard to amicus briefs, Epstein and Kobylka (1992) and Spriggs and Wahlbeck (1997) found that the Supreme Court's majority opinions adopt language and legal rules submitted by interest groups. Specifically, Spriggs and Wahlbeck (1997) examined all party briefs on the merits and amicus briefs filed in the 1992 term. They found that the Court's majority opinions often accept arguments found in amicus briefs, using information from 54.2 percent of petitioner amicus briefs and 43.2 percent of respondent amicus briefs. However, the Court is much less likely to adopt arguments from amicus briefs that provide arguments not found in the party briefs. Thus, they concluded that amici influence is based on reiterating party arguments rather than conveying independent information.

Relating to oral arguments, Johnson's (2001) analysis indicates that the Court focuses a major portion of its opinions on issues that are discussed during oral arguments. He found that, in cases without amicus participation, one third of all the majority syllabi points refer to issues raised by the Court *only* during oral arguments, and in cases with amici, 25 percent of syllabi points do so. Thus, he concluded that "oral arguments provide an independent source of information that the justices ultimately use when making substantive decisions" (Johnson 2001: 346).

Corley, Collins, and Calvin (2011) found that the justices systematically incorporate language from lower court opinions into the Court's majority opinions based on their perceptions as to whether the lower court opinions will enhance their ability to make effective law and policy. Utilizing plagiarism detection software, they found that the justices are especially likely to borrow from lower court opinions that are written by prestigious judges. Moreover, the justices are particularly likely to borrow language from published lower court opinions versus unpublished opinions. Finally, they found that Supreme Court majority opinions use more language from lower court majority opinions than separate opinions, in addition to relying more on U.S. Courts of Appeals opinions than U.S. District Court opinions.

Scholars have also examined the language choices that judges make. Hume (2006) investigated whether U.S. Supreme Court justices use opinion content strategically to enhance the legitimacy of case outcomes. Specifically, he focused on rhetorical sources, such as the Federalist Papers, Blackstone's *Commentaries on the Laws of England*, and the writings of Thomas Jefferson and John Locke. He found that justices do cite rhetorical sources with greater frequency when the legitimacy of their decisions is lowest, such as when they are overturning precedents, invalidating laws, or facing opposition from other justices. Hume (2006) also found that opinion writers respond to the use of rhetorical sources by other justices since citations to rhetorical sources were more likely in dissents when majority opinion writers also used them. Corley, Howard, and Nixon (2005) similarly found that the Federalist Papers were cited strategically by the justices. Specifically, they found that a minimum winning coalition vote, formal alterations of precedent, the exercise of judicial review, and dueling citations all led to an increased probability of a citation to the Federalist Papers. Given that there is a heightened need to assert legitimacy to the other justices or to the other institutions of government and the public in these situations, it makes sense to cite an authoritative source such as the Federalist Papers.

Owens, Wedeking, and Wohlfarth (2013) investigated whether justices strategically write more complex opinions to prevent negative review from a politically hostile Congress. They argued that members of Congress face significant time and resource constraints that force them to consider electoral and transactional opportunity costs. Complex opinions increase the costs of congressional review and, accordingly, decrease the likelihood that they will review the decision. They examined the readability of 500 randomly selected Supreme Court majority opinions published between the 1953 and 2009 Court terms and found that as the Court's majority coalition in a case becomes increasingly distant ideologically from the relevant pivot points of Congress, justices craft less readable opinions. Thus, they concluded that the justices have the ability to manipulate the readability of their opinions in order to evade legislative review.

A recent study analyzed the clarity of Supreme Court opinions from 1983 to 2007 (Owens and Wedeking 2011). They measured the cognitive complexity of each opinion using Linguistic Inquiry and Word Count (LIWC), a content-analysis program that examines the words people use. LIWC assigns each word of a text to a defined dimension categorized by independent examiners. They employed ten LIWC indicators connected with cognitive complexity: causation, insight, discrepancy, inhibition, tentativeness, certainty, inclusiveness, exclusiveness, negations, and percentage of words containing six or more letters. They found that certain justices systematically author the clearest opinions, while others tend to write the most complex opinions. Justices Scalia and Brennan consistently wrote the clearest majority opinions while Justice Ginsburg wrote the most complex. They also found that ideology does not predict opinion clarity since conservative and liberal justices were equally likely to author clear opinions. They also found that dissents are more clearly written than majority opinions and that criminal procedure cases are the most clearly written types of cases. Finally, they found that justices write more complex opinions when the size of the majority opinion increases and when the Court alters one of its precedents.

After the process of opinion drafting (and redrafting as part of the bargaining and negotiation process) concludes, the final opinion that secures the support of at least five justices is the majority opinion of the Court. There are some instances in which no one opinion secures a majority of votes from among the justices. For example, six justices may agree as to the appropriate outcome in a case but only four of those six agree as to the rationale. In this case, the opinion agreed to by those four justices is the opinion of the Court but it is a plurality opinion, rather than a majority opinion. Plurality opinions do not occur frequently but they do result in a non-trivial number of the Court's cases. What makes plurality opinions vexing for lower courts trying to discern the dictates of their judicial superior and lawyers trying to provide sound guidance to their clients is that they leave ambiguous what the actual rule of law is. Corley et al. (2010) tested three possible explanations for plurality decisions—a lack of social consensus, "hard" cases, and strategic interactions during opinion writing. They found that the probability of a plurality opinion increases when the Court reviews politically salient and constitutional issues, and when there was dissensus on the lower court, while it decreases when the chief assigns the opinion and when the Court is ideologically heterogeneous.

Whether the opinion of the Court is a majority opinion or a plurality opinion, that opinion represents "the law" as determined by the Supreme Court. While it is true that the opinion of the Court determines who wins and who loses in the instant case, the true import of the opinion lies in the legal precedent set by it.

Although many studies on opinion writing rely on old data because the judicial papers of the justices are unavailable after the 1993 term, there is no reason to believe the modern Court behaves substantially differently from the Burger Court or early Rehnquist Court; thus, these studies are still relevant to understanding the opinion-writing process, from opinion assignment to the content of opinions. Furthermore, given the advances in content analysis software, there continue to be new and creative ways to analyze opinion writing, especially when it comes to the content of opinions. Some areas that remain open to research are coding opinions on a liberal to conservative scale, and coding whether the opinion is written narrowly or broadly.

References

Benesh, S. C., Sheehan, R. S., and Spaeth, H. J. 1999. "Equity in Supreme Court Opinion Assignment." *Jurimetrics* 39(4): 377–89.

Black, R. C., Johnson, T. R., and Wedeking, J. 2012. *Oral Arguments and Coalition Formation on the U.S. Supreme Court: A Deliberate Dialogue*. Ann Arbor, MI: University of Michigan Press.

Bonneau, C. W., Hammond, T. H., Maltzman, F., and Wahlbeck, P. J. 2007. "Agenda Control, the Median Justice, and the Majority Opinion on the U.S. Supreme Court." *American Journal of Political Science* 51(4): 890–905.

Brenner, S. 1980. "Fluidity on the United States Supreme Court: A Reexamination." *American Journal of Political Science* 24: 526–35.

Brenner, S. 1982. "Fluidity on the Supreme Court: 1956–1967." *American Journal of Political Science* 26: 388–90.

Brenner, S. 1984. "Issue Specialization as a Variable in Opinion Assignment on the U.S. Supreme Court." *Journal of Politics* 46(4): 1217–25.

Brenner, S., and Spaeth, H. J. 1986. "Issue Specialization in Majority Opinion Assignment on the Burger Court." *Western Political Quarterly* 39(3): 520–7.

Brenner, S., and Spaeth, H. J. 1988. "Majority Opinion Assignments and the Maintenance of the Original Coalition on the Warren Court." *American Journal of Political Science* 32(1): 72–81.

Brenner, S., Hagle, T., and Spaeth, H. J. 1990. "Increasing the Size of the Minimum Winning Coalitions on the Warren Court." *Polity* 23(2): 309–18.

Carruba, C., Friedman, B., Martin, A. D., and Vanberg, G. 2012. "Who Controls the Content of Supreme Court Opinions?" *American Journal of Political Science* 56(2): 400–12.

Corley, P. C. 2008. "The Supreme Court and Opinion Content: The Influence of Parties' Briefs." *Political Research Quarterly* 61(3): 468–78.

Corley, P. C. 2010. *Concurring Opinion Writing on the U.S. Supreme Court*. Albany, NY: SUNY Press.

Corley, P. C., Sommer, U., Steigerwalt, A., and Ward, A. 2010. "Extreme Dissensus: Explaining Plurality Decisions on the United States Supreme Court." *The Justice System Journal* 31(2): 180–200.

Corley, P. C., Collins, P. M., Jr., and Calvin, B. 2011. "Lower Court Influence on U.S. Supreme Court Opinion Content." *Journal of Politics* 73(1): 31–44.

Corley, P. C., Howard, R. M., and Nixon, D. C. 2005. "The Supreme Court and Opinion Content: The Use of the Federalist Papers." *Political Research Quarterly* 58(2): 329–40.

Dorff, R. H., and Brenner, S. 1992. "Conformity Voting on the United States Supreme Court." *Journal of Politics* 54: 762–75.

Epstein, L., Landes, W. H., and Liptak, A. 2014. "The Decision to Depart (or Not) from Constitutional Precedent: An Empirical Study of the Roberts Court." Unpublished paper prepared for the *NYU Law Review's* symposium, "Testing the Constitution: The Empirics of Constitutional Doctrine."

Epstein, L., and Knight, J. 1998. *The Choices Justices Make*. Washington, DC: Congressional Quarterly Inc.

Epstein, L., and Kobylka, J. F. 1992. *The Supreme Court and Legal Change: Abortion and the Death Penalty*. Chapel Hill, NC: University of North Carolina Press.

Garner, B. A. 2010. "Justice John Paul Stevens." *The Scribes Journal of Legal Writing* 41–50, 42. Available at: http://legaltimes.typepad.com/files/garner-transcripts-1.pdf.

Ginsburg, R. B. 1990. "Remarks on Writing Separately." *Washington Law Review* 65: 133–50.

Hagle, T. M., and Spaeth, H. J. 1991. "Voting Fluidity and the Attitudinal Model of Supreme Court Decision Making." *Western Political Quarterly* 44(1): 119–28.

Howard, J. W., Jr. 1968. "On the Fluidity of Judicial Choice." *American Political Science Review* 62(1): 43–56.

Hume, R. J. 2006. "The Use of Rhetorical Sources by the U.S. Supreme Court." *Law & Society Review* 40(4): 817–43.

Johnson, T. R., Springs, J. F., II, and Wahlbeck, P. J. 2005. "Passing and Strategic Voting on the U.S. Supreme Court." *Law & Society Review* 39(2): 349–78.
Johnson, T. 2001. "Information, Oral Arguments, and Supreme Court Decision Making." *American Politics Research* 29(4): 331–51.
Johnson, T. 2004. *Oral Arguments and Decision Making on the United States Supreme Court.* Charlottesville, VA: University of Virginia Press.
Kagan, E. 2012. "Conversation with Supreme Court Justice Elena Kagan," C-SPAN, September 20. Available at: http://www.c-span.org/video/?308291-1/conversation-supreme-court-justice-elena-kagan.
Lupu, Y., and Fowler, J. H. 2013. "Strategic Citations to Precedent on the U.S. Supreme Court." *Journal of Legal Studies* 42: 151–86.
Maltzman, F., Spriggs, J. F., II, and Wahlbeck, P. J. 2000. *Crafting Law on the Supreme Court: The Collegial Game.* New York, NY: Cambridge University Press.
Maltzman, F., and Wahlbeck, P. J. 2004. "A Conditional Model of Opinion Assignment on the Supreme Court." *Political Research Quarterly* 57(4): 551–63.
Maltzman, F., Wahlbeck, P. J. 1996. "Strategic Policy Considerations and Voting Fluidity on the Burger Court." *American Political Science Review* 90(3): 581–91.
Martin, A. D., Quinn, K. M., and Epstein, L. 2005. "The Median Justice on the U.S. Supreme Court." *North Carolina Law Review* 83(5): 1275–322.
Maveety, N., Turner, C. C., and Way, L. B. 2010. "The Rise of the Choral Court: Use of Concurrence in the Burger and Rehnquist Courts." *Political Research Quarterly* 63(3): 627–39.
Owens, R. J., and Wedeking, J. P. 2011. "Justices and Legal Clarity: Analyzing the Complexity of U.S. Supreme Court Opinions." *Law & Society Review* 45(4): 1027–61.
Owens, R. J., Wedeking, J., and Wohlfath, P. C. 2013. "How the Supreme Court Alters Opinions Language to Evade Congressional Review." *Journal of Law and Courts* 1(1): 35–59.
Ray, L. K. 1990. "The Justices Write Separately: Uses of the Concurrence by the Rehnquist Court." *University of California, Davis Law Review* 23: 777–831.
Rohde, D. W., and Spaeth, H. J. 1976. *Supreme Court Decision Making.* San Francisco, CA: W.H. Freeman.
Rosenthal, J. S., and Yoon, A. H. 2011. "Judicial Ghostwriting: Authorship on the Supreme Court." *Cornell Law Review* 96(6): 1307–44.
Scalia, A. 1994. "The Dissenting Opinion." *Journal of Supreme Court History* 19: 33–44.
Segal, J. A., and Spaeth, H. J. 2002. *The Supreme Court and the Attitudinal Model Revisited.* New York, NY: Cambridge University Press.
Sill, K. L., Ura, J. D., and Haynie, S. L. 2010. "Strategic Passing and Opinion Assignment on the Burger Court." *The Justice System Journal* 31(2): 164–79.
Smith, M. R. 2012. "Alito Says Supreme Court Misunderstood by Media." September 12. Available at: http://www.boston.com/news/local/rhode-island/2002/09/14/alito-says-surpeme-court-misunderstood-media/omnoFr6jnCEhI2cKDMX9I/story.html.
Spriggs, J. F., II, and Wahlbeck, P. J. 1997. "*Amicus Curiae* and the Role of Information at the Supreme Court." *Political Research Quarterly* 50(2): 365–86.
Wahlbeck, P. J., Spriggs, J. F., II, and Sigelman, L. 2002. "Ghostwriters on the Court? A Stylistic Analysis of U.S. Supreme Court Opinion Drafts." *American Politics Research* 30: 166–92.
Wahlbeck, P. J., Spriggs, J. F., II, and Maltzman, F. 1999. "The Politics of Dissents and Concurrences on the U.S. Supreme Court." *American Politics Research* 27(4): 488–514.

Wallace, C. 2012. "Justice Antonin Scalia on Issues Facing SCOTUS and the Country," *Fox News Sunday*, July 29. Available at: http://www.foxnews.com/on-air/fox-news-sunday/2012/07/29/justice-antonin-scalia-issues-facing-scotus-and-country.

Ward, A., and Weiden, D. L. 2006. *Sorcerers' Apprentices: 100 Years of Law Clerks at the United States Supreme Court*. New York, NY: New York University Press.

Way, L. B., and Turner, C. C. 2006. "Disagreement on the Rehnquist Court: The Dynamics of Supreme Court Concurrence." *American Politics Research* 34: 292–318.

Woodward, B., and Armstrong, S. 1979. *The Brethren: Inside the Supreme Court*. New York, NY: Avon Books.

Cases Cited

Bowers v. Hardwick, 478 U.S. 186 (1986).

Katz v. United States, 389 U.S. 347 (1967).

Lawrence v. Texas, 539 U.S. 558 (2003).

CHAPTER 11

VERTICAL *STARE DECISIS*

THOMAS G. HANSFORD

Of the numerous ways in which courts are thought to be different from other policy-making institutions, the purported existence and importance of the norm of *stare decisis* is particularly intriguing. The strongest version of this norm requires that when deciding cases judges follow previously established precedents, i.e., legal rules indicating the relevance of different case facts and setting forth legal tests or consequences that accompany these facts. Even though both judges (Knight and Epstein 1996; Phelps and Gates 1991) and the public (Scheb and Lyons 2001) indicate that precedent is an important factor in judicial decision-making, one of the fascinating aspects of *stare decisis* is that it is simply a norm and thus judges can opt to ignore relevant precedent without clear formal consequences. To the extent that judges are policy-motivated it is puzzling that they would regularly choose to self-impose a constraint on their decisions, even though adherence to precedent might contribute to collective goals such as judicial efficiency (Landes and Posner 1976), predictability (Stevens 1983), clarity (Bueno de Mesquita and Stephenson 2002), compliance (Rasmusen 1994), and legitimacy (Hansford and Spriggs 2006).

There are two types of *stare decisis* that can operate in a judicial hierarchy: horizontal and vertical. The former refers to the following of precedents established by the same court. For instance, horizontal *stare decisis* implies that a three-judge panel deciding a case for a U.S. Court of Appeals should follow precedents established by previous decisions of this court. Vertical *stare decisis*, however, involves a lower court following the precedents set by a higher court and is typically seen as the stronger version of the norm. It could be said that horizontal *stare decisis* makes the following of precedent *desirable* while vertical *stare decisis requires* that the High Court precedent is followed, though there is still a lack of formal sanctioning even in the vertical version.

The purpose of this chapter is to critically assess the current state of the literature on vertical *stare decisis*. I begin with a discussion of how *stare decisis* does, or does not, fit with the principal–agent framework that is often used as a starting point for theories of the relationship between high and low courts. I then assess the various approaches to testing for the existence of vertical *stare decisis* and consider the factors that might condition the strength of this constraint. The punch line here is that there is a good deal of evidence that is consistent with the claim that High Court precedent constrains lower court decision-making, though this evidence is not as conclusive as it might first appear. There is also ambiguity regarding the precise causal mechanism at work. This chapter then considers recent scholarship focused on the potential for bottom-up influences on the operation of precedent in a judicial hierarchy.

As should be implied by the preceding, the scope of this chapter is limited and will not consider several important, thriving areas of research on *stare decisis* and precedent. The focus on vertical *stare decisis* means that influential studies of the effect of precedent on U.S. Supreme Court decision-making (e.g., Bailey and Maltzman 2011; Bartels 2009; Richards and Kritzer 2002; Spaeth and Segal 1999) will receive little attention. It will also become quickly clear that the studies discussed here almost exclusively examine U.S. federal courts, though many of the conclusions drawn likely apply to state courts too. Finally, as discussed in more detail later, this chapter addresses vertical *stare decisis*, which is not the same thing as the purely preference-driven principal–agent model employed in many studies of judicial hierarchy (e.g., Haire, Songer, and Lindquist 2003; Owens and Black 2012; Randazzo 2008).

Stare Decisis and the Principal–Agent Model

By definition, vertical *stare decisis* can only exist in a judicial hierarchy and scholars typically approach such hierarchies from the principal–agent perspective (e.g., Beim, Hirsch, and Kastellec 2014; Carrubba and Clark 2012; Haire, Songer, and Lindquist 2003; Lax 2012; Songer, Segal, and Cameron 1994; Westerland et al. 2010). It is thus instructive to consider how precedent fits into existing principal–agent theories of judicial hierarchies. Though there are key differences in the specific models that have been advanced, all principal–agent models assume that the High Court (i.e., the principal) has the ultimate policy-making authority but effectively delegates much of this authority to lower courts (i.e., the agents) as they are the first, and often only, courts to resolve new legal disputes. The High Court monitors these decisions and reverses them when it desires, though this monitoring is imperfect due to the information asymmetry between a lower court deciding a case and the High Court for which this case is but one of hundreds or thousands of cases that could be reviewed. Lower court preferences can differ from those of the High Court, which means that imperfectly monitored lower courts may decide cases in a way that conflicts with the policy or preferences of their judicial principal.[1]

Many of the specific models of hierarchy developed or tested do not actually incorporate vertical *stare decisis*, however. Instead, these models consider whether lower courts decide cases in a manner consistent with the High Court's *current preferences* over legal/policy outcomes (e.g., Haire, Songer, and Lindquist 2003; Klein 2002; Owens and Black

2012; Randazzo 2008). The High Court monitors the lower courts and reverses decisions that deviate from its preferences. If these judicial agents dislike being reversed then they avoid reversals by falling in line with the High Court's preferences. To be clear, vertical *stare decisis* is not a component of this subset of principal–agent models, as lower courts are guided by the current preferences, not the precedent, of the High Court.

Other principal–agent-inspired studies of judicial hierarchies implicitly incorporate vertical *stare decisis* and test the extent to which lower courts follow High Court precedent (e.g., Baum 1980; Songer, Segal, and Cameron 1994; Songer and Sheehan 1990). But studies in this vein struggle to specify exactly why lower courts follow High Court precedent. If lower courts only follow High Court precedent when the current High Court is supportive of the precedent, then it is High Court preferences, not precedent, that really matter (Westerland et al. 2010). On the other hand, why would lower courts follow a High Court precedent that is no longer compatible with High Court preferences? For vertical *stare decisis* to exist in a meaningful sense, lower courts must be swayed by High Court precedent absent any influence of current High Court preferences. The nature of the mechanism that would cause this type of preference-free precedential influence has yet to be nailed down, a topic to which I return later.

In sum, researchers usually view the operation of judicial hierarchies through the principal–agent lens and the preference-driven versions of these models imply the non-existence of the venerated, and purportedly strong, norm of vertical *stare decisis*. The models that assume or test the effect of High Court precedent on lower court decision-making have yet to clearly identify why policy-motivated judges would be constrained by High Court precedent that runs contrary to both their preferences and those of the High Court.

Evidence for the Existence of Vertical *Stare Decisis*

Setting aside for now theoretical concerns about either the uncomfortable relationship between *stare decisis* and principal–agent models or the causal mechanism leading High Court precedent to act as an independent constraint on lower court decision-making, I now turn to empirical efforts to test the presence of this constraint. Each approach conceptualizes the operation of precedent somewhat differently, though all the approaches generally yield results implying that lower courts are to some degree constrained by High Court precedent.[2]

Changes in the Direction of Lower Court Decisions

If High Court precedent governs lower court behavior, then the establishment of a new precedent could lead to changes in the directionality of lower court decisions. The first wave of studies examining the relationship between High Court decisions and lower court behavior adopts this approach. Typically, these studies examine the effect of a single Supreme Court decision (or very limited set of decisions) on the ideological direction of subsequent lower court decisions in the relevant issue area. For example, Songer and Haire (1992) find that the *Miller v. California* (1973) decision increased the probability of appeals courts deciding obscenity cases in a conservative manner. Songer and Sheehan (1990) find a similar sort of effect for libel decisions in wake of *New York Times v. Sullivan* (1964), though there is less evidence for the impact of *Miranda v. Arizona* (1966) on appeals court decisions regarding self-incrimination.[3]

These are often referred to as compliance studies and it could be the case that the compliance in question is with the relevant Supreme Court precedent; an interpretation supportive of the existence of vertical *stare decisis*. But, it is also possible that the directionality of lower court decisions immediately following a Supreme Court decision is more a function of the signaled ideological location of the contemporary Court on the particular legal issue. This approach cannot rule out the very real possibility that lower courts are responding to information about the Court's ideological location more so than the precedent, per se. This latter interpretation is more consistent with preference-based hierarchical control than precedent-based *stare decisis*.

Consistent Use of Case Facts

Any given precedent can be viewed as identifying the set of relevant case facts for deciding a legal dispute and attaching a consequence to these facts. If a precedent indicates that the presence of fact *X* ought to lead to (or increase the probability of) outcome *Y* and in subsequent lower court decisions there is a positive correlation between the presence of *X* and outcome *Y*, then this might be taken as evidence of the lower courts following High Court precedent.[4] This is the approach adopted by Songer, Segal, and Cameron's (1994) influential study of Supreme Court control of the U.S. Courts of Appeal in which they find that search and seizure decisions made by appeals courts are similarly influenced by the case facts that predict Supreme Court decisions in this issue area.[5]

This result is consistent with the claim that lower courts follow High Court precedent, but it is far from conclusive due to the issue of behavioral equivalence. After all, the attitudinal model also points to the importance of case facts in judicial decision-making (Segal and Spaeth 2002). For instance, case facts indicating the intrusiveness of the search will influence the decisions of purely preference-motivated judges. Thus, evidence that lower court judges use the same case facts as Supreme Court justices do when deciding a certain type of case does not necessarily indicate any sort of precedent-based constraint.

More recently, scholars have sought to discriminate between precedent-driven and preference-driven use of case facts by employing what is termed the jurisprudential regimes approach (Richards and Kritzer 2002).[6] This approach involves testing whether landmark precedents alter the relevance and impact of different case facts in the determination of subsequent court decisions. Luse et al. (2009), for example, assess the importance of case facts indicated as relevant by the *Lemon v. Kurtzman* (1971) precedent for Establishment Clause decisions in the appeals courts. While they find evidence that *Lemon*-relevant case facts are significant predictors of post-*Lemon* appeals court decisions, they do not test whether these case facts also predicted appeals court outcomes before the *Lemon* decision. Again, this raises the question of whether similar usage of case facts might simply result from case facts indicating the location of the case on a policy dimension.

Constraining Ideological Decision-Making

Perhaps a more compelling way to conceive of the effect of High Court precedent is as a constraint on the influence of the policy preferences of lower court judges on their decisions. Scholars can then test whether the existence of governing High Court precedent conditions the effect of judicial ideology on decision-making in lower courts. The advantage to this approach is that it both avoids the behavioral equivalence problem of case-fact-based studies and clearly models precedent as a constraint. The issue with this approach, however, is that it is difficult for the researcher to reliably determine whether a relevant precedent exists or not. There is a risk to relying on a lower court opinion as a guide to whether there is relevant precedent or if the case is one of first impression. Judges avoiding a precedent are unlikely to broadcast this fact. There is also the oft-noted possibility that relevant precedents are heterogeneous to the point where judges are relatively unconstrained. Lindquist and Cross (2005), for instance, find that precedent might decrease the importance of judicial ideology but more precedent actually leads to less constraint.

Perhaps owing to the difficulty in systematically determining the degree to which precedent ought to constrain judicial preferences in specific cases, outside of the Lindquist and Cross (2005) study there have not been many efforts to directly test this conditioning effect of precedent. McKenzie's (2012) study of legislative redistricting decisions is one of the few recent exceptions, as he finds that clearer Supreme Court precedents reduce the importance of the partisan leanings of district court judges deciding subsequent cases in this particularly political issue area.[7] Here, precedential clarity is coded based on a largely subjective assessment of the relative precision of Supreme Court precedent in one person, one vote cases (more clear) and Voting Rights Act cases (less clear). Alternatively, researchers can employ computational linguistics methods to assess the certainty (Corley and Wedeking 2014) or complexity (Owens and Wedeking 2011) of the language of the precedent establishing majority opinions.

Other studies reveal patterns of results that are circumstantially consistent with the claim that precedent diminishes the effect of judicial ideology. For instance, judicial preferences matter more as you move up the U.S. judicial hierarchy (Epstein, Landes, and Posner 2013; Zorn and Bowie 2010), which is compatible with the claim that precedent might bind more as you move down. There is also evidence that appeals court decisions producing opinions that focus primarily on law tend to exhibit less ideological influence than decisions that focus on facts (Smith 2014). This pattern is not direct evidence of *stare decisis*, but is compatible with it.

Lower Court Treatment of High Court Precedent

The above approaches all treat the direction of the lower court decisions as a dependent variable that might be explained, one way or the other, by High Court precedent. Court opinions regularly reference precedent and often do so in a manner indicative of whether the court is relying or building on a precedent to reach an outcome, or instead circumventing a precedent by distinguishing it or otherwise indicating its inapplicability. These explicit treatments of precedent offer an alternative window into how precedent might shape judicial decision-making and serve as the dependent variable in numerous studies of judicial hierarchy, particularly ones interested in the role of precedent (Corley 2009; Johnson 1979; Kassow, Songer, and Fix 2012; Landes and Posner 1976; Westerland et al. 2010).

While many of these studies focus on the conditions that increase the prevalence of positive or negative uses of High Court precedent, there is evidence that lower courts generally follow Supreme Court precedent. Songer and Sheehan (1990), for instance, show that appeals courts largely followed the *Miranda* and *New York Times* precedents.[8] A more comprehensive examination of lower federal court usage of Supreme Court precedent reveals that lower courts typically treat these precedents positively, as opposed to negatively (Hansford and Spriggs 2006). Over time, however, the balance of lower court treatment of a precedent does even out with positive and negative treatments occurring at approximately the same frequency once a precedent is more than twenty years old (Hansford and Spriggs 2006: 117).

Again, though, this evidence should be approached with a degree of skepticism owing to two issues. First, it is possible that lower court judges are more reluctant to note in their opinions that they are circumventing a Supreme Court precedent than they are to claim that they are following a precedent. It could also be the case that lower courts are quicker to cite and apparently follow High Court precedents that allow for greater discretion. Precedents that dictate specific outcomes, on the other hand, might be avoided. Either pattern of behavior could pose a problem for citation or treatment-based measures of precedential constraint. Second, lower court treatment of precedent might be conditioned by the extent to which this precedent represents the contemporary preferences of the Court and thus is more indicative of preference-based deference than anything truly driven by precedent (Westerland et al. 2010).

It could be fruitful for future research to attempt to identify situations in which a lower court follows a Supreme Court precedent with which both the lower court and current Supreme Court might disagree. These could be viewed as instances in which a Court precedent is actually constraining the lower court. Such situations could be further probed by examining whether the explicit following of precedent corresponds with decisions of a direction disfavored by both the lower court and Supreme Court. For instance, if conservative lower court judges follow a liberal Supreme Court precedent and reach a liberal outcome while the current median justice is relatively conservative, this would seem to be precedent-based constraint. Alternatively, do lower courts "follow" ideologically distant precedents but still reach outcomes predicted by the preferences of the judges? This would indicate either disingenuous usage of precedent or that the policy consequences of the precedent have drifted or are unintended (see Hansford, Spriggs, and Stenger 2013).

Furthermore, it might be illuminating to study precedent in a court system in which a lower court is expected to follow High Court precedent but is not subject to reversal by that court. Of course, this is not the case in the U.S. federal court system, nor is it the case in most judicial hierarchies. Interestingly, though, the California state court system mandates vertical *stare decisis* without the threat of reversal by the precedent-setting High Court. Specifically, all the superior courts (i.e., trial courts) in California are supposed to follow the precedent set by any California appeals court, regardless of whether the superior court is within the geographic area covered by the appeals court.[9] Thus, superior courts are expected to follow the precedents set by courts that cannot reverse them. To the extent that superior courts outside of a circuit follow precedent set by that circuit's appeals court, this could be considered evidence of true vertical *stare decisis*.

Regardless of the specific court system under analysis, research using references to precedent as indications of the use of precedent might benefit from recent advances in computational text analysis. These modern tools could be used to better assess the degree to which a lower court case is similar (based on the text of the opinions) to a precedent-setting High Court case and thus ought to be using the precedent. Sentiment analysis could also provide an alternative, formalized measure of how lower court opinions use or treat High Court precedent.

The Conditionality of Constraint?

While not dispositive, the studies discussed above point towards the general conclusion that lower courts often follow or are otherwise influenced by High Court precedent, which in turn supports the existence of vertical *stare decisis*. As I have emphasized, however, alternative, preference-based explanations have not been ruled out. Given that any apparent precedent-based influence is not uniform, the next logical step for the literature has been to examine the conditions that amplify or minimize the extent of this influence or constraint. Much of the evidence of the conditionality of the relationship between Supreme Court precedent and lower court decision-making implies that it could be preferences, not *stare decisis* per se, that actually drive lower court usage of precedent. For example, one widely hypothesized predictor of lower court use of High Court precedent is the extent to which the precedent is compatible with the policy preferences of the judges on the lower court (e.g., Kassow, Songer, and Fix 2012). Obviously, though, precedent treatment driven by the preferences of the lower courts is hardly compatible with vertical *stare decisis*. In this section, I consider three other sets of variables that might condition the constraining effect of precedent.[10]

Number of Relevant Precedents

Judges note that there are often a number of competing precedents that could be used to help decide a case or justify an outcome (e.g., Posner 2008: 45; Wald 1995). The extent to which any one High Court precedent constrains lower court decision-making should thus depend upon whether it is *the* precedent on the specific legal issue at hand or one of several possibly relevant precedents that each might point towards different decisions. Ironically, this implies that the more precedent a High Court has generated the less constraint this body of precedent will impose upon lower courts, assuming that there is some heterogeneity in these precedents. Lindquist and Cross (2005) test this implication and find that the more precedent that exists in a specific issue area, the less constrained the decisions of appeals court judges. This result suggests that particularly consistent or singular precedent can act as a meaningful constraint on judicial behavior.

The Precedent-Setting Case

Researchers contend that there are a number of characteristics of the precedent-setting case that might influence subsequent usage of the precedent. Most of these characteristics can be considered indicators of clarity or certainty of the precedent, or commitment to the precedent by the precedent-setters. The typical argument is that the clearer the precedent and the greater the level of High Court commitment to the precedent, the more that lower courts will be constrained by the precedent. There is evidence, for example, that plurality opinions of the Supreme Court are less likely to be followed by appeals courts than those established by majorities (Corley 2009). A recent, innovative study by Corley and Wedeking (2014) uses modern linguistic software to directly measure the certainty of the language in Supreme Court opinions and finds that linguistic certainty increases the positive usage of the precedent by the appeals courts, though Staton and Vanberg (2008) point out that a High Court might deliberately be vague when it expects noncompliance. Whether the precedent establishes a rule or a standard might also contribute to clarity and thus constraint on lower courts, but this choice could again be endogenous to the anticipated behavior of lower courts (Jacobi and Tiller 2007).

Beyond these endogeneity concerns, it is not at all clear that Supreme Court commitment to a precedent at the time it is established is a conditioning factor that implies the operation of vertical *stare decisis*. Lower courts could simply be responding to the anticipated probability of being reviewed and reversed by a preference-driven Supreme Court. Similarly, the importance of opinion clarity could be consistent with either preference- or precedent-based lower court compliance.

Subsequent High Court Support for the Precedent

The posture of the High Court towards one of its existing precedents also affects how lower courts use the precedent. The more that the Supreme Court treats a precedent positively (i.e., by following the precedent) instead of negatively (e.g., by limiting or distinguishing the precedent), the more that lower federal courts (Hansford and Spriggs 2006) and state courts (Kassow, Songer, and Fix 2012) will follow the precedent. The clearest expression of disapproval of a precedent occurs when the Supreme Court formally overrules a precedent, and these overrules cause appeals courts to quickly cease any reliance on the precedent (Benesh and Reddick 2002).[11]

Supreme Court treatments of precedent are explicit indications of how the Court views one of its existing precedents. It is also conceivable that lower courts attempt to anticipate the Court's as of yet unexpressed orientation towards one of its precedents and adjust their decisions accordingly.[12] To test this possibility, Westerland et al. (2010) model lower court treatment of Supreme Court precedent as a function of the ideological distance between the contemporary Court and the precedent and find support for this relationship. This result implies that lower courts are more concerned with the current Court's preferences than the directives of an existing precedent. This raises a puzzle—if the initial precedent has little to no bite, then why does the Supreme Court's expressed orientation towards it matter? Why would the Court bother treating an existing precedent by, for example, limiting or overruling it?

The Mechanism Underlying *Stare Decisis*

The research discussed above reveals that lower courts use and are possibly constrained by High Court precedent, but the inconclusiveness of the evidence on the second point and the conditionality of any precedent influence point towards some uncertainty regarding the influence of true vertical *stare decisis*. Which raises the theoretical question, why would a judge follow a precedent that leads to an outcome less-preferred by the judge? Put differently, to the extent that precedent actually operates as a constraint on judicial decision-making, what is the causal mechanism for this constraint? Numerous mechanisms have been posited and they can be roughly categorized as sincere and instrumental.

There are two variants of the sincere mechanism. First, some scholars argue that in addition to any policy goals that judges may have they also pursue legal goals (see Baum 1998; Klein 2002), which include adherence to precedent (Cross 2005). There is a potential tension here, though, since the more that a judge values law and legal precedent, the more this judge might want to shape precedent instead of simply following it. Posner (2008) points out that the more a precedent-minded judge binds herself to existing case law, the less consequential her decisions will be for the development of legal doctrine. There is also something inherently circular and unsatisfying in the argument that judges follow precedent because it is what they want to do.

The second variant of the sincere mechanism is that precedent-oriented behavior is not a goal but is instead part of a judge's fundamental conception of what they do on the bench. This could be a termed a role-theoretic mechanism or it could be said that "adhering to precedents created by a higher court is one of the rules of the judicial 'game' that judges internalize" (Posner 2008: 45). Whether, how, and when this deference to precedent becomes internalized is unclear, however, and likely warrants further exploration.

Many researchers assume that judges do not sincerely prefer to be constrained but instead act as if constrained for instrumental reasons. There are four main instrumental explanations for *stare decisis* or *stare decisis*-like behavior, the first of which is that it is more efficient to follow precedent than to treat each case as one of first impression (Posner 2008). Judicial efficiency could be viewed as a collective goal or as an individual-level motivation. Posner (1995), for example, argues that by following precedent a judge can maximize her leisure time.

Another way of conceptualizing efficiency as a motivation for *stare decisis* is to draw the parallel between *stare decisis* and incrementalism in policy-making (Shapiro 1965). The theory of incrementalism contends that cognitive limitations make it impractical to regularly make wholly *de novo* policy decisions and thus the starting point for any policy at time t is the policy at $t-1$. It is important to point out, though, that if *stare decisis* is simply a form of policy incrementalism then this undercuts the supposed uniqueness of this norm and implies that policy making in the courts is akin to budgeting or other types of policy-making. Typical conceptions of *stare decisis* imply that it must be more than just incrementalism at work.[13]

A second type of instrumental explanation for the existence of *stare decisis* contends that adherence to precedent increases the ultimate impact that court decisions will have. This can be due to increases in intrajudicial compliance owing to the precedent-induced legal clarity (Bueno de Mesquita and Stephenson 2002) or reciprocity (Rasmusen 1994). Alternatively, judges concerned with the ultimate influence that their decisions have could adhere to precedent in order to maximize the perceived legitimacy of their decisions or their court (Hansford and Spriggs 2006; Knight and Epstein 1996). The public expects courts to base their decisions on precedent, not preferences, and thus might be more inclined to view courts and their decisions as legitimate when it appears that *stare decisis* is operative.[14] There are potential issues with this mechanism, though. The appearance of adhering to precedent is not the same thing as a judge being truly constrained by precedent. Furthermore, to the extent that the concern is with the legitimacy of the institution, as compared to specific decisions, a collective action problem exists in which there is a common good (judicial legitimacy) but any one decision matters little in terms of the extent to which this common good is realized. Meanwhile, there is the individually incurred cost of following precedent when the judge would prefer not to.

A third instrumental mechanism might be particularly relevant for vertical *stare decisis*. It could be the case that lower courts follow High Court precedent because to do otherwise would increase the likelihood of review and reversal by the High Court. For High Court precedent to exert independent influence, however, the threat of reversal would need to be tied to use of precedent about which the High Court is indifferent or even displeased. There is little evidence of this type of High Court behavior. In addition, it is not clear that lower court judges are generally all that concerned with reversal by a higher court (Cross 2005; Klein 2002; Luse et al. 2009; cf. Randazzo 2008).

A fourth, related mechanism involves the connection between precedent and the individual reputations and career aspirations of judges (Epstein and Knight 2013). Miceli and Cosgel (1994), for example, theorize that for reputational reasons judges will avoid deviating from precedent if that precedent is valued by other judges. If, however, the precedent is not valued then there is a reputational incentive to deviate from the precedent.[15] This latter behavior is clearly not consistent with *stare decisis*. Furthermore, to the extent that reputational concerns lead to the former behavior it cannot truly be said that this is *stare decisis* in action. The reputation-motivated judge is only following a precedent because of the preferences of others regarding this precedent.

In sum, there are theoretical issues with each of these proposed mechanisms that might drive *stare decisis*. Empirical work has not yet sorted this out either, in part because it is even more difficult to identify the mechanism than it is to establish the degree to which precedent acts as a constraint on behavior.

Reversing the Causal Arrow

All the work discussed thus far emphasizes the top-down nature of judicial hierarchies and focuses on the extent to which High Court precedent, in combination with or independent of High Court preferences, constrains the decisions made by lower courts. The traditional conception of vertical *stare decisis*, after all, implies that precedent and precedent-induced influence is a one-way street. Recent research, however, investigates the possibility that there could be a meaningful bottom-up component to the operation of judicial hierarchies, thus implying a more interesting informational or strategic relationship between High Court, lower court, and the use of precedent.

It could be the case, for instance, that a High Court takes into account whether lower courts will follow a particular precedent when deciding whether to establish the precedent in the first place (Jacobi and Tiller 2007; Lax 2012). To the extent that this occurs, then it is anticipated lower court behavior that is driving precedent creation, instead of the reverse, traditional relationship. This is not just an interesting theoretical insight; it also implies that tests for the presence of precedent-influenced behavior in the lower courts could suffer from a form of endogeneity that might bias results in the direction of overstating the existence of vertical *stare decisis*.

Other recent studies argue that a High Court can learn from lower court decisions and thus there is an important bottom-up informational component to judicial hierarchies that has consequences for precedent. A High Court can learn from lower court conflict in a specific legal issue area (Clark and Kastellec 2013) or use the language found in lower court opinions to help craft precedent-setting opinions (Corley, Collins, and Calvin 2011). Hansford, Spriggs, and Stenger (2013) theorize that the type of lower court judges using a precedent can inform the High Court about the current policy consequences of the precedent. The High Court will then take this information into account when deciding whether to curtail the reach of the precedent. Their empirical analysis supports the claim that information about precedent moves up the judicial hierarchy.

Finally, Hansford and Spriggs (2014) investigate usage of landmark Supreme Court precedents in all levels of U.S. federal courts in an effort to assess whether attention to these precedents is dictated by the Court (i.e., a top-down model of attention to precedent) or by a bottom-up process in which lower court judges, perhaps spurred by litigants, drive attention to precedent.[16] The preliminary results reveal that while the Supreme Court may exert some top-down control of the federal judicial agenda, there is at least as much evidence of lower courts, district courts in particular, playing an important role in influencing attention to precedent at the Court. Thus, while a good deal of research demonstrates that the Supreme Court may have some top-down control over *how* the lower courts decide cases, it appears that attention to precedent can flow upward in the judicial hierarchy.

Conclusion

The principle of *stare decisis* is thought to be one of the core features of the American judicial system and a primary determinant of case outcomes. From either a normative or positive perspective, the vertical form of *stare decisis* should be the strongest version of this foundational norm as lower courts ought to be guided by the directives of higher courts. Research on the operation of precedent in the U.S. court system has produced a substantial body of knowledge about how the hierarchical nature of this system influences the decisions made by the different levels of court. Many questions regarding vertical *stare decisis* largely still remain, however. These include very basic ones, such as to what extent does High Court precedent systematically constrain lower court decision-making in a manner that is independent of current High Court preferences? As I have discussed at length in this chapter, there exists a great deal of evidence consistent with the predictions derived from *stare decisis* models. But, the inability to rule out reasonable alternative explanations for these patterns in the data leaves the existence of genuine precedent-based constraint an open question. The precise mechanism that causes any such constraint is also still largely unknown, as is whether such a mechanism is truly consistent with precedent-induced constraint.

As scholars seek to more conclusively identify the presence and determinants of vertical, precedent-based influences on lower court decisions, they will need to keep in mind recent research indicating that various decision-making influences may flow both up and down a judicial hierarchy. Of course, allowing for the possibility of a bottom-up component to the operation of precedent will only further complicate efforts to identify precedent effects, which already face several challenges. Nonetheless, developing a fuller understanding of the dynamic operation of precedent in a judicial hierarchy would represent a particularly important advance in the literature on courts.

Notes

1. An application of the principal–agent model to elected state courts may need to add a second principal: the voters. Voters may have a preference for the following of precedent in the abstract (Scheb and Lyons 2001), though it is likely that voters would also prefer that unpopular precedents be ignored. Interestingly, Comparato and McClurg (2007) find that more evidence for the influence of Supreme Court precedent in non-elected state supreme courts (c.f., Kassow, Songer, and Fix 2012).
2. Unfortunately, some of the more compelling approaches used to examine horizontal *stare decisis* at the Supreme Court are inapplicable in the context of vertical constraint. Spaeth and Segal (1999) use a powerful and innovative research design to test whether the justices are constrained by precedent when they vote on the merits. They compare the votes cast by justices in landmark cases with those cast by the same justices in subsequent progeny cases and find that dissenters in the landmark cases rarely switch to the majority position. Because lower-court judges do not cast votes in precedent-setting cases, this approach cannot be used to examine vertical *stare decisis.* Bailey and Maltzman (2011) utilize the positions taken by members of Congress to identify what preference-based decision-making looks like in a given Supreme Court case, thus allowing them to estimate the effect of legal factors such as precedent. Members of Congress will not publicize positions on enough lower federal court cases to make this approach useful for estimating vertical precedent-based constraint.
3. Cross (2005) essentially employs a roughly similar version of this approach by using the lagged median of the Supreme Court as an indicator of the overall location of its existing precedent and finds that lagged Court preferences predict appeals court decisions.
4. This approach was first applied in efforts to assess whether Supreme Court decisions are influenced by existing Court precedent (see George and Epstein 1992; Segal 1984).
5. Comparato and McClurg (2007) use a similar approach while examining whether state supreme courts adhere to U.S. Supreme Court precedent.
6. Lax and Rader (2010) question the existence of meaningful jurisprudential regimes at the Supreme Court.
7. Focusing on horizontal *stare decisis* at the Supreme Court, Bartels (2009) uses an analogous approach and examines whether the level of scrutiny dictated by a precedent conditions the importance of ideology in determining decisions.
8. Though they use somewhat different terminology, Kilwein and Brisbin's (1997) study of state supreme court adoption of the heightened scrutiny standard suggests that these lower courts largely followed Supreme Court precedent.

9. See *Cuccia v. Superior Court*, 153 Cal. App. 4th 347, 353–4 (2007); *Auto Equity Sales, Inc. v. Superior Court*, 57 Cal. 2d 450, 455 (1962).
10. Though it does not cleanly fit into one of the three types of variable discussed below, it should be noted that the age of a precedent might affect its applicability to current disputes and thus condition the degree to which it constrains judges (Landes and Posner 1976).
11. Brent (1999) provides evidence that appeals courts also respond to whether Congress is supportive or hostile towards a precedent when deciding cases that could be governed by the precedent.
12. Consistent with this argument, Kastellec (2011) suggests that ideological or partisan diversity on a panel might make the panel more attentive to precedent when that precedent is supported by the entire circuit or the Supreme Court.
13. A related justification for the existence of *stare decisis* is that judges value legal stability and predictability (Posner 2008; Stevens 1983). Or, put somewhat differently, the norm of *stare decisis* causes case law to evolve relatively slowly, since *stare decisis* makes legal innovations more costly (Fernandez and Ponzetto 2012).
14. Survey data indicates that Americans want courts to base decisions on precedent (Scheb and Lyons 2001). There is less evidence that adherence to precedent is a particularly important determinant of how particular decisions are viewed (Nicholson and Hansford 2014; Zink, Spriggs, and Scott 2009).
15. Levy (2005) similarly contends that an ambitious judge will try to make a name for herself through legal innovation instead of adherence to precedent.
16. Other studies of agenda-setting in a judicial hierarchy focus on attention to issues, not precedents (Hurwitz 2006; Peters 2007; Rice n.d.).

References

Bailey, M. A., and Maltzman, F. 2011. *The Constrained Court: Law, Politics, and the Decisions Justices Make*. Princeton, NJ: Princeton University Press.

Bartels, B. L. 2009. "The Constraining Capacity of Legal Doctrine on the U.S. Supreme Court." *American Political Science Review* 103(3):474–95.

Baum, L. 1980. "Response of Federal District Judges to Court of Appeals Policies: An Exploration." *Western Political Quarterly* 33(2):217–24.

Baum, L. 1998. *The Puzzle of Judicial Behavior*. Ann Arbor, MI: University of Michigan Press.

Beim, D., Hirsch, A. V., and Kastellec, J. P. 2014. "Whistleblowing and Compliance in a Judicial Hierarchy." *American Journal of Political Science* 58(4): 904–18.

Benesh, S. C., and Reddick, M. 2002. "Overruled: An Event History Analysis of Lower Court Reaction to Supreme Court Alteration of Precedent." *Journal of Politics* 64(2): 534–50.

Brent, J. 1999. "An Agent and Two Principals: U.S. Courts of Appeals Responses to *Employment Division, Department of Human Resources v. Smith* and the Religious Freedom Restoration Act." *American Politics Quarterly* 27: 236–66.

Bueno de Mesquita, E., and Stephenson, M. 2002. "Informative Precedent and Intrajudicial Communication." *American Political Science Review* 96: 755–66.

Carrubba, C. J., and Clark, T. S. 2012. "Rule Creation in a Political Hierarchy." *American Political Science Review* 106(3): 622–43.

Clark, T. S., and Kastellec, J. P. 2013. "The Supreme Court and Percolation in the Lower Courts: An Optimal Stopping Model." *Journal of Politics* 75(1): 150–68.

Comparato, S. A., and McClurg, S. D. 2007. "A Neo-Institutional Explanation of State Supreme Court Responses in Search and Seizure Cases." *American Politics Research* 35(5): 726–54.

Corley, P. C. 2009. "Uncertain Precedent: Circuit Court Responses to Supreme Court Plurality Opinions." *American Politics Research* 37(1): 30–49.

Corley, P. C., Collins, P. M., Jr., and Calvin, B. 2011. "Lower Court Influence on U.S. Supreme Court Opinion Content." *Journal of Politics* 73(1): 31–44.

Corley, P. C., and Wedeking, J. 2014. "The (Dis)Advantage of Certainty: The Importance of Certainty in Language." *Law & Society Review* 48: 35–62.

Cross, F. B. 2005. "Appellate Court Adherence to Precedent." *Journal of Empirical Legal Studies* 2: 369–405.

Epstein, L., and Knight, J. 2013. "Reconsidering Judicial Preferences." *Annual Review of Political Science* 16: 11–31.

Epstein, L., Landes, W. M., and Posner, R. A. 2013. *The Behavior of Federal Judges: A Theoretical and Empirical Study of Rational Choice*. Cambridge, MA: Harvard University Press.

Fernandez, P. A., and Ponzetto, G. A. M. 2012. "Stare Decisis: Rhetoric and Substance." *Journal of Law, Economics & Organization* 28(2): 313–36.

George, T. E., and Epstein, L. 1992. "On the Nature of Supreme Court Decision Making." *American Political Science Review* 86: 323–37.

Haire, S. B., Songer, D. R., and Lindquist, S. 2003. "Appellate Court Supervision in the Federal Judiciary: A Hierarchical Perspective." *Law & Society Review* 37(1): 143–68.

Hansford, T. G., and Spriggs, J. F., II. 2006. *The Politics of Precedent on the U.S. Supreme Court*. Princeton, NJ: Princeton University Press.

Hansford, T. G., and Spriggs, J. F., II. 2014. "Attention to Precedent in a Judicial Hierarchy." Paper presented at the Annual Meeting of the Southern Political Science Association, New Orleans, LA.

Hansford, T. G., Spriggs, J. F., II., and Stenger, A. 2013. "The Information Dynamics of Vertical *Stare Decisis*." *Journal of Politics* 75(4): 894–906.

Hurwitz, M. 2006. "Institutional Arrangements and the Dynamics of Agenda Formation in the U.S. Supreme Court and Courts of Appeals." *Law & Policy* 28(3): 321–44.

Jacobi, T., and Tiller, E. H. 2007. "Legal Doctrine and Political Control." *Journal of Law, Economics & Organization* 23(2): 326–45.

Johnson, C. A. 1979. "Lower Court Reactions to Supreme Court Decisions: A Quantitative Examination." *American Journal of Political Science* 23: 792–804.

Kassow, B., Songer, D. R., and Fix, M. P. 2012. "The Influence of Precedent on State Supreme Courts." *Political Research Quarterly* 65(2): 372–84.

Kastellec, J. P. 2011. "Hierarchical and Collegial Politics on the U.S. Courts of Appeals." *Journal of Politics* 73(2): 345–61.

Kilwein, J. C., and Brisbin, R. A., Jr. 1997. "Policy Convergence in a Federal Judicial System: The Application of Intensified Scrutiny Doctrines by State Supreme Courts." *American Journal of Political Science* 41: 122–48.

Klein, D. E. 2002. *Making Law in the United States Courts of Appeals*. New York, NY: Cambridge University Press.

Knight, J., and Epstein, L. 1996. "The Norm of *Stare Decisis*." *American Journal of Political Science* 40: 1018–35.

Landes, W. M., and Posner, R. A. 1976. "Legal Precedent: A Theoretical and Empirical Analysis." *Journal of Law & Economics* 19: 249–307.

Lax, J. R. 2012. "Political Constraints on Legal Doctrine: How Hierarchy Shapes the Law." *Journal of Politics* 74(3): 765–81.

Lax, J. R., and Rader, K. T. 2010. "Legal Constraints on Supreme Court Decision Making: Do Jurisprudential Regimes Exist?" *Journal of Politics* 72(2): 273–84.

Levy, G. 2005. "Careerist Judges and the Appeals Process." *The RAND Journal of Economics* 36(2): 275–97.

Lindquist, S. A., and Cross, F. B. 2005. "Empirically Testing Dworkin's Chain Novel Theory: Studying the Path of Precedent." *New York University Law Review* 80: 1156–206.

Luse, J. K., McGovern, G., Martinek, W. L., and Benesh, S. C. 2009. "Such Inferior Courts ... Compliance by Circuits with Jurisprudential Regimes." *American Politics Research* 37(1): 75–106.

McKenzie, M. J. 2012. "The Influence of Partisanship, Ideology, and the Law on Redistricting Decisions in Federal Courts." *Political Research Quarterly* 65: 799–813.

Miceli, T. J., and Cosgel, M. M. 1994. "Reputation and Judicial Decision-Making." *Journal of Economic Behavior and Organization* 23: 31-51.

Nicholson, S. P., and Hansford, T. G. 2014. "Partisans in Robes: Party Cues and Public Acceptance of Supreme Court Decisions." *American Journal of Political Science* 58(3): 620–36.

Owens, R. C., and Black, R. J. 2012. "Consider the Source (and the Message): Supreme Court Justices and Strategic Audits of Lower Court Decisions." *Political Research Quarterly* 65(2): 385–95.

Owens, R. J., and Wedeking, J. P. 2011. "Justices and Legal Clarity: Analyzing the Complexity of Supreme Court Opinions." *Law & Society Review* 45(4): 1027–61.

Peters, C. S. 2007. "Getting Attention: The Effect of Legal Mobilization on the U.S. Supreme Court's Attention to Issues." *Political Research Quarterly* 60: 561–72.

Phelps, G. A., and Gates, J. B. 1991. "The Myth of Jurisprudence: Interpretive Theory in the Constitutional Opinions of Justices Rehnquist and Brennan." *Santa Clara Law Review* 31: 567–96.

Posner, R. A. 1995. *Overcoming Law*. Cambridge, MA: Harvard University Press.

Posner, R. A. 2008. *How Judges Think*. Cambridge, MA: Harvard University Press.

Randazzo, K. A. 2008. "Strategic Anticipation and the Hierarchy of Justice in U.S. District Courts." *American Politics Research* 36(5): 669–93.

Rasmusen, E. 1994. "Judicial Legitimacy as a Repeated Game." *Journal of Law, Economics & Organization* 10: 63–83.

Rice, D. 2014. "The Impact of Supreme Court Activity on the Judicial Agenda: Calling to Action or Settling of the Law." *Law & Society Review* 48(1): 63–90.

Richards, M. J., and Kritzer, H. M. 2002. "Jurisprudential Regimes in Supreme Court Decision Making." *American Political Science Review* 96(2): 305–20.

Scheb, J. M., and Lyons, W. 2001. "Judicial Behavior and Public Opinion: Popular Expectations Regarding the Factors that Influence Supreme Court Decisions." *Political Behavior* 23: 181–94.

Segal, J. A. 1984. "Predicting Supreme Court Decisions Probabilistically: The Search and Seizure Cases, 1962–1981." *American Political Science Review* 78: 891–900.

Segal, J. A., and Spaeth, H. J. 2002. *The Supreme Court and the Attitudinal Model Revisited*. New York, NY: Cambridge University Press.

Shapiro, M. 1965. "Stability and Change in Judicial Decision-Making: Incrementalism or *Stare Decisis*?" *Law in Transition Quarterly* 2: 134–57.

Smith, J. L. 2014. "Law, Fact, and the Threat of Reversal from Above." *American Politics Research* 42(2): 226–56.

Songer, D. R., and Haire, S. 1992. "Integrating Alternative Approaches to the Study of Judicial Voting: Obscenity Cases in the U.S. Courts of Appeals." *American Journal of Political Science* 36: 963–82.

Songer, D. R., Segal, J. A., and Cameron, C. M. 1994. "The Hierarchy of Justice: Testing a Principal–Agent Model of Supreme Court–Circuit Court Interactions." *American Journal of Political Science* 38: 673–96.

Songer, D. R., and Sheehan, R. S. 1990. "Supreme Court Impact on Compliance and Outcomes: Miranda and *New York Times* in the United States Courts of Appeals." *Western Political Quarterly* 43: 297–316.

Spaeth, H. J., and Segal, J. A. 1999. *Majority Rule or Minority Will*. New York, NY: Cambridge University Press.

Staton, J. K., and Vanberg, G. 2008. "The Value of Vagueness: Delegation, Defiance, and Judicial Opinions." *American Journal of Political Science* 52: 504–19.

Stevens, J. P. 1983. "The Life Span of a Judge-made Rule." *New York University Law Review* 58: 1–21.

Wald, P. M. 1995. "The Rhetoric and the Results of Rhetoric: Judicial Writings." *University of Chicago Law Review* 62: 1371–419.

Westerland, C., Segal, J. A., Epstein, L., Cameron, C. M., and Comparato, S. 2010. "Strategic Defiance and Compliance in the U.S. Courts of Appeals." *American Journal of Political Science* 54(4): 891–905.

Zink, J. R., Spriggs, J. F., II, and Scott, J. T. 2009. "Courting the Public: The Influence of Decision Attributes on Individuals' Views of Court Opinions." *Journal of Politics* 71(3): 909–25.

Zorn, C., and Bowie, J. B. 2010. "Ideological Influences on Decision Making in the Federal Judicial Hierarchy: An Empirical Assessment." *Journal of Politics* 72(4): 1212–21.

CHAPTER 12

LAW IN JUDICIAL DECISION-MAKING

DAVID KLEIN

DOES the law play a role in judges' decisions? Quite often, yes. The amount of intellectual effort that has gone into generating that answer to that question would likely stun and dismay most outsiders. After all, law is what judges do, isn't it? Would intelligent people spend thousands of hours trying to determine whether religion plays a role in clerics' actions or whether senators are influenced by politics? Perhaps not, but it would be a mistake to think that the scholars responsible for that tremendous effort undertook it mindlessly. Their actions can be explained by two important facts. First, the stakes involved in the question of law's influence are high. Second, the role of law turns out to be not nearly as straightforward nor as easily demonstrated as one might first think.

That said, it is hard to deny that there is something fundamentally unsatisfying about the state of our understanding, and there seems to be a widespread feeling in the law and courts community that we have reached a point of rapidly diminishing returns in our study of this issue. In the remainder of this chapter, I will review how we reached this point, consider reasons for dissatisfaction with the current state of things, and offer suggestions for moving forward.

Before proceeding, it is important to note that most examples in the chapter will reflect the fact that empirical research on the law's influence has focused overwhelmingly on U.S. courts. I do not mean to imply that the question is any less important in other countries or in the context of international law, and most of the ideas in the chapter should readily transfer to other settings.

CONTEXT AND MOTIVATIONS

Virtually all knowledgeable observers today would agree that judging is not simply a matter of applying readily ascertained legal rules to individual cases; in many cases judges must exercise independent judgment that is inevitably shaped by their personalities, experiences, and worldviews. In fact, this basic truth has been recognized by thoughtful lawyers and judges for many years (Tamanaha 2010). But widespread recognition of the truth does not entirely prevent lawyers and, especially, judges from pretending otherwise when it suits them.

The pretense that judicial decision-making can be accomplished purely through value-free analysis of legal materials often appears in judicial confirmation battles, where presidents and senators purport to care only about nominees' character and "judicial philosophy," not their ideology. Worse yet, the nominees typically join the charade. The most notorious recent example is John Roberts' opening-statement analogy: "Judges are like umpires. Umpires don't make the rules; they apply them."[1] Another example, Elena Kagan's statement that, "My politics would be, must be, have to be, completely separate from my judgment," (Burek 2010) and her reluctance to share her policy views with the Judiciary Committee, seemed especially egregious in light of her criticisms of Ruth Bader Ginsburg and Stephen Breyer for the same kind of behavior (Kagan 1995).

While most visible in confirmation hearings, self-serving statements about the degree to which judges are constrained by law abound in judicial opinions as well. This is very troubling, not only because it is unseemly for people entrusted with enormous responsibility to deceive those who entrust them with it, but because it allows judges to dodge responsibility for the policy decisions they make ("The law made me do it!").

The ascendance of the "attitudinal model" of judicial decision-making (and its cousin the "strategic model") among researchers in the second half of the twentieth century can be understood as a reaction against this kind of judicial prevarication. Researchers, many of them political scientists, seemed to feel that the best antidote to judicial attempts to fool the public was a mountain of rigorous evidence demonstrating that ideology plays a crucial role—or, to use the terms more commonly employed in legal circles, that politics trumps law—in judges' decisions, not only at the U.S. Supreme Court (e.g., Segal and Spaeth 1993, 2002), but in other courts in the United States and around the world.

The effort that has gone into locating evidence that law matters to judges' decisions must be understood in the context of this mountain of evidence pointing in the other direction. Many scholars, even some with considerable sympathy for the attitudinalists' project and methods (e.g., Baum 1997; Posner 2008) have been concerned that the corrective has gone too far—that a picture of judging in which decisions are driven by little more than personal moral and policy views and in which the most important variable in determining a case outcome is the identity of the judge(s) deciding it, is distorted and misleading.

There are a number of reasons to think this even in light of all the evidence of ideology's effects. For one thing, the picture is a bad match for what lawyers and judges, even at their most self-aware and sincere, seem to think they are doing (Dworkin 1986; Gillman 2001). It is one thing to believe that they are willing to delude others (or even themselves) on occasion, another to imagine that they inhabit a fantasy world. Furthermore, correspondence between judges' ideologies and votes is not conclusive proof that their decisions are driven by ideology. It is at least conceivable that liberal and conservative judges gravitate toward different approaches to the law independently of the specific policies they prefer and that honest application of these approaches tends to produce decisions in line with their policy preferences. Perhaps most importantly, even if personal attitudes dominate judges' decisions in some cases, law still could have a controlling influence in others.

Empirical Studies of Law's Influence

These objections to purely attitudinal accounts of judging have struck many scholars as compelling. However, believing that law is important to judges' decisions is not the same as showing it, and demonstrating the influence of law has turned out to be quite difficult. Consider the most direct possible test: identify the legally best answer to a question in a case and see whether judges choose that answer even when it is inconsistent with their personal preferences. The first problem this approach runs into is the very one that has fueled so many doubts about law's influence over the years—that in many cases, especially the most interesting ones, there is no obviously best answer. Even when it is reasonable to think one answer is clearly better than another, the researcher must find a valid, reliable method of identifying it, most likely involving multiple expert and unbiased coders. Although this approach has been employed with some success (e.g., Gilbert 2011), the difficulties involved have kept it from playing a major role in the debate over law's influence.

Other approaches being less direct, their inferences are more open to question, and the evidence frequently points in more than one direction. For instance, a few scholars have undertaken the intensive coding needed to determine whether judges' choices of interpretive methods, such as originalism, are at all independent of their policy leanings (Phelps and Gates 1990; Gates and Phelps 1996; Howard and Segal 2002; Benesh and Czarnezki 2009). The studies, which have focused primarily on the U.S. Supreme Court (Benesh and Czarnezki 2009 is the exception), have yielded very little evidence that choice of method drives case outcomes rather than the other way around.

On the other hand, studies of precedent have uncovered substantial evidence of law's influence, especially, though not solely, in studies of trial and intermediate appellate courts. This proviso requires some elaboration before the overview can continue. The most famous exposition of the attitudinal model, in Segal and Spaeth (1993, 2002), was always directed foremost at the U.S. Supreme Court. Several special features of that court combine to attenuate the impact of law and enhance the impact of ideology. The justices, like other federal judges but few state court judges, serve for life (impeachment being extremely unlikely) and so can consult their own preferences in making decisions without fear of losing their jobs. They, like many state Supreme Court judges but unlike lower court judges, can choose which cases to hear, eliminating most of the cases that present straightforward legal questions where most lawyers would agree on the answer.

And they, like state supreme court justices in some, but not all, cases, cannot have their decisions reversed by a higher court. Thus, there is reason to think that ideology will play an especially large role, and law an especially small one, at the Supreme Court.

Empirical evidence accords with logical expectations. For instance, Pinello (1999) in a large meta-analysis, found that ideology is a better predictor of votes at the U.S. Supreme Court than at state courts or lower federal courts. Zorn and Bowie (2010) demonstrated that case selection is not entirely responsible for this effect by tracing cases that made their way all the way through the federal judicial system to the Supreme Court. Even in this subset of cases, ideology was a stronger predictor of votes at the Supreme Court level than at district or circuit courts. Although neither study directly assesses the impact of law, it seems reasonable to assume that law fills at least some of the space left by ideology's diminished influence.

More direct evidence of law's impact on lower court decisions comes from studies of how lower courts respond to precedents from higher courts. Studies have consistently shown lower court movement in response to changes in higher court doctrines (e.g., Gruhl 1980; Johnson 1987; Songer and Haire 1992; Benesh and Reddick 2002). Larger-scale studies have revealed that lower court decisions typically track ideological trends in higher courts fairly well (e.g., Songer, Segal, and Cameron 1994; Rowland and Carp 1996) and that positive treatment of precedents by the Supreme Court increases the probability of positive treatment by lower courts even controlling for lower court ideology (Hansford and Spriggs 2006; Westerland et al. 2010).

Returning to the Supreme Court, the best known study of precedent there points in the other direction. Spaeth and Segal (1999) asked how justices treated opinions from which they had dissented when those opinions appeared before them later as relevant precedents. Would they put aside their objections and respect *stare decisis* or reject the ruling they disagreed with even though it was now the law? While it was not unheard of for justices to accept the force of an opinion they disliked, and some justices did it quite often, they far more often refused to accede.

While the Spaeth and Segal study cast serious doubt on the influence of *stare decisis*, it nevertheless demonstrated that it exerts some force, even in those instances where it is least likely to—that is, where a justice has directly considered and previously rejected a ruling. Studies coming at precedent from different angles have contributed additional evidence that precedent matters.

Hansford and Spriggs (2006), for example, found that the "vitality" of precedent, important to federal district and circuit judges, also counts with the justices themselves: they are more likely to accord positive treatment to precedents that have previously been treated positively by the Court. Bailey and Maltzman (2011), employing highly sophisticated measures of justices' ideologies and the ideological implications of the cases before them, tested whether justices were responsive to precedents in cases where those precedents were seriously contested. They found that the precedents exerted significant effects on the decisions of some, though not all, justices.

Other studies of precedent have begun by recognizing that precedent can operate subtly and indirectly, not so much directing judges to a particular answer as guiding them to think about problems in certain ways or to give more or less weight to certain considerations. Richards and Kritzer's (2002; Kritzer and Richards 2003) analyses of legal "regimes" centered on key cases that shifted doctrine in major areas of constitutional law. The authors found that the effects of various case factors on justices' votes changed in the ways suggested by those key cases, indicating that justices allowed precedent to shape the way they approached cases.

Even the subtle method of Richards and Kritzer requires a researcher to make judgments about the content of the law in order to determine whether judges are responding to it. Bartels (2009) largely avoided this difficulty in his study of First Amendment decision-making, though at the expense of requiring a greater inferential leap. He assessed the role of ideology in justices' decisions before and after a key decision establishing that "content-based" restrictions on speech, unlike "content-neutral" restrictions, should be subjected to strict scrutiny. Because strict scrutiny reduces judges' discretion, application of it should attenuate the influence of ideology. Bartels' finding that ideology did not predict voting as well in cases involving content-based restrictions suggests that justices take the law in this area seriously.

If willing to take an even less direct approach, one can look for evidence of law's effect in the influence of other actors on judges. For instance, consider the exceptional litigation success of the Solicitor General's office (Black and Owens 2012) and other highly experienced Supreme Court lawyers (McGuire 1993), success that cannot be explained entirely by the strategic (or lucky) choice of positions that the justices already favor. A highly plausible explanation of this success is that the justices take these lawyers' arguments more seriously than other lawyers', whether because greater experience and skill yields superior arguments or because they earn the justices respect and trust over time.

Recent studies in this spirit include Lindquist and Klein (2006) and Collins (2008). Lindquist and Klein, investigating legal issues that had divided lower courts, found that the Supreme Court was more likely to choose the position supported by a larger number of circuits and by more highly regarded circuit judges. Collins, analyzing all cases with identifiable liberal and conservative positions, found that justices were more likely to vote in favor of the position supported by more amicus curiae briefs. These findings, like those on lawyer success rates, could conceivably be explained in attitudinal terms: the justices might find their arguments convincing on policy, rather than legal grounds. But this reading is implausible for precisely the reason policy attitudes play such an important role at the Supreme Court—because they are typically so strong and easily accessible in the cases the justices hear. Especially as all of these studies controlled for justices' ideology, among other things, it seems more reasonable to view the findings as evidence that the justices are moved by legal reasoning.[2]

A common theme running through recent studies of the Supreme Court is that the law is likely to have a greater influence in some cases than in others. This is especially apparent in studies comparing unanimous with non-unanimous decisions (Edelman, Klein, and Lindquist 2012; Epstein, Landes, and Posner 2012; Corley, Steigerwalt, and Ward 2013) and decisions following oral argument with summary decisions (Masood and Songer 2013). Orally argued cases that result in divided votes tend to get the most attention from scholars. These studies together suggest that we would see more of a balance of law and attitudes at the Supreme Court if we did not restrict our attention in this way. At the same time that they do not come close to showing that law's influence at the Supreme Court is constant or pervasive.

Obstacles to Further Progress

This modesty in claims is typical of scholarship on law's effects. I suspect that the authors of all the studies cited above would agree that there are many cases, especially but not solely at the Supreme Court, where the law plays little or no role in judges' decisions.

But perhaps this concedes too much. Perhaps we would find more evidence of the law's influence if we knew better where and how to look. Scholars who incline toward this view might point out that even the more subtle approaches described above take a stunted view of law. Take a judge who, despite her reservations about the purpose of a particular statute, works hard to make the ruling that best serves that purpose. Or what of the judge who, despite his discomfort with a particular governmental practice, sustains it in light of a long tradition of acceptance by the community? Both judges would have excellent claims to be deciding according to the law, but how would this show up in the kinds of studies I have been describing?

When we reflect on the sources of law—texts, norms, even ideas—it is easy to see how empirical studies of readily observable behavior, like votes, could fail to capture some effects of law. Our best chances to see the full extent of law's influence on judges is through intensive examinations of the reasons judges offer and the considerations they point to in their opinions and comparisons of these with reasons and considerations found in legal sources at the time (e.g., Gillman 1993; Cushman 1998; Kahn 1999). Unfortunately, even such studies have only a limited capacity to change the larger picture. For one thing, they are so labor-intensive that even the most ambitious can cast light on only a small area of judicial decision-making. More importantly, they run into two fundamental problems that bedevil all empirical research on judges' behavior.

The first of these is immediately apparent to anyone who ventures into the territory of legal theory: there is no consensus or even-near consensus as to what law is. Everyone can agree that the typical statute, constitution, or administrative rule counts as law. But do all enactments that occur through accepted procedures deserve to be called "law"? What about those passed by morally repugnant regimes like Nazi Germany? Or what about statutes that are inconsistent with a constitution or administrative rules that are inconsistent with statutes? On the other side, what else besides enactments should count as law? Presumably past decisions by courts often should, but what about community norms, principles of fairness, moral rules? Scholars have struggled mightily to answer these questions. Consider just the immense body of scholarship inspired by Hart's *The Concept of Law* (1961), itself by no means the first major attempt to define law. As hard as it can be to say definitively what the law requires in a given case, the task becomes impossible if we cannot even agree on what constitutes law.

The second inescapable problem is behavioral equivalence—the fact that individual actions and even whole patterns of judicial behavior can often be explained equally well in either attitudinal or legal terms, however one defines law. Take, for example, Justice's Brennan's insistence that the death penalty was unconstitutional in any circumstances. Is that stance better explained by his aversion to the death penalty or by a sincere belief, independent of his views on capital punishment, that the Constitution is centrally concerned with protecting human dignity? Reasonable people will disagree not only about the answer but about how to reach an answer. Note that this problem cuts in both directions: sometimes what we take to be ideological consistency might really be driven by legal reasons, and sometimes ostensibly legal considerations mask the attitudinal considerations that are really driving the decision. But the important point for this essay is that behavioral equivalence limits our ability to draw confident inferences about the importance of law even where claims of its importance are highly plausible.

This overview of research progress and prospects is not entirely discouraging. Although attitudinalism's corrective to self-serving judicial claims once threatened to leave us with a permanently distorted picture of decision-making, concerted efforts to gauge law's importance have brought greater balance, persuading even some skeptics (e.g., Epstein and Knight 2013) that in building models of decision-making we should take seriously judges' claims to care about doing right by the law. Moreover, we have deepened our understanding of how the effects of law and attitudes vary across courts and across types of cases.

Nevertheless, frustration is common among scholars working in or interested in this area. One reason for dissatisfaction is that the conclusions I just described seem to differ little from what people's intuitions would have told them in the first place. Of course, intuitions are faulty, as social scientists often feel compelled to point out, and they are not entitled to much respect unless backed up by rigorous evidence. Furthermore, as noted earlier, these intuitions have been challenged at times from two directions, by practitioners claiming that judges can routinely disregard personal values entirely in reaching decisions and by scholars claiming that they almost never can (or at least almost never do). Still, it is hard to maintain that the payoff in terms of knowledge is sufficient reward for the immense effort that has gone into acquiring it.

But I suspect that there is an even more important reason for dissatisfaction, a reason that also explains why the question of law's influence has attracted such attention—namely, that we have made little progress on the tremendously consequential normative question underlying the main empirical (and theoretical) questions. Consider debates in legal theory over the status of moral principles. Why are Ronald Dworkin (1978, 1986) and his supporters not content simply to say that deciding cases sometimes requires judges to rely on broad moral principles; why insist that reliance on certain moral principles—when properly done—should be understood as a form of legal reasoning, the principles themselves being sources of law? Why has so much ink been spilled attacking, defending, or refining these claims?

There are probably a number of reasons, but one of them undoubtedly is the same reason that judges so often are moved to insist that their decisions are driven by law: a belief that decisions based on the law are—and are seen as—more proper, more entitled to respect, more legitimate than decisions that are not.

For most people, whether or not they are academics and/or members of the legal community, law is special. Most believe that a command's status as law adds an additional moral reason to whatever other reasons one might have to obey it. If, as Fuller (1958) argued against Hart, Nazi statutes were not in fact laws, then the moral (though not the practical) calculus for citizens of Nazi regimes was much easier—they had no moral reasons to obey statutes or regulations that were even slightly unjust. But if those statutes or regulations did have a valid claim to the title of "law," then moral reasons for obeying the law in general would have to be weighed against the moral reasons for disobeying these specific laws.

Judges' professional obligations vis-à-vis their governments are not quite the same as their obligations as citizens. Still, law's status has obvious implications for their behavior. Thus, the Hart–Fuller debate about Nazi law repeatedly returns to the question of how a judge in a Nazi regime should act, and issues of judicial decision-making are frequently at or near the heart of writings in legal theory. More broadly, the role of "judge" is almost universally understood to entail some specific obligations with respect to law. Almost all of us would agree at least that judges are obligated to take law seriously and that judges who willfully disregard the law to reach decisions they prefer will often deserve our opprobrium.

Empirical scholars may shy away from addressing normative questions directly and may be committed to minimizing the influence their normative positions have on their analyses. But there is no reason to think that their personal criteria for evaluating judicial performance differ systematically from the criteria of other informed observers. Furthermore, it seems highly likely that what draws most empirical scholars to the study of judicial decision-making in the first place is an intense interest in the quality and legitimacy of that decision-making. And so it is natural that they would think about how empirical evidence can be brought to bear in evaluating judicial decision-making and that in doing so they would focus on the role of law.

As we have seen, however, assessing the role of law is a maddeningly difficult enterprise. Here, then, is what I take to be the other major source of frustration at the state of our knowledge and the obstacles to further progress. If all we can say is that law is often important to judges' decisions, we are not in a position to make (or enable others to make) meaningful appraisals of their performance.

A New Direction

Closer inspection reveals some grounds for optimism. For it turns out that we have not always been careful to distinguish the motivating question—to what extent judges act appropriately in deciding cases—from the empirical question—to what extent judges base their decisions on law. This would not be a mistake if appropriateness depended entirely on adherence to the law. But despite vast efforts by many scholars to define law so that the set of "legal" grounds available for decision exactly coincides with the set of grounds on which judges can validly rest a decision, several decades of debate have not yielded anything approaching a consensus that they are right. Nor is it easy to imagine consensus emerging in the future, for the disagreement goes to the level of basic premises. One can agree that judges are obligated to respect the law when it speaks clearly, while denying—as it seems a great many scholars, lawyers, and judges do—that judges who bring in considerations from outside the law in hard cases are necessarily acting inappropriately.

Consider a judge in a difficult contract dispute who asks what fairness would seem to require, a judge who looks to considerations of justice in choosing a criminal sentence, or a judge deciding a novel intellectual property issue who asks which decision is likely to bring greater benefits to society in the long run. While anyone could imagine disagreeing with exactly how the judges worked through or weighted those considerations, only some people would rule the considerations strictly out of bounds. Many others would agree that there are at least some circumstances in which those judges could be seen as acting properly. Now, one could maintain that judges are acting properly in those circumstances precisely because the grounds relied on actually constitute law in those circumstances. But at least for purposes of evaluating judicial decisions, this seems unnecessary and confusing.[3]

In my view, renewed progress is most likely to come if scholars begin by recognizing a) that the fundamental normative concern motivating many empirical studies is whether judges are relying on appropriate considerations in making their decisions, and b) that the set of appropriate considerations is not exhausted by what are commonly understood as legal considerations. This approach would not entail putting the question of law's influence entirely to one side; it would simply treat that question as one among several. Nor would it necessarily bring rapid advances in our understanding; interesting questions about judicial behavior just aren't easy to answer. But it holds considerably more promise of real gains than a continued focus on law does. How might this approach proceed?

Among theorists who agree with Dworkin and like-minded scholars that judicial decision-making cannot be confined to sources that are uncontroversially legal in nature but balk at their attempts to stretch the definition of law to include considerations of moral or political theory, two responses are most common. One, associated with Hart and his followers, is to distinguish sharply between cases where ordinary legal materials provide significant guidance and cases where they do not, with judges having broad discretion to act as they see fit in the latter. The disadvantage of this approach for our purposes is obvious: it provides little help in evaluating judges' decisions in difficult cases. The other response is to go Dworkin one better and deny that there is such a thing as distinctively "legal" reasoning (e.g., Alexander and Sherwin 2008). This approach does not deny that traditional legal materials do and should often play an important role in judge's decisions, but it does not assign them any special status. Legal decision-making is simply a form of practical reason, employing the same techniques and materials that one finds in other forms of practical reason.

It would be a mistake to think that proponents of this view must throw up their hands and treat all judicial decisions as equally sound. In fact, they often take great pains to point out that some reasons and some lines of argument will be much stronger than others even under this approach (e.g., Posner 2003, 2013). Nevertheless, I think the approach ultimately does risk sacrificing something important. To see why, consider Posner's criticism of Justice Scalia's decisions in *McDonald v. City of Chicago*[4] and *Arizona v. United States*[5] (Posner 2013: 217–19).

Both cases involved the subordination of states to the federal government. In *Arizona*, Scalia argued against the preemption of state laws directed at illegal immigrants, supporting his position with, in Posner's characterization, a "passionate paean to states' rights" (p. 219). Yet in *McDonald*, Scalia joined the majority in extending the reach of the Second Amendment to state laws, seriously restricting their power to regulate handguns. Posner concludes the discussion this way: "I don't understand how Scalia's votes in these two cases can be reconciled on any grounds other than his personal values—a liking for guns … and an intense dislike of illegal immigrants" (p. 219).

This last line does not read as mere disagreement with Scalia's reasoning; one gets the impression that Posner is taking Scalia to task for failing to perform his job properly. Even if Posner did not intend this, readers who accept his interpretation are likely to feel that way. The dominant response elicited by the discussion is not that Scalia reasoned poorly, but that he acted badly—that while his arguments might or might not deserve criticism, he as a judge does.

Imagine instead that Scalia had decided both cases for the state and local governments and had done so on the grounds that democracy is better served by maintaining strong state and local governments, which tend to be more responsive to constituents and less dangerous than the federal government. Doubtless many people would consider this an inadequate reason for decision, and some might go so far as to call it inappropriate. But few would be inclined to react as strongly as if they believed his decisions were based on animus toward a particular group.

The first key intuition here is that some reasons strike us, not only as weaker than others, but as less proper. Of course, this can hold true for decision-making in many spheres. A legislator or even an ordinary citizen would probably be open to greater criticism for basing a position on animus than on a principled distinction between levels of government. But it is not hard to think of examples where judges are held to a different standard. Consider taking a position because it is favored by one's political party or by many of one's neighbors. For a legislator to act on either of those reasons would hardly raise an eyebrow. A judge who did so would invite harsh censure. The second key intuition, then, is that the appropriateness of different considerations is bound up with the role of judge.

It may well be that the judging-as-practical-reason approach can accommodate these intuitions. But in any case it seems wise for empirical researchers wishing to speak as effectively as possible to normative concerns to respect the widely held assumption that legal reasoning should be special in at least some way.

At this point, it might feel like we have come full circle, realizing now that we were too hasty in rejecting the sharp distinction between law and not-law. But that is not the case. In fact, we can now see an additional reason for eschewing that approach when attempting to evaluate judging. Categorizing considerations as law or not-law encourages us to think of reasons as either in or out, appropriate or not. This fails to reflect the nuance of our actual thinking, in which we tend to recognize degrees of appropriateness.

Let us return to Scalia's actual and hypothetical decisions in *McDonald*. Imagine a truly neutral observer who had no feelings one way or the other about gun control but was able to observe Scalia's other decisions. Almost certainly the hypothetical decision would reflect better on Scalia in the observer's eyes than the actual decision. But this would be true even if the observer considered both grounds to be extralegal and dubious. Slightly altering the hypothetical might clarify the point. Again imagine that Scalia voted in support of Chicago, though now because he felt that state and local governments were more trustworthy when it came to making gun control policy. This reason would have little claim to be law-based, but it would still likely strike most people as a more acceptable reason than distaste for Chicago's gun control policy would be. Or consider again Posner's take on Scalia's motivations in *McDonald* and *Arizona*—an affinity for guns and an aversion to illegal immigrants. Surely neither motivation could be regarded as law-based under any respectable theory. But that does not mean we would evaluate them the same. Deciding a case on the basis of how comfortable one is with guns is inappropriate; deciding based on how one feels about a group is apt to be regarded as reprehensible.

At the risk of belaboring the point, let us consider some other comparisons. Which is worse, deciding in a way that promotes what you (though not necessarily others) view as the proper balance of power between the executive and legislative branch or deciding according to the wishes of most people in your political party? Virtually everyone would say that the latter is worse; in fact, it seems terrible in comparison. But now compare deciding according to the wishes of your political party with deciding in the way that provides you with the greatest financial benefit or that does the greatest harm to a litigant you dislike. Suddenly partisan voting doesn't seem all that bad. The point is that we do not naturally tend toward absolute judgments in this area. Reasons are not simply acceptable or unacceptable; they are more or less acceptable. And note again that our ability to discriminate does not depend on categorizing some reasons as legal and others as extralegal. We have no trouble discriminating between reasons that are all obviously extralegal.

Here, then, is another argument for moving away from questions about whether judicial decisions are based on law and asking instead how appropriate or inappropriate the grounds judges rely on in their decisions are. Not only does the latter question speak more directly to the underlying normative issue, but it better captures the nuances of our thinking about it.

One possible objection to this move is that it calls for empirical scholars to make normative judgments. As damaging as this objection might be in other contexts, it is not particularly compelling in this one. "Law" is a normatively loaded and fiercely contested concept. As soon as empirical researchers choose a conception of it, they necessarily take sides, perhaps unwittingly and surely with limited awareness of the broader implications of their position. At least when we ask directly about appropriateness we can be more sure of what we are doing. And so even research that simply relied on our intuitions would begin from at least as strong a foundation as empirical work on law.

However, we need not rest on our own intuitions. For one thing, we can consult the intuitions of the general public. Studies like those of Scheb and Lyons (2001) and Gibson and Caldeira (2011) can provide revealing insights into what ordinary people think should go into judges' decisions. For instance, while large majorities of Scheb and Lyons' respondents said that partisanship and ideology should have no impact, they were far more accepting of decisions based on the "judges' views of what's best for the public" (p. 125). True, there is no particular reason to think that ordinary citizens' intuitions are necessarily superior to empirical researchers'. On the other hand, it is not safe to assume that empirical researchers are representative of the general population, and—this is the important point—the law judges make is binding on everyone in society, not just those who study courts closely. It seems eminently reasonable to consult the views of those subject to the law when assessing the legitimacy of judges' behavior.

We can also look again to legal theory. Even if legal theorists are unable to agree on what law is, there is considerable agreement regarding the key challenges faced by legal systems and some fundamental things citizens should expect from a legal system. Beginning from those, it should not be difficult to generate at least some non-controversial evaluative statements about judicial decision-making. There is not space in this chapter for a proper analysis, but even a cursory one should be sufficient to demonstrate the possibilities.

Let us begin with four fairly self-evident statements about courts. 1) Their decisions are typically made in the context of concrete cases involving litigants with major stakes in the outcome. 2) In a non-trivial proportion of cases, the best answer is not easy to discern, whether because the law is ambiguous or undeveloped or because it is unclear how best to apply the law to the issues raised by the case. 3) The answers given by courts can change the law of their jurisdictions. 4) That law is binding on all people in that jurisdiction, regardless of whether they had any connection to the case, and will continue to be binding on them until changed by some governmental authority.

Focusing on the last two statements first, we can immediately see the force of Wechsler's (1959) admonition that legal reasoning "must be genuinely principled, resting with respect to every step which is involved in reaching judgment on analysis and reasons quite transcending the immediate result that is achieved" (p. 15) The more a decision deviates from this standard, relying on reasons that work for this case only, the less likely it is that the resulting law will serve the population at large well moving forward and thus the less appropriate the decision is.

The first and fourth statements point toward the necessity for stability and predictability in the law. This is vitally important for the parties to a case. As Dworkin (1978: 84) points out, "if a judge makes new law and applies it retroactively in the case before him, then the losing party will be punished, not because he violated some duty he had, but rather a new duty created after the event." Decisions applying new law retroactively also undercut the ability of individuals (Scalia 1989) and societies (Shapiro 2011) to engage in effective planning. Presumably no one would argue that judges should always refrain from making new law or that all decisions should apply prospectively only. But most would agree that weighing fairness and reliance considerations is essential to good judicial decision-making.

The discussion so far points to some questions researchers might consider asking instead of "Are judges following the law or their attitudes?" How broadly applicable are the principles on which judges rest their decisions? How consistently do they follow those principles in other cases? How carefully do they weigh the possibility of disruptive effects on society and unfairness to litigants in deciding whether to adhere to precedent? Other possibilities include:

- How well do judges understand the empirical conditions relevant to the issues they are deciding? How much effort do they put into understanding those conditions? These questions build on an insight from Posner (2013: 83): "The perception of the [Supreme] Court as a political court in most constitutional cases and many nonconstitutional ones derives from the fact that the Justices form confident views without any empirical basis for them." One of the things that can make a judicial decision difficult is uncertainty about the effect it will have on people's situations in a complex world. The good judge will work hard to acquire reliable information about current conditions and possible effects, drawing on the expertise of others where appropriate, rather than rest on facile assumptions.
- To what extent do a judge's decisions reflect positive or negative attitudes toward a group to which a litigant belongs? Deciding on the basis of attitudes toward groups violates judges' duty of fairness toward both the individuals involved in the case and citizens in society at large.
- To what extent and how frequently do the moral and policy views a judge brings to bear in making a decision deviate from those of the general population? In keeping with the spirit of this entire chapter, this question begins with the realist assumption that moral and policy views will inevitably enter into judicial decisions but rejects the inference that therefore "anything goes." Moral and policy questions are often very difficult, and it can be especially tricky to discern the best answer in the unique circumstances of one particular case (Schauer 1991, 2006). For this reason, one crucial function of law is to decide key questions in advance, taking them out of the hands of individual decision-makers in unique circumstances (Shapiro 2011). Recognizing this, good judges will require exceptionally strong reasons before deciding on the basis of views that most others do not share.

- How thoroughly does a judge consider the reasons for and against a given position? Few norms are more fundamental to the legal process than evenhandedness in the evaluation of cases. This norm begins in recognition of the stakes for the parties, regardless of how far-reaching the implications of the case; fairness to the parties requires that their arguments be heard and taken seriously. It also reflects the understanding that cases that make it to court, especially to the appellate level, are rarely entirely one-sided. Even when one party clearly has the more credible argument, there are typically some non-trivial considerations favoring the other party. Even observers who differ greatly as to the merits of the different legal positions will still often be able to agree whether a judge has respectfully weighed the reasons on both sides and therefore whether the judge's opinion is itself worthy of respect.[6]

It would be foolish to pretend that questions of this sort can be easily answered. But I submit that they are no harder to answer than ones empirical researchers currently struggle with. In fact, progress is already underway in some areas, for instance in research on judicial independence around the world that asks to what extent judges kowtow to those who control their job prospects and in studies of state courts in the United States that ask whether campaign contributions for judicial elections influence judges' votes.

Most importantly, questions like these would get more directly at the underlying concern motivating much research into law's role in judicial decision-making—to what extent judges are performing their jobs properly and their decisions are entitled to our respect. Ultimately, our best hope for advancing the project of understanding law's influence might be to come at it from new angles.

Notes

1. http://www.nytimes.com/2005/09/13/politics/politicsspecial1/13ctext.html?pagewanted=all. The widespread mockery of Roberts might be unfair. Assuming there exists a baseball league where umpires are authorized to decide which pitches they will call and which they will ignore, to amend the definition of balls and strikes at will, and to announce the definition after the pitch has been called—and where the teams have a large and not necessarily equal say in who the umpires will be—then the analogy may well be apt.
2. Collins' finding that the predictive value of ideology weakens as the number of amicus briefs grows gives us additional reason to think that amicus briefs' effects occur through legal persuasion. Additional evidence of this, from in-depth analyses of group arguments and justices' responses in two areas of law can be found in Epstein and Kobylka (1992).
3. More than that, it can be pernicious, providing a rhetorical device for judges to hide behind when they disagree with each other (Geyh 2012). Rather than do the hard work of demonstrating that my argument is sounder than yours, I accuse you of acting outside the law. Your reasons, being illegitimate, are entitled to no respect, so I win. Of course, this would be a reasonable enough argument if your reasons clearly were illegitimate. But as typically employed by judges, the argument serves only to obfuscate.
4. 130 S. Ct. 3020 (2010).
5. 132 S. Ct. 2492 (2012).

6. Like other questions discussed in this chapter, this one presents considerable methodological challenges. Here efforts by political psychologists at coding "integrative complexity" (e.g. Conway et al. 2014) might point a way toward overcoming them.

References

Alexander, L., and Sherwin, E. 2008. *Demystifying Legal Reasoning.* New York, NY: Cambridge University Press.

Bailey, M. A., and Maltzman, F. 2011. *The Constrained Court: Law, Politics, and the Decisions Justices Make.* Princeton, NJ: Princeton University Press.

Bartels, B. L. 2009. "The Constraining Capacity of Legal Doctrine on the U.S. Supreme Court." *American Political Science Review* 103: 474–95.

Baum L. 1997. *The Puzzle of Judicial Behavior.* Ann Arbor, MI: University of Michigan Press.

Benesh, S. C., and Czarnezki, J. J. 2009. "The Ideology of Legal Interpretation." *Journal of Law and Policy* 29: 113–32.

Benesh, S. C., and Reddick, M. 2002. "Overruled: An Event History Analysis of Lower Court Reaction to Supreme Court Alteration of Precedent." *Journal of Politics* 64: 534–50.

Black R. C., and Owens, R. J. 2012. *The Solicitor General and the United States Supreme Court:Executive Branch Influence on Judicial Decisions.* Cambridge: Cambridge University Press.

Burek, J. 2010. "Elena Kagan Confirmation Hearings: Do Her Politics Really Matter?" *Christian Science Monitor.* Available at: http://www.csmonitor.com/Commentary/Editorial-Board-Blog/2010/0630/Elena-Kagan-confirmation-hearings-Do-her-politics-really-matter.

Corley, P. C., Steigerwalt, A., and Ward, A. 2013. *The Puzzle of Unanimity: Consensus on the United States Supreme Court.* Stanford, CA: Stanford University Press.

Collins, P. M., Jr. 2008. *Friends of the Supreme Court: Interest Groups and Judicial Decision Making.* Oxford: Oxford University Press.

Conway, L. G., Conway, K. R., Gornick, L. J., and Houck, S. C. 2014. "Automated Integrative Complexity." *Political Psychology* 35: 603–24.

Cushman, B. 1998. *Rethinking the New Deal Court: The Structure of a Constitutional Revolution.* Oxford: Oxford University Press.

Dworkin, R. 1978. *Taking Rights Seriously.* Cambridge, MA: Harvard University Press.

Dworkin, R. 1986. *Law's Empire.* Cambridge, MA: Harvard University Press.

Edelman P. H., Klein, D. E., and Lindquist, S. A. 2012. "Consensus, Disorder, and Ideology on the Supreme Court." *Journal of Empirical Legal Studies* 9: 129–48.

Epstein, L., and Knight, J. 2013. "Reconsidering Judicial Preferences." *Annual Review of Political Science* 16: 11–31.

Epstein, L., and Kobylka, J. F. 1992. *The Supreme Court and Legal Change: Abortion and the Death Penalty.* Chapel Hill, NC: University of North Carolina Press.

Epstein, L., Landes, W. M., and Posner, R. A. 2012. "Are Even Unanimous Decisions in the United States Supreme Court Ideological?" *Northwestern University Law Review* 106: 699–714.

Fuller, L. L. 1958. "Positivism and Fidelity to Law: A Reply to Professor Hart." *Harvard Law Review* 71: 630–72.

Gates, J. B., and Phelps, G. A. 1996. "Intentionalism in Constitutional Opinions." *Political Research Quarterly* 49(2): 245–61.

Geyh, C. G. 2012. "Can the Rule of Law Survive Judicial Politics?" *Cornell Law Review* 97: 191–253.

Gibson, J. L., and Caldeira, G.A. 2011. "Has Legal Realism Damaged the Legitimacy of the U.S. Supreme Court?" *Law & Society Review* 45: 195–219.

Gilbert, M. D. 2011. "Does Law Matter? Theory and Evidence from Single-Subject Adjudication." *Journal of Legal Studies* 40: 333–65.

Gillman, H. 1993. *The Constitution Besieged: The Rise and Demise of Lochner Era Police Power Jurisprudence*. Durham, NC: Duke University Press.

Gillman, H. 2001. "What's Law Got to Do with It? Judicial Behavioralists Test the 'Legal Model' of Judicial Decision Making." *Law and Social Inquiry* 26: 465–504.

Gruhl, J. 1980. "The Supreme Court's Impact on the Law of Libel: Compliance by Lower Federal Courts." *Western Political Quarterly* 33: 502–19.

Hansford, T. G., and Spriggs, J. F., II. 2006. *The Politics of Precedent on the U.S. Supreme Court*. Princeton, NJ: Princeton University Press.

Hart, H. L. A. 1961. *The Concept of Law*. Oxford: Oxford University Press.

Howard, R. M., and Segal, J. A. 2002. "An Original Look at Originalism." *Law and Society Review* 36: 113–38.

Johnson, C. A. 1987. "Law, Politics, and Judicial Decision Making: Lower Federal Court Uses of Supreme Court Decisions." *Law & Society Review* 21: 325–40.

Kagan, E. 1995. "Confirmation Messes, Old and New." *University of Chicago Law Review* 62: 919–42.

Kahn, R. 1999. "Interpretive Norms and Supreme Court Decision Making: The Rehnquist Court on Privacy and Religion." In *Supreme Court Decision Making: New Institutionalist Approaches*, edited by C. W. Clayton and H. Gillman. Chicago, IL: University of Chicago Press, 175–99.

Kritzer, H. M., and Richards, M. J. 2003. "Jurisprudential Regimes and Supreme Court Decision Making: The Lemon Regime and Establishment Clause Cases." *Law & Society Review* 37: 827–40.

Lindquist, S. A., and Klein, D. E. 2006. "The Influence of Jurisprudential Considerations on Supreme Court Decision-Making: A Study of Conflict Cases." *Law & Society Review* 40: 135–62.

McGuire, K. T. 1993. *The Supreme Court Bar: Legal Elites in the Washington Community*. Charlottesville, VA: University Press of Virginia.

Masood, A. S., and Songer, D. R. 2013. "Reevaluating the Implications of Decision-Making Models: The Role of Summary Decisions in US Supreme Court Analysis." *Journal of Law and Courts* 1: 363–89.

Phelps, G. A., and Gates, J. B. 1990. "The Myth of Jurisprudence: Interpretive Theory in the Constitutional Opinions of Justices Rehnquist and Brennan." *Santa Clara Law Review* 31: 567–96.

Pinello, D. R. 1999. "Linking Party to Judicial Ideology in American Courts: A Meta-Analysis." *Justice System Journal* 20: 219–54.

Posner, R. A. 2003. *Law, Pragmatism, and Democracy*. Cambridge, MA: Harvard University Press.

Posner, R. A. 2008. *How Judges Think*. Cambridge, MA: Harvard University Press.

Posner, R. A. 2013. *Reflections on Judging*. Cambridge, MA: Harvard University Press.

Richards, M. J., and Kritzer, H. M. 2002. "Jurisprudential Regimes in Supreme Court Decision Making." *American Political Science Review* 96: 305–20.

Rowland, C. K., and Carp, R. A. 1996. *Politics and Judgment in Federal District Courts.* Lawrence, KS: University Press of Kansas.

Scalia, A. 1989. "The Rule of Law as a Law of Rules." *University of Chicago Law Review* 56(4): 1175–88.

Schauer, F. 1991. "Rules and the Rule of Law." *Harvard Journal of Law and Public Policy* 14: 645–94.

Schauer, F. 2006. "Do Cases Make Bad Law?" *University of Chicago Law Review* 73: 883–918.

Scheb, J. M., II, and Lyons, W. 2002. "Judicial Behavior and Public Opinion: Popular Expectations Regarding the Factors That Influence Supreme Court Decisions." *Political Behavior* 23: 181–94.

Segal, J. A., and Spaeth, H. J. 1993. *The Supreme Court and the Attitudinal Model.* New York, NY: Cambridge University Press.

Segal, J. A., and Spaeth, H. J. 2002. *The Supreme Court and the Attitudinal Model Revisited.* New York, NY: Cambridge University Press.

Shapiro, S. J. 2011. *Legality.* Cambridge, MA: Harvard University Press.

Songer, D. R., and Haire, S. 1992. "Integrating Alternative Approaches to the Study of Judicial Voting: Obscenity Cases in the U.S. Courts of Appeals." *American Journal of Political Science* 36: 963–82.

Songer, D. R., Segal, J. A., and Cameron, C. M. 1994. "The Hierarchy of Justice: Testing a Principal–Agent Model of Supreme Court–Circuit Court Interactions." *American Journal of Political Science* 38: 673–96.

Spaeth, H. J., and Segal, J. A. 1999. *Majority Rule or Minority Will: Adherence to Precedent on the U.S. Supreme Court.* New York: Cambridge University Press.

Tamanaha, B. Z. 2010. *Beyond the Formalist-Realist Divide.* Princeton, NJ: Princeton University Press.

Wechsler, H. 1959. "Toward Neutral Principles of Constitutional Law." *Harvard Law Review* 73: 1–35.

Westerland C., Segal, J. A., Epstein, L., Cameron, C. M., and Comparato, S. 2010. "Strategic Defiance and Compliance in the U.S. Courts of Appeals." *American Journal of Political Science* 54: 891–905.

Zorn, C., and Bowie, J. B. 2010. "Ideological Influences on Decision Making in the Federal Judicial Hierarchy: An Empirical Assessment." *Journal of Politics* 72: 1212–21.

Other Readings

Braman, E. 2009. *Law, Politics, and Perception: How Policy Preferences Influence Legal Reasoning.* Charlottesville, VA: University of Virginia Press.

Lindquist, S. A., and Cross, F. B. 2005. "Empirically Testing Dworkin's Chain Novel Theory: Studying the Path of Precedent." *New York University Law Review* 80: 1156–206.

CHAPTER 13

THE STRATEGIC ANALYSIS OF JUDICIAL BEHAVIOR AND THE SEPARATION OF POWERS

CHAD L. WESTERLAND

THE assertion that judges have policy preferences is no longer a controversial claim. But once we accept the premise of a policy-pursuing judge, we need to understand how judges work to realize favorable policy outputs and outcomes. The strategic analysis of judging focuses on the interdependent nature of political decision-making. These strategic models of judicial decision-making are the most important innovation in judicial research in the last thirty years. Formal models have become more sophisticated, and the variety and quality of quantitative and qualitative evidence has improved greatly.

The attitudinal model and the strategic model have much in common. The major distinction between the two approaches is a different understanding of the institutional context of judging. The attitudinal model (Segal and Spaeth 2002) is an institutional model; it posits that the independence of the U.S. Supreme Court allows justices to pursue their ideological preferences largely without concern for the potential responses outside of the Court. Simply put, the institutional position of the Court allows for strategic sincerity. From the strategic perspective, ideological preferences are no less important. However, the institutional landscape is arrayed in a way that constrains how judges can pursue those preferences (Epstein and Knight 1998). If a sincerely preferred outcome of the Court will result in a legislative reprisal, then the Court would be better off issuing a moderated decision closer to legislative preferences. Each model generates these different predictions precisely because of a different understanding of institutional constraints.

In this chapter, I use the separation of powers (SOP) literature to explore how well the strategic accounts explain judicial behavior. I first offer a brief explanation for the general absence of strategic models in the early judicial behavior literature. I then explain the basic SOP model and highlight the key institutional assumptions that motivate the major variants of the model. A review of the empirical literatures reveals a tremendous amount of progress in the past twenty-five years. Empirical support for the classic statutory SOP model remains elusive, but the same cannot be said for newer institutional legitimacy models. I conclude with several suggestions for future research.

Strategic Approaches to Judicial Behavior

The prominence of the strategic framework for judicial behavior might be easy to take for granted now, but its rise as a dominant analytic framework is a relatively recent development. While a full intellectual history is beyond the scope of this chapter,[1] the strategic model of judicial decision-making is best understood as a reaction to the attitudinal model. Early classics such as Pritchett's *The Roosevelt Court* (1948), Murphy's *Elements of Judicial Strategy* (1964), and Schubert's *The Judicial Mind* (1965) all explicitly assumed policy-pursuing judges as a starting point for their investigations. Schubert, Pritchett, and Murphy were in some ways speaking the same language about goal-oriented actors, but the socio-psychological strands of Pritchett's and Schubert's work had the most important initial impact. Schubert's behavioral insights in particular greatly influenced other early attitudinal studies (Spaeth 1972). From this perspective, judicial decisions are best understood as a response to case facts (the stimulus) based on the attitudes of the judge. Even as later work refined these ideas with work from economics (Rohde and Spaeth 1976), the attitudinal model of Segal and Spaeth (1993, 2002) retained its behavioral roots.[2]

The strategic perspective, especially as advanced by Murphy, was lost in the debate between the attitudinal model and the legal model. Murphy's work did not have the impact of similar early rational choice applications, such as Downs (1957) or Riker (1962). This was not just because the field was preoccupied with the attitudinal versus legal model debate, and by extension, the debate on how to conduct social science. As important and insightful as *The Elements of Judicial Strategy* remains fifty years later, it forgoes the type of formal analysis conducted by both Downs and Riker. In *Elements*, just about any decision a justice makes could be "strategic." It would be false to claim that predictions cannot be derived from Murphy, but the work as a whole is presented almost as a cautious hypothetical.[3] Although the attitudinal model is also not derived from formal equilibrium analysis, it nonetheless provides falsifiable propositions that are amenable to empirical testing. This was a major early advantage for the behavioralist approach.

By the time scholars brought their attention fully to the strategic model an impressive body of evidence for the attitudinal model had been amassed. The reintroduction of the strategic analysis of judicial decision-making acknowledged the attitudinal model as critical starting point but presented it as a fundamentally incomplete explanation.

Judges, like all political actors, certainly have preferences and goals, but from a rational choice perspective, that claim by itself is not very interesting. Attitudes are essential, as strategic considerations do not make much sense absent clearly defined preferences.[4] But the institutional rules and norms that constrain those attitudes and the interdependent nature of political choices are what matter most. Picking up where Murphy left off, Epstein and Knight (1998) argue that every aspect of Supreme Court decision-making should be viewed through a strategic lens. Justices have short-term goals, and the pursuit of these goals involves a series of interdependent choices. The strategic literature quickly developed along two largely separate lines of inquiry—models of strategic interaction between the justices (internal models) and models of the strategic interaction between the Court and non-judicial actors (external models). The internal models are primarily concerned with how justices constrain one another during the opinion-writing process (Maltzman, Spriggs, and Wahlbeck 2000). The external constraints literature focuses mostly on SOP games. The SOP literature developed rapidly in the late 1980s and was in fact responsible for launching the general interest in strategic models of judicial decision-making.

Not surprisingly, the foundations of the separation of powers model begin with Murphy's *The Elements of Judicial Strategy*. While much of his analysis concerns intra-Court politics, Murphy devotes two chapters in *Elements* to exploring how a justice might consider legislative or executive preferences when making a decision. Murphy identifies two broad dimensions of strategic considerations: ensuring a decision is followed and preventing a negative response. As already noted, Murphy avoids any precise behavioral predictions, but the innovation of Murphy's work was simply to acknowledge the possibility that the Court might anticipate Congressional or executive responses to its decisions. Many of Murphy's insights are still fundamental components of the strategic models of the Court's inter-branch relationships, but twenty-five years would pass before his insights were formalized.

Brian Marks's dissertation (1989) ignited widespread interest in the SOP model and strategic judicial decision-making more broadly. For Marks, the Court is actually non-strategic and has fully exogenous preferences; his focus was instead on why Congress was unable to overturn the Court's decision in *Grove City College v. Bell* (1986). But the "Marksist" framework was quickly used as the foundation for the classic statutory SOP model. The importance of the approach for the broader study of judicial behavior is obvious, as the statutory SOP model has critical implications for attitudinal model's predictions about the merits vote. Under the assumptions of the SOP model, voting sincerely on the merits will not result in the best possible policy outcome for the Court. Thus, the SOP model is framed as a more complete alternative to the attitudinal model.

In the remainder of the chapter, I review the assumptions motivating different variants of the SOP model and detail a major empirical problem that must be solved if the model is to be tested. Along the way, I highlight several of the key findings from the literature and suggest possible avenues for future scholarship.

The Strategy of SOP

The basic insight of the SOP model relies on a straightforward application of spatial voting (Marks 1989; Ferejohn and Shipan 1990; Ferejohn and Weingast 1990; Gely and Spiller 1990; Spiller and Gely 1992). Figure 13.1 presents the simplest formulation of the SOP game. The medians of the Court (C), House (H), and Senate (S) are arrayed in a single policy dimension. A Court that finds itself located between the medians of both the House and the Senate is free to act sincerely. In this scenario, the Court's ideal point falls within the set of Pareto optimals and thus cannot be overturned without making one chamber worse off than the policy at the Court's ideal point. If the Court finds itself either to the right or to the left of both chambers, then Congress can overturn a decision rendered at the Court's ideal point. In the hypothetical arrangement in the bottom of Figure 13.1, the best the Court can do is to set policy at the Senate's ideal point. Otherwise, the House can offer an alternative that will be acceptable to the Senate but that is further away from the Court's ideal point than if the Court were to set policy at the Senate's ideal point. The SOP model may be presented with greater complexity without changing the general point that the Court faces constraints that may produce strategic decisions. For example, different pivotal players (committee chairs, filibuster veto points, executive preferences, etc.) can easily be added to the model without changing the basic predictions. Recent models have included public support for either the Court or a specific decision (Vanberg 2005; Clark 2011). The general contribution from this refinement is that if the public views the Court favorably as an institution, then the Court may be able to achieve better policy outcomes even when in conflict with the legislature. But all SOP models point to an unavoidable conclusion: a rational, policy-oriented Court's decisions are conditional on the alignment of the preferences of actors (political branches, public opinion) outside of the Court.

The setup of the basic SOP model requires a series of assumptions about the nature of the interaction between the Court and external actors. Two key core assumptions are (1) a common policy space across institutions and (2) perfect information about preferences. The legislature is usually given the last move and the costs of proposing and

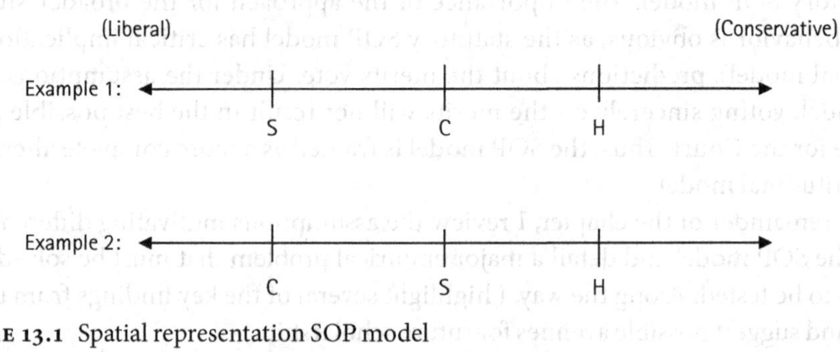

FIGURE 13.1 Spatial representation SOP model

Source: Author.

passing overriding legislation are assumed to be minimal. The legislature must also be able to overturn the Court's decision via regular legislation. This assumption can be recast slightly by recognizing that the Court usually cannot enforce its own decisions. Even if an unpopular decision is not overturned, it may simply be ignored and not implemented by the political branches. A variant of the standard SOP model posits that Congressional control over many of the sources of the Court's institutional power (appellate jurisdiction, funding, etc.) will ensure that the Court does not stray too far from legislative preferences. This formulation does not require that the Court makes precise predictions about the location of a potential policy response from Congress. Instead, the Court must gauge its ideological position relative to the rest of the political environment and determine whether a sincere decision would be divergent enough as to generate an attack on the Court itself.

The key difference between the attitudinal model and the strategic model involves a disagreement about how to understand the Court's institutional context. The attitudinal model finds fault with many of the standard SOP assumptions (Segal and Spaeth 2002: 105–10) and instead argues that the Court's control over its docket, its position at the top of the judicial hierarchy, its lack of electoral accountability, and its ability to review override attempts and to base its decisions on constitutional rather than statutory grounds all create a largely independent Court. The Court's institutional legitimacy is also mostly taken for granted in the attitudinal model. The key point (and one that is all too often forgotten in the literature) is that the attitudinal model does not deny that justices are strategic actors. Rather, the model argues that the Court's unique institutional position means that, more often than not, the Court's optimal strategy is strategic sincerity (Segal 1997; Segal and Spaeth 2002).

Previous work has carefully catalogued concerns regarding the assumptions underlying the strategic model (Segal 1997; Segal and Spaeth 2002), but it is nonetheless worthwhile to explore these various assumptions a little further. The key question at the heart of all strategic formulations of judicial behavior is whether or not judges are actually better off by voting in a manner contrary to their sincere preferences. The standard SOP model provides crisp predictions about when this will be the case and about the Court's optimal behavior. Working through the theoretical underpinnings of the SOP model helps us to understand how prevalent strategic behavior might be.

SOP models begin with the assumptions that the Court and other political actors are operating on the same policy dimensions and all actors have perfect information about each player's preferences. Usually the model is presented as a single policy dimension, but this is certainly not a requirement (Gely and Spiller 1990). The key is that the SOP model only makes sense if all of the actors understand the policy space in the same basic terms. This is generally not a point of contention between the attitudinal and strategic perspectives, but the low-dimensional, shared policy space assumption has serious implications for the viability of SOP models. If the Court's decision-making space consists of a large number of dimensions, then the assumption of perfect information about preference alignments is harder to maintain. Even with perfect information, the strategic considerations facing all of the actors become increasingly complex as the number of dimensions grows. Recent work by Lauderdale and Clark (2014) identifies twenty-four politically relevant dimensions to Supreme Court decisions.[5] The median of the Court may or may not be the same across these dimensions (see also Lauderdale and Clark 2012), and many of the individual cases may be a mix of issues (Lauderdale and Clark 2014: 765). A high dimensional policy space is not necessarily incompatible with SOP models, but at the very least, it would provide an opportunity for the Court to combine issues strategically in order to avoid reversal, thus minimizing the relevance of SOP considerations.

The assumption of a low dimensional policy space does have a great deal of empirical support. A single dimension seems to explain a large percentage (80–90 percent) of both Congressional and Supreme Court decisions (Poole and Rosenthal 1997; Grofman and Brazil 2002; Martin and Quinn 2002). Yet even if this is the case, the dimension may not be identical for each branch. This is most relevant for reconciling legal models of decision-making with SOP models. Judges who are meaningfully constrained by legal values but who are simultaneously constrained by Congress pose an interesting problem. In the most methodologically sophisticated study of the legal model to date, Bailey and Maltzman (2008, 2011) identify three legal values (*stare decisis*, judicial restraint, strict constructivism) that constrain judicial decision-making. Judicial restraint means judges will defer to electorally accountable branches of government and is compatible within the SOP framework. Less clear is the fit of *stare decisis* and strict constructivism. Consider a case where justice makes a decision that is unpalatable to Congress but is in line with a strict constructivist interpretation. Neither the legal model nor the SOP literature offers clear predictions for the case when legal values require judges to make decisions contrary to the preferences of the legislative branch. A strategic judge might use the language of *stare decisis* or strict constructivism to ward off a legislative response, but that shifts legal values from a general constraint on judicial behavior to a strategic tool that enables the realization of preferred policy outcomes.

Another requirement of the SOP model is that the Court needs complete and perfect information about legislative preferences. The Court must also make a prediction about how those preferences translate into policy outputs. The Court's ability to identify the policy preferences of pivotal players in the legislative process is likely an innocuous assumption. Reasonably anticipating the outcome of legislative process is far more challenging. The basic SOP model in Figure 13.1 omits all internal structure within Congress, omits the president as a veto player, and assumes that opportunity and transaction costs of passing legislation are negligible enough for the Court to think an override would be imminent. These assumptions all concern the relative ease with which legislation can be passed. With respect to the internal structure of Congress, Congressional scholars still have no consensus on whether gatekeeping power exists in Congress or if it does, who has it (Cox and McCubbins 2005; Crombez, Groseclose, and Krehbiel 2006; Shepsle and Weingast 1987). Empirical tests of SOP models tend to account for this by operationalizing a wide range of legislative models (Bergara, Richman, and Spiller 2003; Segal, Westerland, and Lindquist 2011), but the general point is that committee chairs, party leaders, filibusters in the Senate, and the presidential veto all enable the obstruction of legislation. The more veto points in the process, the harder it will be to enact an override. A rational, strategic Court might very well look at the legislative process and decide it is willing to take its chances on an override.

If an override does manage to pass, SOP models further assume that this action ends the SOP game. But there is no substantive reason to give Congress the last move. Override legislation is still potentially subject to review by the Court. In fact, a Court with the last move could effectively constrain Congressional decision-making, which is consistent with the findings of Martin (2001). Further, Carrubba and Zorn (2010) show that the president's role in implementing policy makes the executive branch a plausible last mover in the SOP game. This leads to an increase in the Court's discretion if the president's ideal point is outside the Congressional Pareto set. Assuming Congress has the last move also obscures the fact that the Court has nearly complete control over its docket. The Court might strategically delay hearing a case with the hopes of facing a more sympathetic legislature. This would have a substantial effect on the strategy of deciding what cases to hear (Owens 2010), though the vote on the merits would still end up as sincere.

The original formulation of the SOP model is also limited to the Court's statutory decisions (Eskridge 1991a, 1991b; Ferejohn and Weingast 1992). As a result, one of the key initial critiques of the statutory SOP model is that the Court can simply shift its decision from statutory to constitutional grounds (Segal 1997). This has the effect of insulating the decision from override because Congress cannot reverse the decision with simple legislation (but see Meernik and Ignani 1997). However, subsequent models indicate that the constitutional SOP game poses a more serious problem for the Court (Epstein, Knight, and Martin 2001). While the Court's constitutional decisions may be safe from legislative overrides, the Court's institutional power may be at risk. The costs of an institutional attack on the Court are certainly higher than whatever loss the Court might realize if a lone decision is overturned. Congress has a wide range of tools with which it attacks the Court (Rosenberg 1992), including the ability to withdraw appellate jurisdiction or to cut the judiciary's budget. Congressional attempts to curb the Court's power are not uncommon (Chutkow 2008; Clark 2009), and even if Congress does not ultimately pass court-curbing legislation, the mere introduction of such laws might provide important signals that the Court's legitimacy might be at risk (Clark 2011). The constitutional SOP thus reformulates the statutory model by focusing on the motivation of the Court to maintain its institutional power and status rather than the Court's worry about legislative preferences over a particular decision (Segal, Westerland, and Lindquist 2011).

Formal presentations of the constitutional SOP model generally include public opinion as an additional component of the game, though the basic logic is in no way limited to constitutional decisions (Clark 2011). Unlike the elected branches, the Court cannot make appeals to a democratic mandate to marshal support for its decisions. This suggests that the maintenance of diffuse (institutional) support is an essential concern for the Court. Decisions that stray too far beyond what is acceptable to the public may erode the Court's public standing. For Vanberg (2005), public opinion provides the opportunity for either the legislature or the Court to ignore the preferences of the other branch, at least as long as the public is in a position to know about the Court's decisions. In a transparent policy environment, a Court that diverges from legislative preferences can oppose the legislature if the public supports the Court's position. While public opinion is fixed in Vanberg's model, Staton (2010) allows judicial decisions to influence public opinion, and Clark (2011) does the same for legislative decisions. To be sure, identifying and disentangling the causal links between the outputs of political institutions and public opinion is a major challenge, but these models do not necessarily hinge on assumptions about the formation of public opinion. As long as the Court believes that it lacks support in the broader political environment, it will need to bring its decisions in line or risk losing its institutional legitimacy.

Before turning to the assumptions and predictions of the attitudinal model, a general point of clarification about the differences between the statutory and constitutional SOP models is necessary. The initial SOP models account for the possibility of a Congressional override. Since the Congress cannot readily override Court decisions with simple legislation, the SOP game made sense as a model of statutory decisions. But as the literature has developed, the two general types of SOP models are better conceptualized as an override/rational anticipation model and an institutional legitimacy model. A Court constrained by fear of Congress overturning the Court's specific policy, whether in statutory or constitutional decisions, is motivated by the classic, "statutory" SOP model. A Court that fears losing its legitimacy or incurring a costly attack on its institutional powers, again regardless of whether it is a constitutional or statutory decision, is motivated by the institutional maintenance model.

For the attitudinal model, the Court's institutional protections (no electoral or political accountability, life tenure, docket control, no ambition for other offices) promote institutional independence (Segal and Spaeth 2002: 92–7). The forward-thinking, rational justice in the attitudinal model surveys the political landscape and sees no credible threats either to a specific decision or to the institutional legitimacy of the Court. Additionally, given that the Senate must confirm a presidential nominee to the Court, the likelihood that the Court will have preferences that diverge from that of the other branches is quite low (Dahl 1957). As a result, the Court will be free to be strategically sincere.

We are left with three competing predictions from the SOP and attitudinal models. If the classic statutory model holds, the Court will need to account for legislative preferences over the policy at stake before the Court. The Court is motivated by preventing a worse policy outcome upon legislative review of the Court's decision. The constitutional/institutional legitimacy model suggests that the Court will not necessarily be attentive to specific Congressional preferences but will instead be concerned with its overall relative ideological position in the American political system. A Court that diverges generally from public opinion and/or the preferences of the political branches will have to limit its decisions or risk losing institutional legitimacy and power. The attitudinal model argues that Court's institutional position is likely to be relatively secure and that the political branches will be unable to respond effectively to the Court's decisions. As a result, knowing judicial policy preferences (and case facts) will be sufficient; non-judicial preferences will not constrain the Court.

Testing the SOP Model

The early SOP models generated clear predictions about the need for the Court to consider legislative preferences, but the empirical evidence from these studies is mixed at best. In part, this is because initial examinations were limited in the scope of case selection and the type of evidence used to test the model. Most importantly, comparable, cross-institutional preference measures had not been fully developed. Testing the SOP model requires accurate placement of the actors within the policy space. Without comparable preference measures, conclusions about the SOP model are nearly impossible to make.

The initial formalizing of the SOP game usually was not accompanied by empirical tests of the model. The supporting evidence for the early SOP models tended to involve the application of the model only to one or two Supreme Court cases or issue areas. As noted earlier, Marks's (1989) classic study shows why the alignment of preferences in Congress delayed an override of the Court's decision in *Grove City College v. Bell* (1986). Gely and Spiller (1990) expand Marks's formal specification and apply it to both *Grove City* and *MVMA of the United States v. State Farm Mutual Automobile Insurance et al.* (1983). Eskridge (1991a, 1991b) examines civil rights cases, but his qualitative account of a constrained Court does not necessarily support the conclusions of the SOP model (see Segal and Spaeth 2002: 327–31). In the early large-scale, comprehensive statistical analyses, the statutory SOP model did not fare well, especially in comparison to attitudinal explanations of Supreme Court decisions (Segal 1997; Segal 1999; Segal and Spaeth 2002).

Caution is warranted in drawing strong conclusions from these early tests because directly comparable preference measures are a necessary requirement for a systematic test of the SOP model. This is the most daunting challenge to designing valid tests of the SOP model. The earlier literature relied primarily on Americans for Democratic Action (ADA) scores to measure legislative preferences combined with some type of imputation method to generate ADA scores for the Court (Spiller and Gely 1992). Another approach is taken by Segal (1997), whose study assumed that ADA scores are directly comparable to the Segal-Cover (1989) measures of Supreme Court ideology. If an ADA score of 15 does not have precisely the same meaning as a Segal-Cover score of 15, then we cannot identify when the Court actually is constrained by Congress. Without the development of preference measures that allow an apples-to-apples comparison across time and institutions, empirical tests of the SOP model have only limited utility (see Bailey 2007).

Two more recent solutions to the scaling problem have been adopted in the SOP literature. Epstein, Martin, Segal, and Westerland (2007) bridge Martin-Quinn Supreme

Court ideal point estimates into Poole and Rosenthal's Common Space (Martin and Quinn 2002; Poole and Rosenthal 1997; Poole 1998). Nominees to the Supreme Court who fall under Moraski and Shipan's (1999) unconstrained regime are assigned the president's first-dimension Common Space score for their first year on the Court. By regressing a nonlinear transformation of that Common Space score on the corresponding Martin-Quinn score (MQ) for the unconstrained nominees, a bridging equation that maps the Martin-Quinn space to the Common Space is estimated.[6] The Common Space scores are explicitly designed to be directly comparable across time and across the House, Senate, and the president, just as the MQ scores are directly comparable across time. The resulting Judicial Common Space (JCS) scores provide reliably comparable measures that can be used to test SOP models.

The technique advanced by Bailey (2007) relies on positions taken by Supreme Court, Congress, and the president in order to generate a set of "bridging" observations. The logic is that if a member of Congress files an amicus brief in a Supreme Court case, we can assume we know how that member would decide the case if he or she sat on the Supreme Court. The bridging observations are then incorporated into a larger data set with Supreme Court votes and Congressional roll call votes. The full data set allows the estimation of ideal points that are directly comparable across time and space.[7] Bailey (2007) finds that the Court is almost never the ideologically extreme branch. The exceptions to this are "rather short lived or minor" (Bailey 2007: 443). Beyond generating directly comparable measures of revealed preferences, the underlying statistical model can be extended to incorporate parameters for legal or political constraints (Bailey and Maltzman 2008, 2011).

Both approaches have been used to test SOP models. For example, Segal, Westerland, and Lindquist (2011) employ the JCS scores to compare the rational anticipation and institutional maintenance versions of the constitutional SOP model. The mapping of MQ scores into Poole-Rosenthal's Common Space allows for three important quantities to be calculated. First, it becomes possible to estimate the probability that a member of the Court would have voted for the challenged legislation when proposed. Second, the probability that the contemporaneous Congress would still support the enacted legislation can be estimated. Finally, the relative ideological positions of the Court and Congress can be identified. Segal, Westerland, and Lindquist find clear support for both the attitudinal model and the institutional maintenance model, but none for the rational anticipation model. While the Court's preferences are a consistent and strong predictor of the decision to strike federal legislation, the Court is less likely to do so as it becomes more ideologically distant from Congress, the president, and the judiciary chairs in both chambers, regardless of the legislative preferences over the enacted legislation. Another example of the use of JCS scores to test the SOP model is the Owens (2010) study, which finds no evidence that the SOP model constrains the Court's decisions to hear cases. Owens argues persuasively that the agenda stage is most likely to reveal strategic SOP considerations, which makes this an especially important finding. Hall (2014) recasts the SOP model as a concern over policy implementation. Lateral cases, defined by Hall as all non-criminal or civil liability cases, require support from non-judicial actors for implementation purposes and as a result, the Court is hypothesized to be more constrained in these types of cases. Hall tests this theory with the JCS scores and finds that fear of nonimplementation, rather than fear of an explicit institutional attack, serves to constrain Supreme Court decisions.

Bailey and Maltzman (2008, 2011) use the scaling mechanism outlined in Bailey (2007) to test both the legal model and SOP model. Concerning the SOP model, they find that many justices' revealed preferences are constrained by Congress and the president in both constitutional and statutory cases. If the Court median is outside the Pareto set, some justices seem to moderate their overall preferences. As with their tests of the legal model, Bailey and Maltzman find substantial variation across justices for the effect of the SOP constraint. Clark (2009) uses the Bailey scores to supplement his test of whether or not an increase in the frequency of introduced court-curbing legislation reduces the likelihood that the Court will strike legislation. Court-curbing legislation is hypothesized to serve as a crucial signal to the Court about the status of its legitimacy, a conclusion that Clark's findings support. Segal and Westerland (2005) also test the constitutional SOP model with an early version of Bailey scores but do not find any evidence of legislative constraint. The JCS and Bailey scores are still relatively new, but both approaches have already allowed for sounder empirical tests of the SOP model.

So what conclusions can be drawn from the SOP literature? The combination of increasingly persuasive formalizations of the SOP game with more robust empirical tests has resulted in substantial advances in the literature. Overall, the classic statutory SOP model still has extremely limited empirical support. We have almost no systematic evidence that Court anticipates an override based on specific legislative preferences in either statutory or constitutional cases. Spiller and Gely (1992) and Bergara, Richman, and Spiller (2003) find systematic evidence that the Court is constrained by Congress in statutory decisions. However, neither paper controls for contemporary Congressional preferences over the enacted legislation and both have serious research design issues (see Segal and Spaeth 2002: 331–41). The general absence of support for the statutory SOP model is not for a lack of testing; Segal (1997, 1999), Spriggs and Hansford (2001), Sala and Spriggs (2004), Owens (2010), Segal, Westerland, and Lindquist (2011) all fail to find support for the override model. Harvey and Friedman (2006) find support for the override constitutional model, but the effects of Congressional constraint are not strong.

While the empirical evidence for the classic override/statutory SOP model remains limited, the institutional maintenance SOP model has fared better (Clark 2009, 2011; Segal, Westerland, and Lindquist 2011). The initial tests of these models suggest a Court that is constrained by its political environment but in a clearly different way than is assumed by the classic SOP model. The tests of the institutional maintenance model suggest a Court that worries about its institutional standing but generally does not fear having its decisions overturned. Clark (2011) finds support for his institutional legitimacy model in both statutory and constitutional decisions. This highlights the importance of being clear about whether the Court is constrained by the override game or the institutional legitimacy game, regardless of whether or not the study involves constitutional or statutory decisions. For example, Bailey and Maltzman (2011) find systematic evidence of Congressional constraint in both models of statutory cases and all cases. These results are motivated by the classic statutory override SOP model, but their operationalization and interpretation of their model are far more in line with institutional maintenance models. Bailey and Maltzman include an SOP measure in their ideal point model that is coded as 1 if the Court median is to the left of Congress, −1 if to the right, and 0 otherwise. Their results show that some justices will moderate their views toward Congressional preferences if the Court median is out of the Pareto set.[8] Bailey and Maltzman argue that at least for the justices with a significant (and correctly signed) SOP effect, fear is motivating the deference to Congress. But is it fear of having the decision overturned or fear of an institutional attack? The Bailey and Maltzman analysis supports the latter, not the former. Nothing in their model demonstrates fear of a specific override. However, the finding that some members of the Court will moderate their preferences if the Court is an ideological outlier is fully compatible with the institutional legitimacy SOP model.

Finally, it must be noted that the one inescapable conclusion from the SOP literature is the importance of judicial policy preferences. The individual variation observed with respect to the influence of strategic considerations does not hold for ideological preferences. Even in models that find support for the SOP model, judicial ideology is still a statistically significant and substantively meaningful predictor of judicial decisions (Clark 2011; Segal, Westerland, and Lindquist 2011).

Remaining Puzzles and Future Directions

One of the themes that arises in the work on strategic constraints of judicial behavior is that justices vary greatly in the extent to which their decisions appear constrained, and the SOP literature is no different. This poses two related questions about strategic judicial decision-making. First, if it is strategic for a particular justice to be constrained, then why is it not strategic for all justices to be constrained? One of the clear advantages of the formal specifications of the SOP game is that the predictions are applicable to all justices. But the empirical findings are consistent only with respect to the inconsistency with which justices are constrained. Bailey and Maltzman (2011) believe that this heterogeneity is "common sense" because "justices are influenced in different ways by any given factor" (p. 106). But if it is rational to anticipate Congressional preferences, why do so many justices seem oblivious to this constraint? The literature has yet to offer any good solution to this puzzle. We do not yet have a good answer for why some justices are strategic and others are not, but trying to answer that question quickly leads to a related concern. A theory that requires nine specifications for the Court at any given time is not a theory of anything. Reconciling a general approach to Supreme Court behavior with a coherent way of understanding the cross-justice variation is a non-trivial problem for the strategic literature. Of course, the same variation on the effect of ideology on Supreme Court behavior is not observed, as policy preferences consistently explain the decisions of all of the justices.

We also need a better empirical understanding of the development of institutional legitimacy and how it fluctuates over time. The Court's independence has certainly not been constant. Strategic accounts of decisions such as *Marbury v. Madison* (1803) demonstrate perfectly the logic of the SOP model in action (Clinton 1994; Knight and Epstein 1996), but the Marshall Court faced a very different set of institutional constraints than the modern Court. Is the type of strategic calculation in *Marbury* less likely once the Court reaches some threshold of legitimacy (Gibson, Caldeira, and Baird 1998)? Recent formal work shows how initial restraint by a judiciary can lead to greater independence and legitimacy (Carrubba 2009). The prevailing historical account of the institutional development of the American judiciary suggests that strategic politicians used courts to entrench policies or to accomplish goals that otherwise might have been difficult to realize (Gillman 2002; Crowe 2012). What implications, if any, might that have for how SOP games evolve over time?

The SOP literature is also just beginning to account for the strategic interplay between the Court and public opinion. Ura and Wohlfarth (2010) show that the Court's institutional growth is a function of public support. This potentially recasts the institutional maintenance model as a game of proactively building and growing legitimacy rather than fearing its loss. The Court also seems to have some ability to change public opinion. Ura (2014) finds that the Court is capable of shaping long-term public opinion even when the Court suffers a short-term backlash from a specific decision. Of course, many others find that the causal arrow moves in the opposite direction (McGuire and Stimson 2004; Friedman 2009). The SOP literature can do more to account for the strategic interplay between the Court and public opinion. A notable exception is Staton's (2006, 2010) work on the strategic use of going public with decisions.

The entire discussion thus far has either implicitly or explicitly assumed that "the Court" in the SOP game is the U.S. Supreme Court and "the legislature" is Congress. When limited in this way, the debate between competing models is over the consequences of a fixed institutional context. Moving beyond the Supreme Court–Congress case has the result of varying the institutional arrangements. The SOP literature can expand in at least two ways from a narrow casting of the field. First, we might consider the SOP model for other American courts. Within the federal court system, many assumptions of the SOP model should apply to Courts of Appeals judges as well. The preliminary work on Congressional constraint on Courts of Appeals decision-making has mixed findings (Cross and Tiller 1998; Brent 1999; Revesz 2001; Cross 2007). A part of the difficulty is the need to identify a theoretical account of SOP considerations in conjunction with the judicial hierarchy models. State courts also have promise for the study of SOP models (Brace, Hall, and Langer 2001; Langer 2002), but the institutional legitimacy model has yet to be tested at the state level. State judicial elections have fascinating implications for judicial legitimacy (Gibson 2012), but how this might translate into a state-level SOP game remains unknown.[9]

Even more importantly, the study of the SOP model in a cross-national context has a great deal of potential. This is not to suggest a new avenue but rather a recognition of how important the comparative study of SOP models has been (and likely will be moving forward). Some of the most important contributions to the SOP literature in the past ten to fifteen years have been developed outside of the American institutional context. Vanberg's (2005) influential model of judicial review is tested with the German Constitutional Court, and Staton (2010) builds on the Vanberg model and applies it in Mexico. Using data from Argentina, Helmke (2002) shows that the Argentine Supreme Court strategically defects from regimes that begin to lose power. These studies all have unique formal specifications of the SOP game and careful empirical tests of the models, and as a result, constitute major contributions to our general understanding of judicial institutions.

Conclusion

One way to characterize the debate about judicial behavior is as a direct competition between attitudinal and strategic models. The progress from Murphy's seminal account of judicial strategy to now is remarkable. The strategic analysis of judicial behavior and SOP games has generated both sophisticated models and empirical tests. So what is the lesson from the SOP literature? Is the Supreme Court primarily attitudinal or strategic? The most consistent finding in the SOP literature is the major role attitudes play in explaining decisions. Acknowledging that political preferences matter to Supreme Court justices is far from path breaking, but that does not mean it is any less valid. We simply do not have evidence that the Supreme Court ignores its political preferences because of SOP considerations. This is not to minimize the importance of strategic considerations, but instead is to reaffirm the centrality of the attitudinal model for the U.S. Supreme Court.

At the same time, a growing consensus is emerging regarding the institutional legitimacy variant of the SOP model. The strategic maintenance of judicial power and institutional legitimacy seems to clearly shape U.S. Supreme Court behavior. One of the more interesting points from the SOP literature is the great irony that the Court's pursuit of political preferences is likely contingent on the perception of the Court as a neutral apolitical institution (Clark 2011). The implications of the strategic pursuit of judicial independence have not been fully explored, but this is just one example of the continuing vibrancy of the study of strategic judicial behavior.

Notes

1. See Epstein and Knight (2000).
2. Consider Segal and Spaeth's summary of their version of the attitudinal model: "Rehnquist vote[d] the way he [did] because he [was] extremely conservative; Marshall voted the way did because he was extremely liberal" (Segal and Spaeth 2002: 86).

3. The preface in *Elements* is largely a reassurance that Murphy is not destroying the rule of law by using the words like "bargaining" or by using the papers of deceased justices for data.
4. It is likely not an accident that the strategic models rose to prominence only after decades of extensive empirical testing of the attitudinal model. After all, if we cannot agree that Supreme Court justices have preferences in the first place, it is hard to have a conversation about strategic decision-making.
5. These techniques have yet to be applied to Congressional roll-call data, but there is no reason to expect the legislative policy space to have many fewer dimensions than the Supreme Court's policy space.
6. More precisely, a tangent transformation of the Common Space score for the regression is used. The transformation is necessary because CS scores are bounded between –1 and 1, while the MQ scores are theoretically unbounded. See Sala and Spriggs (2004) for an example of a linear transformation of MQ scores into Common Space.
7. See Bailey (2013) for a comprehensive comparison of his scores with the MQ scores and Ho and Quinn (2010) for a review of conceptual and statistical issues in using MQ scores.
8. Interestingly, some justices, most notably Frankfurter, have a positive SOP effect, meaning they vote more liberally when the SOP model predicts they should vote more conservatively.
9. A hurdle (to say the least) to studying SOP models at the state level is the difficulty with generating directly judicial and legislative preference measures over a substantial period of time.

References

Bailey, M. A. 2007. "Comparable Preference Estimates across Time and Institutions for the Court, Congress, and Presidency." *American Journal of Political Science* 51: 433–48.

Bailey, M. A. 2013. "Is Today's Court the Most Conservative in Sixty Years? Challenges and Opportunities in Measuring Judicial Preferences." *Journal of Politics* 75: 821–34.

Bailey, M. A., and Maltzman, F. 2008. "Does Legal Doctrine Matter?" *American Political Science Review* 102: 369–84.

Bailey, M. A., and Maltzman, F. 2011. *The Constrained Court: Law, Politics, and the Decisions Justices Make.* Princeton, NJ: Princeton University Press.

Bergara, M., Richman, B., and Spiller, P. T. 2003. "Modeling Supreme Court Strategic Decision Making: The Congressional Constraint." *Legislative Studies Quarterly* 28: 247–80.

Brace, P., Langer, L., and Hall, M. G. 2001. "Placing Courts in State Politics." *State Politics and Policy Quarterly* 1: 81–108.

Brent, J. C. 1999. "An Agent and Two Principles: U.S. Courts of Appeals Responses to *Employment Division, Department of Human Resources v. Smith* and the Religious Freedom and Restoration Act." *American Politics Quarterly* 27: 236–66.

Carrubba, C. J. 2009. "A Model of the Endogenous Development of Judicial Institutions in Federal and International Systems." *Journal of Politics* 71: 55–69.

Carrubba, C. J., and Zorn, C. 2010. "Executive Discretion, Judicial Decision Making, and Separation of Power in the United States." *Journal of Politics* 72: 812–24.

Chutkow, D. M. 2008. "Jurisdiction Stripping: Litigation, Ideology, and Congressional Control of the Courts." *Journal of Politics* 70: 1053–64.

Clark, T. S. 2009. "The Separation of Powers, Court-Curbing, and Judicial Legitimacy." *American Journal of Political Science* 53: 971–89.

Clark, T. S. 2011. *The Limits of Judicial Independence*. New York, NY: Cambridge.
Clinton, R. L. 1994. "Game Theory, Legal History, and the Origins of Judicial Review." *American Journal of Political Science* 38: 255–302.
Cox, G., and McCubbins, M. 2005. *Setting the Agenda: Responsible Party Government in the U.S. House of Representatives*. New York, NY: Cambridge University Press.
Crombez, C., Groseclose, T., and Krehbiel, K. 2006. "Gatekeeping." *Journal of Politics* 68: 322–34.
Cross, F. B. 2007. *Decision Making in the U.S. Courts of Appeals*. Palo Alto, CA: Stanford University Press.
Cross, F. B., and Tiller, E. H. 1998. "Judicial Partisanship and Obedience to Legal Doctrine: Whistleblowing on the Federal Courts of Appeals." *Yale Law Journal* 107: 2155–76.
Crowe, J. 2012. *Building the Judiciary: Law, Courts, and the Politics of Institutional Development*. Princeton, NJ: Princeton University Press.
Dahl, R. 1957. "Decision Making in a Democracy: The Supreme Court as a National Policy Maker." *Journal of Public Law* 6: 179–295.
Downs, A. 1957. *An Economic Theory of Democracy*. New York, NY: Harper & Row.
Epstein, L., Martin, A. D., Segal, J. A., and Westerland, C. 2007. "The Judicial Common Space." *Journal of Law, Economics, & Organization* 23: 303–25.
Epstein, L., and Knight, J. 1998. *The Choices Judges Make*. Washington, DC: CQ Press.
Epstein, L., and Knight, J. 2000. "Toward a Strategic Revolution in Judicial Politics: A Look back, a Look ahead." *Political Research Quarterly* 53: 625–61.
Epstein, L., Martin, A. D., and Knight, J. 2001. "The Supreme Court as a Strategic National Policymaker." *Emory Law Review* 50: 583–612.
Eskridge, W. N., Jr. 1991a. "Reneging on History? Playing the Court/Congress/President Civil Rights Game." *California Law Review* 79: 613–64.
Eskridge, W. N., Jr. 1991b. "Overriding Supreme Court Statutory Decisions." *Yale Law Journal* 101: 331–417.
Ferejohn, J., and Shipan, C. 1990. "Congressional Influence on Bureaucracy." *Journal of Law, Economics, & Organization* 6: 1–20.
Ferejohn, J., and Weingast, B. 1992. "Limitation on Statutes: Strategic Statutory Interpretation." *Georgetown Law Journal* 80: 565–82.
Friedman, B. 2009. *The Will of the People: How Public Opinion Has Influenced the Supreme Court and Shaped the Meaning of the Constitution*. New York, NY: Farrar, Straus and Giroux.
Gely, R., and Spiller, P. T. 1990. "A Rational Choice Theory of Supreme Court Decision Making with Applications to the *State Farm* and *Grove City* Cases." *Journal of Law, Economics, & Organization* 12: 263–79.
Gibson, J. L. 2012. *Electing Judges: The Surprising Effects of Campaigning on Judicial Legitimacy*. Chicago, IL: University of Chicago Press.
Gibson, J. L., Caldeira, G. A., and Baird, V. 1998. "On the Legitimacy of National High Courts." *American Political Science Review* 92: 343–58.
Gillman, H. 2002. "How Political Parties Can Use the Courts to Advance their Agendas: Federal Courts in the United States, 1875–1819." *American Political Science Review* 96: 511–24.
Grofman, B., and Brazill, T. 2002. "Identifying the Median Justice on the Supreme Court." *Public Choice* 112: 55–79.
Hall, M. E. K. 2014. "The Semiconstrained Court: Public Opinion, the Separation of Powers, and the U.S. Supreme Court's Fear of Nonimplementation." *American Journal of Political Science* 58: 352–66.

Harvey, A., and Friedman, B. 2006. "Pulling Punches: Congressional Constraints on the Supreme Court's Constitutional Rulings." *Legislative Studies Quarterly* 31: 533–62.

Helmke, G. 2002. "The Logic of Strategic Defection: Court-Executive Relations in Argentina under Dictatorship and Democracy." *American Political Science Review* 96: 291–303.

Ho, D. E., and Quinn, K. M. 2010. "How Not to Lie with Judicial Votes." *California Law Review* 98: 813–76.

Knight, J., and Epstein, L. 1996. "On the Struggle for Judicial Supremacy." *Law & Society Review* 30: 87–130.

Langer, L. 2002. *Judicial Review in State Supreme Courts: A Comparative Study*. Albany, NY: SUNY Press.

Lauderdale, B., and Clark, T. S. 2012. "The Supreme Court's Many Median Justices." *American Political Science Review* 106: 847–66.

Lauderdale, B. E., and Clark, T. S. 2014. "Scaling Politically Meaningful Dimensions Using Texts and Votes." *American Journal of Political Science* 58: 754–71.

Maltzman, F., Spriggs, J. F., and Wahlbeck, P. J. 2000. *Crafting Law on the Supreme Court: The Collegial Game*. Cambridge: Cambridge University Press.

Marks, B. A. 1989. "A Model of Judicial Influence on Congressional Policy-Making: *Grove City College v. Bell*." Ph.D. dissertation, Washington University.

Martin, A. D. 2001. "Congressional Decision Making and the Separation of Powers." *American Political Science Review* 95: 361–78.

Martin, A. D., and Quinn, K. M. 2002. "Dynamic Ideal Point Estimation via Markov Chain Monte Carlo for the U.S. Supreme Court, 1953–1999." *Political Analysis* 10: 134–53.

McGuire, K. T., and Stimson, J. A. 2004. "The Least Dangerous Branch Revisited: New Evidence on Supreme Court Responsiveness to Public Preferences." *Journal of Politics* 66: 1018–35.

Meernik, J., and Ignani, J. 1997. "Judicial Review and Coordinate Construction of the Constitution." *American Journal of Political Science* 41: 447–67.

Moraski, B. J., and Shipan, C. R. 1999. "The Politics of Supreme Court Nominations: A Theory of Institutional Constraints and Choices." *American Journal of Political Science* 43: 1069–95.

Murphy, W. 1964. *Elements of Judicial Strategy*. Chicago, IL: University of Chicago Press.

Owens, R. J. 2010. "The Separation of Powers and Supreme Court Agenda Setting." *American Journal of Political Science* 54: 412–27.

Poole, K. T. 1998. "Recovering a Basic Space from a Set of Issue Scales." *American Journal of Political Science* 42: 954–93.

Poole, K. T., and Rosenthal, H. 1997. *Congress: A Political-Economic History of Roll Call Voting*. Oxford: Oxford University Press.

Pritchett, C. H. 1948. *The Roosevelt Court: A Study in Judicial Politics and Values, 1937–1947*. New York, NY: Macmillan.

Revesz, R. L. 2001. "Congressional Influence on Judicial Behavior? An Empirical Examination of Challenges to Agency Action in the D.C. Circuit Court." *New York University Law Review* 6(4): 1100–41.

Rhode, D. W., and Spaeth, H. J. 1976. *Supreme Court Decision Making*. San Francisco, CA: W. H. Freeman.

Riker, W. H. 1962. *The Theory of Political Coalitions*. New Haven, CT: Yale University Press.

Rosenberg, G. N. 1992. "Judicial Independence and the Reality of Judicial Power." *Review of Politics* 54: 369–98.

Sala, B. R., and Spriggs, J. F. 2004. "Designing Tests of the Supreme Court and the Separation of Powers." *Political Research Quarterly* 57: 197–208.

Segal, J. A. 1997. "Separation of Power Games in the Positive Theory of Congress and Courts." *American Political Science Review* 91: 28–44.
Segal, J. A. 1999. "Supreme Court Deference to Congress: An Examination of the Marksist Model." In *Supreme Court Decision Making: New Institutional Approaches*, edited by C. W. Clayton and H. Gillman. Chicago, IL: University of Chicago Press, 237–53.
Segal, J. A., and Cover, A. D. 1989. "Ideological Values and the Votes of U.S. Supreme Court Justices." *American Political Science Review* 83: 557–65.
Segal, J. A., and Spaeth, H. J. 1993. *The Supreme Court and the Attitudinal Model*. New York, NY: Cambridge University Press.
Segal, J. A., and Spaeth, H. J. 2002. *The Supreme Court and the Attitudinal Model Revisited*. New York, NY: Cambridge University Press.
Segal, J. A., and Westerland, C. 2005. "The Supreme Court, Congress, and Judicial Review." *North Carolina Law Review* 83: 1323–52.
Segal, J. A., Westerland, C., and Lindquist, S. A. 2011. "Congress, the Supreme Court, and Judicial Review: Testing a Constitutional Separation of Powers Model." *American Journal of Political Science* 55: 89–104.
Schubert, G. 1965. *The Judicial Mind*. Evanston, IL: Northwestern University Press.
Shepsle, K. A., and Weingast, B. R. 1987. "The Institutional Foundations of Committee Power." *American Political Science Review* 81: 85–104.
Spaeth, H. 1972. *An Introduction to Supreme Court Decision Making*, rev. ed. New York, NY: Chandler Publishing.
Spiller, P. T., and Gely, R. 1992. "Congressional Control or Judicial Independence: The Determinants of U.S. Supreme Court Labor-Relations Decisions." *RAND Journal of Economics* 23: 463–92.
Spriggs, J. F., and Hansford, T. G. 2001. "Explaining the Overruling of U.S. Supreme Court Precedent." *Journal of Politics* 63: 1091–111.
Staton, J. K. 2006. "Constitutional Review and the Selective Promotion of Case Results." *American Journal of Political Science* 50: 98–112.
Staton, J. K. 2010. *Judicial Power and Strategic Communication in Mexico*. New York, NY: Cambridge University Press.
Ura, J. D. 2014. "Backlash and Legitimation: Macro Political Responses to Supreme Court Decisions." *American Journal of Political Science* 58: 110–26.
Ura, J. D., and Wohlfarth, P. C. 2010. "'An Appeal to the People': Public Opinion and Congressional Support for the Supreme Court." *Journal of Politics* 72: 939–56.
Vanberg, G. 2005. *The Politics of Constitutional Review in Germany*. New York, NY: Cambridge University Press.

CHAPTER 14

JUDICIAL REVIEW

TOM CLARK

COURTS around the world often exercise the power to make declarations about the constitutionality of laws passed, and actions taken, by other branches of government. The process of allowing judges to review laws and actions is known as "judicial review" and constitutes an aspect of the judicial process to which scholars have paid great attention. Although judicial review comprises only one piece of the total body of nearly all courts' dockets, some of the most politically salient and contentious decisions courts have made around the world are cases of judicial review. In this chapter, I first provide a brief overview of the practice of judicial review and what it entails. I then describe the origins of judicial review, starting with its intellectual roots in documents like the Magna Carta and leading up through the early years of the U.S. Constitution and following through the spread throughout the world of the contemporary, common practice. Next, I describe research on judicial review, examining both normative, philosophical work and more positive, empirical work. I conclude with some remarks on the current state of interest and knowledge about judicial review.

WHAT IS JUDICIAL REVIEW?

In resolving disputes, between individuals, between individuals and the government, or between branches or levels of the government, courts must interpret the law and apply it to the question at hand in the case. Sometimes, though, there is conflict within the law. Two laws may prescribe inapposite actions. Particularly when those laws are hierarchically related—as in when a statute is in conflict with a constitution—judges exercise judicial review when they decide whether the "lower" law is invalid because of its inconsistency with the "higher" law. Below, I describe the emergence and evolution of this practice, but it is important to note at the outset that its intellectual roots lie in the observation that courts must interpret the law to apply it to individual cases, and it is unavoidable that at times some laws, because they were written at different times, for different purposes, or even intentionally, may conflict with each other. When one of those laws in a constitutional document—a law supreme to other laws, then it seems courts must opt to enforce the constitution rather than the legally inferior law.

A related issue concerns the locus of judicial review authority. In many common law systems, for example, any court with jurisdiction in a particular case may be competent to exercise judicial review. In other systems, though, judicial review is reserved to a designated court, perhaps one with a specialized constitutional function. Decentralized judicial review creates some opportunities, such as facilitating the adjudication of rights claims efficiently, without having to go to a special court. However, at the same time that opportunity creates the risk of disparate law governing different cases. A contemporary example concerns the state of same-sex marriage in the United States. In 2014, there were several cases pending before state and federal courts, challenging the constitutionality of state-level bans on same-sex marriage. Many judges, mostly federal judges, have declared those bans unconstitutional, though their decisions only have authority in their geographically defined jurisdictions. Therefore, whereas same-sex couples in Pennsylvania benefit from a federal judge's opinion that bans on same-sex marriage violate the US Constitution, similar individuals in states like Georgia have not yet won such a case. Thus, whereas it is relatively easy for anyone affected to challenge the constitutionality of the same-sex marriage ban, there is not a uniform voice of constitutional law for the entire country.

At an opposite end of the spectrum are places like France, which traditionally did not have any possibility for judicial review in the context of individual cases. Prior to 2009, any law, once enacted and promulgated by the executive, could not be reviewed for its constitutionality. (Since the founding of the Fifth Republic, the particular circumstances under which a law might be challenged—and by whom—gradually evolved to a more permissive standard, even while retaining a strict prohibition on challenging laws as they are applied.) Since 2009, there has been a possibility of judicial review, through a procedure known as the *question prioritaire de constitutionnalité*, or QPC. QPC cases are decided only by the Conseil Constitutionnel and must be first verified by one of the high courts—administrative or judicial—and referred to the Conseil Constitutionnel. In other words, constitutional challenges are centralized in a single body and must pass through a series of demanding procedural tests and convince high judges of their importance before being addressed.

There are, moreover, other models of judicial review. In much of Latin America, for example, the *recurso de amparo* is essentially the most common form of judicial review and is open to citizens with low barriers. In Costa Rica, Sala IV of the Supreme Court of Justice has authority over constitutional claims, but it is easy to file a claim with the court. In some jurisdictions, like Colombia, these complaints number over 400,000 per year, as contrasted with the small numbers—one hundred or so—of constitutional claims adjudicated in places like the United States, France, or Chile. While there are important differences in how constitutional courts hear and process constitutional cases, the key issue here is that there is marked variation in what constitutional courts do with constitutional challenges.

In the next section, I describe the intellectual origins and spread of judicial review. In part, this history helps account for the different styles of judicial review, though there is more than historical accident to explain why some places exercise diffuse judicial review whereas others exercise centralized review, and why some places have extensive constitutional dockets whereas others have massive dockets.[1]

Origins of Judicial Review

While the modern practice of judicial review has its origins in the federal and state judiciaries of the United States during the Founding era, the intellectual roots trace as far back as the Magna Carta. The Magna Carta was an agreement during the early thirteenth century between the king of England and the people of England that identified a number of principles limiting government power—in effect, rights. While debate exists about whether the Magna Carta in fact imposed meaningful limits on the monarch, the principle that government action may be limited by *ex ante* written agreements is at the core of judicial review. And, the Magna Carta has lived on as the symbol of government limited by written accord.

That principle would play a central role in the American Founding. The idea of writing a constitution that delegates government powers was to create an accountable government of limited powers, the implication being that exercises of authority in contravention of the constitution would be illegitimate. Who, though, would decide when government action crosses a constitutional line? That question, many have argued, was unresolved in the Constitution and remained a topic of speculation during the early years of the American Constitution. During the first decade of its existence, the U.S. Supreme Court reviewed the constitutionality of Acts of Congress as well as acts of state legislatures. However, it was not until the famous case of *Marbury v. Madison* (1803) that the Supreme Court first decided, in a formal opinion, that an Act of Congress was prohibited by the Constitution and therefore was not to be given effect.

Marbury is among the most famous cases in the history of American constitutional law. At stake in that case were a number of connected issues regarding early power struggles in America. However, the politically salient issue, from history's perspective, concerns judicial appointments made by President Adams during his last days in office. The 1800 presidential election was a bitter one, pitting Adams and the Federalists against Thomas Jefferson and the Republicans. The dividing cleavage in this battle was the role, size, and strength of the federal government. Whereas Adams favored a strong national government, Jefferson thought the federal government should be sharply limited and prioritized states' rights. In the wake of the election, but before the end of Adams' term, there were a number of federal judicial posts that were vacant, including positions as Justices of the Peace in Washington, DC. Adams set out to fill them before leaving office. One judge, William Marbury, was nominated and confirmed to be Justice of the Peace in Washington, DC, the day before Jefferson was sworn in. However, Jefferson refused to deliver the paperwork to Marbury, who then sued James Madison, in his capacity of Secretary of State, seeking a *writ of mandamus*. Marbury brought the case directly to the U.S. Supreme Court.

When they considered the case, the justices faced a difficult situation.[2] If the Court were to rule against Jefferson and order Madison to deliver Marbury's commission, there was a real chance that Jefferson would defy the Court and potentially retaliate. If the Court were to rule against Marbury, it would concede a political battle over the limits on executive power, implicitly limit the role of the Court in government, and make a decision that appeared, on its face, wrong. The genius of the Court's decision in this case lies in its elegant solution. Led by Chief Justice John Marshall (who was a cousin and staunch political adversary of Jefferson), the Supreme Court held that (1) Marbury deserved to have his commission delivered by Madison but (2) the Supreme Court did not have the authority to grant the writ of *mandamus*, because the provision of the Judiciary Act of 1789 that was unconstitutional. The reason for holding the law unconstitutional was that, on Marshall's reading of the law, it impermissibly created new original jurisdiction for the Supreme Court. The law could only give the Supreme Court appellate jurisdiction over writs of mandamus. The reason was that the Constitution clearly specifies which types of cases the Supreme Court can hear on "original" jurisdiction (meaning they can begin at the Supreme Court) and which types of cases the Supreme Court can only hear as an appellate court (meaning they must start elsewhere and work their way up to the Supreme Court). Because the Judiciary Act created a new type of original jurisdiction (i.e., the writ of mandamus)[3] the Act was inconsistent with the Constitution and therefore must be set aside. With this decision, Marshall not only took the high road on the political controversy—he was able to say that Marbury was in the right—but he also avoided the political conflict and turmoil that would follow if Jefferson ignored the Court's order. However, perhaps more important, Marshall was able to establish the authority to exercise judicial review and declare Acts of Congress unconstitutional (and, seemingly, to oversee the executive branch). It may not have been a novel idea, but its use in this situation and the assent it attained from the elected branches marked the beginning of a judicial practice that has deepened and spread throughout the world ever since.

Since Marbury, the use and practice of judicial review has grown in depth and breadth. In the United States, federal courts continued to review the constitutionality of laws throughout the nineteenth century, though for most of that time declined to invalidate any as unconstitutional. There are, to be sure, notable exceptions, such as the U.S. Supreme Court's decision in *Scott v. Sanford*, which invalidated the Missouri Compromise and is often credited with rendering unavoidable the Civil War. At the same time, judicial review began to spread to other parts of the world. Perhaps most important was the development of the writ of *amparo* in Mexico, which was an attempt to "introduce the basic principles of judicial review of the constitutionality of laws" in Mexico (Zamudio 1979: 309). Mexico's innovation was to create a writ by which citizens could go to court to enforce individual rights against the government. And, the Mexican innovation has been attributed to the American experience, as recounted through de Tocqueville's account of American politics and read by Mexican political figures. Moreover, just as in the American experience, the extent and import of judicial review has grown as the courts have extended the practice and attained political assent. Indeed, Mexican Constitution, both in the 1857 Constitution and during subsequent revisions, embodies the practice and subordinate laws have been written to formalize the practice (Staton 2010; Zamudio 1979: 315–16).

Throughout the nineteenth century, the practice of judicial review continued to spread throughout the world, especially through Latin America. The Mexican *amparo* served as a model for countries establishing constitutions and the rule of law through much of the twentieth century, especially South and Central American states. Today, most of the Latin American countries have a procedure like *amparo* to enable citizens to file constitutional claims before constitutional courts (e.g., Brewer-Carías 2009). Further abroad, places like Spain and the Philippines have adopted the *amparo* with similar outcomes—massive amounts of constitutional complaints being brought to a specialized constitutional tribunal.[4]

At the same time, during the twentieth century, there was yet another period during which new constitutions were written—some at the end of World War II and others after the collapse of the Soviet Union—and many of the new constitutions adopted or created forms of judicial review that had by then become typical of Western systems with constitutional courts (see, e.g., Ginsburg 2008). Earlier in the twentieth century, after World War I, there was a smaller, but similar, spread of constitutional courts, including a Supreme Court in the Weimar Republic and a constitutional court in Austria. The 1920 Austrian constitution is often cited as one prototype for modern European constitutional courts.[5] The German case provide an interesting comparison to the Latin American *amparo*. In many ways, the intent is the same. The *Constitutional Complaint*, as it is known in Germany, provides a very flexible mechanism for bringing a complaint about an unconstitutional law to the German courts. However, as contrasted with Costa Rica and similar states with *amparo*, the constitutional complaint has relatively demanding standards. Not just anyone can bring a constitutional complaint at any time; instead there are restrictions and conditions that must be satisfied, which resemble in many aspects the American "case and controversy."[6] Crucially, whereas the case and controversy rule is a judicially created doctrine in the United States, grounded in Article III, Section 2, of the Constitution, other countries often have more elaborate rules set out in their constitutions themselves. These rules may enumerate the kinds of claims that can be brought and/or the procedure for bringing constitutional cases. Moreover, whereas judicial review in the United States is a practice grounded in constitutional theory and judicial interpretation, in many countries judicial review is a process specifically authorized and detailed in the constitutions themselves. This is particularly true in most new constitutions.

Indeed, the prevalence of judicial review to a political culture in which individual rights are prominent or even central can be detected in twenty-first-century European politics. Supra-national institutions, such as the European Court of Human Rights and the European Court of Justice exist in large part to exercise a version of judicial review in which grievances about the conflict between laws can be resolved.

RESEARCH ON JUDICIAL REVIEW

Two areas of research on judicial review have dominated the literature during much of the past one hundred years. Unfortunately, these literatures too often have not spoken directly to each other, though there are natural connections and important lessons that transcend the research programs (see, e.g., Friedman 2005).

Normative Concerns

Scholars of judicial review have puzzled at least since the end of the nineteenth century over the tension between a commitment to protecting individual rights via judicial review on one hand and the principle of democratic self-governance and accountability on the other hand. Commonly referred to as the "counter-majoritarian difficulty" (e.g., Bickel 1962),[7] the central puzzle can be summarized as follows. The signature intellectual feature of constitutionalism emerging from the era marked by the American and French Revolutions was that of liberal constitutionalism and the idea that one could create a government of limited powers. Liberal constitutionalism developed to entail two competing goals—government by majority rule and the protection of unalienable rights. A government of limited powers became synonymous with the idea of a written constitution and could, in theory, provide the basis for limiting the power of the people. The authority of the state would be under popular control, but there would be limits to the purposes to which that authority could be put. However, an inherent tension emerges in that any government powerful enough to carry out the powers of the state is also powerful enough to abuse individual rights, especially minority rights. How can one reconcile a commitment to giving the power of the state to elected majorities with the commitment to limit the power of those majorities? Clearly, something must give.

The innovation of judicial review provides a way to balance those goals. If the will of the people is to be limited by a written constitution, then there ought to be an institution or body responsible for identifying instances of transgression. Moreover, that body ought to be as removed from the elected majority as possible, for fear that the interpreter of government power be bound up with the government itself. The judiciary is the branch of government that is not directly accountable to the public (with limited exceptions, including many U.S. states, where judges are elected) and is charged not with making policy but with interpreting policy as made by legislative and executive officials in the process of applying those policies to individual cases. As John Marshall famously claimed in *Marbury*, in justifying the Supreme Court's authority to invalidate a law via judicial review, "It is emphatically the province and duty of the judicial department to say what the law is. Those who apply the rule to particular cases, must of necessity expound and interpret that rule. If two laws conflict with each other, the courts must decide on the operation of each."

The logic of Marshall's claim is elegant. Courts are the institution charged with resolving disputes in individual cases. Doing so requires the capacity to interpret the law; it is a logical corollary of that responsibility. At the same time, it is unavoidable that at times, two laws will come into conflict. Courts must, therefore, have the capacity to decide what to do in such instances, which entails setting aside one law in favor of another. That this logical conclusion points to, of necessity, the authority to exercise judicial review follows directly from the principle that a constitution is the supreme law of the land.

However, as the use of judicial review by the judiciary grew over the course of the nineteenth century, scholars became increasingly concerned about the potential for the courts to usurp government authority and undermine the principle of self-government. As I explain later in this chapter, this period also marked the rise of legal realism, the view that judges do not merely interpret and apply the law as disinterested, neutral arbiters, but instead impose their own worldviews through the interpretation of the law. By the end of the nineteenth century, scholars were engaged in a heated debate about the conditions under which courts may legitimately exercise the power of judicial review. James Bradley Thayer published a landmark law review in 1893, entitled "The Origin and Scope of the American Doctrine of Constitutional Law," which opened with the observation that state constitutions did not bestow upon the federal judiciary the power to declare legislation unconstitutional (Thayer 1893: 129). Thayer then criticizes the use of judicial review as being prone to abuse and inadequate for addressing the democratic deficiencies which defenders of minority rights argue is the justification for judicial review.

However, Thayer's observation, rather than marking a point of resolution of the counter-majoritarian tension, would mark the beginning of a deep, complex intellectual struggle over judicial review. The early years of the twentieth century would witness increased "activism" by the U.S. Supreme Court, with important decisions such as *Lochner v. New York* serving as rallying calls for those concerned with judicial usurpation of policy-making powers, only a decade after Thayer's essay.

Lochner was a case that came to the Supreme Court in 1904 and was decided in 1905. The issue was the following. The New York state legislature had enacted the Bakeshop Act in 1895. The law was meant to regulate the hours and sanitary conditions in bakeries. It is important to keep in mind the broader context in which this all took place. The late-nineteenth century was a period of considerable immigration and also of industrialization. Many unions worked to push for legislation to protect whites against immigrant labor (see, e.g., Kersch 2004). During these years, Upton Sinclair wrote *The Jungle*, which portrayed the unsanitary and dangerous working conditions immigrants found themselves in. It was under these circumstances that the Bakeshop Act imposed on bakers a limit of ten working hours per day and a weekly maximum of sixty hours. Lochner was a bakery owner convicted of violating the Bakeshop Act by allowing an employee to work over the limits. When the Supreme Court took up the Lochner case, it did so in the context of heated politics surrounding economic regulation, industrialization, and immigration. Conservatives of the time widely advanced a theory of "laissez-faire economics," which held that the best policy is for government to stay out of regulating industry. Liberals, by contrast, adopted the view that with industrialization came relationships between employees and employers that were not just inherently unequal but prime to foster exploitation of the employee.

Its decision, which was decided by a 5–4 majority, held that the Bakeshop Act was unconstitutional because it violated a "liberty to contract" created by the Fourteenth Amendment. In the Court's view, individuals were free to contract with employers, and restrictions on the working arrangements to which they could contract violated their liberty. The Court's opinion claimed that being a baker is not hazardous to one's health and that there is no reason why the State should be allowed to regulate baking. Justices Harlan and Holmes each wrote dissenting opinions, and Justice Holmes is perhaps the most often quoted. His dissent begins:

> This case is decided upon an economic theory which a large part of the country does not entertain. If it were a question whether I agreed with that theory, I should desire to study it further and long before making up my mind. But I do not conceive that to be my duty, because I strongly believe that my agreement or disagreement has nothing to do with the right of a majority to embody their opinions in law. It is settled by various decisions of this court that state constitutions and state laws may regulate life in many ways which we, as legislators, might think as injudicious, or, if you like, as tyrannical, as this, and which, equally with this, interfere with the liberty to contract. Sunday laws and usury laws are ancient examples. A more modern one is the prohibition of lotteries. The liberty of the citizen to do as he likes so long as he does not interfere with the liberty of others to do the same, which has been a shibboleth for some well-known writers, is interfered with by school laws, by the Post Office, by every state or municipal institution which takes his money for purposes thought desirable, whether he likes it or not. The Fourteenth Amendment does not enact Mr. Herbert Spencer's Social Statics.[8]

The last line, referring to Spencer's *Social Statics* refers to a mid-nineteenth-century libertarian political philosophy treatise by Herbert Spencer. Holmes' opening paragraph was deeply incisive. He accuses the majority of using judicial review to pursue its own policy agenda. He also claims, presumably correctly, that the policy agenda advanced by the Court in the majority opinion was one of great public division. By claiming that the Fourteenth Amendment does not enact *Social Statics*, Holmes directly accuses the majority of trying to read into the Constitution a deeply divisive political philosophy of libertarianism. Following *Lochner*, reaction was at first mild but within months grew increasingly fierce. Libertarians rushed to praise the decision, whereas progressives and labor unions quickly denounced the decision (Bernstein 2005: 1500–1). Moreover, the course of history has had its way with *Lochner*, as it has become a symbol for conservative judicial activism and an expression to refer to the worst uses of judicial review. The critical point, though, is that with *Lochner*, the tension between judicial review and democratic governance was laid bare for the public, in the context of a national policy debate, for the second time in a half century. Moreover, the Court's increased use of judicial review since the growth of the nation after the Civil War and with industrialization meant that this was not just an aberration like the *Dred Scott* case but was instead a fundamental tension in the Constitution with which we would have to wrestle.

Following *Lochner*, however, the Court's laissez-faire approach to economic regulation persisted, as it increasingly brought the power of judicial review to bear on state regulations of employment conditions. Led by four justices known as the "Four Horsemen," the Court developed a doctrine of substantive due process that would make it difficult for states or Congress to regulate the economy. The doctrine of substantive due process, coupled with a narrow reading of congressional powers under the Commerce Clause, would lead the Court, during the New Deal, into perhaps its greatest confrontation with the elected branches and a larger political battle about the role of judicial review in society.

Still the Court's interpretation of the due process and commerce clauses did not spark the ire that it would during the 1930s. The Great Depression and New Deal legislative program that followed would mark an important point in the normative debate over judicial review. The Supreme Court, in reviewing President Roosevelt's legislative efforts to overcome the depression, would adopt a rather suspect approach and invalidated a number of key provisions of the New Deal program. That those efforts were sometimes divided, and divided along generational and partisan lines, served to underscore the inherent difficulty associated with giving judges appointed to lifetime tenure an effective veto over elected majorities. If large legislative majorities could not enact regulatory legislation in a time of national—and, international—economic crisis because it did not comport with "out-of-date" understandings of the economy and the Constitution's provisions pertaining thereto, then what had become of the principle of self-government. Was the American experience now one of a juristocracy, rather than a republican democracy? This question motivated a significant period of criticism of the Supreme Court (see, Clark 2011: ch. 2). Indeed, it is notable that one of the earliest Gallup public opinion polls ever taken asked the public whether the Constitution should be amended to limit or take away the Court's power to declare Acts of Congress unconstitutional. Fifty-nine percent of those who responded thought so (Clark 2011).

However, while the Supreme Court did ultimately back down from its skeptical stance against the elected branches (more on this below), normative concern about the practice of judicial review continued. Indeed, in one watershed decision, *US v. Carolene Products* (1938), the Supreme Court noted (in the famous footnote 4 of the majority opinion) that it would shift its strictest applications of judicial review to specific kinds of cases—most specifically, those involving discrimination against "discrete and insular minorities." Most notably, when the Supreme Court, in 1954, held unconstitutional the practice of racially segregating public schools, intellectuals were thrust into a difficult position. Liberals who had argued forcefully against the use of judicial review to invalidate legislation during the 1930s were now faced with a use of judicial review of which they morally approved. How could one square a desire to approve of *Brown v. Board of Education* with an intellectual position that calls for limiting judicial activism against the government?

In perhaps one of the most famous and important arguments on this subject, Alexander Bickel argued that the Supreme Court should exercise its "passive virtues" to decline to review cases where there are other branches or institutions more adequately prepared to resolve the controversy. Only when an issue is such that only the judiciary can be the one to resolve an inequity or injustice should the Court resort to constitutional judicial review. Bickel's prescription, though, turned out to be insufficient just over a decade later when it seemed to justify the Court's decision in *Roe v. Wade*, invalidating outright prohibition of abortion. Academics set out to outline a prescription for the use of judicial review that would simultaneously permit the Court's invalidation of school segregation and proscribe the Court's invalidation of abortion restrictions.

Among these proposals, John Hart Ely's *Democracy and Distrust* (1980) is perhaps the most significant. Ely proposes that courts should be able to use judicial review when the inequities or rights violations are appropriate for judicial remedy, but only when those rights violations undermine the democratic process. In Ely's view, the Constitution's paramount goal is to ensure participation and democratic equality, when a majoritarian act is designed to inhibit or have the effect of inhibiting equal political participation, the Court should step in to correct the violation. Leveling the playing field, so to speak, allows the democratic process to work so that the majority can rule, but requires that minority voices and viewpoints be given their place in policy-making.

By the end of the twentieth century, however, debate moved away from an argument about the conditions that justify the exercise of judicial review to one about the role of myriad institutions in constitutional interpretation. The idea of "departmentalism" took hold, with scholars arguing that legislatures, executives, courts, and even the public all have a role in interpreting the Constitution. In this view, judicial decisions are but one part of a constitutional dialogue (see, e.g., Murphy 1986; Alexander and Schauer 1997; Whittington 2009). Others, including Tushnet (2000) and Kramer (2004) famously called for the people to engage in robust constitutional discourse to protect their rights themselves, rather than relying on the courts to do so. Eisgruber (2001) and Peretti (1999) argued that courts should engage in explicitly political judicial review in order to encourage and facilitate constitutional debate and respect for minority rights.

Debate about the appropriate role of judicial review in a democratic society continues. Of late, though, it has largely moved from a scholarly debate about the normative desirability of a counter-majoritarian check to a partisan debate about "judicial activism." The phrase is one we hear often in political debates and the media, though it is rarely well conceptualized. Usually, it is used to criticize judicial decisions with which one disagrees. To conservatives, the Supreme Court's decision to invalidate a portion of the Defense of Marriage Act was an example of "liberal judicial activism," whereas the preceding day's decision to invalidate the Voting Rights Act was a victory for liberty, "restor[ing] constitutional order."[9] To liberals, the Voting Rights Act case was the worst kind of judicial activism,[10] whereas the DOMA decision as a triumph for equality.[11] Whether this debate is in the spirit of what scholars of constitutional theory have hoped for remains to be seen.

Empirical Patterns

Turning from normative to empirical scholarship on judicial review, there are (at least) two important issues to which research speaks. The first concerns how judicial review acts as a tool for conflict between the branches. The second examines how larger democratic institutions shape the consequences of judicial review. The empirical research, especially that motivated by the latter set of issues, has moved in recent years to speak more closely to the normative literature.

Beginning in the mid-twentieth century, scholars began to study the use of judicial review in the context of the countermajoritarian difficulty from a quantitative perspective. In a landmark study, Robert Dahl identified every instance in which an Act of Congress was struck down as unconstitutional (by the U.S. Supreme Court) and asked whether it seemed the Court was acting as an unduly anti-majoritarian Court (Dahl 1957). Dahl's finding is that legislation is very commonly invalidated within four years of enactment, and when legislation is struck down, enacting majorities usually have an opportunity to revisit the subject and pass new legislation. One reason, Dahl argues, is that 73 percent of Supreme Court vacancies take place within two years of the most recent vacancy. As a consequence, the Supreme Court is generally part of the dominant governing coalition.

While in many senses preliminary and less sophisticated than subsequent studies of judicial review, Dahl's analysis highlights an important point that goes to the heart of normative debates about judicial review. Whereas the practice of judicial review might in theory be in tension with ideals of democratic majoritarianism, the method by which judges are selected implies a level of democratic representation on the courts that mitigates that tension.

While others have criticized Dahl's study on various grounds—notably, Casper (1976) argues that by excluding Supreme Court review of state legislation, Dahl underestimates the Court's countermajoritarianism—the crucial point remains unchallenged. However, it is important to note that the late twentieth century witnessed a period of relatively slow turnover on the Court. What is more, modern Supreme Court justices are increasingly insulated from the political process; with the retirement of Justice O'Connor in 2006, the Supreme Court had not a single member who had ever held elected office.

Indeed, Dahl's thesis has served as a starting point for countless studies of judicial review. Scholars have probed the determinants of judicial votes to invalidate legislation (e.g., Howard and Segal 2004; Harvey and Friedman 2006; Lindquist and Solberg 2007; Keith 2008; Clark and Whittington n.d.) and largely concluded, not surprisingly, the decision to invalidate legislation is heavily attributed to attitudinal factors that influence most judicial choices (e.g., Segal and Spaeth 2002; Lindquist and Cross 2009) but that may be a modern-day phenomenon (see Epstein and Landes 2012).

Of course, these observations simply raise additional, empirically-driven concerns about the counter-majoritarian difficulty. If courts exercise judicial review in seemingly ideological ways, even if the majority selects who is on the court, does this not undermine the representative ideal? A series of studies I refer to collectively as "separation of powers analyses" look directly at this problem. The question motivating these studies is whether the courts are constrained by the elected branches. To the extent judicial review is limited by the authority of the elected branches, while one might worry more about the integrity of minority rights, majoritarian policy-making might find itself on stronger ground.

Many separation of powers analyses have studied statutory interpretation, though some of been concerned directly with judicial review. In these studies, a variety of theoretical mechanisms might constrain the use of judicial review. Epstein, Knight, and Martin (2001) argued, and Segal, Westerland and Lindquist (2011) demonstrate that the Supreme Court will exercise self-restraint when it is worried that Congress will diminish the Court's power, through budgetary or similar means. Similarly, Vanberg (2005) argues that public support is critical to the meaningful exercise of judicial review. Because courts do not have the power to enforce their own decisions, they rely on political will to enforce their decisions; if elected officials decide to stand up against the courts, the whether the public supports the court or the elected officials will be the deciding factor for who "wins" in such a confrontation. A crucial component to Vanberg's theory is that disputes between the courts and elected branches may involve complicated, or obtuse legal questions. The consequence is that the public will sometimes understand the issue at hand and sometimes not; the courts and elected officials must incorporate this prospect into their calculation about what will happen if they conflict. Staton (2010) extends that logic to examine how courts may engage with the public in order to clarify the issues at hand, through, for example, direct media action to inform the public. Clark (2011) proposes an alternative extension, claiming that political posturing by elected representatives, in the form of criticism of the Court, can be useful for figuring out where the public stands. The reason is, Clark observes, elected officials have a more direct connection with the public than the courts and therefore better information about whether the public will side with them in the event of a conflict with the courts.

Coming full circle to the Dahlian framework, Friedman (2010) documents an ongoing, consistent pattern by which the courts respond to and in turn mold public opinion about hotly-debated policy and constitutional questions. The bottom line is that over time, public opinion affects judicial review in such a way that the meaning of the Constitution, as interpreted through judicial decisions, will in fact reflect popular opinion (Friedman 2010, 367–8). Thus, in many ways, the initial observation from Dahl still dominates the way in which scholars study the empirical use of judicial review. Judges may exercise judicial review in an ideologically-driven way, but the court is not entirely divorced from democratic accountability. Regular appointments to the courts by elected representatives (Dahl 1957), institutional oversight and power (Segal, Westerland, and Lindquist 2011; Rosenberg 1992), and the ultimate authority of the public will over both legislatures and courts (Vanberg 2005) combine to create a system in which courts are simply part of a system of governance in which constitutional interpretation must take place, and institutional structures are designed to facilitate incorporating public sovereignty into the meaning of our laws.

Conclusion

Judicial review is an important institution in a liberal representative democracy. It provides a mechanism by which violations of constitutional rights or limitations can be addressed and remedied. The spread of the practice during the nineteenth and twentieth centuries has rendered it an omnipresent feature of modern democracy. However, with the rise of judicial review has come a series of normative and empirical debates about the use and practice of judicial review. Scholars have pondered how we can square judicial review with a commitment to majority rule, a question that really goes to the heart of the practice of liberal representative democracy. Empirical scholars have asked how, in practice, judicial review takes place in societies with powerful majoritarian institutions. These debates and lines of inquiry have been particularly acute in the context of constitution-writing and state-building that has characterized the last decade of the twentieth century and beginning of the current century. Perhaps even more so in an age where the tension between state power and individual rights have been in particular relief.

Notes

1. For one account of the tradeoffs and motivations behind different styles of constitutional dockets, see Clark and Staton (2015).
2. For an overview of the strategic dilemma and a discussion of the problems confronting the justices, see Clinton (1994) and Knight and Epstein (1996).
3. An interesting question concerns the implications of a similar action in which states or foreign ambassadors are the subjects of the lawsuit. In this instance, a plausible reading of the Constitution would enable the Court to take original jurisdiction over the case.
4. For a detailed description of the ruse of judicial review in democratic systems during the twentieth century, see Ginsburg (2003: ch. 1).
5. The so-called Kelsenian constitutional court derives its name from Hans Kelsen, the author of several constitutions, notably the Austrian Constitution, during the early twentieth century.
6. For a thorough overview of the spread of judicial review and its various forms, see Ginsburg (2008).
7. On the centrality of this debate to academic study of judicial review, see, for example, Friedman (2002).
8. *Lochner v. New York* 198 U.S. 45, 75 (1905) (Holmes, J., dissenting).
9. See, e.g., http://www.cato.org/blog/supreme-court-restores-constitutional-order-strikes-down-outdated-voting-rights-act-provision.
10. http://blog.constitutioncenter.org/2013/09/the-voting-rights-decision-as-a-clear-example-of-judicial-activism/.
11. http://www.huffingtonpost.com/2012/06/01/doma-unconstitutional-ruling_n_1560780.html.

References

Alexander, L., and Schauer, F. 1997. "On Extrajudicial Constitutional Interpretation." *Harvard Law Review* 110(7): 1359–87.

Bernstein, D. E . 2005. "*Lochner v. New York*: A Centennial Retrospective." *Washington University Law Review* 83(5):1469–527.

Bickel, A. 1962. *The Least Dangerous Branch: The Supreme Court at the Bar of Politics*. New Haven, CT: Yale University Press.

Brewer-Carías, A. R. 2009. *Constitutional Protection of Human Rights in Latin America: A Comparative Study of Amparo Proceedings*. New York, NY: Cambridge University Press.

Casper, J. D. "The Supreme Court and National Policy Making." *The American Political Science Review* 70(1): 50–63.

Clark, T. S. 2011. *The Limits of Judicial Independence*. Cambridge: Cambridge University Press.

Clark, T. S., and Staton, J. K. 2015. "An Informational Model of Constitutional Jurisdiction." *Journal of Politics* 77(3): 589–607.

Clark, T. S., and Whittington, K. E. n.d. "Ideology, Partisanship, and Judicial Review of Acts of Congress, 1790–2006." Emory University working paper.

Clinton, R. L. 1994. "Game Theory, Legal History, and the Origins of Judicial Review: A Revisionist Analysis of *Marbury v. Madison*." *American Journal of Political Science* 38(2): 285–302.

Dahl, R. A. 1957. "Decision-Making in a Democracy: The Supreme Court as a National Policy-Maker." *Journal of Public Law* 6(2): 279–95.

Eisgruber, C. L. 2001. *Constitutional Self-Government*. Cambridge, MA: Harvard University Press.

Ely, J. H. 1980. *Democracy and Distrust: A Theory of Judicial Review*. Cambridge, MA: Harvard University Press.

Epstein, L., Knight, J., and Martin, A. 2001. "The Supreme Court as a Strategic National Policy Maker." *Emory Law Journal* 50(2): 583–611.

Epstein, L. and Landes, W. M. 2012."Was There Ever Such a Thing as Judicial Self-Restraint?" *California Law Review* 100: 557–78.

Friedman, B. 2002. "The Birth of an Academic Obsession: The History of the Countermajoritarian Difficulty, Part Five." *Yale Law Journal* 112(1): 153–529.

Friedman, B. 2005. "The Politics of Judicial Review." *Texas Law Review* 84(2): 257–337.

Friedman, B. 2010. *The Will of the People*. New York, NY: Farrar, Straus and Giroux.

Ginsburg, T. 2003. *Judicial Review in New Democracies: Constitutional Courts in Asian Cases*. New York, NY: Cambridge University Press.

Ginsburg, T. 2008. "The Global Spread of Constitutional Review," in *The Oxford Handbook of Law and Politics*, edited by G. A. Caldeira, K. E. Whittington, and R. D. Keleman. New York, NY: Oxford University Press.

Harvey, A., and Friedman, B. 2006. "Pulling Punches: Congressional Constraints on the Supreme Court's Constitutional Rulings, 1987–2000." *Legislative Studies Quarterly* 31(4): 533–62.

Howard, R. M., and Segal, J. A. 2004. "A Preference for Deference? The Supreme Court and Judicial Review." *Political Research Quarterly* 57(1): 131–43.

Keith, L. C. 2008. *The U.S. Supreme Court and the Judicial Review of Congress*. New York, NY: Peter Lang.

Kersch, K. I. 2004. *Constructing Civil Liberties: Discontinuities in the Development of American Constitutional Law*. New York, NY: Cambridge University Press.

Knight, J., and Epstein, L. 1996. "On the Struggle for Judicial Supremacy." *Law & Society Review* 30(1): 87–120.

Kramer, L. D. 2004. *The People Themselves: Popular Constitutionalism and Judicial Review*. New York, NY: Oxford University Press.

Lindquist, S. A., and Cross, F. B. 2009. *Measuring Judicial Activism*. Oxford: Oxford University Press.

Lindquist, S. A., and Solberg, R. S. 2007. "Judicial Review by the Burger and Rehnquist Courts: Explaining Justices' Responses to Constitutional Challenges." *Political Research Quarterly* 60(1): 71–91.

Murphy, W. F. 1986. "Who Shall Interpret? The Quest for an Ultimate Constitutional Interpreter." *Review of Politics* 48(3): 401–23.

Peretti, T. J. 1999. *In Defense of a Political Court*. Princeton, NJ: Princeton University Press.

Rosenberg, G. N. 1992. "Judicial Independence and the Reality of Political Power." *Review of Politics* 54: 369–98.

Segal, J. A., and Spaeth, H. J. 2002. *The Supreme Court and the Attitudinal Model Revisited*. New York, NY: Cambridge University Press.

Segal, J. A., Westerland, C., and Lindquist, S. A. 2011. "Congress, the Supreme Court, and Judicial Review: Testing a Constitutional Separation of Powers Model." *American Journal of Political Science* 55(1): 89–104.

Staton, J. K. 2010. *Judicial Power and Strategic Communication in Mexico*. New York, NY: Cambridge University Press.

Thayer, J. B. 1893. "The Origin and Scope of the American Doctrine of Constitutional Law." *Harvard Law Review* 7(3): 129–56.

Tushnet, M. 2000. *Taking the Constitution away from the Courts*. Princeton, NJ: Princeton University Press.

Vanberg, G. 2005. *The Politics of Constitutional Review in Germany*. New York, NY: Cambridge University Press.

Whittington, K. E. 2009. *The Political Foundations of Judicial Supremacy*. Princeton, NJ: Princeton University Press.

Zamudio, H. F. 1979. "A Brief Introduction to the Mexican Writ of *Amparo*." *California Western International Law Journal* 9(2): 306–48.

CHAPTER 15

THE ROLE OF PERSONAL ATTRIBUTES AND SOCIAL BACKGROUNDS ON JUDGING

TRACEY E. GEORGE AND TAYLOR GRACE WEAVER

PRESIDENT Richard Nixon, frustrated after two failed Supreme Court nominations, sought the counsel of his new Chief Justice, Warren Burger.[1] Chief Justice Burger recommended his closest friend, Eighth Circuit Judge Harry Blackmun, for the seat (Greenhouse 2005: 46). Burger and Blackmun were best friends. They both grew up poor in a working-class, Catholic St. Paul neighborhood. And they both considered themselves modestly conservative and Republican. Burger naturally expected Blackmun to be an ally on the Court. As Linda Greenhouse wrote in her Blackmun biography, the relationship between Burger and Blackmun was "encrusted with a lifetime of shared experiences and mutual expectations" (Greenhouse 2005: 186). But, instead of becoming Court allies, the men became alienated, disagreeing in half of the Supreme Court's rulings by their last term together. We can think of other jurists who were surprising rivals, or unexpected supporters, on the bench. Our surprise arises from our belief—like that of Chief Justice Burger—that common backgrounds produce common judicial views and actions.

The social background theory of judges seeks to leverage the idea that we are a product of our identity and our experiences—nature and nurture—to create a theory of judicial decision-making. Social background theory, as defined here, includes research that hypothesizes and tests the influence of factors like personal attributes and experience on judicial behavior. Attributes can include race, gender, sexual orientation, sexual identity, religion, and socioeconomic background. Experience can include education, occupation, and political activism. Social background theory treats these factors as an explanation for a judge's actions. Political party affiliation or appointing president, by contrast, are generally used as proxies for a judge's unstated attitudes or policy preferences, and thus neither political party affiliation or appointing president is within the scope of social background theory as covered here. We can return to Burger and Blackmun to examine the characteristics which might be relevant under a social background approach.

In the beginning, the media called Chief Justice Burger and Justice Blackmun the "Minnesota Twins." Everyone focused on their commonalities, brushing aside their differences. Despite their personal similarities, their paths to the Supreme Court diverged in several respects. While Burger stayed in Minneapolis after high school to work and take pre-law undergraduate classes at night at the University of Minnesota, Blackmun won a scholarship which took him to Harvard University for college and then law school. Burger never finished college, but did secure a law degree from an unaccredited night law school (which later became William Mitchell College of Law). Burger practiced law and became active in both state and national Republican Party politics, which lead to jobs in Washington at the U.S. Department of Justice and later a seat on the U.S. Court of Appeals for the DC Circuit. After graduating from Harvard Law School, Blackmun returned to Minnesota to clerk for an Eighth Circuit judge and turned down an offer to work for the federal government in DC for posts first at a Minneapolis law firm and later as in-house counsel at the Mayo Clinic in Rochester, Minnesota. Like Burger, Blackmun did accept an appointment to the federal appellate bench—the Eighth Circuit—but his experiences on that collegial, Midwestern court were far different from Burger's on the highly politicized and contentious DC Circuit.

Social background theory allows us to hypothesize a relationship between the lives of judges like Justice Blackmun and Chief Justice Burger and their judicial rulings. We can determine whether and how the differences outweighed the similarities in their rulings as justices. In this chapter, we offer an overview of what we know about the influence of social background on judicial behavior. The first part explores the source and development of social background theory through four eras. The second part briefly assesses the contributions and limitations of the theory. The third part introduces our proposal for where social background theory should go from here.

This chapter focuses only on those studies that have taken a (principally) positive approach to the examination of how personal attributes and social backgrounds affect judging. Unlike normative inquiries that address how judges *ought* to engage in judicial decision-making, the positive studies examined in this chapter use various empirical tools to assess judicial outputs, ultimately offering a theory for how judges *do* engage in judicial decision-making. That said, normative and positive theories intersected and influenced each other, making prescription sometimes relevant to understanding description. Therefore, we consider related normative theories when they inform our understanding of the positive theory.

The Source and Development of Social Background Theory

The idea that judicial decisions are the product of the person making the decision is not new. President George Washington considered a candidate's background when deciding whether to nominate him to a judicial opening. Then as now, presidents and other elected leaders wanted judges with whom they shared much in common in the belief that their peers were more likely to rule the *right* way. This focus has been most visible since the 1930s because of President Franklin Roosevelt's highly visible and strategic use of judicial nominations and because the federal courts themselves became more visible due to landmark legislation expanding and modernizing the federal judicial system. Studies of courts and judges became more sophisticated and complex in response to these two watershed developments, and the social background theory was one result.

Social background theory formalizes and tests the intuition that jurists' attributes and experiences will affect their rulings. The origins and development of social background scholarship is closely tied to the broader evolution of legal scholarship and social scientific research. We examine the source and development of the theory by looking at its four stages or waves: Legal Realism, behavioralism, new institutionalism, and computation. We assign each stage to a specific time period, marking the beginning and key stage of growth for each specific approach. While all four approaches continue in some form today, formative development generally occurred in the initial twenty-year to thirty-year period. But, the ideas and scholarship discussed here continue to have an impact on social background scholarship.

Carrying out the Positive Agenda of Legal Realism: 1930s–1950s

Social background theory developed alongside and was influenced by the rise of Legal Realism. Legal Realists, beginning in the 1930s, adopted as a normative paradigm the observation that judges cannot make decisions without being strongly influenced by their personal perceptions—that judges cannot be wholly "impartial" (Frank 1930; Llewellyn 1930). This idea stood in sharp contrast to the classical understanding of judicial thought—that jurists, through thoughtful reasoning, could arrive at a certain and universal legal truth—that had previously dominated legal scholarship. Accordingly, the ideas and advocacy of Realists like Jerome Frank, Karl Llewellyn, and Thurman Arnold drastically altered the course of legal education and the development of legal scholarship (Kalman 1986). At the same time, social scientists sought to test positive hypotheses mirroring what lawyers and judges were claiming should influence judicial decisions. Together these developments came to lay a foundation for modern social background theory.

During the early 1930s, economist Walton Hamilton, one of the leaders of Legal Realism at Yale Law School, helped to spur the growth of Legal Realism by offering an empirical account to match the movement's normative judicial philosophy. (Gordon 2004; Schlegel 1995: 19–20, 218). Although Hamilton is more commonly remembered today for bringing institutional economics to substantive law, he was invited to write the Judicial Process chapter in the 1932 edition of the *Encyclopedia of the Social Sciences*. In it, Hamilton defined "judicial process" as the "intellectual procedure by which judges decide cases" and entailed "all the ways of the mind, deliberate and subconscious, and all of the elements in personality, profession and environment which impel toward judgment" (Hamilton 1933: 450). Although his description is at a high level of abstraction, his characterization of judicial decisions as the product of "personality, profession and environment" is both a departure from contemporary thought and a precursor of social background theory.

Even before Hamilton's influential chapter appeared, political scientist Charles Grove Haines argued that judges necessarily evaluate cases through a lens formed by experience and training (Haines 1922). Haines's argument is principally normative, advocating for the recognition that judges and courts are political actors and thus the selection of judges should include a consideration of a judge's background and personality. But, he goes farther by offering a list of factors such as education, socio-economic class, and professional occupation which may impact how a judge rules.

In 1933, three legal scholars presented one of the first tests of Hamilton's and Haines's social background hypotheses. Struggling with many of the same questions facing the broader Legal Realist movement, the researchers juxtaposed the long-standing notion that "we have a government of laws, and not men," against the commonly held belief among prosecutors and criminal defense attorneys that criminal trial judges were either "tough" or "lenient" in sentencing. The authors looked at six judges' sentencing decisions during a nine-year period and found appreciable differences between judges in sentences handed down for nineteen commonly occurring crimes. After ruling out traditional explanations for these variations, the authors were left with the conclusion that "what determines whether a judge will be severe or lenient is to be found in the environment to which the judge has been subjected previous to his becoming an administrator of sentences" (Gaudet, Harris, and St. John 1933: 814). While the authors did not attempt to construct a general theory of judicial behavior, their research question and design augured a shift in how scholars looked at courts and judges.

Political scientist C. Herman Pritchett was the first to propose a general positive theory of judicial behavior. Pritchett, quoting Hamilton's observation that judicial process is a product of the individual judge as much as the law, aimed to empirically test jurisprudential theories that "take into account [the] personal element in the judicial interpretation and making of law" (Pritchett 1941: 890). He asserted that if U.S. Supreme Court justices disagreed about the outcome in a case, then the division could be attributed to the justices' "conscious or unconscious preferences and prejudices." In an article and later a book, he mapped the justices' votes and found interesting patterns including voting blocs and revealed preferences as to public policy (Pritchett 1948). Pritchett did not link the justices' votes to specific background characteristics, but he provided a reason to try to do so and a way to do it.

Courts scholars quickly recognized Pritchett's work as a springboard for exciting new lines of inquiry. They understood, however, that any theory linking judicial decisions to judges' underlying preferences and prejudices would need to be rooted in the behavioral sciences, where psychologists had already sought to offer systematic explanations of human behavior. By intentionally connecting the study of legal phenomena to the work of social psychologists like Louis Thurstone, Clyde Coombs, and Louis Guttman, judicial process scholars began to fashion a behavioral approach to the study of judicial decision-making, ushering in a new era in the study of judicial process.

The Behavioral Agenda in the Social Sciences: 1950s–1970s

Glendon Schubert was one of the most influential pioneers in the application of behavioralism to the study of law and courts, creating a behavioral theory of judging while also documenting this new approach to the study of judging (see, e.g., Schubert 1963). Schubert saw behavioral theory in courts studies as a product of both an evolving and richer understanding of the legal process and a growing interest in scientific methods among academics studying courts (Schubert 1965). Together, these shifts fueled a move away from the previous focus on "prescriptive norms" to "a new approach" which he termed "behavioral jurisprudence" (Schubert 1968: 407). To appreciate the significance of this shift, consider how researchers would treat a disagreement between judges hearing the same case. A traditionalist would seek to *reconcile* the conflict to construct a coherent body of legal doctrine. Behavioralists would instead *exploit* the conflict to discover how differences between the judges might be affecting their votes.

The behavioral approach is marked by the construction (sometimes explicit, sometimes implied) of a "stimulus-response" model to explain judicial rulings. A case is a set of stimuli. The judge's decision is the response. Behavioralists focused on the step between stimulus and response. That transition, unlike the stimulus or the response, cannot be directly observed; thus, a theory had to be constructed to explain it. The flexibility of the stimulus-response model allowed for different lines of scholarly inquiry. Some scholars chose to consider a specific set of general demographic variables and how they played out across a wide range of cases. Others focused instead on a specific set of cases, allowing them to explore background variables which were more closely connected to the issue.

Taking a subject-matter focused approach, a behavioralist could use the stimulus-response model to answer the riddle which troubled those three scholars back in 1933: Why were some judges sentencing harshly and others leniently in response to the same case facts. The criminal violation would be the stimulus and the judge's sentence the response. Beverly Blair Cook, for example, looked at federal trial judges' sentencing of draft dodgers during 1972—a time of intense debate regarding the legitimacy of military conscription and the Vietnam War (Cook 1973). She found significant disparities in sentences and, like the 1933 study, a distribution of judges from more to less severe. She hypothesized that numerous independent variables including, significantly for social background theory, the characteristics of the judge accounted for the variance. She specifically looked at whether the judge's life made him more or less sympathetic to the draft dodger. She found that judges with substantial military service were, contrary to her initial expectations, less punitive than judges with no prior military service while judges with draft-age sons were more severe. Stuart Nagel also looked at criminal cases but focused on appellate judges' rulings on defense claims (Nagel 1962a). His dependent variable was the percentage of criminal appeals in which a judge voted for the defense. Among other findings, he discovered that former prosecutors were significantly less likely to favor the criminally accused over the state while Catholics were more sympathetic than Protestants to the accused.

Cook was not the only scholar who sought to explain court decisions on hotly contested issues of the period. Recognizing the courtroom as a key battlefield of the civil rights movement, Kenneth Vines asked what factors made judges more likely to support the civil rights claims of African Americans. He examined 250 race segregation and discrimination cases decided in federal trial courts in twenty-eight Southern judicial districts from 1954 to 1962 (Vines 1964). Vines categorized each judge based on the relative frequency with which the judge ruled in favor of an African American party. Having ordered the judges from most to least likely to support civil rights claims, Vines observed commonalities within each category and differences between categories. He found that judges who attended law school and/or practiced in the South were more likely to oppose civil rights claims than those who did not. While the results were not statistically significant because of the limited number of southern trial judges who had left the south for training or work, the distribution was sufficiently stark to prompt Vines to observe that southern judges' votes could be seen as a product, in part, of the fact that their "legal development ... has taken place within the framework of the Southern political system and very largely within the state containing the district of their appointment" (Vines 1964: 352).

Michael W. Giles and Thomas G. Walker looked at the most momentous set of civil rights rulings of the twentieth century: racial desegregation of public schools (Giles and Walker 1975). Examining 151 school districts under active court supervision, the authors hypothesized that the data would indicate higher rates of ongoing segregation in the schools actively monitored by the judges with southern backgrounds. While the data mostly failed to support the authors' predictions, the study did show that *where* a judge was educated mattered. Consistent with Vines's earlier work on all civil rights cases, Giles and Walker discovered that the average level of segregation allowed by judges who attended Southern universities for both college and law school was significantly higher than the level allowed by those judges that were educated outside the South.

Where many scholars used the new behavioral lens to analyze highly politicized issues in courts (see, e.g., Ulmer 1973), others set out to examine a broader range of cases. These models often lost some explanatory value by using broader demographic categories. But the general models gained explanatory power and statistical strength by looking at more cases and judges. Sheldon Goldman, for example, focused on the U.S. Courts of Appeals, which he viewed as a troublingly understudied part of the federal judiciary. Goldman evaluated the relationship between an array of background variables and individual judges' votes in a subset of cases where a relationship could theoretically exist (Goldman 1969). In his initial study of non-unanimous cases and unanimous reversals from 1961–4 and, again later, in a second set drawn from 1965–71, Goldman found that for certain characteristics and certain sets of issues, social background appeared to explain appellate judge's votes (Goldman 1966, 1975). For example, he found that Catholics were more likely than non-Catholics to favor the underdog but discerned no difference between elite-educated and non-elite-educated judges or between judges with or without prior judicial or prosecutorial experience.

A person's race and gender obviously impacts her experiences and views of the world; thus, a judge's race and gender would seem likely to affect how a judge processes case stimuli to reach a result. Behavioralists tested this hypothesis by looking at the small but growing number of women and minorities serving as judges in the 1960s and 1970s. But, they were able to find little if any effect. Herbert Kritzer and Thomas Uhlman looked at criminal sentences imposed by male and female judges for violent crimes, predicting that female judges would impose relatively longer sentences on rapists than did their male colleagues (Kritzer and Uhlman 1977). But, they uncovered no difference between women and men. Uhlman in a separate study looked at criminal sentencing and race. He found no difference between white judges and black judges, but he did find that both groups imposed harsher sentences on black defendants than on white ones (Uhlman 1979).

While these studies only offer a glimpse into the development of behavioral legal scholarship, they are representative of the larger body of work developing during this period in several respects. First, these studies lent empirical support to the idea that judicial determinations by trial and appellate judges were influenced by a judge's attitudes and experiences. Second, and just as importantly, not every attribute or experience was found to influence judicial decisions. In fact, the relationships between observed attributes and judicial decisions were subtler than most behavioralists initially hypothesized. Finally, when a relationship was found, these studies showed that the relationship between the personal attribute or experience and the judge's ruling was stronger when the background factor was salient to a contested issue (Nagel 1962b, 1969; Tate 1981).

As Sidney Ulmer explained, however, a constraint awaited behavioralists who narrowed their inquiry too greatly in the hopes of highlighting points of greatest saliency (Ulmer 1986). He specifically challenged behavioral works that were defined entirely by the time period under study. While such studies offered insights into time sensitive relationships between social background factors and judicial decisions, they did little for the theoretical development of social background theory and were more akin to descriptive pieces on "particular courts at particular points in time" (Ulmer 1986: 958). For example, Vines's exploration of the influence of personal attributes and experiences on the decision-making of Southern district court judges seems defined by the times. Just as racial attitudes changed across the country, so did the attitudes prevailing in colleges and law schools. The composition of Southern law schools' faculties and student bodies changed too. While nearly all law professors in the 1950s and 1960s were from the region where their law school was located, they were increasingly educated at elite law schools by the 1970s and certainly by the 1980s. Southern students too were more aware of and engaged with the national debate over civil rights as a result of the dramatic expansion in television and telecommunications. Vines's attribution of anti-civil rights decisions to "unsophisticated" southerners would be unpersuasive as a theoretical account today.

In highlighting the limitations of discrete individualized studies, scholars like Ulmer anticipated a shift in the explication and application of social background theory. This next wave of scholarship deliberately builds upon earlier behavioral advances. Behavioral jurisprudence allowed scholars to study judicial decision-making scientifically. That is, they could propose a falsifiable hypothesis and test it against the evidence, typically judges' rulings. Knowledge would be built systematically based on proof rather than intuition. The next generation of scholarship sought to build on this important foundation through the construction of a much more complex theory of judicial behavior which took into account ideas developing in economics and political science under a broad label of organizational or institutional theory.

Institutional Economics: 1970s–1990s

Behavioral jurisprudence greatly expanded our understanding of how an individual judge's rulings may be a direct product of the judge's background and attributes. But its focus on the individual judge was both a strength and a weakness. The focus on judges rather than courts was a strength because it revealed the role of the personal in the judicial process. But it was a weakness because judges, of course, make their decisions in a rich and varied context that includes other actors, the institutional setting, and judges' personal goals. This broader context may affect how a judge's social background translates to judicial actions. Stated differently, judicial behavior is the product of the interaction between the judge's characteristics and the setting in which she is working. The next wave of social background research drew on institutional economics to construct a more fully developed theory of how individual judges make decisions in a complex setting.

An institutional economic account of judicial behavior is grounded upon two distinct observations. First, that the nature of the judicial process may alter how background and attributes influence a judge, producing an indirect or otherwise subtle, yet significant, effect. Second, that a judge's personal characteristics may affect a range of actions beyond votes in cases. These two important insights prompt the following questions: How does the setting in which decisions are made affect the influence of background and attributes upon judicial actions? Does social background theory predict different effects for different types of decisions such that some attributes only impact certain categories of actions? We consider in turn how judicial process scholars answered each question.

Judicial decisions are subject to three major constraining forces: superiors, colleagues, and law. We begin by considering the effect of superiors. American judges operate in a hierarchy where superior courts can reverse lower courts. Trial judges can be reversed by appellate judges, intermediate appellate judges by supreme court judges. Judges are aware of the risk of reversal. Sincere (or naïve) judges will simply vote their preferences without regard to the possibility of reversal, but strategic judges will take the risk into account when making decisions.

Behavioralists assumed that judges were sincere, and therefore they expected that any hypothetical relationship between a judge's personal characteristics and a case stimulus would be direct and readily observable in the judge's response. Many behavioralists, for example, studied criminal sentences to see whether specific judicial characteristics such as race, prior prosecutorial experience, and gender impacted the sentences judges imposed, but most studies failed to find any relationship. Institutional theorists looked not only at direct effects—do female judges impose harsher sentences than male judges on rapists or do African American judges impose lighter sentences than white judges on African American defendants--but also looked for indirect effects that may be the product of strategic judging.

For example, the federal sentencing guidelines provide a sentence range for each offense of conviction. In a given case, a lenient trial judge may initially be inclined to grant a defendant's request for a downward departure to produce a penalty that the judge believes is merited. Although such departures are allowed under the law, it may be the case that the reviewing appellate court is controlled by conservative judges who routinely reverse downward departures. Thus, the strategic judge will choose another method, one aimed at producing a sentence which is close to the downward-departed sentence, while remaining near enough to the guideline range so as to avoid reversal. The judge may do this, for example, by dismissing a more serious charge (or ruling inadmissible evidence to support it), leaving a lesser count. Even though the lesser count carries a harsher guidelines penalty than the initial downward-departed sentence she was inclined to impose on the serious charge, the judge recognizes that this outcome is a better result than the guidelines' sentence for the more serious charge, which would potentially be handed down should she be reversed. Ultimately, if a study only looked at the judge's sentence, it would not appear lenient because it is the standard sentence for the crime of conviction. But, if alternative methods of achieving a lighter sentence were taken into account, then the study would reveal that the attribute does have the hypothesized effect (see, e.g., Schanzenbach and Tiller 2007).

Collegiality, like hierarchy, is a hallmark of the American judicial system. Appellate judges work on panels. Thus, a judge's vote is a product not only of her background but also the influences of her peers and the necessity of reaching a collective decision. This fact has numerous implications for social background theory in terms of both constructing an explanation for why there would be an effect and measuring the hypothesized effect. For example, the impact of one's background may be mitigated by a need to compromise such that a judge's personal characteristics may be less significant when the judge faces the choice of accommodating the majority in order to remain part of it (and thereby have some impact on the ruling) or instead dissenting (Maltzman, Spriggs, and Wahlbeck 2000). Alternatively, the impact of background may not be visible if measured by comparing judges. In a collegial court, a judge's salient personal attribute may affect the votes of colleagues who lack that attribute, such that male judges on a panel with a female judge may be more sensitive to women's claims when facing sex-salient questions (Boyd, Epstein, and Martin 2010).

The most fundamental constraint on judicial behavior is the law itself (George and Epstein 1992; Ashenfelter, Eisenberg, and Schwab 1995: 281). Strategic theorists hypothesize that when the law grants discretion to the judge—either explicitly through the relevant standard or implicitly through the lack of precedent—the judge has greater freedom to act and thus is more likely to be affected by personal attributes. While behavioralists often used broad measures of outcomes that were unresponsive to nuances in legal doctrine or to the way in which a legal question was presented to the court, institutional scholars refined how judicial actions were measured to recognize that the law itself frames the questions presented to the court and thus the impact of professional and personal backgrounds on judges' actions. Goldman's research on the courts of appeals, for example, categorized labor law rulings as either pro-union or anti-union. He failed to find a strong relationship between social background and labor law rulings (Goldman 1966). James Brudney, Sara Schiavoni, and Deborah Merritt, writing more than thirty years later, refined the outcome measure by dividing labor law cases based on the specific statutory provision under consideration on the theory that the influence of a background variable depends upon the nature and stance of the union's position (Brudney, Schiavoni, and Merritt 1999). By doing so, they revealed that certain characteristics—like religion and college selectivity (which was viewed as a proxy for socio-economic status)—were strongly associated with pro-union votes on certain claims but not others. Thus, the refinement revealed that the hypothesized relationship did exist when specific questions were presented to the court. Likewise, Andrew Morriss, Michael Heise, and Gregory Sisk found that race did not explain whether federal trial judges ruled that the Sentencing Guidelines were unconstitutional but did explain the reason given to support the ruling with black judges more likely to rely on due process principles and white judges more likely to cite separation of powers (Morriss, Heise, and Sisk 2005; Sisk, Heise, and Morriss 1998).

New Institutionalists recognized that judges make many decisions beyond the ultimate ruling in a case and began examining the full range of actions taken by judges. For example, judges have discretion about writing and publishing opinions to explain their rulings. Appellate judges choose whether to join an opinion written by a co-panelist or instead to write a separate opinion. Judges who had jobs or education which involved substantial individual writing would seem more likely to opt to write separately as would judges who routinely operated independently rather than on a team. Virginia Hettinger, Stefanie Lindquist, and Wendy Martinek found that federal courts of appeals judges with prior appellate court experience were more likely than other judges to write a concurrence rather than join the majority, but that federal appellate judges with prior trial experience did not appear less likely than other judges to go along with a colleague's majority (Hettinger, Lindquist, and Martinek 2006). One of the authors of the current chapter found that academics who have significant writing experience and are unaccustomed to accommodating other's views were likely to continue to issue solo-authored written work—now judicial opinions—when they became appellate judges (George 2001). Similarly, Merritt and Brudney found that courts of appeals judges who went to elite law schools were more likely than non-elite graduates to publish their own opinions

(Merritt and Brudney 2001). Christina Boyd, however, failed to find that elite education or law professor experience produce a higher publication rate for federal *trial* judges who can resolve disputes without issuing written opinions (Boyd 2015).

Judges also take significant actions outside a specific dispute. The most fundamental decision is whether to continue to serve as a judge. Albert Yoon has conducted extensive studies of federal judicial tenure. He found that women and black judges served much shorter terms than their male and non-black colleagues on both district and appellate courts (Yoon 2003). (While gender and race affected how long a judge served, the judge's prior wealth appeared to have little effect across the sample.) But, women and black judges who served as chief judge were much more likely than male and white judges to complete their leadership term (George and Yoon 2008). Thus, Yoon has found that race and gender effects that have been observed in the labor market generally also are manifest in the judicial labor market.

Institutional theory brought greater richness to the theoretical account of how social background and personal attributes impact judge's behavior. The examples outlined here highlight the variety of research questions and hypotheses which courts scholars have examined. By 2000, the institutional account was a well-accepted understanding of how social background variables could influence the work of judges and courts. Around the same time, the capacity and speed of computers and the availability of new computational methods grew dramatically, bringing tremendous changes to the way scholars study courts.

Sophisticated Methods and New Technologies: 1990s to present

The sophistication and complexity of the federal judicial appointment process has increased with the growing power and prestige of the federal bench and the expanding diversification of potential nominees. Likewise, tools and methods for studying federal judges have become more complex and sophisticated with expanded computer power, evolving statistical models, and growth in multi-user databases. Scholars have been able to test for the effects of social background factors in ever more refined and creative ways by leveraging these new tools. The development of social background *theory* often took a backseat to methods and data during the most recent stage of development.

Multi-user databases are data sets which are designed to facilitate and encourage analysts other than just the creators to use them. When behavioralists or institutionalists sought to test the research questions which they posed, they typically would collect data by identifying and coding cases and also assembling relevant details in judicial biographies. They only recorded the information which they needed for the research project on which they were working. This research-question-centered approach to the construction of data sets is not efficient: the marginal cost of collecting all usable information from each case and biography is lower than the marginal benefit to the scholarly community interested in the same cases or judges but asking different questions.

As Lee Epstein has observed, "we ought to amass large databases so rich in content that multiple users, even those with distinct projects, can draw on them" (Epstein 2000: 225). The problem, of course, is that the marginal costs of creating the data set would be borne by the original researcher and the marginal benefits would accrue to everyone.

Harold Spaeth saw the solution to this collective action problem in the creation of a multi-user database on the U.S. Supreme Court which would be funded by the National Science Foundation (Spaeth and Segal 2000). The data set first became available in the late 1980s, and has been expanded and improved over time. The widespread use of the U.S. Supreme Court Data Base as well as the creation of other databases picked up speed in the 1990s and 2000s. The internet's growth has had a profound impact on the role of multi-user databases in judicial research. Scholars can easily share, locate, and download databases. Digital dockets and archives accessible through web portals have decreased the costs of accessing information to include in data sets. Multi-user databases have played an important role in the development of social background theory. For example, prior research found little relationship between the race of a judge and her decisions. Adam Cox and Thomas Miles, however, uncovered a sizable effect in voting rights cases—where minority judges were more than twice as likely to side with minority plaintiffs—by using Ellen Katz's voting rights database which included the universe of such disputes (Cox and Miles 2008).

The dramatic expansion in computer memory capacity and processor speed has inspired scholars to develop models and methods which capitalize on these technological improvements. One such example is textual statistical analysis. Appellate judges offer written explanations for their decisions. Scholars in the past who wanted to examine opinions for patterns which could reveal something about the judge's thinking and possibly be attributed to personal characteristics of the judge would have to read and hand code each opinion. This time-consuming process necessarily limited the number of cases which could be included in any study. Today, software makes it possible to consistently gather information across large numbers of opinions. The text analysis program scans the opinion's text for common patterns, allowing the researcher to find salient factors much more quickly, efficiently, and reliably than collecting information by hand (Williams and George 2014: 441–2). This and other automated coding techniques can be used to capture basic variables of interest from large caches of information (Sen 2015). Maya Sen exploited this method to collect judicial reversal data from Westlaw for over one thousand judges, finding that black district judges were more likely than white judges to be reversed by courts of appeals judges (who sit in panels which are almost always majority-white) even controlling for non-race-based reasons for reversal.

An exciting and impressive array of new methodologies and data sources have been developed since 1990. Network analysis, which visualizes and analyzes connections between judges through their actions, has revealed, among other things, peer effects within the courts which could serve as the basis for testing whether pre-judicial experiences dictate a judge's influence on others (Katz and Stafford 2010). Markov chain Monte Carlo (MCMC) methods allow scholars to run repeated simulations on data to better measure judicial preferences (Martin and Quinn 2002). Social background variables are regularly included in scholarship utilizing these innovative approaches.

The Strengths and Weaknesses of the Theory

It is difficult to imagine a world in which legal scholars neglected to study the notion that judges, like all other men and women, are influenced by their attributes and previous experiences. But while its most basic premise is intuitive, social background theory rests on years of preceding developments in legal, sociological, and psychological scholarship. In fact, it is social background theory's history of intentional scholarly integration that presents it with unique opportunities going forward.

Contemporary social background scholarship, however, routinely suffers from two significant weaknesses. First, while the empirical methods have become more sophisticated and the data sets richer, the theoretical models have become thinner. Theory feels post hoc (and even ad hoc) and less coherent. Arguments are elliptical, failing to explicate important steps in the logical reasoning to get from what we know about people and courts separately to a persuasive hypothesized relationship between them. Facts without theory do not add to our understanding of law or legal systems (see, e.g., Gibson 1983). Second, the sophisticated statistical models often overemphasize measurable and sortable attributes at the expense of other ineffable ones that might be more useful or relevant. Both of these weaknesses reflect a greater, but tractable, problem: Judicial process scholars regularly fail to offer a narrative to support their hypotheses. Herman Pritchett, Glendon Schubert, and Beverly Blair Cook were storytellers: Each told a story about how and why judges' decisions were influenced by their earlier experiences, political allegiances, and colleagues on the bench. That story provided the link between the evidence offered, how it proved a fact, and how that fact was material to the research question.

Theories of Relevance

The first principle of evidence law, which governs the admission of evidence at trial, is relevancy. Evidence must be relevant in order to be admissible. Relevance is necessary, but not sufficient. The question of whether evidence is relevant serves as the preliminary and often decisive inquiry in litigation.

The fundamental relevancy principle applies with equal force to evidence offered in academic research. That is, scholarly evidence should be relevant in order to be admissible to the world of ideas and the body of scholarship. Academic publication of irrelevant evidence wastes time and other scarce resources. And, it may undermine the development of valid theories by misleading or distracting other scholars. The rigorous enforcement of a relevancy requirement would strengthen and improve social background scholarship.

The test of relevance in academic scholarship is in essence the same as the test of relevance in law. "Evidence is relevant if it has any tendency to make more or less probable the existence of a fact that is of consequence in determining the action" (Federal Rule of Evidence 401). Relevance therefore requires both probativeness ("any tendency to make more or less probable the existence of a fact") and materiality ("a fact that is of consequence in determining the action"). Evidence is relevant if (1) it proves a fact and (2) that fact is material to the legal action. In law, the two requirements are known as "logical" relevance and "legal" relevance, respectively. In scholarship, they could be described as logical relevance and scholarly relevance.

The power of a simple relevancy test can be seen through its application to Christina Boyd, Lee Epstein, and Andrew Martin's influential 2010 study, "Untangling the Causal Effects of Sex on Judging." Their article uses sophisticated methods to test a question which has animated social background research since at least the 1970s: Are women judges different from men? They sought to test whether female judges decided sex discrimination cases differently from male judges ("individual effects") and whether male judges behaved differently in such cases when a co-panelist was female ("panel effects"). If we apply the relevancy requirement, we see two theories of relevance undergird their study. A judge's sex (evidence) makes it more (or less) likely than it would be without the evidence that the judge has experienced sex discrimination (fact) which means that the judge will be more (or less) receptive to sex discrimination claims (research question). If the judge is a woman, she is more likely to have experienced sex discrimination and will be more receptive to such claims. If a judge is male, he is less likely to have experienced sex discrimination and will be less receptive to such claims. The authors also hypothesize that a female judge sitting on a panel with a male judge (evidence) makes it more likely than it would be if the panel were all male that the male judge will hear arguments from another judge in support of a sex discrimination claim (fact) which makes it more likely the male judge will vote in favor of the plaintiff (research question). Focusing on their theory of relevancy allows us to test its persuasiveness and coherency. Are we persuaded that experiencing sex discrimination affects a person's receptivity to such claims? That a person who has likely experienced sex discrimination is more likely than someone who has not to make an argument to her colleagues during conference in support of a claim? That a judge is more persuaded by arguments made by a colleague than made by parties? More importantly, because their hypotheses are supported by a compelling theory of relevancy, their results succeed in demonstrating that the sex of a judge matters in sex discrimination cases. And, it serves as a model for how scholars should begin their social background research.

Conclusion

When he was nominated to the Court, Justice Harry Blackmun's mother warned him that his appointment would change his relationship with his best friend, Chief Justice Warren Burger. Blackmun recalled responding " 'Mother, it just can't. We've been friends for a long time.' 'Well, you wait and see,' his mother replied" (Greenhouse 2005: 51). During his confirmation hearing, Justice Blackmun testified that he and Burger expected that at times they would disagree (Greenhouse 2005: 51). But, Blackmun did not expect the conflict that would grow between them. They not only took different substantive positions, they also carried out their work in markedly different ways.

Social background theory helps us to understand why the two justices could share so many experiences and attributes yet behave so differently on the Court. Chief Justice Burger lacked the elite credentials of his colleagues on the DC Circuit and the Supreme Court, but he brought the ideological perspective and strategic outlook of a party activist, which were only strengthened by his bruising experience on the DC Circuit. Justice Blackmun had the Harvard degrees, circuit clerkship, and elite practice background, but no prior political experience. His erudite approach was only strengthened by his service on the collegial Eighth Circuit. Court observers at the time knew about these differences, but were inattentive to them. Today, however, their effects seem almost as inevitable to us as they did to Theo Blackmun on the eve of her son's appointment.

Note

1. Nixon's first appointment to the Court was Burger, who was confirmed as Chief Justice on June 9, 1969. Two months later, Nixon had an opportunity to name an Associate Justice, but his first two attempts—Fourth Circuit Judge Clement Haynsworth Jr. and Fifth Circuit Judge G. Harrold Carswell—were each rejected by the Senate.

References

Ashenfelter, O., Eisenberg, T., and Schwab, S. 1995. "Politics and the Judiciary: The Influence of Judicial Background on Case Outcomes." *Journal of Legal Studies* 24(2): 257–81.

Boyd, C. L. 2015. "Opinion Writing in the Federal District Courts." *Justice System Journal* 36(3): 254–73.

Boyd, C. L., Epstein, L., and Martin, A. D. 2010. "Untangling the Causal Effects of Sex on Judging." *American Journal of Political Science* 54(2): 389–411.

Brudney, J. J., Schiavoni, S., and Merritt, D. J. 1999. "Judicial Hostility toward Labor Unions? Applying the Social Background Model to a Celebrated Concern." *Ohio State Law Journal* 60(5): 1675–771.

Cook, B. B. 1973. "Sentencing Behavior of Federal Judges: Draft Cases—1972." *University of Cincinnati Law Review* 42: 597–633.

Cox, A. B., and Miles, T. J. 2008. "Judging the Voting Rights Act." *Columbia Law Review* 108(1): 1–54.

Epstein, L. 2000. "Social Science, the Courts, and the Law." *Judicature* 83(5): 224–27.

Federal Rules of Evidence, 28 U.S.C. Appendix (as amended 2014).

Frank, J. 1930. *Law and the Modern Mind.* Gloucester, MA: Peter Smith.

Gaudet, F. J., Harris, G. S., and St. John, C. W. 1933. "Individual Differences in the Sentencing Tendencies of Judges." 23: 811–18.

George, T. E. 2001. "Court Fixing." *Arizona Law Review* 43(1): 9–62.

George, T. E., and Epstein, L. 1992. "On the Nature of Supreme Court Decision Making." *American Political Science Review* 86(2): 323–37.

George, T. E., and Yoon, A. H. 2008. "Chief Judges: The Limits of Attitudinal Theory and Possible Paradox of Managerial Judging." *Vanderbilt Law Review* 61(1): 1–61.

Gibson, J. L. 1983. "From Simplicity to Complexity: The Development of Theory in the Study of Judicial Behavior." *Political Behavior* 5(1): 4–49.

Giles, M. W., and Walker, T. G. 1975. "Judicial Policy-Making and Southern School Segregation." *The Journal of Politics* 37(4): 917–36.

Goldman, S. 1966. "Voting Behavior on the United States Courts of Appeals, 1961–1964." *American Political Science Review* 60(2): 374–83.

Goldman, S. 1969. "Backgrounds, Attitudes, and the Voting Behavior of Judges: A Comment on Joel Grossman's Social Backgrounds and Judicial Decisions." *Southern Political Science Association* 31: 214–22.

Goldman, S. 1975. "Voting Behavior on the United States Courts of Appeals: Revisited." *American Political Science Review* 69: 491–506.

Gordon, R. W. 2004. "Professors and Policy-Makers: Yale Law School Faculty in the New Deal—and after." In *History of Yale Law School: The Tercentennial Lectures*, edited by A. T. Kronman. New Haven, CT: Yale University Press.

Greenhouse, L. 2005. *Becoming Justice Blackmun: Harry Blackmun's Supreme Court Journey.* New York: Times Books (Henry Holt and Company).

Haines, C. G. 1922. "General Observations on the Effects of Personal, Political, and Economic Influences in the Decisions of Judges." *Illinois Law Review* 17: 96–116.

Hamilton, W. H. 1933. "Judicial Process." In *Encyclopaedia of the Social Sciences*, Vol. 8, edited by E. R. A. Seligman and A. Johnson. New York, NY: Macmillan, 450–7.

Hettinger, V. A., Lindquist, S. A., and Martinek, W. L. 2006. *Judging on a Collegial Court: Influences on Federal Appellate Decision Making.* Charlottesville, VA: University of Virginia Press.

Kalman, L. 1986. *Legal Realism at Yale, 1927–1960.* Chapel Hill, NC: University of North Carolina Press.

Katz, D. M., and Stafford, D. K. 2010. "Hustle and Flow: A Social Network Analysis of the American Federal Judiciary." *Ohio State Law Journal* 71(3): 457–509.

Kritzer, H. M., and Uhlman, T. M. 1977. "Sisterhood in the Courtroom: Sex of Judge and Defendant in Criminal Case Disposition." *The Social Science Journal* 14(2): 77–88.

Llewellyn, K. N. 1930. "A Realistic Jurisprudence: The Next Step." *Columbia Law Review* 30: 431–65.

Maltzman, F., Spriggs, J. F., II, and Wahlbeck, P. J. 2000. *Crafting Law on the Supreme Court: The Collegial Game.* New York, NY: Cambridge University Press.

Martin, A. D., and Quinn, K. M. 2002. "Dynamic Ideal Point Estimation via Markov Chain Monte Carlo for the U.S. Supreme Court, 1953–1999." *Political Analysis* 10(2): 134–53.

Merritt, D. J., and Brudney, J. J. 2001. "Stalking Secret Law: What Predicts Publication in the United States Courts of Appeals?" *Vanderbilt Law Review* 54(1): 71–121.

Morriss, A. P., Heise, M., and Sisk, G. C. 2005. "Signaling and Precedent in Federal District Court Opinions." *Supreme Court Economic Review* 13: 63–97.

Nagel, S. S. 1962a. "Judicial Backgrounds and Criminal Cases." *The Journal of Criminal Law, Criminology, and Police Science* 53: 333–9.

Nagel, S. S. 1962b. "Testing Relations between Judicial Characteristics and Judicial Decision-Making." *The Western Political Quarterly* 15: 425–37.

Nagel, S. S. 1969. *The Legal Process from a Behavioral Perspective*. Homewood, IL: Dorsey Press.

Pritchett, H. C. 1941. "Divisions of Opinion Among Justices of the U.S. Supreme Court, 1939–1941." *American Political Science Review* 35: 890–8.

Pritchett, H. C. 1948. *The Roosevelt Court: A Study in Judicial Politics and Values, 1937–1947*. New York, NY: Macmillan.

Schanzenbach, M. M., and Tiller, E. H. 2007. "Strategic Judging under the U.S. Sentencing Guidelines: Positive Political Theory and Evidence." *Journal of Law, Economics & Organization* 23: 23–56.

Schlegel, J. H. 1995. *American Legal Realism and Empirical Social Science*. Chapel Hill, NC: University of North Carolina Press.

Schubert, G. 1963. "Behavioral Research in Public Law." *American Political Science Review* 57: 433–45.

Schubert, G. 1965. *The Judicial Mind: The Attitudes and Ideologies of Supreme Court Justices, 1946–1963*. Evanston, IL: Northwestern University Press.

Schubert, G. 1968. "Behavioral Jurisprudence." *Law & Society Review* 2: 407–28.

Sen, M. 2015. "Is Justice Really Blind? Race and Reversal in US Courts." *Journal of Legal Studies* 44: S187–S228.

Sisk, G. C., Heise, M., and Morriss, A. P. 1998. "Charting the Influences on the Judicial Mind: An Empirical Study of Judicial Reasoning." *NYU Law Review* 73: 1377–498.

Spaeth, H. J., and Segal, J. A. 2000. "The U.S. Supreme Court Judicial Data Base: Providing New Insights into the Court." *Judicature* 83(5): 228–35.

Tate, C. N. 1981. "Personal Attribute Models of Voting Behavior of U.S. Supreme Court Justices: Liberalism in Civil Liberties and Economics Decisions, 1946–1978." *American Political Science Review* 75: 355–67.

Uhlman, T. 1979. *Racial Justice: Black Judges and Defendants in an Urban Trial Court*. Lexington, MA: Lexington Books.

Ulmer, S. S. 1973. "Social Background as an Indicator of the Votes of Supreme Court Justices in Criminal Cases: 1947–1956 Terms." *American Journal of Political Science* 17: 622–30.

Ulmer, S. S. 1986. "Are Social Background Models Time-Bound?" *The American Political Science Review* 80: 957–68.

Vines, K. N. 1964. "Federal District Judges and Race Relations Cases in the South." *The Journal of Politics* 26(2): 337–57.

Williams, M. S., and George, T. E. 2013. "Who Will Manage Complex Litigation? The Decision to Transfer and Consolidate Multidistrict Litigation." *Journal of Empirical Legal Studies* 10(3): 424–61.

Yoon, A. H. 2003. "Love's Labor's Lost? Judicial Tenure among Federal Court Judges: 1945–2000." *California Law Review* 91(4): 1029–60.

CHAPTER 16

IDEOLOGY AND PARTISANSHIP

JUSTINE D'ELIA-KUEPER AND JEFFREY A. SEGAL

EVER since the work of legal realists (Frank 1949; Llewellyn 1931) and behaviorists (Rhode and Spaeth 1976; Segal and Spaeth 1993, 1996, 2002; Segal and Howard 2002) debunked the myth that the Court substantially adhered to the legal model of decision-making, in which the justices were largely guided by precedent, legal texts, and the intent of the founders (Bailey and Maltzman 2011; Kahn 1999; Scalia and Garner 2012), scholars have been interested in how the personal attributes of the justices affect their decision-making.[1] The justices' party affiliation and ideology are two of the most studied of these personal attributes. Due to the overlap or "behavioral equivalence" between party and ideology, however, it has always been hard for scholars to examine separately the influence of party and ideology on the justices' decisions. In fact, many scholars have simply relied upon the party of the justice or the party of the appointing president as a proxy for ideology (Pinello 1999). Recently the Court has become more even more polarized, and the overlap between the party and ideology of the justices has grown noticeably larger, with conservative Republican appointees voting as a block in opposition to liberal Democratic appointees. Despite this, however, there has been an emerging interest in identifying the unique contributions that both party and ideology make in shaping the justices' voting behavior. Scholars have made some progress in this respect by identifying a subset of cases, often related to election law, where partisan and ideological considerations sometimes conflict, meaning a liberal decision actually threatens the Democratic Party's electoral interests and vice versa (Lloyd 1995; Gillman 2001a; Kopko 2008, 2010; McKenzie 2012). Future research on the effects of party and ideology on the Court should continue in this vein until the independent effects of party and ideology are better understood. Additionally, work examining the causes behind the increased polarization of the Court, and specifically, how the increased polarization of the Senate may affect polarization on the Court, also has the potential to contribute greatly to the literature.

Demonstrating an Effect of Ideology on the Court

Prior to the rise of the attitudinal model of judicial decision-making (Segal and Spaeth 1993, 2002), it was largely assumed that judges made decisions based largely on the facts of the case and the applicable law (Bailey and Maltzman 2011; Kahn 1999; Scalia and Garner 2012). Under this legal model of decision-making, the legal doctrine or principle clearly determined the outcome, leaving little discretionary space that would enable the justices to vote in accordance with their policy preferences. The attitudinal model, on the other hand, posited that the justices would consider their own personal preferences as well as the facts of the case when making decisions (Segal and Spaeth 1993, 2002). Early work in support of the attitudinal model, however, was hampered because no independent measure of judicial ideology had yet been developed (Rohde and Spaeth 1976; Schubert 1959, 1965, 1974; Spaeth 1979). Earlier scholars had used data-reduction techniques, such as cumulative scaling, multidimensional scaling, or factor analysis of the justices' votes, to derive measures of judicial ideology. Explaining votes from those measures created serious endogenity problems, because scholars were essentially using votes to predict votes (a modern version of this is the widely used Martin-Quinn ideal point estimates).[2] While the attitudinal model was controversial at first (Mendelson 1963, 1966, Tanenhaus 1966; Friedman 2006; Gillman 2001b), ultimately scholarship demonstrating the weakness of the legal model as a predictor of judicial voting behavior (Rhode and Spaeth 1976; Segal and Spaeth 1993, 1996, 2002; Segal and Howard 2002), combined with strong empirical evidence supporting the attitudinal model (Segal and Spaeth 1993, 2002), gradually generated increasing scholarly acceptance of the latter. The Supreme Court's clearly partisan decision in *Bush v. Gore* may have also played a role in increasing widespread acceptance of the model among scholars.[3]

The most prominent proponents of the attitudinal model, Segal and Spaeth (1993, 2002) argued that the Supreme Court's institutional rules and structure—including the fact that the Court's decisions are not subject to appeal, the justices' lack of electoral accountability or ambition for higher office, and the justices' discretionary docket—foster an environment that leaves the justices highly susceptible to being influenced by their own partisan and ideological preferences. Empirically, Segal and Cover (1989) developed the first measure of the justices' ideology that is exogenous to their votes by content coding newspaper editorials published at the time of the judge's nomination. Using this new measure, Segal and Cover found that this exogenous measure of judicial ideology did correlate very highly ($r = 0.80$) with the judge's later voting behavior in civil liberties cases (Segal and Cover 1989).

These initial studies, however, were limited to Supreme Court justices. Additionally, because much of the theory in support of the attitudinal model was based on conditions unique to the Supreme Court (i.e., lifetime appointments, discretionary docket, life tenure etc.), it was not immediately obvious that the attitudinal model would explain the behavior of lower court judges equally well. Since then scholars have shown that lower court judges are also vulnerable to the influence of ideology (Emmert and Traut 1994; Sunstein, Ellman, and Schkade 2004). Using party of the appointing president as a proxy for ideology, these studies demonstrate that partisan and ideological considerations do affect, albeit to a lesser extent, the votes of federal court of appeals judges across a wide array of issue areas. Additionally, they demonstrate that the effect of ideology upon the judges is heightened when the entire panel is of the same party and depressed when there are judges of both parties serving on the panel (Sunstein, Ellman, and Schkade 2004). This study is limited, however, because it measures ideology only indirectly through party.

Giles, Hettinger, and Pepper (2001) employ a different methodology to measure lower court judges' ideological preferences based on the Poole and Rosenthal Common Space scores[4] for elected officials involved in the federal court appointment process. Giles, Hettinger, and Pepper rely on two basic assumptions to calculate judicial scores from the Common Space scores. First, they assume that the actors involved in the nomination process want to appoint judges who share their ideological predispositions, and second, they assume that the Senate norm of courtesy holds.[5] Thus their ideological scores for court of appeals judges are calculated based on the Common Space score of the nominee's home state senator, if either of them belong to the president's party or the average of their scores if both belong to the president's party. If neither of the home state senators are from the president's party then the president's score is used. Using these scores, Segal (2008) found a correlation of 0.47 with the civil liberties votes of judges who cast at least twenty such votes in the U.S. Appeals Court Database.[6] As Segal reports, "Although the fit is pretty good—indeed it would be hard to imagine any other variable that explains so substantial a proportion of the judges' voting behavior—obviously much more is at work on the Court of Appeals than just ideology" (p. 28).

Traut and Emmert (1998) also study the effect of ideology on lower court judges, but they focus on state supreme court justices and employ a measure of ideology constructed in manner similar to the Segal-Cover scores. Specifically, because they are interested in California Supreme Court judges, they code the editorial content of the *Los Angeles Times* and the *San Francisco Chronicle* to arrive at a measure of judicial ideology for each of the justices serving on the California Supreme Court between 1979 and 1990. They then use this measure of ideology, combined with indicators for the facts of the case, to predict judicial votes in death penalty cases. They find a strong impact of judicial ideology, with conservative judges being significantly more likely than liberal judges to vote to uphold the death penalty. These findings reinforce the idea that the influence of ideology on judicial decision-making is not just limited to the justices serving on the U.S. Supreme Court (Traut and Emmert 1998).

Using a different measure, Brace, Langer, and Hall (2000), find that while judicial preferences may have some effect on judicial decision-making at the state supreme court level the effect is often quite small across a wide array of different issue areas.

Brace, Langer, and Hall (2000) devise a unique measure of judicial preferences, the party-adjusted judicial ideology (PAIJD) scores. The PAIJD scores reflect both the judge's party as well as the ideology of the state at the time of the judge's selection. Furthermore, Brace, Langer, and Hall, distinguish between the different methods of judicial selection by giving more weight to elite ideology in judicial appointment states and citizen ideology in judicial election states. Using this innovative measure, Brace, Langer, and Hall (2000) find that judicial preferences may affect judicial decision-making on state supreme courts, but even though their measure of judicial preferences explains more than party alone, there is still a lot of unexplained variance. This indicates that although judicial preferences may play a role in judicial decision-making in the states, there are other factors that are clearly important as well (Brace, Langer, and Hall 2000).

Party as a Proxy for Ideology

Although scholars were often interested in the effects of the ideology on the decision-making of judges, many scholars instead measured the effect of the judge's party identification on their decision-making (Pinello 1999). These scholars relied on party to serve as an indirect measure of judicial ideology, perhaps because of the inherent difficulties and complexities associated with measuring judicial ideology independently of party. Even after the Segal-Cover scores provided a reliable measure of ideology for Supreme Court justices, scholars may have continued to use party as a substitute for judicial ideology, especially in studies of lower court judges for which Segal-Cover scores are not available and for which similar scores cannot be calculated without a great a good deal of time and investment (Pinello 1999). This practice was so ubiquitous that Pinello (1999) identified at least 140 studies, articles, dissertations, books, etc. that used party as a proxy measure for judicial ideology. In his meta-analysis, Pinello (1999) concluded that there is a positive relationship between a judge's party and ideology. Specifically, he shows that Democratic judges are indeed more liberal than are Republican judges. Additionally, he finds that this relationship is stronger in the federal courts than in the state courts, with party explaining roughly 31 percent of the variance in judicial ideology for state court judges compared to 48 percent for federal court judges. These finding suggest that there is some validity in using party as a proxy measure for ideology (Pinello 1999). The drawback of this approach, however, is that it does not allow scholars to study the separate effects of party and ideology on the judges. It also does not distinguish between judges of the same party. Consider for example the considerable ideological differences that exist between Justice Stevens and Justice Thomas despite the fact that they are both Republicans. Similarly, there were considerable ideological differences between Justices Brennan and Powell, though both were Democrats.

Identifying the Unique Contributions of Party and Ideology on the Court

Because partisan and ideological considerations often overlap and lead judges to the same outcome, it may not be immediately obvious why it is worthwhile to identify whether it is party or ideology that judges ultimately rely on to reach their decision. However, this view assumes that one is concerned only with the final decision of the judges and not with the process that they used to reach their decisions. If one is concerned with the process, however, then it becomes very important to deduce whether judges' decisions are shaped by their partisan or ideological biases. This is because while people expect judges to be influenced by their own ideology and values when making decisions they do not expect or approve of judges making decisions based solely on partisan motivations (Gillman 2001a). Gillman (2001a) refers to the former as "high politics" and the latter as "low politics." Similar findings at the congressional level, suggest that this phenomena extends beyond just the courts (Carson, Koger, Lebo, and Young 2010). When it comes to politics, it seems, that people may view a commitment to ideology as principled, but are likely to view reliance on party negatively (Carson, Koger, Lebo, and Young 2010). Thus although only rarely will the outcome of judicial votes change depending on whether judges look to their party or ideology to influence their decision, the normative implications for the Court are very different depending on whether partisan or ideological considerations are found to be paramount (Gillman 2001a).

Although it had been quite common for scholars to use party as a proxy for ideology in their models of judicial decision-making, the idea that party and ideology might have separate influences on the justices has come to be recognized by scholars (Lloyd 1995; Kopko 2008, 2010; McKenzie 2012). Referring to psychological theory, scholars have noted that belonging to a party may have important psychological effects on the judges that can naturally be expected to affect their decision-making above and beyond its indirect effect through shaping the judges' policy preferences (Lloyd 1995; Kopko 2008, 2010; McKenzie 2012). Lloyd (1995) argues that the judges' party may act as a reference group for them, and thus the judges may have a sincere desire to see their party succeed both electorally and in terms of the policy it supports. Additionally, work on social identity theory suggests that if judges identify strongly with their parties they may be reluctant to harm them by handing down decisions that are unfavorable to them (Kopko 2008). In addition to partisanship (e.g., Lloyd 1995), a study by Epstein, Parker, and Segal (2013) does provide support for in-group bias as applied to ideology, by showing that the Supreme Court justices exhibit behavior consistent with in-group bias in the resolution of First Amendment free speech cases. Specifically, they find that liberal justices are not always more supportive of free speech as was initially assumed (e.g., Schubert 1965; Rohde and Spaeth 1974), but that the liberal justices are markedly more supportive of free speech claims made by liberal speakers compared to conservative speakers (see Haidt 2012). The conservative justices, on the other hand, exhibit the opposite behavior favoring free speech claims more often if the speech is conservative and less often if not.

In lower state courts, judges may have more tangible reasons for voting in ways that benefit their party. In states where judges are elected on partisan ballots, they may be more likely to vote in a way that benefits their party because they anticipate needing the money and support of their party in future electoral contests (Kopko 2008). There is, however, a separate line of thought that argues that the influence of partisanship upon judges will be limited. This is because judges have an incentive to protect the legitimacy of their institutions, and judicial legitimacy is thought to suffer when partisanship is seen as a basis for the court's decisions (Gillman 2001a). This view, however, assumes that judges are cognizant of the potential influences of their party on their decision-making and thus can actively block it. If the influence of party happens at an unconscious level, however, then judges may not be able to resist its influence no matter how motivated they are to protect the legitimacy of their institutions (Braman 2009; Lodge and Taber 2013).

Although there are some strong theoretical reasons for expecting party to have independent effects from ideology on judicial decision-making, research in this area has been difficult due to methodological issues. Essentially the problem with trying to separate out the effects of party and ideology on judicial decision-making has been that normally partisan and ideological considerations influence judges in the same direction. Thus it becomes both theoretically and methodologically difficult to determine whether it is the justices' party or personal beliefs that led them to their decision. Gillman (2001a) draws a theoretical distinction by arguing that decisions based on partisan, rather than ideological decisions, are characterized by shallow legal reasoning employed solely for the purpose of reaching one's preferred partisan outcome. Based on this definition he argues that partisan decisions can be identified when judges make decisions consistent with their party that are not supported by opposing partisans, and are inconsistent with the legal reasoning they have used in past cases (Gillman 2001a). Recently scholars have also begun to make some progress towards empirically identifying the effects of party, separate from ideology, by studying a unique subset of cases in which partisan considerations and ideological considerations point to different outcomes. These cases mostly deal with election laws (Lloyd 1995; Gillman 2001a; Kopko 2008, 2010; McKenzie 2012). With respect to the constitutionality of majority minority districts, for example, a liberal judge is predisposed to rule in favor of these districts, whereas a Democratic judge may be tempted to rule against them, because it is widely demonstrated that majority minority districts may cause the Democratic Party to lose seats by packing its voters into one district (Swain 1993; Lublin 1997; Bositis 1998; Handley, Grofman, and Arden 1998; Clayton 2000).

Perhaps one of the most well-known examples of election law cases where partisan and ideological considerations clearly came into conflict is the litigation surrounding the 2000 election. These cases were unique, because they all had clear partisan implications as the decisions reached literally had the power to throw the outcome of the presidential election to either Bush or Gore (Gillman 2001a). Gillman (2001a) conducts an in-depth case study of this conflict and argues that while judges on the lower courts and even the Florida Supreme Court did not seem to exhibit overtly partisan behavior, even in cases with very favorable conditions for partisan influence, the same cannot be said for the justices of the U.S. Supreme Court. Gillman reaches this conclusion by showing that the behavior of the judges on the lower courts ultimately fail to meet the three conditions for partisan behavior defined above. Firstly, he notes that there are many examples of lower court judges writing or signing on to opinions that were contrary to the opinions that would have been expected of them if they were thinking only of their party. For example, even though the majority of the Florida Supreme Court was composed of Democratic judges only two of the five decisions handed down by it favored Democratic presidential candidate, Al Gore. Additionally, many of the decisions reached in the lower courts did not split along party lines, but rather were supported by judges of both parties. This provides evidence that the legal reasoning employed in these cases was sincere. Lastly, the decisions reached by the Florida Supreme Court, were markedly consistent with the principles it had enunciated in prior cases. These findings combine to suggest that the behavior of the lower court judges in these cases was not primarily motivated by partisan concerns (Gillman 2001a).

In contrast, Gillman (2001a) argues that the decisions of the U.S. Supreme Court appear far more partisan. Decisions reached by the Supreme Court, for instance, were much more likely to split among partisan lines. In *Bush v. Gore* the five conservative justices voted to stop the recounts thus ensuring a Bush victory, while the four liberal justices dissented. Thus not only were the justices split on partisan lines, no judge supported the legal reasoning of the opposing party. Gillman also characterized the decision as partisan, because the legal reasoning employed by the five conservative justices was not supported by existing precedent and was also a dramatic departure from anything they would have previously argued. To highlight the insincerity of the legal reasoning applied by the conservative justices, Gillman notes the conservative justices included language in the decision purposefully limiting its impact on future cases. Specifically, they wrote, "Our consideration is limited to the present circumstances, for the problem of equal protection in election processes generally presents many complexities" (*Bush v. Gore*, 531 U.S. 98, 109 (2000) as quoted in Gillman 2001a: 87). Many legal commentators believe this language was included because the conservatives were fearful of appearing too supportive of equal protection arguments, which if carried out logically would allow for more federal intervention into the state's administration of elections, something the conservatives were keen to avoid (Gillman 2001a). Although Gillman persuasively argues that the decision of the Supreme Court in *Bush v. Gore* was partisan, he does not believe that this is the normal practice of the Court. Specifically, he points to unanimous decisions of the Court in two other cases that clearly had strong partisan implications *Clinton v. Jones*, where the Court allowed a lawsuit against Clinton to continue, and in *United States v. Nixon*, which required President Nixon to turn over the Watergate tapes. Thus it would premature to conclude that the justices are systematically influenced by their partisanship on the basis of *Bush v. Gore* alone

(Gillman 2001a). This highlights the need for more systematic studies on the same question.

One of the first studies to do this more systematically is the work of Lloyd (1995). Lloyd (1995) examined the effect of the U.S. District courts judges' party on their votes in reapportionment cases. Specifically, he codes for whether or not the judge is of the same party as the legislature responsible for drawing up the plan. Controlling for the facts of the case and judicial ideology, he estimated the effects of belonging to the party that drew up the plan on the probability that the judge will vote to uphold the plan. He finds that while partisan considerations do play a role, because judges are more likely to uphold plans proposed by their partisans rather than opposing partisans, its role is limited, as judges of both parties are more likely to uphold nonpartisan plans than partisan ones. Specifically, judges are 0.55 times more likely to strike down a plan proposed by members of the opposite party than a nonpartisan plan and only 0.25 more likely to strike down an in-party plan again compared to a nonpartisan plan (Lloyd 1995).

Kopko (2008) also finds that party may not have the largest influence on judges even in election law cases. Specifically, Kopko (2008) studied litigation surrounding Nader's 2004 effort to be placed on the general election ballot. According to Kopko, Democrats did not want Nadar to appear on the ballot, because they feared he would attract votes from people who typically vote Democratic. Republicans also saw the possibility of Nader draining support from usual Democratic voters, and thus worked hard to secure Nader a place on the ballot (Kopko 2008). As these disputes ultimately wound up in the courts and the partisan implications of the outcome are clear, they provide good test cases to determine if judges strategically act in a manner that benefits their own party (Kopko 2008). What Kopko (2008) finds, however, is that judges were influenced more by the decision of the state election authorities as to whether or not Nadar should be allowed on the ballot than by their own partisan biases. Thus he concludes that, at least in these cases, judges did not base their decisions on partisan considerations (Kopko 2008).

Some research has suggested that the effects of partisanship may be conditioned by the type and facts of the case and by the composition of the panel (Kopko 2010; McKenzie 2012). Kopko (2010) studied the effect of party on three different types of election law cases: redistricting, campaign finance, and right to association cases. While specifically controlling for judicial preferences, he finds an independent effect of party only in campaign finance cases. In redistricting cases, however, he finds that there may be an effect of party, but only when the entire three-judge panel is of the same party (Kopko 2010). Additionally, McKenzie (2012) finds an independent effect of partisanship on judicial redistricting decisions when the facts of the case leave room for ambiguity, such as in Voting Rights Act racial gerrymandering cases. If the facts of the case, however, clearly point to one outcome, such as in one person one vote cases, then this is the decision reached regardless of party (McKenzie 2012). These results suggest that while party can sometimes have an independent effect on judicial decision-making the relationship is dependent on the type of case and is more nuanced than previously thought (Kopko 2010; McKenzie 2012).

As a result of these newer studies we know now quite a bit more about the independent effects of party on judicial decision-making. For example, we know that in certain circumstances, judges do act as partisans, deciding cases in a way that benefits their party. We also know, however, that in other instances when the law is clear, judges act more like neutral arbitrators who impartially apply the law to the case at hand (McKenzie 2012). While work in this field has come a long way, many questions still remain unanswered. For example, we still do not know if party independently affects decision-making in cases that are not about election laws. We also do not know if certain judges are more inclined to consider their party when making decisions than are others and what might explain these differences. Additionally, we do not know if party has always been a factor in judicial decision-making or if this is a relatively new phenomenon. One reason to believe that the effect of party has increased is that we have in the past had political eras with many liberal Republicans. We have also had many conservative (mostly southern) Democrats. Certainly partisan polarization characterizes legislative elites in the United States today (Poole and Rosenthal 1997; Fiorina 1986; Abramowitz 2010) and ordinary citizens too (Abramowitz 2010). Far less effort has gone into the question as to whether judicial elites are similarly polarized, especially at the Supreme Court. As noted above, the mass public much more readily accepts an ideological Supreme Court than it would a partisan Supreme Court. Partisan polarization on the Court will make it much more likely that it will be seen in a partisan manner.

Increasing Polarization of the Court

Since the 2010 resignation of liberal Republican Justice John Paul Stevens, the Court has been perfectly divided by party so that no Republican appointees are more liberal than any Democratic appointees and vice versa (Segal, Westerland, and Lindquist 2010; Devins and Baum 2014; Liptak 2014). Additionally, Devins and Baum (2014) found that the ideological difference between the voting record of Republicans and Democrats on the Court is growing, while the ideological difference between co-partisans is decreasing, which is largely a result of the disappearance of moderate justices in each party. Another way to gauge the increasing partisanship of the Court is to examine the alignment of the justices on case decisions. Early on in the Court's history most of its decisions were unanimous. Thus we can be fairly confident that the early Court was not polarized (Devins and Baum 2014; Liptak 2014). Additionally, even when dissents did occur they did not often split the Court along party lines (Devins and Baum 2014; Liptak 2014). This held true about until about 2010, when many more major cases began to split the Court by party (Devins and Baum 2014; Liptak 2014). As the polarization of the Court is not projected to decrease any time in the near future, it is vital to understand the causes behind the increasing polarization of the Court (Devins and Baum 2014).

One of the main factors behind the increasing polarization of the Court is thought to be a change in presidents' nomination strategies. In the past, presidents considered many factors in addition to the nominee's ideology when identifying potential nominees (Epstein and Segal 2005; Yaloff 1999). More recently, however, ideology has become the paramount, if not the only, consideration of presidents when choosing their nominees (Devins and Baum 2014; Liptak 2014). This alone is not entirely responsible for the polarization of the Court, however (Devins and Baum 2014; Liptak 2014). The increasing ability of presidents to find reliable partisans to nominate also contributes by reducing the chances that a Republican president will mistakenly appoint a liberal, as Nixon did with his appointment of Blackmun to the Supreme Court, and vice versa for Democratic presidents, as occurred when Kennedy nominated Justice White (Devins and Baum 2014; Liptak 2014). It has become easier for presidents to find reliable partisans to nominate, because now more than in the past, president are selecting appointees from the federal court of appeals who have long records of decisions that can be examined for ideological consistency (Devins and Baum 2014; Liptak 2014).

Another factor to blame for the increasing polarization of the Court may be the increasing tendency of the justices to befriend their fellow partisans, thus isolating themselves from opposing viewpoints (Devins and Baum 2014; Liptak 2014). This is evident in the recent trend of justices hiring only law clerks who also share their partisanship (Devins and Baum 2014; Liptak 2014). It can also be seen by the tendency of the justices to speak predominantly in front of favorable audiences and to consume news that is slanted in favor of their party (Devins and Baum 2014; Liptak 2014). Additionally, the social circles of the justices from different parties rarely overlap anymore as they did in the past, when Justice Scalia remembers going to bipartisan social events that he says do not exist anymore (Devins and Baum 2014; Liptak 2014).

Another possible cause of increasing polarization on the Court is the increasing polarization in the Senate. Given the fact that justices are nominated by the president and confirmed by the Senate, the impact of party on the justices should roughly reflect the amount of partisan division at the time of the justices' appointment. For example, the Senate confirmed Justice Stevens, a liberal Republican, at a time when there were many liberal Republicans in the Senate. Similarly, the Senate confirmed Lewis Powell at a time when conservative Democrats were fairly common. Given growing party polarization in Congress over the last thirty years, we should expect a relatively tighter fit between party and voting behavior on the Court in 2010 than we would find in 1994 (Abramowitz 2010).

We begin to examine this by looking at the overlap between (1) partisanship in a Senate from not too long ago, the 98th (1983–5) Senate and the justices serving ten years later, i.e., on the 1994 Term of the Court, and (2) partisanship in a much more recent Senate, the 107th Senate (2001–3) and the justices serving on the 2010 Term.[7] As Figure 16.1 shows, there was a fair amount of overlap in partisanship in the 98th Senate. There were several Democrats (Republicans) to the right (left) of several Republicans (Democrats). Ten years later, we find, based on the Martin-Quinn ideal point scores, Republican Justice Stevens to be the most liberal member of the Court while Republican Justice David Souter falls to the left of Democratic Justice Stephen Breyer (see Figure 16.2).

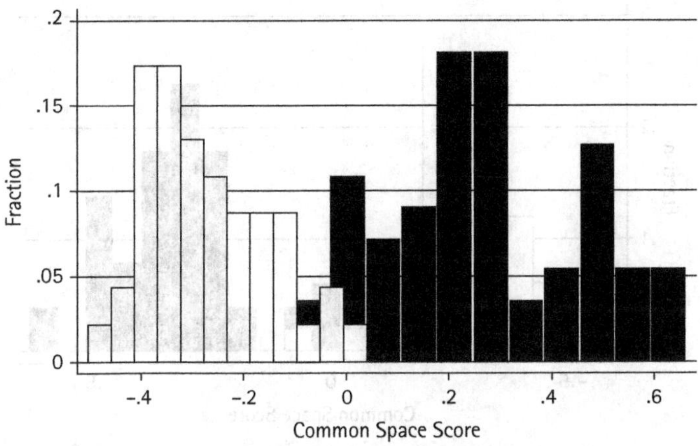

FIGURE 16.1 Distribution of ideal points by party, 98th Senate

Source: http://voteview.com.

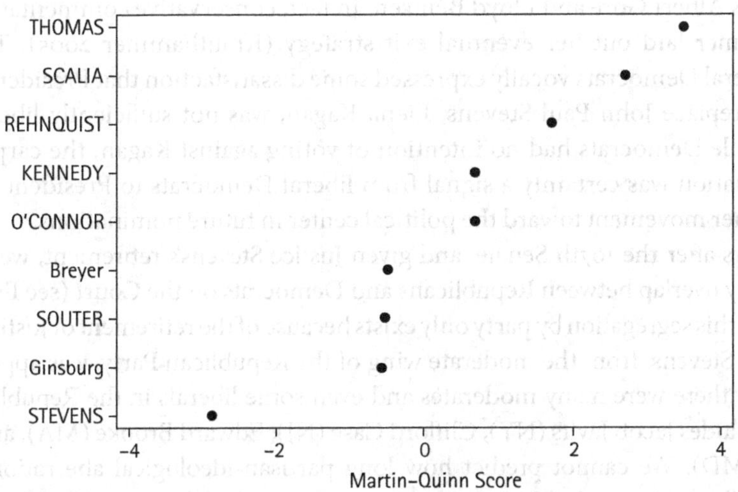

FIGURE 16.2 Partisan polarization and ideology of the justices, 1994 term

Source: Andrew Martin and Kevin Quinn, http://mqscores.berkeley.edu/.
Note: Scores based on 2010 Martin-Quinn ideal point estimates; legend: nominees by Republican presidents in CAPS.

By the 107th Senate, we observe far less overlap between Republicans and Democrats (see Figure 16.3). The increasing homogeneity of the Republican Party since the 1980s, combined with the battle cry "No More Souters" should make it increasingly difficult for a Republican president to nominate a Supreme Court justice who overlaps ideologically with Democratic justices. While Bush's Supreme Court nominee, Harriet Miers's, lack of qualifications no doubt hurt her chances for confirmation, her failure was certainly aided and abetted by conservatives who were not certain about her ideological purity, given ambiguous statements about abortion rights and past political contributions to

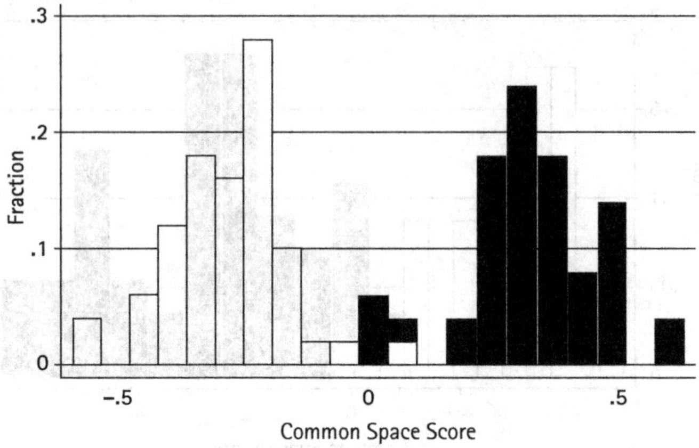

FIGURE 16.3 Distribution of ideal points by party, 107th Senate

Source: http://voteview.com.

Democrats Albert Gore and Lloyd Bentsen. In fact, conservative commentator Charles Krauthammer laid out her eventual exit strategy (Krauthammer 2005). To a lesser extent, liberal Democrats vocally expressed some dissatisfaction that President Obama's choice to replace John Paul Stevens, Elena Kagan, was not sufficiently liberal (Baker 2010). While Democrats had no intention of voting against Kagan, the carping about her nomination was certainly a signal from liberal Democrats to President Obama to resist further movement toward the political center in future nominations.

Ten years after the 107th Senate, and given Justice Stevens's retirement, we no longer observe any overlap between Republicans and Democrats on the Court (see Figure 16.4). To be sure, this segregation by party only exists because of the retirement of Justice Stevens, but Justice Stevens, from the moderate wing of the Republican Party, was appointed at a time when there were many moderates and even some liberals in the Republican Party. The list includes Jacob Javits (NY), Clifford Case (NJ), Edward Brooke (MA), and Charles Mathias (MD). We cannot predict how long partisan-ideological aberrations such as Stevens will remain on the Court once that partisan-ideological package largely disappears from the Senate, only that with some undetermined lag that it will happen. This preliminary look at the data suggests that there is some relationship between the polarization in the Senate and the polarization on the Court.

Other work also points to a relationship between the polarization of the Senate and the polarization of the Court. Esptein, Segal, Lindstaedt, and Westerland (2006) analyze the confirmation votes of senators and find that the importance of the ideological distance between the senator and the nominee has increased in recent nominations (see also Cameron, Kastellec, and Park 2013; Devins and Baum 2014). Party has also become a more important voting cue. Since the 1993 nomination of Ruth Bader Ginsburg to the Supreme Court, only two out of 336 votes against Ginsburg or the five subsequent nominees came from senators of the president's party (Nelson's vote against Kagan and Chafee's vote against Alito).[8] Although the fact that opposing partisans are more likely

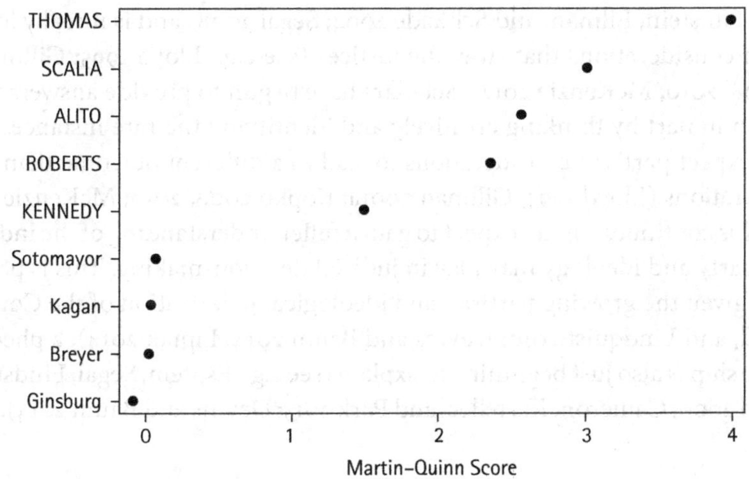

FIGURE 16.4 Partisan polarization and ideology of the justices, 2010 term

Source: Andrew Martin and Kevin Quinn, http://mqscores.berkeley.edu/.

Note: Scores based on 2010 Martin-Quinn ideal point estimates; legend: nominees by Republican presidents in CAPS.

to vote against nominees may not initially seem surprising, it does represent an important break from the past where most Supreme Court nominees where accorded high levels of bipartisan support (Devins and Baum 2014). Additionally, a counterfactual analysis, conducted by Cameron, Kastellec, and Park (2013), predicted that Senate confirmation votes would be less contentious had the Senate remained less polarized. These results suggest that in a less polarized Senate more nominees could have been confirmed and that the confirmation of other nominees would have been less controversial than they were in reality (Cameron, Kastellec, and Park 2013).

Scholars have only just begun to analyze systematically how polarization in the Senate may affect polarization on the Court. Our preliminary look at the data showing a temporal correlation and other early work on this topic (Cameron, Kastellec, and Park 2013), however, provide initial support for the idea. A more full understanding of how the effects of party and ideology in the Senate affect the influence of party and ideology on the Court would be an important contribution to the field. Thus future work should consider more explicitly how polarization in the Senate may bleed over and cause polarization on the Court. The implications of a more polarized Court, particularly with regards to the legitimacy of the Court, should be examined more fully as well.

Scholarship on the effect of party and ideology on the Court has evolved a long way from the early debates in the literature about whether or not party or ideology had any influence on judicial decision-making (see e.g., Mendelson 1963, 1966; Tanenhaus 1966; Friedman 2006; Gillman 2001b: Frank 1949: Llewellyn 1931; Rhode and Spaeth 1976; Segal and Spaeth 1993, 1996, 2002; Segal and Howard 2002). For the most part, scholars have now come to accept the fact that partisan and ideological considerations do matter and have begun to ask more interesting and nuanced questions, such as when do party and ideology matter most (see e.g., Emmert and Traut 1994; Brace, Langer, and

Hall 2000; Sunstein, Ellman, and Schkade 2004; Segal 2008) and is it really ideological or partisan considerations that sway the justices (see e.g., Lloyd 1995; Gillman 2001a; Kopko 2008, 2010; McKenzie 2012). Scholars have begun to provide answers to the latter question in part by thinking creatively and identifying the rare instances in which we would expect partisan considerations to lead to a different outcome than ideological considerations (Lloyd 1995; Gillman 2001a; Kopko 2008, 2010; McKenzie 2012). As work like this continues we can expect to gain a fuller understanding of the independent roles that party and ideology may play in judicial decision-making. This is particularly important given the growing partisan and ideological polarization of the Court (Segal, Westerland, and Lindquist 2010; Devins and Baum 2014; Liptak 2014), a phenomenon that scholarship is also just beginning to explain (see e.g., Esptein, Segal, Lindstaedt, and Westerland 2006, Cameron, Kastellec, and Park 2013; Devins and Baum 2014).

Notes

1. We thank Alan Champlin for research assistance.
2. http://mqscores.berkeley.edu/.
3. 531 U.S. 98 (2000). Again, while we have not systematically studied this, it seems to us that comments about the attitudinal model on the lawcourt-l (lawcourt-l@unt.edu) and conlawprof (conlawprof@lists.ucla.edu) listservs went from "dead wrong" prior to *Bush v. Gore* to "everyone knows that" sometime after the case.
4. Poole and Rosenthal (1997).
5. The Senate norm of courtesy calls for the president to give senators of his party input on judicial nominations arising in their state (Giles, Hettinger, and Peppers 2001).
6. Songer, U.S. Appeals Court Database. Available at: http://artsandsciences.sc.edu/poli/juri/appct.htm.
7. This section follows Segal, Westerland, and Lindquist (2010).
8. Data updated by Chad Westerland and authors from Epstein and Segal (2005).

References

Abramowitz, A. 2010. *The Disappearing Center: Engaged Citizens, Polarization, and American Democracy*. New Haven, CT: Yale University Press.

Bailey, M. A., and Maltzman, F. 2011. *The Constrained Court: Law, Politics, and the Decisions Justices Make*. Princeton, NJ: Princeton University Press.

Baker, P. 2010. "Kagan Nomination Leaves Longing on the Left." *The New York Times*, May 10. Available at: http://www.nytimes.com/2010/05/11/us/politics/11nominees.html.

Bositis, D. A. 1998. "The Future of Majority-Minority Districts and Black and Hispanic Legislative Representation." In *Redistricting and Minority Representation: Learning from the Past, and Preparing for the Future*, edited by D. A. Bositis. Maryland: University Press of America, Inc. and Washington, DC: The Joint Center for Political and Economic Studies, 9–42.

Brace, P., Langer, L., and Hall, M. G. 2000. "Measuring the Preferences of State Supreme Court Judges." *The Journal of Politics* 62(2): 387–413.

Braman, E. 2009. *Law, Politics, and Perception: How Policy Preferences Influence Legal Reasoning*. Charlottesville, VA: The University of Virginia Press.

Cameron, C. M., Kastellec, J. P., and Park, J. 2013. "Voting for Justices: Change and Continuity in Confirmation Voting 1937–2010." *Journal of Politics* 75(2): 283–99.

Carson, J. L., Koger, G., Lebo, M. J., and Young, E. 2010. "The Electoral Costs of Party Loyalty in Congress." *American Journal of Political Science* 54(3): 598–616.

Clayton, D. M. 2000. *African Americans and the Politics of Congressional Redistricting*. New York, NY: Garland Publishing.

Devins, N., and Baum, L. 2014. "Split Definitive: How Party Polarization Turned the Supreme Court into a Partisan Court." William and Mary Law School, Research Paper No. 09-276.

Emmert, C. F., and Traut, C. A. 1994. "The California Supreme Court and the Death Penalty." *American Politics Research*, 22(1): 41–61.

Epstein, L., Parker, C. M., and Segal, J. 2013. "Do Justices Defend the Speech They Hate? In Group Bias, Opportunism, and the First Amendment." Paper presented at the annual meeting of the American Political Science Association, Chicago.

Epstein L., Lindstaedt, R., Segal, J. A., and Westerland, C. 2006. "The Changing Dynamics of Senate Voting on Supreme Court Nominees." *Journal of Politic*, 68: 296–307.

Epstein, L., and Segal, J. A. 2005. *Advice and Consent: The Politics of Judicial Appointments*. New York, NY: Oxford University Press.

Fiorina, M. P. 1986. "Legislator Uncertainty, Legislative Control, and the Delegation of Legislative Power." *Journal of Law, Economics, & Organizations* 2: 33–51.

Frank, J. 1949. *Law and the Modern Mind*. New York, NY: Coward-McCann.

Friedman, B. 2006. "Taking Law Seriously." *Perspectives on Politics* 4(2): 261–76.

Giles, M. W., Hettinger, V., and Peppers, T. 2001. "Picking Federal Judges: A Note on Policy and Partisan Selection Agendas." *Political Research Quarterly* 54(3): 623–41.

Gillman, H. 2001a. "*The Votes that Counted: How the Court Decided the 2000 Presidential Election*. Chicago, IL: The University of Chicago Press.

Gillman, H. 2001b. "What's Law Got to Do with It? Judicial Behavioralists Test the 'Legal Model' of Judicial Decision Making." *Law & Social Inquiry* 26(2): 465–504.

Haidt, J. 2012. *The Righteous Mind*. London: Penguin Group.

Handley, L., Grofman, B., and Arden, W. 1998. "Electing Minority-Preferred Candidates to Legislative Office: The Relationship between Minority Percentages in Districts and the Election of Minority-Preferred Candidates." In *Race and Redistricting in the 1990s*, edited by B. Grofman. New York, NY: Agathon Press, 13–38.

Kahn, R. 1999. "Institutionalized Norms and Supreme Court Decision-Making: The Rehnquist Court on Privacy and Religion." In *Supreme Court Decision Making: New Institutionalized Approaches*, edited by C. W. Clayton and H. Gillman. Chicago, IL: University Press, 175–98.

Kopko, K. C. 2008. "Partisanship Suppressed: Judicial Decision-Making in Ralph Nader's 2004 Ballot Access Litigation." *Election Law Journal* 7(4): 301–24.

Kopko, K. C. 2010. "The Effect of Partisanship in Election Law Judicial Decision-Making." PhD dissertation, Ohio State University.

Krauthammer, C. 2005. "Miers: The Only Exit Strategy." *The Washington Post*, October 21. Available at: http://www.washingtonpost.com/wp-dyn/content/article/2005/10/20/AR2005102001635.html.

Liptak, A. 2014. "The Polarized Court." *The New York Times*, May 10. Available at: http://www.nytimes.com/2014/05/11/upshot/the-polarized-court.html?_r=3.

Llewellyn, K. 1931. "Some Realism about Realism: Responding to Dean Pound." *Harvard Law Review* 44(8): 1237–64.

Lloyd, R. D. 1995. "Separating Partisanship from Party in Judicial Research: Reapportionment in the U.S. District Courts." *American Political Science Review* 89(2): 413–20.

Lublin, D. 1997. *The Paradox of Representation: Racial Gerrymandering and Minority Interests in Congress*. Princeton, NJ: Princeton University Press.

Lodge, M., and Taber, C. S. 2013. *The Rationalizing Voter*. New York, NY: Cambridge University Press.

McKenzie, M. J. 2012. "The Influence of Partisanship, Ideology, and the Law on Redistricting Decisions in Federal Courts." *Political Research Quarterly* 65(4): 799–813.

Mendelson, W. 1963. "The Neo-Behavioral Approach to the Judicial Process: A Critique." *American Political Science Review* 57: 593–603.

Mendelson, W. 1966. "An Open Letter to Professor Spaeth and his Jurimetrical Colleagues. *Journal of Politics* 28: 429–32.

Pinello, D. R. 1999. "Linking Party to Judicial Ideology in American Courts: A Meta-analysis." *The Justice System Journal* 20(3): 219–54.

Poole, K. T., and Rosenthal, H. 1997. *Congress: A Political-Economic History of Roll Call Voting*. New York: Oxford University Press.

Rohde, D. W., and Spaeth, H. J. 1976. *Supreme Court Decision Making*. San Francisco W.H. Freeman.

Scalia, A., and Garner, B. A. 2012. *Reading Law: The Interpretation of Legal Texts*. St. Paul: Thomson/West.

Schubert, G. 1959. *Quantitative Analysis of Judicial Behavior*. Glencoe, IL: The Free Press.

Schubert, G. 1965. *The Judicial Mind: The Attitudes and Ideologies of Supreme Court Justices, 1946-1963*. Evanston: Northwestern University Press.

Schubert, G. 1974. *The Judicial Mind Revisited: A Psychometric Analysis of Supreme Court Ideology*. New York, NY: The Free Press.

Segal, J. A. 2008. "Judicial Behavior." In *The Oxford Handbook of Law and Politics*, edited by K. E. Whittington, R. D. Kelemen, and G. A. Caldeira. New York: Oxford University Press, 19–33.

Segal, J. A., and Cover, A. D. 1989. "Ideological Values and the Votes of U.S. Supreme Court Justices." *The American Political Science Review* 83 (2): 557–65.

Segal, J. A., and Howard, R. M. 2002. "An Original Look at Originalism." *Law & Society Review* 36 (1): 113–38.

Segal, J. A., and Spaeth, H. J. 1993. *The Supreme Court and the Attitudinal Model*. New York: Cambridge University Press.

Segal, J. A., and Spaeth, H. J. 1996. "The influence of Stare Decisis on the Votes of United States Supreme Court Justices." *American Journal of Political Science* 40 (4): 971–1003.

Segal, J. A., and Spaeth, H. J. 2002. *The Supreme Court and the Attitudinal Model Revisited*. New York: Cambridge University Press.

Segal, J. A., Westerland, C., and Lindquist, S. A. 2010. Are Supreme Court Justices Legislators in Robes? Evidence from Judicial Review of Federal Enactments. Paper presented at the Annual Meeting of the Midwest Political Science Association.

Songer, D. R. U.S. Appeals Court Database. Available at http://artsandsciences.sc.edu/poli/juri/appct.htm.

Spaeth, H. 1979. *Supreme Court Policy Making*. San Francisco, CA: W.H. Freeman and Company.

Sunstein, C. R., Schkade, D., and Ellman, L. M. 2004. "Ideological Voting on Federal Courts of Appeals: A Preliminary Investigation." *Virginia Law Review* 90 (1): 301–54.

Swain, C. M. 1993. Black Faces, Black Interests: The Representation of African Americans in Congress. Cambridge: Harvard University Press.

Tanenhaus, J. 1966. The Cumulative Scaling of Judicial Decisions. *Harvard Law Review*, 79: 1583–94.

Traut, C. A., and Emmert, C. F. 1998. "Expanding the Integrated Model of Judicial Decision Making: The California Justices and Capital Punishment." *The Journal of Politics* 60(4): 1166–80.

Yalof, D. A. 1999. *Pursuit of Justices*. Chicago: University of Chicago Press.

CHAPTER 17

THE ECONOMIC ANALYSIS OF JUDICIAL BEHAVIOR

LEE EPSTEIN AND JACK KNIGHT

IN the study of judicial behavior, "economics" has multiple meanings. Many scholars view it through a conceptual lens, grounding their studies on the assumption that the judge is a "rational maximizer of his ends in life, his satisfactions—or ... his 'self-interest'" (Posner 2011: 3).[1] A second group might claim that work exploring economics as a substantive matter—say, a paper on the effect of the economy on judicial decisions—qualifies as an economic study of judging. Still others might emphasize methodology, focusing on whether the research employs the tools of mathematics or econometrics.

We limit our discussion here to research falling into the first group—to studies proceeding from the assumption of rationality, regardless of their methodological approach. By trimming our chapter in this way, we do not mean to deprecate the other two types; ours is a decision of necessity. Because most important studies of judicial behavior fit into at least one of the three categories, including the full range of "economic" work would require not a chapter but an entire Handbook. For the same reason, we exclude work related to but not squarely focused on the behavior of judges such as studies of litigants and lawyers (including the selection of cases for litigation) (e.g., Priest and Klein 1984; Hubbard 2013a) and the large literature on judicial appointments that explores the choices made by rational politicians (e.g., Segal, Cameron, and Cover 1992; Moraski and Shipan 1999).

For a number of reasons, though, our choices aren't especially limiting. First, rational choice studies of judicial behavior vary in approach. Some are purely theoretical; others are mostly empirical. And even within these categories there is variation. On the theoretical side, there are scholars who explore how the individual judge acts *parametrically* to maximize her preferences. If the judge desires to make more money, she might write a novel assuming she has weighed her own costs (e.g., time away from her judicial work) and benefits; in other words, she is the variable and all others, the constants (Elster 1983). Other studies of judicial behavior—perhaps the great majority—invoke *non-parametric* rational choice models. Strategic accounts belong in this category because they assume that goal-directed judges operate in a strategic or interdependent decision-making context, regardless of the judges' specific motivation. Then, within the class of strategic accounts there are studies that undertake formal equilibrium analysis (e.g., Anderson and Tahk 2007; Cameron et al. 2000) and there are studies that use economic theories to reason by analogy (e.g., Songer et al. 1994, Westerland et al. 2010). Empirical work too comes in many shades, from large-*n* studies that invoke complex methods (Epstein et al. 2005; Black and Owens 2016) to largely descriptive or historical case studies (Brams 1990; Knight and Epstein 1996). Exemplars of all theoretical and empirical types appear in this essay, reflecting our belief that there are many ways to incorporate assumptions of rationality into research on the choices judges make (Epstein and Knight 2000).

A second way our focus on rational choice studies of judicial behavior isn't especially limiting is that the targets are many in number. Though the early studies focused on the U.S. Supreme Court (Murphy 1962, 1964; Schubert 1958), modern-day scholars have paid as much if not more attention to lower federal court judges (e.g., Kastellec 2007, Beim, Hirsch, and Kastellec 2014) and judiciaries in the U.S. states (e.g., Huber and Gordon 2007; Berdejo and Yuchtman 2013) and abroad (e.g., Staton 2010; Helmke 2005; Vanberg 2005). Our essay considers all of these developments.

Third, because rational choice accounts of judicial behavior are hardly the sole province of economists, the scholars and their studies vary considerably. Murphy, a political scientist, produced a path-marking book, *Elements of Judicial Strategy* (1964), which portrayed U.S. Supreme Court justices as strategic actors who seek to maximize their policy preferences (see also Schubert 1958). Decades later, Eskridge (1991), a law professor, developed an account of statutory interpretation in which judges are more concerned with the preferences and likely actions of contemporaneous elected actors than with the legislature that enacted the law. The studies we cite in this essay demonstrate this disciplinary diversity, with their authors hailing from business and law schools and from departments of economics, political science, and psychology. They also span the globe, from the United States of course but also Latin America, Europe, and the Middle East. (As an aside, bringing together these literatures in one essay is, we hope, an important contribution in and of itself. Because of the number of disciplines engaged in the study of judicial behavior, the right hand doesn't always know what the left hand is doing, even when they are writing on the same topics.)

Finally, even focusing exclusively on rational choice studies, the range of topics is impressive. There are many ways to splice and dice them but these six stand out: (1) the judge: motivations, careers and performance; (2) selection and retention of judges; (3) opinions and precedent; (4) collegial courts; (5) the hierarchy of justice; and (6) external actors.

In what follows we consider the literature on each, with the caveat that these topics are hardly mutually exclusive. Because this is abundantly clear from the discussion that follows, only a few examples suffice to make the point. Consider, first, Cross and Tiller's (1998: 2156) important study "Judicial Partisanship and Obedience to Legal Doctrine," which argues that the presence of a "whistleblower"—a judge "whose policy preferences differ from the majority's and who will expose the majority's manipulation or disregard of the applicable legal doctrine" to a higher court—can constrain his or her colleagues from behaving in accord with their own preferences. This study started a now large literature on panel effects, and so we discuss it in the section on collegial courts. Yet because the mechanism triggering the effect is the lower court judges' fear of reversal by a higher court, the chapter implicates the hierarchy of justice (relations between lower and upper courts) too. Then there is Ramseyer and Rasmussen's (2001) research on Japanese judges, which suggests that the judges' careers hinge on deference to the government. This study could fit within the scope of the topic, selection and retention of judges, but it also speaks to the judges' interest in promotion and other careerist motivations.

With this (long!) windup in mind, let's turn to the research. For each topic, we discuss the literature and offer some thoughts on future directions. In the last section we are even more specific, emphasizing two promising opportunities for scholars to pursue.

The Judge: Motivations, Careers, and Performance

As the subheading suggests, studies in this area explore features of individual judges—with a central question being, "What do judges want?" This is a reasonable starting point because rational choice accounts assume that actors make decisions consistent with their goals and interests. We say that judges or any other actors make rational decisions when they choose a course of action that they believe satisfies their desires most efficiently. To give meaning to this assumption—essentially, that judges maximize their preferences—we must identify the judges' goals. If we do not, our explanations become a tautology because we can always claim that a judge's goal is to do exactly what we observe her doing (Ordeshook 1992).

Political scientists have long had a ready and singular answer to the question of the judges' desires: it's all politics, stupid! That is, on the standard political science account of judicial behavior, judges hope to bring the law in line with their own policy or ideological values.[2] Because many political science studies continue to analyze the behavior of U.S. Supreme Court justices, we don't think an emphasis on policy preferences is especially misguided. From Pritchett (1941) to Segal and Spaeth (2002) to Epstein, Landes, and Posner (2013), scholars have offered plausible (although somewhat distinct) reasons and mounds of data for thinking that ideology plays a very substantial role in the choices *justices* make.

It's also worth pointing out that U.S. Supreme Court justices are hardly unique in this regard. Grendstad et al.'s (2015) wonderful study of the Norwegian Supreme Court demonstrates that justices appointed by social democratic governments are significantly more likely to find for the litigant pursuing a "public economic interest" than are their non-socialist counterparts. Ideology (as measured by the appointing regime) plays a bigger role in these decisions than most any other factor that Grendstad et al.

considered. Hönnige (2009) found that ideology helps predict the votes of judges serving on the French and German Supreme Courts (see also Hanretty 2012). And, in their study of Spanish Constitutional Court judges, Garoupa et al. (2013: 516) discovered that under certain conditions, "the personal ideology of the judges does matter," which led them to "reject the formalist approach taken by traditional constitutional law scholars in Spain."

At the same time, though, these very studies demonstrate that ideological (or partisan) motivations have their limits—and not only for judges outside the United States. As so much research has shown, there is hardly a perfect correlation between ideology and voting: far short of 0 percent of the votes cast by liberal justices (however measured) are conservative; and far short of 100 percent of the conservative judges' votes are conservative (see even Segal and Spaeth 2002). Moreover, once we move down the judicial hierarchy to the U.S. Courts of Appeals and district courts, ideology carries even less weight (see, e.g., Epstein, Landes, and Posner 2013). In other words, however useful ideology is for understanding judicial behavior, it cannot be the only motivation for explanations of the judges' choices.

Recognition of this fact has led law professors, economists, judges, and even some political scientists to challenge the standard political science approach to judicial motivations. These scholars assert that more realistic conceptions of judicial behavior must take into account the judges' desire to maximize their preferences over a set of personal factors (while also attending to the political scientists' emphasis on ideology and the law community's interest in legal motivations). According to Epstein, Landes, and Posner (2013; see also Epstein and Knight 2013), personal factors (most of which also have implications for ideological and legal goals) include:

1. job satisfaction, which we take to mean the internal satisfaction of feeling that one is doing a good job as well as the more social dimensions of judicial work, such as relations with other judges, clerks, and staff (see Baum 2006; Caldeira 1977; Drahozal 1998; Gulati and McCauliff 1998; Shapiro and Levy 1995)
2. external satisfactions that come from being a judge, including reputation, prestige, power, influence, and celebrity (see Drahozal 1998; Miceli and Cosgel 1994; Schauer 2000; Shapiro and Levy 1995; Whitman 2000)
3. leisure, such that at some point, "the opportunity cost of foregone leisure exceeds the benefits to the judge of additional time spent making decisions" Drahozal (1998: 476; see also Klein and Hume 2003).
4. salary/income, in that all else equal, judges like most of us, prefer more salary, income, and personal comfort to less (see, e.g., Baum 2006)
5. promotion.

We flesh out these possibilities in Epstein and Knight (2013). But let us provide a flavor of the analysis by focusing on the last motivation: promotion. This would seem to be an important factor influencing the personal utility that judges derive from their work. It could be coincident with policy preferences: the higher judges sit in the hierarchy, the more important the cases they hear and the greater the opportunity to influence the law. Promotion also tends to increase job satisfaction, prestige and reputation, and, of course, salary.

To explore the possible effects of this motivation, Epstein, Landes, and Posner (2013) compared federal judges with some realistic chance of promotion to those without much hope of advancement to determine whether the former "audition" for their next job. Epstein et al. hypothesized that the auditioners would impose harsher sentences on criminal defendants to avoid being tagged as soft on crime. The data supported their hypothesis.

We think these results, along with other studies of promotion effects (e.g., Cohen 1991; Sisk et al. 1998; Taha 2004; Gaille 1997; Ramseyer and Rasmussen 2001; Salzberger and Fenn 1999; Black and Owens 2016), do more than flesh out a particular element in the judge's personal utility function; they provide sufficient evidence of the importance of personal motivations to pose a serious challenge to the (un)realist(ic) conception of judicial behavior that generations of political scientists have assumed in their work on law and legal institutions. The findings also of course should invite more creative research on the general topic of judicial motivations.

Selection and Retention of Judges

Societies have devised an impressive array of institutions to govern the selection and retention of judges—from life tenure to a single nonrenewable term to periodic elections and re-election by the electorate. And a substantial body of work considers the decisions of the actors who select (or retain) the judges (e.g., in the United States, the president and Senate for federal judges, and governors, legislatures, commissions, and voters for state judges; see Gibson 2012; Cameron et al. 1990).

The economic literature on judicial behavior is more concerned with whether and how these various institutions affect the choices judges make—and so is related to important work on *judicial independence*. We (and others) define this term as the ability of judges to behave sincerely without fear of reprisal and with some confidence that political actors will enforce their decisions (see, e.g., Ríos-Figueroa and Staton 2014). So defined, we might expect that forcing judges to face the electorate or the legislature for renewal—relative to providing them with life tenure—would lead to a more dependent judiciary; the opportunity costs for voting on the basis of sincere preferences are higher. A life-tenured system, in contrast, should lead to a more independent judiciary, with judges freer to vote as they desire.

The empirical literature provides strong support for these expectations. Consider, for example, a classic article by two economists, Tabarrok and Helland (1999). Focusing on U.S. states that elect their judges, the authors examined whether tort awards were higher in cases brought by an in-state plaintiff against an out-of-state defendant. They predicted that elected judges would be more likely than appointed judges to rule in favor of plaintiffs because "redistribut[ing] wealth from out-of-state businesses to in-state plaintiffs" would help them win re-election (p. 157).[3] Using a variety of statistical methods, Tabarrok and Helland report that their hypothesis held: "the expected total award in ... elected states with out-of-state defendants is approximately $240,000 higher than in other states" (p. 186).

Similarly, in the criminal context research shows the judges who face the electorate to retain their jobs are especially tough on defendants, in part because the public (yet again) doesn't like judges who are softies. Gordon and Huber (2004: 247), for example, found that as retention elections for Pennsylvania trial court judges grew closer, the judges were significantly harsher on defendants. Overall, they "attribute at least 1,818 to 2,705 years of incarceration to the electoral dynamic." Berdejo and Yuchtman (2013) reached much the same conclusion. Their analysis of sentences imposed by 265 trial court judges in Washington State shows that sentences are significantly longer "at the end of a judges' political cycle than [at] the beginning."

This is just the tip of the iceberg. Study after study confirms that elected judges engage in sophisticated behavior designed to please their constituents—whether ruling for in-state plaintiffs or against criminal defendants. (For work on civil cases, see, e.g., Kang and Shepherd 2011; Canes-Wrone, Clark, and Park 2012; Caldarone, Canes-Wrone, and Clark 2009; Helland and Tabarrok 2002. On criminal cases, see, e.g., Gordon and Huber 2007; Hall 1987; Brace and Hall 1997; Brace and Boyea 2008).

These results are not too surprising: when societies subject their judges to reelection, they are presumably trying to induce accountability. But what of life-tenured judges? Oddly, research has shown that U.S. Supreme Court justices tend to vote as their appointing president would—almost as if the president appointed himself to the Court (Epstein and Segal 2005; Segal et al. 2000). Perhaps this recurring pattern reflects some perceived benefit (and minimal costs) of loyalty on the part of life-tenured justices (Epstein and Posner 2015). Or perhaps life-tenured justices feel free to vote sincerely (without fear of reprisal) because they share the preferences of the regime that appointed them.

But therein lies the rub for life-tenured schemes. Although they are designed to induce judicial independence, once the appointing regime changes, the institutional framework can produce the opposite effect, or at least cause substantial trouble for the judges. Some, though limited, evidence (not to mention famous anecdotes)[4] shows that as a life-tenured Court ages, attacks from the elected branches follow—with the judges ultimately caving to the pressure (Epstein, Knight, and Shvetsova 2002). Seen in this way, nonrenewable terms, which many European countries use for their constitutional court judges, may be a better mechanism than life tenure for inducing judicial independence. But we need far more work, necessarily comparative work, to get a better handle on this.

Opinions and Precedent

In the course of deciding cases, judges face countless choices, including, in many societies, whether to join the majority or write separately and then how to craft their opinions. A great deal of research makes use of rational choice to analyze these decisions. Such is Epstein, Landes, and Posner's (2011) study, which takes up the puzzle of why judges do not always dissent when they disagree with the majority. The basic argument is that dissents impose substantial collegiality costs on the other judges on the panel by making them work harder (e.g., more work), while the benefits of dissenting (e.g., future citations) are few. Although "dissent aversion" is stronger in the federal circuits than in the U.S. Supreme Court, there is some evidence that it exists there too, especially in cases in which the ideological stakes are low. (But see Beim, Hirsch, and Kastellec 2015, Lindquist et al. 2007, and Black and Owens 2012, all presenting evidence that the benefits may be more substantial than Epstein, Landes, and Posner posited.)

Other studies focus on opinions of the court, and consider how they make use of precedent and other traditional legal materials. In the formal economics literature, there is a debate of long standing over the extent to which reputation- or power-seeking judges ought to be followers (apply existing doctrine) or more avant-garde. Levy (2005) takes the latter position, contending that judges motivated by esteem should be less willing to follow precedent to show that they are more capable than their predecessors. Creating new precedents, on this account, can also generate citations and other accolades. On the other side, Landes and Posner (1976: 273) note that if judges regularly choose to reject existing doctrine, the "precedential value of [their] own decisions would be reduced." Of course, this could lead to rogue judges—those who feel free to disregard all precedents in their quest for power (or policy). But on Landes and Posner's account appellate review keeps the system in check. Judges who are too innovative run the risk of seeing their decisions overturned, which can harm their reputation.

Staton and Vanberg (2008) also analyze majority opinions but are less concerned with the internal context of judging—adhering to precedent or grappling with colleagues—than with external context. They want to know why judges sometimes write vague opinions when they could be more decisive. The answer the researchers derive is interesting: assuming that the costs to implementers of deviating from a clear court decision are higher than the costs of deviating from a vague decision (because non-compliance is easier to detect), a court facing "friendly" implementers will write clear opinions. Clarity increases pressure for—and thus the likelihood of—compliance. But when the probability of opposition from implementers is high, clarity could be costly to the judges; if policymakers were determined to defy even a crystal clear decision, they would highlight the relative lack of judicial power. To soften the anticipated resistance, courts may be purposefully vague.

Staton and Vanberg provide several examples of their theory in action (e.g., *Brown v. Board of Education* (*Brown II*) (1955)), but more systematic follow-ups now exist. Black et al. (2016) show that justices strategically craft language in their opinions, adjusting the level of clarity to correspond to their assessment of the likelihood of noncompliance by external actors, including federal agencies and the states. Corley and Wedeking (2014) find that lower courts are more likely to follow Supreme Court decisions that are written at higher degrees of certainty. And there is now also work on how lower court judges write opinions to insulate themselves from reversal (Boyd 2015a; Hinkle 2016; Hinkle et al. 2012; Smith and Tiller 2002). In addition to serving as an antidote to the long-suffering study of judicial implementation and compliance, this new line of work on opinion writing provides a link between the internal and external contexts of this important facet of judging.

Collegial Courts

There is a large literature exploring relations among judges who serve on the same court. Many studies focus on so-called panel, collegial, or peer effects, asking whether the case's outcome (or a judge's vote) would have been different had a single judge, and not a panel, decided the case (Kastellec 2007)—and, if so, why? As we noted earlier, the foundational work is Cross and Tiller's (1998) article, which argues that the presence of a "whistleblower" on a judicial panel can constrain his colleagues from voting sincerely. Some studies find evidence of this phenomenon while bringing more nuance to the Cross/Tiller account (e.g., Kastellec 2007, 2011; Beim and Kastellec 2014); others offer different explanations for moderation among judges serving on an ideologically mixed panel—including "dissent aversion."

Cross and Tiller's study and work following from it focus on the U.S. courts of appeals, where judges decide cases in panels of three (except in those cases heard en banc). Collegial effects, though, are not limited to courts that sit in panels. Consider Caldeira, Wright, and Zorn's (1999) justifiably famous analysis of case selection in the Supreme Court. The authors show that justices are less likely to vote to grant certiorari (agree to hear a case) when they think they will be on the losing side if certiorari is granted, even if they would like to reverse the decision below (sometimes called a "defensive denial"). Caldeira et al. also supply evidence of "aggressive grants": voting to hear a case when the justice agrees with the lower court's decision because he believes that the majority of the other justices do too.

Work on case selection is ongoing (e.g., Black and Owens 2009; Benesh et al. 2002), as are related studies on the role of threshold requirements. Following from Riker's (1984, 1986) analysis of the "art of manipulation," scholars have explored whether and to what extent judges raise questions about standing, mootness, and the like to turn around a seemingly foregone loss (e.g., Black et al. 2013; Epstein and Shvetsova 2002; Goelzhauser 2011; Staudt 2004). Much of this work focuses on collegial courts—where, for example, a judge might seek to kick a case on mootness because he thinks his colleagues will affirm when he wants to reverse. But there are also studies of trial court judges exploring why and how they embrace doctrines that limit judicial workloads to maximize leisure (especially if they have heavy dockets). We think here of research assessing the impact of the U.S. Supreme Court's decisions in *Bell Atlantic Corp. v. Twombly* (2007) and *Ashcroft v. Iqbal* (2009) ("Twiqbal"), which made it easier for district courts to dismiss cases before any pretrial discovery (for a review of the studies see Engstrom 2013). Though *Twombly* alone "precipitated no significant change in dismissal rates" (Hubbard 2013b), *Iqbal* did, perhaps because it clarified *Twombly's* reach. In the post-*Iqbal* period (June 2009 to June

2010), the predicted probability of dismissal increased by somewhere between 35 and 49 percent relative to their pre-*Iqbal* levels (Epstein, Landes, and Posner 2013).

Once judges have agreed to resolve disputes, research has demonstrated that they try to influence one another through memoranda (Maltzman et al. 2000; Epstein and Knight 1998; Spriggs et al. 1999). Other research suggests that group effects also play a role in the Chief Justice's assignment of the majority opinion (Maltzman and Wahlbeck 1996; Lazarus 2015; Wahlbeck 2006). A formal model developed by Lax and Cameron (2007: 293), for example, yields a prediction that the Chief Justice will favor justices more (ideologically) extreme than himself in part because "more extreme writers must invest more heavily in judicial craftsmanship, in order to hold the majority."

All in all, these studies demonstrate that group or collegial effects are hardly limited to panels on circuit courts. Whether voting on certiorari or the merits of cases, bargaining or assigning opinions, they show that a judge's choices might have been different if the outcome depended only on his vote and not on the votes of his other colleagues.

Hierarchy of Justice

Research on the hierarchy of justice explores interactions between higher and lower courts and so is related to work on the collegial court. The efficacy of whistleblowing, for example, hinges on the ability of a higher court to reverse the decision of a lower court.

Many of the studies make use of principal–agent theory, which, in this literature, assumes heterogeneous ideological preferences between upper and lower court judges and emphasizes how a higher court can extract conformity from a lower court with different preferences (Westerland et al. 2010: 891–2). More concretely, the typical starting point in these studies is that lower court judges no less than higher court judges are interested in etching their political values into law. But lower court judges face a substantial constraint in their quest to do so: the possibility of sanctioning from a higher court. To the extent that higher courts (at least in the United States) cannot hire, fire, promote, demote, financially reward, or penalize members of trial or intermediate courts, the studies propose various mechanisms for keeping the lower courts honest, including strategic auditing (e.g., Spitzer and Talley 2000; Cameron, Segal, and Cover 2000), implicit tournaments among lower courts (e.g., McNollgast 1995), en banc review (Clark 2009b; Giles et al. 2006, 2007), the articulation of rules rather than standards (Smith and Todd 2015), and, of course, whistleblowing (Lindquist, Haire, and Songer 2007; Black and Owens 2012; Kastellec 2007; Beim, Hirsch, and Kastellec 2015). Much of the empirical work assessing these mechanisms focuses on review by the U.S. Supreme Court (or circuits *en banc*) of decisions reached by appellate panels. But there is a growing literature showing that trial court judges alter their behavior to avoid reversal by intermediate appellate courts (e.g., Boyd 2015b; Randazzo 2008; Epstein, Landes, and Posner 2013).

Other research, though rarer, reverses the usual approach to lower-higher court relations and attends to the fact that lower court judges are fully capable of limiting the commands of higher courts by avoiding, limiting, or even defying them—as many did with the U.S. Supreme Court's desegregation decisions. In these studies, the limitation imposed by the hierarchy of justice "comes full circle": higher courts "must take into account the reaction of inferior judges, and lower courts must attempt to divine the counter-reaction" of superior courts (Murphy 1959: 1031). Perhaps this is why lower court criticism of Supreme Court precedents seems associated with the justices' willingness to depart from them (Hansford and Spriggs 2008; Epstein, Landes, and Liptak 2015). At the very least these studies illustrate the truly interactive nature of judicial hierarchy and highlight yet another important avenue for future research on strategic judicial decision-making.

External Actors

Much of the work on the relationship between courts and external actors—especially elected officials— bears a family resemblance to the hierarchy of justice studies in that it too uses a strategic framework to explore their interactions. In this literature, the judges must attend to the preferences and likely actions of the government if they are to achieve their goals (e.g., Eskridge 1991; Ferejohn and Weingast 1992; Gely and Spiller 1990). If the judges do not, they run the risk of retaliation from elected actors, thereby making it difficult for them to establish enduring policy, maintain legitimacy, or whatever else their objectives may be.

Most of the early empirical work assessing this claim focused on cases of statutory interpretation, on the theory that when federal judges interpret statutes, Congress can override their interpretations by enacting new laws. The results assessing this expectation are mixed and debates (apparently) continue (e.g., compare Bergara, Richman, and Spiller 2003; Spiller and Gely 1992; Eskridge 1991; Sala and Spriggs 2004; Segal 1997).

In *The Choices Justices Make* (1998) and elsewhere (Epstein, Knight, and Martin 2001), we extended the argument to cases involving constitutional interpretation. Our contention was (and is) that although Congress cannot pass legislation to overturn constitutional judicial decisions (but see Meernik and Ignagni 1997), it can take aim at courts in other ways: withdrawing their jurisdiction, eradicating judicial review, approving constitutional amendments to overturn decisions, slashing their budget, and impeaching judges (Rosenberg 1992). As a result, we speculated (but only partially tested) the idea that the Court must be equally if not more vigilant in attending to the preferences of elected actors in constitutional cases.

Subsequent work has shown this to be a promising hypothesis. From Clark's (2009a) important study, we know that congressional threats are not merely theoretical: Members of Congress introduced more than 900 court-curbing proposals between 1877 and 2008. More to the point, Clark's work, along with an equally important article by Segal et al. (2011), demonstrates that when Congress threatens the Supreme Court's authority, the Court cowers, either exercising greater judicial self-restraint or reaching decisions closer to congressional preferences. Related research also suggests that under certain circumstances, the Court will duck constitutional cases (Goelzhauser 2011).

These studies focus on the United States. Helmke's (2002, 2005) work on Argentina draws attention to the fact that in many parts of the developing world, governments have taken even more radical steps to tame their courts, with sanctions ranging from impeachment, removal, and court-packing to criminal indictment, physical violence, and even death. Her study and many others running along similar lines show that judges respond to these potential threats by defecting against the old regime (Helmke 2002, 2005), avoiding cases that may contribute to further escalation (Epstein, Knight, and Shvetsova 2002), going public (Gauri et al. 2015; Staton 2010) and passing up posts on apex courts altogether (Basabe-Serrano 2012), among other strategies.

This line of research focuses most directly on the relations between courts and executives/legislatures. There is also a substantial body of work that explores the relationship between courts and the American people—specifically, the extent to which the public constrains judicial decisions. Using qualitative data and historical methods, Friedman (2009) provides an unequivocal answer to the question of whether "we the people" influence the Supreme Court: we do. Many large-*n* studies agree (e.g., Giles et al. 2008; McGuire and Stimson 2004; Mishler and Sheehan 1996). At the risk of generalizing, they tend to find that when the "mood of the public" is liberal (conservative), the Court is significantly more likely to issue liberal (conservative) decisions.

But *why* is the real question. Friedman offers a response straight out of the strategic literature: the justices bend to the will of the people because the Court requires public support to remain an efficacious branch of government. We agree with his response; and the existing quantitative studies could be read to support this view. But even we must admit that the findings are consistent with another mechanism: that "the people" include the justices. On this account, the justices do not respond to public opinion directly but rather respond to the same events or forces that affect the opinion of other members of the public. Or, to quote Cardozo (1921: 168), "the great tides and currents which engulf the rest of men do not turn aside in their course and pass the judges by." That's why Epstein and Martin (2010) titled their paper (written for a symposium on Friedman's book), "Does Public Opinion Influence the Supreme Court? Possibly Yes (But We're Not Sure Why)."[5] (By the way, the same problem of behavioral equivalence arises in work on macroevents, e.g., war: Do judges strategically retreat from war-related cases [or otherwise rubber stamp the government] or are they too swept in rally-round-the-flag effects?)

What's Next?

However extensive the economics literature on judging, many more studies will inevitably follow. In what directions are scholars heading (or should they head)? There are many possibilities but in the interest of space we note two: one mostly theoretical, the other empirical.

Beginning with the theoretical, we have emphasized studies assuming that judges are rational actors. To us, this is a reasonable assumption, or at least it gets us pretty far in understanding judicial behavior. But it will not get us all the way. It is just too late in the day to question the decades' worth of studies showing that in many situations, people rely heavily on their intuitions to make fast decisions without much effort. Social psychologists tell us that these responses are not always wrong or even unhelpful (Wistrich et al. 2015). But we also know that unchecked by deliberative assessments, they can lead to mistakes and biased decisions (Thaler 2015; Kahneman 2011).

Although judges may think they can "suppress or convert" their intuitions, prejudices, sympathies, and the like into rational decisions (Wistrich et al. 2015: 862), this is not so. Experiments conducted on thousands of judges by Rachlinski et al. demonstrate that judges respond more favorably to litigants they like or with whom they sympathize (e.g., Wistrich et al. 2015), are affected by anchors in making numeric estimates (e.g., Rachlinski et al. 2015), and fall prey to hindsight bias when assessing probable cause (e.g., Rachlinski et al. 2015). In short, it turns out that judges are human too (see also Rachlinski et al. 2009, 2011; Guthrie, et al. 2001, 2007, along with work by Braman 2009; Landsman and Rakos 1994; Simon and Scurich 2013).

To the extent that judges are influenced by their emotions, intuitions, and prejudices, it will complicate their ability to make rational decisions. And thus it complicates our efforts to explain their behavior. There is no getting around the fact that these factors can distort purely rational or strategic decision-making. The interesting research questions relate to how much these non-rational factors alter what we would expect to see if we assume that judges are acting rationally. One possibility would be to compare the predictions of strategic analysis with the data on actual judicial decisions. This would give us a better sense of the extent to which these non-rational factors influence the judges' choices.

As should be obvious, we take the experimental evidence quite seriously, but some members of the legal community (especially judges) do not; they complain that the experiments are artificial and do not capture the real courtroom environment. This counsels for observational studies—that is, studies making use of data that the world, not the researchers, have created. These are not easy to do, but neither are they impossible, as Shayo and Zussman's (2011) study of Israeli small claims courts demonstrates. More to the point, we think they are crucial: should the experimental and the observational converge, we can have more confidence in our conclusions.

That's the theoretical point; the more empirical avenue concerns our targets of inquiry. At the outset, we noted that they have expanded from an exclusive focus on the U.S. Supreme Court to lower courts and courts outside the United States. Our discussion of the existing literature provides ample proof of this claim. Today, there is almost no corner of the world whose judges are not under analysis by some scholar somewhere. Through these analyses, we have learned a great deal about the choices of judges in other societies of course, but also about our own judges. For example, to understand the effect of life tenure on judging, we need points of comparison. Research on the state courts provides some, but moving to a comparative context provides even more. The world-wide variation of judicial selection-retention mechanisms is so high that it is hard to imagine one that does not exist.

The comparative advantage in illuminating judicial behavior is now so well understood that we've already said too much. Worth emphasizing, though, is that the data infrastructure has not kept pace with the interest. Instead of creating modern, reliable, maintainable, and sustainable large-scale public databases with crucial information about world's courts, judges, and judicial decisions, scholars have worked in isolation building one-off (or otherwise limited) data sets designed for particular projects and centered on particular courts, countries, or regions. The "one-off" approach has its benefits of course. But it also has substantial costs, ultimately impeding the march toward knowledge, innovation, and invention. These costs include the massive duplication of effort, inefficiencies, and dated (if not downright unreliable) measures and data.

Moving the field forward requires the development of at least two large-scale and sustainable databases, one focused on the institutional features of courts throughout the world and the other, on case-level data. Sure, we understand that scholars will raise questions about the kinds of institutional detail and case-based information we should collect, just as they did when Spaeth, Songer, and others built their databases and other infrastructure for the analysis of the U.S. federal judiciary. The answer to these questions is simple: public databases are foundational, not comprehensive. By design scholars should be able to adapt and build on them to suit their own needs. Very few studies published on the U.S. Supreme Court, for example, use Spaeth et al.'s U.S. Supreme Court Database "as is"; their authors backdate data, recode categories, and add variables. And so it will be for global databases.

The same answer holds for questions about conceptualization. We know that there is much hand-wringing in the comparative analysis of judicial behavior over how to define and measure even basic concepts (e.g., judicial independence). If the past is any indication, waiting around for scholars to agree will continue to impede innovation and invention. It would be better to focus on the provision of basic data—facts about the world—that scholars can develop in ways they think appropriate. We believe there is widespread agreement on the importance of at least some of these facts. Falling into this category are, among other institutional details, legal family, number of judges, judicial/constitutional review power, tenure, budget, and salaries. As for case-level data, the parties, the year of decision, the judges, separate opinions, and the disposition would seem rudimentary.

Building this infrastructure sooner rather than later will have great payoffs for the analysis (economic or otherwise) of judicial behavior. Not only will it advance knowledge but it also has the potential to bring together diverse communities of scholars worldwide—goals on which we all can agree.

Notes

1. This chapter draws on some of our other work on judicial behavior, including Epstein (2013), Epstein and Knight (2013), Epstein (2016). Epstein thanks the National Science Foundation, the John Simon Guggenheim Foundation, and Washington University in St. Louis for supporting her research on law, legal institutions, and judicial behavior.
2. The idea here is that judges want the law to reflect their preferred policy positions. To assess empirically the judges' policy positions, political scientists use partisan measures (e.g., the party affiliation of the judge or the appointing president) and ideological measures (e.g., the Segal-Cover [1989] or Martin-Quinn [2002] scores). For a review, see Epstein et al. (2012). This is why the political science literature tends to treat political goals, policy goals, ideological goals, and partisan goals as interchangeable terms.
3. The story is a little more complicated than this because Tabarrok and Helland (1999) compared awards in partisan-elected states (where judges identify their partisan affiliation), nonpartisan states (where judges run for reelection but not on a partisan ballot), and non-elected states.
4. The battle between FDR and the Supreme Court is the most obvious example. For a terrific empirical account, see Ho and Quinn (2010).
5. For a possible answer (supportive of Friedman's argument), see Casillas et al. (2011).

References

Anderson, R., IV, and Tahk, A. M. 2007. "Institutions and Equilibrium in the United States Supreme Court." *American Political Science Review* 101: 811–25.

Basabe-Serrano, S. 2012. "Judges without Robes and Judicial Voting in Contexts of Institutional Instability: The Case of Ecuador's Constitutional Court, 1999–2007." *Journal of Latin American Studies* 44: 127–61.

Baum, L. 2006. *Judges and their Audiences: A Perspective on Judicial Behavior*. Princeton, NJ: Princeton University.

Beim, D., Hirsch, A. V., and Kastellec, J. P. 2015. "Signaling and Counter-Signaling in the Judicial Hierarchy: An Empirical Analysis of En Banc Review." *American Journal of Political Science* 60(2): 490–580.

Benesh, S. C., Brenner, S., and Spaeth, H. J. 2002. "Aggressive Grants by Affirm-Minded Justices." *American Politics Research* 30: 219–34.

Berdejó, C., and Yuchtman, N. M. 2013. "Crime, Punishment and Politics: An Analysis of Political Cycles in Criminal Sentencing." *Review of Economics and Statistics* 95: 741–56.

Bergara, M., Richman, B. D., and Spiller, P. T. 2003. "Modeling Supreme Court Strategic Decision Making: The Congressional Constraint." *Legislative Studies Quarterly* 28: 247–80.

Black, R. C., and Owens, R. J. 2009. "Agenda Setting in the Supreme Court: The Collision of Policy and Jurisprudence." *Journal of Politics* 71: 1062–75.

Black, R. C., and Owens, R. J. 2012. "Consider the Source (and the Message): Supreme Court Justices and Strategic Audits of Lower Court Decisions." *Political Research Quarterly* 65: 385–95.

Black, R. C., and Owens, R. J. 2016. "Courting the President: How Circuit Court Judges Alter their Behavior for Promotion to the Supreme Court." *American Journal of Political Science* 60: 30–43.

Black, R. C., Schutte, C. R., and Johnson, T. R. 2013. "Trying to Get What You Want: Heresthetical Maneuvering and U.S. Supreme Court Decision Making." *Political Research Quarterly* 66: 818–29.

Black, R. C. et al. 2016. *U.S. Supreme Court Opinions and their Audiences.* Cambridge: Cambridge University Press.

Boyd, C. L. 2015a. "Opinion Writing in the Federal District Courts." *Justice System Journal* 36: 254–73.

Boyd, C. L. 2015b. "The Hierarchical Influence of Courts of Appeals on District Courts." *Journal of Legal Studies* 44: 113–41.

Brace, P., and Boyea, B. 2008. "State Public Opinion, the Death Penalty, and the Practice of Electing Judges." *American Journal of Political Science* 52: 360–72.

Brace, P., and Hall, M. G. 1997. "The Interplay of Preferences, Case Facts, Context, and Rules in the Politics of Judicial Choice." *Journal of Politics* 59: 1206–31.

Braman, E. 2009. *Law, Politics, and Perception: How Policy Preferences Influence Legal Reasoning.* Charlottesville, VA: University of Virginia Press.

Brams, S. J. 1990. *Negotiation Games.* New York, NY: Routledge.

Caldarone, R., Canes-Wrone, B., and Clark, T. S. 2009. "Partisan Signals and Democratic Accountability: An Analysis of State Supreme Court Abortion Decisions." *Journal of Politics* 29: 560–73.

Caldeira, G. A. 1977. "Incentives of Trial Judges and the Administration of Justice." *Justice System Journal* 3: 163–80.

Caldeira, G. A., Wright, J. R., and Zorn, C. J. W. 1999. "Sophisticated Voting and Gate-Keeping in the Supreme Court." *Journal of Law, Economics, & Organization* 15: 549–72.

Cameron, C. M., Cover, A. D., and Segal, J. A. 1990. "Senate Voting on Supreme Court Nominees: A Neoinstitutional Model." *American Political Science Review* 84: 525–34.

Cameron, C. M., Segal, J. A., and Songer, D. 2000. "Strategic Auditing in a Political Hierarchy: An Informational Model of the Supreme Court's Certiorari Decisions." *American Political Science Review* 94: 101–16.

Canes-Wrone, B., Clark, T. S., and Kwang, J. 2012. "Judicial Independence and Retention Elections." *Journal of Law, Economics, & Organization* 28: 211–34.

Cardozo, B. N. 1921. *The Nature of the Judicial Process.* New Haven, CT: Yale University Press.

Casillas, C. J., Enns, P. K., and Wohlfarth, P. C. 2011. "How Public Opinion Constrains the Supreme Court." *American Journal of Political Science* 55: 74–88.

Clark, T. S. 2009a. "The Separation of Powers, Court Curbing, and Judicial Legitimacy." *American Journal of Political Science* 53: 971–89.

Clark, T. S. 2009b. "A Principal–Agent Theory of En Banc Review." *Journal of Law, Economics, & Organization* 25: 55–79.

Cohen, M. A. 1991. "Explaining Judicial Behavior or What's 'Unconstitutional' about the Sentencing Commission?" *Journal of Law, Economics, & Organization* 7: 183–200.

Corley P. C., and Wedeking, J. 2014. "The (Dis)Advantage of Certainty: The Importance of Certainty in Language." *Law & Society Review* 48: 35–62.

Cross, F. B., and Tiller, E. 1998. "Judicial Partisanship and Obedience to Legal Doctrine: Whistleblowing on the Federal Courts of Appeals." *Yale Law Journal* 107: 2155–76.

Drahozal, C. R. 1998. "Judicial Incentives and the Appeals Process." *SMU Law Review* 51: 469–503.

Elster, J. 1983. *Explaining Technical Change*. Cambridge: Cambridge University Press.

Engstrom, D. F. 2013. "The *Twiqbal* Puzzle and Empirical Study of Civil Procedure." *Stanford Law Review* 65: 1203–48.

Epstein, L. ed. 2013. *The Economics of Judicial Behaviour.* Cheltenham: Edward Elgar.

Epstein, L. 2016. "Some Thoughts on the Study of Judicial Behavior." *William & Mary Law Review* 57(6): 201–73.

Epstein, L., Ho, D. E., King, G., and Segal, J. A. 2005. "The Supreme Court during Crisis." *New York University Law Review* 80: 1–116.

Epstein, L., and Knight, J. 1998. *The Choices Justices Make.* Washington, DC: CQ Press.

Epstein, L., and Knight, J. 2000. "Toward a Strategic Revolution in Judicial Politics: A Look back, a Look ahead." *Political Research Quarterly* 53: 625–61.

Epstein, L., and Knight, J. 2013. "Reconsidering Judicial Preferences." *Annual Review of Political Science* 16: 19.1–19.21.

Epstein, L., Knight, J., and Martin, A. D. 2001. "The Supreme Court as a *Strategic* National Policymaker." *Emory Law Journal* 50: 583–611.

Epstein, L., Knight, J., and Shvetsova, O. 2002. "The Role of Constitutional Courts in the Establishment and Maintenance of Democratic Systems of Government." *Law & Society Review* 35: 117–64.

Epstein, L., Landes, W. M., and Posner, R. A. 2011. "Why (and When) Judges Dissent." *Journal of Legal Analysis* 3: 101–37.

Epstein, L., Landes, W. M., Posner, R. A. 2013. *The Behavior of Federal Judges.* Cambridge, MA: Harvard University Press.

Epstein, L., Liptak, A., and Landes, W. M. 2015. "The Decision to Depart (or Not) from Precedent." *New York University Law Review* 90: 1115–19.

Epstein, L., and Martin, A. D. 2010. "Does Public Opinion Influence the Supreme Court? Possibly Yes (But We're Not Sure Why)." *University of Pennsylvania Journal of Constitutional Law* 13: 263–81.

Epstein, L., Martin, A. D., Quinn, K., and Segal, J. A. 2012. "Ideology and the Study of Judicial Behavior." In *Ideology, Psychology, and Law*, edited by Jon Hanson. Oxford: Oxford University Press, 705–28.

Epstein, L., and Posner, E. 2015. "Supreme Court Justices' Loyalty to the President." Available at: http://papers.ssrn.com/sol3/papers.cfm? abstract_id=2702144.

Epstein, L., and Segal, J. A. 2005. *Advice and Consent.* Oxford: Oxford University Press.

Epstein, L., and Shvetsova, O. 2002. "Heresthetical Maneuvering on the U.S. Supreme Court." *Journal of Theoretical Politics* 14: 93–122.

Eskridge, W. N., Jr. 1991. "Overriding Supreme Court Statutory Interpretation Decisions." *Yale Law Journal* 101: 331–455.

Ferejohn, J. A., and Weingast B. R. 1992. "A Positive Theory of Statutory Interpretation." *International Review of Law and Economics* 12: 263–79.

Friedman, B. 2009. *The Will of the People.* New York, NY: Farrar, Straus and Giroux.

Gaille, S. S. 1997. "Publishing by United States Court of Appeals Judges: Before and after the Bork Hearings." *Journal of Legal Studies* 26: 371–6.

Garoupa, N., Gomez-Pomar, F., and Grembi, V. 2013. "Judging under Political Pressure: An Empirical Analysis of Constitutional Review Voting in the Spanish Constitutional Court." *Journal of Law, Economics, & Organization* 29: 513–34.

Gauri, V., Staton, J. K., and Cullell, J. V. 2015. "The Costa Rican Supreme Court's Compliance Monitoring System." *Journal of Politics* 77(3): 774–86.

Gely, R., and Spiller, P. T. 1990. "A Rational Choice Theory of Supreme Court Statutory Decisions with Applications to the State Farm and Grove City Cases." *Journal of Law, Economics, & Organization* 6: 263–300.

Gibson, L. 2012. *Electing Judges*. Chicago, IL: University of Chicago Press.

Giles, M. W., Blackstone, B., and Vining, R. L. 2008. "The Supreme Court in American Democracy: Unraveling the Linkages between Public Opinion and Judicial Decision Making." *Journal of Politics* 70: 293–306.

Giles, M. W., Hettinger V. A., Zorn, C., and Peppers, T. C. 2007. "The Etiology of the Occurrence of En Banc Review in the U.S. Court of Appeals." *American Journal of Political Science* 51: 449–63.

Giles, M. W., Walker, T. G., and Zorn, C. 2006. "Setting a Judicial Agenda: The Decision to Grant En Banc Review in the U.S. Courts of Appeals." *Journal of Politics* 68: 852–66.

Goelzhauser, G. 2011. "Avoiding Constitutional Cases." *American Politics Research* 39: 483–511.

Gordon, S. C., and Huber, G. A. 2007. "The Effect of Electoral Competitiveness on Incumbent Behavior." *Quarterly Journal of Political Science* 2: 107–38.

Grendstad, G., Shaffer, W. R., and Waltenburg, E. 2015. *Policy Making in an Independent Judiciary: The Norwegian Supreme Court*. Colchester: ECPSR.

Gulati, M., and McCauliff, C. M. A. 1998. "On Not Making Law." *Law & Contemporary Problems* 61: 157–228.

Guthrie, C., Rachlinski J. J., and Wistrich A. J. 2001. "Inside the Judicial Mind." *Cornell Law Review* 86: 777–830.

Guthrie, C., Rachlinski J. J., and Wistrich A. J. 2007. "Blinking on the Bench: How Judges Decide Cases." *Cornell Law Review* 93: 1–43.

Hall, M. G. 1987. "Constituent Influence in State Supreme Courts: Conceptual Notes and a Case Study." *Journal of Politics* 49: 1117–24.

Hanretty, C. 2012. "Dissent in Iberia: The Ideal Points of Justices on the Spanish and Portuguese Constitutional Tribunals." *European Journal of Political Research* 51: 671–92.

Hansford, T. G., and Spriggs, J. F. 2006. *The Politics of Precedent on the U.S. Supreme Court*. Princeton, NJ: Princeton University Press.

Helland, E., and Tabarrok, A. 2002. "The Effect of Electoral Institutions on Tort Awards." *American Law and Economics Review* 4: 341–70.

Helmke, G. 2002. "The Logic of Strategic Defection: Court-Executive Relations in Argentina under Dictatorship and Democracy." *American Political Science Review* 96: 291–303.

Helmke, G. 2005. *Courts under Constraints: Judges, Generals, and Presidents in Argentina*. Cambridge: Cambridge University Press.

Hinkle, R. K. 2016. "Strategic Anticipation of En Banc Review in the U.S. Courts of Appeals." *Law & Society Review*, forthcoming.

Hinkle, R. K., Martin, A. D., Shaub, J. D., and Tiller, E. H. 2012. "A Positive Theory and Empirical Analysis of Strategic Word Choice in District Court Opinions." *Journal of Legal Analysis* 10: 407–44.

Ho, D. E., and Quinn, K. M. 2010. "Did a Switch in Time Save Nine?" *Journal of Legal Analysis* 2: 69–113.

Hönnige, C. 2009. "The Electoral Connection: How the Pivotal Judge Affects Oppositional Success at European Constitutional Courts." *Western European Politics* 32: 963–84.

Hubbard, W. H. J. 2013a. "An Empirical Study of the Effect of *Shady Grove v. Allstate on Forum Shopping* in the New York Courts." *Journal of Law, Economics & Policy* 10: 151–72.

Hubbard, W. H. J. 2013b. "Testing for Change in Procedural Standards, with Application to *Bell Atlantic v. Twombly*." *Journal of Legal Studies* 42: 35–68.

Huber, G. A., and Gordon, S. C. 2004. "Accountability and Coercion: Is Justice Blind When It Runs for Office?" *American Journal of Political Science* 48: 247–63.

Iaryczower, M., and Katz, G. 2015. "More than Politics: Ability and Ideology in the British Appellate Committee." *Journal of Law, Economics, & Organization*, forthcoming.

Kahneman, D. 2011. *Thinking, Fast and Slow.* New York: Farrar, Straus and Giroux.

Kang, M. S., and Shepard, J. M. 2011. "The Partisan Price of Justice: An Empirical Analysis of Campaign Contributions and Judicial Decisions." *New York University Law Review* 86: 69–130.

Kastellec, J. P. 2007. "Panel Composition and Judicial Compliance on the U.S. Courts of Appeals." *Journal of Law, Economics and Organization* 23: 421–41.

Kastellec, J. P. 2011. "Hierarchical and Collegial Politics on the U.S. Courts of Appeals." *Journal of Politics* 73: 345–61.

Klein, D. E., and Hume, R. J. 2003. "Fear of Reversal as an Explanation of Lower Court Compliance." *Law & Society Review* 37: 579–606.

Knight, J. and Epstein, L. 1996. "On the Struggle for Judicial Supremacy." *Law & Society Review* 30: 87–130.

Landes, W. M., and Posner, R. A. 1976. "Legal Precedent: A Theoretical and Empirical Analysis." *Journal of Law and Economics* 19: 249–307.

Landsman, S., and Rakos, R. F. 1994. "A Preliminary Inquiry into the Effect of Potentially Biasing Information on Judges and Jurors in Civil Litigation." *Behavioral Sciences & the Law* 12: 113–26.

Lax, J. R., and Cameron, C. M. 2007. "Bargaining and Opinion Assignment on the U.S. Supreme Court." *Journal of Law, Economics, & Organization* 23: 276–302.

Lazarus, R. J. 2015. "'Back to Business' at the Supreme Court: The 'Administrative' Side of Chief Justice Roberts." *Harvard Law Review Forum* 129: 33–93.

Levy, G. 2005. "Careerist Judges and the Appeals Process." *Rand Journal of Economics* 36: 275–97.

Lindquist, S. A., Haire, S. B., and Songer, D. R. 2007. "Supreme Court Auditing of the U.S. Courts of Appeals: An Organizational Perspective." *Journal of Public Administration Research and Theory* 17: 607–24.

Maltzman, F., Spriggs, J. F., Wahlbeck, P. J. 2000. *Crafting Law on the Supreme Court: The Collegial Game.* New York, NY: Cambridge University Press.

Maltzman, F., and Wahlbeck, P. J. 1996. "May It Please the Chief? Opinion Assignments in the Rehnquist Court." *American Journal of Political Science* 40: 421–43.

McGuire, K. T., and Stimson, J. A. 2004. "The Least Dangerous Branch Revisited: New Evidence on Supreme Court Responsiveness to Public Preferences." *Journal of Politics* 66: 1018–35.

McNollgast. 1995. "Politics and the Courts: A Positive Theory of Judicial Doctrine and the Rule of Law." *Southern California Law Review* 68: 1631–83.

Meernik, J., and Ignagni, J. 1997. "Judicial Review and Coordinate Construction of the Constitution." *American Journal of Political Science* 41: 447–67.

Miceli, T. J., and Metin, M. C. 1994. "Reputation and Judicial Decision-Making." *Journal of Economic Behavior & Organization* 23: 31–51.

Mishler, W., and Sheehan, R. S. 1996. "Public Opinion, the Attitudinal Model, and Supreme Court Decision Making: A Micro-Analytic Perspective." *Journal of Politics* 58: 169–200.

Moraski, B. J., and Shipan, C. R. 1999. "The Politics of Supreme Court Nominations: A Theory of Institutional Constraints and Choices." *American Journal of Political Science* 43: 1069–95.

Murphy, W. F. 1959. "Lower Court Checks on Supreme Court Power." *American Political Science Review* 53: 1017–31.

Murphy, W. F. 1962. *Congress and the Supreme Court*. Chicago, IL: University of Chicago Press.

Murphy, W. F. 1964. *Elements of Judicial Strategy*. Chicago. IL: University of Chicago Press.

Oredeshook, P. 1992. *A Political Theory Primer*. New York, NY: Routledge.

Posner, R. A. 2011. *Economic Analysis of Law*. 8th ed. New York, NY: Aspen.

Pritchett, C. H. 1941. "Divisions of Opinion among Justices of the U.S. Supreme Court, 1939–1941." *American Political Science Review* 35: 890–98.

Priest, G., and Klein, B. 1984. "The Selection of Disputes for Litigation." *Journal of Legal Studies* 14: 1–55.

Rachlinski, J. J. et al. 2009. "Does Unconscious Racial Bias Affect Trial Judges?" *Notre Dame Law Review* 84: 1195–246.

Rachlinski, J. J., Guthrie, C., and Wistrich, A. J. 2011. "Probable Cause, Probability, and Hindsight." *Journal of Empirical Legal Studies* 8: 72–98.

Rachlinski, J. J., Guthrie, C., and Wistrich, A. J. 2015. "Can Judges Make Reliable Numeric Judgments? Distorted Damages and Skewed Sentences." *Indiana Law Journal* 90: 695–739.

Ramseyer J. M., and Rasmussen, E. B. 2001. "Why Are Japanese Judges so Conservative in Politically Charged Cases?" *American Political Science Review* 95: 331–44.

Randazzo, K. A. 2008. "Strategic Anticipation and the Hierarchy of Justice in the U.S. District Courts." *American Politics Research* 36: 669–93.

Riker, W. H. 1984. "The Heresthetics of Constitution-Making: The Presidency in 1787, with Comments on Determinism and Rational Choice." *American Political Science Review* 78: 1–16.

Riker, W. H. 1986. *The Art of Political Manipulation*. New Haven, CT: Yale University Press.

Ríos-Figueroa, J., and Staton, J. K. 2014. "An Evaluation of Cross-National Measures of Judicial Independence." *Journal of Law, Economics, & Organization* 30: 104.

Rosenberg, G. N. 1992. "Judicial Independence and the Reality of Political Power." *Review of Politics* 54: 369–98.

Sala, B. R., and Spriggs, J. F. 2004. "Designing Tests of the Supreme Court and the Separation of Powers." *Political Research Quarterly* 57: 197–208.

Salzberger, E., and Fenn, P. 1999. "Judicial Independence: Some Evidence from the English Court of Appeal." *Journal of Law and Economics* 42: 831–47.

Schauer, F. 2000. "Incentives, Reputation, and the Inglorious Determinants of Judicial Behavior." *University of Cincinnati Law Review* 68: 615–36.

Schubert, G. 1958. "The Study of Judicial Decision-Making as an Aspect of Political Behavior." *American Political Science Review* 52: 1007–25.

Segal, J. A. 1997. "Separation-of-Powers Games in the Positive Theory of Congress and Courts." *American Political Science Review* 91: 28–44.

Segal, J. A., Cameron, C. M, and Cover, A. D. 1992. "A Spatial Model of Roll Call Voting: Senators, Constituents, Presidents, and Interest Groups in Supreme Court Confirmations." *American Journal of Political Science* 36: 96–121.

Segal, J. A., and Spaeth, H. J. 2002. *The Supreme Court and the Attitudinal Model Revisited*. Cambridge: Cambridge University Press.

Segal, J. A., Timpone, R. J., and Howard, R. M. 2000. "Buyer Beware? Presidential Success through Supreme Court Appointments." *Political Research Quarterly* 53: 557–73.

Segal, J. A., Westerland, C., and Lindquist, S. 2011. "Congress, the Supreme Court, and Judicial Review: Testing a Constitutional Separation of Powers Model." *American Journal of Political Science* 55: 89–104.

Shapiro, S. A., and Levy, R. E. 1995. "Judicial Incentives and Indeterminacy in Substantive Review of Administrative Decisions." *Duke Law Journal* 44: 1051–80.

Shayo, M., and Zussman, A. 2011. "Judicial Ingroup Bias in the Shadow of Terrorism." *Quarterly Journal of Economics* 126: 1447–84.

Simon, D., and Scurich, N. 2013. "Judicial Overstating." *Chicago-Kent Law Review* 88: 411–31.

Sisk, G. C., Heise, M., and Morris, A. P. 1998. "Charting the Influences on the Judicial Mind: An Empirical Study of Judicial Reasoning." *New York University Law Review* 73: 1377–500.

Smith, J. L., and Tiller, E. H. 2002. "The Strategy of Judging: Evidence from Administrative Law." *Journal of Legal Studies* 31: 61–82.

Smith, J. L., and Todd, J. A. 2015. "Rules, Standards, and Lower Court Decisions." *Journal of Law and Courts* 3: 257–75.

Songer, D. R., Segal, J. A., and Cameron C. M. 1994. "The Hierarchy of Justice: Testing a Principal–Agent Model of Supreme Court–Circuit Court Interactions." *American Journal of Political Science* 38: 673–96.

Spiller, P. T., and Gely, R. 1992. "Congressional Control or Judicial Independence: The Determinants of U.S. Supreme Court Labor-Relations Decisions, 1949–1988." *RAND Journal of Economics* 23: 463–92.

Spitzer, M., and Talley, E. 2000. "Judicial Auditing." *Journal of Legal Studies* 29: 649–83.

Spriggs, J. F., II, Maltzman, F., and Wahlbeck, P. J. 1999. "Bargaining on the U.S. Supreme Court: Justices' Responses to Majority Opinion Drafts." *Journal of Politics* 61: 485–506.

Staton, J. K. 2010. *Judicial Power and Strategic Communication in Mexico*. Cambridge: Cambridge University Press.

Staton, J. K., and Vanberg, G. 2008. "The Value of Vagueness: Delegation, Defiance, and Judicial Opinions." *American Journal of Political Science* 52: 504–19.

Staudt, N. 2004. "Modeling Standing." *New York University Law Review* 79: 612–84.

Tabarrok, A., and Helland, E. 1999. "Court Politics: The Political Economy of Tort Awards." *Journal of Law and Economics* 42: 157–88.

Taha, A. E. 2004. "Publish or Paris? Evidence of How Judges Allocate their Time." *American Law and Economics Review* 6: 1–27.

Thaler, R. H. 2015. *Misbehaving: The Making of Behavior Economics*. New York, NY: Norton.

Vanberg, G. 2005. *The Politics of Constitutional Review in Germany*. Cambridge" Cambridge University Press.

Wahlbeck, P. J. 2006. "Strategy and Constraints on Supreme Court Opinion Assignment." *University of Pennsylvania Law Review* 154: 1729–55.

Westerland, C., Segal, J. A., Epstein, L., Cameron, C. M., and Comparato, S. 2010. "Strategic Defiance and Compliance in the U.S. Courts of Appeals." *American Journal of Political Science* 54: 891–905.

Whitman, D. G. 2000. "Evolution of the Common Law and the Emergence of Compromise." *Journal of Legal Studies* 29: 753–81.

Wistrich, A. J., Rachlinski, J. J., and Guthrie, C. 2015. "Heart versus Head: Do Judges Follow the Law or Follow their Feelings?" *Texas Law Review* 93: 855–923.

PART IV

JUDGES AND THEIR PUBLICS

CHAPTER 18

JUDGES AND THEIR AUDIENCES

LAWRENCE BAUM

How are judges influenced by the world outside their courts? Among scholars who study judging in the United States,[1] there are two standard conceptions of the relationship between judges and their environments. In this chapter I offer a third conception, one that rests on different premises about judicial behavior.

The first of the two standard conceptions treats judges as essentially independent of their environments. The traditional version of this conception depicted judges as people who focus on the job of applying the law properly to the cases they decide. Such judges ignore other considerations, including any potential influences from outside their courts, with the exception of ideas and information that help them to interpret the law well.

Because this traditional version treated judges as single-minded in pursuing good law, it faded with the rise of the legal realist movement that emphasized the role of non-legal considerations in judges' choices (Rumble 1968). This version survives primarily in judges' public descriptions of their own decision-making, such as Chief Justice John Roberts's well-known analogy between judges and baseball umpires at his Senate confirmation hearing (U.S. Senate 2005: 55). But the traditional version of this conception was replaced by another version, one that focused on the Supreme Court. In what became known as the attitudinal model of judging (Segal and Spaeth 2002), scholars argued that justices' life terms and other attributes of the Court provide justices with nearly complete insulation from their political environment. As a result, they are free to make decisions that accord with their conceptions of good public policy.

The attitudinal model gained wide support among the many political scientists who study the Supreme Court. It continues to shape scholars' views of judicial behavior, but its conception of judges' relationships with their environments is not as widely adopted as it once was. One reason is that students of judicial behavior increasingly give attention to lower federal courts and state courts, and the attitudinal model was never intended to apply fully to those courts. More fundamentally, political scientists and legal scholars have gravitated to a different view, one that has become the most influential conception of judges' relationship with their environments.

This second conception is part of what is usually called the strategic model of judging (see Epstein and Knight 2000).[2] Like the attitudinal model, the strategic model begins with the premise that judges care most about making good policy.[3] But to achieve this end, according to the strategic model, judges cannot simply reach the decisions that best accord with their policy preferences. For one thing, such decisions might trigger actions by the other branches of government that effectively reverse a court's decision. Similarly, decisions by lower court judges that accord with their preferences might trigger reversals of their decisions by higher courts. Further, disapproval of a court's decisions potentially weakens its institutional position. Congress might limit the Supreme Court's jurisdiction, or the general public might withdraw the support for the Court that fosters compliance with its decisions. On a different level, judges below the Supreme Court might jeopardize their chances of promotion to higher courts, and judges who lack life terms might be denied new terms. In turn, these consequences would limit judges' opportunity to act as policymakers or eliminate that opportunity altogether.

For all these reasons, according to this conception, judges must sometimes deviate from the decisions that they most prefer in order to maximize their ability to shape public policy. They might do so by modifying a decision to reduce the chances that it will be overturned or by avoiding decisions that would arouse unhappiness in the other branches or the general public.

In this chapter I argue for a third and quite different conception of the relationship between judges and their environments.[4] This conception departs from the assumptions of the attitudinal and strategic models about judges' motivations.[5] In this conception, judges care a good deal about what people think of the decisions they reach. But in contrast with the other conceptions, the regard of other people is not just a means for judges to achieve other ends that are important to them, such as achieving good policy and maintaining their judicial careers.

Rather, judges care about whether they are liked and respected by others as a goal in itself. And because this is an important goal for judges, they are motivated to reach decisions that they think will please the individuals and groups whose regard they care most about—what I call their audiences. One way to describe the difference between the strategic conception and this alternative conception is that in the alternative conception, judges respond to their audiences not just for instrumental reasons but also—and perhaps primarily—for personal reasons.

This third conception rests on three realities about judges. First, judges are fundamentally like other people, and one of the most powerful human motivations is a desire for the approval of other people. Much of what people do can be understood as self-presentation aimed at achieving that approval (Goffman 1959; Schlenker and Pontari 2000). It would be surprising if this were not true of judges.

Second, as a group judges are even more concerned with winning the approval of others than are people in general. Many if not most lawyers who become judges make a financial sacrifice to do so, and that is especially true of judges on the highest courts.

Further, becoming a judge can be a difficult and unpleasant process. The people who are willing to accept those negatives are likely to be people for whom the status and prestige that judgeships provide are especially attractive. For the same reason, the kinds of people who become judges are likely to be very interested in winning approval for their work on the bench.

Finally, the judges who are of greatest interest to scholars and other observers of the courts—Supreme Court justices—are relatively free from the forms of self-interest that constrain most other people. That freedom allows them to pursue goals that are unconnected with concrete self-interest. Some of those goals involve the satisfaction that judges derive from taking positions that accord with what they see as good law or good policy. As the strategic model suggests, justices also get satisfaction from helping to achieve good law or policy in the Court or the larger world of government.

The justices' interest in popularity and respect from people whose approval they care about is another goal that may affect their choices as decision makers. In practice, this goal interacts with goals related to making good law or good policy, moderating or reinforcing their effects. That interaction is apparent in the ways that elite groups may influence the justices and other judges, discussed later in this chapter.

To the extent that judges use their votes and opinions to win approval from people outside the courts, their actions are not necessarily conscious and deliberate. Indeed, it is probably unusual for judges to recognize that this goal affects their behavior. In this respect, judges' interest in the regard of other people is probably similar to most other considerations that affect their choices as decision makers.

This third conception of the relationship between judges and their environments is reflected in some research and writing about judging,[6] but it does not play a substantial role in the study of judicial behavior. One reason is its departure from widely accepted assumptions about judges' motivations. Another reason is that the effects of an interest in the regard of other people are less concrete, more complex, and thus more difficult to analyze than the effects of strategic efforts to advance policy goals. But I think that this conception captures an important reality about judging and thus helps in understanding judicial behavior. In this chapter I use it to probe relationships between judges and the world outside the courts.

Elected Judges, Interest Groups, and the General Public

Even federal judges who hold their positions for life might act on their interest in promotion to a higher court, an interest that is widely held (Kozinski 2004: 1104). Some studies have found evidence that judges on the federal district courts and courts of appeals are influenced by their interest in promotion when they decide certain kinds of cases (e.g., Morriss, Heise, and Sisk 2005; Budziak 2013). But career considerations are considerably stronger for judges whose tenure in office is insecure. Most of those judges sit in state courts and face periodic elections of one type or another.

Scholars and other commentators have given considerable attention to elections as a concern for state judges. In part, this attention flows from the increased level of activity and intensity of electoral contests for positions on state supreme courts in the past two decades. One feature of that development has been a growing mobilization of interest groups to elect judges who are sympathetic to the groups' positions, an effort that often means targeting incumbent justices whose decisional records displease a group (Tarr 2012: ch. 3).

As in other elections, interest groups participate in Supreme Court elections primarily through financial contributions to candidates and independent expenditures. Large-scale funding of candidates comes primarily from the competing sides in personal injury (tort) law: labor unions and the lawyers who represent tort plaintiffs on one side and business and professional groups and the lawyers who defend against tort suits on the other (Semple et al. 2010: 38–54). Not surprisingly, there is a strong relationship between state justices' sources of funding and their decisional records in tort law and other fields of concern to the same interests (e.g., Kang and Shepherd 2011). The tendency of financial contributors to support candidates who already agree with their position in tort law is not easy to distinguish empirically from the independent effects of contributions on judges' decisions. But it seems likely that some independent effects occur, primarily by strengthening justices' pre-existing tendencies to support one of the two sides in personal injury cases.[7]

Electoral campaigns against Supreme Court justices often center on votes and opinions by those justices that can be portrayed negatively. Opposing candidates and interest groups usually focus on votes that favor criminal defendants, especially votes to overturn death sentences. Thus justices might seek to avoid votes that could provide ammunition to electoral opponents.

At least some justices do act to minimize the chances that they will gain a reputation as unfavorable to the death penalty (Hall 1995; Canes-Wrone, Clark, and Kelly 2014). One early spur to adopt such behavior was the highly visible defeats of three California Supreme Court justices in their 1986 retention elections,[8] defeats driven largely by their votes to overturn death sentences in high proportions of cases (Wold and Culver 1987). The prospect of facing the voters may influence justices' choices on other issues that are highly salient to the public, such as abortion (Canes-Wrone, Clark, and Park 2012).

Changes in the conduct of electoral campaigns for seats on state supreme courts have not extended much into lower courts. The scope of contests for positions on intermediate appellate courts, for instance, has not grown appreciably and remains relatively small (Frederick and Streb 2011). Judges on the largely invisible intermediate courts ordinarily have little reason to fear electoral opposition based on their decisions. The work of trial judges is not so invisible, especially in rural areas, but these judges are not often attacked by election opponents on the basis of their decisions. Those trial judges who run in retention elections ordinarily face no organized opposition and win by comfortable margins (Aspin 2011), so they usually have little reason to fear electoral defeat for any reason.[9]

Because of their relative safety, the responses of lower-court judges to the prospect of election are of particular interest. There has been little inquiry into those responses, but two meticulous studies of criminal sentencing produced striking evidence. Huber and Gordon (2004) found that Pennsylvania trial judges, who are subject to retention elections, moved toward tougher sentences as those elections neared. In Kansas, where some judicial districts use partisan elections and others use retention elections, Gordon and Huber (2007) found a similar temporal pattern in the partisan-election districts but not in the retention-election districts.

There is a need for considerable caution in interpreting findings for only two states,[10] but these two studies are intriguing for the questions they raise. The broad question is why trial judges would change their sentencing behavior as elections come closer even though they are unlikely to face opposition and even less likely to lose their seats (Breslin 2010: 903; Gordon and Huber 2007: 112 n. 8).

At least part of the answer to that question lies in the multiple reasons why elections are important to judges. The strategic conception suggests that judges care about elections because they can continue to shape legal policy only if they remain in office. Undoubtedly, this is one reason that some judges worry about electoral defeat. But maintaining their positions is important to judges largely because of the value of those positions in themselves. In turn, that value rests heavily on the prestige that attaches to being a judge. Because staying in office is so important, risk-averse judges might be swayed by an impending election even if there seems little reason for fear. And changes in sentencing behavior may protect some judges who otherwise would suffer defeats, an effect that would be obscured by the dearth of actual defeats.

Election results are also the most visible indicator of a judge's degree of success. Defeat is a sign of failure, even if that failure has little or nothing to do with a judge's performance in office. Moreover, the higher the proportion of the vote that a judge receives, the stronger the judge's sense of having achieved public approval. As a result, even judges who have no reason to fear electoral defeat may still act in ways that potentially increase their share of the vote.

A subsidiary question is why Kansas judges who face partisan elections and Pennsylvania judges who face retention elections respond to the prospect of facing the voters, but not Kansas judge who face retention elections. One reason may lie in the structure of the system for selection of Pennsylvania judges. A judge's first election is partisan, before the retention elections that follow. Thus, like the Kansas judges in partisan-election districts, Pennsylvania judges have experience in "real" elections, and they were willing to run in those elections. Because of this orientation toward the electorate, they may be especially prone to see the share of the vote that they receive as an indication of public support for them.

Thus, judges' interest in the regard of other people magnifies the relevance of elections to them. In turn, their decisions are more susceptible to influence from the general public and from interest groups that participate in judicial elections than they would be if re-election were only a means to the end of shaping judicial policy.

The Supreme Court, the Other Branches, and the General Public

Among judges in the United States, members of the U.S. Supreme Court in the current era are unique or close to unique in the near-absence of concern about continuation of judicial tenure and securing other positions. Yet adherents to the strategic model of judging treat the justices as highly sensitive to their political environment as a means to advance their policy goals.

As noted earlier, these scholars emphasize two types of strategic behavior by justices that are aimed at the political world around them (Epstein and Knight 1998: ch. 5). The first involves adjustment of decisions to avoid negative responses from the president and Congress that would weaken or negate those decisions. The most direct and most common form of such responses is reversal of the Court's interpretations of statutes through adoption of new statutes. The second type of strategic behavior involves avoidance of decisions that would lead to weakening of the Supreme Court as an institution and thus its capacity to make effective policy. The other branches could limit the Court's jurisdiction or withhold their support in securing implementation of the Court's decisions. If the general public disapproves of the Court's decisions, the Court's general legitimacy might decline and with it the willingness of public officials to comply with its decisions.

Most studies of both types of strategic behavior are correlational. Some studies examine whether the ideological content of justices' votes or the Court's collective decisions shifts with the ideological positions of the other branches or the general public. Other studies ask whether justices or the Court are less likely to strike down laws when the political environment is relatively unfavorable to the Court or to its policy positions. The findings of such studies are sensitive to methodological choices, especially the measurement of variables. Largely as a result, there is considerable variation in these findings.

This variation is most evident in the sets of studies that probe for a systematic relationship between the ideological content of Court policy and the preferences of the other branches or the general public, controlling for the justices' own preferences. Some studies that analyze the relationship between Court and the other branches in statutory interpretation find that the justices respond to the ideological positions of the president and Congress as a means to reduce the chances that their decisions will be overridden (e.g., Bergara, Richman, and Spiller 2003); others do not (e.g., Segal 1997). Most studies of the relationship between the "public mood," defined in ideological terms, and the Court's mix of liberal and conservative decisions find a relationship between the two. But they disagree about whether this relationship reflects responsiveness to the public or instead the effects of developments and trends in society on both the public and the justices (e.g., Giles, Blackstone, and Vining 2008; Casillas, Enns, and Wohlfarth 2011). The best judgment about these sets of studies is that the case has not been proved in either direction (see Epstein and Martin 2010).

A related but somewhat different question is whether justices act cautiously when they are considering decisions that could arouse conflict with the other branches, such as striking down major federal legislation, or decisions that are likely to be met with strong disapproval in the general public. Robert McCloskey's (1960) classic history of the Supreme Court and some more recent qualitative studies (Rosen 2006; Friedman 2009) conclude that the justices do behave with caution in those circumstances. Rosen and Friedman argue that this caution effectively makes the Court a majoritarian institution. Other scholars disagree with this conclusion (Pildes 2010). Some quantitative studies of the Court's exercise of judicial review indicate that the justices consider potential damage to their public standing and the likelihood of push-back from Congress in that subset of decisions (e.g., Clark 2011; Harvey 2013; see Segal, Westerland, and Lindquist 2011; Lindquist and Corley 2013). Both the qualitative and quantitative evidence is subject to multiple interpretations, and here too no strong conclusions are yet possible.

If the picture remains clouded, there is enough evidence of influence for the other branches and the general public that the implications of this evidence merit consideration. Why would the justices depart from the decisions that they see as most desirable on the basis of prospective reactions from their political environment?

There are reasons to question whether such departures would constitute good policy-oriented strategy on the part of the justices. Action by Congress and the president to overturn a decision is typically difficult to predict before the Court actually reaches the decision. Moreover, such action usually leaves policy no further from the justices' preferences than it would be if the Court had reached a different decision. For those reasons, regular efforts to avoid decisions that might trigger legislative overturning seem unnecessary and perhaps counterproductive.

Under extreme circumstances it makes sense for the justices, or at least the Court's pivotal justices, to retreat in the face of a threat to the Court's institutional position from Congress and the president. But those extreme circumstances are rare (Glick 2009). Similarly, the justices seldom seem to have good reason to forgo decisions they prefer to make because such decisions do not accord with the views of majorities in the general public. A single decision or even a set of decisions seldom usually has little effect on support for the Court.[11] Further, reduced public support does not necessarily weaken the Court as a policymaker. The substantial decline in public approval of the Court that has occurred in recent years, which is probably a product of negative attitudes toward government in general, does not detract from the Court's capacity to secure compliance with its decisions (see Posner 2013: 304–5).[12]

But if we move beyond strategy to consider the justices' interest in approval from other people, influence from the other branches and the general public becomes more plausible. It is likely that some justices—perhaps most justices—dislike criticism and disapproval of their decisions even if those negative responses do no harm to the Court and its policies. Justices might perceive the enactment of bills that override statutory decisions as a sign that they erred, even if the net effect on public policy is minimal. The introduction of bills in Congress to weaken the Court might bother the justices because of the criticism those bills reflect even if their enactment into law is very unlikely. And denunciations by members of Congress and polls indicating that a decision elicited widespread opposition in the general public may be hurtful in themselves.

In other words, the justices may want to avoid negative reactions from their political environment simply because those reactions are unpleasant, creating a situation of conflict and detracting from the justices' desire to think of themselves as well respected. If that motivation seems weak because it is unconnected with concrete self-interest, it should be noted that the same is true of acting to advance certain policy goals or to interpret the law properly.

Ascertaining the influence of the general public and the other branches of government on the choices of Supreme Court justices is a highly challenging task, and identifying the sources of that influence is no easier. Thus, any conclusions about this influence must be quite tentative. To the extent that influence does occur, however, there is no reason to assume that it occurs solely for strategic reasons. Indeed, the justices' concern with how they are regarded by people outside the Court may be the most powerful motivation for attentiveness to the Court's political environment.

Judges and Elite Groups

Judges may have good reason to take the general public and policymakers in the other branches into account when they reach decisions. But these are seldom the most salient audiences to judges at a personal level.[13] Judges are likely to care considerably more about the regard with which they are held by several other sets of people.

Perhaps most obvious are judges' families, friends, and acquaintances. For many judges, a large portion of these people are in the legal profession. This profession and the segments of it that are most relevant to judges can be a key audience, because lawyers are in an especially good position to evaluate judges' work. As people who have been active in politics and public policy, many judges also identify with political and ideological groups. And for the most visible judges, especially Supreme Court justices, the mass media and the legally oriented news media may be important as visible reviewers of their performance.

This is a rather disparate set of groups. What they have in common is that people in those groups are overwhelmingly part of the social, economic, and political elites in the United States. Thus the people whom judges know personally and those whose opinions matter most to them are not a representative sample of the country as a whole. This is an important reality, because the collective views of elite groups often diverge from those of the public as a whole. When the two do converge, influence from elites can move judicial policy toward the opinions of the public as a whole. As a result, the influence of elites looks like influence from the general public. But sometimes the effect of elite influence will be to draw judges away from majority positions in the public (see Baum and Devins 2010).

The possible effect of judges' orientation toward elite groups has received less attention from scholars than it has from people in the political and legal worlds. In particular, political conservatives have described what they perceive as the influence of elites that have a liberal ideological orientation on decision-making by Supreme Court justices. In this narrative, some justices with conservative policy preferences move to the left because of their desire to win the approval of liberal elite audiences.

This narrative goes back at least as far as President Richard Nixon, who expressed concern about the influence of what he identified as the liberal social elite of Washington, DC (Reeves 2001: 338; Greenhouse 2005: 48). The narrative gained adherents with the growing disappointment of conservatives that the long string of Republican appointments to the Supreme Court between 1969 and 1991 did not move the Court's policies more sharply in a conservative direction. Some of those disappointed conservatives identified the source of the problem as the unexpected moderation or even liberalism of Republican appointees such as Harry Blackmun (in his later years on the Court), John Paul Stevens, Anthony Kennedy, and David Souter. And in turn, these conservatives argued, these moderate or liberal stances largely reflected the influence of liberal elite groups whose approval these justices sought. These groups included the reporters who regularly cover the Supreme Court and elite segments of the legal profession (e.g., Bryden 1992; Eastland 1993; Sowell 1994).

There is evidence that some justices appointed by Republican presidents between the 1950s and the 1990s indeed moved to the left over the course of their tenure on the Supreme Court (Baum 2006: 145–9). Of course, this pattern does not establish that these justices were responding to liberal elite audiences. The relative moderation of several Republican appointees since the 1950s reflects appointment politics to a considerable degree (Devins and Baum 2017), and there may be an element of chance to the number of Republican appointees who were less conservative than expected.

Even so, the assumption that underlies the narrative of disappointed conservatives—that judges are subject to influence from salient elite audiences—has a firm basis. It is noteworthy that the adherents to this narrative include some federal appellate judges and former judges (Kleinfeld 1993–4: 18; *Legal Times* 1992: 16–17; Bork 2003: 9–10). The perspectives of these judges might be biased by their unhappiness with the stances taken by more liberal colleagues, but they are also in a good position to observe the forces that shape the positions of judges on the highest courts.

Moreover, if we move away from the broad sweep of the conservative narrative to more specific influences, it is not unreasonable to conclude that elite audiences help to shape judges' thinking about the issues they address. The decisions of federal judges on discrimination based on sexual orientation and on prohibitions of same-sex marriage undoubtedly have been shaped by the growing elite consensus in favor of equality in this area. Indeed, Justice Antonin Scalia pointed to that influence in dissenting opinions (*Romer v. Evans* 1996: 636; *Lawrence v. Texas* 2003: 602). The revolution in judicial policy on sex discrimination in the 1970s resulted largely from changes in thinking about gender roles that were especially pronounced among well-educated people, those with whom judges were most likely to interact.

Of course, elite groups in American society are hardly homogeneous in their views. Those commentators who believe that elite audiences draw Supreme Court justices toward more liberal positions do not argue otherwise. But they see liberalism as dominant in sectors such as legal academia and the news media that cover the Court, so that justices who seek the respect of people in those sectors are pulled more strongly in one direction than the other. What we know about the distribution of opinion in these sectors provides some support for that perception (Merritt 1978: 780 n. 54; Rothman and Lichter 1985; McGinnis, Schwartz, and Tisdell 2005).

However, the elite world that is relevant to Supreme Court justices and other judges has changed in important ways over the past few decades (Devins and Baum 2017: 32–8). With the increased mobilization of conservatives and the growing polarization of politics at the elite level,[14] there are substantial and clearly identified conservative audiences to which judges can orient themselves.

This is especially evident in the legal world. Conservative law students and professors who felt isolated and beleaguered created the Federalist Society to provide institutional support for their views, and the Society has been highly successful in serving that function (Teles 2008; Hollis-Brusky 2015). Indeed, visible ties to the Federalist Society have become an important credential for lawyers who seek federal appellate judgeships in Republican administrations (Scherer and Miller 2009). Law schools with a conservative orientation and other institutions such as the Volokh Conspiracy blog and conservative public interest law firms also applaud judicial conservatism. Thus, a judge who seeks reinforcement and support from elite legal audiences today hardly needs to adopt a liberal stance in order to get them. On the liberal side, the American Constitution Society developed as a counterpart to the Federalist Society (Baldas 2004). Although the ACS has not achieved anything like the importance of the Federalist Society, it too provides reinforcement for judges who stand on its ideological side (see Ginsburg 2003).

Similar changes have occurred in the news media. If the "mainstream media" once leaned subtly but firmly in a liberal direction, the proliferation of new media with unsubtle and even firmer ideological commitments has created a quite different situation. The national presence of the *Wall Street Journal* and the success of Fox News, to take two important examples, ensure that major court decisions will be evaluated very visibly from conservative perspectives as well as liberal ones. Thus the judge who seeks favorable coverage from the news media need not focus on liberal news outlets.

These changes are part of a more general polarization that has widened the gap between liberal and conservative segments of political and social elites. To an increased extent in the current era, conservatives and liberals, including judges, live in separate worlds (see Fisher 1995; Lithwick 2013). Justice Scalia touched on this development in his comments on social life in Washington, DC: "When I was first in Washington, and even in my early years on this Court, I used to go to a lot of dinner parties at which there were people from both sides. Democrats, Republicans … It doesn't happen anymore" (Senior 2013: 27).

Changes in the judicial selection process reinforce these developments. More than in past eras, the lawyers who are chosen as federal judges tend to be firmly committed to the ideological leaning of their appointing president's party. With these firm commitments, reinforced by supportive audiences, judges are less susceptible to influences that would move them away from their pre-existing ideological tendencies. This change is symbolized by the fact that the liberal–conservative division on the Supreme Court since 2010 falls along party lines, with all the justices appointed by Republican presidents on one side and all the Democratic appointees on the other side. Those conservatives who were frustrated by the moderation or liberalism of some justices appointed by Republican presidents from the 1950s on have little cause for unhappiness today, except for the liberal positions that Justice Anthony Kennedy takes on some issues.[15]

How much difference do these elite audiences make for judges' decisions? From one perspective, their influence would seem quite marginal. When people become judges, they typically hold deeply rooted attitudes on many issues. On federal appellate courts, judges are relatively free from the day-to-day constraints on judges in trial courts[16] and the career concerns of judges who lack life terms. As a result, it would appear, Supreme Court justices and judges on the federal courts of appeals can take the course they prefer, constrained only (if at all) by strategic considerations as they seek the most effective ways to put their conceptions of good law or good policy into effect. Given that reality, how much could Ruth Bader Ginsburg or Samuel Alito, to take two examples, be swayed by an interest in the regard of other people?

This perspective makes considerable sense, but there is an important reality that it does not capture. If judges are indeed like other people in seeking popularity and respect, that goal inevitably will affect their choices as decision makers. Thus it is plausible that a left-leaning elite world in the second half of the twentieth century exerted an influence on the thinking of some Supreme Court justices. At the least, that world provided encouragement for justices who moved to the left primarily for other reasons. As Justice Harry Blackmun moved away from the conservatism that characterized his early years on the Supreme Court, the praise he received from liberal audiences gave him support he needed and sought as he took his new course (e.g., Greenhouse 2005: 223–4).

But what about the more polarized elite world of the present era? It would seem that judges are now less subject to influence because they can choose audiences that applaud what they are already doing. The conservative judges who have associations with the Federalist Society, for instance, receive reinforcement from like-minded members of the legal community (see Mauro 2013).

Yet justices' interest in maintaining approval from like-minded audiences can exert an influence by discouraging them from straying from the fold on cases that people on the left and right care most about. Had Clarence Thomas or Antonin Scalia voted against the claims of George W. Bush in *Bush v. Gore* (2000), their interactions with fellow conservatives would have become considerably less comfortable. The vitriol directed at John Roberts by some conservatives after his decisive vote for the validity of the Affordable Care Act in *National Federation of Independent Business v. Sebelius* (2012) makes it clear that justices can sometimes withstand the prospect of that reaction, but it also indicates the price that justices today (especially conservative justices) may pay for such apostasy. It is understandable if justices are sometimes swayed by that consideration.[17]

Even in this polarized era, judges' interest in the regard of others may have effects other than ideological reinforcement. Justice Kennedy has won considerable praise for his opinions opposing discrimination based on sexual orientation, praise that he seems to enjoy considerably (Liptak 2013). Thus he has an incentive to adhere to that position, although that incentive might be outweighed by other considerations in any specific case.

For Justice Scalia, the same interest may have had a more complicated effect. His desire to portray himself as someone who stood above ideology gave him an incentive to take what are considered liberal positions on certain issues, positions that he could cite in support of his argument that he decides based on legal rather than policy considerations. His references at public appearances to his votes to strike down prohibitions of flag burning (e.g., Fuchs 2014) and to his votes in favor of criminal defendants on certain issues (e.g., de Jaager 2012) underlined the strength of that incentive. At the same time, his ties to conservative audiences may have made it more difficult for him to adopt liberal positions on the issues that are of the greatest concern to those audiences. Supreme Court justices are unique in their visibility among elite groups. As a result, judges on other courts have smaller and somewhat different audiences. But they are subject to the same kinds of influences, as they seek to maintain and build positive regard from the individuals and groups that are important to them. When judges' personal audiences exert strong and one-sided influence, such as the pressure that most Southern federal district judges felt during the 1950s and 1960s on civil rights issues, their impact is clear (Peltason 1971).

Occasionally, as in that example, this influence might be the most powerful force shaping judges' choices. More often, personal audiences exert a less decisive impact on justices' positions. But that impact can be substantial, even if it is difficult to separate from the effect of judges' own preferences. A full theory of judicial decision-making needs to take it into account.

Conclusions

The introduction to this chapter referred to alternative conceptions of the relationship between judges and their environments. One conception, dominant among scholars today, posits that judges respond to their environments for strategic reasons—primarily to advance their policy goals. In contrast, the conception that I have presented posits that judges respond to their environments largely because they care about the regard in which they are held by salient audiences for its own sake.

It is impossible now, and probably will remain impossible, to compare the explanatory power of these two conceptions with any precision. But I think it clear that at the least, an audience-based conception fills important gaps in a strategic conception of judging. For one thing, it helps in understanding why judges take the general public and the other branches of government into account. There are times when elected judges have good reason to fear that voters will remove them from office, and there are times when judges have good reason to fear that legislatures will take action to damage their courts. However, there is evidence that judges are sometimes responsive to their political environment even when they have little reason for fear. Judges' interest in popularity and respect provides an incentive for them to avoid criticism and to maintain a sense that they are well regarded by people elsewhere in government and in the general public. Thus it provides a needed explanation for their attentiveness to the public and the other branches of government.

Further, an audience-based conception directs attention to key elements of judges' environments that receive little or no attention in strategic accounts of judging. Like other people, judges have powerful reasons to care about the regard in which they are held by others who are important to them personally. And this is true even if those others have no impact on their careers or on the success of the policies they favor. As a result, the choices of judges as policymakers may be shaped subtly—and, occasionally, unsubtly—by the influence of audiences that range from family members to ideological groups with which they identify. For this reason as well, attention to judges' personal interest in the regard of other people can provide a better understanding of judicial behavior.

Notes

1. This chapter focuses on judges in the United States. The relevance of the perspective offered in the chapter to judges in other nations depends in part on the extent of judicial independence in a particular nation.
2. The other key part is strategic action to influence collective decisions within a court. I leave that part aside in order to focus on the relationship between judges and the environments of courts.
3. However, judges who care most about making good law could also be analyzed in strategic terms.
4. For an earlier version and more extensive presentation of this conception, see Baum (2006).
5. In that respect this conception is part of the body of work that considers the operation and impact of judicial goals other than making good law or good policy. Early examinations of this broader array of goals include Posner (1993) and Baum (1994); Epstein, Landes, and Posner (2013: ch. 1) provide a valuable framework and analysis for this broader array. Judges' interest in the regard of other people, the emphasis of this chapter, is only one of the goals that merit greater attention from scholars. Of these goals, however, it is the one that is most directly relevant to the impact of judges' environments on their choices as decision makers.
6. Examples include Miceli and Cosgel (1994); Gulati and McCauliff (1998); Schauer (2000); and Yates, Moeller, and Levey (2013). There is other work on judicial behavior that gives some attention to judges' interest in popularity and esteem (e.g., Posner 1995: 119; Drahozal 1998: 475; Epstein and Knight 2013: 20–1).
7. Scholars and commentators have given considerable attention to another question about the effects of campaign contributions: whether justices are more likely to side with specific litigants or lawyers who have contributed to them, all else being equal (e.g., McCall 2003; Cann, Bonneau, and Boyea 2012). Largely because of the difficulty of isolating the causal impact of contributions, the strength of these effects and the conditions under which they occur remain uncertain.

8. In retention elections, voters vote "yes" or "no" on retaining a judge in office. In the preponderance of states that use retention elections, a judge must gain a simple majority of votes to win retention.
9. Trial judges might have reason to fear public reactions to occasional high-profile cases, especially in states in which judges can face opposing candidates (rather than retention elections). This fear undoubtedly helps to explain a pattern that Supreme Court Justice Sonia Sotomayor noted in an opinion: Alabama trial judges override jury recommendations against the death penalty more than ten times as often as they override recommendations for the death penalty (*Woodward v. Alabama*, 2013: 449).
10. A study by another pair of authors found that sentences by trial judges in the state of Washington, selected in nonpartisan elections, tended to become heavier as elections approached—though not for judges who retired rather than run for re-election (Berdejó and Yuchtman 2013). This finding is consistent with the pattern that Gordon and Huber found for judges with experience in "regular" elections.
11. Support for the Court has multiple dimensions and can be measured in several ways (Gibson, Caldeira, and Spence 2003). I am thinking primarily of the Court's perceived legitimacy as an institution (Gibson and Caldeira 2009: ch. 3).
12. It is quite possible that risk-averse justices exaggerate the fragility of public support for the Court as an institution. That risk aversion probably helps to explain justices' expressions of worry about maintaining support (Clark 2011: 68–71). Even so, it seems unlikely that justices would often modify their positions in cases solely because of concern about the Court's standing as an institution.
13. Neal Devins has played an important part in development of the ideas presented in this section.
14. Political polarization has multiple aspects. The aspect most relevant to changes in elite influence on judges is affective polarization: increased strength of people's personal identifications with one side of the political spectrum and negative feelings about the other side (Iyengar, Sood, and Lelkes 2012).
15. However, Chief Justice Roberts has been criticized by some conservatives for what they view as signs of undue moderation, especially his decisive vote to uphold a key provision of the health care plan sponsored by President Obama in *National Federation of Independent Business v. Sebelius* (2012). One commentator lamented that "we need jurists" who have "the intestinal fortitude not to be swayed by pressure from *The New York Times*, the Georgetown cocktail circuit, and the legal academy" (Thiessen 2012; see Yoo 2012).
16. In particular, sentencing decisions in federal and state trial courts are affected heavily by plea bargains and by prosecutors' recommendations.
17. See criticism of Chief Justice Roberts discussed earlier.

References

Aspin, L. 2011. "The 2010 Judicial Retention Elections in Perspective: Continuity and Change from 1964 to 2010." *Judicature* 94: 218–32.

Baldas, T. 2004. "Law School Turf War Ignites." *National Law Journal* April 26: 1, 12.

Baum, L. 1994. "What Judges Want: Judges' Goals and Judicial Behavior." *Political Research Quarterly* 47: 749–68.

Baum, L. 2006. *Judges and their Audiences: A Perspective on Judicial Behavior*. Princeton, NJ: Princeton University Press.

Baum, L., and Devins, N. 2010. "Why the Supreme Court Cares about Elites, Not the American People." *Georgetown Law Journal* 98: 1515–81.

Berdejó, C., and Yuchtman, N. 2013. "Crime, Punishment, and Politics: An Analysis of Political Cycles in Criminal Sentencing." *Review of Economics and Statistics* 95: 741–56.

Bergara, M., Richman, B., and Spiller, P. T. 2003. "Modeling Supreme Court Strategic Decision Making: The Congressional Constraint." *Legislative Studies Quarterly* 28: 247–80.

Bork, R. H. 2003. *Coercing Virtue: The Worldwide Rule of Judges*. Washington, DC: AEI Press.

Breslin, D. M. 2010. "Judicial Merit-Retention Elections in Pennsylvania." *Duquesne Law Review* 48: 891–907.

Bryden, D. P. 1992. "Is the Rehnquist Court Conservative?" *The Public Interest* (Fall): 73–88.

Budziak, J. 2013. "Blind Justice or Blind Ambition? The Influence of Promotion on Decision Making in the U.S. Courts of Appeals." *Justice System Journal* 34: 295–320.

Canes-Wrone, B., Clark, T. S., and Kelly, J. P. 2014. "Judicial Selection and Death Penalty Decisions." *American Political Science Review* 108: 23–39.

Canes-Wrone, B., Clark, T. S., and Park, J. K. 2012. "Judicial Independence and Retention Elections." *Journal of Law, Economics, & Organization* 28: 211–34.

Cann, D. M., Bonneau, C. W., and Boyea, B. D. 2012. "Campaign Contributions and Judicial Elections in Partisan and Nonpartisan Elections." In *New Directions in Judicial Politics*, edited by K. T. McGuire. New York, NY: Routledge, 38–52.

Casillas, C. J., Enns, P. K., and Wohlfarth, P. C. 2011. "How Public Opinion Constrains the U.S. Supreme Court." *American Journal of Political Science* 55: 74–88.

Clark, T. S. 2011. *The Limits of Judicial Independence*. New York, NY: Cambridge University Press.

De Jaager, J. 2012. "Justice Scalia Comes Home to the Law School," *The Record Online*. University of Chicago Law School, Spring. Available at: http://www.law.uchicago.edu/alumni/magazine/spring12/scalia.

Devins, N., and Baum, L. 2017. "Split Definitive: How Party Polarization Turned the Supreme Court into a Partisan Court." *Supreme Court Review*.

Drahozal, C. R. 1998. "Judicial Incentives and the Appeals Process." *SMU Law Review* 51: 469–503.

Eastland, T. 1993. "The Tempting of Justice Kennedy." *American Spectator* February: 32–7.

Epstein, L., and Knight, J. 1998. *The Choices Justices Make*. Washington, DC: CQ Press.

Epstein, L., and Knight, J. 2000. "Toward a Strategic Revolution in Judicial Politics: A Look back, a Look ahead." *Political Research Quarterly* 53: 625–61.

Epstein, L., and Knight, J. 2013. "Reconsidering Judicial Preferences." *Annual Review of Political Science* 16: 11–31.

Epstein, L., and Martin, A. D. 2010. "Does Public Opinion Influence the Supreme Court? Possibly Yes (But We're Not Sure Why)." *University of Pennsylvania Journal of Constitutional Law* 13: 263–81.

Fisher, M. 1995. "The Private World of Justice Thomas." *Washington Post*, September 11, 1995: B1.

Frederick, B., and Streb, M. J. 2011. "The Cost of Going for the Gavel: Individual Candidate Spending in Intermediate Appellate Court Elections." *Justice System Journal* 32: 25–43.

Friedman, B. 2009. *The Will of the People: How Public Opinion Has Influenced the Supreme Court and Shaped the Meaning of the Constitution*. New York, NY: Farrar, Straus and Giroux.

Fuchs, E. 2014. "Justice Scalia Says He Would Jail This 'Bearded Weirdo' if He Were King." *Business Insider*, March 26. Available at: http://www.businessinsider.com/scalia-talks-texas-v-johnson-at-brooklyn-law-2014-3.

Gibson, J. L., and Caldeira, G. A. 2009. *Citizens, Courts, and Confirmations: Positivity Theory and the Judgments of the American People*. Princeton, NJ: Princeton University Press.

Gibson, J. L., Caldeira, G. A., and Spence, L. K. 2003. "Measuring Attitudes toward the United States Supreme Court." *American Journal of Political Science* 47: 354–67.

Giles, M. W., Blackstone, B., and Vining, R. L., Jr. 2008. "The Supreme Court in American Democracy: Unraveling the Linkages between Public Opinion and Judicial Decision Making." *Journal of Politics* 70: 293–306.

Ginsburg, R. B. 2003. "Looking beyond our Borders: The Value of a Comparative Perspective in Constitutional Adjudication," speech to the national conference of the American Constitution Society, August 2. Available at: americanconstitutionsociety.org/pdf/Ginsburg transcript final.pdf.

Glick, D. 2009. "Conditional Strategic Retreat: The Court's Concession in the 1935 Gold Clause Cases." *Journal of Politics* 71: 800–16.

Goffman, E. 1959. *The Presentation of Self in Everyday Life*. New York, NY: Doubleday.

Gordon, S. C., and Huber, G. A. 2007. "The Effect of Electoral Competitiveness on Incumbent Behavior." *Quarterly Journal of Political Science* 2: 107–38.

Greenhouse, L. 2005. *Becoming Justice Blackmun: Harry Blackmun's Supreme Court Journey*. New York, NY: Times Books.

Gulati, M., and McCauliff, C. M. A. 1998. "On *Not* Making Law." *Law and Contemporary Problems* 61 (Summer): 157–228.

Hall, M. G. 1995. "Justices as Representatives: Elections and Judicial Politics in the American States." *American Politics Quarterly* 23: 485–503.

Harvey, A. 2013. *A Mere Machine: The Supreme Court, Congress, and American Democracy*. New Haven, CT: Yale University Press.

Hollis-Brusky, A. 2015. *Ideas with Consequences: The Federalist Society and the Conservative Counterrevolution*. New York, NY: Oxford University Press.

Huber, G.A., and Gordon, S. C. 2004. "Accountability and Coercion: Is Justice Blind When It Runs for Office?" *American Journal of Political Science* 48: 247–63.

Iyengar, S., Sood, G., and Lelkes, Y. 2012. "Affect, Not Ideology: A Social Identity Perspective on Polarization." *Public Opinion Quarterly* 76: 405–31.

Kang, M. S., and Shepherd, J. M. 2011. "The Partisan Price of Justice: An Empirical Analysis of Campaign Contributions and Judicial Decisions." *New York University Law Review* 86: 69–130.

Kleinfeld, A. J. 1993–4. "Politicization: From the Law Schools to the Courts." *Academic Questions* 6 (Winter): 9–19.

Kozinski, A. 2004. "The *Real* Issues of Judicial Ethics." *Hofstra Law Review* 32: 1095–106.

Legal Times. 1992. "Attacking Activism, Judge Names Names." June 22: 14–17.

Lindquist, S. A., and Corley, P. C. 2013. "National Policy Preferences and Judicial Review of State Statutes at the United States Supreme Court." *Publius* 43: 151–78.

Liptak, A. 2013. "Surprising Friend of the Gay Rights Movement in the Highest of Places." *New York Times*, September 2: A10.

Lithwick, D. 2013. "No. No. Not That I Know of." *Slate*, October 7. Available at: http://www.slate.com/articles/news_and_politics/jurisprudence/2013/10/scalia_interview_in_new_york_magazine_the_conservative_justice_reveals_his.html.

Mauro, T. 2013. "Joyous Justice Thomas Speaks to Federalist Society." *The BLT: The Blog of Legal Times*, November 15. Available at: http://legaltimes.typepad.com/blt/2013/11/joyous-justice-thomas-speaks-to-federalist-society.html.

McCall, M. 2003. "The Politics of Judicial Elections: The Influence of Campaign Contributions on the Voting Patterns of Texas Supreme Court Justices, 1994–1997." *Politics and Policy* 31: 314–43.

McCloskey, R. G. 1960. *The American Supreme Court*. Chicago, IL: University of Chicago Press.

McGinnis, J. O., Schwartz, M. A., and Tisdell, B. 2005. "The Patterns and Implications of Political Contributions by Elite Law School Faculty." *Georgetown Law Journal* 93: 1167–212.

Merritt, D. J. 1998. "Research and Teaching on Law Faculties: An Empirical Exploration." *Chicago-Kent Law Review* 73: 765–821.

Miceli, T. J., and Coşgel, M. M. 1994. "Reputation and Judicial Decision-Making." *Journal of Economic Behavior and Organization* 23: 31–51.

Morriss, A. P., Heise, M., and Sisk, G. C. 2005. "Signaling and Precedent in Federal District Court Opinions." *Supreme Court Economic Review* 13: 63–97.

Peltason, J. W. 1971. *Fifty-Eight Lonely Men: Southern Federal Judges and School Desegregation*. Urbana, IL: University of Illinois Press.

Pildes, R. H. 2010. "Is the Supreme Court a 'Majoritarian' Institution?" *Supreme Court Review* 2010: 103–58.

Posner, R. A. 1993. "What Do Judges and Justices Maximize? (The Same Thing Everybody Else Does)." *Supreme Court Economic Review* 3: 1–41.

Posner, R. A. 1995. *Overcoming Law*. Cambridge, MA: Harvard University Press.

Posner, R. A. 2013. "The Supreme Court and Celebrity Culture." *Chicago-Kent Law Review* 88: 299–305.

Reeves, R. 2001. *President Nixon: Alone in the White House*. New York, NY: Simon & Schuster.

Rosen, J. 2006. *The Most Democratic Branch: How the Courts Serve America*. New York, NY: Oxford University Press.

Rothman, S., and Lichter, S. R. 1985. "Personality, Ideology and World View: A Comparison of Media and Business Elites." *British Journal of Political Science* 15: 29–49.

Rumble, W. E., Jr. 1968. *American Legal Realism: Skepticism, Reform, and the Judicial Process*. Ithaca, NY: Columbia University Press.

Schauer, F. 2000. "Incentives, Reputation, and the Inglorious Determinants of Judicial Behavior." *University of Cincinnati Law Review* 68: 615–36.

Scherer, N., and Miller, B. 2009. "The Federalist Society's Impact on the Federal Judiciary." *Political Research Quarterly* 62: 366–78.

Schlenker, B. R., and Pontari, B. A. 2000. "The Strategic Control of Information: Impression Management and Self-Presentation in Daily Life." In *Psychological Perspectives on Self and Identity*, edited by A. Tesler, R. B. Felson, and J. M. Suls. Washington, DC: American Psychological Association, 199–232.

Segal, J. A. 1997. "Separation-of-Powers Games in the Positive Theory of Congress and Courts." *American Political Science Review* 91: 28–44.

Segal, J. A., and Spaeth, H. J. 2002. *The Supreme Court and the Attitudinal Model Revisited*. New York, NY: Cambridge University Press.

Segal, J. A., Westerland, C., and Lindquist, S. A. 2011. "Congress, the Supreme Court, and Judicial Review: Testing a Constitutional Separation of Powers Model." *American Journal of Political Science* 55: 89–104.

Semple, J., Skaggs, A., Blitzer, J., and Casey L. 2010. *The New Politics of Judicial Elections 2000–2009*. New York, NY: Justice at Stake Campaign.

Senior, J. 2013. "In Conversation: Antonin Scalia." *New York Magazine*, October 7: 23–7, 80–1.
Sowell, T. 1994. "Blackmun Plays to the Crowd." *St. Louis Post-Dispatch*, March 4: 7B.
Tarr, G. A. 2012. *Without Fear or Favor: Judicial Independence and Judicial Accountability in the States*. Stanford, CA: Stanford University Press.
Teles, S. M. 2008. *The Rise of the Conservative Legal Movement: The Battle for Control of the Law*. Princeton, NJ: Princeton University Press.
Thiessen, M. A. 2012. "Why Are Republicans So Awful at Picking Supreme Court Justices?" *Washington Post*, July 7: A15.
U.S. Senate. 2005. *Confirmation Hearing on the Nomination of John G. Roberts, Jr. to be Chief Justice of the United States*. 109th Congress, 1st Session.
Wold, J. T., and Culver, J. H. 1987. "The Defeat of the California Justices: The Campaign, the Electorate, and the Issue of Judicial Accountability." *Judicature* 70: 348–55.
Yates, J., Moeller, J., and Levey, B. 2013. "'For the Times They Are A-Changin': Explaining Voting Patterns of U.S. Supreme Court Justices through Identification of Micro-Publics." *Brigham Young University Journal of Public Law* 28: 117–43.
Yoo, J. 2012. "Chief Justice Roberts and his Apologists." *Wall Street Journal*, June 29.

Cases Cited

Bush v. Gore. 2000. 531 U.S. 98.
Lawrence v. Texas. 2003. 539 U.S. 558.
National Federation of Independent Business v. Sebelius. 2012. 183 L. Ed. 2d 450.
Romer v. Evans. 1996. 517 U.S. 620.
Woodward v. Alabama. 2013. 187 L. Ed. 2d 449.

CHAPTER 19

INTEREST GROUPS AND THE JUDICIARY

JARED PERKINS AND PAUL M. COLLINS, JR.

SCHOLARSHIP on the role of interest groups in American politics tends to focus most heavily on the legislative, executive, and electoral arenas. For example, research investigates the ability of groups to shape legislative outcomes, regulatory policy, and political campaigns (for a review, see Baumgartner and Leech 1998; Hojnacki et al. 2012). Though it may not be as visible as these other outlets, interest groups have long participated in the judiciary, particularly at the U.S. Supreme Court. In doing so, groups recognize that, like the legislative and executive branches, the courts are policy-making institutions. Accordingly, their decisions are capable of affecting a wide range of behavior, including how police officers question suspects, the rights of same-sex couples to marry, the constitutionality of affirmative action and health care programs, and the ability of governments to confiscate private property.

The purpose of this chapter is to address the state of academic scholarship on interest group litigation in the American judiciary. We begin by exploring the three primary means by which organizations engage the courts: case sponsorship, amicus curiae participation, and intervention. Next, we discuss topics relevant to each of these methods of litigation by considering venue selection and coalition activity, followed by a treatment of extrajudicial lobbying. In addition to reviewing scholarship in each area, we also provide a critical analysis of existing research for the purpose of establishing the limitations of our current knowledge of interest group litigation. Our hope is that, by shining light on theoretical and empirical weaknesses of existing research, as well as overlooked avenues of study, we will identify opportunities for future scholars to advance our understanding of organizational litigation.

Case Sponsorship

The earliest academic work on interest group litigation focused on how, and to what effect, organizations brought cases into the courts for the purpose of challenging various policies (e.g., Cortner 1964, 1968; Vose 1955, 1959). Interest groups do this in two ways. First, if the group can obtain standing to sue, the group will generally bring a lawsuit as a party to the litigation. In order to obtain standing, the organization must demonstrate that an actual controversy exists that will impair its interests (Orren 1976; Scheppele and Walker 1991). Alternatively, if the group cannot obtain standing, it can file a lawsuit on behalf of an individual (or group of individuals) who has standing to sue. In this capacity, the group directs the litigation on behalf of the individual (at both the trial and appellate levels), including providing attorneys, research and clerical personnel, and other resources. In exchange, the organization uses the case to further its goals. Case sponsorship is an extremely resource intensive form of litigation as it takes years to litigate cases into the appellate stages, potentially costing hundreds of thousands to millions of dollars (e.g., O'Connor 1980; Wasby 1995). It is for this reason that some groups wait until cases have reached the appellate stages to sponsor litigation, working with, or taking the case over from, the attorneys who litigated it at the trial court.

There are several notable examples of interest groups successfully employing case sponsorship in the pursuit of their goals. For example, the NAACP and the NAACP Legal Defense Fund (LDF) used planned litigation to effectively challenge school segregation, restricted covenants, and other race-based statutes (Vose 1955, 1959; Wasby 1984, 1985, 1995). Similarly, women's rights organizations, such as the National Organization for Women and the American Civil Liberties Union Women's Rights Project, successfully fought an array of gender discrimination policies in the courts (Cowan 1976; O'Connor 1980). More recently, a variety of organizations representing the interests of lesbian, gay, bisexual, and transgender Americans have utilized case sponsorship to litigate issues including adoption, marriage, and hospital visitation (e.g., Pinello 2003; Rubenstein 1999).

Despite these prominent illustrations of group success, it is not clear whether case sponsorship is an effective litigation strategy. Most of the evidence we have on the topic is from case studies that may have been chosen precisely because they demonstrate the triumphs of interest groups. As Segal and Spaeth (1993: 241) note, "Few people want to spend a year or two studying losing litigators." Related, our understanding of this strategy is circumscribed by the fact that most studies focus on a single case or issue area, which may not be generalizable to other areas of litigation. Third, it is not entirely evident why we should expect groups to be especially effective litigators. Presumably, organizations will be successful because they carefully select cases and bring a great deal of expertise and resources to the table, making them repeat players (e.g., Epstein and Rowland 1991; Galanter 1974). Yet, this expectation remains largely untested and is confounded by the fact that groups frequently challenge the policies of governments, who also have ample expertise and resources (Sheehan, Mishler, and Songer 1992). Finally, our knowledge is limited because studies very rarely compare the success of litigants sponsored by organized interests to those without such support. Of those that have, the results have been mixed. For example, Epstein and Rowland (1991) demonstrate that interest groups are no more likely to win federal district court cases than other types of litigants, and Tauber (1998) shows that sponsorship by the NAACP LDF does not influence the outcome of capital punishment cases in the U.S. courts of appeals. Conversely, George and Epstein (1992) provide evidence that U.S. Supreme Court death row appeals sponsored by interest groups are more likely to be decided in favor of the inmate.

Though case sponsorship is typically associated with organized interest groups, there has been a recent trend of individuals supplanting the role of groups in some situations and sponsoring cases themselves. For example, in *District of Columbia v. Heller* (2010), the Supreme Court determined that the Second Amendment established an individual right to keep and bear arms. This case was sponsored not by a pro-Second Amendment group, but by Robert Levy, a lawyer and senior fellow at the Cato Institute. Levy organized and personally financed the case owing to his academic interest in constitutional issues, rather than because of a particular devotion to gun rights (Liptak 2007). Another interesting phenomenon involves a small group of Washington lawyers arguing an increasingly large number of cases before the Supreme Court (Biskupic, Roberts, and Shiffman 2014; Lazarus 2008; McGuire 1993). In so doing, these elite attorneys—who often represent business interests—sometimes perform a role similar to interest groups by taking cases over from other attorneys once they reach the Supreme Court. Further investigation into these relatively recent developments is certainly warranted.

It is also interesting to note that, compared to the study of amicus curiae briefs, there is a dearth of recent scholarship on case sponsorship, despite the fact that this strategy has become more common over time (Epstein 1993). In part, we suspect this is due to the fact that it is more difficult to collect data on case sponsorship than amicus curiae briefs. Such is the case because one cannot necessarily read a judicial opinion and determine that a case was sponsored by an interest group. Further, the rigorous analysis of case sponsorship often entails studying litigation at multiple levels of the judicial system, and sometimes in both state and federal courts. In addition to being a time-consuming endeavor, this requires an understanding of multiple layers of the legal system that many scholars lack.

Despite this, it is clear that case sponsorship is a powerful tool at the disposal of interest groups and we hope to see a resurgence of scholarship devoted to this most significant topic. In addition to addressing some of the limitations of existing research discussed above, we also encourage researchers to include a broader set of organizations in their studies. In particular, we think it will be useful to focus attention, not just on civil rights and liberties organizations, but also on groups whose goals implicate other issue areas, such as economic policies (e.g., Franklin 2009). Further, there has been little scholarly attention focused on class action lawsuits organized by interests groups (e.g., Scheppele and Walker 1991). Through these lawsuits, organizations consolidate the claims of dozens (or even thousands) of individuals into a single lawsuit. The expectation is that, by combining claims, the class action may result in higher damage awards than would be expected from a single lawsuit (e.g., Coffee 1995). Lastly, we believe that large-scale investigations into how groups select cases for sponsorship are warranted (e.g., Scheppele and Walker 1991). Though we have a fairly good knowledge of how particular organizations choose cases for planned litigation, it is not clear how generalizable these studies are to the broader interest group population. To be sure, we recognize that such studies are very time-consuming and resource-intensive to conduct. However, they have the potential to shed a great deal of light on how and why interest groups use the court system in the pursuit of their goals.

Amicus Curiae Briefs

Research on interest group amicus curiae activity is by far the most well-developed literature on organizational litigation. Through this technique, organizations submit legal briefs to courts providing judges with information regarding the application of legal standards, the interpretation of precedent, the perspectives of other actors in the American political system, as well as their views of the broader economic, legal, and policy implications of a decision (Collins 2008a). Amicus curiae translates literally to "friend of the court" in Latin, suggesting that the briefs provide neutral information that helps educate judges. However, they are, in fact, adversarial weapons, urging courts to decide in favor of one litigant or the other (Banner 2003; Krislov 1963).

Research on amicus participation takes a variety of forms. Numerous studies provide information on the overall amount of amicus activity in various courts, and address the identity of the organizations that file amicus briefs. These studies reveal that the number of amicus briefs filed has increased steadily over time (e.g., Collins 2008a; Corbally, Bross, and Flango 2004; Epstein 1994; Kearney and Merrill 2000; Laroche 2009; Martinek 2006; O'Connor and Epstein 1982). Today, it is the rare case that does not have amicus briefs in the U.S. Supreme Court. Other studies address the types of organizations that participate as amici. Generally speaking, a diverse assortment of groups file amicus briefs, and the amicus environment in the courts is quite pluralistic when compared to organizational participation in the executive and legislative branches (Caldeira and Wright 1990; Collins and Solowiej 2007; Collins 2008a; Collins and Martinek 2010a; Epstein 1994).

While the literatures on these topics are fairly saturated, they overwhelmingly focus on federal appellate courts, especially the U.S. Supreme Court. Given this, it would be useful to devote more research to understanding the volume of amicus activity and the types of organizations that file amicus briefs in state courts and the federal district courts. The question of who files amicus briefs is particularly important because most theories of amicus influence posit that judges are provided with a diverse assortment of information (Collins 2008a; Hansford 2004; Kearney and Merrill 2000; Spriggs and Wahlbeck 1997). Presumably they would not be privy to such varied information if the amicus environment was homogenous, or had an elitist bent.

Another body of research addresses why interest groups participate as amicus curiae. These studies reveal that groups file amicus briefs in an attempt to further their policy goals, and that membership groups are also attentive to organizational maintenance concerns (Hansford 2004a, 2004b; Martinek 2006; Solberg and Waltenburg 2006; Scheppele and Walker 1991; Solowiej and Collins 2009). As it relates to the pursuit of policy goals, organizations are attracted to cases that have far-reaching policy implications, such as those involving important constitutional questions, the exercise of judicial review, and civil rights and liberties policies (Martinek 2006; Provost 2011; Salzman, Williams, and Calvin 2011; Solowiej and Collins 2009). In addition, groups are more likely to file amicus briefs when the information environment at the court is relatively poor, as in cases featuring complex legal questions or inexperienced counsel (Hansford 2004a; Martinek 2006; Solowiej and Collins 2009). Further, groups participate as amici in an effort to counteract the lobbying efforts of their opponents (Epstein 1985; Hansford 2011; Solowiej and Collins 2009; Teles 2008). In terms of maintaining the organization, membership groups are especially interested in cases that allow them to increase publicity for their causes, particularly those generating media attention that touch on the concerns of the their members (Hansford 2004a, 2004b; Koshner 1998; Solberg and Waltenburg 2006).

Though this is an important and growing corpus of research, it is almost entirely concentrated on federal appellate courts, particularly the U.S. Supreme Court. It is clear that, in order to understand group motivations for filing amicus briefs, we must move beyond the almost myopic focus on the Supreme Court. In addition, it would be useful to have more information on why groups file amicus briefs at particular stages of litigation. This will shed light on, for example, whether interest groups enter litigation at the intermediate appellate level and then continue to file amicus briefs at the court-of-last-resort level. On the one hand, this seems to be a useful strategy since groups can easily revise their amicus briefs for submission to a different court and because amicus participation in an intermediate appellate court can increases the chances that a higher court will review the case (Hagle and Spaeth 2009). On the other hand, groups filing amicus briefs at the intermediate court of appeals level run the risk that a higher court will not accept the case for review and there is an increased financial burden in participating in multiple judicial venues. Finally, we encourage scholars to devote more attention to ascertaining the weight that membership groups place on pursuing their policy goals relative to attending to organizational maintenance issues. For example, some argue that maintaining the group represents a goal (Koshner 1998; Solberg and Waltenburg 2006), while others view it as a constraint that only membership-based groups face (Collins 2008a; Hansford 2004a, 2004b). Far from being mere semantics, this distinction can make a real difference in terms of how we approach the study of amicus curiae participation.

A voluminous amount of scholarship has been devoted to ascertaining the influence of amicus briefs. Groups can file amicus briefs at two stages of decision-making. At the agenda-setting stage (when judges determine which cases will receive their full attention), groups urge courts to grant or deny a petition for review. At the merits stage (when judges decide the outcome of cases), organizations advocate for courts to rule in favor of a particular litigant. Beginning with the agenda-setting stage, research by Caldeira and Wright (1988) shows that the number of amicus briefs filed with a certiorari petition is a significant determinant in the U.S. Supreme Court's decision to review a case (see also McGuire and Caldeira 1993). In addition, Black and Boyd (2013) provide evidence that Supreme Court justices are more likely to add cases accompanied by amicus briefs to their discuss list (the group of cases the justices discuss amongst themselves prior to voting to grant or deny certiorari). Amicus briefs are argued to influence judges' selection of cases because they provide reliable signals regarding the broader economic, legal, and social impact of a decision, thus making review more likely.

Although it is has become the conventional wisdom that amicus briefs filed at the certiorari stage in the Supreme Court enhance the likelihood that a case will be accepted for review, most of the studies on which this wisdom is based focus on a single term or a single issue area. Accordingly, it would be useful to provide more longitudinal examinations into this relationship. Because the number of amicus briefs filed with the Court has increased over time, it is plausible that the effect of these briefs on certiorari decisions has lessened in more recent years. In addition, research on amicus influence on agenda-setting focuses entirely on the U.S. Supreme Court. Since many state courts of last resort enjoy discretionary jurisdiction, it will prove useful to apply the insights garnered from this literature to state high courts. Finally, because studies that examine why groups file amicus briefs overwhelmingly focus on the merits stage, it will be beneficial to investigate the decisions of groups to participate at the agenda-setting stage.

There is a vast literature on amicus influence on judicial decision-making at the merits stage. One line of research attempts to determine whether amicus briefs influence the likelihood of litigation success, i.e., whether a particular party wins or loses (Collins 2004; Collins and Martinek 2010b; Comparato 2003; Kearney and Merrill 2000; Laroche 2009; McGuire 1990, 1995; Songer and Kuersten 1995; Songer and Sheehan 1993). Based on the idea that amicus briefs provide judges with persuasive information that helps buttress the arguments of the litigants they support, several of these studies show that amicus support increases litigation success. That is, as the number of amicus briefs supporting a litigant increase, so too does the chances of that litigant winning the lawsuit (e.g., Collins 2004; Collins and Martinek 2010b; Songer and Kuersten 1995).

Others approach the question of amicus influence by exploring the ability of amicus briefs to influence the ideological direction of case outcomes and judicial votes (Box-Steffensmeier, Christenson, and Hitt 2013; Collins 2007, 2008a; Collins and Martinek 2015). These studies are premised on the idea that, because interest groups are most concerned with the broader policy outcomes of a decision, we are best served by studying the ideological direction of those decisions, instead of whether a particular litigant won or lost the case. Collins (2008a) finds that amicus briefs influence the ideological direction of the justices' votes, with conservative briefs shaping the voting behavior of liberal justices and vice-versa. This finding demonstrates that amicus briefs can influence judges across ideological lines (see also Box-Steffensmeier, Christenson, and Hitt 2013).

A third means to study amicus influence at the merits stage involves analyzing how amici contribute to judicial opinions. This is an especially important avenue of study since opinions provide the rational for judges' decisions, establishing rules and tests that provide guidelines for the behavior of judges, elected officials, and the American public. Several studies demonstrate that judges cite amicus briefs in their opinions and adopt the arguments of amici (Alger and Krislov 2004; Chauncey 2004; Collins, Corley, and Hamner 2015; Day 2001; Kearney and Merrill 2000; Kolbert 1989; Manz 2002; Samuels 1995; Spriggs and Wahlbeck 1997; Wofford 2015). For example, Behuniak-Long (1991) found that amicus briefs filed in *Webster v. Reproductive Health Services* (1989) shaped the content of the majority opinion, as well as that of the concurring and dissenting opinions. Similarly, Epstein and Kobylka (1992) provide compelling evidence that amicus briefs were influential in shaping the Supreme Court's death penalty and abortion litigation, and Samuels (2004) provides similar evidence with respect to the Court's privacy decisions. Moreover, studies show that amicus briefs increase the chances that judges will write concurring and dissenting opinions (Collins 2008b; Rebe 2013). Such is the case because amicus briefs provide numerous alternative perspectives on the outcomes of cases, creating ambiguity in judges' already uncertain decision-making, while providing them with substantial foundations for concurring and dissenting opinions.

Scholarship on amicus influence on judicial decision-making on the merits has provided a variety of insights into how friends of the court shape judicial behavior. Yet, some areas are less well developed than others. First, as with interest group litigation research in general, it focuses overwhelmingly on the U.S. Supreme Court. Though such studies have shed tremendous light on our understanding of amici, we need to look to other venues to test the generalizability of theories developed in the Supreme Court. This is especially true for research that explores the influence of amicus briefs on the ideological direction of votes and decisions, as well as that investigating amicus influence on opinion content, which focuses almost entirely on the Supreme Court.

Second, the theoretical motivation for these studies is not as well developed as it could be. While there is agreement that amicus briefs are influential because they provide judges with information, little attention has been paid to determining whether particular types of information are more useful than others. This is a particularly important point since amicus briefs supply judges with a wide variety of information and there is good reason to believe that some types of information are more useful than others (e.g., Collins, Corley, and Hamner 2014; Spriggs and Wahlbeck 1997). For example, a survey of Supreme Court law clerks shows that they pay particular attention to amicus briefs providing social scientific data and that amicus briefs are most beneficial in highly technical cases (Lynch 2004; see also Flango, Bross, and Corbally 2006).

Third, our collective understanding of amicus influence would benefit from a consideration of particular aspects of amicus briefs, including their quality and the identity of the amici (e.g., Box-Steffensmeier, Christenson, and Hitt 2013). Similar to interest group scholarship more broadly, research on amicus briefs tends to operationalize amicus influence using the presence or amount of amicus activity, heeding little attention to the quality of the argumentation in the amicus brief or the identity of the amici.[1] Because not all amicus briefs are created equal, future scholars would be well advised to heed greater attention to capturing these attributes.

Fourth, a greater consideration of how the influence of amicus briefs might be enhanced or attenuated would be useful. With a few exceptions (e.g., Collins 2008a; Box-Steffensmeier, Christenson, and Hitt 2013; Collins and Martinek 2015), most studies of amicus influence fail to consider how judges of various ideological stripes might differently respond to amicus briefs. Because there is substantial evidence that receivers are active participants in persuasion (e.g., Crano and Prislin 2006), there is good reason to believe that judges might have varied reactions to amicus briefs. Similarly, interviews with clerks and judges reveal that they believe that amicus briefs are especially useful in particular types of cases, such as complex and technical disputes (Flango, Bross, and Corbally 2006; Lynch 2004; Simard 2008). Conversely, because judges rely more on their attitudes in especially salient cases (Collins 2008c), the influence of amicus briefs might be lessened in such high-profile controversies. A careful consideration of how such factors might mediate the effect of amicus briefs will surely enhance our understanding of friends of the court.

Lastly, there are two types of amicus participation that have gone largely overlooked by scholars. Although rare, from time to time judges invite interest groups to participate as amici curiae. Such invitations might be issued when a litigant refuses to defend a law or an unfavorable lower court decision, or when the court believes that the amicus can provide especially valuable information (e.g., Black and Owens 2012; Goldman 2011). Given that these amicus briefs are filed at the invitation of the court, it seems that judges would be particularly receptive to the information supplied in them. Second, some amicus "briefs" are not briefs at all, but are instead letters or written comments that are submitted to judges. These tend to be much shorter than traditional amicus briefs, usually constituting only a few pages. As far as we can tell, these are most commonly submitted at the trial court level and it is at the discretion of the judge as to whether they become a formal part of the case record. Although uncommon, these forms of amicus participation offer additional opportunities for interest group involvement in the courts. Accordingly, we believe that they deserve some scholarly attention.

Intervention

Without a doubt, the most underdeveloped literature on interest group litigation involves intervention. As intervenors, organizations can enter into a lawsuit that has already commenced at either the trial or appellate levels. Although they are not technically parties to the litigation, intervenors are authorized to make motions, introduce new legal arguments, and present evidence and witnesses at trials (Hall 2012; White 2002). While this is seemingly an attractive strategy for organizations (mimicking in many ways case sponsorship), the requirements for obtaining intervener status are rather amorphous and do not seem to be applied consistently. For example, despite the fact that the Federal Rules of

Civil Procedure detail the conditions under which organizations might obtain intervenor status as a matter of right (in addition to providing guidelines for discretionary intervention), judges treat such requests for intervention as if they are discretionary (Hilliker 1981; Tobias 1991).

The small body of research devoted to intervention focuses primarily on the requirements for intervention, and how these rules are applied (Appel 2000; Hall 2012; Hilliker 1981; Tobias 1991). Much of this scholarship is prescriptive, suggesting best practices to clarify the confusing nature of the requirements for obtaining intervenor status (e.g., Gardner 2002; Vreeland 1990; White 2002). Thus, there is a plethora of opportunities to expand on our understanding of interest group intervention. For example, we know little about how successful organizations are at obtaining intervenor status and what happens when intervenor status is denied. It seems that groups would turn to the amicus brief (Hilliker 1981), but there is little empirical evidence on this point. Moreover, there is scant research on the frequency of intervention, the categories of organizations that successfully become intervenors, or the types of information these groups provide courts. Further, evidence with respect to the influence of intervenors on judicial decisions and opinions is sorely lacking. Thus, we believe that increased attention to the study of interest group intervention will benefit our collective knowledge of group litigation.

Venue Selection

How interest groups choose judicial venues to participate in is a topic relevant to the study of all forms of organizational litigation. Though there is a relatively large literature on why litigants bring cases into the legal system (e.g., Cooter and Rubinfeld 1989; Priest and Klein 1984), there is not nearly as much research on how interest groups select venues for litigation, whether through sponsorship, amicus participation, or intervention. Much of this scholarship focuses on why organizations choose to pursue their goals in the legal system, as opposed to other venues, such as the legislative and executive branches (Engel 2007; Hansford 2004b; Holyoke 2003; Rubin, Curran, and Curran 2001; Scheppele and Walker 1991). However, a few studies explore why groups opt to litigate at different levels of the legal system, including choosing between federal and state courts (Rubenstein 1999; see also Howard 2007).

The question of why groups select certain venues for litigation is a significant one, speaking directly to concerns about interest group influence on the judiciary. For example, if organizations "cherry pick" venues for participation in which judges are likely to rule in their favor—regardless of their participation—this indicates that the groups were not likely influential, despite the appearance of their "success." Thus, it would be useful to approach the study of group influence as a two-stage selection model. For example, the first stage might capture venue selection, with the second stage examining whether the organization was successful in that venue (e.g., Nicholson and Collins 2008). Moreover, venue selection decisions tell us a great deal about how organizations approach the legal system. For example, though it is believed that groups prefer to litigate in venues with the potential for the broadest policy impact (Wasby 1995), such a strategy is accompanied by risks. In particular, while a victory in a venue with nationwide jurisdiction is a huge achievement, a loss can be devastating to the organization, setting it back years in the pursuit of its policy goals. Finally, studies of venue selection across institutions enhance our understanding of how groups view litigation relative to other strategies, such as lobbying legislators or bureaucrats. Insofar as it is important to more closely connect the study of interest group litigation to the scholarship on interest groups more generally (Collins 2008a), venue selection studies can play a key role in this.

Coalition Formation

Similar to venue selection, research on why interest groups work alone or together is relevant to the study of all forms of litigation, although amicus coalitions have garnered the most scholarly attention. Regarding alliance formation, we have a basic understanding of the types of amici that work together (Caldeira and Wright 1990; Collins and Solowiej 2007; see also Box-Steffensmeier and Christenson 2014). For example, these studies show that groups of the same organizational type are inclined to work together in coalitions (e.g., corporations form alliances with other corporations). Yet, because these studies address coalitional activity as only a small part of the more general analysis of amicus activity, they do not speak to the frequency with which different group types work together and what coalitional amicus activity looks like as a whole.

Another line of research explores why groups opt to join coalitions or work alone (e.g., Box-Steffensmeier and Christenson 2014; Whitford 2003). These studies reveal that organizations tend to join coalitions because it allows them to pool their resources while influencing public policy. In other words, it is a low-cost means to lobby the courts. However, the research on litigation coalitions is far less developed than studies of coalition formation in other venues, particularly in legislative settings (e.g., Hojnacki 1997, 1998; Hula 1999). Among other topics, we have only a limited of knowledge of how coalitions form, why organizations opt to join specific coalitions, the means by which work and resources are allocated in coalitions, and how groups claim credit for coalitional victories. We suspect that the use of interviews and surveys will be particularly useful tools for addressing such questions.

Moreover, we have only scratched the surface in our understanding of how turf wars develop between possible coalition partners. As noted above, *District of Columbia v. Heller* was financed by Robert Levy. As part of the litigation strategy, Levy fought the National Rifle Association's (NRA) direct involvement in the case, stating that he did not want the case "to be identified with the usual gun lobby groups" (Teichner 2008). In addition to refusing requests from NRA lawyers to not file the lawsuit in the first place, Levy challenged the organization's attempt to consolidate *Heller* with a similar case filed by the NRA (Gibeaut 2007). Though Wasby (1995) sheds a great deal of insight into the inter-organizational dynamics at play in race relations litigation from the late 1960s to the 1980s, there has been scant attention devoted to this important line of inquiry beyond this.

Finally, there is a very small body of research that investigates the effect of coalitional amicus activity. Collins (2004) evaluated whether the number of interest groups cosigning amicus briefs influence Supreme Court decision-making. Though he provided evidence that the justices responded to the number of briefs filed in a case, he found no support that the size of group coalitions affected litigant success. This suggests that amicus briefs are influential, not because they signal broad support for a cause, but instead because of their legal and policy arguments. In addition, Spriggs and Wahlbeck (1997) found that no relationship exists between the size of amicus coalitions and the adoption of arguments from amicus briefs into Supreme Court majority opinions.

Nonetheless, it would be useful to expand on such studies before shutting the door on the idea that coalition size might matter. For example, Box-Steffensmeier, Christenson, and Hitt (2013) provide evidence that amici who are central actors in coalitions are especially influential in certain circumstances. Though this does not speak to coalition size, it does suggest that judges might pay attention to the identity of coalition members (see also Simard 2008). In addition to these studies that focus on judicial decision-making, Lynch (2004) interviewed Supreme Court law clerks, who overwhelmingly indicated that they would prefer to see more collaboration among amici. This was especially true if this resulted in fewer overall briefs, with those submitted being of higher quality. Further, a very large majority of clerks indicated that they would give special attention to amicus briefs filed by ideologically diverse coalitions. We are certain that applying these insights to the study of the influence of coalitional amicus briefs will prove highly useful.

Extrajudicial Lobbying

Thus far, we have focused on the various methods that are available to organizations to participate directly in the American legal system. Though these are the primary tools at the disposal of groups, it is important to note that there are methods that groups can employ outside of the legal arena in an attempt to influence judicial decisions. Chief among these is making campaign donations to candidates for state judicial offices. Because most state judges are elected in some way, organizations regularly contribute to their political campaigns in hopes of influencing who sits on the state bench and the decisions those judges render.

Though this is a common strategy for groups, there is relatively little research on this topic. We have some knowledge of the types of groups that give to political campaigns and the influence of money on campaigns themselves (Bonneau and Hall 2009; Champagne 2001; Streb 2007), but our understanding of whether campaign donations influence litigation outcomes is more circumscribed. Presumably, groups donate to judicial campaigns with the expectation that a quid pro quo relationship will exist. That is, a group provides campaign funding and, in return, expects some level of favorable treatment from the judge whose campaign the organization funded. Indeed, there is some evidence in support of this relationship (Cann 2007; Cann, Bonneau, and Boyea 2012; Kang and Shepherd 2011; McCall 2008; McCall and McCall 2006; Waltenburg and Lopeman 2000; Ware 1999).

As a growing body of research, this literature is still developing into its own. Because the question of whether campaign contributions influence judicial decision-making speaks to the very impartiality of the American legal system, this is clearly an area worthy of investigation. As it continues to grow, we encourage researchers to focus their studies beyond the analysis of a single state. Because this topic touches on such a sensitive area (the impartiality of judges), it is important that we make our studies as generalizable as possible. Moreover, employing data from multiple states will allow researchers to investigate whether institutional variation among states conditions the effect of money on judicial decisions (Cann, Bonneau, and Boyea 2012; Kang and Shepherd 2011).

In addition, we advocate for the adoption of techniques such as those used by Cann (2007) to address questions of causality. Consider, for example, two states of the world. In the first, groups donate money in an effort to receive favorable rulings. In the second, groups donate money to reward judges who are ideologically supportive of the groups' preferred policies. A correlation between donations and the outcomes of judicial decisions supports both narratives, but does not indicate that the donations *caused* the judge to behave in a particular manner. Due to this, it is important that researchers are attentive to causality concerns that can be addressed through techniques such as the use of selection and instrumental variable models.

Another strategy available to groups involves participating in the selection of federal judges. Because federal judges are appointed by the president and confirmed by the Senate, there are numerous access points available to groups. For example, some groups lobby executive and legislative branch officials who are active in the selection of federal judges. Others testify before the Senate Judiciary Committee and take public positions on behalf of, or in opposition to, a nominee (e.g., Bell 2002; Caldeira and Wright 1998; Scherer 2005; Scherer, Bartels, and Steigerwalt 2008; Segal, Cameron, and Cover 1992; Steigerwalt 2010; Vining 2011). This is a relatively well-established body of research that has reached consensus on a good number of points. For example, it is clear that groups are very active in federal judicial selection and also that group lobbying and testimony can influence the fate of a nominee in the Senate. Yet, our knowledge of other issues is not quite as clear, such as the diversity of the organizations that participate, whether some strategies are more useful than others (e.g., lobbying individual senators versus testifying before the Judiciary Committee), and how groups select which nominees they will support or oppose. In addition, we know very little about how interest groups form coalitions for the purpose of influencing federal judicial selection.

The final extrajudicial strategy we wish to discuss involves interacting with judges outside of the confines of their selection or litigation. This typically involves groups inviting judges to often lavish resorts to give speeches or teach courses and substantially remunerating them for their time (*The New York Times* 2006; *The Washington Post* 2011; see also Black, Owens, and Armaly 2016).[2] Although attending such junkets do not appear to violate any federal laws, it certainly gives rise to numerous ethnical concerns. Equally importantly, this type of extrajudicial activity provides a host of avenues for future research. Among other questions, investigating the types of organizations and judges that participate in these junkets is important, as is unearthing how much judges are remunerated for their attendance. Moreover, the question of what groups expect from these events is significant. For example, do groups invite judges in hopes they will receive favorable outcomes in future cases, do they invite them to reward like-minded jurists, or are their other reasons motivating this choice? As with campaign contributions, this is an extremely important area of investigation as it gets at the heart of questions about judicial impartiality.

Conclusions

Although scholars and the public tend to give short shrift to how interest groups use the courts in pursuit of their goals, it is clear that litigation is a powerful tool at the disposal of interest groups. Indeed, many of the U.S. Supreme Court's most significant decisions in the past century featured substantial involvement by interest groups, including *Brown v. Board of Education* (1954), *Mapp v. Ohio* (1961), and *Grutter v. Bollinger* (2003). In this chapter, we have reviewed academic research on interest group litigation for the purpose of highlighting the current state of our knowledge and suggesting directions for future research. As we have argued, there are only a small number of areas in which continued labors are unlikely to bear additional fruits. Chief among these is the literature that examines the volume of amicus activity at the U.S. Supreme Court, and the types of organizations that file amicus briefs in that institution. In addition, we have a solid understanding of the litigation activities of particular organizations, such as the NAACP LDF.

As it relates to suggestions for future scholarship, we have identified numerous opportunities for advancement, a few of which bear emphasizing. First, due to the almost myopic focus on the U.S. Supreme Court, much of what we know about interest group litigation comes from studies of that venue. Accordingly, we encourage scholars to look beyond the Supreme Court and center their studies on other federal and state judiciaries (as well on foreign judicial bodies). Second, there has been little systematic attention as to why organizations choose venues for litigation, or why they opt to pursue particular litigation strategies (e.g., O'Connor 1980; Scheppele and Walker 1991). Moreover, it is not evident whether certain litigation methods are more effective than others. Third, because scholars have focused on how groups pursue their goals in the legal system, they have given little attention to the effects of extrajudicial lobbying methods, such as inviting judges on lucrative junkets. Finally, the vast majority of research on the influence of interest groups considers how judges respond to group litigation. This ignores the fact that judges' law clerks are often the first, and sometimes the only, eyes on legal documents, such as amicus briefs, as well as the important roles these clerks play in drafting judicial opinions (Lynch 2004; Ward and Weiden 2006). We are confident that our understanding of interest group litigation will be greatly enhanced by developing and testing theoretical expectations for how relatively green law clerks respond to interest group litigation.

Notes

1. A clear exception to this is the voluminous literature on the US Solicitor General (e.g., Bailey, Kamoie, and Maltzman 2005; Black and Owens 2012; Deen, Ignagni, and Meernik 2003; Nicholson and Collins 2008; O'Connor 1983; Pacelle 2003).
2. In addition, groups sometimes organize mass mailings or petition drives in an attempt to influence judicial decisions, and hold vigils outside of courts (Vose 1958). Because there is little reason to believe that such techniques have the potential to be influential, we mention them only in passing.

References

Alger, J., and Krislov, M. 2004. "You've Got to Have Friends: Lessons Learned from the Role of Amici in the University of Michigan Cases." *Journal of College and University Law* 30(3): 503–29.

Appel, P. A. 2000. "Intervention in Public Law Litigation: The Environmental Paradigm." *Washington University Law Review* 78(1): 215–311.

Banner, S. 2003. "The Myth of the Neutral Amicus: American Courts and their Friends, 1790–1890." *Constitutional Commentary* 20(1): 131–50.

Bailey, M. A., Kamoie, B., and Maltzman, F. 2005. "Signals from the Tenth Justice: The Political Role of the Solicitor General in Supreme Court Decision Making." *American Journal of Political Science* 49(1): 72–85.

Baumgartner, F. R., and Leech, B. L. 1998. *Basic Interests: The Importance of Groups in Politics and in Political Science.* Princeton, NJ: Princeton University Press.

Behuniak-Long, S. 1991. "Friendly Fire: Amici Curiae and *Webster v. Reproductive Health Services*." *Judicature* 74: 261–70.

Bell, L. C. 2002. *Warring Factions: Interest Groups, Money, and the New Politics of Senate Confirmation*. Columbus, OH: Ohio State University Press.

Biskupic, J., Roberts, J., and Shiffman, J. 2014. "At America's Court of Last Resort, a Handful of Lawyers Now Dominates the Docket." *Reuters*. Available at: http://www.reuters.com/investigates/special-report/scotus/.

Black, R. C., and Boyd, C. L. 2013. "Selecting the Select Few: The Discuss List and the U.S. Supreme Court's Agenda-Setting Process." *Social Science Quarterly* 94(4): 1124–44.

Black, R. C., and Owens, R. J. 2012. *The Solicitor General and the United States Supreme Court: Executive Branch Influence and Judicial Decisions.* New York, NY: Cambridge University Press.

Black, R. C., Owens, R. J., and Armaly, M. T. 2016. "A Well-Traveled Lot: A Research Note on Judicial Travel by U.S. Supreme Court Justices." *Justice System Journal* 37(4): 367–84.

Bonneau, C. W., and Hall, M. G. 2009. *In Defense of Judicial Elections.* New York, NY: Routledge.

Box-Steffensmeier, J. M., and Christenson, D. P. 2014. "The Evolution and Formation of Amicus Curiae Networks." *Social Networks* 36: 82–96.

Box-Steffensmeier, J. M., Christenson, D. P., and Hitt, M. P. 2013. "Quality over Quantity: Amici Influence and Judicial Decision Making." *American Political Science Review* 107(3): 446–60.

Caldeira, G. A., and Wright, J. R. 1988. "Organized Interests and Agenda Setting in the U.S. Supreme Court." *American Political Science Review* 82(4): 1109–27.

Caldeira, G. A., and Wright, J. R. 1990. "Amici Curiae before the Supreme Court: Who Participates, When, and How Much?" *Journal of Politics* 52(3): 782–806.

Caldeira, G. A., and Wright, J. R. 1998. "Lobbying for Justice: Organized Interests, Supreme Court Nominations, and United States Senate." *American Journal of Political Science* 42(2): 499–523.

Cann, D. M. 2007. "Justice for Sale? Campaign Contributions and Judicial Decisionmaking." *State Politics & Policy Quarterly* 7(3): 281–97.

Cann, D. M., Bonneau, C. W., and Boyea, B. D. 2012. "Campaign Contributions and Judicial Decisions in Partisan and Nonpartisan Elections." In *New Directions in Judicial Politics*, edited by K. T. McGuire. New York, NY: Routledge, 38–52.

Champagne, A. 2001. "Interest Groups and Judicial Elections." *Loyola of Los Angeles Law Review* 34(4): 1391–409.

Chauncey, G. 2004. "What Gay Studies Taught the Court." *GLQ: A Journal of Gay and Lesbian Studies* 10(3): 509–38.

Coffee, J. C., Jr. 1995. "Class Wars: The Dilemma of the Mass Tort Class Action." *Columbia Law Review* 95(6): 1343–465.

Collins, P. M., Jr. 2004. "Friends of the Court: Examining the Influence of Amicus Curiae Participation in U.S. Supreme Court Litigation." *Law & Society Review* 38(4): 807–32.

Collins, P. M., Jr. 2007. "Lobbyists before the U.S. Supreme Court: Investigating the Influence of Amicus Curiae Briefs." *Political Research Quarterly* 60(1): 55–70.

Collins, P. M., Jr. 2008a. *Friends of the Supreme Court: Interest Groups and Judicial Decision Making*. New York, NY: Oxford University Press.

Collins, P. M., Jr. 2008b. "Amici Curiae and Dissensus on the U.S. Supreme Court." *Journal of Empirical Legal Studies* 5(1): 143–70.

Collins, P. M., Jr. 2008c. "The Consistency of Judicial Choice." *Journal of Politics* 70(3): 861–73.

Collins, P. M., Jr., Corley, P. C., and Hamner, J. 2014. "Me Too? An Investigation of Repetition in U.S. Supreme Court Amicus Curiae Briefs." *Judicature* 97(5): 228–34.

Collins, P. M., Jr., Corley, P. C., and Hamner, J. 2015. "The Influence of Amicus Curiae Briefs on U.S. Supreme Court Opinion Content." *Law & Society Review* 49(4): 917–44.

Collins, P. M., Jr., and Martinek, W. L. 2010a. "Who Participates as Amici Curiae in the U.S. Courts of Appeals?" *Judicature* 94(3): 128–36.

Collins, P. M., Jr., and Martinek, W. L. 2010b. "Friends of the Circuits: Interest Group Influence on the U.S. Courts of Appeals." *Social Science Quarterly* 91(2): 397–414.

Collins, P. M., Jr., and Martinek, W. L. 2015. "Judges and Friends: The Influence of Amici Curiae on U.S. Court of Appeals Judges." *American Politics Research* 43(2): 255–82.

Collins, P. M., Jr., and Solowiej, L. A. 2007. "Interest Group Participation, Competition, and Conflict in the U.S. Supreme Court." *Law & Social Inquiry* 32(4): 955–84.

Comparato, S. A. 2003. *Amici Curiae and Strategic Behavior in State Supreme Courts*. Westport, CT: Praeger.

Cooter, R. D., and Rubinfeld, D. L. 1989. "Economic Analysis of Legal Disputes and their Resolution." *Journal of Economic Literature* 27(3): 1067–97.

Corbally, S., Bross, D. C., and Flango, V. E. 2004. "Filing of Amicus Curiae Briefs in State Courts of Last Resort: 1960–2000." *Justice System Journal* 25(1): 39–56.

Cortner, R. C. 1964. *The Wagner Act Cases*. Knoxville, TN: University of Tennessee Press.

Cortner, R. C. 1968. "Strategies and Tactics of Litigants in Constitutional Cases." *Journal of Public Law* 17(2): 287–307.

Cowan, R. B. 1976. "Women's Rights through Litigation: An Examination of the American Civil Liberties Union Women's Rights Project." *Columbia Human Rights Review* 8(2): 373–412.

Crano, W. D., and Prislin, R. 2006. "Attitudes and Persuasion." *Annual Review of Psychology* 57(January): 345–74.

Day, J. G. 2001. "Words that Counted—A Vignette." *Case Western Reserve Law Review* 52(2): 373–4.

Deen, R. E., Ignagni, J., and Meernik, J. 2003. "The Solicitor General as Amicus, 1953–2000: How Influential?" *Judicature* 87(2): 60–71.

Engel, S. M. 2007. "Organizational Identity as a Constraint on Strategic Action: A Comparative Analysis of Gay and Lesbian Interest Groups." *Studies in American Political Development* 21(1): 66–91.

Epstein, L. 1985. *Conservatives in Court*. Knoxville, TN: University of Tennessee Press.

Epstein, L. 1993. "Interest Group Litigation during the Rehnquist Court Era." *Journal of Law and Politics* 9(4): 639–717.

Epstein, L. 1994. "Exploring the Participation of Organized Interests in State Court Litigation." *Political Research Quarterly* 47(2): 335–51.

Epstein, L., and Kobylka, J. F. 1992. *The Supreme Court and Legal Change: Abortion and the Death Penalty*. Chapel Hill, NC: University of North Carolina Press.

Epstein, L., and Rowland, C. K. 1991. "Debunking the Myth of Interest Group Invincibility in the Courts." *American Political Science Review* 85(1): 205–17.

Flango, V. E., Bross, D. C., and Corbally, S. 2006. "Amicus Curiae Briefs: The Court's Perspective." *Justice System Journal* 27(2): 180–90.

Franklin, D. L. 2009. "What Kind of Business-Friendly Court—Explaining the Chamber of Commerce's Success at the Roberts Court." *Santa Clara Law Review* 49(4): 1019–61.

Galanter, M. 1974. "Why the 'Haves' Come out ahead: Speculations on the Limits of Legal Change." *Law & Society Review* 9(1): 95–160.

Gardner, A. M. 2002. "An Attempt to Intervene in the Confusion: Standing Requirements for Rule 24 Intervenors." *University of Chicago Law Review* 69(2): 681–703.

George, T. E., and Epstein, L. 1992. "On the Nature of Supreme Court Decision Making." *American Political Science Review* 85(2): 205–17.

Gibeaut, J. 2007. "A Shot at the Second Amendment." *ABA Journal*. Available at: http://www.abajournal.com/magazine/article/a_shot_at_the_second_amendment/.

Goldman, B. P. 2011. "Should the Supreme Court Stop Inviting Amici Curiae to Defend Abandoned Lower Court Decisions?" *Stanford Law Review* 63(4): 907–72.

Hagle, T. M., and Spaeth, H. J. 2009. "The Presence of Lower-Court Amici as an Aspect of Supreme Court Agenda Setting." *Justice System Journal* 30(1): 1–13.

Hall, M. I. 2012. "Standing of Intervenor-Defendants in Public Law Litigation." *Fordham Law Review* 80(4): 1539–84.

Hansford, T. G. 2004a. "Information Provision, Organizational Constraints, and the Decision to Submit an Amicus Curiae Brief in a U.S. Supreme Court Case." *Political Research Quarterly* 57(2): 219–30.

Hansford, T. G. 2004b. "Lobbying Strategies, Venue Selection, and Organized Interest Involvement at the U.S. Supreme Court." *American Politics Research* 32(2): 170–97.

Hansford, T. G. 2011. "The Dynamics of Interest Representation at the U.S. Supreme Court." *Political Research Quarterly* 64(4): 749–64.

Hilliker, D. 1981. "Rule 24: Effective Intervention." *Litigation* 7(3): 21–3.

Hojnacki, M. 1997. "Interest Groups' Decisions to Join Alliances or Work Alone." *American Journal of Political Science* 41(1): 61–87.

Hojnacki, M. 1998. "Organized Interests' Advocacy Behavior in Alliances." *Political Research Quarterly* 51(2): 437–59.

Hojnacki, M., Kimball, D. C., Baumgartner, F. R., Berry, J. M., and Leech, B. L. 2012. "Studying Organizational Advocacy and Influence: Reexamining Interest Group Research." *Annual Review of Political Science* 15: 379–99.

Holyoke, T. T. 2003. "Choosing Battlegrounds: Interest Group Lobbying across Multiple Venues." *Political Research Quarterly* 56(3): 325–36.

Howard, R. M. 2007. "Controlling Forum Choice and Controlling Policy: Congress, Courts, and the IRS." *Policy Studies Journal* 35(1): 109–23.

Hula, K. 1999. *Lobbying Together: Interest Group Coalitions in Legislative Politics*. Washington, DC: Georgetown University Press.

Kang, M. S., and Shepherd, J. M. 2011. "The Partisan Price of Justice: An Empirical Analysis of Campaign Contributions and Judicial Decisions." *New York University Law Review* 86(1): 69–130.

Kolbert, K. 1989. "The *Webster* Amicus Curiae Briefs: Perspectives on the Abortion Controversy and the Role of the Supreme Court." *American Journal of Law and Medicine* 15(2): 153–68.

Koshner, A. J. 1998. *Solving the Puzzle of Interest Group Litigation*. Westport, CT: Praeger.

Krislov, S. 1963. "The Amicus Curiae Brief: From Friendship to Advocacy." *Yale Law Journal* 72(4): 694–721.

Kearney, J. D., and Merrill, T. W. 2000. "The Influence of Amicus Curiae Briefs on the Supreme Court." *University of Pennsylvania Law Review* 148(3): 743–853.

Laroche, M. 2009. "Is the New York State Court of Appeals Still 'Friendless?' An Empirical Study of Amicus Curiae Participation." *Albany Law Review* 72(3): 703–61.

Lazarus, R. J. 2008. "Advocacy Matters before and within the Supreme Court: Transforming the Court by Transforming the Bar." *Georgetown Law Journal* 96(5): 1488–564.

Liptak, A. 2007. "Carefully Plotted Course Propels Gun Case to Top." *New York Times*. Available at: http://www.nytimes.com/2007/12/03/us/03bar.html?_r=0.

Lynch, K. J. 2004. "Best Friends? Supreme Court Law Clerks on Effective Amicus Curiae Briefs." *Journal of Law and Politics* 20(1): 33–75.

Manz, W. H. 2002. "Citations in Supreme Court Opinions and Briefs: A Comparative Study." *Law Library Journal* 94(2): 267–300.

Martinek, W. L. 2006. "Amici Curiae in the U.S. Courts of Appeals." *American Politics Research* 34(6): 803–24.

McCall, M. M. 2008. "The Politics of Judicial Elections: The Influence of Campaign Contributions on the Voting Patterns of Texas Supreme Court Justices, 1994–1997." *Politics and Policy* 31(2): 314–43.

McCall, M. M., and McCall, M. A. 2006. "Campaign Contributions, Judicial Decisions, and the Texas Supreme Court: Assessing the Appearance of Impropriety." *Judicature* 90(5): 214–25.

McGuire, K. T. 1990. "Obscenity, Libertarian Values, and Decision Making in the Supreme Court." *American Politics Quarterly* 18(1): 47–67.

McGuire, K. T. 1993. *The Supreme Court Bar: Legal Elites in the Washington Community*. Charlottesville, VA: University of Virginia Press.

McGuire, K. T. 1995. "Repeat Players in the Supreme Court: The Role of Experienced Lawyers in Litigation Success." *Journal of Politics* 57(1): 187–96.

McGuire, K. T., and Caldeira, G. A. 1993. "Lawyers, Organized Interests, and the Law of Obscenity: Agenda Setting in the Supreme Court." *American Political Science Review* 87(3): 746–55.

New York Times, The. 2006. "Justice and Junkets," January 27.

Nicholson, C., and Collins, P. M., Jr. 2008. "The Solicitor General's Amicus Curiae Strategies in the Supreme Court." *American Politics Research* 36(3): 382–415.

O'Connor, K. 1980. *Women's Organizations' Use of the Courts*. Lexington, MA: Lexington Books.

O'Connor, K. 1983. "The Amicus Curiae Role of the U.S. Solicitor General in Supreme Court Litigation." *Judicature* 66(5): 256–64.

O'Connor, K., and Epstein, L. 1982. "Amicus Participation in the U.S. Supreme Court: An Appraisal of Hackman's Folklore." *Law & Society Review* 16(2): 311–20.

Orren, K. 1976. "Standing to Sue: Interest Group Conflict in the Federal Courts." *American Political Science Review* 70(3): 723–41.

Pacelle, R. L. 2003. *Between Law and Politics: The Solicitor General and the Structuring of Race, Gender, and Reproductive Rights Litigation*. College Station, TX: Texas A&M University Press.

Pinello, D. R. 2003. *Gay Rights and American Law*. New York, NY: Cambridge University Press.

Priest G. L., and Klein, B. 1984. "The Selection of Disputes for Litigation." *Journal of Legal Studies* 13(1): 1–55.

Provost, C. 2011. "When to Befriend the Court? Examining State Amici Curiae Participation before the U.S. Supreme Court." *State Politics & Policy Quarterly* 11(1): 4–27.

Rebe, R. 2013. "Amicus Curiae and Dissenting Votes at the Texas Supreme Court." *Justice System Journal* 34(2): 171–88.

Rubenstein, W. B. 1999. "The Myth of Superiority." *Constitutional Commentary* 16(3): 599–626.

Rubin, P. H., Curran, C., and Curran, J. F. 2001. "Litigation versus Legislation: Forum Shopping by Rent Seekers." *Public Choice* 107(3/4): 295–310.

Salzman, R., Williams, C. J., and Calvin, B. T. 2011. "The Determinants of the Number of Amicus Briefs Filed before the U.S. Supreme Court, 1953–2001." *Justice System Journal* 32(3): 293–313.

Samuels, S. U. 1995. "Amici Curiae and the Supreme Court's Review of Fetal Protection Policies." *Judicature* 78(5): 236–41.

Samuels, S. U. 2004. *First among Friends: Interest Groups, the U.S. Supreme Court, and the Right to Privacy*. Westport, CT: Praeger.

Scheppele, K. L., and Walker, J. L. 1991. "The Litigation Strategies of Interest Groups." In *Mobilizing Interest Groups in America: Patrons, Professions, and Social Movements*, edited by J. L. Walker, Jr. Ann Arbor, MI: University of Michigan Press, 157–83.

Scherer, N. 2005. *Scoring Points: Politicians, Activists, and the Lower Federal Court Appointment Process*. Palo Alto, CA: Stanford University Press.

Scherer, N., Bartels, B. L., and Steigerwalt, A. 2008. "Sounding the Fire Alarm: The Role of Interest Groups in the Lower Federal Court Confirmation Process." *Journal of Politics* 70(4): 1026–39.

Segal, J. A., Cameron, C. M., and Cover, A. D. 1992. "A Spatial Model of Roll Call Voting: Senators, Constituents, Presidents, and Interest Groups in Supreme Court Confirmations." *American Journal of Political Science* 36(1): 96–121.

Segal, J. A., and Spaeth, H. J. 1993. *The Supreme Court and the Attitudinal Model.* Cambridge: Cambridge University Press.

Sheehan, R. S., Mishler, W., and Songer, D. R. 1992. "Ideology, Status, and the Differential Success of Direct Parties before the Supreme Court." *American Political Science Review* 86(2): 464–71.

Simard, L. S. 2008. "An Empirical Study of Amici Curiae in Federal Court: A Fine Balance of Access, Efficiency, and Adversarialism." *Review of Litigation* 27(Summer): 669–711.

Solberg, R., and Waltenburg, E. N. 2006. "Why Do Interest Groups Engage the Judiciary? Policy Wishes and Structural Needs." *Social Science Quarterly* 87(3): 558–72.

Solowiej, L. A., and Collins, P. M., Jr. 2009. "Counteractive Lobbying in the U.S. Supreme Court." *American Politics Research* 37(4): 670–99.

Songer, D. R., and Kuersten, A. 1995. "The Success of Amici in State Supreme Courts." *Political Research Quarterly* 48(1): 31–42.

Songer, D. R., and Sheehan, R. S. 1993. "Interest Group Success in the Courts: Amicus Participation in the Supreme Court." *Political Research Quarterly* 46(2): 339–54.

Spriggs, J. F., II, and Wahlbeck, P. J. 1997. "Amicus Curiae and the Role of Information at the Supreme Court." *Political Research Quarterly* 50(3): 365–86.

Steigerwalt, A. 2010. *Battle over the Bench: Senators, Interest Groups, and Lower Court Confirmations.* Charlottesville, VA: University of Virginia Press.

Streb, M., J., ed. 2007. *Running for Judge: The Rising Political, Financial, and Legal Stakes of Judicial Elections.* New York, NY: New York University Press.

Tauber, S. C. 1998. "On Behalf of the Condemned? The Impact of the NAACP Legal Defense Fund on Capital Punishment Decision Making in the U.S. Courts of Appeals." *Political Research Quarterly* 51(1): 191–219.

Teichner, M. 2008. "Targeting the Supreme Court." *CBS News.* Available at: http://www.cbsnews.com/news/targeting-the-supreme-court/.

Teles, S. M. 2008. *The Rise of the Conservative Legal Movement: The Battle for Control of the Law.* Princeton, NJ: Princeton University Press.

Tobias, C. 1991. "Standing to Intervene." *Wisconsin Law Review* 1991(3): 415–63.

Vining, R. L. 2011. "Grassroots Mobilization in the Digital Age: Interest Group Response to Supreme Court Nominees." *Political Research Quarterly* 64(4): 790–802.

Vose, C. E. 1955. "NAACP Strategy in the Covenant Cases." *Case Western Reserve Law Review* 6(2): 101–45.

Vose, C. E. 1958. "Litigation as a Form of Pressure Group Activity." *Annals of the American Academy of Political and Social Science* 319(September): 20–31.

Vose, C. E. 1959. *Caucasians Only: The Supreme Court, the N.A.A.C.P., and the Restrictive Covenant Cases.* Berkeley, CA: University of California Press.

Vreeland, C. 1990. "Public Interest Groups, Public Law Litigation, and Federal Rule 24(a)." *University of Chicago Law Review* 57(1): 279–310.

Waltenburg, E. N., and Lopeman, C. S. 2000. "Tort Decisions and Campaign Dollars." *Southeastern Political Review* 28(2): 241–63.

Ward, A., and Weiden, D. L. 2006. *Sorcerers' Apprentices: 100 Years of Law Clerks at the United States Supreme Court.* New York, NY: New York University Press.

Ware, S. J. 1999. "Money, Politics and Judicial Decisions: A Case Study of Arbitration Law in Alabama." *Journal of Law & Politics* 15(4): 645–86.

Wasby, S. L. 1984. "How Planned Is Planned Litigation?" *American Bar Foundation Research Journal* 9(1): 83–138.
Wasby, S. L. 1985. "Civil Rights Litigation by Organizations." *Judicature* 68(9): 337–52.
Wasby, S. L. 1995. *Race Relations Litigation in an Age of Complexity*. Charlottesville, VA: University of Virginia Press.
Washington Post, The. 2011. "The Justices' Junkets," February 20.
White, K. C. 2002. "Rule 24(A) Intervention of Right: Why the Federal Courts Should Require Standing to Intervene." *Loyola of Los Angeles Law Review* 36(Fall): 527–63.
Whitford, A. B. 2003. "The Structures of Interest Coalitions: Evidence from Environmental Litigation." *Business and Politics* 5(1): 45–64.
Wofford, C. B. 2015. "Assessing the Anecdotes: Amicus Curiae, Legal Rules, and the U.S. Supreme Court." *Justice System Journal* 36(3): 274–94.

Cases Cited

Brown v. Board of Education, 347 U.S. 483 (1954).
Grutter v. Bollinger, 539 U.S. 306 (2003).
Mapp v. Ohio, 367 U.S. 643 (1961).
Webster v. Reproductive Health Services, 492 U.S. 490 (1989).

CHAPTER 20

THE RELATIONSHIP BETWEEN COURTS AND LEGISLATURES

THOMAS M. KECK

POLICY outcomes in the United States are routinely shaped by interactions between judicial and legislative institutions. In some respects, this state of affairs was anticipated by those who designed the unusually fragmented system of political authority that has characterized the U.S. government from the beginning. Writing in *The Federalist No. 78*, Alexander Hamilton described courts as bulwarks of a limited Constitution, emphasizing that state and federal legislatures would sometimes threaten the public will or private rights and that the independent judiciary would be in position to thwart these encroachments. Assuming that institutional conflict would be the driving force in American politics, Hamilton defended the controversial design of the federal courts, which were to be staffed by life-tenured judges with the power to invalidate legislative acts that conflict with the Constitution.

At first glance, the relationship between courts and legislatures in the twenty-first century looks rather different. Courts still thwart the legislative will on occasion, but when they do so, it often appears that partisan and ideological (rather than institutional) conflicts are the driving force, with liberal legislators and judges uniting in pursuit of one set of policies and conservative legislators and judges uniting in pursuit of another. Hamilton's vision of institutional conflict between judges defending constitutional principle and legislators pursuing short-term preferences has not disappeared, but it sits in uneasy tension with the partisan and ideological conflicts that have been layered atop it.

As a result, some modern scholarship on courts has suggested that the founding design of institutionally fragmented government power is no longer particularly consequential (if it ever was), because judges generally unite with their partisan allies in the elected branches. A different scholarly tradition, however, has emphasized that the fragmented institutional structure significantly complicates the policy process, with potential normative costs in terms of blurred lines of political accountability but perhaps some countervailing benefits in terms of increased points of access to the policy process, particularly for organized groups of like-minded political actors.

This chapter surveys four contexts in which social scientists and legal scholars have tried to make sense of these institutional interactions. First, some scholars have sought to explain when and why Supreme Court justices (and judges more generally) exercise the power of judicial review. Of course, as Jonathan Casper and Martin Shapiro pointed out decades ago, an exclusive focus on decisions invalidating statutes on constitutional grounds ignores many other significant expressions of judicial power (Casper 1976: 56–60; Shapiro 1964). Nevertheless, exercises of judicial review are often important in their own right and have an additional layer of symbolic import as they (at least theoretically) reflect the pinnacle of judicial power. As such, they are likely to remain the focus of significant scholarly attention for the foreseeable future. A separate and distinct, though overlapping, group of scholars has examined the political foundations of judicial power over time, emphasizing that courts have developed, retained, and expanded the authority to alter policy outcomes only because (and to the extent that) governing legislative coalitions have supported these developments. This body of scholarship is often characterized as a regime politics account of the courts. A third group of scholars has examined the range of legislative responses to assertions of judicial power, emphasizing that the judicial interpretation or even invalidation of a legislative policy is often far from the final word on the policy conflict in question. Taking this perspective a step further, a fourth group of scholars has advocated an "interbranch perspective" on the contemporary policy process, an approach that has significant potential to advance our substantive understanding of judicial politics and to facilitate more and better conversations between scholars of courts and legislatures.

Judicial Review of Legislation

The question of when and why judges invalidate democratically enacted statutes has long been a central preoccupation of judicial politics scholarship in the United States. Hamilton characterized judicial review as a mechanism for enforcing long-term constitutional principle in the face of the countervailing short-term preferences of governing legislative majorities. But at least since an influential 1957 article by Robert Dahl, a "central expectation of the political analysis of judicial review … [has been] that the Supreme Court will use its constitutional veto to obstruct the policies of its ideological foes and validate the policies of its ideological friends" (Whittington and Clark 2009: 1). On Dahl's account, the indeterminacy of constitutional law left the justices with sufficient discretion to pursue their own policy preferences, and the dynamics of the judicial appointment process made it likely that those preferences would reflect the values of the governing partisan coalition (Dahl 1957). As a result, most exercises of judicial review were far from countermajoritarian. To the contrary, Dahl argued that the only time we should expect the Court to invalidate a recently enacted and substantively significant federal statute is during the short-lived transitional periods that follow a national partisan realignment, at which time a majority legislative coalition representing the new partisan order is likely to face a majority judicial coalition representing the old.

Dahl's basic observation regarding the incidence of federal judicial review is now somewhat dated. Writing in 1957, he observed that for the Court's history to date, federal judicial review had been rare and largely insignificant, with the single exception of the New Deal period, when a conservative Court invalidated multiple pieces of significant legislation recently enacted by a Democratic Congress. Subsequent accounts have made clear that federal judicial review was more common in the Court's first 150 years than Dahl indicated. For example, the standard story that the Court invalidated only two federal statutes before the Civil War is wrong (Whittington 2009). Counting not just *Marbury v. Madison* (1803) and *Dred Scott v. Sandford* (1857), but also decisions that invalidated statutes as applied in particular circumstances or that interpreted statutes to rule out certain constitutionally questionable applications, Keith Whittington has identified twenty cases in which the Court enforced constitutional limits on federal legislative authority during this period, along with forty-two others in which the Court considered but rejected such constitutional challenges. (Even counting only decisions invalidating federal statutes on their face, Whittington indicates that the correct number for the pre-Civil War Court is five rather than two (2009: 1327).) By the time of *Dred Scott*, the Court routinely considered constitutional challenges to federal statutes, and though it continued to reject most such challenges, the pace of judicial review had begun to quicken (Whittington 2009: 1325–6).

Twentieth-century patterns of judicial review were likewise somewhat different than Dahl's account might lead us to expect. The frequency of federal judicial review increased on the Warren Court in the 1950s and 1960s and again on the Rehnquist Court in the 1990s and 2000s, in both cases exceeding the New Deal period in the rate of decisions invalidating federal statutes (though not in terms of the significance of the invalidated statutes, where the anti-New-Deal Court remains unsurpassed) (Casper 1976; Keck 2004). This rate then declined under the leadership of Chief Justice John Roberts during the early twenty-first century, approaching historically low levels of federal judicial review (Whittington 2014). Patterns of judicial review of state legislation have been broadly similar, though the timing of particular cycles of increase or decrease does not always match up precisely. For example, on the Warren Court, judicial review of state legislation increased earlier and more sharply than judicial review of federal legislation, and on the Rehnquist and Roberts Courts, judicial review of state legislation declined earlier and more sharply than judicial review of federal legislation (Whittington 2014).

Beyond the incidence of judicial review, Dahl's account of its functions and causes has spawned a wide range of scholarly examinations. His central claims have been tested most systematically by Whittington and Tom Clark, who perhaps surprisingly find no clear partisan effects on the exercise of judicial review. In other words, they find that "the Court rejects the policies of its own party as often as the policies of the opposite party" (Whittington and Clark 2009: 2). Using more sophisticated measures of the ideological distance between the enacting Congress and the invalidating Court, Whittington and Clark (2009: 22–3) find that facial invalidations of federal statutes do increase as that distance increases, but other scholars have marshaled significant evidence that Dahl went too far in dismissing the potentially countermajoritarian character of judicial review. In one notable critique that remains largely unanswered, Casper made clear that the Court's post-1957 decisions invalidating federal statutes appeared to include more instances of the Court challenging the preferences of the national governing coalition than Dahl's account would have predicted (1976: 52–4). More recently, Matthew E. K. Hall and Thomas M. Keck have echoed Casper's argument that a great many of the Court's decisions invalidating federal statutes seem inexplicable as efforts to promote the interests of the governing regime (Hall 2012; Keck 2007a).[1]

Indeed, for the period 1981–2006, close to 50 percent of the Court's federal judicial review decisions involve statutes that were enacted by a bipartisan congressional coalition and then invalidated by a bipartisan judicial coalition (Keck 2007a: 327). Careful tracing of historical processes may uncover evidence that some of these decisions nevertheless represent examples of certain justices trying to promote the interests of their partisan and ideological allies in Congress, but the better explanation for the full pattern is that the justices are acting on the basis of multiple competing motivations, only some of which are captured by the concept of regime preferences. After all, the well-known fragmented character of the U.S. policy process renders judicial institution-building just as challenging as other types of policy-making (Crowe 2012). Most of the time, governing coalitions lack sufficient authority to fully (re)create the judiciary in their image, which may leave judges with significant room to maneuver (Keck and McMahon 2016).

In addition to challenging Dahl's characterization of the Court's decisions invalidating federal statutes, Casper pointed out that Dahl's failure to examine decisions invalidating state and local statutes led him to miss many potentially significant instances in which the Court altered policy outcomes (1976: 57–60). Regime politics scholars have long observed that the judicial review of state and local statutes can serve a regime-supporting function, with the federal courts invalidating statutes that represent local outliers from the national consensus (Klarman 1996; Powe 2000; Whittington 2005a). Matthew E. K. Hall and Ryan C. Black (2013) have argued that the Court more often invalidates state statutes that are close to the national governing consensus than those that are outliers, but it is clear that some of the modern Court's most well-known instances of judicial review fit the description of suppressing local outliers. Consider, for example, the Court's decisions regarding sexual privacy in *Griswold v. Connecticut* (1965) and *Lawrence v. Texas* (2003), each of which invalidated a legislative restriction on private consensual sexual activity that most states had already decriminalized.[2]

Legislative Efforts to Empower the Courts

A key premise of much scholarship on the Court is that the Court and Congress should be understood as opposed to one another, with each institution competing to establish federal policy on its own terms. Dahl's account fundamentally challenged this premise, and in a series of influential articles in the 1990s and 2000s, Whittington, Howard Gillman, and Mark Graber called further attention to the political foundations of judicial review, in the sense that the institution was created and maintained via conscious choices made by elected legislators (Gillman 2002, 2003, 2004, 2006a, 2006b; Graber 1993, 1995, 1998, 2000, 2003, 2005; Whittington 2005a, 2005b, 2009). Influential normative treatments of judicial review had long characterized this key feature of judicial power as fundamentally opposed to legislative authority, even if it was nonetheless sometimes democratically legitimate, as when judges were trying to clear the channels of political change (Bickel 1986; Ely 1980). But Gillman, Graber, Whittington, and other regime politics scholars have documented repeated examples in which governing partisan coalitions actively sought to empower federal judges to settle key policy and political conflicts. This phenomenon dates to the earliest days of the republic, as the members of Congress who drafted and enacted the Judiciary Act of 1789 clearly assumed that federal courts would exercise the power of judicial review and used this landmark statute to grant the federal jurisdiction necessary for them to do so (Crowe 2012: 29–43; Graber 2003). Since that first statute, governing legislative majorities have repeatedly found it in their interest to expand the size and jurisdiction of the federal courts (Crowe 2012; Gillman 2002). And even during periods of institutional stability rather than change, governing coalitions have regularly signaled to sympathetic members of the federal judiciary that it would be helpful for the judges to settle certain pending issues (Graber 1993; Lemieux and Lovell 2010; Whittington 2005a). Judges have sometimes heeded these signals, as "the Supreme Court has often used the power of judicial review to advance rather than to obstruct the political projects of political leaders" (Whittington 2009: 1259). This dynamic operates at the state as well as the federal level, as Scott Barclay's work on the state constitutional politics of same-sex marriage demonstrates that legislators sometimes empower courts on the assumption that they will exercise judicial review in ways that the legislators support, and they sometimes even signal judges that particular exercises of judicial review would be welcome (2010).

This regime politics perspective on the political foundations of judicial power has led a number of scholars to advance Dahlian accounts of the Court's exercise of judicial review. Regarding the pre-Civil War Court, for example, Whittington emphasizes that "the Court used judicial review to work with, rather than against, Congress during this period to construct a new national government. The Court never created serious obstructions to important policies favored by active majorities when reviewing federal laws before the Civil War. The Court established the power of judicial review by using it.

But the Court used it to validate congressional actions or correct congressional errors, not to block what Congress was vested in trying to accomplish" (2009: 1329; see also Graber 1993; Whittington 2005b: 823–4).

The claim that judicial power develops and survives only because (and to the extent that) legislators and other power holders tolerate it has been developed most fully in the U.S. context by Justin Crowe and in the comparative context by Ran Hirschl. Crowe has emphasized that Article III of the original Constitution left open multiple key questions regarding the institutional structure of the federal courts, including the size of SCOTUS, the very existence of lower federal courts, and the jurisdiction of all of them (2012: 27–8). On Crowe's account, when members of Congress have stepped in to fill this void—from the Judiciary Act of 1789 through the Foreign Intelligence Surveillance Act of 1978—they have usually had a complex mix of goals in mind, including a desire to ensure a well-functioning legal system, but the mix has virtually always included partisan and ideological motivations. For example, legislators have regularly sought to expand federal judicial power to "[entrench] their policy preferences past the duration of the current political regime"; "to shift particular classes of disputes from hostile forums where their interests are unlikely to be represented to friendlier forums more receptive to their desired ends"; and to provide a venue into which divisive issues can be diverted, "thereby enhancing electoral prospects by sidestepping contentious and coalition-disrupting political decisions" (2012: 11–12).

In the comparative context, Hirschl has likewise emphasized that the post-World War II proliferation of written bills of rights, enforced by independent constitutional courts, has come about largely because existing power holders believed that such courts would more often than not advance the power holders' own preferred policy visions (2004). In a helpful summary of this body of work, Graber has emphasized that:

> Judicial review is established and maintained by elected officials. Adjudication is one of many means politicians and political movements employ when seeking to make their constitutional visions the law of the land. Elected officials provide vital political foundations for judicial power by creating constitutional courts, vesting those courts with jurisdiction over constitutional questions, staffing those courts with judges prone to exercising judicial power, assisting or initiating litigation aimed at having those courts declare laws unconstitutional, and passing legislation that encourages justices to make public policy in the guise of statutory or constitutional interpretation. (2005: 427–8)

Some scholars sympathetic to the regime politics approach have retained an emphasis on the possibility of relatively independent judicial action under certain conditions. As Whittington has noted with regard to *Lochner*-era judicial review:

> The Court's decisions against the government were less reflections of a party platform than of a legal sensibility. Insulated from political pressures and immersed in

> legal tradition, the Court was less likely than Congress to look with approval on the suspension of traditional elements of criminal due process or backdoor efforts to raise revenue or to extend federal police powers.
>
> (2005b: 856–7)

Keck has advanced a similar account of First Amendment free speech decisions during the Rehnquist era, as have Keck and Kevin J. McMahon with regard to abortion rights decisions during the Rehnquist and Roberts eras (Keck 2007a; Keck and McMahon 2016; see also Miller 2009: 33–5).

Nonetheless, the driving logic of the regime politics approach is a principal–agent account of Congress–Court relations. Gillman has articulated this logic most explicitly, arguing "that the expansion of federal judicial power in the late-nineteenth century is best understood as the sort of familiar partisan or programmatic entrenchment that we frequently associate with legislative delegations to executive or quasi-executive agencies." Much of this expansion "resulted from the passage of two key pieces of legislation … that were part of the Republican Party's efforts to restructure national institutions better to facilitate national economic development." This agenda eventually led to a well-known "expansion of federal administrative capacity," but before the administrative state took hold, "economic nationalists were successful at promoting large-scale enterprise by extending more reliable legal institutions to investors and producers who operated within a national market." Federal judges were "the principal agents of this agenda" (2002: 512–13). Again, the key insight that has emerged from this body of literature is that Congress often seeks to empower the courts, and that it does so because it hopes that judges will serve as effective agents of congressional will. Some regime politics accounts have acknowledged that there have likewise been regular congressional attempts to limit judicial power, but they have argued that "very few [such attempts] have been successful in any meaningful sense." Indeed, the "developmental path for judicial capacity … has been overwhelmingly, though not irreversibly, upward," largely because legislators "have often viewed the judiciary as a potential partner in, rather than an obstacle to, their governing coalitions" (Crowe 2012: 17).

Legislative Efforts to Constrain the Courts

While regime politics scholars emphasize legislative efforts to empower the courts, other scholars have long emphasized legislative efforts to constrain the courts. The Madisonian design of the Constitution sought to preserve the judicial independence emphasized by Hamilton, but it also provided a number of mechanisms by which Congress might check objectionable patterns of decisions issuing from the federal courts. Article III prohibits Congress from reducing federal judicial salaries, but by declining to index such salaries to inflation, Congress remains free to exert some economic pressure on judges. Article II gives Congress the power to remove federal judges by impeachment, though one of the earliest exercises of this power produced an entrenched norm against using it to remove judges because of dissatisfaction with the ideological or partisan tenor of their decisions (Whittington 1999: 20–71). Congress's most significant power over the federal courts derives from the Article III provisions regarding jurisdiction. Indeed, from the beginning, Congress has regularly responded to unwanted judicial decisions by considering (and occasionally enacting) bills that withdraw certain subjects from the courts' purview (Miller 2009: 156–84; Murphy 1962). As Clark (2011) has emphasized, such court-curbing bills are primarily position-taking endeavors by legislators, designed to signal to voters that the legislators are doing something about some set of objectionable court decisions.

As Clark has likewise emphasized, such bills also serve as signals to the justices regarding levels of public support for the Court. If the justices are strategic actors, then it is possible that they respond to such signals by refraining from exercising judicial review in instances where they otherwise might have done so (Clark 2011: 23). A substantial body of literature explores the justices' responses to such external signals and constraints (Bailey and Maltzman 2011: 95–120; Epstein and Knight 1998: 138–81; for a critique, see Gillman 2004: 376–7). This strategic model serves in some ways as the mirror image of the literature on the political construction of judicial power described above. Where regime politics scholars emphasize legislative signals to judges that their active exercise of judicial review in particular circumstances would be received favorably, advocates of the strategic model tend to emphasize situations in which judges would like to actively assert their authority in ways that are contrary to legislative preferences, but the legislators discourage such decisions by signaling the costs to the courts that may result.

While broad curbs on judicial authority have long been theoretical possibilities, most congressional responses to the courts have consisted of narrower efforts to respond to individual decisions with legislation that would push policy back in Congress's preferred direction. Federal legislators have successfully used the constitutional amendment process to reverse a constitutional decision issued by the Court only four times, though such reversals occur much more regularly with regard to state constitutional decisions issued by state high courts. Consider, for example, the enactment of Proposition 8 by California voters in November 2008, which amended the state constitution to reverse a holding by the California Supreme Court that had legalized same-sex marriage earlier in the year.[3] This reversal was part of a broader state constitutional backlash that followed a series of marriage equality decisions issued by state high courts.[4] The principal reason that this phenomenon occurs so much more often at the state than the federal level is that most state constitutions are significantly easier to formally amend than is the federal constitution.

Short of a constitutional amendment, however, Congress has a variety of additional tools available for altering or even reversing the policies that result from the Court's constitutional holdings. Dahl characterized such congressional responses as evidence of judicial weakness, arguing that the Court's rare constitutional invalidations of significant federal statutes were often effectively reversed and hence that the Court "by itself ... is almost powerless to affect the course of national policy" (1957: 293). Updating Dahl's data, Joseph Ignagni and James Meernik (1994) found that Congress had reversed the policy results of thirteen of the sixty-five federal judicial review decisions issued from 1954 to 1990. They also found that Congress had reversed the policy results of 4.6 percent of the Court's decisions invalidating state laws during that period (Meernik and Ignagni 1995: 52). As Bethany Blackstone and J. Mitchell Pickerill have emphasized, however, judges and legislators are often interested in different things (Blackstone 2013; Pickerill 2004). Legislators tend to focus on their policy priorities and the political gains they anticipate from pursuing those priorities, while judges are sometimes more preoccupied with the technical requirements of legal doctrine. As such, it is often possible for both judges and legislators to have their way, with Congress responding to an exercise of federal judicial review in ways that achieve at least some of Congress's original policy goals without directly challenging the Court's legal holding. As Blackstone puts it, most congressional responses to exercises of judicial review "attempt to partially or fully reverse the Court's policies while simultaneously working within the bounds of the legal rules announced by the Court" (2013: 200).

Consider, for example, the Rehnquist Court's invalidation of the Gun Free School Zones Act for exceeding the scope of congressional power to regulate interstate commerce.[5] Congress responded by enacting a revised statute that applied only to guns that had traveled in interstate commerce, and the federal courts responded in turn by upholding this revised law.[6] Dahl might characterize this episode as evidence of the Court's insignificance, but as Casper (1976: 62) notes, the policies that emerge from such processes of institutional interaction are often significantly different than the status quo ante. In other words, it is true that judicial decisions on controversial policy questions are often far from final, but the same is true for legislative enactments on controversial policy questions. In a fragmented system of political authority, no institution has the final word; instead, policy emerges from a never-ending process of institutional interaction (Casper 1976: 61–2; Keck 2014).

Such institutional interactions have drawn particular scholarly attention in the context of the Court's statutory interpretation decisions, where congressional authority to respond to the courts is at its apex. These decisions represent the justices' efforts to clarify the meaning of federal statutory law as applied to a particular legal conflict. If the justices adopt an interpretation that is inconsistent with the preferences of current or future Congresses, the legislators can fully reverse the holding via a new statutory enactment, as when a Democratic Congress reversed the Roberts Court's holding in *Ledbetter v. Goodyear* (2007) by enacting the Lily Ledbetter Fair Pay Act.[7] The presence of multiple veto points within the federal legislative process will often allow supporters of the Court's decision to prevent such legislative overrides, but as William Eskridge (1991) and Jeb Barnes (2004a) have shown, Congress succeeds on this front with some regularity.

In a widely influential study, Eskridge documented that each Congress from the 94th through the 101st (1975–1990) overrode an average of twelve statutory decisions issued by the Supreme Court and thirty-five issued by federal courts as a whole (1991: 338).

Updating and extending Eskridge's data, Lawrence Baum and Lori Hausegger reported that at least 5.6 percent of the Court's statutory decisions during its 1978–89 Terms were overridden by Congress in whole or in large part (2004: 111). On Eskridge's account, "congressional overrides are most likely when a Supreme Court interpretation reveals an ideologically fragmented Court, relies on the text's plain meaning and ignores legislative signals, and/or rejects positions taken by federal, state, or local governments" (1991: 334).

Carrying Eskridge's account a step further, Barnes examined the process of legislative and judicial interactions in a random sample of 100 override bills enacted from 1974 to 1990. Drawing on these data, Barnes argued that just over half of the override bills succeeded in increasing judicial consensus in Congress's intended direction. In other words, when the federal courts divide on the meaning of an existing statute (or when they coalesce around an interpretation that Congress rejects), Congress sometimes steps in to clarify the law, and Congress is often successful in this regard (2004a: 84–96). Then again, Barnes's data also made clear that Congress fails in this regard almost half the time. In other words, the federal courts regularly persist in enforcing interpretations of federal statutory law that Congress has attempted to correct. Such judicial persistence sometimes results from weak congressional signals issuing from an override bill that includes vague or contradictory provisions. At other times, it results from partisan judicial resistance to congressional policy goals; Barnes' data suggest that such resistance is particularly likely on politically divisive issues involving the legal rights of discrete and insular minorities (2004a: 123–8, 169–71).

Thus, even in a context where congressional authority to reverse the decisions of federal courts is unambiguous, and even in cases in which Congress has run the gauntlet of the fragmented legislative process to enact such a reversal, the policy outcomes that result are often those that were adopted by the courts. We should also expect federal judicial decisions to shape policy outcomes in a large number of cases in which members of Congress try but fail to enact an override.

Courts and the Policy Process

Building on these insights, a distinct though overlapping group of scholars has pointed toward a research enterprise that emphasizes the ongoing—indeed, never-ending—interaction between judicial and legislative institutions in the policy process. Once again, Casper's response to Dahl is a helpful starting point. In addition to criticizing Dahl for ignoring the Court's decisions involving judicial review of state legislation and statutory interpretation of federal legislation, Casper objected that Dahl overemphasized congressional reversals of the Court's decisions involving judicial review of federal legislation. Casper agreed with Dahl that the Court is generally unable to shape policy outcomes "by itself," but observed that the same is true with regard to all other policy-making institutions in the famously fragmented American policy-making system (Casper 1976: 61; see Dahl 1957: 293). The Court is unable to dictate policy outcomes on its own, but like other key institutions in the U.S. constitutional system, it has the capacity to influence policy processes and outcomes in a variety of ways—for example, by forcing long-ignored issues onto the agenda of other policymakers or by drawing public attention to political movements in ways that attract new resources and supporters (1976: 60–3). A wide range of scholarship has followed Casper's lead in trying to integrate the study of courts into broader accounts of the policy process in the United States. This emerging literature is part of a broader policy-focused (or Schattschneiderian) turn in American politics scholarship (Hacker and Pierson 2014).

One line of research has built on Dahl's skeptical account of judicial influence, with Gerald Rosenberg famously describing the Court as a "hollow hope" for social movements. Rosenberg's initial account emphasized the Court's limited capacity to enforce compliance with its controversial holdings, and he subsequently observed that some exercises of judicial review prove so controversial that they spark a political backlash that effectively reverses the courts' decisions (Rosenberg 1991, 2008: 339–429; see also Klarman 2004, 2005).

A separate line of research has followed Casper by conducting case studies of judicial-legislative interactions that appear to show a greater degree of judicial influence on policy outcomes than Dahl and Rosenberg acknowledged. Early examples of this approach include Walter Murphy and Martin Shapiro's examinations of congressional interactions with the Warren Court (Murphy 1962; Shapiro 1964). More recent examples include influential works by Barnes (2011), Malcolm Feeley and Edward Rubin (1998), and Shep Melnick (1983, 1994). Melnick's studies have demonstrated that the modern welfare regulatory state provides routine opportunities for federal judges to intervene in policy conflicts between federal legislators and administrative agencies, and that a great many of these interventions go unaddressed (or only partly addressed) by Congress. Like Barnes and Eskridge, Melnick acknowledges that Congress regularly overrides statutory interpretations issued by federal courts, but emphasizes that enacting such overrides "is seldom easy and ... usually takes several years. Those who favor the courts' interpretation can often block remedial legislation or demand concessions. By altering the policy status quo, the courts inevitably affect the bargaining power of various legislative factions." As a result, "one would be hard-pressed to find a major domestic policy area in which statutory interpretation by the federal courts did not play a significant role in shaping the activities of government" (1994: 6–7). Drawing on case studies of judicial/legislative interactions with regard to Aid to Families with Dependent Children, food stamps, and educational services for children with disabilities, Melnick makes clear that the fragmented nature of the policy process effectively "insulate[s many] judicially initiated [reforms] from legislative revision" (1994: 114).

One key part of Melnick's story, subsequently elaborated by Tom Burke and Sean Farhang, is that Congress in the 1960s and 1970s repeatedly enacted sweeping welfare and regulatory statutes that delegated substantial enforcement authority to the courts (Melnick 1994: 25–34, 140–59, 175–9; Burke 2002; Farhang 2010; see also Kagan 2001; 2004: 28–30; Mulroy 2012). This sort of congressional delegation may reflect both strategic considerations (such as insulating implementation from political opponents or reining in subnational government actors) and fiscal considerations (such as privatizing the costs of implementation in an era of budgetary austerity). Both sets of factors are likely to persist for the foreseeable future. From this angle, the modern Court's statutory interpretation decisions are sometimes explicable on grounds similar to those emphasized by the regime politics account of constitutional development. That is, active assertions of judicial power—even those that appear at first glance opposed to legislative authority—are sometimes traceable to and supported by legislative preferences. But as with the constitutional decisions emphasized by the regime politics literature, the Court's statutory decisions will sometimes depart from legislative preferences as well. As such, any comprehensive account of the Court's institutional power must include an examination of its ability to alter policy outcomes via federal statutory interpretation (Casper 1976: 56–7).

The case studies conducted by Melnick and like-minded scholars are methodologically well suited to advancing our understanding of the processes by which judicial and legislative (and administrative) actors interact in pursuit of particular policy goals, but it is also important for scholars to examine what might be thought of as "medium-N" groups of cases—groups that are small enough to capture some of the benefits of case studies with regard to tracing causal processes, but large enough to reveal "recurring patterns within the ongoing, inter-branch dialogue that defines—and refines—American law and policy-making" (Barnes 2004a: 195; see also Kapiszewski 2011; Keck 2007a: 324).

Barnes and Mark Miller have gone the furthest in urging scholars to explicitly adopt an interbranch perspective on the policy process (Barnes and Miller 2004). On Barnes's description, this approach "holds that American politics and policy making emerge from the continuing interaction among 'separated institutions sharing power' [and that] this intricate dispersal of power creates a complex and shifting web of relations among various centers of power." Rather than "focus[ing] on the behavior of any single actor or on any one point in the process ... the central task is to understand the shifting relationships among these actors across policy areas and over time" (2007: 27–8).

Barnes characterizes some well-known regime politics studies as examples of interbranch analysis (2007: 31–3), and the two approaches do share some key similarities. Both bodies of literature typically involve a shift in the unit of analysis "from judicial decisions in individual cases to patterns of rule application over time and across policy areas" (Barnes 2004a: 195). In addition, both tend to "recast legal processes in political terms," while also "underscor[ing] how courts perform basic political functions differently than other policy-making forums" (Barnes 2007: 37). But regime politics scholars themselves have not typically adopted the language of interbranch analysis, and most scholars who do use this language have produced studies that depart from regime politics accounts in some key respects. The departure rests in part on different substantive areas of focus, with regime politics scholars most often writing about constitutional decisions issued by the Supreme Court and interbranch analysis scholars most often writing about decisions issued by lower courts on complex issues of welfare and regulatory policy (Barnes 2007: 33–4). But the two approaches also evince some theoretical differences that have not yet been adequately explored.

As noted above, the regime politics accounts rest implicitly on a principal–agent conception of the relationship between legislatures and courts, though they typically do not use the formal language in which principal–agent theory is most often deployed. But one of the key lessons of the interbranch perspective on policy-making is that the principal–agent model does not adequately capture the complex interactions among multiple policymakers in the United States. As Burke emphasizes, the problem with principal–agent theory as applied to statutory interpretation is that there are both too many principals and too many agents (2004: 137). More generally, "there is no hierarchy of lawmakers in the American system of separated institutions sharing power and there are a welter of competing agents empowered to give laws meaning in the decentralized American administrative state" (Barnes and Miller 2004: 11; see also Kagan 2001, 2004). As Barnes notes, "the implicit goal [of the framers' design] was to create dynamic tension among redundant branches facing countervailing political pressures and not an orderly division of labor between elected principals and appointed agents" (2004b: 47).

Rather than seeking to assess the degree to which judges behave as faithful agents of their legislative principals, interbranch scholars generally emphasize that "courts [serve] as an alternative political forum for ... interests who [face] political obstacles in the elective branches of government" (Kagan 2004: 17). Interests that lose in court regularly appeal to legislators for relief and interests that lose in the legislatures regularly appeal to courts in turn. Indeed, interests that are winning in one set of institutions regularly appeal to the other set to expand and consolidate their victories. These dynamics have received the greatest scholarly attention in the contexts of welfare and regulatory policy, where interests regularly appeal their legislative and/or judicial defeats to executive branch regulators as well (Kagan 2004; Melnick 1994). But similar dynamics also play out in constitutional law (Kagan 2004: 21–4; Keck 2014). In a yet further departure from the principal–agent perspective, interbranch scholars have emphasized that judge-made law (much of it emerging from organized litigation) deeply shapes congressional (and administrative) policy discourse (Barnes 2011; Barnes and Burke 2015; Shapiro 1968; Silverstein 2009). From this angle, the so-called agents are influencing their principals as much as the reverse.

Whither the Field?

One key implication of both the regime politics accounts of constitutional development and the interbranch accounts of the policy process is that judicial politics should be understood as part of democratic politics, rather than external to it. As Barnes puts it, "federal courts and agencies should not be seen as exceptions to democratic rule in the United States, simply because their members are not elected. Instead, appointed federal judges and bureaucrats are part of the accepted fabric of American democracy that includes a wide range of policy forums, each of which is designed to give voice to different types of factions and respond to different types of political resources" (2004b: 44; see also Barnes and Burke 2015; Crowe 2012: 22; Keck 2014).

An additional and related shared theme is that empirical inquiries into the behavior of judges and the operation of courts should be designed in ways that inform important normative questions about what we might want judges and courts to do. The regime politics approach developed in part as an effort to debunk the countermajoritarian difficulty by making clear that active assertions of judicial power sometimes have substantial democratic support (Keck 2007b). The leading advocate of the interbranch perspective has emphasized that "the crucial issue in evaluating contemporary interbranch relations is ... whether—and under what conditions—interbranch relations promote important democratic outcomes, such as open deliberation and coalition-building among varied interests" (Barnes 2004b: 37). Barnes himself has concluded that "inter-branch policy-making [regularly] promotes broad political participation," including by groups representing the public interest and/or relatively powerless segments of society, though he and Burke have also noted the ways in which adversarial legalism tends to individualize interests and exacerbate political conflict (Barnes 2004a: 187–9; Barnes and Burke 2015). Other scholars have emphasized other downsides of fragmented authority, such as blurred lines of political accountability that make it harder for ordinary citizens to hold policymakers responsible for objectionable policies (Lovell 2003). Either way, fragmented authority has long been a central feature of the U.S. policy process, and judicial institutions have long played a key role in the operation of this process. These facts provide a fruitful ground for scholarly investigations that continue to advance our understanding and evaluation of courts and judges.

Acknowledgments

The author would like to thank Jeb Barnes and Logan Strother for helpful comments on earlier drafts.

Notes

1. Note also Whittington and Clark's finding that decisions to invalidate a statute as applied are not influenced by the ideological distance between the Court and the enacting Congress, though they are influenced by the distance between the Court and the governing president at the time of judicial consideration. This finding suggests that the justices may be more likely to invalidate statutes as applied when they fear that the current executive will support applications that the justices do not favor (2009: 24–5).
2. *Griswold v. Connecticut*, 381 U.S. 479 (1965); *Lawrence v. Texas*, 539 U.S. 558 (2003).
3. In re Marriage Cases, 43 Cal.4th 757 (Cal. 2008).
4. In addition to the California holding, the most notable of these decisions were *Baehr v. Lewin*, 74 Haw. 530 (Haw. 1993); *Baker v. State of Vermont*, 170 Vt. 194 (Vt. 1999); *Goodridge v. Department of Public Health*, 440 Mass. 309 (Mass. 2003); and *Varnum v. Brien*, 763

N.W.2d 862 (Iowa 2009). On the backlash that was sparked by these decisions, see Klarman (2005); Rosenberg (2008); for an alternative account of the aftermath of these decisions, see Keck (2009).

5. *United States v. Lopez*, 514 U.S. 549 (1995).
6. *United States v. Danks*, 221 F.3d 1037 (8th Cir. 1999), cert. denied, *Danks v. United States*, 528 U.S. 1091 (2000).
7. *Ledbetter v. Goodyear Tire & Rubber Co.*, 550 U.S. 618 (2007).

References

Bailey, M. A., and Maltzman, F. 2011 *The Constrained Court: Law, Politics, and the Decisions Justices Make*. Princeton, NJ: Princeton University Press.

Barclay, S. 2010. "In Search of Judicial Activism in the Same Sex Marriage Cases: Sorting the Evidence from Courts, Legislatures, Initiatives and Amendments. *Perspectives on Politics* 8(1): 111–26.

Barnes, J. 2004a. *Overruled? Legislative Overrides, Pluralism, and Contemporary Court–Congress Relations*. Stanford, CA: Stanford University Press.

Barnes, J. 2004b. "Adversarial Legalism, the Rise of Judicial Policymaking, and the Separation-of-Powers Doctrine." In *Making Policy, Making Law: An Interbranch Perspective*, edited by M. C. Miller and J. Barnes. Washington, DC: Georgetown University Press, 35–52.

Barnes, J. 2007. "Bringing the Courts Back in: Interbranch Perspectives on the Role of Courts in American Politics and Policy Making." *Annual Review of Political Science* 10: 25–43.

Barnes, J. 2011. *Dust-up: Asbestos Litigation and the Failure of Commonsense Policy Reform*. Washington, DC: Georgetown University Press.

Barnes, J., and Burke, T. 2015. *How Policy Shapes Politics: Rights, Courts, Litigation, and the Struggle over Injury Compensation*. New York, NY: Oxford University Press.

Barnes, J. and Miller, M. C. 2004. "Putting the Pieces Together: American Lawmaking from an Interbranch Perspective." In *Making Policy, Making Law: An Interbranch Perspective*, edited by M. C. Miller and J. Barnes. Washington, DC: Georgetown University Press, 3–12.

Baum, L., and Hausegger L. 2004. "The Supreme Court and Congress: Reconsidering the Relationship." In *Making Policy, Making Law: An Interbranch Perspective*, edited by M. C. Miller and J. Barnes. Washington, DC: Georgetown University, 107–22.

Bickel, A. M. 1986. *The Least Dangerous Branch: The Supreme Court at the Bar of Politics*, 2nd ed. New Haven, CT: Yale University Press.

Blackstone, B. 2013. "An Analysis of Policy-Based Congressional Responses to the U.S. Supreme Court's Constitutional Decisions." *Law and Society Review* 47:1 (March): 199–228.

Burke, T. F. 2002. *Lawyers, Lawsuits and Legal Rights: The Struggle over Litigation in American Society*. Berkeley, CA: University of California.

Burke, T. F. 2004. "The Judicial Implementation of Statutes: Three Stories about Courts and the Americans with Disabilities Act." In *Making Policy, Making Law: An Interbranch Perspective*, edited by M. C. Miller and J. Barnes. Washington, DC: Georgetown University Press, 123–39.

Casper, J. D. 1976. "The Supreme Court and National Policy Making." *American Political Science Review* 70 (March): 50–63.

Clark, T. S. 2011. *The Limits of Judicial Independence*. New York, NY: Cambridge University Press.

Crowe, J. 2012. *Building the Judiciary: Law, Courts, and the Politics of Institutional Development*. Princeton, NJ: Princeton University Press.

Dahl, R. A. 1957. "Decision-Making in a Democracy: The Supreme Court as a National Policy Maker." *Journal of Public Law* 6: 279–95.

Ely, J. H. 1980. *Democracy and Distrust: A Theory of Judicial Review*. Cambridge, MA: Harvard University Press.

Epstein, L. and Knight, J. 1998. *The Choices Justices Make*. Washington, DC: CQ.

Eskridge, W. N., Jr. 1991. "Overriding Supreme Court Statutory Interpretation Decisions." *Yale Law Journal* 101: 331–455.

Farhang, S. 2010. *The Litigation State: Public Regulation and Private Lawsuits in the United States*. Princeton, NJ: Princeton University Press.

Feeley, M. M., and Rubin, E. L. 1998. *Judicial Policy Making and the Modern State: How the Courts Reformed America's Prisons*. New York, NY: Cambridge University Press.

Gillman, H. 2002. "How Political Parties Can Use the Courts to Advance their Agendas: Federal Courts in the United States, 1875–1891. *American Political Science Review* 96(3): 511–24.

Gillman, H. 2003. "Robert G. McCloskey, Historical Institutionalism, and the Arts of Judicial Governance." In *The Pioneers of Judicial Behavior*, edited by N. Maveety. Ann Arbor, MI: University of Michigan, 336–60.

Gilman, H. 2004. "Martin Shapiro and the Movement from 'Old' to 'New' Institutionalist Studies in Public Law Scholarship." *Annual Review of Political Science* 7: 363–82.

Gilman, H. 2006a. "Regime Politics, Jurisprudential Regimes, and Unenumerated Rights." *University of Pennsylvania Journal of Constitutional Law* 9(October): 107–19.

Gilman, H. 2006b. "Party Politics and Constitutional Change: The Political Origins of Liberal Judicial Activism." In *The Supreme Court and American Political Development*, edited by R. Kahn and K. I. Kersch. Lawrence, KS: University Press of Kansas, 138–68.

Graber, M. A. 1993. "The Non-Majoritarian Difficulty: Legislative Deference to the Judiciary." *Studies in American Political Development* 7(Spring): 35–73.

Graber, M. A. 1995. "The Passive-Aggressive Virtues: *Cohens v. Virginia* and the Problematic Establishment of Judicial Power." *Constitutional Commentary* 12: 67–92.

Graber, M. A. 1998. "Federalist or Friend of Adams: The Marshall Court and Party Politics." *Studies in American Political Development* 12(Fall): 229–66.

Graber, M. A. 2000. "The Jacksonian Origins of Chase Court Activism." *Journal of Supreme Court History* 25: 17–39.

Graber, M. A. 2003. "Establishing Judicial Review: Marbury and the Judicial Act of 1789." *Tulsa Law Review* 38(Summer): 609–50.

Graber, M. A. 2005. "Constructing Judicial Review." *Annual Review of Political Science* 8: 425–51.

Hacker, J. S., and Pierson, P. 2014. "After the 'Master Theory': Downs, Schattschneider, and the Rebirth of Policy-Focused Analysis." *Perspectives on Politics* 12(Sept.): 643–62.

Hall, M. E. K. 2012. "Rethinking Regime Politics." *Law and Social Inquiry* 37(Fall): 878–907.

Hall, M. E. K., and Black, R. C. 2013. "Keeping the Outliers in Line: Judicial Review of State Laws by the U.S. Supreme Court." *Social Science Quarterly* 94(2): 395–409.

Hamilton, A. 1788. *The Federalist, No. 78*. Available at: http://www.constitution.org/fed/federa78.htm.

Hirschl, R. 2004. *Towards Juristocracy: The Origins and Consequences of the New Constitutionalism*. Cambridge, MA: Harvard University Press.

Ignagni, J., and Meernik, J. 1994. "Explaining Congressional Attempts to Reverse Supreme Court Decisions." *Political Research Quarterly* 47: 353–71.

Kagan, R. A. 2001. *Adversarial Legalism: The American Way of Law*. Cambridge, MA: Harvard University Press.

Kagan, R. A. 2004. "American Courts and the Policy Dialogue: The Role of Adversarial Legalism." In *Making Policy, Making Law: An Interbranch Perspective*, edited by M. C. Miller and J. Barnes. Washington, DC: Georgetown University Press, 13–34.

Kapiszewski, D. 2011. "Tactical Balancing: High Court Decision Making on Politically Crucial Cases." *Law & Society Review* 45(June): 471–506.

Keck, T. M. 2004. *The Most Activist Supreme Court in History: The Road to Modern Judicial Conservatism*. Chicago, IL: University of Chicago Press.

Keck, T. M. 2007a. "Party, Policy, or Duty: Why Does the Supreme Court Invalidate Federal Statutes?" *American Political Science Review* 101(May): 321–38.

Keck, T. M. 2007b. "Party Politics or Judicial Independence: The Regime Politics Literature Hits the Law Schools." *Law and Social Inquiry* 32(Spring): 511–44.

Keck, T. M. 2009. "Beyond Backlash: Assessing the Impact of Judicial Decisions on LGBT Rights." *Law & Society Review* 43 (1): 151–85.

Keck, T. M. 2014. *Judicial Politics in Polarized Times*. Chicago, IL: University of Chicago Press.

Keck, T. M., and McMahon, K. J. 2016. "Why *Roe* Still Stands: Abortion Law, the Supreme Court, and the Republican Regime." *Studies in Law, Politics & Society* 70: 33–83.

Klarman, M. J. 1996. "Rethinking the Civil Rights and Civil Liberties Revolutions." *Virginia Law Review* 82(February): 1–67.

Klarman, M. J. 2004. *From Jim Crow to Civil Rights: The Supreme Court and the Struggle for Racial Equality*. New York, NY: Oxford University Press.

Klarman, M. J. 2005. "*Brown* and *Lawrence* (and *Goodridge*)." *Michigan Law Review* 104(December): 431–89.

Lemieux, S. E., and Lovell, G. 2010. "Legislative Defaults: Interbranch Power Sharing and Abortion Politics." *Polity* 42(April): 210–43.

Lovell, G. I. 2003. *Legislative Deferrals: Statutory Ambiguity, Judicial Power, and American Democracy*. New York, NY: Cambridge University Press.

Meernik, J., and Ignagni J. 1995. "Congressional Attacks on Supreme Court Rulings Involving Unconstitutional State Laws." *Political Research Quarterly* 48: 43–59.

Melnick, R. S. 1983. *Regulation and the Courts: The Case of the Clean Air Act*. Washington, DC: Brookings.

Melnick, R. S. 1994. *Between the Lines: Interpreting Welfare Rights*. Washington, DC: Brookings.

Miller, M. C. 2009. *The View of the Courts from the Hill: Interactions between Congress and the Federal Judiciary*. Charlottesville, VA: University of Virginia Press.

Mulroy, Q. 2012. "Public Regulation through Private Litigation: The Regulatory Power of Private Lawsuits and the American Bureaucracy." Ph.D. dissertation, Columbia University (February).

Murphy, W. F. 1962. *Congress and the Court: A Case Study in the American Political Process*. Chicago, IL: University of Chicago Press.

Pickerill, J. M. 2004. *Constitutional Deliberation in Congress*. Durham, NC: Duke University Press.

Powe, L. A., Jr. 2000. *The Warren Court and American Politics*. Cambridge, MA: Harvard University Press.

Rosenberg, G. N. 1991. *The Hollow Hope: Can Courts Bring about Social Change?* Chicago, Il: University of Chicago Press.

Rosenberg, G. N. 2008. *The Hollow Hope: Can Courts Bring about Social Change?* rev. ed. Chicago, IL: University of Chicago Press.

Shapiro, M. 1964. *Law and Politics in the Supreme Court: New Approaches to Political Jurisprudence*. New York, NY: Free Press of Glencoe.

Shapiro, M. 1968. *The Supreme Court and Administrative Agencies*. New York: Free Press.

Silverstein, G. 2009. *Law's Allure: How Law Shapes, Constrains, Saves, and Kills Politics*. New York, NY: Cambridge University Press.

Whittington, K. E. 1999. *Constitutional Construction: Divided Powers and Constitutional Meaning*. Cambridge, MA: Harvard University Press.

Whittington, K. E. 2005a. "Interpose your Friendly Hand: Political Supports for the Exercise of Judicial Review by the United States Supreme Court." *American Political Science Review* 99(4): 583–96.

Whittington, K. E. 2005b. "Congress before the Lochner Court." *Boston University Law Review* 85(June): 821–58.

Whittington, K. E. 2009. "Judicial Review of Congress before the Civil War." *Georgetown Law Journal* 97(June): 1257–331.

Whittington, K. E. 2014. "The Least Activist Supreme Court in History? The Roberts Court and the Exercise of Judicial Review." *Notre Dame Law Review* 89(May): 2219–52.

Whittington, K. E., and Clark, T. S. 2009. "Ideology, Partisanship, and Judicial Review of Acts of Congress, 1789–2006." Available at: http://papers.ssrn.com/sol3/papers.cfm?abstract_id=1475660.

CHAPTER 21

COURTS AND EXECUTIVES

JEFFREY L. YATES AND SCOTT BODDERY

William Howard Taft was both our twenty-seventh president and the tenth Chief Justice of the U.S. Supreme Court—the only person to have ever held both high positions in our country. He once famously commented that "presidents may come and go, but the Supreme Court goes on forever" (Pringle 1998). His remark reminds us that presidents serve only four-year terms (and are now limited to two of them), but justices of the Supreme Court are appointed for life and leave a legacy of precedent-setting cases after departing the High Court. Of course, presidents also leave a legacy of important decisions, not the least of which being their appointment of federal judges.

Just as presidents cast an influence on the federal judiciary and the direction of American legal policy-making through judicial appointment (and other means), federal judges help shape the Constitutional parameters and contours of the executive branch, as well as its powers and policies, through their jurisprudence. From the High Court's rebuke of president Harry Truman's assertion of executive power in the *Steel Seizure Case* to President Barack Obama's "calling out" the Supreme Court regarding the *Citizens' United* ruling on the First Amendment rights of corporations—the relationship and interactions between the two primary institutions are important, at times volatile, and always intriguing.

Although executive-courts phenomena lend themselves well to empirical investigation and scholarship they are perhaps understudied relative to other topics in American politics and law. This is unfortunate as these interactions and related policy outcomes provide fruitful lines of inquiry for scholars interested in the dynamics of American government and law.

In this chapter we examine and analyze empirical studies addressing the intersection of courts and executives and explore multiple aspects of the dynamics and nuances involved in direct and indirect interactions between these two federal branches. In the section that follows we explore the literature on the formal powers of the president and how courts have shaped and adjusted the legal authority and reach of the president. We further investigate how executives can influence legal policy through less direct pathways such as agenda-setting. In the next section we consider how presidents have helped shape the landscape of American law through the appointment of judicial actors and the politics of the federal judicial selection process. Finally, we address the president's legal arm—the Solicitor General's Office—and investigate the office's influence on Supreme Court policy-making.[1]

Defining the Executive: Courts on the Formal Powers of the President

The Constitutional foundations of the executive and judicial branches are not set forth in a tremendous amount of detail. Time and practice have helped inform our understanding of the relationship. Although the judiciary was originally considered the 'least dangerous branch' that wielded 'neither the purse nor the sword' (Hamilton 1788), the power dynamics between the executive and the judicial branch have emerged over time as more balanced and nuanced than these early assertions might have portended. Prominent in most scholars' minds is Chief Justice John Marshal's positioning of the Supreme Court as the ultimate interpreter of the Constitution in *Marbury v. Madison* (1803) through his jousting with President Thomas Jefferson. Knight and Epstein (1996) explain that the confrontation between Jefferson and Marshal highlight well the fluid and incremental process whereby democracy is institutionalized. They further note:

> The major long-term consequence of the Jefferson-Marshall interaction was a restructuring of the institutional division of labor among the branches ... The Supreme Court's authority for judicial review emerged, not because of some complex intentional design and not because of some brilliant strategic move by Marshall in the face of overwhelming political opposition, but merely because it was politically viable at the time. The lesson for contemporary efforts to institutionalize democracy through constitutional design is that such efforts are merely the first, and tentative, steps in an ongoing political game.
>
> (1996: 113–14)

Certainly *Marbury* helped solidify judicial review power for the Court, but legal institutions remain dependent on executive branch actors to implement and bring to policy fruition their legal edicts. This fact makes direct interactions between courts and executives—in which courts rule on the powers of the executive—especially intriguing. The somewhat uncomfortable nature of this situation is highlighted by the situation the High Court faced in *U.S. v. Nixon* in which, during oral arguments before the justices, President Nixon's counsel vacillated when directly asked if the executive would comply with an order from the Court (to turn over information). In an interview years later, former justice Lewis Powell noted, "one has to wonder what would have happened if Nixon had said what President Jackson said on one occasion, 'You have your decree, now enforce it.' We had 50 'police' officers, but Nixon had the First Infantry Division"

(Powell 1995: 173). Of course, Nixon did in fact follow the Court's ruling and such a confrontation was ultimately avoided.

Assessments of the appropriate scope and reach of presidential power and action have varied considerably, even among those who have held the position. William Howard Taft's view of the executive role was one of constraint. He opined:

> The true view of executive functions ... is, as I conceive it, that the President can exercise no power which cannot be fairly and reasonably traced to some specific grant of power or justly implied and included within such grant as proper and necessary.
>
> (Biskupic and Witt 1997: 169)

On the other end of the spectrum rests the view of Theodore Roosevelt that the executive stands as an active steward of the public well-being and, as such, must be free to have far-reaching powers. He argued that:

> Every executive officer ... was a steward of the people ... My belief was that it was not only his right but his duty to do anything that the needs of the nation demanded unless such action was forbidden by the Constitution or by the laws ... In other words, I acted for the public welfare ... whenever and in whatever manner was necessary, unless prevented by direct constitutional or legislative provision.
>
> (1997: 170)

Judicial assessments of the parameters of presidential power have led to productive lines of research. Early treatments of the limits of executive authority focused on formal Constitutional provisions and Court opinions on the reach of the executive with the general consensus being that the president has fared well over time and has generally been afforded greater deference in foreign policy and defense matters relative to domestic policy concerns (e.g. Corwin 1984; Rossiter 1951; Schubert 1957; Scigliano 1971). As the study of both the presidency and the judiciary progressed, scholars endeavored to provide more social-science-oriented approaches to assaying courts' treatment of the limits of executive power.

In 1989 Ducat and Dudley's seminal study on the topic systematically examined federal district court cases pertaining to core aspects of presidential legal concerns—the lawful reach of executive power and relevant limits. In assessing the decisions of district court judges they found that there were indeed "two presidencies" in executive power jurisprudence—consistent with Aaron Wildavsky's (1966) broader thesis on the U.S. presidency and Justice Sutherland's majority opinion analysis of the domestic-foreign policy contextual aspects of the law of presidential power in *United States v. Curtis-Wright Export Corp.* (1936).

Ducat and Dudley found that in cases involving foreign policy the executive was afforded much more deference by district court judges than in domestic policy cases. In break out analyses, they found that theoretically interesting political factors such as a presidents' prestige (public approval levels), whether a judge was appointed by the president whose powers were at issue, and the specific type of power involved helped to explain executive success in domestic cases, but that none of these considerations mattered in foreign policy litigation outcomes before the district courts. Regarding this distinction, Ducat and Dudley concluded that "presidential leadership on the home front depends upon his persuasive power backed by his public prestige. In this area, district court judges have not acted much differently from other officeholders with whom the president deals" (1989: 116).

Their study design was later extended to U.S. Supreme Court justice voting by Yates and Whitford (1998) who advanced alternative measurement and specification strategies. Their study confirmed Ducat and Dudley's primary finding that the president is afforded more deference in foreign policy presidential power cases (but cf. King and Meernik 1999; Clark 2006) and they also found that justices' votes were influenced by justices' ideological preferences and upward trends in presidents' public approval. More recently, Robinson (2012) examined High Court justices' votes in an updated data set of presidential power cases and found that justices' background socialization, more specifically justice executive branch experience and the length of that experience, were associated with voting outcomes that favor deference to the president when core powers are at issue.

Certainly, differences of opinion exist on the proper scope and limits of executive power. Construction of a doctrinal matrix that makes sense of courts' jurisprudence on presidential power has been a popular scholarly endeavor (e.g. Chemerinsky 1983), but perhaps one that appropriately considers historical and political context rather than strictly legal considerations. In the section that follows, we turn our attentions to executive–court interactions that have less to do with addressing the formal powers of office and more to do with battles over policy and the direction of U.S. governance and policy-making.

The "Less Formal" Powers: Inter-Branch Deference, Persuasion, and Potential Threat

The executive and judiciary have multiple pathways of interaction, but one of the more interesting occurs when the executive's bureaucratic arm—the federal agencies—appear before the courts, most notably, before the U.S. Supreme Court. The federal bureaucracy provides the president with one of the most effective means of implementing their desired policy changes since most legislation affords a good degree of implementation discretion by the agencies. Further, policy scholars argue that federal agencies have become more "politicized" over time as executives are held accountable by the public, yet sometimes find their policy goals thwarted by Congress. In contrast, the federal agencies provide perhaps a more receptive avenue for effecting the type of change on which executives will stake their re-election and legacy aspirations (e.g. Moe 1991). The acknowledged proposition that presidents attempt to make their policy mark through agencies is outlined well in one of the Court's opinions, authored by Justice William Rehnquist:

> The agencies' changed view of the standard seems to be related to the election of a new President of a different political party ... A change in administration brought about by people casting their votes is a perfectly reasonable basis for an executive agency's reappraisal of the costs and benefits of its programs and regulations.
>
> (*Motor Vehicle Manufacturing Association v. State Farm Mutual Insurance*, 463 U.S. 59 (1983))

Of course, the courts are responsible for reviewing agency action and thus presidents must deal with judicial monitoring of their policy implementation agents. Federal agency litigation in the Supreme Court has long been a topic of interest to judicial politics scholars, with most studies finding that they fare pretty well, overall. Traditional social science accounts of the federal agency experience before the High Court often focused on the type of agency involved—social versus economic—with the thesis being that social agencies handled more salient or volatile concerns and were likely to fare worse.

Sheehan (1990) argued persuasively that this distinction was not as important as the ideological direction of the agency's position relative to the ideology of the Court. In follow-up work he found that the distinction between independent and executive agency mattered, with independent agencies—often quasi-judicial in character and typically more removed from executive politics—winning more before the Court (Sheehan 1992). However, he again found that the biggest driver of agency success in such litigation was ideology—when agencies (executive or independent) were bringing cases that were antagonistic to the Court's aggregate policy preferences, they fared worse. Yates (1999) added a nuance to this thesis, finding that justices' votes on agencies that were more proximate to the president (cabinet-level agencies vs. independent agencies) were conditioned on presidential public standing (i.e., public approval). Justices' votes on agencies were also found to be influenced by the type of subject matter they dealt with—agencies charged with foreign policy concerns fared better than those whose work focused on domestic matters.

Finally, Richards, Smith, and Kritzer (2006) added an interesting wrinkle to the Supreme Court's treatment of federal agencies story by evaluating the impact of jurisprudent regimes on agency Court outcomes. Specifically, they were interested in the effect of the Court's decision in *Chevron U.S.A. v. Natural Resources Defense Counsel, Inc. et al.* (467 U.S. 865 (1984)) on justices' subsequent voting in agency cases. In *Chevron*, the Court addressed the issue of what should be the proper amount of deference that courts should afford to the statutory interpretations of federal agencies. The majority opinion, authored by Justice John Paul Stevens, set forth the Court's standard for doing so in the absence of clear congressional intent:

> If, however, the court determines Congress has not directly addressed the precise question at issue, the court does not simply impose its own construction on the statute, as would be necessary in the absence of an administrative interpretation. Rather,

> if the statute is silent or ambiguous with respect to the specific issue, the question for the court is whether the agency's answer is based on a permissible construction of the statute.
>
> (467 U.S. 842–3)

Richards et al. found that even though judicial ideology or attitudes still did much to explain justice voting, the Court's adjustment in legal regime (standard of review) on agency cases has a substantively interesting effect on justices' propensity to afford deference to agencies. Moreover, consistent with the *Chevron* holding, this deference was constrained in cases in which Congress's intent was more clear and in cases dealing with rule-making (hence involving higher stakes) (2006: 456–62).

Another important dynamic in U.S. Supreme Court–executive relations is issue attention and agenda-setting. Executive branch influence on Supreme Court case selection is addressed in our discussion on the Solicitor General, but here we are interested in broader-level matters regarding issue attention and problem-solving focus. Those who study governance have appropriately acknowledged the centrality of problem and issue attention and agenda-setting for policy-making. Institutions identify and pursue issues, or social/economic problems and engage in complex cue-taking relationships.

The Supreme Court's issue agenda has long been a topic of interest for legal and social science scholars. As Pacelle (1991), Perry (1991), and others have noted, the High Court's selection of issues to adjudicate from the thousands of petitions for certiorari it receives is one of the most important decisions that it makes. Of course, the president's time, resources, and political capital to expend on issues is also finite and involves opportunity costs. Executive or Supreme Court identification and recognition of a social or economic concern gives it public validation and promotion as an important matter that all political actors must either address or risk becoming less relevant in the arena of public debate. How these two primary institutions come to choose what broad issues and problems to focus their attentions on has been a recurring research question (e.g. Caldeira 1981; Pacelle 1991; Cohen 1997; Hill 1998; Flemming, Wood, and Bohte 1997; Edwards and Wood 1999; Yates, Whitford, and Gillespie 2005). Studies testing whether these two branches of the federal government actually influence each other's issue attentions have been more rare.

Whether primary federal institutions (president, Congress, and Supreme Court) and the general public (systemic) are related and affect one another was the central question addressed by Flemming, Wood, and Bohte (1997). They employed vector autoregression methods to assess macrodynamic shifts in attention to policy issues. Their areas of interest were civil rights, civil liberties, and environmental issues. They found that the Court's focus on civil rights and civil liberties influenced the executive's attention to those policy matters, but that there was no such effect with regard to environmental concerns. In contrast, they found that presidential attention to all three policy issues had no influence on Court attentions. Presidents' issue attentions were also affected by Congress (civil liberties and environmental) and system (public) emphasis (environmental) whereas Court issue priorities were influenced by Congress' (civil liberties and civil rights) issue attention.

Later work has found that High Court attentions (to criminal justice policy issues) is influenced by expressed presidential issue emphasis (Yates, Whitford, and Gillespie 2005) and that executive issue priorities are influenced by Court issue agenda signaling (Yates and Whitford 2005). Certainly, future research might explore the stream of issues that compete for the attentions of government institutions and the public and media stage. As social media becomes increasingly pervasive, the battle over what public concerns gain the eyes and ears of public leaders becomes more complex and perhaps is influenced not only by the relevant actors and institutions themselves, but also by the manner in which communication takes place.

Finally, a river of scholarly research has explored the possibility that political institutions and their actors operate in a sophisticated, forward-thinking manner, in that they anticipate the potentially threatening or contrarian reactions of other relevant policy actors and adjust their policy decisions accordingly. Of course, two of those political institutions (and their policy-making actors) are the judicial and executive branches. Studies exploring this rational choice approach to explaining institutional political phenomena are plentiful and typically consider the executive and judiciary as part of a larger game that also includes Congress and the public (e.g. Eskridge 1991; Epstein and Knight 1998; Segal 1997; Martin 2001; Curry, Pacelle, and Marshall 2008; Lindquist and Corley 2011).

However, Baum (2006) asserts that, on balance, the empirical findings of these studies supporting the existence of such strategic actions are decidedly mixed. He further argues convincingly that parsing such effects from alternative judicial motivations can be problematic and that there are theoretical and pragmatic concerns with the proposition of systemic threat driving judges' decisions. Still, he leaves the door open to the possibility of such strategic action by judges, noting: "Undoubtedly some judges at some times act on their fear of negative consequences from displeasing other branches. Yet their incentives to take this course are limited in important respects, and by no means do judges automatically bend under pressure. Action to avoid or defuse conflict with other branches is episodic, and it may be exceptional as well" (2006: 81). Baum's concerns about the viability of a systemic impact on judicial actions are noteworthy, however Epstein and Knight (1998) and others have made a convincing case that Supreme Court justices at least consider and discuss (with each other) the potential reactions of other branches to Court action on occasion.

There also exists the possibility that presidents are influenced by either the persuasion or potential threat of judges. Certainly executives react to judicial action and, in fact, use the "bully pulpit" regularly to discuss judicial matters. Perhaps the most memorable instance of this in recent years was President Obama's state of the union rebuke of the High Court's decision in *Citizens United v. Federal Election Commission*. But how often does the executive actually address such matters in public rhetoric? Blackstone and Goelzhauser (2014) explore presidential rhetoric regarding the U.S. Supreme Court. They analyze such rhetoric from 1929 to 2011 and find that presidents delivered over six-thousand sentences concerning the High Court during that time, for an average of seventy-four sentences a year. Presidents' gave an average of twenty-three positive statements regarding the Court per year and thirty-eight negative statements (critical of the Court or its actions) with the balance being described as neutral.

Thus, we can at least surmise that presidents pay relatively close attention to the Court and its dealings and regularly expend valuable public-speaking time discussing it. But executive branch action is often employed through agency action and the Court regularly rules on such actions. Hence, scholars studying the intersection of Court jurisprudence and presidential policy implementation make a strong argument that the Supreme Court (and lower courts) wield a viable tool in influencing the course of executive branch governance through judicial decisions. For example, Spriggs (1996) finds that federal agencies did adjust their policy-making in response to decisions made by the Court, but that the degree to which they adjusted their actions was influenced by the specificity of the Court's majority opinion, among other important considerations.

The Power of Appointment—Can Presidents Mold the Judiciary?

In announcing his 2009 appointment of now associate justice Sonia Sotomayor, President Obama began his public statement by observing "of the many responsibilities granted to a president by our Constitution, few are more serious or more consequential than selecting a Supreme Court justice. The members of our highest court are granted life tenure, often serving long after the presidents who appointed them."[2] His remark outlines well the profound policy implications of presidential Court appointments. Historically, such presidential appointments have reflected a mix of personal and professional motivations by the executive as well as concerns over the reality of the ideological politics surrounding such important decisions (Epstein and Segal 2005).

Of course, such appointments must pass the gauntlet of Senate confirmation, but the power of appointment provides presidents with the opportunity to potentially make substantively significant inroads on the character of policy-making within the judicial branch of government. In this section we first examine the politics of U.S. Supreme Court selection and how presidential appointment decisions may impact the High Court's policy-making. We then turn to the lower federal courts, exploring the dynamics of staffing the nation's federal district and intermediate appellate courts and the policy implications of these choices. Finally, we consider diversity and policy outcomes that have resulted in the lower courts through presidential appointment decisions.

The federal Constitution's provisions regarding how Supreme Court justices are selected underwent a number of revisions and were the topic of much debate by the Founders. While some favored a legislatively driven selection mechanism, others preferred one tilted toward the executive—and in the end they settled on the Article II (section 2) language granting the president the power to nominate and, "by and with the advice of the Senate" to appoint "judges of the Supreme Court." Though the role of the Senate and the appropriate bases for confirmation decisions have been a subject of debate, the executive has largely been successful in getting nominees confirmed for the nation's High Court.

To consider the first step of this process (nomination choice), we turn to Moraski and Shipan's (1999) oft-cited study on the dynamics of executive nominations to the High Court. They explored nominations to the Court from 1949 to 1994 and postulated that presidents acted in a forward-thinking, strategic manner in choosing who to nominate. Their empirical findings revealed that presidents were cognizant of the relative preferences and ideological character of both the Senate and continuing members of the Court and that in certain contexts their nomination choices were influenced by these considerations. Thus, political concerns cast an influence on who ultimately ascends the Court before a single confirmation vote is cast in the Senate.

Once a president has nominated a potential justice for the Court, they often engage in the process of "selling" their choice to both the Senate and the public. Maltese (1995) maintains that the "selling" of Supreme Court nominees has changed over time as modern presidents increasingly "go public" with their preferred judicial candidates, as opposed to earlier executives. He notes, "for many years presidents felt that it was inappropriate to comment publicly on their Supreme Court nominees. To do so would be to stoop to 'politics' in a process that was supposed to be untainted by political considerations" (1995: 447). He argues that the executive's increased willingness to speak publicly about their candidates is likely part of a broader "public presidency" phenomenon. It also likely reflects the increasing attention that politicians pay to media concerns and public sentiment.

Taking this line of reasoning a step further, Johnson and Roberts (2004) explored the determinants of presidential "selling" of Supreme Court nominees via public rhetoric. They analyze the content of presidential statements on nominees from 1949 to 1994 and focus on three primary types of statements: 1) those espousing the nominee's qualifications, 2) those claiming that the public favors the nominee, and 3) those encouraging the Senate to act fairly and quickly. As might be expected, most of the presidents public comments concerned promoting the nominee's qualities and qualifications (followed by statements pressuring the Senate and then claims regarding public opinion). They found that ideological conflict with the Senate (distance between nominee and Senate filibuster pivot; distance between Court median and filibuster pivot; and distance between president and filibuster pivot) led to increased rhetoric on nominees by presidents. Such rhetoric was also influenced by the president's relative public prestige (popular presidents were less likely to go public), nomination timing, and Senate delay on confirmation. But did these executive appeals to the public have an effect on Senate confirmation outcomes? Johnson and Roberts found that presidents' rhetorical efforts did in fact have a payoff as such statements cast a meaningful influence on senators' votes on Supreme Court nominees.

It is likely that executives' public campaigns for High Court candidates are here to stay, as such battles over nominations increasingly end up getting played out in the media and social forums. Of course, the success of presidents' nominees before the

Senate can turn on a number of executive-oriented factors, beyond presidential rhetoric. For instance, even though presidents with high public approval are by no means assured of Senate success, their nominees do, on average, fare better before the Senate than those of less popular presidents (Epstein and Segal 2005: 108). Future research might do well to consider the relevant political context and presidents' personal motivations in such nomination/confirmation scenarios. For example, presidents who have previously experienced a failed or divisive nomination may be more apt to make concessions on their next appointment attempt. In similar vein, Senate confirmations may be less salient and accordingly less volatile in times in which media and public attention are drawn to other compelling political or social events that compete with confirmation hearings for social agenda space.

The attention and tumult over Supreme Court selection leads many to wonder what impact, if any, such personnel decisions have on U.S. legal policy. Do executives leave a lasting policy legacy through their Supreme Court appointments? Historical accounts provide anecdotal evidence of executive policy success as well as some presidents' bitter disappointments in their appointees (Epstein and Segal 2005). Gates and Cohen (1988) found that presidents generally enjoyed policy agreement with the justices they appointed in the area of racial equality cases. In a subsequent study, Segal, Timpone, and Howard (2000) assayed this general premise, examining presidents' appointments to the Court from 1937 to 1994. They were not only concerned with overall president-appointee policy agreement, but whether such agreement fluctuated over time—the idea being that justices' policy druthers might approximate their appointing presidents' preferences early on, but then "drifted" over time. Using a measure of presidential ideology derived from a survey of political scientists, they find general concordance between presidents and their appointed justices in civil liberties and economic cases. However, such agreement disintegrated over time, with executive–justice concordance dissipating after the first four years of justice tenure on the High Court in civil liberties cases and after ten years of judicial service in economic cases.

Krehbiel (2007) argued that presidents could make significant policy gains through Supreme Court appointments, but his empirical findings suggested that the political circumstances necessary to effectuate such an impactful judicial appointment rarely presented themselves. In a more recent study Epstein, Landes, and Posner found that Supreme Court justices exhibited substantial "ideological divergence" from their appointing presidents over time, with these effects being mitigated by executives' choice of justices who had prior government service. They found similar ideological divergence effects concerning executive nominations to the U.S. Courts of Appeals (2013: 119–22). Given that average life spans are increasing and many justices serve as long as health permits, this drifting of justices' voting (from presumed orientation during appointment and confirmation) has caused some to question the democratic nature of High Court policy-making as the electoral connection becomes more tenuous (Sharma and Glennon 2013).

High Court judicial selections garner plentiful media attention and can provide high political drama. However, it is arguably the case that greater cumulative policy inroads are made by presidents through their lower federal court appointments. Presidents' may not experience the level of scrutiny on these nominations as they do with regard to the High Court, however political dynamics still persist in lower court selections. Consternation over executive nominations and delay in confirmations of lower federal court judges have increased in recent decades (Scherer 2005). Presidents appear to be ready, willing, and able to bring the bully pulpit to bear in promoting such lower court nominations. Holmes (2008) finds that presidents have increasingly gone public on behalf of their lower court nominees over time and explains that this trend may be part of a strategy aimed at elite interests rather than simply securing the confirmation of nominees. She notes:

> The context of these references does not always appear to be aimed toward shifting mass public attitude toward a nominee or securing confirmation for that specific individual. Rather, presidents often utilize these nominees in public discourse to achieve other goals, including appealing to organized groups, women and minorities, or partisan campaign supporters.
>
> (2008: 119–20)

One aspect of the lower court selection process that is less relevant for the Supreme Court (at least since President Eisenhower) has been executive use of recess appointments to place jurists on the federal bench. Graves and Howard (2010) examine all judicial appointments made during Senate recess from 1789 to 2004. They find that presidents' use of recess appointments has declined substantially since the administration of President Kennedy as Senate recesses have grown shorter. Further, presidents use such appointments in a political strategic fashion and active presidents are more apt to take advantage of recess opportunities for appointment (2010: 650). Finally, there is also some evidence to suggest that presidents act strategically in their nomination of lower court judges—carefully timing their nominations (relative to the date of vacancy) in order to facilitate a nominee-friendly confirmation environment—with certain institutional constraints, of course (Massie, Hansford, and Songer 2004).

Appointments to the lower federal courts provide presidents with substantial opportunities to influence the law as trial and intermediate appellate courts represent the final disposition for the vast majority of litigated matters. But, are those opportunities actually realized in lower court policy-making? Rowland, Songer, and Carp (1988) examined the policy-making of the nominees of presidents Nixon, Reagan, and Carter in criminal justice cases. They found important differences among the appointed justices, both in the federal district courts and in the courts of appeals, with Reagan's judges deciding cases significantly more conservatively than Carter's judges (with Nixon falling between the two). Goldman (1997) suggests that presidents have competing goals in appointing lower court judges, with some presidents focusing on partisan considerations (e.g., gaining political capital) as others were primarily interested in shaping the ideological contours of the federal judiciary.

Certainly, some executives were mainly interested in advancing personal goals (e.g., increasing gender and racial diversity). A host of studies have addressed the latter proposition regarding diversity.[3] Kimel and Randazzo (2012) assay the appointment propensities of recent presidential administrations (William Clinton, George W. Bush, and Barack Obama) and address how these presidents' nomination policies have impacted diversity in the federal lower courts. They find that Obama nominated more minorities for the bench (35 percent) than Clinton (24 percent) or Bush (17 percent) as well as the most female jurists (46 percent, with Clinton at 29 percent and Bush at 22 percent). Examining a subset of nominees for which ideological scores were available, they find that Obama's nominees were more moderate than either the Bush or Clinton nominee's scores—suggesting that Obama pursued a rather pragmatic approach to diversifying the federal lower courts. All three presidents enjoyed fairly high levels of confirmations success for their nominations, with Clinton being the most successful overall (81 percent confirmed), followed by Bush (78 percent) and Obama (74 percent). Finally, Collins (2009, 2010) demonstrates that presidents can significantly change the partisan makeup of the U.S. Courts of Appeals through appointment, and, accordingly, the policy-making jurisprudence of the intermediate court.

The President's Lawyer—the Supreme Court and the Solicitor General

We would certainly be remiss if we did not discuss the storied relationship between the High Court and the president's legal arm, the Office of the Solicitor General (OSG). The OSG is a creature of the Federal Judiciary Act of 1870 which created both the Department of Justice and the OSG. This act came in response to a burgeoning workload that had been heaped upon the Attorney General as the nation and its legal issues expanded and other attempts to solve the workload issue had proven problematic (Black and Owens 2012: 11–14). The OSG is the primary legal advocate for the executive branch and U.S. government before the Supreme Court. Its duties with regard to the nation's High Court include, among others: a) the selection of cases for petitioning for certiorari (when the United States is a direct litigant); b) representing the United States on the merits of the case (again, when the United States is a direct litigant); c) drafting and filing amicus curiae when the government is an interested party; d) authorizing other interested actors to submit amicus curiae briefs (when the United States is a direct litigant) (Salokar 1992).

To say that the OSG occupies a curious place in U.S. law and politics would be an understatement. The Court relies on the OSG to provide reliable and informative views (e.g., submission of amicus curiae briefs). At the same time, the Solicitor General (SG) is an executive appointee and even though SGs can and do depart from presidents' policy views in their role, studies typically find a congruence between the OSG's positions and executives' preferences, as we might intuitively surmise (e.g. Yates 2002; Black and Owens 2012). On this "dual identity" dynamic, President Ronald Reagan's SG, Rex Lee, commented that:

> On the one hand, I am a presidential appointee, a part of the president's team. I very much believe in the president's program and I want to do what I can to help advance it... On the other hand, I am also an officer of the Court. And the relationship between the solicitor general and the Supreme Court is one that knows no counterpart.
>
> (Witt 1986: 120)

Lee's comment prompts the question of whether the OSG carries special influence with the Court. A number of rationales for such possible influence have been posited—deference to the executive branch; reputation and credibility that have been developed over time; and resource advantages, to name a few. Undoubtedly, the OSG has had tremendous success before the Court along multiple dimensions—certiorari petition outcomes, on the merits outcomes, and amicus activity—as a bevy of studies on the matter have confirmed (e.g. Caplan 1987; Salokar 1992; Segal 1990; Zorn 2002; Pacelle 2003; Black and Owens 2012). But does this success necessarily demonstrate that the OSG carries any special influence or sway with the nation's High Court? Are there perhaps other considerations that may lead to its success?

One consideration is legal experience. McGuire (1998) makes a convincing argument that much of the SG's success in the U.S. Supreme Court is due to differential levels of experience in litigating cases before the High Court—the SG has, in the typical situation, more experience than opposing counsel—and accordingly, wins more often. In similar fashion, Zorn (2002) makes the case that the SG's success before the Court can be partially attributed to the OSG's meticulous and strategic selection of the cases it chooses to argue before the Court (from the relatively large pool of cases that could be pursued). On the other hand, Black and Owens (2012) use a case-matching strategy to assess SG fortunes before the Court that takes into account some of these considerations (e.g., attorney experience) and conclude that the SG does carry unique influence with the Court across a number of dimensions. They reason that the credibility of the OSG as an informative, reliable, and principled officer of the Court is key to this relationship. Wohlfarth's (2009) study provides some support for this proposition. He finds that the SG wins less before the Court when its litigation efforts become more politicized. Suffice it to say, these research efforts are certainly not the end of this debate and scholars will certainly continue to investigate the roots of the OSG's success with the nation's High Court.

As presidents continue to push the parameters of presidential power in an attempt to appease the sometimes unreasonable demands of the citizenry to promote the public well-being, interactions with courts will likely increase—both in number and in salience. The U.S. Supreme Court is also increasingly perceived by the public as a political, rather than purely policy-neutral, institution. Thus, matters such as presidential judicial appointments and the OSG's activities before the High Court will likely find themselves more and more as the media's top news stories.

With this in mind, the dynamics between executives and courts bring to bear some of the fundamental questions of our Constitutional tradition—what is the place of each of these institutions in guiding the direction of U.S. life? To what degree does each provide a meaningful check on congressional power in the policy arena? And what happens regarding policy enforcement when the president and the Court strongly disagree? These questions and others offer rich opportunities for further scholarship as we strive to better understand how U.S. political power is shared and policy made.

Notes

1. We focus here on studies involving the interplay between the American president and the federal courts (primarily the U.S. Supreme Court). We acknowledge that an intriguing, but relatively limited, literature addresses interactions between state executives and courts (e.g. Schorpp 2012; Johnson 2014).
2. http://www.whitehouse.gov/the_press_office/Remarks-by-the-President-in-Nominating-Judge-Sonia-Sotomayor-to-the-United-States-Supreme-Court.
3. Kimel and Randazzo (2012) provide a useful review of the many studies commenting on political concerns that may influence the development of diversity on the federal bench.

References

Baum, L. 2006. *Judges and their Audiences: A Perspective on Judicial Behavior*. Princeton, NJ: Princeton University Press.

Biskupic, J., and Witt, E. 1997. *Congressional Quarterly's Guide to the U.S. Supreme Court*, 3rd ed. Washington, DC: Congressional Quarterly.

Black, R., and Owens, R. 2012. *The Solicitor General and the United States Supreme Court: Executive Influence and Judicial Decisions*. New York, NY: Cambridge University Press

Blackstone, B., and Goelzhauser, G. 2014. "Presidential Rhetoric toward the Supreme Court." *Judicature* 97: 179–87.

Caldeira, G. 1981. "The United States Supreme Court and Criminal Cases, 1935–1976: Alternative Models of Agenda Building." *British Journal of Political Science* 11: 449–70.

Caplan, L. 1987. *The Tenth Justice: The Solicitor General and the Rule of Law*. New York, NY: Alfred A. Knopf.

Chemerinsky, E. 1983. ""Controlling Inherent Presidential Power: Providing a Framework for Judicial Review." *Southern California Law Review* 56: 863–911.

Clark, T. 2006. "Judicial Decision-Making during Wartime." *Journal of Empirical Legal Studies* 3: 397–419.

Cohen, J. 1997. *Presidential Responsiveness and Public Policy-Making*. Ann Arbor, MI: University of Michigan Press.

Collins, T. 2009. "Balancing the Scales or Stacking the Deck? The President's Ability to Appoint Majorities on the Circuit Courts of Appeals." *White House Studies* 8: 431–46.

Collins, T. 2010. "Is the Sum Greater than its Parts? Circuit Court Composition and Judicial Behavior in the Courts of Appeals." *Law & Policy* 32: 434–53.

Corwin, E. 1984. *The President: Office and Powers, 1787–1984: History and Analysis of Practice and Opinion*. New York, NY: New York University Press.

Curry, B., Pacelle, R., and Marshall, B. 2008. "An 'Informal and Limited Alliance': The President and the Supreme Court." *Presidential Studies Quarterly* 38: 223–47.

Ducat, C., and Dudley, R. 1989. "Federal District Judges and Presidential Power during the Postwar Era." *Journal of Politics* 51: 98–118.

Edwards, G., and Wood, B. D. 1999. "Who Influences Whom? The President, Congress, and the Media." *American Political Science Review* 93: 327–44.

Epstein, L., and Knight, J. 1998. *The Choices Justices Make*. Washington, DC: CQ Press.

Epstein, L., Landes, W., and Posner, R. 2013. *The Behavior of Federal Judges: A Theoretical and Empirical Study of Rational Choice*. Cambridge, MA: Harvard University Press.

Epstein, L., and Segal, J. 2005. *Advice and Consent: The Politics of Judicial Appointments*. New York, NY: Oxford University Press.

Eskridge, W. 1991. "Reneging on History? Playing the Court/Congress/President Civil Rights Game." *California Law Review* 79: 613–84.

Flemming, R., Bohte, J., and Wood, B. D. 1997. "One Voice among Many: The Supreme Court's Influence on Attentiveness to Issues in the United States, 1947–92." *American Journal of Political Science* 41: 1224–50.

Gates, J., and Cohen, J. 1988. "Presidents, Supreme Court Justices, and Racial Equality Cases: 1954–1984." *Political Behavior* 10: 22–36.

Goldman, S. 1997. *Picking Federal Judges: Lower Court Selection from Roosevelt through Reagan*. New Haven, CT: Yale University Press.

Graves, S., and Howard, R. 2010. "Ignoring Advice and Consent? The Uses of Judicial Recess Appointments." *Political Research Quarterly* 63: 640–53.

Hamilton, A. 1788. *The Federalist, No. 78*. Available at: http://www.constitution.org/fed/federa78.htm.

Hill, K. Q. 1998. "The Policy Agendas of the President and the Mass Public: A Research Validation and Extension." *American Journal of Political Science* 42: 1328–34.

Holmes, L. 2008. "Why "Go Public"? Presidential Use of Nominees to the U.S. Courts of Appeals." *Presidential Studies Quarterly* 38: 110–22.

Johnson, G. 2015. "Executive Power and Judicial Deference: Judicial Decision Making on Executive Power Challenges in the American States." *Political Research Quarterly* 68: 128–41.

Johnson, T., and Roberts, J. 2004. "Presidential Capital and the Supreme Court Confirmation Process." *Journal of Politics* 66: 663–83.

Kimel, T. J., and Randazzo, K. 2012. "Shaping the Federal Courts: The Obama Nominees." *Social Science Quarterly* 93: 1243–50.

King, K., and Meernik, J. 1999. "The Supreme Court and the Powers of the Executive: The Adjudication of Foreign Policy." *Political Research Quarterly* 52: 801–24.

Knight, J., and Epstein, L. 1996. "On the Struggle for Judicial Supremacy." *Law & Society Review* 30: 87–120.

Krehbiel, K. 2007. "Supreme Court Appointments as a Move-the-Median Game." *American Journal of Political Science* 51: 231–40.

Lindquist, S., and Corley, P. 2011. "The Multiple-Stage Process of Judicial Review: Facial and As-Applied Constitutional Challenges to Legislation before the U.S. Supreme Court." *Journal of Legal Studies* 40: 467–502.

Maltese, J. 1995. "Speaking out: The Role of Presidential Rhetoric in the Modern Supreme Court Confirmation Process." *Presidential Studies Quarterly* 25: 447–55.

Martin, A. 2001. "Congressional Decision Making and the Separation of Powers." *American Political Science Review* 95: 361–78.

Massie, T., Hansford, T., and Songer, D. 2004. "The Timing of Presidential Nominations to the Lower Federal Courts." *Political Research Quarterly* 57: 145–54.

Moe, T. 1991. "The Politicized Presidency." In *The Managerial Presidency*, edited by J. Pfiffner. Pacific Grove: Brooks/Cole Publishing, 144–61.

Moraski, B., and Shipan, C. 1999. "The Politics of Supreme Court Nominations: A Theory of Institutional Constraints and Choices." *American Journal of Political Science* 43: 1069–95.

Pacelle, R. 1991. *The Transformation of the Supreme Court's Agenda: From the New Deal to the Reagan Administration*. Boulder, CO: Westview Press.

Pacelle, R. 2003. *Between Law and Politics: The Solicitor General and the Structuring of Race, Gender, and Reproductive Rights Litigation*. College Station, TX: Texas A&M University Press.

Perry, H. W. 1991. *Deciding to Decide: Agenda Setting in the United States Supreme Court*. Cambridge, MA: Harvard University Press.

Powell, L. 1995. "The Supreme Court and the Presidency." In *Problems and Policies of American Presidents*, edited by K. Thompson. Lanham, MD: University Press of America.

Pringle, H. 1998. *The Life and Times of William Howard Taft*, vol. i. Newtown, CT: American Political Biography Press.

Richards, M., Smith, J., and Kritzer, H. 2006. "Does *Chevron* Matter?" *Law & Policy* 28: 444–69.

Robinson, R. 2012. "Executive Branch Socialization and Deference on the U.S. Supreme Court." *Law & Society Review* 46: 889–921.

Rossiter, C. 1951. *The Supreme Court and the Commander in Chief*. Ithaca, NY: Cornell University Press.

Rowland, C.K., Songer, D., and Carp, R. 1988. "Presidential Effects on Criminal Justice Policy in the Lower Federal Courts: The Reagan Judges." *Law & Society Review* 22: 191–200.

Salokar, R. 1992. *The Solicitor General: The Politics of Law*. Philadelphia, PA: Temple University Press.

Scherer, N. 2005. *Scoring Points: Politicians, Activists, and the Lower Federal Court Appointment Process*. Stanford, CA: Stanford University Press.

Schubert, G. 1957. *The Presidency in the Courts*. Minneapolis, MN: University of Minnesota Press.

Segal, J. 1990. "Supreme Court Support for the Solicitor General: The Effect of Presidential Appointments," *Western Political Quarterly* 43: 137–52.

Segal, J. 1997. "Separation-of-Powers Games in the Positive Theory of Congress and Courts." *American Political Science Review* 91: 28–45.

Segal, J., Timpone, R., and Howard, R. 2000. "Buyer Beware? Presidential Success through Supreme Court Appointments." *Political Research Quarterly* 53: 557–73.

Sharma, H., and Glennon, C. 2013. "A Case for Supreme Court Term Limits? The Changing Ideological Relationship between Appointing Presidents and Supreme Court Justices." *Politics & Policy* 41: 267–97.

Scigliano, R. 1971. *The Supreme Court and the Presidency*. New York, NY: Free Press.

Schorpp, S. 2012. "Strategic Anticipation of Noncompliant Governors: State Supreme Court Behavior in Response to the Political Environment." *Justice System Journal* 33: 275–93.

Sheehan, R. 1990. "Administrative Agencies and the Supreme Court: A Reexamination of the Impact of Agency Type on Decisional Outcomes." *Western Political Quarterly* 43: 875–85.

Sheehan, R. 1992. "Federal Agencies and the Supreme Court." *American Politics Quarterly* 20: 478–500.

Spriggs, J. 1996. "The Supreme Court and Federal Administrative Agencies: A Resource-Based Theory and Analysis of Judicial Impact." *American Journal of Political Science* 40: 1122–51.

Wildavsky, A. 1966. "The Two Presidencies." *Trans-Action* 4: 7–14.

Witt, E. 1986. *A Different Justice: Reagan and the Supreme Court*. Washington, DC: Congressional Quarterly Press.

Wohlfarth, P. 2009. "The Tenth Justice? Consequences of Politicization in the Solicitor General's Office." *Journal of Politics* 71: 224–37.

Yates, J. 2002. *Popular Justice: Presidential Prestige and Executive Success in the Supreme Court*. Albany, NY: State University of New York Press.

Yates, J. 1999. "Presidential Bureaucratic Power and Supreme Court Justice Voting." *Political Behavior* 21: 349–66.

Yates, J., and Whitford, A. 1998. "Presidential Power and the United States Supreme Court." *Political Research Quarterly* 51: 539–50.

Yates, J., and Whitford, A. 2005. "Institutional Foundations of the President's Issue Agenda." *Political Research Quarterly* 58: 577–85.

Yates, J., Whitford, A., and Gillespie, W. 2005. "Agenda Setting, Issue Priorities and Organizational Maintenance: The US Supreme Court, 1955 to 1994." *British Journal of Political Science* 35: 369–81.

Zorn, C. 2002. "U.S. Government Litigation Strategies in the Federal Appellate Courts." *Political Research Quarterly* 55: 145–66.

CHAPTER 22

COVERING THE COURTS

RORIE SOLBERG

How We Study the Media

The Founding Fathers recognized the media as a key component of democracy, enshrining freedom of the press in the First Amendment along with other individual freedoms related to expression. The framers of our government understood that a free media was essential to the success of their democratic experiment. The founders believed an independent Supreme Court was equally essential. However, it is unlikely that they foresaw the importance of the relationship that would develop between these two institutions. For the Court, the media's transmission of information to the public is especially consequential to institutional credibility. The Supreme Court, as we know by rote, has "neither the power of the purse nor the sword" and therefore is reliant upon the good will of the public for its exalted position in our system.[1] As the public gains most of its information about government actions and policies via the media, any understanding of our political institutions, and perhaps especially the Supreme Court as the Court ensures it is woefully ill-equipped to communicate directly, is incomplete without the concomitant study of the media's coverage of those institutions.

It is perhaps to state the obvious that the media's most fundamental role in our political system is to act as a producer of information to the public—directing the flow of news about the various political institutions' decisional behavior, outputs, and composite personalities to its audience. In performing this role, the media frames governmental activities and decisions—painting a picture or molding the presentation in a way that affects the public's perception of and support for those institutions (see, e.g., Hibbing and Theiss-Morse 1995).[2]

Yet, the Court eschews direct contact with the public—communicating its policies to the public only through orders and opinions rife with legalese, difficult prose, and erudite references. The Court, then, by default allows the media to act as its interpreter (with little or no assistance coming from the Court in this endeavor). The framing the media places on its interpretation is vital to a healthy and legitimate Supreme Court. Not surprisingly, therefore, what the media chooses to cover about the Court and how the media performs that coverage have been central concerns of Court scholars. In these studies the media's coverage is the dependent variable—the object that is to be explained, that is, what does the media cover or report about the Court's activity and why? The understanding of dynamics of media coverage and how it represents the Court sits at the heart of this line of inquiry. In general, this work on the media coverage of the Court is focused heavily on the print media, with some attention provided to the major broadcast networks, news magazines, and more recently to additional outlets like CNN or Fox News. It is worth bearing in mind that all we know about the media's coverage of the Court may be reaching its shelf life as newspapers approach extinction, a greater variety of channels fragment the audience, and social media takes on the role of disseminating information to the public.

A second rich vein of analysis has been to study the media's coverage of the Supreme Court for its instrumental value in understanding judicial legitimacy or other aspects of judicial behavior. Can media coverage affect the public's view of the Court or its outputs? And does media coverage affect the decision-making of the justices? Given the role the mass media plays in our political system described above, it is no wonder that the work of reporters finds its way into many of our studies of judicial politics. When examining the role or power of the Court in our system—the ability of the Court to maintain its legitimacy and pass that legitimacy onto its specific decisions—the media's coverage of the Court serves as an integral part of the examination (see Franklin and Kosaki 1989; Mondak 1994; Clawson and Waltenburg 2003, 2008; Clawson, Strine, and Waltenburg 2003). Media coverage of the Court has been equally useful for understanding the public's support for it as an institution overall—that is, the public's diffuse support for the Court (Baird and Gangl 2006; Gibson and Caldeira 2011; Woodson, Gibson, and Lodge 2012; Johnston and Bartels 2010). In this subset of work, the media coverage is an independent variable—a key concept to understanding a different political phenomenon or behavior.

Obviously, these two streams of research cross paths as scholars establish that there are different media frames associated with the Court or its outputs, and these different frames might affect the public's perception of the Court and/or its policies. Again, a frame is created by the various decisions made by journalists and editors on how to portray each individual story and institution. Just as the frame of a painting can alter the experience of the observer, media frames can influence the conclusions of the media's audience. The research of Clawson and her various coauthors is an excellent example of a research program that combines examining the media as an independent and dependent variable. Beginning with content analyses of the mainstream and specialized media, she demonstrates the presence of qualitatively different frames across the different types of media sources (Towner, Clawson, and Waltenburg 2006; Clawson, Strine, and Waltenburg 2003). In subsequent research, she incorporates these frames into experimental stimuli to test whether different media frames affect the Court's capacity to legitimize policies (Clawson and Waltenburg 2003, 2008). In the end, Clawson and her colleagues' work suggests that the frame placed on information, and the differences in the frames used by the mainstream and Black or Hispanic press, may affect audience perceptions of the Court. For example, in their 2003 study, Clawson and Waltenburg examine the framing of a major affirmative action decision. In the mainstream media, the case was framed as one of disallowing the allocation of government resources for reasons other than merit. In speaking of the outcome, this group of media discussed the end of racial preferences and reverse discrimination. The decision was a net gain in terms of moving toward a color-blind society and the stories were riddled with quotes from the majority justices. Yet, in the Black press the decision was couched as a setback not a move forward. Unlike the mainstream media's propensity to quote Justice Sandra Day O'Connor's phrase, "The Constitution protects persons, not groups," the Black media turned to Black leaders instead, quoting Jesse Jackson as saying, "While we react to those wearing white sheets, those wearing black robes are killing our dreams and our justice." In turn, these altered perceptions potentially can have consequences for the Court's overall reservoir of public support (but see Gibson, Caldeira and Spence 2003).

Finally, there is another body of literature on media coverage of the Court that is more instrumental. This research uses the media coverage as a tool when trying to measure elusive concepts like case salience or complexity. Gauging these abstract concepts often require creative operationalization. Thus the attention the media provides a case has often served as a proxy for salience (e.g., Epstein and Segal 2000). Here the media serves as leverage for scholars and provides a foothold or part of an index as we work toward measurements that are useful when explaining a variety of political behaviors—measurements with greater construct validity.

In the review that follows, I chart these different bodies of research literature on the media and the Supreme Court. I begin by describing what we know about the media's coverage of the Court—that is, the research literature that treats the coverage itself as the phenomenon of interest. What does the media choose to cover? How accurately or fully does it report on these phenomena? And what is the nature or tone of this coverage? I then turn my attention to the scholarship that treats the media's coverage of the Court as an explanatory or control variable. First, I consider the literature that examines the effect of the media's coverage on public attitudes toward the Court and/or its outputs. The media coverage in these studies serves as an independent variable of interest; however, the study is not focused on describing or explaining the coverage itself. Second I discuss other works that consider the media as an independent variable that systematically affects judicial behavior. Again, here the media is only one of the potential forces examined to explain judicial behavior. This review concludes with studies that employ the media in the operationalization of concepts consequential to judicial politics.

Media Coverage as the Dependent Variable

What Gets Covered?

As previously mentioned, the breadth and scope of media examined in this literature is generally narrow, often limited in terms of type of medium, number of outlets, and/or amount of time that is examined. Quite frankly, the task of data collection tends to limit the systematic exploration of media coverage of the Court. Recent innovations in machine coding, however, potentially provide access to oceans of data for analysis. Many extant studies describe the content of the coverage, as well as how well and how accurately the coverage represents the work of the Court. In general, studies since the 1970s have found the media's coverage to be wanting, rendering a distorted, incomplete, or even erroneous image of the Court's work. For one thing, the Court's decisional docket is not fully covered. Many scholars examining various types of media—newspapers, news magazines, broadcast networks—and sometimes using longer periods of time all conclude that what the media covers is only an abridged version of the composition of the Court's docket. In other words, the reality of the Court's work and the reality of the media's total coverage do not match (see Ericson 1977; Solimine 1980; Katsh 1983; Tarpley 1984; Larson 1985; O'Callaghan and Dukes 1992; Bowles and Bromley 1992; Larson 1995;, Slotnick and Segal 1998; Spill and Oxley 2003; Stoutenborough, Haider-Markel, and Allen 2006; and Solberg and Waltenburg 2014b).

As Larson (1985) notes, however, scholars should not be too quick to blame the media for what they consider to be poor coverage of the Court and its business. What to cover and how much coverage to provide a case or the institution is a complicated calculus that involves a variety of factors. Accordingly, some scholars have attempted to identify the nature of those cases that seem to warrant greater media attention. Relying on the concept of "news pegs," Solberg and Waltenburg find that the major national newspapers do indeed make different calculations in terms of which cases deserve extended coverage (2014b).[3] Examining five separate Terms of the Court (1976, 1985, 1989, 1996, and 2006) and three major newspapers (*The New York Times, The Washington Post,* and the *Los Angeles Times*), Solberg and Waltenburg identified only sixty-two news pegs over all of these terms and media; moreover, the different newspapers did not necessarily focus on the same cases. This finding may have implications for those scholars utilizing media coverage as a measure of case salience if their measure does not account for unique editorial decisions. For example, if a measure of salience depends solely on the appearance of a case on the front page of one major paper, the measure will be affected by the editorial decisions of that paper and the findings discussed here suggest that editorial decisions across major papers regarding which cases deserve coverage do not always converge.

Continuing in this vein, Solberg and Waltenburg explore the coverage of "landmark" cases, as identified in Congressional Quarterly's *Guide to the U.S. Supreme Court* (2010). Their findings regarding the varied editorial decisions hold. Very few of these cases generate enough newsworthiness to become a news peg, let alone to achieve peg status across all three national newspapers, although Solberg and Waltenburg do find a temporal dimension (i.e., an increasing rate/scope of coverage over time) seemingly at work. In later Terms of the Court, these legally and politically salient cases receive a great deal more coverage (17 percent, 27 percent, 24 percent, 55 percent, and 52 percent of all case coverage in the 1975, 1985, 1989, 1996, and 2006 Terms of the Court respectively). It is interesting to speculate on the reason for this change. One possibility is that Court reporters are simply getting better at recognizing landmark rulings, particularly as this group of elite reporters obtains greater legal education before covering the Court (Davis 1994). Another possible reason is that the increasingly limited space provided for reporting on the Court coupled with a dramatically decreased number of decisions by the Court forces media convergence on a few key issues and cases.

If landmark status per se, does not fully account for higher levels of media coverage, what case characteristics are associated with media attention? Most frequently, the legal issue addressed in the dispute determines news coverage. Specifically, decisions dealing with the First Amendment, civil rights and liberties, and criminal justice get the lion's share of ink or air (Franklin and Kosaki 1995; O'Callaghan and Dukes 1992; Solberg and Waltenburg 2014b). These findings have remained consistent despite the dramatic reduction in the frequency of the Court's merits decisions in more recent Terms (Franklin and Kosaki 1995; Collins and Cooper 2012; Johnson and Socker 2012; Solberg and Waltenburg 2014b).

These are especially salient and polarizing social topics with activated constituencies arrayed on both sides, and therefore they play into the media's emphasis on drama with concomitant winners and losers (see, e.g., Boykoff and Boykoff 2007). Indeed, Solberg and Waltenburg (2014b) have shown that political and/or popular salience is a better indicator of likely coverage than the amount of cases in any particular issue area. Using the Supreme Court Database's "Issue" codes,[4] Solberg and Waltenburg find that decisions about the First Amendment, privacy, and criminal rights issues are more likely to find their way into reporter's columns, even though these issues do not necessarily account for the largest share of the Court's docket (see Tables 3.4a through 3.4f). Linos and Twist (2013) find that coverage of salient issues increases as the issue remains on the public agenda or when an initially salient case is challenged in progeny cases. *Roe, Bakke, Buckley,* and *Bowers* all received less coverage than their subsequent challenges. Solberg and Waltenburg (2014a) also find that the *Roe* decision received less coverage than subsequent abortion decisions in their extensive look at media coverage of Justice Blackmun. Ura (2009), however, suggests that a nonrecursive relationship might be at work, inasmuch as the Court foists these issues onto the media's agenda by changing the status quo (see also Flemming, Bohte, and Wood 1997; Flemming, Wood, and Bohte 1999).

Other scholars have found that media attention is more pronounced when the story is "homegrown" (Franklin and Kosaki 1995; Hoekstra 2003; Haider-Markel, Allen, and Johansen 2006; Davis 1994) or has appeal to select readership. In several studies Clawson and her coauthors have shown that the specialized media tends to pitch stories that are of particular relevance and appeal to their audiences (Clawson, Strine, and Waltenburg 2003; Towner, Clawson, and Waltenburg 2006; Clawson and Waltenburg 2009). Without this local or niche angle, however, coverage is generally anemic. It tends to emphasize results in terms of winners and losers and pays little heed to a decision's consequences given the fullness of time or to any broader underlying issues (Shaw 1981).

In terms of relaying the content of the Court's decisions to the public, the media again falls short. The media does not often provide insight into the rationale for any individual decision, eschewing the legal justifications proffered by the majority in support of the final outcome. When such references are reported, the references focus on justifications discussing either the demands of the Constitution, founders' intent, or legal precedent (Spill and Oxley 2003: Solberg and Waltenburg 2014b).

Just as the media's coverage of the Court's outputs is apt to be incomplete and driven by specific issues or events, so too is the media's attention to individual justices. Certain moments in a justice's career life cycle—nominations and confirmations, resignations or death—or a close association with a given case or precedent (e.g., Justice Blackmun and abortion, Chief Justice Rehnquist and the Clinton impeachment) that attract media attention. Otherwise, the justices attract little in the way of media notice particularly when compared to coverage of the president or leaders of Congress.[5] This is true for both the print and electronic media (Solberg and Waltenburg 2014a, 2014b; Diascro 2008).

How Is the Coverage?

Although in general the media's coverage of the Court, its work, and its members are both myopic and anemic, we do know that there is appreciable variation in the *quality* of the coverage. Simply put, some media and some reporters do better than others. Newspapers out cover broadcast media; Court reporters are more thorough than generalists; national papers provide more coverage than local or regional papers; and *The New York Times* deserves its title of "paper of record" in terms of its coverage of the Supreme Court (see Spill and Oxley 2003; Segal and Slotnick 1998; Davis 1987; Solberg and Waltenburg 2014b).

Reporters assigned to the Supreme Court as their main beat are an elite group oftentimes possessing some type of legal training (Davis 1994). The majority of reporters that may cover the Court from time to time, on the other hand, have little or no background in the law or the judicial process (see Grey 1968, MacKenzie 1979, and Shaw 1981, but see LaRowe 2010 and Davis 2014 for the suggestion that this is changing). Not surprisingly, then, Court reporters' coverage of the Court is different from their staff or wire service counterparts. They tend to provide more information on a decision and its rationale than other reporters, and they write more frequently on the Court and cover more cases as well. Court reporters' stories, however, are not significantly longer on average than the stories of non-beat reporters. The similarity in average story length is a consequence of the beat reporters filing more stories. These additional stories tend to concern less consequential cases and therefore are shorter, thereby bringing down the average length (Spill and Oxley 2003).

For the most part, smaller local newspapers do not cover the Court well. In many instances, they utilize wire services and often edit down the longer wire stories to reduce the amount of information provided (Spill and Oxley 2003). However, when a case has a local connection, Hoekstra (2003) and Davis (1994) find that the local papers do a more thorough job. Hale (1999, 2006), Yanus (2009), and Vining and Wilhelm (2010) find that the likelihood of coverage in local papers increases when the decision reported is constitutional, when the paper is locally owned, and if dissenting votes or amicus participation accompany the Court ruling.

What Is the Tone of the Coverage?

Traditionally, the media's coverage of the Court has been highly positive and deferential, emphasizing the notion that the Court is a unique institution in the political system, and the justices are merely objective interpreters of the Constitution, the nation's "sacred text" (Spill and Oxley 2003). Davis (1994) provides a variety of explanations for this tone. These include the Court's control over the information released about its decisions and actions and a tendency of the journalists covering the Court to become captured by it. According to Davis, these journalists perceive the Court as a critical institution to American democracy. Therefore, they promote the myth of the Court as the neutral interpreter of the Constitution and adopt the role of the Court's protector (see also Spill and Oxley 2003).

This tendency among the media toward deference and an emphasis on the non-political aspects of the Court's outputs and the justices' behaviors may be changing, however. As Gibson and Caldeira note, we "live in an era in which nearly all observers of the legal process acknowledge the key role of ideology and political values in the decision-making processes of the U.S. Supreme Court (2011: 195). And this certainly seeps into the media's coverage. Contrary to the expectations that one might have given the myth of court, Spill and Oxley (2003) find that neither broadcast news nor non-beat reporters are especially deferential to the justices.

Moreover, these reporters tend to focus more on the social and/or political implications of a case rather than its legal implications. In an examination of two national newspapers from 1997 to 2004, LaRowe (2010) found that Court reporters produced stories significantly more negative in tone than their non-beat counterparts. Interestingly, despite their tendency towards some sort of legal training, he also found that the Court reporters included fewer discussions of the legal implications of a decision in their stories than did the non-beat reporters. And in the most comprehensive analysis to date, Solberg and Waltenburg, examining the coverage of three national newspapers and one broadcast network over six terms between 1975 and 2009 (two terms each for the past three Chief Justices) find that the content of stories, including references to the political aspects of Court decisions, has changed (2014b). Specifically, they show that references to political justifications for a decision increase appreciably across the time period. Importantly, they also find that these references to political justifications are not crowding out the mentions of legal justifications. Thus, there seems to be a braiding of a "political" Court with the traditional legal characterization.

Media Coverage of the Court as an Independent Variable

As was noted above, that there is a tone to the media's coverage of the Court may have important implications for how the public perceives the Court and its outputs. Indeed, as early as 1964, Newland recognized the link between the media, the Court, and the Court's legitimacy, and a number of scholars have attempted to measure whether media frames bear upon the public's attitudes. This research literature can be divided into two general groups—one assessing media frames and the Court's capacity to legitimate policies and one assessing media portrayals of the Court and the Court's institutional legitimacy.

The Media and the Court's Legitimizing Capacity

Studies examining the effect of media frames on the public's attitudes toward Court decisions generally have found that differences in the media's coverage have a systematic effect on public opinion. In a carefully constructed experiment, Clawson and Waltenburg (2003, 2008), using stimuli derived from the different ways in which the mainstream and Black press frame Court affirmative action decisions, show that the nature of the frame affects an individual's willingness to support or accept the decision. Subjects exposed to the stimulus derived from the Black press frame, with its more critical portrayal of the Court's opinion, were appreciably less likely to support the ruling. Moving outside of the laboratory setting, Stoutenborough, Haider-Markel, and Allen arrive at a similar conclusion. Examining public attitudes towards homosexual relations following the Court's *Lawrence v. Texas* decision, they find the Court's pro-gay rights decision did not increase public support for homosexual relations "because media coverage of the decision turned negative and provided mixed signals by highlighting Justice Scalia's dissenting opinion" (2006: 431). However, in an experiment in which he manipulated the wording of *The New York Times* stories on specific Court decisions, Mondak fails to find an effect of the nature of media reports on the Court's capacity to legitimate policies: "Variance in media reports does not limit the Court's power of legitimation" (1994: 689).

It is not only the nature or tone of the media's coverage of the Court decision that affects the public's opinion about a Court policy, however; these studies show that individual context (e.g., demographic attributes, preexisting attitudes) conditions the effect of media reports as well. And this makes good sense. After all, studies of media effects have shown individual context and prior attitudes matter (Erbring, Goldenberg, and Miller 1980; Bartels 1993), and several studies of the Court's persuasive effect find that individuals do not react uniformly to a Court pronouncement validating a policy (Franklin and Kosaki 1989; Johnson and Martin 1998; Hoekstra and Segal 1996). Preexisting attitudes toward the policy or attitudes toward the Court can moderate individual responses to the Court's decision and subsequently diminish the ability of the Court to use the media to legitimize its pronouncements and/or the media's ability to undercut the Court's reservoir of public support.

The Media and the Court's Institutional Credibility

It is well established that those individuals who possess more knowledge of the Supreme Court tend to have greater levels of diffuse support for it (see, e.g., Gibson and Caldeira 2011: 200). Gibson and Caldeira (2009) have offered "Positivity Bias Theory" as an explanation for this condition. In simplest terms, the theory holds that exposure to information about the Court augments the Court's legitimacy because the information is seeded with messages and symbols that the Court is a unique institution in the political system, one deserving of respect (see also Gibson, Caldeira, and Spence 2003; Woodson, Gibson, and Lodge 2012; Gibson and Nelson 2014). This suggests that media reports about the Court or the judicial system may contribute to the Court's diffuse support provided the news stories include the appropriate symbols. Caldeira and Gibson (1986) have shown that as coverage of the Court increases so too does public support for it.

Some recent scholarship, however, has tempered this conclusion. The type of media (and therefore the tone of the message), the presence or absence of legal justifications (legal symbolism), reference to political motivations, and the mention of dissents all appear to affect diffuse or overall support for the Court as an institution (see Johnston and Bartels 2010; Nie and Waltenburg 2014; Baird and Gangl 2006; Christenson and Glick 2014; Zink, Spriggs, and Scott 2009; Linos and Twist 2013). Now, in some sense many of these media story elements—political motivations or references to dissenting opinions—run contrary to the myth that the Court is not "just another political institution" (Scheb and Lyons 2001: 181–2) as this type of information is normal fare in coverage of the other branches of government. And according to Gibson and Caldeira, this is where the Court gets into trouble: "To the extent that there is a threat to [the Court's diffuse support], it comes from events that challenge the view of the Court as a uniquely nonpolitical political institution" (2011: 200). In other words, the more the coverage of the Court mirrors the coverage of representative institutions, the more fragile the Court's stockpile of general or diffuse support from the public.

The Media and Judicial Behavior

That media coverage can affect public attitudes toward the Court and its outputs suggests that it may affect the justices' decisional behavior as well. Soundings on the public mood, concerns over personal reputation, or a need for respect and approval from particular "audiences" might result in the justices' attention and response to the media. For example, Davis (2011) writes that individual justices have become more willing to engage the media in order to defend the institution, explain themselves, or enter into policy debates. Baum (2006) categorizes the news media as an important policy group that disseminates information about a justice's behaviors. Since justices would prefer to have positive reviews of their work, they "could act on that interest, consciously or unconsciously, in making decisions" (Baum 2006: 138). Baum, in fact, tests this possibility by looking at a so-called Greenhouse effect, referring to the potential influence of veteran and Pulitzer Prize-winning Court reporter Linda Greenhouse. The Greenhouse effect reveals a liberal drift among justices embedded in a liberal social environment. He finds some evidence consistent with the Greenhouse effect and concludes it "should not be dismissed out of hand" (p. 151).

The Media as a Means of Operationalization

Finally, there are instances where the study of the media coverage of the Court is simply a means to an end. Students of the Court devote a great deal of time to analyzing judicial behavior. And, in deciphering the components driving judicial behavior, scholars often hypothesize that case salience will affect decision-making. As case salience is a complex and subjective distinction to place on any given case, Epstein and Segal (2000) spent some time examining the various operationalizations for salience used by political scientists. They find all previous measures to be unacceptable for a variety of reasons and offer an alternative: the front page of *The New York Times*. Thus, the study of this one newspaper's coverage of the Court becomes essential to fruitful research into judicial decision-making. Scholars readily accepted this measure and employed it in a series of studies (e.g., Bailey, Kamoie, and Maltzman 2005; Baird 2004; Giles, Blackstone, and Vining 2008; McAtee and McGuire 2007; Unah and Hancock 2006; Choi, Gulati, and Posner 2010; Casillas, Enns, and Wohlfarth 2011; Posner, Epstein, and Landes 2013). Collins and Cooper (2012) improve on this measure by expanding it beyond the front page and *The New York Times*. Clark, Lax, and Rice (2014 newsletter) also use newspaper coverage to model a different measure of case salience—one that tracks the coverage of the case throughout its lifetime before the Court.[6] Given the findings of Solberg and Waltenburg (2014b) regarding the reduction in coverage of Court decisions over time and the discrepancies in national newspaper convergence on which cases are "front-page worthy," scholars are likely to continue to modify and improve upon this measure.

Concluding Thoughts

As noted earlier, though the field of media coverage of the Court is well tilled, the knowledge gained may be expiring. As social networks usurp traditional and online media sources as the conduit for information, examining the trail of coverage may be more appropriate for understanding what information truly is disseminated. Do we need to follow the "shares," "likes," and "tweets" to determine salience? The questions new media offer are ripe for investigation. Even though there is a tendency for news media to focus on a few salient issues or over-cover these issues when the whole of the Court's docket is considered, is this trend likely to change in the world of social media? Will the "home-grown" effect disappear as individuals are less likely to be aware of cases before the Court that might be relevant to their geographical area? We have documented that most media do a shallow job of covering the Court and its work and leave most of the public woefully less informed about the totality of the Court's work or the breadth and scope of many of its decisions. Will this assessment change in light of the coverage provided via new media? Or does the magic of social networking mean that critical information or at least the decisions in major cases are disseminated more rapidly? Will most users be only a few degrees separated from a reputable legal source? Will dissent receive greater coverage? Will reporters take more time to delineate the rationales for a justice's decision when the constraints of column inches or airtime are removed (if indeed they are removed)?

This new frontier does not stop at the descriptive phase, however. If the tone of media coverage and/or the frame of that coverage can affect the specific or diffuse support for the Court, or affect the Court's capacity as a legitimizing body, then the importance of investigations into the new media becomes important for the role the Court plays in our polity. Some questions for future research follow upon the descriptive questions mentioned above. Are the frames placed on stories by the media exacerbated or mitigated by the comments that follow? Or perhaps there is some kind of systematic credibility measure for comments (number of likes etc.) that might give us a handle on how specific and diffuse support of the Court are now built. Indeed, instead of a "Greenhouse effect" we may have a "Facebook effect."

In terms of the tone of coverage, there is evidence that the tone of coverage may be important. In the world of social media, the tone of coverage is combined with the tone of comments. If the presentation of a dissenting opinion affects support, what is the effect of a significant number of negative (or positive) reactions by your network? Are dissents more likely to get greater coverage on new media thus extending this effect?

Solberg and Waltenburg (2014a, 2014b) find that there is a braiding of the legal and political portrayals of the Court in the more contemporary coverage. One might ask if this trend continues on the new media? Or perhaps more importantly, we might investigate how the combined messages are processed by the public. Does this dual portrayal affect institutional credibility? It certainly seems to affect how the public perceives the justices and their work.[7] However, this conclusion must be verified empirically. A theoretic or perhaps normative question would be whether the mediating role of the media in generating specific support for the Court is troubling for the Court or our system in general.

It is not just specific support that media coverage may influence. Diffuse or general support for the institution should be enduring (Bartels 1993), yet experimental designs, by their very nature, often require or expect immediate or rapid change. This tool, then, is well employed for studies of specific support for Court decisions (i.e., support for an individual decision), but we need an alternative for studying the marked decrease in institutional support for the Court.

As coverage of the Court evolves to match the way in which society obtains and processes information, our studies and our questions must likewise evolve. Understanding how the news media has covered the Court is intrinsically and instrumentally important to the study of judicial politics; however, the rapid and extensive changes in the realm of media means that as scholars, in some ways, we are starting from scratch.

But start from scratch we must. The medium may change from newspapers or broadcast/cable television delivery to dissemination of information via Facebook or Twitter, the scholarly questions driving these inquiries remain. After all, new technologies and changes in our methods for disseminating and receiving information do not alter the role the Court plays in our democracy nor do these changes reduce the effects of Supreme Court decisions on the meaning of various statutes and constitutional phrases. Indeed, the Court is poorly designed for interacting with the news media and these deficiencies will likely be exacerbated in the areas of social media where questions of judicial ethics collide with the distribution of information. Unlike members of Congress or the administration, blogs, podcasts, or YouTube channels do not appear to be viable venues for members of the judiciary given the constraints of judicial ethics (see http://www.ncsc.org/~/media/Files/PDF/Topics/Center%20for%20Judicial%20Ethics/Social-media-and-judicial-ethics.ashx; last accessed March 30, 2015). To continue to understand how the public receives and processes information about the Court and how these same phenomena affect the Court, its decisions and its legitimacy, we must continue to examine how the Court is covered and the influence of that same coverage.

Notes

1. "The judiciary, on the contrary, has no influence over either the sword or the purse; no direction either of the strength or of the wealth of the society; and can take no active resolution whatever. It may truly be said to have neither FORCE nor WILL, but merely judgment ..." *Federalist* 78.
2. e.g., if a story is presented as positive or negative is a basic type of framing (i.e., the glass is half full or half empty). The positive story leads to positive affect and vice versa.
3. A news peg is a concept developing from the media's characteristic event-oriented coverage. As such, any Supreme Court decision could serve as a news peg because it provides

attention to that case or issue that the media may incorporate in that day's news. However, here we require more than basic coverage of a case to reach the threshold of a news peg. We define a peg as a case that generates sustained media focus on the case or the underlying issue. Sustained focus is operationalized as a case that receives at least 1.5 standard deviations of coverage greater than the mean for all cases provided media attention during that October Term of the Court.

4. See http://scdb.wustl.edu/documentation.php?s=1.
5. Davis (2011), however, shows that there is a growing willingness of some justices to directly engage the media.
6. See also Cooper and Collins; Lewis and Vining and Wilhelm in the same volume also discussing the value of media coverage in the creation of measures of case salience.
7. See "Have American Politics Killed the Impartial Supreme Court?" Available at: http://www.washingtonpost.com/blogs/the-fix/wp/2014/05/08/have-american-politics-killed-the-impartial-supreme-court/.

References

Bailey, M. A., Kamoie B., and Maltzman F. 2005. "Signals from the Tenth Justice: The Political Role of the Solicitor General in Supreme Court Decision Making." *American Journal of Political Science* 49: 72–85.

Baird, V. A. 2004. "The Effect of Politically Salient Decisions on the US Supreme Court's Agenda." *Journal of Politics* 66(3): 755–72.

Baird, V. A., and Gangl, A. 2006. "Shattering the Myth of Legality: The Impact of the Media's Framing of Supreme Court Procedures on Perceptions of Fairness." *Political Psychology* 27(4): 597–614.

Bartels, L. M. 1993. "Messages Received: The Political Impact of Media Exposure." *American Political Science Review* 87(02): 267–85.

Baum, L. 2006. *Judges and their Audiences: A Perspective on Judicial Behavior*. Princeton, NJ: Princeton University Press.

Bowles, D. A., and Bromley, R. V. 1992. "Newsmagazine Coverage of the Supreme Court during the Reagan Administration." *Journalism & Mass Communication Quarterly* 69(4): 948–59.

Boykoff, M. T., and Boykoff, J. M. 2007. "Climate Change and Journalistic Norms: A Case-Study of US Mass-Media Coverage." *Geoforum* 38(6): 1190–204.

Caldeira, G. A., and Gibson, J. L. 1992. "The Etiology of Public Support for the Supreme Court." *American Journal of Political Science* 36(3): 635–64.

Casillas, C. J., Enns, P. K., and Wohlfarth, P. C. 2011. "How Public Opinion Constrains the US Supreme Court." *American Journal of Political Science* 55(1), 74–88.

Choi, S. J., Gulati, G. M., and Posner, E. A. 2010. "Professionals or Politicians: The Uncertain Empirical Case for an Elected Rather Than Appointed Judiciary." *Journal of Law, Economics, & Organization* 26(2): 290–336.

Christenson, D. P., and Glick, D. M. 2015. "Chief Justice Roberts' Health Care Decision Disrobed: The Microfoundations of the Court's Legitimacy." *American Journal of Political Science* 59(2): 403–18.

Clark, T., Lax, J., and Rice D. 2014. "Measuring Salience as a Latent Variable." *Law & Courts Newsletter* 24(2): 8–10.

Clawson, R. A., Strine, H. IV, and Waltenburg, E. N. 2003. "Framing Supreme Court Decisions" The Mainstream versus the Black Press. *Journal of Black Studies* 33(6): 784–800.

Clawson, R. A., and Waltenburg, E. N. 2003. "Support for a Supreme Court Affirmative Action Decision: A Story in Black and White." *American Politics Research* 31(3): 251–79.

Clawson, R. A., and Waltenburg, E. N. 2008. *Legacy and Legitimacy: Black Americans and the Supreme Court*. Philadelphia, PA: Temple University Press.

Collins, T. A. and Cooper, C. A. 2012. "Case Salience and Media Coverage of Supreme Court Decisions: Toward a New Measure." *Political Research Quarterly* 65: 396–407.

Davis, R. 1987. "Lifting the Shroud: News Media Portrayal of the US Supreme Court." *Communications and the Law* 9: 43–59.

Davis, R. 1994. *Decisions and Images: The Supreme Court and the Press*. Englewood Cliffs, NJ: Prentice-Hall.

Davis, R. 2011. *Justices and Journalists: The US Supreme Court and the Media*. New York, NY: Cambridge University Press.

Diascro, J. S. 2008. "Legacy of Chief Justice Rehnquist: A View from the Small Screen." *Judicature* 92(3): 106–17.

Epstein, L., and Segal, J. A. 2000. "Measuring Issue Salience." *American Journal of Political Science* 44(1): 66–83.

Erbring, L., Goldenberg, E. N., and Miller, A. H. 1980. "Front-Page News and Real-World Cues: A New Look at Agenda-Setting by the Media." *American Journal of Political Science* 24: 16–49.

Ericson, D. 1977. "Newspaper Coverage of the Supreme Court: A Case Study." *Journalism Quarterly* 54(3): 605–7.

Flemming, R. B., Bohte, J., and Wood, B. D. 1997. "One Voice among Many: The Supreme Court's Influence on Attentiveness to Issues in the United States, 1947–92." *American Journal of Political Science* 41(4): 1224–50.

Flemming, R. B., Wood, B. D., and Bohte, J. 1999. "Attention to Issues in a System of Separated Powers: The Macrodynamics of American Policy Agendas." *Journal of Politics* 61(1): 76–108.

Franklin, C. H., and Kosaki, L. C. 1995." Media, Knowledge, and Public Evaluations of the Supreme Court." In *Contemplating Courts*, edited by L. Epstein. Washington, DC: CQ Press.

Franklin, C. H., and Kosaki, L. C. 1989. "Republican Schoolmaster: The US Supreme Court, Public Opinion, and Abortion." *The American Political Science Review* 83(3): 751–71.

Gibson, J. L., and Caldeira, G. A. 2009. *Citizens, Courts, and Confirmations: Positivity Theory and the Judgments of the American People*. Princeton, NJ: Princeton University Press.

Gibson, J. L., and Caldeira, G. A. 2011. "Has Legal Realism Damaged the Legitimacy of the US Supreme Court?" *Law & Society Review* 45(1): 195–219.

Gibson, J. L., Caldeira, G. A., and Spence, L. K. 2003. "Measuring Attitudes toward the United States Supreme Court." *American Journal of Political Science* 47(2): 354–67.

Gibson, J. L., and Nelson, M. J. 2014. "Is the US Supreme Court's Legitimacy Grounded in Performance Satisfaction and Ideology?" *American Journal of Political Science* 59(1): 162–74.

Giles, M. W., Blackstone, B., and Vining, R. L. 2008. "The Supreme Court in American Democracy: Unraveling the Linkages between Public Opinion and Judicial Decision Making." *The Journal of Politics* 70(2): 293–306.

Grey, D. L. 1968. *The Supreme Court and the News Media*. Evanston, IL: Northwestern University Press.

Haider-Markel, D. P., Allen, M. D., and Johansen, M. 2006. "Understanding Variations in Media Coverage of US Supreme Court Decisions Comparing Media Outlets in their Coverage of Lawrence v. Texas." *The Harvard International Journal of Press/Politics* 11(2): 64–85.

Hale, F. D. 1999. "Chief Justices' Perceptions of News Coverage of State Supreme Courts." *Newspaper Research Journal* 20: 17–28.

Hale, F. D. 2006. "Newspaper Coverage Limited for State Supreme Court Cases." *Newspaper Research Journal* 27: 6–17.

Hibbing, J. R., and Theiss-Morse, E. 1995. *Congress as Public Enemy: Public Attitudes toward American Political Institutions*. Cambridge: Cambridge University Press.

Hoekstra, V. J. 2003. *The Supreme Court and Local Public Opinion*. New York, NY: Cambridge University Press.

Hoekstra, V. J., and Segal, J. A. 1996. "The Shepherding of Local Public Opinion: The Supreme Court and Lamb's Chapel." *Journal of Politics* 58(4): 1079–102.

Johnson, T., and Socker, E. 2012. "Actions, Factions, and Interactions: Newsworthy Influences on Supreme Court Coverage." *Social Science Quarterly* 93(2): 434–63.

Johnson, T. R., and Martin, A. D. 1998. "The Public's Conditional Response to Supreme Court Decisions." *American Political Science Review* 92(2): 299–309.

Johnston, C. D., and Bartels, B. L. 2010. "Sensationalism and Sobriety Differential Media Exposure and Attitudes toward American Courts." *Public Opinion Quarterly* 74: 260–86.

Katsh, E. 1983. "Supreme Court Beat: How Television Covers the US Supreme Court." *Judicature* 67: 6–11.

LaRowe, N. 2010. "On and off the Supreme Court Beat: A Content Analysis of Newspaper Coverage of the Supreme Court from 1997–2004." *APSA 2010 Annual Meeting Paper*.

Larson, S. G. 1985. "How the *New York Times* Covered Discrimination Cases." *Journalism Quarterly* 62: 894–6.

Larson, S. G. 1995. "The Content of Supreme Court Coverage: Making Sense of the Relationship between the Media and Public Confidence." *Southeastern Political Review* 23(2): 231–44.

Linos, K., and Twist, K. 2013. "Endorsement and Framing Effects in Experimental and Natural Settings: The Supreme Court, the Media and the American Public." University of California at Berkeley Public Law Research Paper (2223732).

MacKenzie, J. P. 1979. "Closed Courtrooms." *ABA Journal* 65: 52–5.

McAtee, A., and McGuire, K. T. 2007. "Lawyers, Justices, and Issue Salience: When and How Do Legal Arguments Affect the US Supreme Court?" *Law & Society Review* 41(2): 259–78.

Mondak, J. J. 1994. "Policy Legitimacy and the Supreme Court: The Sources and Contexts of Legitimation." *Political Research Quarterly* 47(3): 675–92.

Newland, C. A. 1964. "Press Coverage of the U.S. Supreme Court." *Western Political Quarterly* 17: 15–36.

Nie, M., and Waltenburg, E. N. 2014. "Media Impact on Diffuse Support for the Supreme Court: The Black Media." Paper prepared for presentation at the annual meeting of the Midwest Political Science Association, Chicago, IL.

O'Callaghan, J., and Dukes, J. O. 1992. "Media Coverage of the Supreme Court's Caseload." *Journalism & Mass Communication Quarterly* 69(1): 195–203.

Posner, R. A., Epstein L., and Landes, W. M. 2013. "How Business Fares in the Supreme Court." *Minnesota Law Review* 97: 1431–72.

Savage, D. 2010. *Guide to the U.S. Supreme Court*, 5th ed. Washington, DC: Congressional Quarterly Press.

Scheb, J. M., and Lyons, W. 2001. "Judicial Behavior and Public Opinion: Popular Expectations Regarding the Factors that Influence Supreme Court Decisions." *Political Behavior* 23: 181–94.

Shaw, D. 1981. "Media Coverage of the Courts: Improving but Still Not Adequate." *Judicature* 65: 18–24.

Slotnick, E. E., and Segal, J. A. 1998. *Television News and the Supreme Court: All the News That's Fit to Air?* New York, NY: Cambridge University Press.

Solberg, R. L., and Waltenburg, E. N. 2014a. "Constructing Harry Blackmun." In *Covering the United States Supreme Court in the Digital Age*, edited by R. Davis. New York, NY: Cambridge University Press, 109–25.

Solberg, R. L., and Waltenburg, E. N. 2014b. *The Media, The Court, and the Misrepresentation: The New Myth of the Court*. New York, NY: Routledge.

Solimine, M. E. 1980. "Newsmagazine Coverage of the Supreme Court." *Journalism & Mass Communication Quarterly* 57(4): 661–3.

Spill, R. L., and Oxley, Z. M. 2003. "Philosopher Kings or Political Actors: How the Media Portray the Supreme Court." *Judicature* 87: 22–9.

Stoutenborough, J. W., Haider-Markel, D. P., and Allen, M. D. 2006. "Reassessing the Impact of Supreme Court Decisions on Public Opinion: Gay Civil Rights Cases." *Political Research Quarterly* 59(3): 419–33.

Tarpley, J. D. 1984. "American Newsmagazine Coverage of the Supreme Court, 1978–81." *Journalism Quarterly* 61(4): 801–26.

Towner, T. L., Clawson, R. A., and Waltenburg, E. N. 2006. "View from Mainstream, Black, and Latino Journalists." *Judicature* 90(3): 120–8.

Unah, I., and Hancock, A. 2006. "US Supreme Court Decision Making, Case Salience, and the Attitudinal Model." *Law & Policy* 28(3): 295–320.

Ura, J. D. 2009. "The Supreme Court and Issue Attention: The Case of Homosexuality." *Political Communication* 26(4): 430–46.

Vining, R. L., and Wilhelm, T. 2010. "Explaining High-Profile Coverage of State Supreme Court Decisions." *Social Science Quarterly* 91(3): 704–23.

Woodson, B., Gibson, J. L., and Lodge, M. 2012. "Judicial Symbols and the Link between Institutional Legitimacy and Acquiescence." *APSA 2012 Annual Meeting Paper*.

Yanus, A. B. 2009. "Full-Court Press: An Examination of Media Coverage of State Supreme Courts." *Justice System Journal* 30(2): 180–95.

Zink, J. R., Spriggs, J. F., II, and Scott J. T. 2009. "Courting the Public: The Influence of Decision Attributes on Individuals' Views of Court Opinions." *Journal of Politics* 71: 909–25.

CHAPTER 23

THE SUPREME COURT AND PUBLIC OPINION

JOSEPH DANIEL URA
AND ALISON HIGGINS MERRILL

In March 2012, the Supreme Court heard oral arguments in *National Federation of Independent Business v. Sebelius* (2012) which considered the constitutionality of a requirement for individuals to purchase health insurance and other provisions in the Patient Protection and Affordable Care Act (ACA). When the justices initially discussed the case in conference, five justices—Alito, Thomas, Kennedy, Scalia, and Roberts—agreed that the individual insurance mandate exceeded Congress's authority under the interstate commerce clause and could not otherwise be justified within the scope of Congress's constitutionally enumerated powers (Crawford 2012). As chief justice, John Roberts was the senior member of this working majority and assigned responsibility for drafting an opinion invalidating the individual mandate.

Over the next several weeks, though, external pressure on the Court to uphold the mandate grew. President Obama publicly asserted that striking down an important pillar of the ACA would be an "unprecedented, extraordinary step," and that his administration was "confident that this [law] will be upheld" (Daly 2012). Senate Judiciary Committee Chairman Patrick Leahy urged Chief Justice Roberts to keep in mind "the proper role of the judicial branch" and "defer to Congress" by upholding the ACA (Mears 2012). Political writers and legal experts claimed that a decision invalidating the ACA would undermine the legitimacy of the Court in the minds of the American people. For example, Elizabetha Wydra wrote in *Politico* that, "the legitimacy of the judiciary is at stake if the justices fail to uphold their duty to follow the law" (2012). Likewise, Akhil Amar Reed said in an interview that a 5–4 ruling against the ACA would show his life to be a "fraud" because "here I was in my silly little office, thinking law mattered, and it really didn't" (Klein 2012).

Amidst these claims, Chief Justice Roberts's opposition to the ACA's mandate for individuals to purchase insurance became "wobbly" (Crawford 2012). Jeffrey Toobin argues that Roberts began to see a decision against the ACA as a threat to "the Court's place as a respected final arbiter of the nation's dispute" by leading "Democrats and perhaps President Obama himself [to] crusade against the Court, eroding its moral if not its legal authority" (2012, see also Christenson and Glick 2014; Franklin 2012; Liptak 2012; Rosen 2012; Roy 2012). Despite intense pressure from other conservative justices on the Court, these doubts eventually crystalized in Chief Justice Roberts's majority opinion upholding the individual mandate under Congress's power to collect taxes (Crawford 2012; Toobin 2012). Though Chief Justice Roberts also made aggressive efforts to lobby other conservatives to join his opinion, at least in part, his overtures were rejected, leading to the 5–4 vote in favor of upholding the individual mandate (Crawford 2012).

While some commentators suggest that Chief Justice Roberts's switch reflected a sincere change of heart about the correct answer to the Constitutional questions presented in *National Federation of Independent Business v. Sebelius* (Walsh 2012), most in-depth journalistic accounts of the Court's decision describe Chief Justice Roberts's behavior as the product of interactions among his political preferences, his views about how the public would react to the decision, and his concern that the public would abandon its faith in the Court in the face of another important case resolved by a bare partisan majority. This narrative points squarely at the important role that public opinion can play in the behavior of the U.S. Supreme Court and raises the same basic questions that confront scholars interested in the reciprocal relationships between constitutional courts and the mass public: How strong is Americans' support for the Supreme Court? What motivates support for the Supreme Court? How does the public's support for the Supreme Court relate to judicial independence? How and under what conditions does the Supreme Court respond to public opinion, and how does the public react to the Court's decisions?

In this chapter, we discuss some answers to these basic questions that emerge from the scholarly literatures linking U.S. public opinion and the Supreme Court. Though political scientists and other researchers increasingly address connections between public opinion and courts in the U.S. states and other nations, the bulk of research on this issue continues to focus on the case of U.S. national politics. Although we draw on these rapidly developing bodies of research, our focus will be the Supreme Court of the United States.

The scientific study of the Supreme Court and public opinion is divided into a pair of overlapping research agendas. The first considers the development of public attitudes about the Supreme Court among the American people and the consequences of those attitudes for judicial behavior and the Court's institutional integrity. The second considers how Americans' policy attitudes influence the behavior of justices and the decisions of the Supreme Court and how the Court's decisions influence public opinion.

We proceed by discussing research on the public's attitudes about judicial legitimacy and how public opinion supports and shapes judicial authority within the separation of powers system. Next, we consider how the Supreme Court influences American's policy attitudes and continue by considering how public opinion shapes the behavior of Supreme Court justices and the decisions of the Court. Finally, we conclude by discussing some promising avenues for continued research on the relationship between courts and public opinion.

Public Support for the Supreme Court

How Strong Is Americans' Support for the Supreme Court?

This question is somewhat more complicated than it might appear. For half a century, political scientists have recognized two classes of attitudes about institutions in general and about constitutional courts in particular: specific support and diffuse support (Easton 1965). As defined by David Easton, specific support refers to "the favorable attitudes and predisposition stimulated by outputs that are perceived by [individuals] to meet their demands as they arise or in anticipation" (1965: 273). In other words, specific support follows from the belief that an institution is producing outcomes consistent with one's interests and preferences. Gibson refers to specific support as "performance satisfaction" (2012: 13).

Conversely, diffuse support refers to "reservoir of favorable attitudes or goodwill that helps members to accept or tolerate outputs to which they are opposed or the effects of which they see as damaging to their wants" (Easton 1965: 273). Diffuse support represents a willingness to accept and abide by an institution's decisions even when those decisions are inconsistent with one's interests and preferences. Gibson equates diffuse support with "legitimacy" and "loyalty" (2012: 17).

Though specific support and diffuse support are discrete concepts, in theory and in practice the two dimensions of public attitudes toward the Supreme Court are linked. There is a significant, positive association across individuals between evaluations of the Supreme Court's performance and beliefs about the Court's legitimacy (Gibson, Caldeira, and Spence 2003b). Those who express the greatest general approval of the Supreme Court also tend to express the most loyalty toward the Court. However, the relationship between these two variables is far from perfect and, as we discuss below, the subject of ongoing scholarly debate. Descriptively, though, strength of Americans' support for the Supreme Court therefore deals with two sets of political attitudes that are related: whether Americans approve of the job the Supreme Court is doing and whether they regard the Court as a legitimate institution even in the face of disagreements with its actions.

The concept of "approval" is one of the closest analogues to specific support utilized in commercial and academic surveys of attitudes towards governing institutions and political figures. A direct way to measure approval is to ask Americans whether they approve of the job the Supreme Court is doing in the same way that they are regularly asked to evaluate presidential job performance. Since 2000, Gallup has at least once a year asked a representative sample of Americans, "Do you approve or disapprove of the way the Supreme Court is handling its job?" Figure 23.1 illustrates the proportion of Gallup respondents who approve of the way the Supreme Court handles its job among respondents who answered yes or no (i.e., excluding those who offered no opinion). For years,

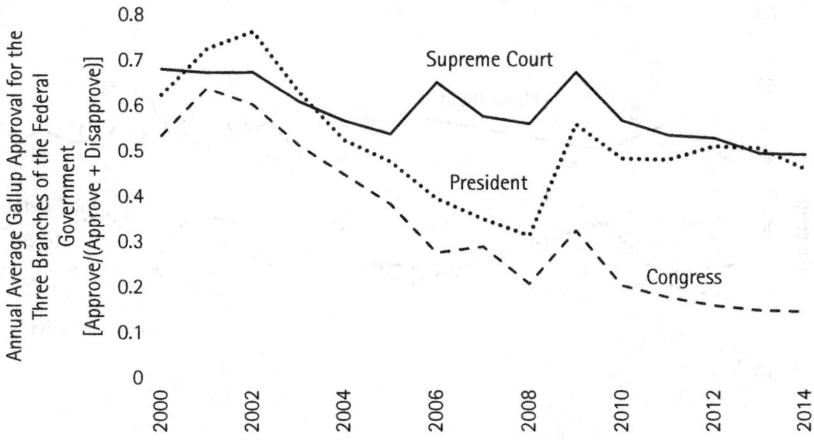

FIGURE 23.1 Approval of the Supreme Court, Congress, and president

Source: Gallup 2000–14.

with more than one survey, the figure shows annual mean approval. For comparison's sake, Figure 23.1 also shows mean annual approval for Congress and the president.

Over the last decade and a half, Americans' approval of the Supreme Court has generally been higher and more stable than their approval of either Congress or the president. Supreme Court approval has been higher than either presidential or congressional approval in eleven of the fourteen years covered by the Gallup data. In that same period, presidential and congressional approval range about 0.45 and 0.49, respectively. In contrast, the difference between the highest and the lowest annual Supreme Court approval measures is only 0.18. Also, though approval of the Supreme Court spiked in a positive direction in 2005 and 2009, the Gallup data show that the Court's approval has generally declined in recent years, especially since 2009. It is unclear whether this decline indicates that Supreme Court approval was unusually high when the Gallup series began in 2000—in which case the decline may simply be a return to normalcy—or whether the apparent downward trend represents a more meaningful rejection of the Court (see Gibson and Caldeira 2009).

A second Gallup question provides additional evidence about Americans' specific support for the Supreme Court and some insight on the recent downward trend in Supreme Court approval. In 1991, 1993, 1995, nearly every year since 2001, Gallup has asked Americans whether they view the Supreme Court as "too liberal, too conservative, or about right?" Figure 23.2 illustrates the Gallup "too liberal, too conservative, or about right" time series from 1991 through 2014.

First, like the Gallup approval data, the ideological evaluations time series shows relatively high and stable support for the Supreme Court. By far, the modal response in each survey implementation is "about right" rather than "too liberal" or "two conservative." Also, only twice since 1991 have less than 40 percent of respondents answered "about right," and only once in that time has "about right" been voiced by 50 percent of survey participants. By and large, "about right" responses bounce around between 40 and 46 percent.

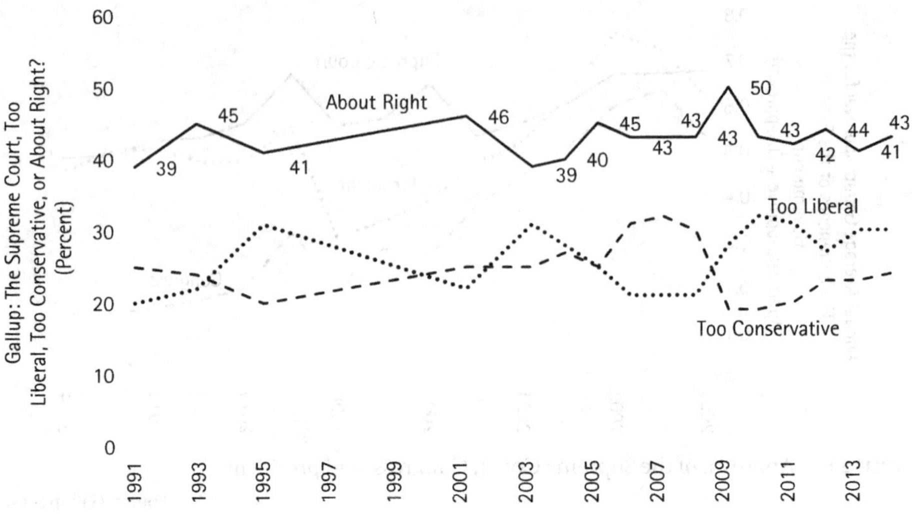

FIGURE 23.2 Ideological evaluations of the Supreme Court

Source: Gallup 1991–2014 with gaps.

Also, nearly as many Americans choose "too conservative" as "too liberal" across the span of this time series. Although there is some potentially consequential variance in the relative size of these groups, they each amount to between 20 and 30 percent of respondents in almost all implementations of these questions. There is a modest trend toward more Americans saying that the Court is either too liberal or too conservative, but this growth had principally come at the expense of the share of those who refuse to answer the question or answer "don't know" rather than from defections from the "about right" category. (This is consistent with growing partisan and ideological polarization in the mass public.) Given that it would be difficult for the Court to move many respondents from the "too liberal" category into the "about right" group without offsetting losses among those switching from "about right" to "too conservative" (and vice versa), the data seem to show that the Court is and has been well centered in the ideological space of American national politics for the past two decades.

Despite the general comparability in the size of the "too liberal" and "too conservative" response categories, it is interesting to note a reasonably strong correspondence between the relative sizes of the "too liberal" and "too conservative" response categories and approval of the Court. As we mentioned above, the Gallup data show a slight decline in approval of the Supreme Court since 2000 that is especially pronounced since 2009. Over the same period, there has also been a shift toward respondents asserting that the Court is "too liberal" rather than "too conservative." Between 2001 and 2014, the correlation between the Supreme Court's annual approval rating and the percentage of respondents claiming that the Supreme Court is "too liberal" is −0.36, while the correlation between its approval rate and the percentage answering "too conservative" is 0.11.

It is difficult to make strong claims on the basis of a decade of annual data points, but the Gallup poll results are consistent with the idea that conservatives and liberals translate their perceptions of the Court's ideological tendencies into approval evaluations differently. Indeed, they suggest that conservatives are more apt to say they disapprove of the Court when it diverges from their ideological preferences than liberals are when the Court diverges from theirs. (Again, this would be consistent with evidence that partisan polarization in the American public has been principally driven by Republicans, e.g., Ura and Ellis 2012). If this is the case, than the recent downturn in support for the Supreme Court may follow from a growing perception that the Supreme Court is slightly out of alignment to the left rather than any change in the total percentage of Americans who believe the Court is out of step with their ideological preferences.

Together, the Gallup approval series and the "too liberal, too conservative, or about right" series indicate that Americans' specific support for the Supreme Court is relatively high and stable. Americans have generally expressed greater approval of either the Supreme Court or Congress over the last decade and a half, and approval of the Supreme Court has been much more stable than approval of the elected branches of the national government. Similarly, a plurality of Americans say that the Supreme Court is neither too liberal nor too conservative. Although the data perhaps suggest a modest decline in specific support for the Supreme Court in recent years, the strength and stability of the Court's public standing are much more notable at this point.

Another survey measure of Americans' evaluations of the Supreme Court deal with the concept of "confidence." The General Social Survey (GSS), for example, which has been fielded roughly every two years since 1973, asks respondents about the level of "confidence" they have in the leaders of various branches of government. Specifically they ask:

> I am going to name some institutions in this country. As far as the people running these institutions are concerned, would you say you have a great deal of confidence, only some confidence, or hardly any confidence at all in them?

Responses to this question call individual attitudes related to both specific support (meeting demands as they arise of in anticipation) and diffuse support (a reservoir of goodwill). Gibson, Caldeira, and Spence (2003b) find that the GSS's confidence question addresses an array of judgments about the Court, including respondents' agreement with the policy implications of Supreme Court decisions and their degree of generalized trust and loyalty for the institution, and many scholars turn to the confidence question, especially as it is implemented by the GSS, to measure the public's broad disposition toward the Supreme Court (e.g., Clark 2009; Durr, Martin, and Wolbrecht 2000; Ura and Wohlfarth 2010). However, the majority of cross-sectional variance in responses to the confidence question appear to be related to specific support (Gibson, Caldeira, and Spence 2003b; see also Durr, Martin, and Wolbrecht 2000).

Among the institutions the GSS inquires about are the Supreme Court, Congress, and the "executive branch of the federal government." The proportion of GSS respondents

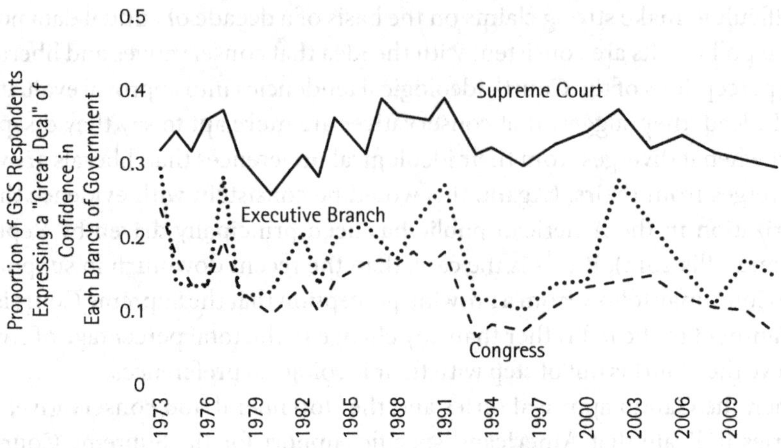

FIGURE 23.3 Proportion of GSS respondents expressing a "great deal" of confidence in each branch of government

Source: GSS 1973–2012 with gaps.

indicating "a great deal of confidence"—the most positive answer choice—in each of the three branches of government from 1973 through 2014 is illustrated in Figure 23.3.

The GSS confidence data show two clear patterns. First, over the last four decades, the American people have consistently expressed a high degree of confidence for the Supreme Court, often higher than for either Congress or the executive branch of government. For example, even during the 1991 and 2002 GSS, which were conducted in the shadows of the first Gulf War and the terrorist attacks of September 11, Americans express more confidence in the Supreme Court than the executive branch.

Second, the public's confidence in both Congress and the executive branch have generally declined in the years covered by the GSS while confidence in the Supreme Court has remained more steady. In 1973, nearly 25 percent of GSS respondents expressed a great deal of confidence in Congress and almost 30 percent expressed a great deal of confidence in the executive branch. In 2012, however, only about 7 percent of Americans had a great deal of confidence in Congress and only 15 percent claimed a great deal of confidence in the executive branch. In contrast, about 32 percent of GSS respondents expressed a great deal of confidence in the Supreme Court in 1973, and, in 2012, that figure remained nearly 30 percent. Although the percentage of Americans expressing a great deal of confidence in the Supreme Court has declined from a high of 40 percent last observed in 1991, the GSS clearly shows the Supreme Court's public standing has been much more robust than the elected branches of the federal government over the last four decades.

Survey data on indicators of the public's specific support for the Supreme Court remains sparse in comparison to data on attitudes toward Congress and, especially, the president. Polling data on diffuse support for the Supreme Court is even more rare. In part, this springs from the difficulty of designing survey measures of legitimacy that get past respondents' short-term judgments about an institution's policy outputs and tap long-term loyalties. Indeed, Gibson, Caldeira, and Spence (2003b) argue that individual survey questions are inadequate for this task. They argue instead for measuring loyalty to the Supreme Court using a battery of questions dealing with support for the structure of the Supreme Court and its role in contemporary American politics (see also Gibson and Caldeira 2009). While this approach is an excellent measurement strategy, it has not often been implemented by either scholars or commercial survey providers. As a result, there are few windows into Americans' deeper loyalty to the Supreme Court.

The data that are available, though, point to the proposition that the "Supreme Court seem[s] to have a fairly broad base of support within the American public" that has remained robust over time (Gibson and Caldeira 2009: 45; see also Caldeira and Gibson 1992; Gibson and Nelson 2014). As Gibson and Caldeira (2009) report, sizeable pluralities of Americans opposed abolishing the Supreme Court altogether or limiting its jurisdiction in surveys conducted in 1987, 1995, 2001, and 2005. Similarly, large majorities of Americans agreed that the Supreme Court can be "trusted to make decisions that are right for the country as a whole" in their 1995, 2001, and 2005 surveys. (The trust question was not included in their 1987 survey.) Although these topline data show some ebb and flow in the precise levels of the public's diffuse support for the Supreme Court, they reliably demonstrate that Americans have expressed much more loyalty to the Court than opposition to it over the last three decades.

Altogether, then, how strong is Americans' support for the Supreme Court? Two answers are evident. First, and most obviously, public support for the Supreme Court is strong and enduring. Although the American people neither universally approve of the Supreme Court nor unanimously embrace its legitimacy, the available survey research record shows that Americans reliably express greater confidence in and approval of the Supreme Court than either of the elected branches of the federal government. Similarly, a healthy plurality consistently regard the Court as "about right" rather than "too liberal" or "too conservative." Moreover, the proportions of those saying the Court is "too liberal" or "two conservative" have typically been comparable across the two-and-a-half decades of available data, indicating the Supreme Court has managed to position itself in the center of Americans' collective political attitudes.

A second answer is that it depends when you ask. Public support for the Supreme Court—like public support for the other branches of national government—is dynamic; it changes over time. Time series of individual survey items indicating various faces of specific support, from "approval" to "confidence" to ideological deviance, as well as available indicators of diffuse support show important changes over time. Moreover, there is evidence that many of these markers of the public's disposition toward the Supreme Court track together longitudinally, revealing a latent dimension of favorableness toward the Supreme Court in American public opinion (Durr, Martin, and Wolbrecht 2000). As we discuss later in this chapter, some of these dynamics relate to the public's systematic responses to Supreme Court decisions and other important elements of the nation's political climate.

The Foundations of Public Support for the Supreme Court

What Motivates Support for the Supreme Court?

Although indicators of both specific support and diffuse support for the Supreme Court have consistently shown widespread confidence in and loyalty to the Court over the last four decades, there is also evidence of substantial longitudinal change in the precise levels of support voiced by Americans. Studies of these aggregate dynamics as well as individual-level expressions of support for the Supreme Court have provided important insights into the political forces that sustain public support for the Court and lead it to change over time. This research includes both points of strong scholarly consensus and ongoing debates.

The standard view is that diffuse support rests on two pillars. The first is that the Court actually exhibits traits that indicate fairness and respect, showing it to be an institution worthy of loyalty. The second is that the Court reliably delivers a basket of decisions that broadly align with public opinion over the long run. Together, these factors lead individuals to develop an enduring loyalty to the Court, which aggregates up into a stable national commitment to judicial independence.

Americans develop loyalty to the Supreme Court as a governing institution through an ongoing process of socialization and experience that reveals the Supreme Court to be worthy of respect and involves both conscious evaluations of the Court and implicit attitudes about the Court. Americans develop loyalty toward the Supreme Court by learning that it strictly adheres to fair procedures, respects dissent, and engages in principled, if political, decision-making (Benesh 2006; Caldeira and Gibson 1992; Gibson 1989; Gibson and Caldeira 2009; Lind and Tyler 1988). This belief is reinforced by repeated exposure to powerful symbols of authority and procedural fairness ranging from the Constitution itself to jurists' black robes and the image of blind justice that inevitably accompany and frame information about the Court and its decisions (e.g., Caldeira and Gibson 1995; Gibson and Caldeira 2009; Gibson, Caldeira, and Baird 1998; Gibson, Caldeira, and Spence 2003b; Gibson, Lodge, and Woodson 2014). The nature of the judicial process and its symbols "[distinguish] courts from other political institutions," even among those who disagree with specific decisions made by the Court (Gibson and Caldeira 2009a: 9). And, as a result, Americans learn to regard the Court as "worthy of more respect, deference, and obedience" than other institutions of national government (Gibson and Caldeira 2009a: 44).

Indeed, learning is a critical component in the development of individual loyalty to the Supreme Court. Although studies of political knowledge have generally concluded that ignorance about politics and government is widespread among Americans (Delli Carpini 2009; Delli Carpini and Keeter 1996), recent research has challenged these findings (Lupia 2006; Mondak and Davis 2001; Krupnikov et al. 2006; Prior 2013; Prior and Lupia 2008). Among these new results, there is strong evidence that Americans are much more knowledgeable about the Supreme Court than previously thought (Caldeira and McGuire 2005; Gibson and Caldeira 2009a, 2009b). These findings suggest that the legitimacy of the Supreme Court rests on a foundation of familiarity with and understanding of the institution among the American people (Gibson 2012; Gibson and Caldeira 2009a, 2009b).

There is clear and convincing evidence of a critical link between public knowledge about courts and the legitimacy of judicial institutions in the public mind (Gibson 2007; Gibson and Caldeira 2009a, 2009b; Gibson, Caldeira, and Baird 1998). Those who know more about courts tend to express higher levels of loyalty to the judiciary than those who know less. Gibson and Caldeira (2009b) have summarized the evidence, "To know courts is to love them" (p. 122).

Though evidence of an individual-level association between political knowledge and judicial legitimacy exists for many democratic countries (Gibson, Caldeira, and Baird 1998), the nexus between knowing and trusting is most thoroughly developed, theoretically and empirically, in the case of Americans and their Supreme Court. Scholars suggest that knowing about the U.S. Supreme Court supports its legitimacy in two ways. First, in learning about the Supreme Court, individuals come to appreciate that the Court's procedures are fair and its decisions are principled, even if they are ideological (Benesh 2006; Caldeira and Gibson 1992; Gibson 1989). This distinguishes the Court from, and perhaps elevates it above, the elected branches of national government in the minds of many individuals, where procedures are strategically manipulated and decision-making is often characterized by partisanship (Gibson, Caldeira, and Spence 2003). Secondly, as individuals learn about the Court, they are exposed to a host of potent legitimizing symbols which surround the Court's public presentation (Gibson et al. 2010). The image of blind justice, justices' black robes, the Court's "marble palace," referring to members of the Court as "justices," and other accoutrement of law and courts activate cognitive processes that create deference to the Supreme Court and may support the public's loyalty to it as an institution.

Diffuse support is reinforced by the Court's delivery of outcomes consistent with Americans' policy preferences. As we showed earlier in this chapter, a sizeable plurality of Americans have judged the Supreme Court's decisions generally to be "about right," rather than "too liberal" or "too conservative" across the two-decade's span of the survey research record (see also McGuire and Stimson 2004; Casillas, Enns, and Wohlfarth 2011; Mishler and Sheehan 1993; Ura and Higgins 2015). This long-established and continuing pattern of consistency between what the American people want and the basket of decisions handed down by the Supreme Court, term after term, creates a "running tally" of favorable considerations about the Supreme Court in Americans' minds (Baird 2001). This bank of goodwill supports broadly positive assessments of the Court and may soften the blow of individual decisions which are contrary to public opinion. In this view, diffuse support for the Supreme Court may decline, but only over the long-run as the Court delivers a body of decisions contrary to the public's demands. This view of diffuse support is evident, for example, in historical patterns of loyalty to the Supreme

Court among African Americans (Gibson and Caldeira 1992). African Americans who were politically socialized during the Warren Court, which was aggressively progressive on issues of racial equality, report more diffuse support for the Supreme Court than earlier or later generations of African Americans.

This second pillar of diffuse support—long-run consistency between Supreme Court decision-making and public opinion—bridges feelings of institutional loyalty and specific support understood as performance approval. Indeed, specific support for the Supreme Court is by definition approval of the Court's decisions. At the individual level, those who agree more strongly with the Supreme Court's decisions express greater approval for and confidence in the Supreme Court, on average, than those who tend to disagree with the Supreme Court's decisions (Casey 1974; Hausegger and Riddle 2004; Murphy and Tanenhaus 1968a, 1968b; Tanenhaus and Murphy 1981). Similarly, at the macro level, the greater the convergence between aggregate liberalism in Supreme Court decisions and liberalism in public mood,[1] the higher the level of public support for the Supreme Court (Durr, Martin, and Wolbrecht 2000).

If the Supreme Court were to begin regularly making a substantial number of decisions that diverged from public opinion, it would hardly be surprising to observe a decline in diffuse support for the Court over the long run. This is consistent with Riker's (1980) observation that, "insofar as a constitutional system supplies an outcome that is not the same as outcomes that might have been obtained from simple majority rule … one can expect that losers on a series of decisions under a particular set of rules will attempt … to change institutions and hence the kind of decisions produced under them" (p. 445).

Recently, though, new evidence indicates that the relationship between specific support and diffuse support may be tighter than the standard view allows. In a prominent set of experiments, Bartels and Johnston (2013) find that disagreement with a salient decision is sufficient to significantly undermine individuals' diffuse support for the Supreme Court. They write, "contrary to conventional wisdom, a potent ideological foundation underlies Supreme Court legitimacy vis-à-vis subjective ideological disagreement with the Court's policy-making" (Bartels and Johnston 2013: 197). Similarly, Scherer and Curry's (2010) experimental study finds evidence that the descriptive representation of African Americans in the federal judiciary is positively associated with federal courts' legitimacy among African Americans and negatively related to courts' legitimacy among whites. They also find that these effects are strongest among ideologically liberal African Americans and conservative whites. The mediating effect of ideology on perceptions of descriptive representation for judicial legitimacy suggests that respondents' expectations about the political implications of the racial composition of the federal bench also shows a connection between (expected) decisions and diffuse support. These experimental results are reinforced by Christenson and Glick's (2015) observational study of responses to the Supreme Court's decision in *National Federation of Independent Business v. Sebelius* (2012). They found that individual-level agreement (or disagreement) with the decision influenced reported levels of diffuse support for the Court. Together, these results offer a stark challenge to conventional legitimacy theory and indicate ongoing scholarly debate about the nature of individual loyalty to the Supreme Court and the nexus between specific support and diffuse support (Gibson and Nelson 2015). Indeed, one of the most valuable contributions of recent research challenging traditional views of attitudes about institutional legitimacy has been to draw renewed attention to the connection between short-term and long-term views of institutions and to spark deeper theoretical and empirical inquiries into the nature of legitimacy.

Public Opinion and Judicial Independence

How Does the Public's Support for the Supreme Court Relate to Judicial Independence?

The U.S. Constitution seemingly reflects a deep ambivalence about judicial authority. On the one hand, the Constitution's supporters favored insulating courts from the pressures of ordinary politics. Hamilton, for example, argued that the "complete independence of the courts of justice is peculiarly essential in a limited Constitution" (*Federalist 78*). On the other hand, they were not shy about the prospect of Congress and the president ignoring the judiciary or punishing judges. Hamilton, again, argued that the Supreme Court constituted by Article III could not encroach on legislative authority because of its "its total incapacity to support its usurpations by force" and Congress's power to "punish [judges'] presumption, by degrading them from their stations" (*Federalist 81*). These competing considerations are evident in the U.S. Constitution, which protects judicial independence while nesting courts in a system of checks and balances.

Thus, although Article III of the U.S. Constitution asserts that federal "judicial power shall extend to all cases, in law and equity, arising under this Constitution, the laws of the United States, and treaties made ... under their authority" it adds, "with such exceptions, and under such regulations as the Congress shall make." Likewise, the Constitution guarantees that federal judges receive compensation for their services, which "shall not be diminished during their continuance in office," and may serve for life during "good behaviour." The Constitution includes no provisions specifying the size, composition, structure, or resources of the federal judiciary, leaving these matters to Congress. In fact, as Geyh (2006) points out, the Constitution puts an array of tools for controlling the federal judiciary at Congress's disposal, including: "impeaching errant judges[,] ... holding their budgets hostage, 'unmaking' federal courts, thwarting the appointment of 'activist' judges, and depriving courts of jurisdiction to hear cases on politically sensitive subjects" (p. 1; see also Ferejohn 1999).

Congressional power to curb or control federal courts was not always a museum piece. The early decades of America's history under the Constitution offers numerous examples of Congress making use of these constitutional prerogatives to undermine or challenge the Supreme Court's authority or independence when it ran afoul of popular majorities (e.g., Kramer 2004; Friedman 2009; Fritz 2008). Some famous examples include disbanding circuit courts (Repeal Act of 1802), postponing a Supreme Court term (Amendatory Act of 1802), impeaching a justice (Samuel Chase in 1804), manipulating the size of the Court (perhaps most cynically in the Judicial Circuits Act of 1866 and the Judiciary Act of 1869), and abrogating a Supreme Court decision with a constitutional amendment (the Eleventh Amendment superseding the Court's holding in *Chisolm v. Georgia* [1793] that Article III, Section 2 of the U.S. Constitution eliminated states' sovereign immunity from private claims).

Indeed, the impulse to curb the Supreme Court when it acted against the preferences of popular majorities persisted well into the twentieth century. Both Presidents Roosevelt, for example, advocated ultimately unsuccessful plans to counter what they saw as excessive judicial independence. During his 1912 bid to return to the White House, Theodore Roosevelt championed a constitutional amendment that would have allowed Congress to overrule Supreme Court decisions that invalidated federal laws. In 1937, Franklin Roosevelt offered a plan that would have allowed him to appoint a new Supreme Court justice for each member of the Court over seventy years and six months old.

These episodes of muscular court-curbing are mostly early deviations from a trend of greater deference to the Supreme Court by Congress and growing judicial independence and institutionalization (Kramer 2004; McGuire 2004; Segal and Spaeth 2002). Yet, they underscore a critical point: judicial authority as it exists in contemporary U.S. politics is a fluid "political construction" rather than a firm constitutional structure (Graber 2005; see also, e.g., Friedman 2009; Lovell 2003; McMahon 2004, 2011; Keck 2004; Kramer 2004; Whittington 2007). In other words, independent judicial authority in the United States was established and is sustained by political processes rather than constitutional fiat.

Moreover, both jurists and scholars of judicial politics have long asserted that there is a critical link between public opinion and judicial authority. This view has been evident in the opinions of the Supreme Court itself for well over a century. In *United States v. Lee* (1882), Justice Miller writes, "[the Supreme Court's] power and influence rest solely upon the public sense of … confidence reposed in the soundness of [its] decisions and the purity of [its] motives." Justice Frankfurter similarly emphasizes that "the Court's authority—possessed of neither the purse nor the sword—ultimately rests on sustained public confidence in its moral sanction" (*Baker v. Carr* 1962). Justice O'Connor, writing in *Planned Parenthood v. Casey* (1992), expresses the same sentiment, "The Court's power lies … in its legitimacy, a product of substance and perception that shows itself in the people's acceptance of the Judiciary as fit to determine what the Nation's law means."

A long line of research in political science and related fields proceeds from the same assumption that public opinion is an important element of the politics of judicial independence. Scholars have often suggested that public support for courts constrains Congress, and legislatures more generally, to accept judicial authority, even when that authority is exercised in a way that works against members' of Congress policy preferences. In other words, when support for courts is sufficiently high, election-minded legislators—who would otherwise prefer to make policy choices without the constraint of judicial review—are induced "to respect judicial decisions as well as the institutional integrity of a court [by t]he fear of … a public backlash" against court-curbing activity

(Vanberg 2001: 347). Durr, Martin, and Wolbrecht therefore note an, "expectation that the Court necessarily depends on public support as a source of institutional legitimacy and political capital" (2000: 775; see also Murphy and Tanenhaus 1968a, 1968b). Likewise, Gibson, Caldeira, and Baird write, "Not even the most powerful courts in the world have the power of the 'purse' or the 'sword' ... Courts are therefore uncommonly dependent on the goodwill of their constituents for ... support" (1998: 343). Segal and Spaeth similarly assert that "the negative political consequences, electoral and otherwise, of limiting judicial independence far outweigh whatever short-run policy gains Congress might gain by reining in the Court" (2002: 94).

In recent years, a growing literature has emerged that extends and refines the basic theoretical claim of a link between public opinion and the institutional capacity of the U.S. Supreme Court and provides systematic empirical evidence linking the Court's public standing with applications of judicial authority. Collectively, this research shows, first, that justices and the leaders of the elected branches of government are aware of the public standing of their institutions and incorporate that information into the calculus of their interactions with one another. As Knight and Epstein point out in their analytic narrative of the strategic interactions between the Supreme Court and the Jefferson administration surround decisions in *Marbury v. Madison* (1803) and *Stuart v. Laird* (1803), "all politicians— ... be they presidents or justices—consider the environment under which they are operating" (1996: 91). In other words, because a "loss of public support ... undermines [a] court['s] capacity to enforce constitutional limits on government, among other things," a court has strong incentives "to engage in deeply political calculations ... to preserve public support for the institution" (Clark 2011: 21–2).

Second, Supreme Court justices act to cultivate the public standing of their institution. These calculations can lead the Supreme Court to constrain itself and avoid challenging congressional authority by invalidating federal laws when its public standing is relatively low (Clark 2011; Hall and Ura 2015). Moreover, as we discuss below, the need to cultivate, or at least preserve, its public standing provides one of the most plausible explanations for the convincing evidence of a reliable association between public mood and ideological patterns in Supreme Court decision-making (Casillas, Enns, and Wohlfarth 2011; Giles, Blackstone, and Vining 2008; Hall 2014; McGuire and Stimson 2004; Mishler and Sheehan 1993, 1996).

Third, because the Supreme Court operates with two other branches of government in a separation of powers system, judicial independence depends on the public's support for the Supreme Court *and* public support for the other branches of government. Ura and Wohlfarth (2010), for example, find that changes in Congress's allocation of resources and discretion to the Supreme Court are significantly related to both public confidence in the Supreme Court and public confidence in Congress. This finding also suggests that public opinion may play an important, although under-appreciated, role in the strategic interactions between the Supreme Court and Congress over the Court's decisions about the constitutionality of federal laws (e.g., Blackstone 2013; Epstein, Knight, and Martin 2001; Fisher 2001; Meernik and Ignagni 1997; Segal 1997; Segal, Westerland, and Lindquist 2011; Segal and Spaeth 2002; but see Marshall 1989).

These basic principles are echoed in a parallel literature in comparative politics dealing with issues of the balance of power among branches of government in separation of powers along with judicial independence. Several studies of Latin American politics, for example, develop formal separation of powers games to identify linkages between the public standing of coordinate branches of government and their ability to establish and preserve institutional independence and political authority (Helmke 2010; Helmke and Staton 2011; Staton 2010; Taylor-Robinson and Ura 2013). Similarly, Vanberg (2001) shows that the German constitutional court is more likely to overturn statutes in cases that have been orally argued, since those "transparent" cases are likely to engender stronger public support.

Together, these findings strongly support the traditional view that the Supreme Court depends on its public standing to protect its decisions and its institutional integrity from encroachment by the elected branches of the national government. However, promising frontiers remain in the study of the role of public opinion in separation of powers systems. In particular, there is much important work to be done to more fully integrate research on the role of public opinion in sustaining judicial independence and the literature on "separation of powers models," which examine how ideological and partisan divisions between the Supreme Court and Congress constrain judicial behavior (e.g., Segal, Lindquist, and Westerland 2011).

The Mass Public's Influence on Judicial Behavior

How and under What Conditions Does the Supreme Court Respond to Public Opinion?

The U.S. Constitution protects the Supreme Court and its justices from the pressures of public opinion to a much greater degree than the president or Congress and its members. For example, the Court's institutional design generally allows justices to select and decide cases in ways that are consistent with their individual policy attitudes (e.g., Segal and Spaeth 2002). However, despite its institutional isolation from public opinion, political scientists have found systematic evidence of a positive association between public opinion liberalism and liberalism in Supreme Court decisions (e.g., Epstein and Martin 2010; Erikson, MacKuen, and Stimson 2002, Flemming and Wood 1997; Mishler and Sheehan 1993, McGuire and Stimson 2004). This evidence reliably shows that greater liberalism in public opinion (generally measured by Stimson's [1999] mood index) in one year predicts that a higher proportion of Supreme Court decisions in the next year will be decided in a liberal direction.[2,3]

Although there is broad agreement that there is an association between the dynamics of public mood and Supreme Court decision-making, scholars disagree about which social and political processes support this relationship. The most common view in the literature is that Supreme Court justices strategically follow public opinion. One form of this argument emphasizes the justices' desire to secure compliance with the decisions from elected officials and the public. Because the "Court requires the cooperation of legislative and executive officials, many of whom are themselves careful auditors of mass opinion ..., the members of the Court must reflect on how well their preferred outcomes will be received and supported by implementers" (McGuire and Stimson 2004: 1022). Mishler and Sheehan (1996: 174) refer to this as "political adjustment" (see also Hall 2011, 2014).

Another view of strategic response theory is that Supreme Court justices follow public opinion in order to sustain the Court's public standing. As we discussed earlier, numerous studies show that Supreme Court decisions that deviate from individuals' preferred outcomes can undermine specific support for the Court, and there is new evidence emerging that these disagreements may undermine diffuse support, as well (Bartels and Johnston 2013; Christenson and Glick 2015; Friedman 2009; Grosskopf and Mondak 1998; Durr, Martin, and Wolbrecht 2000; Hoekstra 2000). Therefore, when the Court issues decisions that deviate from macro-level public preferences, it risks its public approval, and, perhaps, its legitimacy (Mishler and Sheehan 1993, 1996; McGuire and Stimson 2004). Casillas, Enns, and Wohlfarth posit, that in order to maintain high levels of institutional legitimacy, the justices should act strategically through their decisions and avoid regularly making rulings that diverge from public sentiment (2011: 77). In other words, because repeated, discrete blows to the Court's diffuse support can undermine the Court's legitimacy, the Court should account for public opinion when formulating its decisions.

Yet, not all scholars accept the strategic responses hypothesis. Another view is that the Supreme Court follows public opinion as its justices change their own political views as a result of the same processes that influence changes in mass public opinion. Giles, Blackstone, and Vining's (2008) analysis of why Supreme Court decisions appear to correspond with public opinion supports this claim. They conclude that "the direct linkage between public opinion and the voting behavior of justices ... does not arise from the justices' strategic concerns over maintaining legitimacy and compliance among the public ... the most likely explanation is through the mechanism of attitude change" (p. 303).

The available evidence supports no definitive conclusions about the process that connects shifts in public opinion liberalism to changes in ideological patterns in Supreme Court decision-making (Epstein and Martin 2010). However, the literature on the role of public opinion in shaping judicial independence in the separation of powers—which supports the view that the Supreme Court strategically avoids confrontations with Congress when it has lower public standing (Clark 2009, 2011; Hall 2011; Ura and Wohlfarth 2010)—tends to provide additional supporting evidence on the side of some version of the strategic response hypothesis. If the Court's decision-making is sensitive to its public standing, it is somewhat easier to believe that consistency between public mood and Supreme Court decisions follows from the justices' strategic decisions to follow public opinion to protect its approval and legitimacy rather than mere coincidental consistency between the dynamics of public mood and changes in justices' preferences.

Judicial Influence on Mass Political Attitudes

How Does the Public React to the Court's Decisions?

In the middle of the twentieth century, many prominent progressive legal scholars espoused a romantic view of the Supreme Court's role in American national politics. These scholars imagined the Supreme Court as a vital force for positive social and political change. They envisioned the Court as a "republican schoolmaster" that could "transfer to the minds of the citizens the modes of thought lying behind legal language and the notions of right fundamental to the regime" (Lerner 1967: 180) or an "educational body" leading "a vital national seminar" (Rostow 1952: 208). They argued that the moral force of the Supreme Court and Americans' deep loyalty to the Court and the Constitution for which it presumed to speak might "appeal to men's better natures" and remind them of their fundamental commitments to equality and equity "which may have been forgotten in the moment's hue and cry" (Bickel 1986: 26).

A similar view was advanced among political scientists by Robert Dahl. Dahl argued that the Supreme Court enjoyed "unique legitimacy attributed to its interpretations of the Constitution" and reasoned that the Court could confer the legitimacy of the Constitution onto the "policies of the successful [governing] coalition" (1957: 293–4). Although Dahl's argument is, on its face, a narrow claim about the Court's role in reducing the intensity of political conflicts, his conjecture about the Court's influence on the public has often been interpreted as a hypothesis that Supreme Court decisions are persuasive, "shap[ing] policy attitudes on even the most controversial issues" (Hoekstra 2003: 90)—changing "people from segregationists to integrationists, from pro-lifers to pro-choicers," for example (Caldeira 1991: 305).

As we discussed earlier, there is now much evidence that supports Dahl's premise of a unique judicial legitimacy based on the Supreme Court's association with powerful symbols of authority and procedural fairness ranging from the Constitution itself to jurists' black robes and the image of blind justice (e.g., Caldeira and Gibson 1995; Gibson, Caldeira, and Baird 1998; Gibson, Caldeira, and Spence 2003a; Gibson et al. 2010). These symbols are woven into Americans' interactions with courts, and they work to "[distinguish] courts from other political institutions," even among those who oppose the policy implications of specific judicial decisions (Gibson and Caldeira 2009a: 9). These symbols, therefore, reinforce Americans' experiences with the Court that show it to be special, that is "worthy of more respect, deference, and obedience" than other political institutions (Gibson and Caldeira 2009a: 9).

Although there is now strong evidence that Americans are deeply loyal to the Supreme Court, support for the claims that the Supreme Court influences Americans' political views is mixed. Both Franklin and Kosaki's (1989) study of individual responses to *Roe v. Wade* (1973) and Johnson and Martin's (1998) study of reactions to prominent abortion (*Webster v. Reproductive Health Services* 1989) and death penalty cases (*Furman v. Georgia* 1972, *Gregg v. Georgia* 1976, and *McCleskey v. Kemp* 1987) find no evidence of that public opinion shifted toward the policy positions implicit in the Supreme

Court's decisions in the subsequent year (see also Brickman and Peterson 2006). In contrast, Stoutenborough, Haider-Markel, and Allen's (2006) study of public responses to four prominent gay rights cases—*Bowers v. Hardwick* (1986), *Romer v. Evans* (1996), *Boy Scouts of America v. Dale* (2000), and *Lawrence v. Texas* (2003)—shows a range of public opinion effects following from the Supreme Court decision. They find that public support for the Court's position on gay rights increased in response to *Bowers*, decreased in response to *Lawrence*, and was unchanged by *Boy Scouts* and *Romer*. Likewise, in a pair of studies, Marshall (1989, 2008) compares responses to a total of forty-six pre-decision and post-decision survey question pairs (eighteen in the 1989 study and another twenty-eight in the 2008 study), though at substantially variable intervals, dealing with public attitudes on issues before the Court, finding that "poll shifts" away from positions adopted by the Court happen as often as shifts toward the Court's positions.[4]

Additional research has aimed at identifying factors that cause some of the Court's decisions to have a greater impact on public opinion than others. Hoekstra's (2003) analysis of local responses to two civil liberties cases (*Lamb's Chapel v. Center Moriches Union Free High School District* [1993] and *Board of Education of Kiryas Joel v. Grumet* [1994] and two economic cases (*Oklahoma Tax Commission v. Chickasaw Nation* [1995] and *Babbit v. Sweet Home Chapter of Communities for a Great Oregon* [1995] finds that individuals' attitudinal responses to Supreme Court decisions are conditioned by the strength of pre-existing attitudes and also by exposure to information about the Court and its decisions (see also 2000; Hoekstra and Segal 1996). Experimental studies have generally confirmed the conclusions of Hoekstra's observational studies, showing that sufficient information about Supreme Court decisions can be persuasive in some issue domains for which respondents may not have strong prior attitudes (Clawson and Waltenburg 2003; Mondak 1990, 1991, 1992, 1994; Hoekstra 1995; Unger 2008; but see Baas and Thomas 1984).

Finally, Ura (2014) argues that the Supreme Court decisions influence public mood over the long run in ways that are consistent with Dahl's legitimation hypothesis. Ura's analysis of the dynamic relationship between Stimson's (1999) mood index and cumulative Supreme Court liberalism shows that public responses to important Supreme Court decisions are generally marked by a backlash in public opinion in the short term that decays and is replaced by a long-run movement in public opinion toward the positions adopted by the Court. In other words, on average, there is negative reaction in public opinion against important decisions of the Supreme Court. However, these negative responses are relatively short lived. Over the long run, backlash against the Court's decisions tends to be replaced by significant movement toward positions taken by the Supreme Court. The key result of the study is that the Supreme Court generally leads public opinion in an important way—even if there is typically some initial pushback against its decisions in public opinion. This effect is manifest as an incremental, long-run ideological shift toward the cumulative results of Supreme Court decisions.

Scholars have also identified important effects in public opinion related to Supreme Court decisions that are unrelated to legitimation. The most notable of these is Franklin and Kosaki's (1989) finding of "structural responses" in public reactions to Supreme

Court decisions. They argue that Supreme Court decisions may alter the structure of public attitudes on topics related to the Court's actions, even if the aggregate distribution of relevant attitudes is unchanged. For example, they show that *Roe v. Wade* (1973) reinforced social and religious predispositions on abortion attitudes, leading Catholics to become more pro-life and Protestants to become more pro-choice (on average) in the year after the decision. Johnson and Martin (1998) extend this structural response theory, showing that the Court's initial actions on an issue may have structural effects while its subsequent treatment of the same issue may not. Brickman and Peterson (2006), though, contend that the Court's ability to influence the structure of public opinion is conditional on the state of public opinion rather than on the number of times the Supreme Court has addressed an issue. Similarly, Stoutenborough, Haider-Markel, and Allen (2006) show that the existence of structural responses to the Court's gay rights cases are dependent on context and case-specific factors.

Conclusions

In an review of the state of knowledge on courts and public opinion published nearly twenty-five years ago, Caldeira concluded that political scientists "have precious few findings and generalizations planted in solid empirical soil" and "possess even less theoretical understanding" of the links between the judiciary and the mass public (1991: 326–7). In no small part due to the work of Caldeira, his collaborators, and students, as well as the contributions of many others, we find the situation much improved. The increasing availability of high-quality survey data, the growing sophistication and acceptance of experimental research, and the development of new methods of statistical analysis have catalyzed a bright array of empirical research about the reciprocal links between public opinion and judicial behavior. In turn, scholars have developed, tested, and refined basic theoretical frameworks for understanding American's support for courts, the role of public opinion in supporting judicial independence, the influence of public opinion on judicial behavior, and the effect of Supreme Court decisions on public opinion. Active scholarly communities continue to work in each of these areas, and the prospects for continued progress over the next twenty-five years are exceedingly bright.

We see several particularly fruitful paths forward. First, dramatic demographic changes in the United States, especially the rapid growth of communities of immigrants and their families, are creating valuable opportunities to study the socialization processes that contribute to judicial legitimacy. In particular, the rapid growth of the Latino community may provide a unique window into the pathways that have led Americans to embrace and support judicial independence (Fraga et al. 2012).

Second, political scientists will be able to leverage new sources of data on Americans political behaviors and preferences to understand their attitudes about courts. Scholars have already begun to exploit Google search volume data to measure interest in Supreme

Court nominees (Manzano and Ura 2013) and data from posts to Twitter to gauge political responses to Supreme Court decisions (Clark et al. 2014). These types of data, along with tools to organize and analyze them, will open new and exciting frontiers in the study of political behavior in general and to allow scholars of law and courts to broaden and deepen our understanding of individuals' attitudes toward judicial institutions and their responses to judicial decisions.

Third, there are tremendous opportunities to expand research on courts and public opinion outside of the United States. Some of the most valuable of these lie in regions of the world with new and developing democracies, such as Latin America (e.g., Helmke 2010; Helmke and Staton 2011; Staton 2010; Taylor-Robinson and Ura 2013) and Africa (e.g., Aziz 2013, 2014; Gibson and Caldeira 2003; Haynie 2003; Prempeh 2006; VonDoepp 2009, 2013; Widner 2001a, 2001b), and in the Islamic world, where secular courts operate alongside traditional religious courts (e.g., Aldashez et al. 2012; Barnes and Hassan 2007; Kenny 1996; Brown 2007).

Regardless of the particular paths that scientific progress in the study of courts and public opinion may take, continuing to improve our understanding of the linkages between the judiciary and the mass public remains vitally important. We cannot understand the development or practice of American democracy without a firm grasp on the processes that have created and sustained judicial independence, and we will be unable to effectively encourage the development and practice of democracy elsewhere in the world without a deep understanding of the role that courts play in cultivating democratic culture and sustaining other democratic institutions. Continued study in this area, therefore, has critical practical implications for domestic and foreign policymaking in addition to its tremendous value as knowledge for its own sake. It remains worthy of our best efforts.

Notes

1. Policy "mood" indicates Americans' "changing general dispositions" toward a "latent [liberal-conservative] continuum underlying expressed policy preferences" (Stimson 1999: 20–31). Mood represents the nation's level of demand for greater or less liberalism in domestic public policy (Stimson, Erikson, and MacKuen 1995: 544; see also Erikson, Stimson, and MacKuen 2002; Ellis, Ura, and Robinson 2006; Kellstedt, Peterson, and Ramirez 2010; Smith 2000; Stimson 2004; Ura and Socker 2011; Ura 2014). Mood is often measured with Stimson's (1999) *policy mood index*, which is essentially the first principal component of shared longitudinal variance among dozens of time series of survey marginals from major polling organizations collected since the early 1950s.
2. Mishler and Sheehan (1993) argue that there is a seven-year lag between changes in public mood and changes in Supreme Court decision-making. Most subsequent studies have argued for a one-year lag (e.g., Casillas, Enns, and Wohlfarth 2011; Erikson, MacKuen, and Stimson 2002; McGuire and Stimson 2004).
3. Epstein and Martin's (2010) study of the association between public mood and Supreme Court decisions is the most prominent exception to this basic research design. Their study examines the effects of quarterly public mood on the ideological direction of individual

Supreme Court decisions. They nevertheless observe the same basic pattern: greater liberalism in public opinion predicts that individual cases are more likely to be decided in a liberal direction.

4. In addition to prior research addressing public responses to Supreme Court decisions, the literature shows that some salient decisions of the Supreme Court may direct the media's or the public's attention to issues before the Court (e.g., Flemming, Bohte, and Wood 1999; Ura 2009, 2014). This process may create opportunities for the Supreme Court's decisions and its symbols of institutional legitimacy to influence public opinion by heightening information flows that potentially connect the Supreme Court to salient policy questions. This is especially likely for issues on which the public may not have fully "elaborated" opinions (Brickman and Peterson 2006).

References

Aldashev, G., Chaara, I., Platteau, J., and Wahhaj, Z. 2012. "Using the Law to Change the Custom." *Journal of Development Economics* 97(2): 182–200.

Aziz, S. F. 2013. "Bringing down and Uprising: Egypt's Stillborn Revolution." *Connecticut Journal of International Law* 30(1): 1–27.

Aziz, S. F. 2014. "Revolution without Reform? A Critique of Egypt's Election Laws." *George Washington International Law Review* 45(1): 101–83.

Baas, L. R., and Thomas, D. 1984. "The Supreme Court and Policy Legitimation." *American Politics Research* 12(July): 335–60.

Baird, V. A. 2001. "Building Institutional Legitimacy: The Role of Procedural Justice." *Political Research Quarterly* 54(2): 333–54.

Barnes, C., and Hassan, H. 2007. "The Rise and Fall of Mogadishu's Islamic Courts." *Journal of East African Studies* 12: 151–60.

Bartels, B. L., and Johnston, C. D. 2013. "On the Ideological Foundations of Supreme Court Legitimacy in the American Public." *American Journal of Political Science* 57(1): 184–99.

Benesh, S. C. 2006. "Understanding Public Confidence in American Courts." *Journal of Politics* 68(3): 697–707.

Bickel, A. M. 1986. *The Least Dangerous Branch: The Supreme Court at the Bar of American Politics*, 2nd ed. New Haven, CT: Yale University Press.

Blackstone, B. 2013. "An Analysis of Policy-Based Congressional Responses to the U.S. Supreme Court's Constitutional Decisions." *Law & Society Review* 47(1): 199–228.

Brickman, D., and Peterson, D. A. M. 2006. "Public Opinion Reaction to Repeated Events: Citizen Response to Multiple Supreme Court Abortion Decisions." *Political Behavior* 28(March): 87–112.

Brown, N. J. 2007. *The Rule of Law in the Arab World: Courts in Egypt and the Gulf.* New York, NY: Cambridge University Press.

Caldeira, G. A. 1991. "Courts and Public Opinion"." In *The American Courts: A Critical Assessment*, edited by J. B. Gates and C. A. Johnson. Washington, DC: CQ Press, 303–34.

Caldeira, G. A., and Gibson, J. L. 1992. "The Etiology of Public Support for the Supreme Court." *American Journal of Political Science* 36(3): 635–64.

Caldeira, G. A., and Gibson, J. L. 1995. "The Legitimacy of the Court of Justice in the European Union: Models of Institutional Support." *American Political Science Review* 89(June): 356–76.

Caldeira, G. A., and McGuire, K. T. 2005. "What Americans Know about the Courts and Why It Matters." In *Institutions of American Democracy: The Judiciary*, edited by K. L. Hall and K. T. McGuire. New York, NY: Oxford University Press, 262–79.

Casey, G. 1974. "The Supreme Court and Myth: An Empirical Investigation." *Law & Society Review* 8(3): 385–419.

Casillas, C. J., Enns, P. K., and Wohlfarth, P. C. 2011. "How Public Opinion Constrains the U.S. Supreme Court." *American Journal of Political Science* 55(January): 74–88.

Christenson, D. P., and Glick, D. M. 2015. "Chief Justice Roberts's Health Care Decision Disrobed: The Microfoundations of the Supreme Court's Legitimacy." *American Journal of Political Science* 59(2): 403–18.

Clark, T. S. 2009. "The Separation of Powers, Court Curbing, and Judicial Legitimacy." *American Journal of Political Science* 53(4): 971–89.

Clark, T. S. 2011. *The Limits of Judicial Independence*. New York, NY: Cambridge University Press.

Clark, T. S., Staton, J. K., Agchtein, E., and Wang, Y. 2014. "Revealed Public Opinion on Twitter: The Supreme Court of the United States Same Sex Marriage Decisions." Paper presented at the Annual Meeting of the Midwest Political Science Association, Chicago, IL.

Clawson, R. A., and Waltenburg, E. N. 2003. "Support for a Supreme Court Affirmative Action Decision: A Story in Black and White." *American Politics Research* 31(May): 251–79.

Crawford, J. 2012. "Roberts Switched Views to Uphold Health Care Law." *CBS News*, July 2. Available at: http://www.cbsnews.com/news/roberts-switched-views-to-uphold-health-care-law/.

Dahl, R. 1957. "Decision-Making in a Democracy: The Supreme Court as a National Policy Maker." *Journal of Public Law* 6(Fall): 279–95.

Daly, C. 2012. "Obama: Supreme Court Overturning Health Care Would Be 'Unprecedented.'" *CBS News*, April 2. Available at: http://www.cbs.com/news/obama-supreme-curt-overturning-healthcare-would-be-unprecedented/.

Delli Carpini, M. X., and Keeter, S. 1996. *What Americans Know about Politics and Why It Matters*. New Haven, CT: Yale University Press.

Delli Carpini, M. X. 2009. "The Psychology of Civic Learning." In *The Political Psychology of Democratic Citizenship*, edited by E. Borgida, J. L. Sullivan, and C. M. Frederico. New York, NY: Oxford University Press, 23–51.

Durr, R. H., Martin, A. D., and Wolbrecht, C. 2000. "Ideological Divergence and Public Support for the Supreme Court." *American Journal of Political Science* 44(October): 768–76.

Easton, D. 1965. *A Systems Analysis of Political Life*. New York, NY: Wiley.

Ellis, C. R., Ura, J. D., Ashley-Robinson, J. 2006. "The Dynamic Consequences of Nonvoting in American National Elections." *Political Research Quarterly* 59(June): 227–33.

Epstein, L., Knight, J., and Martin, A. D. 2001. "The Supreme Court as a Strategic National Policymaker." *Emory Law Review* 55: 583–611.

Epstein, L., and Martin, A. D. 2010. "Does Public Opinion Influence the Supreme Court? Possibly Yes (But We're Not Sure Why)." *University of Pennsylvania Journal of Constitutional Law* 13: 263–81.

Erikson, R. S., MacKuen, M. B., and Stimson, J. A. 2002. *The Macro Polity*. Cambridge: Cambridge University Press.

Ferejohn, J. 1999. "Independent Judges, Dependent Judiciary: Explaining Judicial Independence." *Southern California Law Review* 72(2/3): 353–84.

Fisher, L. 2001. *Constitutional Conflicts between Congress and the President*. Lawrence, KS: University of Kansas Press.

Flemming, R. B., and Wood, B. D. 1997. "The Public and the Supreme Court: Individual Justice Responsiveness to American Policy Moods." *American Journal of Political Science* 41(April): 468–98.

Flemming, R. B., Wood, B. D., and Bohte, J. 1999. "Attention to Issues in a System of Separated Powers: The Macrodynamics of American Policy Agendas." *American Journal of Political Science* 41(October): 1224–50.

Fraga, L., Garcia, J. A., Hero, R. E., Jones-Correa, M., Martinez-Ebers, V., and Segura, G. 2012. *Latinos in the New Millennium: An Almanac of Opinion, Behavior, and Policy Preferences*. New York, NY: Cambridge University Press.

Franklin, C. H., and Kosaki L. C. 1989. "Republican Schoolmaster: The U.S. Supreme Court, Public Opinion, and Abortion." *American Political Science Review* 83(September): 751–71.

Franklin, D. L. 2012. "Why Did Roberts Do It? To Save the Court." *Slate*, June 28. Available at: http://slate.me/1IdLgTH.

Friedman, B. 2009. *The Will of the People: How Public Opinion Has Influenced the Supreme Court and Shaped the Meaning of the Constitution*. New York, NY: Farrar, Straus and Giroux.

Fritz, C. G. 2008. *American Sovereigns: The People and America's Constitutional Tradition before the Civil War*. New York, NY: Cambridge University Press.

Geyh, C. G. 2006. "Why Courts and Congress Collide, and Why Their Conflicts Subside." *Insights on Law and Society* 7(1): 7–9, 27.

Gibson, J. L. 1989. "Understandings of Justice: Institutional Legitimacy, Procedural Justice, and Political Tolerance." *Law & Society Review* 23(3): 469–96.

Gibson, J. L. 2007. "The Legitimacy of the U.S. Supreme Court in a Polarized Polity." *Journal of Empirical Legal Studies* 4(3): 507–38.

Gibson, J. L. 2008. "Challenges to the Impartiality of State Supreme Courts: Legitimacy Theory and 'New-Style' Judicial Campaigns." *American Political Science Review* 102(1): 59–75.

Gibson, J. L. 2012a. *Electing Judges: The Surprising Effects of Campaigning on Judicial Legitimacy*. Chicago, IL: University of Chicago Press.

Gibson, J. L. 2012b. "Public Reverence for the United States Supreme Court: Is the Court Invincible?" Paper presented at the Conference on Judicial Countermajoritarianism, University of Texas Law School, Austin, TX.

Gibson, J. L., and Caldeira, G. A. 1992. "Blacks and the United States Supreme Court." *Journal of Politics* 54(4): 1120–45.

Gibson, J. L., and Caldeira, G. A. 2003. "Defenders of Democracy? Legitimacy, Popular Acceptance, and the South African Constitutional Court." *Journal of Politics* 65(1): 1–30.

Gibson, J. L., and Caldeira, G. A. 2009a. *Citizens, Courts, and Confirmations: Positivity Theory and the Judgments of the American People*. Princeton, NJ: Princeton University Press.

Gibson, J. L., and Caldeira, G. A. 2009b. "Knowing the Supreme Court? A Reconsideration of Public Ignorance of the High Court." *Journal of Politics* 71(2): 429–41.

Gibson, J .L., Caldeira, G. A., and Spence, L. K. 2003a. "Measuring Attitudes toward the United States Supreme Court." *American Journal of Political Science* 47(2): 354–67.

Gibson, J. L., Caldeira, G. A., Spence, L. K. 2003b. "The Supreme Court and the U.S. Presidential Election of 2000: Wounds, Self-Inflicted or Otherwise? *British Journal of Political* Science 33(4): 535–56.

Gibson, J. L., Caldeira, G. A., Spence, L .K. 1998. "On the Legitimacy of National High Courts." *American Political Science Review* 92(2): 343–58.

Gibson, J. L., and Nelson M. J. 2014. "The Legitimacy of the U.S. Supreme Court: Conventional Wisdoms and Recent Challenges thereto." *Annual Review of Law and Social Science* 10: 201–19.

Gibson, J. L., and Nelson, M. J. 2015. "Is the U.S. Supreme Court's Legitimacy Grounded in Performance Satisfaction and Ideology?" *American Journal of Political Science* 59(1): 162–74.

Gibson, J. L., Lodge, M., and Woodson, B. 2014. "Losing, but Accepting: Legitimacy, Positivity Theory, and the Symbols of Judicial Authority." *Law and Society Review* 48(4): 837–66.

Giles, M. W., Blackstone, B., and Vining, R. L. 2008. "The Supreme Court in American Democracy: Unraveling the Linkages between Public Opinion and Judicial Decision Making." *Journal of Politics* 70(2): 293–306.

Graber, M. A. 2005. "Constructing Judicial Review." *Annual Review of Political Science* 8: 425–51.

Grosskopf, A., and Mondak, J. J. 1998. "Do Attitudes toward Specific Supreme Court Decisions Matter? The Impact of Webster and Texas v. Johnson on Public Confidence in the Supreme Court." *Political Research Quarterly* 51(3): 633–54.

Hall, M. E. K. 2011. *The Nature of Supreme Court Power*. New York, NY: Cambridge University Press.

Hall, M. E. K. 2014. "The Semiconstrained Court: Public Opinion, the Separation of Powers, and the U.S. Supreme Court's Fear of Nonimplementation." *American Journal of Political Science* 58(2): 352–66.

Hall, M. E. K., and Ura, J. D. 2015. "Judicial Majoritarianism." *Journal of Politics* 77(3): 818–32.

Hamilton, A. [1788] 1996a. *Federalist 78*, edited by B. F. Wright. New York, NY: Barnes & Noble Books.

Hamilton, A. [1788] 1996b. *Federalist 81*, edited by B. F. Wright. New York, NY: Barnes & Noble Books.

Hausegger, L., and Riddell, T. 2004. "The Changing Nature of Public Support for the Supreme Court of Canada." *Canadian Journal of Political Science* 37(1): 23–50.

Haynie, S. L. 2003. *Judging in Black and White: Decision Making in the South African Appellate Division, 1950–1990*. New York, NY: Peter-Lang Publishing.

Helmke, G. 2010. "The Origins of Institutional Crises in Latin America." *American Journal of Political Science* 53(3): 737–50.

Helmke, G., and Staton, J. K. 2011. "The Puzzling Judicial Politics of Latin America: A Theory of Litigation, Judicial Decisions, and Interbranch Conflict." In *Courts in Latin America* edited by G. Helmke and J. Rios-Figueroa. New York, NY: Cambridge University Press, 306–31.

Hoekstra, V. J. 1995. "The Supreme Court and Opinion Change: An Experimental Study of the Court's Ability to Change Opinion." *American Politics Quarterly* 23(January): 109–29.

Hoekstra, V. J. 2000. "The Supreme Court and Local Public Opinion." *American Political Science Review* 94(March): 89–100.

Hoekstra, V. J. 2003. Public Reaction to Supreme Court Decisions. New York: Cambridge University Press.

Hoekstra, V. J., and Segal, J. A. 1996. "The Shepherding of Local Public Opinion: The Supreme Court and Lamb's Chapel." *Journal of Politics* 58(4): 1079–102.

Johnson, T. R., and Martin, A. D. 1998. "The Public's Conditional Response to Supreme Court Decisions." *American Political Science Review* 92(June): 299–309.

Keck, T. M. 2004. *The Most Activist Supreme Court in History: The Road to Modern Judicial Conservatism*. Chicago, IL: University of Chicago Press.

Kellstedt, P. M., Peterson D. A. M., and Ramirez, M. D. 2010. "The Macro Politics of a Gender Gap." *Public Opinion Quarterly* 74(March): 477–98.

Kenny, J. 1996. "Sharia and Christianity in Nigeria: Islam and a 'Secular' State." *Journal of Religion in Africa* 26(4): 338–64.

Klein, E. 2012. "Of Course the Supreme Court Is Political." *Wonkblog*, June 21. Available at: http://www.washingtonpost.com/blogs/ezra-klein/wp/2012/06/21/of-course-the-supremecourt-is-political/.

Knight, J., and Epstein, L. 1996. "On the Struggle for Judicial Supremacy." *Law & Society Review* 30(1): 87–120.

Kramer, L. D. 2004. *The People Themselves: Popular Constitutionalism and Judicial Review.* New York, NY: Oxford University Press.

Krupnikov, Y., Levine, A. S., Lupia, A., and Prior, M. 2006. "Public Ignorance and Estate Tax Repeal: The Effect of Partisan Differences and Survey Incentives." *National Tax Journal* 59(3): 425–37.

Lerner, R. 1967. "The Supreme Court as Republican Schoolmaster." *Supreme Court Review* 1967(January): 127–80.

Lind, E. A., and Tyler, T. R. 1988. *The Social Psychology of Procedural Justice.* New York, NY: Plenum.

Liptak, A. 2012. "After Ruling, Roberts Makes a Getaway from Scorn." *The New York Times*, July 2. Available at: http://nyti.ms/1KEvxgK.

Lovell, G. I. 2003. *Legislative Deferrals: Statutory Ambiguity, Judicial Power, and American Democracy.* New York, NY: Cambridge University Press.

Lupia, A. 2006. "How Elitism Undermines the Study of Voter Competence." *Critical Review* 18(1–3): 217–32.

Manzano, S., and Ura, J. D. 2013. "Desperately Seeking Sonia? Latino Heterogeneity and Geographic Variation in Web Searches for Judge Sonia Sotomayor." *Political Communication* 30(1): 81–99.

Marshall, T. 1989. *Public Opinion and the Supreme Court.* New York, NY: Longman.

Marshall, T. R. 2008. *Public Opinion and the Rehnquist Court.* Albany, NY: State University of New York.

McGuire, K. T. 2004. "The Institutionalization of the U.S. Supreme Court." *Political Analysis* 12(2): 128–42.

McGuire, K. T., and Stimson, J. A. 2004. "The Least Dangerous Branch Revisited: New Evidence on Supreme Court Responsiveness to Public Preferences." *Journal of Politics* 66(November): 1018–35.

McMahon, K. J. 2004. *Reconsidering Roosevelt on Race: How the Presidency Paved the Road to Brown.* Chicago, IL: University of Chicago Press.

Mears, B. 2012. "Leahy Urges High Court to 'Do the Right Thing,' Keep Health Care Law." *CNN Politics*, May 15. Available at: http://www.cnn.com/2012/05/15/politics/health-care-reform/.

Meernik, J., and Ignagni, J. 1997. "Judicial Review and Coordinate Construction of the Constitution." *American Journal of Political Science* 41(2): 447–67.

Mishler, W., and Sheehan, R. S. 1993. "The Supreme Court as a Countermajoritarian Institution? The Impact of Public Opinion on Supreme Court Decisions." *American Political Science Review* 87(March): 87–101.

Mishler, W., and Sheehan, R. S. 1996. "Public Opinion, the Attitudinal Model, and Supreme Court Decision Making: A Micro-Analytic Perspective." *Journal of Politics* 58(1): 169–200.

Mondak, J. J. 1990. "Perceived Legitimacy of Supreme Court Decisions: Three Functions of Source Credibility." *Political Behavior* 12(December): 363–84.

Mondak, J. J. 1991. "Substantive and Procedural Aspects of Supreme Court Decisions as Determinants of Institutional Approval." *American Politics Research* 19(April): 174–88.

Mondak, J. J. 1992. "Institutional Legitimacy, Policy Legitimacy, and the Supreme Court." *American Politics Quarterly* 20(4): 457–77.

Mondak, J. J. 1994. "Policy Legitimacy and the Supreme Court: The Sources and Contexts of Legitimation." *Political Research Quarterly* 47(3): 675–92.

Mondak, J. J., and Davis, B. C. 2001. "Asked and Answered: Knowledge Levels When We Won't Take 'Don't Know' for an Answer." *Political Behavior* 23(1): 199–224.

Murphy, W. F., and Tenenhaus, J. 1968a. "Public Opinion and the Supreme Court: The Goldwater Campaign." *Public Opinion Quarterly* 32: 31–50.

Murphy, W. F., and Tenenhaus, J. 1968b. "Public Opinion and the United States Supreme Court: A Preliminary Mapping of Some Prerequisites for Court Legitimation of Regime Change." *Law & Society Review* 2: 357–82.

Prempeh, H. K. 2006. "Marbury in Africa: Judicial Review and the Challenge of Constitutionalism in Contemporary Africa." *Tulane Law Review* 80(4): 1239–324.

Prior, M. 2013. "Visual Political Knowledge: A Different Road to Competence?" *Journal of Politics* 76(1): 41–57.

Prior, M., and Lupia, A. 2008. "Money, Time, and Political Knowledge: Distinguishing Quick Recall and Political Learning Skills." *American Journal of Political Science* 52(1): 169–83.

Riker, W. H. 1980. "Implications from the Disequilibrium of Majority Rule for the Study of Institutions." *American Political Science Review* 74(June): 432–46.

Rosen, J. 2012. "Book Review: 'The Oath: The Obama White House and the Supreme Court' by Jeffrey Toobin." *The Washington Post*, September 14. Available at: http://wapo.st/1Qql090.

Rostow, E. 1952. "The Democratic Character of Judicial Review." *Harvard Law Review* 66(2): 193–224.

Roy, A. 2012. "The Inside Story on How Roberts Changed his Supreme Court Vote on Obamacare." *Forbes*, July 1. Available at: http://onforb.es/1t2nDUt.

Segal, J. A. 1997. "Separation-of-Powers Games in the Positive Theory of Congress and Courts." *American Political Science Review* 91(1): 28-45.

Segal, J. A., and Spaeth, H. J. 2002. *The Supreme Court and the Attitudinal Model Revisited*. New York, NY: Cambridge University Press.

Segal, J. A., Westerland, C., and Lindquist, S. A. 2011. "Congress, the Supreme Court, and Judicial Review: Testing a Constitutional Separation of Powers Model." *American Journal of Political Science* 55(1): 89–104.

Scherer, N., and Curry, B. 2010. "Does Descriptive Race Representation Enhance Institutional Legitimacy? The Case of the U.S. Courts." *Journal of Politics* 72(1): 90–104.

Smith, M. A. 2000. *American Business and Political Power: Public Opinion, Elections, and Democracy*. Chicago, IL: University of Chicago Press.

Staton, J. K. 2010. *Judicial Power and Strategic Communication in Mexico*. New York, NY: Cambridge University Press.

Stimson, J. A. 1999. *Public Opinion in America: Moods, Cycles, and Swings*, 2nd ed. Boulder, CO: Westview.

Stimson, J. A. 2004. *Tides of Consent: How Public Opinion Shapes American Politics*. New York, NY: Cambridge University Press.

Stimson, J. A., Mackuen M. B., and Erikson, R. S. 1995. "Dynamic Representation." *American Political Science Review* 89(September): 543–65.

Stoutenborough, J. W., Haider-Markel D. P., and Allen, M. D. 2006. "Reassessing the Impact of Supreme Court Decisions on Public Opinion: Gay Civil Rights Cases." *Political Research Quarterly* 59(3): 419–33.

Taylor-Robinson, M. M., and Ura, J. D. 2013. "Public Opinion and Conflict in the Separation of Powers: Understanding the Honduran Coup of 2009." *Journal of Theoretical Politics* 25(October): 105–27.

Tenenhaus, J, and Murphy, W. F. 1981. "Patterns of Support for the Supreme Court: A Panel Study." *Journal of Politics* 43(1): 24–39.

Toobin, J. 2012. *The Oath: The Obama White House and the Supreme Court*. New York, NY: Knopf-Doubleday.

Unger, M. A. 2008. "After the Supreme Word." *American Politics Research* 36(5): 750–75.

Ura, J. D. 2014a. "Backlash and Legitimation: Macro Political Responses to Supreme Court Decisions." *American Journal of Political Science* 58(January): 110–26.

Ura, J. D. 2014b. "The Placement of Conflict: The Supreme Court and Issue Attention in the National Media." In *Covering the United States Supreme Court in the Digital Age*, edited by R. Davis. New York, NY: Cambridge University Press, 153–72.

Ura, J. D., and Ellis, C. R. 2012. "Partisan Moods: Polarization and Party Preference Dynamics." *Journal of Politics* 74(1): 277–91.

Ura, J. D., and Higgins, A. 2015. "Signals or Noise? The Influence of Judicial Ideology on Supreme Court Affirmances." Paper presented at the Annual Meeting of the Southern Political Science Association, New Orleans, LA.

Ura, J. D., and Socker, E. M. 2011. "The Behavioral Political Economy of Budget Deficits: How Starve the Beast Policies Feed the Machine." *The Forum* 9(2): Article 7.

Ura, J. D., and Wohlfarth, P. C. 2010. "An Appeal to the People: Public Opinion and Congressional Support for the Supreme Court." *Journal of Politics* 72(4): 939–56.

Vanberg, G. 2001. "Legislative-Judicial Relations: A Game-Theoretic Approach to Constitutional Review." *American Journal of Political Science* 45(2): 346–61.

VonDoepp, P. 2009. *Judicial Politics in New Democracies: Cases from Southern Africa*. New York, NY: Lynne Rienner Publishers.

VonDoepp, P. 2013. "The Rule of Law and the Courts." In *Routledge Handbook of African Politics*, edited by D. Anderson, N. Cheeseman, and A. Scheibler. New York, NY: Routledge, 37–48.

Walsh, K. C. 2012. "Putting the Chief Justice's Switch in Some Recent Historical/Institutional Perspective." *WalshLaw*, July 6. Available at: http://bit.ly/1cxZOC2.

Whittington, K. 2007. *Political Foundations of Judicial Supremacy: The Presidency, The Supreme Court, and Constitutional Leadership in U.S. History*. Princeton, NJ: Princeton University Press.

Widner, J. 2001a. *Building the Rule of Law: Francis Nyalali and the Road to Judicial Independence in Africa*. New York, NY: W. W. Norton and Company.

Widner, J. 2001b. "Courts and Democracy in Postconflict Transitions: A Social Scientist's Perspective on the African Case." *American Journal of International Law* 95(1): 64–75.

Wydra, E. B. 2012. "Supreme Court's Legitimacy at Stake on Affordable Care Act." *Politico*, June 25. Available at: http://www.politico.com/news/stories/0612/77806.html.

Cases Cited

Babbitt, Secretary of the Interior v. Sweet Home Chapter of Communities for a Great Oregon. 1995. 515 U.S. 687.
Baker v. Carr. 1962. 369 U.S. 186.
Board of Education of Kiryas Joel Village School District v. Grumet. 1994. 512 U.S. 687.
Bowers v. Hardwick. 1986. 478 U.S. 186.
Boy Scouts of America v. Dale. 2000. 530 U.S. 640.
Chisholm v. Georgia. 1793. 4 U.S. 419.
Furman v. Georgia. 1972. 408 U.S. 153.
Gregg v. Georgia. 1976. 428 U.S. 163.
Lamb's Chapel v. Center Moriches Free High School District. 1993. 508 U.S. 384.
Lawrence v. Texas. 2003. 539 U.S. 558.
Marbury v. Madison. 1803. 1 Cranch 137.
McCleskey v. Kemp. 1987. 481 U.S. 279.
National Federation of Independent Business v. Sibelius. 2012. 567 U.S. ___.
Oklahoma Tax Commission v. Chickasaw Nation. 1995. 515 U.S. 450.
Planned Parenthood of Southeastern Pennsylvania v. Casey. 1992. 505 U.S. 833.
Roe v. Wade. 1973. 410 U.S. 113.
Romer v. Evans. 1996. U.S. 517 U.S. 620.
Stuart v. Laird. 1803. 1 Cranch 299.
United States v. Lee. 1882. 106 U.S. 196.
Webster v. Reproductive Health Services. 1989. 4492 U.S. 290.

CHAPTER 24

JUDICIAL IMPACT

MATTHEW E. K. HALL

LASTLY, we turn to the most important, common, and dreaded academic question: So what? Judges are driven by these motivations, constrained by those institutions, perhaps even swayed by what they had for breakfast (Pusey 1983: 105–6). So what? What's that got to do with the price of tea in china—or, more appropriately, the price of milk in southern Illinois (*United States v. Carolene Products* 1938)? What are the practical effects of court rulings on society? This "so what" question is the motivating force behind the study of judicial impact.

Conventional wisdom about judicial impact is persistently, conveniently, and maddeningly contradictory. For centuries, scholars and statesmen have been skeptical of judicial power. As Alexander Hamilton argued, the federal "judiciary is beyond comparison the weakest of the three departments of power" and the "least dangerous branch" because it has "no influence over either the sword or the purse; no direction either of the strength or of the wealth of the society" (*Federalist 78*). Many modern political scientists agree: "By itself, the [Supreme] Court is almost powerless to affect the course of national policy" (Dahl 1957: 293). Courts can "be of some use in implementing policies that apply principally to government agencies," but "without the support of the real power holders ... litigation is ineffectual and at times counterproductive. With that support, litigation is unnecessary" (Scheingold 2004: 130). In sum, "U.S. courts can almost never be effective producers of significant social reform. At best, they can second the social reform acts of the other branches of government" (Rosenberg 2008: 422; see also Sweet 2010).

Nevertheless, skeptics of judicial power have consistently faced detractors. Hamilton's predictions of judicial impotence were rebuffed in the *Anti-Federalist Papers*: "The supreme court under this constitution would be exalted above all other power in the government, and subject to no controul" (Yates 1788). The seminal works by Robert Dahl and Gerald Rosenberg, written decades apart, both cast serious doubt on the judiciary's impact. Yet, despite their prominence, these studies have encountered considerable disagreement and criticism (e.g., Casper 1976; Keck 2009; Schultz 1998). In contrast to those classic works, many scholars argue that courts wield significant power over social and policy outcomes (e.g., Hall 2011; Howard and Steigerwalt 2011; McCann 1994; Skowronek 1982).

The schizophrenic state of the impact literature is admittedly convenient for theory building. Should a scholar wish to claim that courts are "uncommonly dependent upon the goodwill of their constituents for both support and compliance" (Gibson, Caldeira, and Baird 1998: 343; see also McGuire and Stimson 2004: 1022) or that Supreme Court "justices lack any real mechanism to enforce their decisions" (George and Epstein 1992: 325; see also Casillas, Enns, and Wohlfarth 2011: 75; Harvey and Friedman 2009: 575), they can do so confident in the literature's support. Should they wish, instead, to claim that "Supreme Court decisions … have broad policy ramifications … [and] guide a wide range of social, economic, and political behavior" (Wahlbeck 1997: 778; see also Carrubba et al. 2012: 400) or that "lower federal courts play a significant role in the creation of public policy" (Giles, Hettinger, and Peppers 2001: 623), they can do so with equal confidence. Because the literature includes a variety of widely contrasting views, it can support almost any theoretical proposition (see, e.g., Wasby 1970: ch. 8). Consequently, these contradictory assumptions may produce ambiguity and inconsistency across the field of judicial politics.

The reality of judicial impact undoubtedly lies between these extreme views. The paragraphs above highlight a few of the more ambitious quotations from prominent sources, but all of these studies present a nuanced view of judicial impact. Even Gerald Rosenberg, in a response to his critics, proclaims, "Of course courts matter! Of course courts influence social change" (Rosenberg 2014). Nonetheless, considerable disagreement obviously exists over the nature of judicial impact. To some degree, this disagreement is driven by a lack of conceptual clarity. Scholars who advance conflicting views of judicial impact are often asking different questions and applying different standards to their analyses. Rather than genuinely disagreeing, many of these studies simply talk past one another. In this chapter, I will discuss some of the conceptual issues that engender confusion and contradictions in the study of judicial impact, and summarize what we know (and do not know) about the impact of courts.

Conceptualizing Judicial Impact

Scholars often frame judicial impact broadly as the role of law in shaping social change. This line of inquiry is motivated by an interest in providing practical advice to advocates of social reform: Is a litigation strategy likely to bring about the desired social change or are non-judicial strategies more likely to prevail? Other studies in this tradition are driven by a desire to understand the role of courts in a democratic system: Do unelected judges exercise truly countermajoritarian influence or are they constrained and powerless, as Hamilton suggested? This conception of impact as the role of law in spurring social change highlights the important theoretical issues at stake. However, "this concept has the weakness of breadth. It refers to a wide range of processes, which are difficult to examine meaningfully as a single phenomenon" (Baum 1976). Consequently, many impact studies complicate and confuse the empirical issues at stake by blurring starkly different empirical questions. In this section, I consider the various empirical questions that fall under the umbrella of judicial impact.

First, some impact studies examine the influence of judicial rulings on the attitudes of elites or the mass public. This form of judicial impact is sometimes described as educating (Franklin and Kosaki 1989: 752), legitimizing (Black 1960; Dahl 1957: 293; Wasby 1970: 14), persuading (Feeley 1973), or "appealing to men's better nature" (Bickel 1986: 26; Funston 1975: 810; Rostow 1952: 208). The literature suggests courts can focus public attention on certain issues (Flemming, Bohte, and Wood 1997), polarize mass opinion (Franklin and Kosaki 1989), and, in some situations, shape popular attitudes (Caldeira 1987; Hoekstra 2000; Hoekstra and Segal 1996; Hume 2013; Johnson and Martin 1998). The Supreme Court, in particular, consistently enjoys a relatively stable level of "diffuse support"—that is, durable, fundamental loyalty to the Court as an institution (Caldeira 1986; Caldeira and Gibson 1992). Consequently, the Court may be able "confer some increment of policy legitimacy" by translating its diffuse support into "specific support" for particular policies (Mondak 1992: 457; Mondak 1990) or at least the acceptance of unpopular rulings (Gibson 1989). "Though public opinion initially pushes back against the Court, over the long run, the authoritative voice of the Supreme Court has the capacity to pull at least some of the disagreeing public toward its decisions" (Ura 2014: 111). See the chapter on public opinion in this handbook for a more extensive discussion of this topic.

Second, impact studies often measure success in terms of litigant goals rather than judicial mandates. For example, the Supreme Court's reapportionment rulings produced dramatic changes in the apportionment of congressional and state legislative districts and "fundamentally altered the structure of power in some of the most important policymaking institutions in the country" (Hall 2011: 102). Yet Rosenberg found that "success with implementation was spotty ... some change did occur. However, it seldom reached the goals for which the reformers had argued" (2008: 299, 302). The proponents of reapportionment hoped that shifting electoral power away from conservative rural districts and toward liberal urban centers would prompt the enactment of new liberal policies, "but the reformers' liberal agenda did not then automatically come to pass" (p. 298).[1] In other words, many studies of law and social change evaluate the degree to which litigants are able to achieve their goals via litigation strategies, but they do not speak to the impact of judicial rulings (after all, the reapportionment decisions never mandated that states enact liberal policies). In short, these studies evaluate the impact of litigation—an important, but conceptually distinct, empirical question.

Third, scholars interested in the long-term impact of litigation often weigh the desired outcomes of a judicial ruling against the unintended consequences and political backlash (e.g., Klarman 2004, 2005). For example, Rosenberg readily acknowledged that several state courts of last resort prompted policy change with regard to gay rights (2008: 353). Yet he concluded that "litigation as a means of obtaining the right to same-sex marriage has not succeeded" because "nowhere in the United States are same-sex couples treated equally with married heterosexual couples" and "there has been a tremendous backlash against same-sex marriage" (pp. 415–16). Of course, Rosenberg's view may have changed in the wake of *United States v. Windsor* (2013) and *Obergefell v. Hodges* (2015); however, as of 2008, he viewed the costs of backlash as outweighing the benefits of same-sex marriage litigation. Similarly, in appraising judicial capacity, Horowitz concluded, "the balance of goal attainment, on the one hand, against the costs and unintended consequences, on the other, remains very difficult to weigh" (1977: 273). Certainly, social reformers should contemplate the possibility of backlash and unintended consequences as they consider litigation, but these potential problems are not unique to courts (Horowitz 1977: 293, 298). Thomas Keck has argued that "all victories by LGBT rights advocates have sparked legal and political countermobilization, regardless of whether the victories occurred through legislative, executive, or judicial channels" (2009: 181). In a similar vein, Lawrence Baum noted that "judicial scholars seldom [consider] whether noncompliance with Supreme Court decisions result[s] chiefly from universal imperfections in implementation rather than special weaknesses of courts" (2003: 172). Accordingly, these studies may say more about policy impact in general than judicial impact in particular.

Fourth, studies of judicially driven social change tend to focus on whether litigation "improves the conditions of [*sic*] disadvantaged groups ... particularly racial minorities, woman, inmates, and people living in poverty" (Epp 2008: 596). For example, Rosenberg defines social reform as "the broadening and equalizing of the possession and enjoyment of what are commonly perceived as basic goods in American society ... rights and liberties, powers and opportunities, income and wealth" (2008: 4). By focusing on reforms that broaden and equalize access to these goods, he deliberately neglects cases in which the courts limit access or create imbalances in access. Consequently, the conclusions of these studies may be limited to certain types of judicial intervention.

Fifth, many impact studies examine how often courts engage in independent policymaking, rather than the effects of those interventions. Do courts frequently attempt to alter public policies via constitutional invalidations, statutory interpretations, and common law rulings? Or do they typically endorse the policies enacted by other officials? If courts merely rubber stamp legislative and executive policies, then they pose no countermajoritarian problem and offer no hope of prompting social reform. Accordingly, many skeptics of judicial power argue that courts have little impact because they rarely try to. For example, Dahl argued that the Supreme Court has little effect on national policy because it rarely invalidates statutes that are supported by the current "lawmaking majority"; he suggests the Court refrains from intervening because it "is inevitably a part of the dominant national alliance ... [and] of course supports the major policies of the alliance" (1957: 291–3; cf. Casper 1976). Similarly, Gerald Rosenberg argued that courts rarely produce social change, in part, because they are constrained by the limited nature of constitutional rights and their lack of independence from political pressure (1992; 2008).[2] As a result, courts seldom, if ever, disturb the status quo.

In contrast, Donald Horowitz (1977) argued that courts drastically expanded their policy-making role during the 1960s and 1970s. More recently, Kevin McGuire (2004) measured the Supreme Court's "legal and political impact" as the frequency with which the Court issues important rulings and exercises judicial review. Using this metric, he found that the Court's "impact" has increased over time as a consequence of its increased institutionalization. Looking more broadly, Thomas Marshall (1989) examined whether Supreme Court rulings are overturned by subsequent constitutional amendments, congressional actions, or Court rulings. He found that rulings tend to prevail when they are unanimous, ideologically liberal, and consistent with public opinion. Robert Hume (2013: chs. 5 and 7) conducted similar analyses on state supreme courts. He concluded that judicial policy innovation largely depends on public opinion, the content of state constitutions, and policy diffusion across states; judicial policy endurance depends on a state's popular initiative and constitutional amendment procedures. Undoubtedly, the frequency with which judges intervene in public policy-making and the propensity of those interventions to endure partially determines the total impact of courts on society. Nonetheless, the degree to which judges are willing to intervene and the effects of those interventions are separate empirical questions.

Finally, many impact studies specifically examine the causal influence of judicial rulings on the behavior of state and private actors (Baum 1976; Canon and Johnson 1998; Hall 2011). In short, when courts say "jump," whose feet leave the ground and how high do they go? Some studies in this genre focus on the concept of judicial power by comparing the judges' intended outcomes of a ruling with the ruling's actual effects (e.g., Hall 2011). But judicial rulings may also have unintended, unanticipated, and indirect consequences, which also reflect the causal effects of judicial rulings on behavior.

Studies that focus narrowly on the causal relationship between judicial rulings and behavior are inherently more limited than research on the use of law as a tool for social reform. Yet, by sacrificing substantive breadth, these studies offer greater conceptual clarity and analytic rigor. Moreover, an emphasis on the causal relationship between judicial rulings and behavior highlights the normative dilemmas associated with judicial power (e.g., the countermajoritarian difficulty and policy-making by unelected judges). In contrast, broader impact studies inherently implicate questions of public opinion, legitimacy, litigant behavior, judicial decision-making, and legal culture. Unfortunately, the simultaneous analysis of these distinct phenomena often blurs the theoretical and empirical issues at stake. The literature on this broader conception of impact as social reform has been ably reviewed in a previous Oxford Handbook by Charles Epp (2008).

Accordingly, this chapter will focus on studies that conceptualize judicial impact narrowly as the causal effects of judicial rulings on behavior. But exactly whose behavior should we expect to change in response to a judicial ruling, and how should we expect their behavior to change? The relevant behavioral responses to judicial rulings can be divided into two categories: (1) implementation, that is, the causal effects of judicial rulings on the behavior of government bureaucrats responsible for putting those rulings into effect, and (2) social outcomes, that is, the causal effects of judicial rulings on the behavior of private actors.

Implementation

Many impact studies examine the influence of judicial rulings on the behavior of government bureaucrats responsible for implementing those rulings, such as lower court judges, police officers, schoolteachers, and other employees in federal, state, or local government agencies. Early implementation research portrayed the U.S. Supreme Court as shockingly ineffective at influencing the behavior of government agents (Baum 2003: 172; Wasby 1970). Public school officials routinely defied the Court's rulings with regard to school desegregation (Blaustein and Ferguson 1973; McKay 1956; Rodgers and Bullock 1976: Rosenberg 2008: ch. 2) and religious activities in public schools (Birkby 1973; Dierenfield 1962; Dolbeare 1973; Laubach 1957; Reich 1968; Way 1968); many teachers continue to violate the school prayer rulings (McGuire 2009). Additionally, law enforcement officials often resisted the implementation of the Court's custodial interrogation rulings, such as *Escobedo v. United Sates* (1964) and *Miranda v. Arizona* (1966; Medalie, Zeitz, and Alexander 1968; Milner 1994; Wald et al. 1966).

However, early implementation research often suffered from problems of selection bias; scholars tended to focus on cases where they expected to find noncompliance (Baum 2003: 172). More recent work concludes that government actors frequently comply with state and federal court rulings (Hall 2011; Howard and Steigerwalt 2011; Keck 2009). In fact, "federal agencies are highly responsive to decisions from the U.S. Courts of Appeals" (Hume 2009: 91; see Spriggs 1996). For example, the courts of appeals appear to strongly influence the behavior of the Internal Revenue Service in conducting audits (Howard and Segal 2002) and the Army Corps of Engineers in granting permits (Canes-Wrone 2003).

Nonetheless, the implementation of judicial rulings is far from perfect. Some rulings prompt swift and decisive action by judges, policymakers, and bureaucrats, while others fall flat. Why are some rulings implemented and others are not? In this section, I attempt to synthesize the most prominent explanations for variation in the implementation of judicial rulings, noting disagreements and contradictions as they arise.

Early studies tended to frame judicial implementation as a unique phenomenon (cf. Baum 1981), but scholars increasingly recognize that judicial implementation shares many features with policy implementation in other domains (Baum 2003: 172–3). In his seminal study on the topic, Michael Lipsky concludes that "policy implementation in the end comes down to the people who actually implement it" (2010: xii). Consequently, the U.S. Supreme Court (as well as any appellate-level court) "is an *implementer-dependent* institution ... the Court, like most political authorities, must rely on other political actors to implement its decisions" (Hall 2011: 16; see also Baum 1981). These other political actors are strategic, meaning that they react to judicial rulings based on the perceived costs and benefits of alternative implementation strategies (Johnson 1979a, 1979b; Rodgers and Bullock 1976; Spriggs 1996; Stover and Brown 1975).[3] A variety of factors potentially influence these perceived costs and benefits (Canon and Johnson 1998; Wasby 1970). The factors most commonly supported by the literature fall generally into four categories: (1) opinion clarity, (2) agency preferences, (3) institutional context, and (4) external pressure.

Opinion Clarity

First, the implementation of a judicial ruling depends in part on the clarity of the message sent by the court's opinion. When courts send unequivocal signals about the types of policy change they desire, those signals tend to prompt change; when courts send ambiguous signals, permit wide discretion, or reveal internal disagreement, bureaucrats are less likely to respond (Baum 1976, 1980a, 1981; Canon and Johnson 1998; Johnson 1979a; Tarr 1977; Wasby 1970). For example, federal administrative agencies are more responsive to a U.S. Court of Appeals decision when the decision includes more explicit instructions with regard to the desired policy change (Spriggs 1996). Agencies are also more responsive when the decision is based on substantive statutory or constitutional grounds (as opposed to procedural issues), because, in these cases, "administrators know that judges expect more than just superficial changes to their policies" (Hume 2009: 85; see also Spriggs 1997; Wasby 1970). Finally, agencies are more responsive when courts reverse, rather than remand, agency decisions, because reversals "send clear signals that [judges] expect policy change" (Hume 2009: 84), whereas "remands provide bureaucracies with greater latitude by ordering them to engage in further proceedings without delineating appropriate outcomes" (Spriggs 1997: 571). Judicial rulings may also prompt more implementation when they include little dissent, because unanimous or near-unanimous decisions indicate legal certainty and little hope of a different outcome in the future (Hume 2009: 87; Wasby 1970). However, several studies fail to confirm this finding in different contexts (Johnson 1979c; Spriggs 1996, 1997; Westerland et al. 2010).

Agency Preferences

An agency's decision to implement a judicial ruling is also influenced by the preferences of individuals in the agency. Administrators and bureaucrats are obviously more likely to implement decisions that comport with their ideological preferences or promote their professional interests (Baum 1976, 1980a; Wasby 1970). In some cases, a judicial ruling might provide political cover for other actors to implement policies that they wanted to implement anyway (Rosenberg 2008). Consequently, federal administrative agencies are less likely to implement a judicial decision when the agency is ideologically distant from the court or the decision asks for a formal rules change. Implementation is also less likely when the decision involves a programmatic issue, such as changing an entire regulatory scheme or administrative process, as opposed to a single decision, because bureaucrats prefer to minimize costs by avoiding large-scale changes (Hume 2009: 84–90; Spriggs 1996, 1997). Additionally, U.S. Supreme Court rulings related to desegregation and school prayer had the least impact in the Deep

South where school board officials, school administrators, and teachers disagreed most vehemently with the decisions (Hall 2011: 127–36; McGuire 2009; Rosenberg 2008: ch. 2). These bureaucratic agents probably resisted implementation due to their strong personal opposition to the rulings.

In some situations, the Supreme Court may be able to persuade bureaucrats on the merits of an issue, thereby altering their preferences. The ability of courts to influence the attitudes of policy implementers has long been thought an important component of judicial impact (Baum 1976), but evidence supporting that proposition has been difficult to attain. Nonetheless, a few studies suggest courts can successfully persuade bureaucrats. For example, when interviewed, administrators report that judicial opinions can sometimes persuade them to change their views on the merits of a decision, "especially when judges direct their attention to arguments or evidence that they have not previously considered" (Hume 2009: 122). Additionally, James Gibson finds that survey respondents are more likely to comply with judicial rulings when they perceive a court as a legitimate institution, and "the United States Supreme Court in particular seems to have some ability to elicit acceptance of public policies that are unpopular with the mass public" (1989: 469). If public officials respond in the same manner, this finding may explain some variation in judicial implementation.

Institutional Context

Implementation decisions also depend on the institutional context in which bureaucratic agents operate. Some agencies are more susceptible to judicially imposed sanctions than others.

Most obviously, implementation requires cooperation from lower court judges (Tarr 1977), and these judges are highly responsive to high court rulings (Sweet 2010). A rich and extensive literature explores the degree to which lower courts comply with high court rulings; this literature is fully reviewed in the chapter on precedent in this handbook. In brief, lower courts tend to faithfully adhere to legal pronouncements issued by their superiors in judicial hierarchies (see Baum 2003; Canon and Johnson 1998). Of course, lower court compliance is not perfect (Bartley 1969; Baum 1978; Canon 1974b; Peltason 1971; Scott 2006), and it may vary depending on characteristics of the precedential opinion and the lower court interpreting the precedent (e.g., Masood, Kassow, and Songer 2013; Masood and Songer 2014). Nonetheless, U.S. Supreme Court rulings strongly influence the behavior of lower federal court judges (Benesh 2002; Brent 1999; Gruhl 1980; Johnson 1987; Songer 1987; Songer, Segal, and Cameron 1994; Songer and Sheehan 1990) and state supreme court judges (Hoekstra 2005; Kassow, Songer, and Fix 2012; Kilwein and Brisbin 1997; Romans 1974; cf. Songer 1988). U.S. district courts also tend to make decisions consistent with U.S. Court of Appeals policies (Baum 1980b).[4] In fact, lower court judges may even anticipate the preferences of higher courts when making their decisions (Kassow, Songer, and Fix 2012; Randazzo 2008). The institutional context of lower courts likely prompt these judges to follow precedent due to a fear of reversal (Caminker 1994; McNollgast 1995; cf. Klein and Hume 2003), reputational concerns (Canon and Johnson 1998: 36), role conceptions (Howard 1981), respect for high court authority (Baum 1977; Pacelle and Baum 1992), or a desire for legal accuracy (Johnson 1987). Consequently, the U.S. Supreme Court's "hierarchical control appears strong and effective" (Westerland et al. 2010: 891; see Cameron, Segal, and Songer 2000).

Some non-judicial agencies are partially dependent on lower courts and, therefore, highly responsive to judicial rulings. The U.S. Supreme Court tends to strongly influence the behavior of non-judicial actors in "vertical" rulings—that is, rulings that can be directly implemented through lower courts in the judicial hierarchy. "Vertical issues usually involve the Court identifying a group of potential criminal defendants as constitutionally immune from criminal prosecution" because law enforcement officials depend on courts to convict criminal defendants (Hall 2011: 16). For example, lower court judges can directly implement *Roe v. Wade* by simply acquitting individuals charged under abortion statutes. In other words, because courts are an integral part of the criminal justice process, they "have direct control over some strategic incentives—they can, for instance threaten to release prisoners if prison conditions are not improved, and they can refuse to accept confessions as evidence if police do not provide the required [*Miranda*] warnings" (Nagel 2001: 57). Therefore, high courts can strongly influence the behavior of law enforcement officials, even when those rulings are highly unpopular (Hall 2011: ch. 5). As a result, decision-making by the U.S. Supreme Court influences the federal incarceration rate (Hall 2015), and both the U.S. Supreme Court and state supreme courts influence state incarceration rates (Hall and Windett 2015).

In contrast, "lateral" rulings involve directives to non-judicial actors who do not rely on courts. For example, the Supreme Court's decision in *Brown v. Board of Education* (1954) required local schools to desegregate. But school officials do not depend on courts because courts are not inherently involved in the public education system. Because courts lack control over direct incentives for school officials, it is more difficult for the judiciary to impose costs and benefits on these actors. Consequently, lateral rulings tend to be successfully implemented only when the decisions are popular among the public; that is, in lateral cases, implementation depends on support from non-judicial actors (Hall 2011).

External Pressure

In some cases, non-judicial bureaucrats do not support a judicial ruling and the courts do not control the necessary strategic incentives to compel implementation. In these instances, other non-judicial actors may be able to prompt implementation by offering incentives or imposing costs on the recalcitrant bureaucrats (Baum 1980a; Nagel 2001; Rosenberg 2008; Stover and Brown 1975; Wasby 1970). A variety of external pressures may encourage implementation of judicial rulings, including financial incentives, coercion from federal officials (Rodgers and Bullock 1976), an individual state's political culture (Hoekstra 2005), public opinion on the specific issue (Hall 2011), and more general social conditions (Nagel 2001).

The classic example of external pressure prompting implementation is the Civil Rights Act of 1964. Many southern public officials fiercely resisted desegregation; a decade after the *Brown* decision, less than 1 percent of African American children in the Deep South attended school with whites (Hall 2011: 127–30; Rosenberg 2008: ch. 2). However, in 1964 the federal government intervened by enacting the Civil Rights Act. The Act empowered the Attorney General to initiate legal action against segregated school districts and—perhaps most importantly—threatened to cut off federal funding for school districts that failed to desegregate. Consequently, the period from 1964 to 1972 saw a dramatic increase in desegregation efforts (Hall 2011: 127–30; Rosenberg 2008: ch. 2), especially in districts where federal or state officials visited the school district, initiated legal action, threatened to terminate funding, or actually cut off funds (Rodgers and Bullock 1976). In other words, the *Brown* decision was implemented in the Deep South only because Congress brought pressure to bear on segregationists.

In addition to pressuring bureaucrats after a judicial ruling is issued, elected officials can actively promote the use of judicial power by legislatively empowering judges, encouraging private litigation, and supporting the expansion of the legal profession (Frymer 2003). Proponents of the "regime politics" approach argue that judicial power is primarily, if not completely, politically constructed; that is, elected officials actively support the creation and maintenance of judicial power in order to serve partisan or ideological interests (Whittington 2007). Judges can then use their power—particularly the power of judicial review—to overcome political obstructions, avoid public blame, address issues unworthy of legislative attention, lend legitimacy, and entrench policies against future changes (Clayton and Pickerill 2004, 2006; Gillman 2002; Graber 1993; Lovell 2003; Whittington 2005, 2007). From this view, courts may exercise extensive influence over social change precisely because elected officials empowered them to do so.

Social Outcomes

The implementation of judicial rulings is often ultimately aimed at altering social outcomes; that is, changing the behavior of private actors. For example, the proponents of *Roe v. Wade* (1973) are likely concerned, first and foremost, with the actual availability of abortion services to women seeking abortion. Accordingly, impact studies often examine the effects of judicial rulings on various social outcomes, such as the frequency with which women obtain abortion procedures. However, social outcomes like the abortion rate usually involve the combined actions of government actors and private actors. For example, the implementation of *Roe* merely requires lower courts to refrain from convicting individuals charged under abortion statutes; it does not require funding for abortions, willing participation by doctors and private clinics, social mores that condone abortions, or any number of other factors that might influence the abortion rate. Consequently, we should not expect the legalization of abortion to lead to the same abortion rate in every state.

In some cases, the disconnect between a judicial ruling and a social outcome is so severe that the social outcome hardly serves as a reliable measure of impact. For example, in the wake of the Supreme Court's decisions protecting flag burning, no person has been convicted under a flag-burning statute and the one person who was in prison for flag desecration was released (Hall 2011: 45). Therefore, the bureaucratic implementation of the decisions was essentially perfect. However, the legalization of flag burning did not prompt a rash of flag burnings as Americans rushed to exercise their new rights. Less than 150 incidents were recorded between 1994 and 2007—a significant increase over the pre-legalization rate, but still a minuscule number compared to the national population (Hall 2011: 45). The Court's decisions were perfectly implemented, but the strong social norm against flag burning prevailed and the change in social behavior was modest. As a result, measuring the effect of court rulings on social outcomes may sometimes provide a skewed picture of judicial impact. Furthermore, there is no reason to think that the justices or the litigants wanted to encourage more flag burnings; therefore, this measure of impact (like many other social outcome measures) is probably not an appropriate test of judicial power.

Nonetheless, the examination of social outcomes offers a fascinating perspective on judicial impact, and a variety of studies adopt this approach. Furthermore, scholars have found ample evidence that some judicial rulings strongly affect a variety of social outcomes. As a result of *Roe v. Wade*, "interstate differences in abortion rates have diminished considerably since 1973" (Hansen 1980: 372) and fewer women must cross state lines to receive an abortion (Hall 2011: 38–44). The Supreme Court's decision in *Citizens United v. Federal Election Commission* (2010) may have increased the stock prices for firms in a majority of regulated industries, especially those headquartered in states with more restrictions on political spending (Burns and Jindra 2013). The Court's criminal justice rulings in *Mapp v. Ohio* (1961) and *Miranda v. Arizona* (1966) may have led to fewer solved crimes and an increased crime rate (Canon 1974a; Cassell and Fowles 1998a, 1998b; Donohue 1998; Nagel 1965); however, these effects diminished over time as law enforcement officials adapted to the new legal rules (Davies 1983; Manwaring 1968). The reapportionment decisions benefited the electoral prospects of non-Southern Democrats and increased average congressional victory margins (Cox and Katz 1999; Cox and McCubbins 2002). These decisions also had a substantial effect on spending for urban versus rural programs at both the state (Ansolabehere, Gerber, and Snyder 2002; Ansolabehere and Snyder 2008) and federal level (McCubbins and Schwartz 1988).

In sum, many judicial rulings have profound effects on social, political, and economic behavior among the mass public. In some cases, the causal link between judicial rulings and social outcomes is clear. More often, though, this link is complicated by a plethora of confounding factors, including public opinion, social mores, economic conditions, and the decisions of other political actors. Studies of judicial implementation can often sidestep these methodological problems by focusing on a narrower range of actors and behaviors.

Unanswered Challenges in the Study of Judicial Impact

In 1976, Lawrence Baum described the preceding two decades as evincing "increasing attention to the process by which Supreme Court decisions are implemented" (1976: 86). However, by 2008, Charles Epp described the study of law as an instrument of social reform as "somewhat moribund" (2008: 610). To be sure, the last few decades saw groundbreaking work on the role of litigation in spurring social change (e.g., Edelman 1990; Epp 1998; Feeley and Rubin 1998; McCann 1994; Rosenberg 1991). Nonetheless, Epp's point was valid: judicial impact was no longer (and perhaps is still not) a "vibrant part of the field of law and courts" (2008: 610). Several recent studies suggest a renewed interest in this important topic (Hall 2011; Howard and Steigerwalt 2011; Hume 2009, 2013; Sweet 2010). However, the success of this research agenda will partially depend on whether the new generation of impact scholars can rise to the challenges posed by those who came before them. The existing literature presents at least four unfinished tasks.

First, almost a half-century ago, Stephen Wasby admonished political scientists to concentrate more on the impact of lower courts (1970: 42; see Barth 1968). Despite his counsel, impact scholars continue to focus primarily on the U.S. Supreme Court (e.g., Hall 2011). A few recent studies have improved on this trend by examining the impact of U.S. Court of Appeals decisions (Canes-Wrone 2003; Hume 2009; Spriggs 1996, 1997) and state supreme court decisions (Hall and Windett 2015; Hume 2013; Keck 2009). Nonetheless, the study of judicial impact could certainly benefit from further inquiry into the effects of lower court decisions, and the discipline should encourage these efforts.

Second, more than a decade ago, Lawrence Baum encouraged impact scholars to consider the "universal imperfections in the implementation process" and explore "the relative success of implementation for legislative and judicial policies" (2003: 173; see Kaufman 1960; Pressman and Wildavsky 1973). Yet most impact studies continue to examine courts in isolation rather than compare the relative influence of legislative, executive, and judicial institutions. One recent study makes a first attempt at this daunting task by comparing the influence of congressional, presidential, and judicial ideology on the federal incarceration rate via their respective control over lower court judges and federal prosecutors (Hall 2014a). However, this preliminary work only takes a rough first cut at this question.

Third, the field must grapple with the complicated conceptual issues that continue to plague the study of judicial impact. The ambiguities and contradictions outlined here are not dissimilar from the concerns Wasby raised decades ago (1970). A major obstacle in this endeavor is the simultaneous desire to both expand and focus the scope of impact research. Studies of reform litigation have broadened our understanding of law as an instrument of social change, but they have also blurred the nature and scope of the impact research agenda. Undoubtedly, the implementation of judicial rulings is closely tied to other aspects of judicial politics (see, e.g., Hall 2014). However, an expanded research agenda demands more analytic rigor in articulating our research questions, defining our theoretical concepts, operationalizing those concepts, and evaluating our findings. If we hope to incorporate broader conceptions of judicial impact via law-related perceptions and norms, the legal environment, and professional networks, we must attend to these methodological demands.

Finally, scholars should continue to work toward a comprehensive theory of judicial impact that explains the relationship between judicial rulings and behavioral responses. Ideally, such a theory would meet several criteria. First, it would operate in concert with broader theories of implementation by building on universal principles of the implementation process, while exploring unique features of the judiciary. Second, it would incorporate institutional, organizational, behavioral, and psychological theories of decision-making by litigants, high court judges, lower court judges, bureaucrats, and private actors, with the understanding that these actors most likely respond to different motivations and pressures in different contexts. Lastly, a comprehensive theory of judicial impact should speak to both practical and normative questions: When should social reformers pursue a litigation strategy and what do the dynamics of judicial impact say about the role of courts in a democracy? Despite the plethora of impressive work on this topic, a theory that meets these criteria is still well out of reach.

Notes

1. Hall (2011) argues that the reapportionment rulings led to significant changes in state and federal legislative behavior (see Ansolabehere, Gerber, and Snyder 2002; Ansolabehere and Snyder 2008; McCubbins and Schwartz 1988).
2. Rosenberg ultimately concludes that the limited nature of constitutional rights is a weak constraint on courts (2008: 421).
3. The proposition that bureaucrats are strategic political actors is common in the judicial impact literature, but this claim is disputed by some bureaucracy scholars (e.g., Golden 2000).
4. Lower court judges may be less responsive when a High Court ruling is extremely controversial (see, e.g., Songer and Sheehan 1990).

References

Ansolabehere, S., Gerber, A., and Snyder, J. 2002. "Equal Votes, Equal Money: Court Ordered Redistricting and Public Expenditures in the American States." *American Political Science Review* 96(4): 767–77.

Ansolabehere, S., and Snyder, J. 2008. *The End of Inequality: One Person, One Vote, and the Transformation of American Politics*. New York, NY: Norton.

Barth, T. 1968. "Perception and Acceptance of Supreme Court Decisions at the State and Local Level." *Journal of Public Law* 17: 308–50.

Bartley, N. V. 1969. *The Rise of Massive Resistance: Race and Politics in the South during the 1950's*. Baton Rouge, LA: Louisiana State University Press.

Baum, L. 1976. "Implementation of Judicial Decisions: An Organizational Analysis." *American Politics Research* 4(1): 86–114.

Baum, L. 1977. "Policy Goals in Judicial Gatekeeping: A Proximity Model of Discretionary Jurisdiction." *American Journal of Political Science* 21(1): 31–6.

Baum, L. 1978. "Lower-Court Response to Supreme Court Decisions: Reconsidering a Negative Picture." *Justice System Journal* 3: 208–19.

Baum, L. 1980a. "The Influence of Legislators and Appellate Courts over the Policy Implementation Process." *Policy Studies Journal* 8(4): 560–74.

Baum, L. 1980b. "Responses of Federal District Judges to Court of Appeals Policies: An Exploration." *Western Political Quarterly* 32(2): 217–24.

Baum, L. 1981. "Comparing the Implementation of Legislative and Judicial Policies." In *The Impact of Supreme Court Decisions: Empirical Studies*, edited by D. A. Mazmanian and P. A. Sabatier. Lexington, MA: Lexington Books, 39–62.

Baum, L. 2003. "The Supreme Court in American Politics." *Annual Review of Political Science* 6: 161–80.

Benesh, S. C. 2002. *The U.S. Court of Appeals and the Law of Confessions: Perspectives on the Hierarchy of Justice*. New York, NY: LFB Scholarly Publishing.

Bickel, A. M. 1986. *The Least Dangerous Branch: The Supreme Court at the Bar of American Politics*, 2nd ed. New Haven, CT: Yale University Press.

Birkby, R. H. 1973. "The Supreme Court and the Bible Belt: Tennessee Reaction to the 'Schempp' Decision." *Midwest Journal of Political Science* 10(3): 304–19.

Black, C. 1960. *The People and the Court: Judicial Review in a Democracy*. New York, NY: Macmillan.

Blaustein, A. P., and Ferguson, C. C. 1973. "Avoidance, Evasion, and Delay." In *The Impact of Supreme Court Decisions: Empirical Studies*, edited by T. L. Becker and M. M. Feeley. 2nd rev. ed. New York, NY: Oxford University Press, 100–9.

Brent, J. C. 1999. "An Agent and Two Principals: U.S. Court of Appeals Responses to *Employment Division, Department of Human Resources v. Smith* and the Religious Freedom Restoration Act." *American Politics Quarterly* 27(2): 236–66.

Burns, N., and Jindra, J. 2013. "Political Spending and Shareholder Wealth: The Effect of the Supreme Court Ruling in *Citizens United*." *American Politics Research* 42(4): 579–99.

Caldeira, G. A. 1986. "Neither the Purse nor the Sword: Dynamics of Public Confidence in the Supreme Court." *American Political Science Review* 80(4): 1209–26.

Caldeira, G. A. 1987. "Public Opinion and the U.S. Supreme Court: FDR's Court-Packing Plan." *American Political Science Review* 81(4): 1139–53.

Caldeira, G. A., and Gibson, J. L. 1992. "The Etiology of Public Support for the Supreme Court." *American Journal of Political Science* 36(3): 635–64.

Cameron, C. M., Segal, J. A., and Songer, D. 2000. "Strategic Auditing in a Political Hierarchy: An Informational Model of the Supreme Court's Certiorari Decisions." *American Political Science Review* 94(1): 101–16.

Caminker, E. H. 1994. "Precedent and Prediction: The Forward-Looking Aspects of Inferior Court Decisionmaking." *Texas Law Review* 73(1): 1–82.

Canes-Wrone, B. 2003. "Bureaucratic Decisions and the Composition of the Lower Courts." *American Journal of Political Science* 47(2): 205–14.

Canon, B. C. 1974a. "Is the Exclusionary Rule in Failing Health? Some New Data and a Plea against a Precipitous Conclusion." *Kentucky Law Journal* 62: 703–7.

Canon, B. C. 1974b. "Organizational Contumacy in the Transmission of Judicial Policies The *Mapp, Escobedo, Miranda*, and *Gault* Cases." *Villanova Law Review* 20: 50–79.

Canon, B. C., and Johnson, B. A. 1998. *Judicial Policies: Implementation and Impact*. 2nd ed. Washington, DC: CQ.

Carrubba, C., Friedman, B., Martin, A., and Vanberg, G. 2012. "Who Controls the Content of Supreme Court Opinions?" *American Journal of Political Science* 56(2): 400–12.

Casillas, C., Enns, P. K., and Wohlfarth, P. C. 2011. "How Public Opinion Constrains the U.S. Supreme Court." *American Journal of Political Science* 55(1): 74–88.

Casper, J. 1976. "The Supreme Court and National Policy Making." *American Political Science Review* 70(1): 50–63.

Cassell, P. G., and Fowels, R. 1998a. "Falling Clearance Rates after Miranda: Coincidence or Consequence?" *Stanford Law Review* 504: 1181–92.

Cassell, P. G., and Fowles R. 1998b. "Handcuffing the Cops? A Thirty-Year Perspective on *Miranda's* Harmful Effects on Law Enforcement." *Stanford Law Review* 50(4): 1055–145.

Clayton, C. W., and Pickerill, J. M. 2004. "Guess What Happened on the Way to the Revolution? Precursors to the Supreme Court's Federalism Revolution." *Publius* 34(3): 85–114.

Clayton, C. W., and Pickerill J. M. 2006. "The Politics of Criminal Justice: How the New Right Regime Shaped the Rehnquist Court's Criminal Justice Jurisprudence." *Georgetown Law Review* 94: 1385–425.

Cox, G. W., and Katz, J. N. 1999. "The Reapportionment Revolution and Bias in U.S. Congressional Elections." *American Journal of Political Science* 43(3): 812–41.

Cox, G. W., and McCubbins, M. D. 2002. *Elbridge Gerrys Salamander: The Electoral Consequences of the Reapportionment Revolution*. New York, NY: Cambridge University Press.

Dahl, R. A. 1957. "Decision-Making in a Democracy: The Supreme Court as a National Policy-Maker." *Journal of Public Law* 6: 279–95.

Davies, T. Y. 1983. "A Hard Look at What We Know (And Still Need to Learn) about the 'Costs' of the Exclusionary Rule: The NIJ Study and Other Studies of 'Lost' Arrests." *American Bar Foundation Research Journal* 8(3): 611–90.

Dierenfield, R. B. 1962. *Religion in American Public Schools*. Washington, DC: Public Affairs.

Dolbeare, K. 1973. "The Supreme Court and the States: From Abstract Doctrine to Local Behavioral Conformity." In *The Impact of Supreme Court Decisions: Empirical Studies*, edited by T. L. Becker and M. M. Feeley. 2nd ed. New York, NY: Oxford University Press.

Donohue, J. J., III. 1998. "Did *Miranda* Diminish Police Effectiveness?" *Stanford Law Review* 50: 1147–80.

Edelman, L. B. 1990. "Legal Environments and Organizational Governance: The Expansion of Due Process in the American Workplace." *American Journal of Sociology* 95(6): 1401–40.

Epp, C. R. 1998. *The Rights Revolution: Lawyers, Activists, and Supreme Courts in Comparative Perspective*. Chicago, IL: University of Chicago Press.

Epp, C. R. 2008. "Law as an Instrument of Social Reform." In *The Oxford Handbook of Law and Politics*, edited by K. E. Whittington, R. D. Kelemen, and G. A. Caldeira. New York, NY: Oxford University Press, 595–693.

Feeley, M. M. 1973. "Power, Impact, and the Supreme Court." In *The Impact of Supreme Court Decisions*, edited by T. L. Becker and M. M. Feeley. 2nd rev. ed. New York, NY: Oxford University Press, 218–29.

Feeley, M. M., and Rubin, E. L. 1998. *Judicial Policy Making and the Modern State: How the Courts Reformed America's Prisons*. New York, NY: Cambridge University Press.

Flemming, R. B., Bohte, J., and Wood B. D. 1997. "One Voice among Many: The Supreme Court's Influence on Attentiveness to Issues in the United States, 1947–1992." *American Journal of Political Science* 41(4): 1224–50.

Franklin, C. H., and Kosaki, L. C. 1989. "Republican Schoolmaster: The U.S. Supreme Court, Public Opinion, and Abortion." *American Political Science Review* 83(3): 751–71.

Frymer, P. 2003. "Acting When Elected Officials Won't: Federal Courts and Civil Rights Enforcement in U.S. Labor Unions, 1935–1985." *American Political Science Review* 97(3): 483–99.

Funston, R. 1975. "The Supreme Court and Critical Elections." *American Political Science Review* 69: 795–811.

George, T. E., and Epstein, L. 1992. "On the Nature of Supreme Court Decision Making." *American Political Science Review* 86(2): 323–37.

Gibson, J. L. 1989. "Understandings of Justice: Institutional Legitimacy, Procedural Justice, and Political Tolerance." *Law & Society Review* 23(3): 469–96.

Gibson, J. L., Caldeira, G. A., and Baird, V. A. 1998. "On the Legitimacy of National High Courts." *American Political Science Review* 92(2): 343–58.

Giles, M. W., Hettinger V. A., and Peppers T. 2001. "Picking Federal Judges: A Note on Policy and Partisan Selection Agendas." *Political Research Quarterly* 54(3): 623–41.

Gillman, H. 2002. "How Political Parties Can Use the Courts to Advance their Agendas: Federal Courts in the United States." *American Political Science Review* 96(3): 511–24.

Golden, M. M. 2000. *What Motivates Bureaucrats? Politics and Administration during the Reagan Years*. New York, NY: Columbia University Press.

Graber, M. A. 1993. "The Nonmajoritarian Difficulty: Legislative Deference to the Judiciary." *Studies in American Political Development* 7(2): 35–73.

Gruhl, J. 1980. "The Supreme Court's Impact on the Law of Libel: Compliance by Lower Federal Courts." *Western Political Quarterly* 33(4): 502–19.

Hall, M. E. K. 2011. *The Nature of Supreme Court Power*. New York, NY: Cambridge University Press.

Hall, M. E. K. 2014. "The Semi-Constrained Court: Public Opinion, the Separation of Powers, and the U.S. Supreme Court's Fear of Nonimplementation." *American Journal of Political Science* 58(2): 352–66.

Hall, M. E. K. 2015. "Testing Judicial Power: The Influence of the U.S. Supreme Court on Federal Incarceration." *American Politics Research* 43(1): 83–108.

Hall, M. E. K. 2017. "Macro Impact: Testing the Causal Paths from U.S. Macro Policy to Federal Incarceration." *American Journal of Political Science*. Available at: http://onlinelibrary.wiley.com/doi/10.1111/ajps.12266/full.

Hall, M. E. K., and Windett, J. H. 2014. "Understanding Judicial Power: Divided Government, Institutional Thickness, and High-Court Influence on State Incarceration." *Journal of Law and Courts* 3(1): 167–91.

Hansen, S. B. 1980. "State Implementation of Supreme Court Decisions: Abortion Rates since *Roe v. Wade*. *Journal of Politics* 42(2): 372–95.

Harvey, A., and Freidman, B. 2009. "Ducking Trouble: Congressionally Induced Selection Bias in the Supreme Court's Agenda." *Journal of Politics* 71(2): 574–92.

Hoekstra, V. J. 2000. "The Supreme Court and Local Public Opinion." *American Political Science Review* 94(1): 89–100.

Hoekstra, V. J. 2005. "Competing Constraints: State Court Responses to Supreme Court Decisions and Legislation on Wages and Hours." *Political Research Quarterly* 58(2): 317–28.

Hoekstra, V. J., and Segal, J. A. 1996. "The Shepherding of Local Public Opinion: The Supreme Court and Lamb's Chapel." *Journal of Politics* 58(4): 1079–102.

Horowitz, D. L. 1977. *The Courts and Social Policy*. Washington, DC: Brookings Institution.

Howard, J. W. 1981. *Courts of Appeals in the Federal Judicial System: A Study of the Second, Fifth, and District of Columbia Circuits*. Princeton, NJ: Princeton University Press.

Howard, R. M., and Stiegerwalt, A. 2011. *Judging Law and Policy: Courts and Policymaking in the American Political System*. New York, NY: Routledge.
Howard, R. M., and Segal, J. A. 2002. "An Original Look at Originalism." *Law & Society Review* 36(1): 113–38.
Hume, R. J. 2009. *How Courts Impact Federal Administrative Behavior*. New York, NY: Routledge.
Hume, R. J. 2013. *Courthouse Democracy and Minority Rights: Same-Sex Marriage in the States*. New York, NY: Oxford University Press.
Johnson, C. A. 1979a. "Judicial Decisions and Organizational Change: A Theory." *Administration & Society* 11(1): 27–51.
Johnson, C. A. 1979b. "Judicial Decisions and Organizational Change: Some Theoretical and Empirical Notes on State Court Decisions and State Administrative Agencies." *Law & Society Review* 14(1): 27–56.
Johnson, C. A. 1979c. "Lower Court Reactions to Supreme Court Decisions." *American Journal of Political Science* 23(4): 792–804.
Johnson, C. A. 1987. "Law, Politics, and Judicial Decision Making: Lower Federal Court Uses of Supreme Court Decisions." *Law & Society Review* 21(2): 325–40.
Johnson, T. R., and Martin, A. D. 1998. "The Public's Conditional Response to Supreme Court Decisions." *American Political Science Review* 92(2): 299–309.
Kassow, B., Songer D. R., and Fix, M. P. 2012. "The Influence of Precedent on State Supreme Courts." *Political Research Quarterly* 65(2): 372–84.
Kaufman, H. 1960. *The Forest Ranger: A Study in Administrative Behavior*. Baltimore, MD: Johns Hopkins University Press.
Keck, T. M. 2009. "Beyond Backlash: Assessing the Impact of Judicial Decisions on LGBT Rights." *Law & Society Review* 43(1): 151–85.
Kilwein, J. C., and Brisbin, R. A. 1997. "Policy Convergence in a Federal Judicial System: The Application of Intensified Scrutiny Doctrines by State Supreme Courts." *American Journal of Political Science* 41(1): 122–48.
Klarman, M. J. 2004. *From Jim Crow to Civil Rights: The Supreme Court and the Struggle for Racial Equality*. New York, NY: Oxford University Press.
Klarman, M. J. 2005. "*Brown* and *Lawrence* (and *Goodridge*)." *Michigan Law Review* 104: 431–89.
Klein, D. E., and Hume, R. J. 2003. "Fear of Reversal as an Explanation of Lower Court Compliance." *Law & Society Review* 37(3): 579–606.
Laubach, J. H. 1957. *School Prayers: Congress, the Courts, and the Public*. Washington, DC: Public Affairs.
Lipsky, M. 2010. *Street-level Bureaucracy: Dilemmas of the Individual in Public Services*. New York, NY: Russell Sage Foundation.
Lovell, G. I. 2003. *Legislative Deferrals: Statutory Ambiguity, Judicial Power, and American Democracy*. New York, NY: Cambridge University Press.
Manwaring, D. 1968. "The Impact of *Mapp v. Ohio*." In *The Supreme Court as Policy-Maker: Three Studies on the Impact of Judicial Decisions*, edited by D. H. Everson. Carbondale, IL: Public Affairs Research Bureau, Southern Illinois University.
Marshall, T. 1989. *Public Opinion and the Supreme Court*. New York, NY: Longman.
Masood, A. S., Kassow, B. J., and Songer, D. R. 2013. "The Impact of Supreme Court Signals and Circuit Effects on Responses to Precedent." Paper presented at the Annual Meeting of the Midwest Political Science, Chicago, IL.

Masood, A. S., and Songer, D. R. 2014. "The Importance of Circuits: Appeals Court Responses to Supreme Court Precedent." Paper presented at the Annual Meeting of the Midwest Political Science, Chicago, IL.

McCann, M. 1994. *Rights at Work: Pay Equity Reform and the Politics of Legal Mobilization*. Chicago, IL: University of Chicago Press.

McCubbins, M. D., and Schwartz, T. 1988. "Congress, the Courts, and Public Policy: Consequences of the One Man, One Vote Rule." *American Journal of Political Science* 32(2): 388–415.

McGuire, K. T. 2004. "The Institutionalization of the U.S. Supreme Court." *Political Analysis* 12(2): 128–42.

McGuire, K. T. 2009. "Public Schools, Religious Establishments, and the U.S. Supreme Court: An Examination of Policy Compliance." *American Politics Research* 37(1): 50–74.

McGuire, K. T., and Stimson, J. A. 2004. "The Least Dangerous Branch Revisited: New Evidence on Supreme Court Responsiveness to Public Preferences." *Journal of Politics* 66(4): 1018–35.

McKay, R. B. 1956. "'With All Deliberate Speed': A Study of School Desegregation." *New York University Law Review* 31: 991–1090.

McNollgast, B. R. 1995. "Politics and the Courts: A Positive Theory of Judicial Doctrine and the Rule of Law." *Southern California Law Journal* 68(3): 1631–83.

Medalie, R. J., Zeitz, L., and Alexander, P. 1968. "Custodial Police Interrogation in our Nation's Capital: The Attempt to Implement *Miranda*." *Michigan Law Review* 66(7): 1347–422.

Milner, N. 1994. *The Court and Local Law Enforcement: The Impact of Miranda*. Beverly Hills, CA: Sage.

Mondak, J. J. 1990. "Perceived Legitimacy of Supreme Court Decisions: Three Functions of Source Credibility". *Political Behavior* 12(4): 363–84.

Mondak, J. J. 1992. "Institutional Legitimacy, Policy Legitimacy, and the Supreme Court." *American Politics Quarterly* 20(4): 457–77.

Nagel, R. F. 2001. "Judicial Power and the Restoration of Federalism." *The Annals of the American Academy of Political and Social Science* 574: 52–65.

Nagel, S. S. 1965. "Testing the Effects of Excluding Illegally Seized Evidence." *Wisconsin Law Review* 1965(2): 283–310.

Pacelle, R. L., Jr., and Baum, L. 1992. "Supreme Court Authority in the Judiciary: A Study of Remands." *American Politics Quarterly* 20(2): 169–91.

Peltason, J. W. 1971. *Fifty-Eight Lonely Men: Southern Federal Judges and School Desegregation*. Urbana, IL: University of Illinois Press.

Pressman, J., and Wildavsky, A. 1973. *Implementation*. Berkeley, CA: University of California Press.

Pusey, M. J. 1983. "Justice Roberts' 1937 Turnaround." *Supreme Court Historical Society Yearbook* 8: 102–7.

Randazzo, K. A. 2008. "Strategic Anticipation and the Hierarchy of Justice in U.S. District Courts." *American Politics Research* 36(5): 669–93.

Reich, D. R. 1968. "The Impact of Judicial Decision Making: The School Prayer Cases." In *The Supreme Court as Policy-Maker: Three Studies on the Impact of Judicial Decisions*, edited by D. H. Everson. Carbondale, IL: Public Affairs Research Bureau, Southern Illinois University, 44–81.

Rodgers, H. R., and Bullock, C. S. 1976. "School Desegregation: A Multivariate Test of the Role of Law in Effectuating Social Change." *American Politics Research* 4(2): 153–76.

Romans, N. T. 1974. "The Role of State Supreme Courts in Judicial Policy Making: *Escobedo, Miranda* and the Use of Judicial Impact Analysis." *Western Political Quarterly* 27(1): 38–59.

Rosenberg, G. N. 1991. *The Hollow Hope: Can Courts Bring about Social Change?* Chicago, IL: University of Chicago Press.

Rosenberg, G. N. 1992. "Judicial Independence and the Reality of Political Power." *Review of Politics* 54(Summer): 369–98.

Rosenberg, G. N. 2008. *The Hollow Hope: Can Courts Bring about Social Change?* 2nd ed. Chicago, IL: University of Chicago Press.

Rosenberg, G. N. 2014. "Ideological Preferences and Hollow Hopes: Responding to Criticism." Available at: http://www.press.uchicago.edu/books/rosenberg/index.html#position3.

Rostow, E. V. 1952. "The Democratic Character of Judicial Review." *Harvard Law Review* 66(Summer): 193–224.

Scheingold, S. A. 2004. *The Politics of Rights: Lawyers, Public Policy, and Political Change.* 2nd ed. New Haven, CT: Yale University Press.

Schultz, D. A., ed. 1998. *Leveraging the Law.* New York, NY: Peter Lang.

Scott, K. M. 2006. "Understanding Judicial Hierarchy: Reversals and the Behavior of Intermediate Appellate Judges." *Law & Society Review* 40(1): 164–91.

Skowronek, S. 1982. *Building a New American State: The Expansion of National Administrative Capacities, 1877–1920.* New York, NY: Cambridge University Press.

Songer, D. R. 1987. "The Impact of the Supreme Court on Trends in Economic Policy Making in the United States Courts of Appeals." *Journal of Politics* 49(3): 830–41.

Songer, D. R. 1988. "Alternative Approaches to the Study of Judicial Impact: *Miranda* in Five State Courts." *American Politics Quarterly* 16(4): 425–44.

Songer, D. R., Segal, J. A., and Cameron, C. M. 1994. "The Hierarchy of Justice: Testing a Principal–Agent Model of Supreme Court–Circuit Court Interactions." *American Journal of Political Science* 38(3): 673–96.

Songer, D. R., and Sheehan, R. S. 1990. "Supreme Court Impact on Compliance and Outcomes: *Miranda* and *New York Times* in the United States Courts of Appeals." *Western Political Quarterly* 43(2): 297–316.

Spriggs, J.F., II. 1996. "The Supreme Court and Federal Administrative Agencies: A Resources-Based Theory and Analysis of Judicial Impact." *American Journal of Political Science* 40(4): 1122–51.

Spriggs, J. F., II. 1997. "Explaining Federal Bureaucratic Compliance with Supreme Court Opinions." *Political Research Quarterly* 50(3): 567–93.

Stover, R. V., and Brown, D. W. 1975. "Understanding Compliance and Non-Compliance with the Law." *Social Science Quarterly* 56(3): 363–75.

Sweet, M. J. 2010. *Merely Judgment: Ignoring, Evading, and Trumping the Supreme Court.* Charlottesville, VA: University of Virginia Press.

Tarr, G. A. 1977. *Judicial Impact and State Supreme Courts.* Lexington, MA: Lexington Books.

Ura, J. D. 2014. "Backlash and Legitimation: Macro Political Responses to Supreme Court Decisions." *American Journal of Political Science* 58(1): 110–26.

Wahlbeck, P. J. 1997. "The Life of the Law: Judicial Politics and Legal Change." *Journal of Politics* 59(3): 778–802.

Wald, M. S., Ayres R., Hess, D. W., Schantz M., and Whitebread, C. H., II. 1966. "Interrogations in New Haven: The Impact of *Miranda.*" *Yale Law Journal* 76: 1519–648.

Wasby, S. L. 1970. *The Impact of the United States Supreme Court: Some Perspectives.* Homewood, IL: Dorsey.

Way, H. F. 1968. "Survey Research on Judicial Decisions: The Prayer and Bible Reading Cases." *Western Political Quarterly* 21(2): 189–205.

Westerland, C., Segal, J. A., Epstein L., Cameron C. M., and Comparato, S. 2010. "Strategic Defiance and Compliance in the U.S. Courts of Appeals." *American Journal of Political Science* 54(4): 891–905.

Whittington, K. E. 2005. "'Interpose your Friendly Hand': Political Supports for the Exercise of Judicial Review by the United States Supreme Court." *American Political Science Review* 99(4): 583–96.

Whittington, K. E. 2007. *The Political Foundations of Judicial Supremacy: The Presidency, the Supreme Court, and Constitutional Leadership in U.S. History*. Princeton, NJ: Princeton University Press.

Yates, R. 1788. "The Power of the Judiciary, Part 1." *New York Journal*, March 20.

Cases Cited

Brown v. Board of Education, 347 U.S. 483 (1954).

Citizens United v. Federal Election Commission, 558 U.S. 310 (2010).

Roe v. Wade, 410 U.S. 113 (1973).

United States v. Carolene Products, 304 U.S. 144 (1938).

United States v. Windsor, 570 U.S. 12 (2013).

PART V

METHODS AND APPROACHES TO STUDYING THE COURTS

CHAPTER 25

COGNITION IN THE COURTS

Analyzing the Use of Experiments to Study Legal Decision-Making

EILEEN BRAMAN

Introduction: Some Thoughts on Evaluating the Value of Experimental Research in Law

Most of our knowledge about the natural world and hard sciences has come from experiments. Experiments are powerful because they allow researchers to isolate and manipulate causal factors (independent variables) so they can observe how target measures (dependent variables) vary, or do not vary, under counter-factual conditions. If a difference in the target measure is observed across treatments where everything but the independent variable has been held constant, we can attribute that difference to the influence of the independent variable on the dependent variable.

Although the logic of experiments is pretty straightforward—and few would deny the contributions of the approach to our knowledge of the physical realm—some question whether experiments can tell us much of anything about more complex social phenomena including aspects of litigation and decision-making. Cases are complex, this argument goes, and so it is either difficult, artificial, or both to investigate the influence of isolated variables without taking into account the larger context in which they are embedded. Legal decision-makers are also complicated; jurors, attorneys, and judges come to the decision task with different social backgrounds, attitudes, and beliefs. Comparing differences among decision-makers is not like measuring how tall identical plant seedlings grow in response to different exposure to light. Finally, specialized rules and norms pervade choices in our legal system, in fact-finding done by jurors, argumentative and strategic choices made by attorneys, and the legal decisions of judges. Some believe it is impossible to account for these specialized rules in an experimental context.

Notwithstanding such concerns, there is a growing group of scholars across disciplines, including law (Robbennolt 2008; Rachlinski et al. 2011; Guthrie et al. 2001, 2007; Kahan et al. 2009, 2012; Simon et al. 2004), economics (Hoffman and Spitzer 1982; Plott and Zeiler 2005), psychology (Pickel 1995; Enlich et al. 2006; Kahneman et al. 1990), and political science (Braman 2006; Braman and Nelson 2007; Guarnaschelli et al. 2000; Bohnet et al. 2001), who conduct experiments relating to law and legal institutions. My goal in this chapter is to discuss some of the basic findings of their research to provide a snapshot of "what we know" from these experimental studies as well as a critical analysis of "what we could be doing better." I also assess our prospects for a unified understanding of legal decision-making in terms of several "cognitively informed" theories developed by researchers doing experimental work (Simon 2004; Robbennolt et al. 2003, 2010; Guthrie et al. 2007; Kahan 2013; Kahan et al. 2009, 2012; Braman 2009).

Addressing Methodological Skepticism

At the outset it is important to acknowledge that researchers have a mixed record in terms of addressing concerns about complexity, artificiality, and the need to account for legal rules in experimental research. Complexity is, perhaps, the easiest to deal with. Cases are no more complicated than the natural phenomena experimental data has been so indispensable for understanding. Moreover, one of the primary benefits of experiments is the "decomposition" of complex processes, in order to isolate and test causal factors among competing alternatives (Arlen and Talley 2008: xvi). Once we understand basic cause-and-effect relationships, our theories and experimental designs can become more refined by identifying boundary conditions and empirical interactions that effectively demonstrate where hypothesized variables are likely to have an effect, and where they are not. This iterative process of experimental investigation and the refinement of theory, based on expected (and often unexpected) findings, is how our understanding of complex processes related to legal phenomena evolves and becomes more sophisticated.

Experiments can also handle the fact the humans bring their own backgrounds, beliefs, and, especially relevant for legal decision-making phenomena, legal training and expertise to the table. Researchers may have little control over the social backgrounds and beliefs of human subjects in an experimental setting, but the experimental method itself helps alleviate concerns that such extraneous factors are driving results in properly conducted study. As long as participants are randomly assigned to conditions, researchers can be confident that individual differences that might affect reasoning processes, such as policy preferences and ideology, are evenly distributed across treatments so that their relative influence is the same. This means observed differences between groups can be attributed to manipulated variables rather than other differences that might be present in the subject pool. Thus, in studies involving human participants *random assignment* to conditions is critical to an experiment's internal validity, or the confidence that a researcher has that she has identified a true causal relationship. Psychologists have long understood this, explaining why experimental methodology has been vital to the "cognitive revolution" in that discipline. The result has been a much richer understanding of individual reasoning processes in social and problem-solving domains (McGraw 2000).

The second concern of artificiality concerns the external validity of experimental research, or how confident researchers can be that their findings apply to decision-makers in the real world.[1] The external validity of an experimental study is related to the *random selection* of subjects from a particular population of interest. For instance, many legal academics would be skeptical that findings from a study involving how undergraduates interpret a statutory provision would tell us anything useful about how judges would interpret that same provision because experimental participants have not been legally socialized. In this way the lack of legal training acts an important difference between experimental participants (undergraduates) and the population of primary interest (judges) suggesting findings may not be transferable because thought processes of each group are likely to be substantially different.

This does not mean, however, that experiments on student subjects are of no value in understanding legal decision-making. Zeiler (2010) effectively argues that concerns about generalization from undergraduate and lay-subject pools may be overdrawn where there is not much reason to think experimental participants think differently about tasks than relevant populations, such as parties involved in litigation. She also points out that the purpose of experimental studies for building theory and demonstrating the *feasibility* of theoretical mechanisms should be considered more seriously in evaluating the worth of experimental research with lay and student samples. Notwithstanding these excellent points, researchers doing work in this area have addressed concerns about the fit between samples and the population by using more sophisticated participants in experimental studies—those who have been legally socialized to "think more like judges," including law students (e.g., Furgeson et al. 2008a; Rowell and Bregant 2014), or attorneys (e.g., Englich et al. 2006). Of course, the best-case scenario is to use judges themselves as experimental subjects. One team of researchers (including Chris Guthrie, a law professor; Jeffrey Rachlinski, a psychologist; and Andrew Wistrich, a magistrate judge) has had a good deal of success in recruiting judges as experimental participants. But some even criticize their studies on the grounds that those participating are different from the general population of judges, and that experimental tasks are often substantially different from how judges engage in decision-making in the real world (see, Schauer 2010; Kysar 2007 for critiques along these lines).

This takes us to the third concern: that the specialized rules and norms, which are so integral to legal decision-making processes, do not really lend themselves to experiments. To this I have two responses. Legal decision-making is, after all, a specialized kind of decision-making; it seems foolhardy to ignore the primary method psychologists use to investigate cognitive processes. Second, our ability to adequately capture aspects of the legal reasoning critically depends on the skill and creativity of scholars involved in experimental research to (1) identify relevant theory from existing disciplines, (2) transfer and operationalize concepts in convincing ways, and (3) create critical tests that effectively measure the influence of hypothesized variables on decision-makers of interest. There is reason for optimism here. As the studies I discuss illustrate, scholars across the disciplines have used clever experimental designs to effectively demonstrate various influences on legal decision-makers. That said, experimental research on legal decision-making is far from perfect and there is much that must be done to improve, build on, and theoretically integrate findings from existing studies. Ironically, our multidisciplinary tradition can cause fragmentation and duplication of effort if we do not look across disciplinary lines to learn from colleagues using similar techniques.

Reviewing Experimental Studies on Legal Cognition

Although it may seem odd to conduct a methodological rather than thematic review of research in the field, the accumulation of knowledge across disciplines suggests the time is right to consider how experimental findings from various studies fit together and contribute to our understanding of law and the judiciary. Moreover, all these studies do have a unifying theme: they concern how individuals *think about* tasks performed in our legal system.

Many of the legal judgments that are the subject of experimental investigation involve the application of specific rules and criteria designed to optimize accuracy or democratic ideals like fairness and liberty. Some of these decision-making conventions date back to our earliest history, adopted because they were *presumed* to improve decision-making or incorporate important democratic values in the pursuit of justice. We now have the science to test such presumptions. Experimental research represents an extremely promising avenue to investigate the influence of appropriate versus inappropriate—accuracy versus error prone—influences on legal choices. Knowing how individuals make legal decisions, and whether specialized rules have their desired influence or tax the capacity of human judgment, is of substantial empirical and normative import.

Clearly there is much to learn from looking at the accumulation of knowledge using experimental methods, but it is also appropriate to say a few words about what this brief survey of a much larger field will not address. Because my primary focus in this chapter is on legal reasoning processes, I do not discuss experimental work that has been done looking at citizen perceptions of judges, courts, and their outputs (see, e.g., Mondak 1994; Gibson 2008; Simon and Scurich 2011; Bartels and Johnson 2012; Braman and Easter 2014). Moreover, although juries make important factual determinations in our legal system and empirical research on jury decision-making goes as far back as the 1950s (e.g., Broder 1958), I do not focus on this research here, as there are already some excellent reviews of experimental findings in this area (MacCoun 1989; Devine et al. 2001; Devine 2012).

I concentrate on research that has been done across disciplines regarding some of the foundational theories and assumptions concerning the thinking of litigants, attorneys, and judges making decisions in legal contexts. Much of this research has been motivated by hypotheses seeking to determine if judges are "better" at avoiding certain cognitive pitfalls than lay decision-makers, so although studies of juror decision tasks are not the focus of this review, I will discuss them where relevant. In the following sections I analyze experimental research that has been done on basic legal presumptions, heuristic processing, and various forms of bias in legal decision-making. The approach has contributed significantly to our knowledge of cognition in the courts, but there is still much that can be done to integrate findings across disciplines and refine our experimental inquiries.

Experimental Work on Legal Presumptions

One of the central principles in legal thinking concerning litigant behavior is from law and economics. The "Coase Theorem" (Coase 1960) holds that the initial choice of who is assigned a right is often arbitrary, and indeed, irrelevant. In the absence of transaction costs, the parties will bargain efficiently so that the party who values the right more will be willing to incur the costs of securing it, and the party who values it less will be willing to forgo the right as long as she is adequately compensated. The Coase Theorem is related to Expected Utility Theory because it assumes that each party will be able to come up with an objective valuation reflecting what the right is worth to them; it also assumes that this valuation will be the same regardless of whether the party is buying or selling that right. Over the past forty years researchers doing experimental work in law and economics have tested this theory with some success, finding that parties can negotiate in various contexts simulating contract and property transactions to reach socially efficient outcomes (Hoffman and Spitzer 1982; Schwab 1988; Croson and Johnston 2000).

Economics experiments testing Coasian intuitions, however, are not without criticism. Studies often involve complex games with decision rules that may be difficult for subjects to understand; and the precise operationalization of concepts is not always agreed upon, even by other experimentalists (see, e.g., Kelman 1985 commenting on Hoffman and Spitzer's study; Plott and Zeiler 2005 controlling for misconceptions among participants about experimental valuation tasks).

In a refreshingly simple study Kahneman, Knetch, and Thaler (1990) illustrate what may be the most serious challenge to Coase Theorem. Drawing from Prospect Theory, they posit that individuals will value identical property differently depending on whether the transaction represents a gain or a loss to them personally. Because individuals tend to feel pain from losses more powerfully than the benefits of gains, Kahneman and his colleagues hypothesize that experimental subjects will require more money to part with an item that they currently possess, than they would be willing to pay to acquire that item if they did not own it. In an experiment involving simple transactions using university mugs and pens, they effectively demonstrate this type of asymmetrical pricing, commonly referred to as the "endowment effect."

This endowment effect has been replicated and tested repeatedly in various experimental contexts (see Arlen and Talley 2008 for review). Its implications have been explored across various fields of law. Buccafusco and Springman (2011), for instance, demonstrate a "creativity effect," where creators value work more than potential purchasers and subsequent owners due to the substantial effort they invested in its production. They conclude that this could create substantial inefficiencies in the intellectual property markets. Braman (2010) theorizes that "third party endowment effects" can influence seemingly neutral legal decisions if judges privilege "status quo" states of ownership over alternative distributions that may be required by the application of relevant legal frameworks.

We also know from experimental research that how instructions are worded can impact damage awards. In a series of studies with lay and law student participants McCafffey, Kahneman, and Spitzer (1995) demonstrate that awards for pain and suffering are substantially higher when decision-makers are told to award the amount of money they would require to "accept an injury" (selling-price perspective), compared to when they are told to award an amount that would make the plaintiff "as fortunate as before the injury happened" (making-the-plaintiff-whole perspective). Again, this challenges a central assumption that individuals will be able to come up with an objective valuation for damages that is not inordinately influenced by other considerations like instruction wording. Inconsistencies may be especially prominent where there is a high degree of incommensurability in the units of loss and compensation—as when plaintiffs are awarded money for non-pecuniary injuries like pain and suffering.

The number and relative nature of alternatives can also influence preferences in decision-making. Kelman, Rottenstreich, and Tversky (1996) investigate "compromise" and "contrast effects" in legal fact-finding showing that an identical alternative may be less attractive to decision-makers when it is presented as a choice between just one other outcome compared to when it represents the "middle ground" between that alternative and a more extreme option. Rachlinski et al. (2013) demonstrate similar contrast effects in judges' assessments of the qualifications of legal experts. And Guthrie (2003) shows how contrast effects created by the generation of options in contact negotiations can sometimes hinder the ultimate goal of parties coming to a mutual and satisfactory "meeting of the minds."

Experimental Work on Heuristics and Other Cognitive Pitfalls

A good deal of experimental work on legal decision-making focuses on discovering whether judges fall victim to "heuristic" biases that have been uncovered in lay populations. Heuristic biases are a result of reasoning shortcuts that are adaptive because they save us substantial cognitive effort, but they are also error prone. Some heuristic strategies are quite pervasive in the way we think. This poses a problem, particularly in tasks like fact-finding where accuracy is the primary goal.

Studies reveal, for instance, that mentioning numbers in certain judgment tasks can have an inordinate influence on decision-makers, even where those numbers are irrelevant.[2] The phenomenon, referred to as "anchoring" has been shown to be incredibly durable across various classes of legally relevant decision-makers and judgment tasks. Scholars have tested the role of anchoring in sentencing (Englich et al. 2006), liability judgments (Guthrie et al. 2001), and settlement determinations (Wistrich et al. 2005). Findings across studies generally indicate that irrelevant numerical starting points can have a strong and consistent influence on such judgments, even where judges are supposed to disregard such information (Wistrich et al. 2005).

Findings about judges' susceptibility to heuristic biases are both interesting and substantively important. Using surveys with simple question manipulations, Guthrie et al. (2001) test the vulnerability of federal magistrate judges to several heuristic biases. They find that judges are susceptible to some biases, but do better than lay decision-makers at avoiding others. Guthrie and his colleagues discover that judges fall victim to anchoring and "hindsight bias"[3] at rates similar to decision-makers in the general population. But, they also find that judges are better at avoiding the "representativeness" heuristic, where individuals commonly discount "base rate," or relevant background information if specific instances of stimuli share characteristics of a target category that are easily called to mind. Sometimes these "representative" characteristics are more diagnostic than others. If something quacks and has a beak it is probably a duck. It is incorrect, however, to conclude that a suspect is engaged in terrorist activities because he has olive skin and comes from the Middle East. Guthrie et al. (2001) find that judges are not perfect, but perform better than average individuals in avoiding the representative heuristic in judgments of civil liability and making other types of "intuitive" mathematical errors that have been identified in the general population (2007).

Research on other relevant biases is harder to summarize because of inconsistent findings across, and sometimes within, studies. The hindsight bias has been investigated in contexts involving jurors' civil liability determinations (Kamin and Rachlinski 1995), the ability of judges to predict outcomes on appeal (Guthrie et al. 2001), and its role in probable cause determinations made before and after the conduct of searches (Rachlinski et al. 2011). In the first two instances knowing the outcome of a case significantly influenced participants' judgments as to whether they would have predicted or made decisions consistent with that outcome. In the probable cause study, however, judges who were given identical facts before and after a search that they were told yielded evidence of criminal activity, made similar judgments about whether those facts provided sufficient probable cause for that search. Thus, hindsight *did not* influence the legal judgments of judicial participants in this instance. Although the authors did find that judges who were told the outcome of the search were more likely to say they would have predicted that result in hindsight.

Experimental work has also been conducted looking at decision-makers' ability to avoid certain kinds of statistical pitfalls. A common finding in experimental studies is that the way DNA evidence is represented can influence judgments of the likelihood that someone is the source of a given sample. Where odds are represented as frequencies (e.g., 1/1000) decision-makers are more likely to consider alternative sources (a state of mind more favorable to defendants) than when they are presented as a probabilities (0.1). Rachlinski et al. (2013) find that judges respond to questions about the likelihood of guilt with patterns that are similar to lay decision-makers (Koehler 2001) when presented with frequentist versus probabilistic framing of DNA evidence.[4]

Distinguishing between Factual and Legal Judgments

Some have criticized experimental work on heuristics on the grounds that scholars do not adequately differentiate between factual and legal decision tasks in their research (Vidmar 1999; Schauer 2010). The criticism is important given the division of labor in our legal system. In jury trials ordinary citizens deliberate to make factual determinations about guilt and liability, but judges issue rulings on legal issues like who qualifies as an "expert" and the admissibility of evidence. Specialized rules must be applied in each context. Lay jurors may be told to disregard particular information they hear at trial or that certain testimony is allowed to be considered for one purpose but not another. In bench trials judges must also adhere to these rules at the same time they make legal determinations using appropriate criteria.[5]

As Friedman (2006) notes, part of the problem in distinguishing between fact and law is that some factual findings have legal significance. Consider, for example, whether a search occurs in a "house" or an "automobile"; Friedman argues, due to the different rights that attach in each context, the determination of search location is more of a legal question than a factual one, although prominent law and courts scholars have characterized it otherwise (see, for instance, Segal and Spaeth 2002).

Similar concerns could be raised about experiments asking judges to make determinations that are generally made by juries but subject to judicial modification, such as the appropriate level of damages for pain and suffering awards (Guthrie et al. 2007, investigating influence of the anchoring on such awards), or decisions made by judges with significant jury input or statutory guidelines limiting their discretion as in criminal sentencing (Englich et al. 2006; Rachlinski et al. 2013, investigating influence of information on cost of incarceration in judges sentencing behavior). Are these legal determinations or factual determinations or some inseparable blending of the two? The issue is complicated by the fact that some decisions made by trial judges, including admissibility determinations, unquestionably involve elements of both fact and law.[6]

Still, the question is theoretically important. While we expect and require that judges make legal determinations in a particular way based on their training and expertise, there may not be any good reason to think they would be less susceptible to cognitive biases than ordinary citizens. Schauer alludes to this in his essay, "Is There a Psychology of Judging?" (2010), noting legal socialization and judicial training does not, as of yet, involve required courses in the avoidance of heuristic biases or advanced statistical training.

Researchers who do this sort of work have convincingly argued that there may be other reasons to expect judges to be less prone to judgment errors. Jurists are generally intelligent and well-educated individuals (Guthrie et al. 2007) and repeated exposure to certain types of decision tasks should help them avoid intuitive and heuristic pitfalls (Guthrie et al. 2001; Wistrich and Rachlinski 2013). Still, Shauer's point about the normative punch of discovering differences between judges and lay decision-makers is apt. Indeed, one could argue that when judges act as fact-finders it is preferable that they act more like "regular folk" to better approximate findings that would be made by a jury of one's peers.

Integrating Influences: Judicial Traits, Context, and Experience

Guthrie and his colleagues eschew such logic, pointing to the fact that heuristic reasoning is error prone. They argue that heuristic biases, whether they are evident in lay or more sophisticated decision-makers, are a threat to the goal of accuracy in legal decision-making. In "Blinking on the Bench" (2007) they set forth a dual process model of legal reasoning where some trial judges are more likely to engage in intuitive, error prone, "Type I" processing, while other judges employ more accurate, in-depth, "Type II" processing.[7]

Guthrie et al. treat the propensity to engage in deeper reasoning as an individual characteristic by categorizing participants according to their scores on a Cognitive Refection Task (CRT). This is somewhat problematic because while it is true that some people are more likely to engage in in-depth processing than others, the *characteristics of the decision task* can also influence the likelihood that someone will engage in deeper processing.

Research shows, for instance, that when a judgment is particularly important or when a decision-maker is accountable for explaining the logic behind a decision to others she is more likely to engage in Type II, in-depth, processing (Eagly and Chaiken 1993; Lerner and Tetlock 1999). Judging and judicial fact-finding are highly structured deliberative processes with important implications for litigants. Even judges who score lower on CRT tasks relative to other judges may be motivated to engage in deeper processing under such circumstances. Guthrie and colleagues do not really deal with how characteristics of the judicial task itself may discourage intuitive reasoning—or why they find intuitive effects more prevalent for some types of judicial decisions than others.

This does not mean that their theory of judging is without merit, only that more can (and should) be done to specify the theoretical conditions where we can expect to see such differences. The approach also seems to take for granted that legal problems have accurate, discoverable, answers. While this may be so with regard to many legal questions, such as whether the defendant in a criminal negligence trial, in fact, ran a red light, there are other questions that fact-finders are often asked to answer that are less clear cut, involving, for instance, the appropriate penalty for such conduct.

Consider the extensive experimental work by Jennifer Robbennolt and her colleagues (2003) on the significance of apologies. She shows that parties in litigation tend to be influenced by the expression of regret. When apologies have certain characteristics indicative of sincerity, the acceptance of responsibility, and remorse individuals are more willing to settle and accept lower amounts to settle disputes in civil litigation. Generally attorneys are not influenced to the same degree by apologies (Robbennolt 2008); studies with judges (Rachlinski et al. 2013) tend to show that apologies do not help in reducing judges' suggested settlements or sentences and can sometimes *hurt* defendants because judges are likely to think apologies are proffered for strategic reasons.

Rachlinski and colleagues (2013) explain this result by positing that judges are somewhat jaded; they are so used to hearing apologies that they lose the effect that they generally have on litigants and victims of crime. If the authors are correct, judicial experience leading to the diminished impact of apologies on their judgments can be characterized as an undesirable normative finding. Do we want judges who are "different" in this regard, or would it be preferable if they were more like lay decision-makers in their willingness to be influenced by regret. Sevier (2014) makes a distinction between the search for "truth" and "justice" in the legal system. Perhaps it is not so bad if judges act like ordinary citizens in decision tasks where justice is the primary goal. Certainly individuals might reach different conclusions with regard to this question, but it is an important normative discussion prompted by experimental research that should be addressed.

Research on Biases in Decision-Making

Perhaps more problematic than research on "cold" heuristic pitfalls that can influence the accuracy of fact-finding is the idea that judges may be motivated to make findings or apply legal criteria in a biased manner depending on how they feel about parties or issues in litigation. Though evidence from psychology suggests judges may engage in this kind of directed decision-making unconsciously (Kunda 1990), these sort of motivations and affectively charged, "hot biases," go to the heart of judges' capacity to act as fair and objective decision-makers in our legal system.

Experimental techniques are well suited for investigating how personal views can interact with case facts and legal authority to influence legal decision-making. Researchers can observe how decision-makers with different views respond to identical parties, evidence, and arguments within conditions *and* how decision-makers with similar views respond across conditions where relevant case facts and legal arguments are manipulated in theoretically relevant ways.

Recent Experimental Work on Racial Bias among Judges

Racial and ethnic biases are particularly important in the fair administration of justice. There are a number of observational studies showing judges can exhibit in-group biases, deciding cases more harshly for litigants who do not share their characteristics (see, e.g., Shayo and Zussman 2010 showing in-bias among Arab and Jewish judges in Israel; see also, Glaeser and Saerdote (2003) demonstrating biases in sentencing depending on the race of the victim).

A recent line of experimental research tries to get at the mechanism behind such behavior to see if judges engage in the same sort of basic racial processing as other individuals. Rachlinski and his colleagues (2009) find that white judges exhibit a preference for white faces that is commonly detected in samples of ordinary citizens through a computerized measure of implicit preferences known as the Implicit Associations Test (IAT). They also find that white judges who have a stronger preference for white faces tend to give harsher sentences to defendants when subliminally primed with adjectives related to African Americans, compared to judges who receive neutral primes. This is true where the race of the defendant is not explicit in scenarios involving juvenile defendants accused of shoplifting and robbery. In a third experimental condition involving battery where the race of the defendant is explicitly manipulated, white judges do not show any preferences attributable to an interaction between IAT scores, priming condition, and the race of the defendant. Black judges that have a preference for black faces, however, tend to give more lenient sentences to African American defendants when primed with black-associated words.

The authors attribute the difference in the behavior of white judges in explicit versus non-explicit scenarios to an effort to compensate for biases where the judges suspect that researchers are studying the influence of race on their decisions. When the race of the defendant is clear there is more of an effort to consciously control biases. They suggest black judges are not similarly motivated where race is explicit because they may be unaware of the subconscious preferences they foster.

Perhaps it is not surprising that judges demonstrate the same implicit biases as others in terms of preferences for black and white faces. That such preferences have the potential to influence sentencing behavior when race is primed is, of course, problematic. But the finding is perhaps less disconcerting if judges can overcome such biases through cognitive effort. In the real world judges are usually aware of the race of the individuals before them. The key seems to be in motivating judges to become aware of such biases and guard against them in their decision-making. Thus, as the authors state, results of this study are "both discouraging and encouraging" (Rachlinski et al. 2009).

Research on Motivated Reasoning

Another type of bias that has been studied in legal decision-making with experimental methods is "motivated reasoning." Psychology reveals that individuals often engage in "goal directed" behavior when making judgments; law and courts scholars have tested the implications of such tendencies in various legal contexts (see, Sood 2013 for review). This particular cognitive phenomenon poses a challenge to normative conceptions of neutral fact-finding and the objective application of legal criteria for several reasons. First, evidence from psychology and political science suggests motivated cognition is ubiquitous. From activities as varied as watching sporting events to the evaluation of scientific research (MacCoun 1998; Lord, Ross, and Lepper 1979) we tend to see things and weigh evidence in ways that are consistent with our prior beliefs and worldviews (Kunda 1990). We do this because it serves the ego in complex ways, either by bolstering the correctness of our own thought processes (Cooper and Fazio 1984; Tesser and Campbell 1983) or reinforcing the attachment to relevant group memberships (Kahan et al. 2009, 2012).

Second, even where decision-makers are seemingly motivated by "accuracy goals," research demonstrates that "directional goals," causing decision-makers to selectively use evidence to reach desired outcomes, can come into play. This suggests that debiasing techniques that are effective in other domains may not be enough to forestall motivated decision processes.[8] Third, research suggests that decision-makers are often unaware of the influence of directional goals on their own perceptions and evaluation of evidence and arguments. So, much like the African American judges described above, jurors and legal decision-makers may not be aware there could be inappropriate factors influencing their seemingly neutral decision processes (see, Braman 2009 and Ferguson et al. 2008a for specific evidence supporting this assertion with regard to the evaluation of legal doctrine).

Very generally research on motivated cognition in legal decision-making falls into two categories: studies involving directional fact-finding[9] (Giner-Sorrolla et al. 2002; Kahan et al. 2009, 2012; Sood and Darley 2012) and those involving motivated reasoning in the use and application of legal criteria (Braman 2006, 2009; Ferguson et al. 2008a; Farnsworth et al. 2010, 2013; Redding and Reppucci 1999). Studies also differ with respect to whether researchers characterize motivated reasoning as preference based, or motivated by the desire to fortify cultural identity memberships.

Evidence of Motivated Reasoning in Fact-Finding

Giner-Sorrola, Chaiken, and Lutz (2002) look at the role of two types of priors in lay judgments about liability in sex discrimination cases: what they call "validity beliefs" and the extent to which decision-makers adhere to "feminist ideology." They hypothesize that validity beliefs, such as "even well-qualified women often cannot get the jobs that they want due to sex discrimination" or "most accusations of gender discrimination are false" act as a kind of fallback assumption in sex discrimination judgments that can be contradicted by evidence if jurors have sufficient time and cognitive resources to consider case facts and testimony. They show that female undergraduates who are under significant time pressure when reviewing evidence rely on validity beliefs more heavily than experimental participants who are not under such pressure.

They also provide evidence that the effect of feminist ideology in discrimination judgments is different. Because ideology is a general cognitive orientation that organizes specific thoughts and belief structures, they argue that rather than acting as a fallback assumption, ideology tends to influence judgments by filtering the interpretation of evidence for participants. They provide evidence of this by coding and analyzing participants' recall of case details and the valance of thoughts related to those facts (Giner-Sorrolla et al. 2002: 515–21).

In a series of clever experiments Sood and Darley (2012) look at citizens' propensity to impute harm in the evaluation of criminal behavior, hypothesizing that individuals are motivated to punish certain deviations from morality. They find experimental participants who are instructed that they must make a finding of "harm" to criminalize conduct are more likely to say the activity of a nudist caused harm to others than those who were not given similar legal instructions. In a follow-up study they find that where the harm requirement was coupled by the nudist expressing views on a sign that were either consistent with, or contrary to, participants' own views on abortion (a factor that should be irrelevant in harm judgments), participants were more likely to impute harm to conduct in conditions where the views expressed were inconsistent with their own. The authors argue this demonstrates that participants are especially motivated to punish individuals who do not share their moral outlook.[10]

Dan Kahan of the Cultural Cognition Project at Yale Law School and his colleagues have an impressive experimental agenda demonstrating the influence of "culturally motivated reasoning" in several legal contexts relevant to fact-finding. Utilizing Wildavsky's (1987) conception of "cultural cognition" and well-worn survey measures of the concept that have been developed since that seminal piece, Kahan and colleagues argue that " 'cultural cognition' is a species of motivated reasoning that promotes congruence between a person's defining group commitments, on one hand, and his or her perceptions of risks and related facts, on the other" (Kahan et al. 2012: 859).

According to cultural cognition theory, people can be aligned along two dimensions reflecting their support for hierarchical versus communitarian social structures (commonly referred to as "grid" orientations) and individualistic versus egalitarian ways of thinking (referred to as "group" orientations). This typology yields four distinct personality types depending where individuals fall on these two dimensions (Hierarchical/Individualists, Hierarchical/Egalitarians, Communitarian/Individualists and Communitarian/Egalitarians). Each type has a specific worldview that dictates the sort of bias he or she might evidence in particular legal domains. According to Kahan and his colleagues, people are motivated to see things consistent with these cultural group biases "to protect individuals' connection to others on whom they depend for material and emotional support" (Kahan et al. 2012: 859).

As these worldviews do not correlate perfectly with traditional left-right political ideologies (or even the more expansive four-group political typologies including, liberals, conservatives, progressives, and libertarians), Kahan and his colleagues painstakingly set forth hypotheses that support motivated reasoning for each cultural cognition group in a series of articles describing studies with national samples related to fact-finding on a variety of legal issues including: whether the victim gave consent in an acquaintance rape scenario (Kahan et al. 2010); whether demonstrators are "intimidating" individuals trying to exercise controversial legal rights (Kahan et al. 2012); and whether or not authorities were justified in the use of deadly force in a salient Supreme Court case (Kahan et al. 2009).[11]

For those uninitiated in cultural cognition theory, some of their hypotheses can seem over drawn and hard to follow. It is not always clear what differentiates views of people sharing some dimensional features but not others in particular subject domains, or reasons some groups should be closer together and others further apart ("semi-polarized" versus "polarized"). Such distinctions seem to come down to which dimension is prioritized in particular issue areas—but here again the logic as to why is not always intuitive. Still, the experimental evidence amassed by Kahan and his colleagues that individuals can view the same facts quite differently, and draw vastly different inferences from those facts depending on how details relate to their cultural group memberships is quite impressive and has extremely important implications for the dissemination of justice in our legal system.

These researchers have also developed a theoretical framework to elaborate on the implications of such biases known as "cognitive illiberalism" (Kahan et al. 2009, 2012). There is a critical aspect to the theory based on the proposition that judges, who are likely to come from particular advantaged backgrounds, privilege their own groups and cultural values relative to other ways of thinking that have equal merit. This is especially evident in an article where Kahan et al. (2009) take Justice Scalia to task for authoring a majority opinion after viewing a videotape of a high-speed chase, stating "no reasonable juror" could credit the defendant's position, that the police were not justified in their use of deadly force. "We are happy to let the videotape speak for itself" (Kahan et al. 2009: 839, quoting Scalia writing for the majority in *Scott v. Harris* 127 S. Ct. 1769, 1775).

In a clever and simply designed study Kahan et al. take Scalia up on the offer. Showing the videotape to a nationally representative sample they demonstrate that, although a majority of citizens agreed with the Court that the defendant's behavior caused danger to the public justifying the use of deadly force, there were a substantial number of citizens (26 percent in their sample of 1,350) who did not share this view. Moreover, the propensity of citizens to agree with the Court's position was predictably related to their cultural cognition group classification (Kahan et al. 2009: 874–9).

One interesting issue this particular research raises is the tension between the sort of empirical evidence academic scholars commonly credit in discovering "what is," and the normative function of judges in declaring "what should be" in a society governed by the rule of law. Although Kahan and colleagues may have effectively demonstrated that it was *the Court* that was being unreasonable in its opinion by neglecting to credit the possibility that others (indeed 26 percent of the population) could possibly see things in a different way, an alternative interpretation of its decision-making is that the justices were setting forth the outer limits of what is acceptable in an ordered society. Again the distinction between fact-finding and legal determinations is relevant; on this view, what looks a lot like a fact-finding task (saying what reasonable people would or would not perceive) might actually involve more of a normative legal judgment (defining the scope of acceptable behavior in society where the authority of police must be respected to enable them to keep order).

Finally, Dan Simon and his colleagues (Simon 2004; Simon et al. 2004; Simon and Holyoak 2002) have done a series of experiments looking at a slightly different type of motivation in fact-finding that has implications for the process of legal decision-making rather than its content. Drawing from cognitive consistency theory they present a theory of "constraint satisfaction" where the authors argue that decision-makers engage in a "bidirectional" reasoning process where they are motivated to achieve maximum coherence in the interpretation of evidence and case facts. They suggest this is an especially useful strategy in complex decision domains where alternative explanations compete for viability.

Using scenarios involving shareholder liability and criminal law they provide evidence that experimental participants converge on judgments over time and that their evaluation of individual pieces of evidence tends to become consistent with emergent decisions over the course of their evaluations. The research has implications for decision-makers' ability to remain neutral over the course of litigation, as evidence presented later in the process may be interpreted in a biased manner to fit emerging conclusions.

Although most of the direct experimental evidence on constraint satisfaction has been acquired with experiments on lay subjects, Simon (2004) and others (Robbennolt et al. 2003, 2010) have theorized about how the logic might similarly apply to judicial reasoning processes. Researchers who do work along these lines posit that decision-makers' (jurors and judges) have multiple goals they are trying to achieve that are conceptually connected in "constraint networks"; moreover, these goals can have different weights for different decision-makers. They are somewhat less clear about what particular constraints are common among decision-makers (but see, Robbennolt et al. 2003 theorizing about possible goals for fact-finders and Robbennolt et al. 2010 doing the same for trial judges) and, perhaps more importantly, how to determine the relative weight individuals place on particular goals. Some might also question whether these conceptual constraint networks are so idiosyncratic, or unique to particular choices and decision-makers, that they frustrate the goal of parsimonious theory-building. Still, if they accurately capture the process of how people go about making complex legal judgments, it seems we stand much to gain from the approach.

Evidence of Motivated Reasoning in the Use and Application of Legal Criteria

A second strain of research on motivated reasoning in legal decision-making has a different focus, looking at the influence of policy preferences or political ideology in the use and application of legal criteria by experimental participants with legal training. These studies are largely driven by findings in behavioral research demonstrating that judges tend to vote disproportionately in ways that are consistent with their political leanings, though they purport to reach judgments through the unbiased application of legal criteria (Prichett 1948; Schubert 1962; Segal and Spaeth 2002).

Short of accusing legal decision-makers of intentionally masking inappropriate political goals behind doctrine, these researchers focus on the fact that judges may be unconsciously predisposed to credit legal arguments, precedent, and statutory interpretations that they agree with over those they do not in deciding adversarial disputes. Indeed, Braman (2009: 36) argues, "motivated reasoning is the best explanation we have to reconcile findings of directed [voting] behavior with indicia that judges use, or believe they are using legal criteria to make decisions."

Although this experimental research has great potential to reveal the link between preferences and their expression in judicial voting behavior, some believe that the major shortcoming of this work is its reliance on law students, rather than judges as study participants. Studies can also vary in the threshold level of legal training required. Farnsworth et al. (2010, 2013) use first-year law students in their studies of the link between preferences and statutory interpretation, while Braman and Nelson (2007), Furgeson et al. (2008a), and Redding and Reppucci (1999) require participants that are further along in their legal education (second year and beyond) theorizing that much of the most important socialization regarding decision-making norms occurs in that first year.

The reluctance to use judges in studies of preference-based decision-making stems from several considerations that perhaps should be overcome in future studies given the success of Rachlinski and colleagues in recruiting judicial samples. First, of course, is the real or presumed assumption that judges will be unwilling to divulge their political preferences on issues involving experimental stimuli. There are ways to ask questions so they are less objectionable and some issues on which judges may be more willing to reveal preferences than others. Redding and Reppucci (1999), for instance, successfully obtained answers to questions on judge's views of the death penalty in their study of decision-makers' willingness to admit social science evidence that either supported or contradicted those views. Moreover, the fact that they found differences between judges and law-student participants on some questions but not others suggests it is important to recruit judges where possible.[12]

A second reason law students are likely utilized in such studies is that they are more accessible to law professor and university researchers than judges who can erect substantial barriers to those seeking to infringe on their time and expertise with experimental research. To overcome such barriers Rachlinski and colleagues recruit judges at judicial conferences in informational sessions where they present research in exchange for judges' voluntary participation in studies fueling such knowledge. Still, the fact that experimental stimuli and case vignettes must be short in such contexts might limit the depth in which one can delve into legal reasoning processes.[13]

Notwithstanding such issues, research on motivated reasoning in the use and application of legal criteria reveals some interesting findings. In a series of studies on statutory interpretation, Farnsworth et al. (2010, 2012) find that those with strong preferences tend to see identical statutory language as less ambiguous than those with weaker preferences and that the way legally trained participants were asked to interpret language modified the role of attitudes in such judgments. Interestingly, in conditions where participants were asked to interpret statutes consistent with legal approaches like "ordinary meaning" or according to the "drafters intent" decision-makers' policy preferences played *more of a role* than where they were asked to interpret the statute as an "ordinary reader of English." The authors suggest that this has relevant implications for how we train and require judges to construe legislative language.

Furgeson et al. (2008a) demonstrate that law students are more likely to credit identical arguments involving legal text and intent regarding how a hypothetical state constitutional provision should be interpreted depending on whether those arguments are consistent with outcomes supporting their preferences for increasing taxes allocated for educational purposes. In a follow up study (2008b) they also provide survey evidence that federal law clerks have preferences for constitutional interpretation that vary systematically with ideology; and undergraduate observers of court outputs tend to support broader conceptions of judicial discretion when experimental conditions expose them to the logic of landmark cases they are likely to agree with compared to those with which they are likely to disagree.

Looking at how decision-making norms can moderate the expression of preference-based decision-making Braman (2009) hypothesizes, and provides evidence illustrating the existence of two particular "mechanisms of motivated reasoning" in legal decision-making: analogical perception (Braman and Nelson 2007) and the relationship between "threshold" issues and feelings about the merits of particular claims in litigation involving multiple issues (Braman 2006). What distinguishes Braman's approach from others who have demonstrated motivated cognition in legal decision-making is that she takes seriously findings from psychology that decision-makers' capacity to engage in directed decision-making is limited. As Kunda writes "people are not at liberty to conclude what they want simply because they want to ... [They] will come to believe what they want only to the extent that reality permits" (1990: 482–3). Braman hypothesizes that objective case facts and norms of appropriate decisional behavior temper the role of policy attitudes in legal decision-making. Her experiments seek to uncover both the avenues of motivated reasoning in legal decision-making, and *their limiting conditions*, to get a better idea of when policy preferences are likely to matter in legal judgments and when they are not.

Braman and Nelson (2007) find that the similarity of proffered precedent to current case facts acts as a limiting factor in judgments about the similarity of case law. Where discrimination cases are very similar to one another on objective dimensions policy preferences do not matter in judging similarity, but where there is some room for ambiguity in similarity judgments, both undergraduate and law-student decision-makers are more likely to see cases that support outcomes they prefer as similar to pending cases than cases that do not support those preferences.

With respect to attitudes in cases involving multiple issues, Braman (2006) finds that how law students feel about views expressed by litigants can influence threshold judgments regarding whether those litigants have suffered an "injury in fact" sufficient to confer standing in a hypothetical case involving a challenge to an ordinance involving free speech. Critically, she also finds that policy preferences have their strongest influence in jurisdictional conditions where there is no precedent on the threshold issue, but that the role of such preferences are significantly tempered where participants must take into account case authority that is directly controlling on the standing question. Braman argues that this demonstrates applicable norms of legal decision-making can blunt attitudinal influence where the law is sufficiently clear.

Supplementing these findings with an open-ended analysis of reasons for their decisions (2009), she finds that law students were largely unaware of the role policy preferences in their seemingly neutral reasoning process. Yet, consistent with motivated reasoning hypotheses, they employed identical legal arguments in systematically different ways depending on how it served their judgments. This was particularly true in experimental conditions where participants were relatively unconstrained by directly controlling jurisdictional authority.

Concluding Thoughts: What We Could Do Better and Prospects for a Unified Theory of Legal Decision-Making

This brief review reveals that researchers from different disciplines and theoretical approaches have creatively used experiments to yield a much richer understanding of how individuals reason about cases in our legal system. But it also suggests that there are several things experimentalists who study legal decision-making could be doing better. Here I will suggest some ways to improve our inquiries.

Over the years several experimental scholars have proposed "cognitively informed" accounts of legal decision-making that should perhaps be better theoretically integrated, or at least delineated in terms of the specific types of decisions and contexts to which they are applicable. Right now there exists a hodge-podge of approaches speaking to different goals and aspects of decision-making depending on which particular feature of legal reasoning researchers choose to emphasize. Research on heuristic biases speaks most directly to accuracy, while work on motivated reasoning is more concerned with the deviations from the goal of neutrality in our adversarial system. Theories involving constraint satisfaction seem concerned with the process of decision-making under conditions of complexity and less occupied with the specific content of those decisions.

In some ways even this categorization of research is overly simplistic and unfair to scholars doing work in the field. All experimentalists are concerned with process; this is why we employ the primary method that allows us to delve inside the "black box" of legal cognition. Moreover, the reason we look at how individuals make decisions in our legal system is because of the implications of such reasoning processes on the quality and content of particular decisions in terms of whether they frustrate or foster normative and democratic goals like decisional accuracy and equality before the law. Although this review has incorporated critiques from scholars that have been critical of the failure of experimental researchers to distinguish between legal reasoning and fact-finding—choices made by lay decision-makers and those with legal training—it is evident that such lines are not always clear cut. Some legal choices like admissibility determinations are imbued with fact and, as was suggested in the discussion of Kahan et al.'s (2009) study, sometimes determinations that seem on their face to be of an entirely factual nature, can have normative legal aspects that law and courts scholars should consider more carefully.

There are some emergent themes about the specific conduct of experimental research and questions we should be investigating. We need to be better about testing a priori limiting conditions rather than coming up with post hoc explanations in our studies for when effects are observed and when they are not. Where findings are unexpected, we need to come up with new hypotheses to test our intuitions about why things happened differently than our theory predicted. Moreover, while it is true that different types of "directional" goals can be problematic because they threaten the normative ideal of objectivity in legal decision-making, researchers could be more careful about demonstrating what those goals are for different types of decision-makers, and what particular needs they fulfill for individuals among competing alternatives. Knowing how decision-makers are served by particular biases will help us to predict where they are likely to occur, where they are not, and perhaps even enable researchers to come up with concrete solutions to forestall particular biases in fact-finding and the application of legal criteria.

So where does this leave us? In their extremely thoughtful review of literature in their own discipline Arlen and Talley (2008) note that researchers' attempts to confirm one of two unified theories in experimental economics generally yield conflicting findings when considered in the aggregate; some studies support Expected Utility approaches, other studies support Prospect Theory. They argue this suggests a need to consider context in decision-making. Of course, this is somewhat surprising coming from law and economics types (and the authors seem to that this is heresy in their field!) On the flip side, we do not want our studies of legal decision processes to be so contextual that they frustrate the goal of parsimonious theory-building and generalization.

Perhaps the goal of achieving a unified theory of legal reasoning is illusory and should not have been anyone's ideal to begin with. Still it seems we could be doing a better job at addressing how what we know about legal cognition relates across individual studies and disciplines—across the goals of accuracy and neutrality that are relevant to different types of decision-makers in our legal system including fact-finders, trial judges, and appellate judges making legal determinations.

More than anything, this review demonstrates that we have learned much from the application of experiments to understand different types of legal decision-making, but such methods have even more potential to inform our knowledge of how individuals perform important tasks in our judicial system. There is no doubt creative researchers will continue to use experimental designs to fulfill this promise.

Acknowledgments

The author would like to thank Dan Kahan, Jeff Rachlinski, Jennifer Robbennolt, Dan Simon, and the editors of this volume for their helpful comments and suggestions on earlier drafts of this chapter.

Notes

1. "Ecological validity," or mundane realism, is a related concern involving how well experimental stimuli and decision tasks approximate real-world judgment contexts.
2. A classic example comes from a study where researchers spin a roulette wheel then ask participants to estimate the percentage of African countries in the United Nations (Tversky and Kahneman 1974). If the number on the wheel is low participants are more likely to give a low estimate compared to conditions where the number on the roulette wheel is higher.
3. This bias involves decision-makers overestimating their a priori ability to predict an event after the event has already occurred.
4. See also, Rowell and Bregant (2014) looking at whether "numeracity," the individual capacity to use and understand numbers, has similar effects for law students as have been found in the general population and testing its influence on the invocation of different legal justifications.
5. See, Pickle (1995) for an example of an experimental investigation of jurors' capacity to disregard inadmissible information, with the surprising finding that giving explanations for inadmissibility may do more harm than good; and Wistrich et al. (2005) for a study of judges ability to do the same in fact-finding and settlement contexts.
6. In judging the admissibility of a confession in a criminal case, for instance, a judge might have to consider whether the defendant was, in fact, advised of his rights and whether the circumstances surrounding the appraisal were "adequate" under applicable law.
7. Dual process models are commonly employed in psychology to describe situations where individuals are more and less likely to engage in an exhaustive search of information and options in decision tasks (see, Eagly and Chaiken 1993 for an early example; Kahneman 2011 for more recent prominent portrayal of such research).
8. See for example, Lord, Lepper, and Preston (1984) demonstrating that reminding decision-makers to "be objective" in the evaluation of scientific evidence is not as effective as asking them to consider the possibility that research could have yielded opposite results.
9. Though here again, the distinction between fact and law is somewhat blurred. Many of the "factual" conclusions researchers investigate have important legal implications, but this

research is generally done with lay participants and does not involve the primary interpretation of text, intent, or legal precedent.

10. See also, Sood (2015) finding differences in lay participants' willingness to apply exceptions to the exclusionary rule in scenarios with identical facts patterns relating to searches involving crimes concerning the sale of medical marijuana versus heroin to high school students.
11. Although the (2009) study is not an experiment, per se, as the researchers ask participants to view a video that was utilized by the Court without any sort of manipulation, the study does tend to demonstrate, consistent with much experimental evidence on motivated reasoning, that people with different worldviews can see the same evidence in vastly different ways.
12. The study revealed law students were more likely to allow preferences to sway admissibility judgments, but judges and law students were similarly influenced by preferences in judging the dispositive weight of social science evidence.
13. Braman (2006), for instance, gave law students a realistic legal brief with arguments on both sides of a case involving multiple issues. The instrument asked closed and open-ended questions about and factors affecting participants' judgments without any imposed time limits. It is unclear whether this type of experimental stimulus could be employed in a more rigidly timed environment.

References

Arlen, J., and Talley, E. 2008. "Introduction." In *Experimental Law and Economics* edited by J. Arlen and E. Talley. Northampton. MA: Elgar Reference, xv–lxi.

Bartels, B., and Johnson, C. 2012. "On the Ideological Foundations of Supreme Court Legitimacy in the American Public." *American Journal of Political Science*. 57: 184–99.

Bohnet, I., Frey, B. S., and Hack, S. 2001. "More Order with Less Law: On Contract Enforcement, Trust and Crowding." *American Political Science Review* 95: 131–44.

Braman, E. 2006. "Reasoning on the Threshold: Testing the Separability of Preferences in Legal Decision-Making." *Journal of Politics* 68(2): 308–21.

Braman, E. 2009. *Law, Politics and Perception: How Policy Preferences Influence Legal Reasoning.* Charlottesville, VA: University of Virginia Press.

Braman, E. 2010. "Searching for Constraint in Legal Decision-Making." In *The Psychology of Judicial Decision-Making*, edited by D. Klein and G. Mitchell. New York, NY: Oxford University Press, 203–18.

Braman, E., and Easter, B. 2014. "Normative Legitimacy: Rules of Appropriateness in Citizens' Assessments of Individual Legal Decisions." *Justice System Journal* 35(3): 239–68.

Braman, E., and Nelson, T. E. 2007. "Mechanism of Motivated Reasoning: Analogical Perception in Discrimination Disputes." *American Journal of Political Science* 51: 940–56.

Broeder, D. W. 1958. "The University of Chicago Jury Project." *Nebraska Law Review* 38: 744–61.

Buccafusco, C., and Springman C. J. 2011. "The Creativity Effect." *Chicago Law Review* 78: 31–52.

Coase, R. H. 1960. "The Problem of Social Cost." *Journal of Law and Economics* 3:1–44.

Cooper, J., and Fazio, R. H. 1984. "A New Look at Dissonance Theory." In *Advances in Experimental Psychology*, Vol. 17, edited by L. Berkowitz. New York, NY: Academic Press, 229–67.

Croson, R., and Johnston, J. S. 2000. "Experimental Results on Bargaining under Alternative Rights Regimes." *Journal of Law, Economics, & Organization* 16: 50–73.

Devine, D. J. 2012. *Jury Decision-making: The State of the Science*. New York, NY: New York University Press.

Devine, D. J., Clayton, L. D., Dunford, B. B., Seying, R., and Pryce, J. 2001. "Jury Decision-making: 45 Years of Empirical Research on Deliberating Groups." *Psychology, Public Policy and Law* 7: 622–727.

Eagly, A. E., and Chaiken, S. "Process Theories of Attitude Formation and Change: The Elaboration Likelihood Model and Heuristic Systematic Models." *The Psychology of Attitudes* (1993): 305–25.

Englich, B., Mussweiler, T., and Strack, F. 2006. "Playing Dice with Criminal Sentences: The Influence of Irrelevant Anchors on Experts Judicial Making." *Personality and Social Psychology Bulletin* 32: 188–200.

Farnsworth, W., Guzior, D., and Malani, A. 2010. "Ambiguity about Ambiguity: An Empirical Inquiry into Legal Interpretation." *Journal of Legal Analysis* 2: 257–300.

Farnsworth, W., Guzior, D., and Malani, A. 2013. "Policy Preferences and Legal Interpretation." *Journal of Law and Courts* 1: 115–38.

Furgeson, J., Babcock, L., and Shane, P. M. 2008a. "Do a Law's Policy Implications Affect Beliefs about its Constitutionality: An Experimental Test." *Law and Human Behavior* 32: 219–27.

Furgeson, J., Babcock, L., and Shane, P. M. 2008b. "Behind the Mask of Method: Political Orientation and Constitutional Interpretive Preferences." *Law and Human Behavior* 32: 502–10.

Friedman, B. 2006. "Taking Law Seriously." *Perspectives on Politics* 4: 261–76.

Gibson, J. L. 2008. "Challenges to the Impartiality of State Courts: Legitimacy Theory and the 'New Style' Judicial Campaigns." *American Political Science Review* 102(1): 59–75.

Giner-Sorolla, R., Chaiken, S., and Lutz, S. 2002. "Validity Beliefs and Ideology Can Influence Legal Case Judgments Differently." *Law and Human Behavior* 26: 507–26.

Glaeser, E. L., and Saerdote, B. 2003. "Sentencing in Homicide Cases and the Role of Vengeance." *Journal of Legal Studies* 32: 363–82.

Guarnaschelli, S., McKelvey, R. D., and Palfrey, T. R. 2000. "An Experimental Study of Jury Decision Rules" *American Political Science Review* 94: 407–23.

Guthrie, C. 2003. "Panacea or Pandora's Box? The Costs of Options in Negotiations." *Iowa Law Review* 88: 601–37.

Guthrie, C., Rachlinski, J. J., and Wistrich, A. J. 2001. "Inside the Judicial Mind." *Cornell Law Review* 86: 777–830.

Guthrie, C., Rachlinski, J. J., and Wistrich, A. J. 2007. "Blinking on the Bench: How Judges Decide Cases." *Cornell Law Review* 93: 1–43.

Hoffman, E., and Spitzer, M. 1982. "The Coase Theorem: Some Experimental Tests." *Journal of Law and Economics* 25: 73–98.

Kahan, D. M. 2010. "Culture Cognition and Consent: Who Percieves What, and Why, in Acquaintance Rape Cases." *University of Pennsylvania Law Review* 158: 729–813.

Kahan, D. M. 2013. "Ideology, Motivated Reasoning and Cognitive Reflection." *Judgment and Decision-making* 8: 407–24.

Kahan, D. M., Hoffman, D. A., and Braman, D. 2009. "Whose Eyes Are You Going to Believe? *Scott v. Harris* and the Perils of Cognitive Illiberalism." *Harvard Law Review* 122: 837–906.

Kahan, D. M., Hoffman, D. A., Braman, D., Evans, D., and Rachlinski, J. J. 2012. "They Saw a Protest: Cognitive Illiberalism and the Speech Conduct Distinction." *Stanford Law Review* 64: 851–906.

Kahneman, D. 2011. *Thinking Fast and Slow*. New York, NY: Macmillan.

Kahneman, D., Knetch, J. L., and Thaler, R. H. 1990. "Experimental Tests of the Endowment Effect and the Coase Theorem." *Journal of Political Economy* 98: 1325–48.

Kamin, K. A., and Rachlinski, J. J. 1995. "Ex Post = Ex Ante: Determining Liability in Hindsight." *Law and Human Behavior* 19: 89–104.

Kelman, M. 1985. "Comment on Hoffman and Spitzers' Experimental Law and Economics." *Columbia Law Review* 85: 1037.

Kelman, M., Rottenstreich, Y., and Tversky, A. 1996. "Context Dependence in Legal Decision-Making." *Journal of Legal Studies* 25: 287–318.

Koehler, J. 2001. "When Are People Persuaded by DNA Match Statistics?" *Law and Human Behavior* 25: 493–513.

Kunda, Z. 1990. "The Case for Motivated Reasoning." *Psycological Bulletin* 108: 480–98.

Kysar, D. 2007. "The Jurisprudence of Experimental Law and Economics." *Journal of Institutional and Theoretical Economics* 163: 187–98.

Lord, C. G., Ross, L., and Lepper, M. R. 1979. "Biased Assimilation and Attitude Polarization: The Effects of Theories on Subsequently Considered Evidence." *Journal of Personality and Social Psychology* 37: 1098–2021.

Lerner, J. S., and Tetlock, P. E. 1999. "Accounting for the Effects of Accountability." *Psychological Bulletin* 125: 255–75.

MacCoun, R. J. 1989. "Experimental Research on Jury Decision-Making." *Jurimetrics Journal* 30: 223–33.

MacCoun, R. J. 1998. "Biases in the Interpretation and Use of Research Results." *Annual Review of Psychology* 49: 259–87.

McCaffery, E. J., Kahneman, D., and Spitzer, M. L. 1995. "Framing the Jury: Cognitive Perspectives on Pain and Suffering Awards." *Virginia Law Review* 81: 1141–87.

McGraw, K. 2000. "Contributions of the Cognitive Approach to Political Psychology." *Political Psychology* 21: 805–32.

Mondak, J. J. 1994. "Policy Legitimacy and the Supreme Court: The Sources and Context of Legitimation." *Political Research Quarterly* 47: 675–92.

Pickel, K. L. 1995. "Inducing Jurors to Disregard Inadmissible Evidence: A Legal Explanation Does Not Help." *Law and Human Behavior* 19: 407–24.

Plott, C. R., and Zeiler, K. 2005. "The Willingness to Pay-Willingness to Accept Gap, the 'Endowment Effect,' Subject Misconceptions, and Experimental Procedures for Eliciting Valuations." *American Economic Review* 95: 530–45.

Pritchett, C. H. 1948. *The Roosevelt Court: A Study in Judicial Politics and Values*. New York, NY: Macmillan Press.

Rachlinski, J. J., Guthrie, C., and Wistrich, A. J. 2013. "Contrition in the Courtroom: Do Apologies Affect Adjudication." *Cornell Law Review* 98: 1189–243.

Rachlinski, J. J., Guthrie, C., and Wistrich, A. J. 2011. "Probable Cause, Probability, and Hindsight." *Journal of Empirical Legal Studies* 8: 72–99.

Rachlinski, J. J., Johnson, S. L., Wistrich, A. J., and Guthrie, C. 2009. "Does Unconscious Racial Bias Affect Trial Judges?" *Notre Dame Law Review* 84: 1195–247.

Rachlinski, J. J., Wistrich, A. J., and Guthrie, C. 2013. "Altering Attention in Adjudication." *University of California Los Angeles Law Review* 60:1586–618.

Redding R. E., and Reppucci, N. D. 1999. "Effects of Lawyers' Socio-Political Attitudes on their Judgments of Social Science in Legal Decision Making." *Law and Human Behavior* 23: 31–54.

Robbennolt, J. K. 2008. "Attorneys, Apologies, and Settlement Negotiation." *Harvard Negotiation Law Review* 13: 349–90.

Robbennolt, J. K., Darley, J. M., and MacCoun, R. J. 2003. "Symbolism and Incommensurability in Civil Sanctioning: Legal Decision-Makers as Goals Managers." *Brooklyn Law Review* 68: 1121–54.

Robbennolt, J. K., MacCoun, R. J., and Darley, J. M. 2010. "Multiple Constraint Satisfaction in Judging." In *The Psychology of Judicial Decision-Making*, edited by D. Klein and G. Mitchell. New York, NY: Oxford University Press, 27–40.

Rowell, A., and Bregnant, J. 2014. "Numeracy and Legal Decision-Making." *Arizona State Law Review* 46: 191.

Schauer, F. 2010. "Is There A Psychology of Judging?" In *The Psychology of Judicial Decision-Making*, edited by D. Klein and G. Mitchell. New York, NY: Oxford University Press, 103–20.

Schubert, G. 1962. "The 1960 Term of the Supreme Court." *American Political Science Review* 56: 90–107.

Schwab, S. 1998. "A Coasean Experiment on Contract Presumptions." *Journal of Legal Studies* 17: 237–68.

Segal, J. A., and Spaeth, H. J. 2002. *The Supreme Court and the Attitudinal Model Revisited.* New York, NY: Cambridge University Press.

Sevier, J. 2014. "The Truth-Justice Trade-Off: Perceptions of Decisional Accuracy and Procedural Justice in Adversarial and Inquisitorial Systems." *Psychology, Social Policy, and Law* 20: 212–61.

Simon, D. 2004. "A Third View of the Black Box: Cognitive Coherence in Legal Decision-Making." *University of Chicago Law Review* 2: 511–86.

Simon, D., and Holyoak, K. J. 2002. "Structural Dynamics of Cognition: From Consistency Theories to Constraint Satisfaction." *Personality and Social Psychology Review* 6: 283–94.

Simon, D., and Scurich, N. 2011. "Lay Judgments of Judicial Decision-Making." *Journal of Empirical Legal Studies* 8: 709–27.

Simon, D., Snow, C. J., and Read, S. J. 2004. "The Redux of Cognitive Consistency Theories: Evidence Judgments by Constraint Satisfaction." *Journal of Personality and Social Psychology* 86: 814–37.

Shayo, M., and Zussman, A. 2010. "Judicial In-Group Bias in the Shadow of Terrorism." *Quarterly Journal of Economics* 126: 1447–84.

Sood, A. M. 2013. "Motivated Cognition in Legal Judgments: An Analytic Review." *Annual Review of Law and Social Science* 9: 307–25.

Sood, A. M. 2015. "Cognitive Cleansing: Experimental Psychology and the Exclusionary Rule." *Georgetown Law Review* 103: 1545–608.

Sood, A. M., and Darley, J. 2012. "The Placidity of Harm in the Service of Criminalization Goals." *California Law Review* 100: 1313–58.

Tesser, A., and Campbell J. 1983. "Self Definition and Self Evaluation Maintenance." In *Psychological Perspectives on the Self*, edited by J. Suls and A. Greenwald. New York: Gilford Press, 1–31.

Tversky, A., and Kahneman, D. 1974. "Judgment under Uncertainty: Heuristics and Biases." *Science* 185: 1124–30.

Vidmar, N. 1999. "Juries Don't Make Legal Decisions and Other Problems: A Critique of Hastie et al. on Punitive Damages." *Law and Human Behavior* 23: 705–14.

Wistrich, A. J., Guthrie, C., and Rachlinski, J. J. 2005. "Can Judges Ignore Inadmissible Information? The Difficulty of Deliberately Disregarding." *University of Pennsylvania Law Review* 153: 1251–345.

Wistrich, A. J., and Rachlinski, J. J. 2013. "How Lawyers' Intuitions Prolong Litigation." *Southern California Law Review* 86: 571–635.

Zeiler, K. 2010. "Cautions on the Use of Economics Experiments in Law." *Journal of Institutional and Theoretical Economics* 166: 178–93.

Other Readings

Casey, P., Burke, K., and Leben, S. 2013. "Minding the Court: Enhancing the Decision-Making Process." *International Journal for Court Administration* February 2013: 1–10.

Hastie, R., Schkade, D., and Payne, J. 1998. "A Study of Juror and Jury Judgments in Civil Cases: Deciding Punitive Damages." *Law and Human Behavior* 22: 287–314.

Kinder, D., and Palfrey, T. R. 1993. "On Behalf of an Experimental Political Science." In *Experimental Foundations of Political Science*, edited by D. Kinder and T. R. Palfrey. Ann Arbor, MI: University of Michigan Press.

Lucas, J., Graif, C., and Lovaglia, M. J. 2006. "Misconduct in the Prosecution of Severe Crimes: Theory and Experimental Test." *Social Psychology Quarterly* 69: 97–107.

CHAPTER 26

NEW MEASUREMENT TECHNOLOGIES

A Review and Application to Nuremberg and Justice Jackson

DANIEL E. HO AND MICHAEL MORSE

When C. Herman Pritchett published his volume on the Vinson Court, Justice Jackson was not amused. Disputing claims about the justice's ideological voting, Jackson wrote privately: "There is a unique way of determining whether a judge is 'liberal.' If he voted for the defendant in any case ... he is called a liberal; if he voted against ... he is called a conservative. [This] seems a rather naive standard" (Domnarski 2006: 36).[1]

Addressing Jackson's skepticism of subjective coding of ideological positions, a vibrant advance in the study of judicial behavior over the past fifteen years has been the development and application of formal measurement technology to quantitatively capture principal dimensions of judicial decision-making. Stemming originally from psychometrics, with antecedents in the Congress literature (see Clinton et al. 2004; Heckman and Snyder 1997; Martin and Quinn 2002; Poole and Rosenthal 1985, 1991, 1997), these methods and extensions have reinvigorated a wide range of research questions about courts.

This chapter provides a critical overview of these new measurement technologies. The second section presents the intuition of the now standard model, with technical details provided in the Technical Appendix. The third section discusses chief advances that have capitalized on this family of measurement techniques. While they are widely employed, the fourth section cautions against naïve reliance on these measures. They are no panacea. Inferences depend critically on qualitative assumptions that should be grounded and defended in a substantive understanding of law.

The fifth section illustrates how more jurisprudentially meaningful data collection coupled with measurement techniques provides one way forward. As a running illustration, we address long-standing questions about how Justice Jackson's one-year absence from the Supreme Court to serve as U.S. chief counsel in the Nuremberg Trial affected his jurisprudence. While many scholars have conjectured about Nuremberg's effect—with one camp asserting fundamental conservative change (e.g., Abraham 1999; Schubert 1965; Rodell 1955) and another positing consistency over time (e.g., Hockett 1990, 1996; Hutchinson 1996)—none have employed modern measurement techniques to study Jackson's voting patterns.[2] We show evidence that Jackson shifted to the right post-Nuremberg. The aggregate pattern, however, may (i) mask a more dramatic shift in economic regulation, and (ii) gloss over the Court's realignment on due process, but such inferences are sharply limited by the quality of extant data.

The Item Response Theoretic Approach

We here discuss informally the item response theoretic (IRT) approach to measuring differences between justices based on judicial voting patterns (Martin and Quinn 2002). As a running example, we use voting data from Justice Jackson's service on the Court from 1941 to 1953. For a spatial voting theory justification, see Clinton et al. (2004). For more extensive elaboration in the context of judicial voting, see Ho and Quinn (2010b). The Appendix provides technical details.

Voting Data

The primary input for IRT models are voting data by a multimember court, most commonly the U.S. Supreme Court. To illustrate, Figure 26.1 plots a representative data set of non-unanimous cases from Justice Jackson's tenure. Cases are sorted chronologically on the x-axis and justices are sorted from date of service on the y-axis. Light grey cells indicate a majority vote and dark grey cells indicate a minority vote, with white indicating that a justice did not vote on the case. As indicated by the white space interrupting his service, Justice Jackson took leave from the Court in the 1945–6 term to serve as U.S. chief counsel in Nuremberg.

The IRT approach models individual votes in cases probabilistically as a function of an underlying dimension (θ) along which the justices are assumed arrayed. This dimension is commonly interpreted to represent the "liberal/conservative" spectrum. Figure 26.2 illustrates the intuition of the probability model at the case level. Each panel plots the justices' positions θ on the x-axis against votes on the y-axis, with the grey bands representing the estimated probability curve along ranges of θ. In *Pence v. United States*, 316 U.S. 332 (1941), the "conservative" majority held that the government was entitled to a directed verdict in its favor, given certain facts about fraud in the government life insurance policy, when the jury had initially ruled in favor of the beneficiary. The slope is positive, with the "liberal" coalition (in an opinion by Justice Murphy, joined by Douglas and Black) dissenting on the grounds that the question of fraud was a jury determination. The next two panels depict

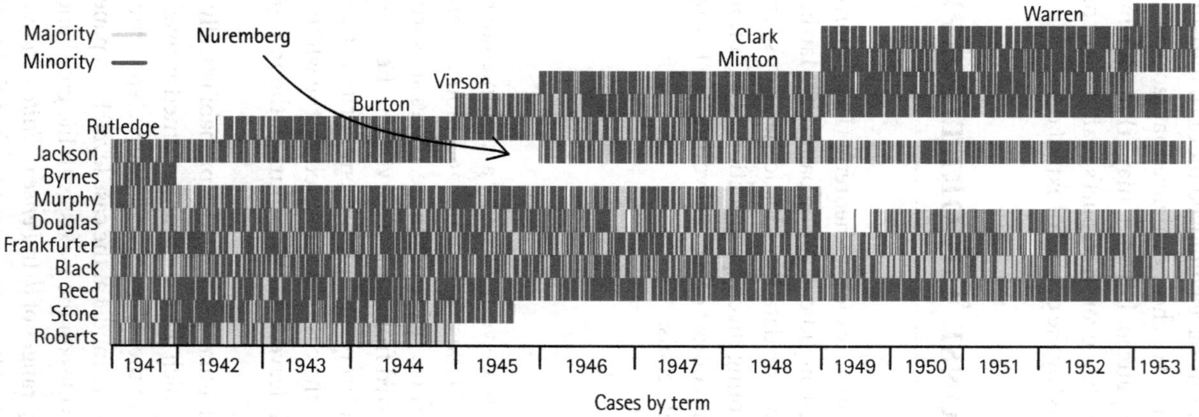

FIGURE 26.1 Votes in all non-unanimous cases for the 1941–53 terms

Source: Authors.

Note: Justices on the *y*-axis are sorted by years of service and cases are sorted by dates of decision. Light (dark) grey cells indicate a majority (minority) vote. The arrow labels the 1945–6 term, during which Justice Jackson took leave from the Court to serve in Nuremberg. The other mid-tenure interruption of judicial votes is for Justice Douglas, who was absent due to an injury for much of the 1949 term.

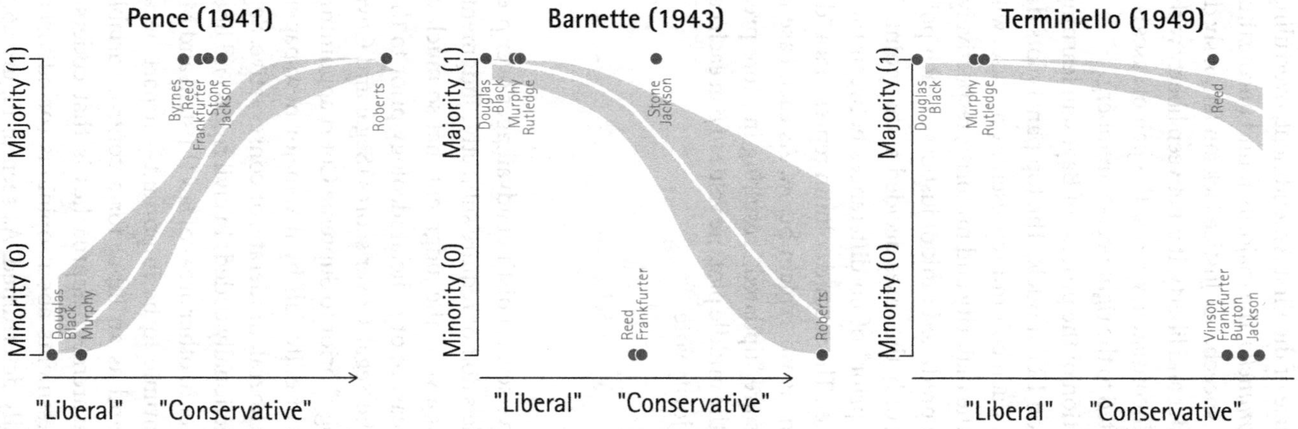

FIGURE 26.2 Illustration of probability (probit) model for judicial votes in three cases

Source: Authors.

Note: Each dot represents the vote of one justice, coded as 1 on the y-axis if for the majority and 0 if for the minority. The x-axis represents the latent dimension, with dots plotting each justice's position. The grey curves plot the predicted probability of a majority vote as a function of the position (with posterior interquartile range). Because Justice Roberts, who is the outlier on the right, retired in 1945, the range of the x-axis is more constrained in the third panel for visibility.

West Virginia State Board of Ed. v. Barnette, 319 U.S. 624 (1943), and *Terminiello v. Chicago*, 337 U.S. 1 (1949), which feature prominently in the scholarship about Justice Jackson. In *Barnette*, Justice Jackson, writing for the majority, found a school's compulsory flag salutation to violate the free speech clause of the First Amendment, overruling an earlier decision by Justice Frankfurter. In *Terminiello*, the majority found unconstitutional a Chicago ordinance banning inflammatory speech, but Justice Jackson famously dissented, writing that "the choice is not between order and liberty. It is between liberty with order and anarchy without either." The apparent inconsistency across this pair of cases is most commonly invoked to argue that Jackson shifted to the right post-Nuremberg.

Figure 26.3 illustrates the intuition of the process of Bayesian learning about the relative placement of justices based on IRT models. The top panel plots data on votes cast chronologically in the 1941 term. Each column represents one case, with light grey and dark grey representing votes for the majority and minority, respectively, by each justice. The bottom panel represents the predicted rank of justices at each point in time—that is, by fitting an IRT model using only the cases decided at that point. The first column of uniform grey represents our "prior" of no differences between the justices, associated with no votes on the top panel. The second column represents a "directional prior," which helps to fix the dimension, as we explain below. As each case is handed down, our beliefs about the parameters are "updated," resulting in more precise distinctions between the justices. The bars in the middle plot the value of β in each case, representing the estimated direction of the majority vote.

Advantages

Formal measurement models have several distinct advantages over previous classifications of justices. First, these models do not require subjective judgments about the "liberal" or "conservative" valence of a vote, the judgment that so much disturbed Justice Jackson. The most prominent measure of judicial ideology prior to the advent of such measurement technology were the Segal-Cover scores (Segal and Cover 1989). Widely deployed as a measure of "ideology" prior to Supreme Court appointment, these scores are based on coding paragraphs of editorials by five major newspapers on the confirmation process of each justice as liberal, moderate, or conservative. Segal-Cover scores predict voting patterns (also directionally coded) in civil rights and liberties cases fairly well, but have less predictive power in other areas of law (Epstein and Mershon 1996).

While Segal-Cover scores continue to be important—in part because using votes simultaneously as an outcome and as an input for a control variable of ideology is problematic—the virtue of measurement approaches is that coders do not have to make potentially subjective assessments about opinions (or editorials). The valence of case slope is instead empirically determined. As seen in Figure 26.3, it is, nonetheless, necessary to impose additional, albeit weaker, assumptions to assure "rotational invariance"—that is, to make sure that the dimension does not flip. One convention is

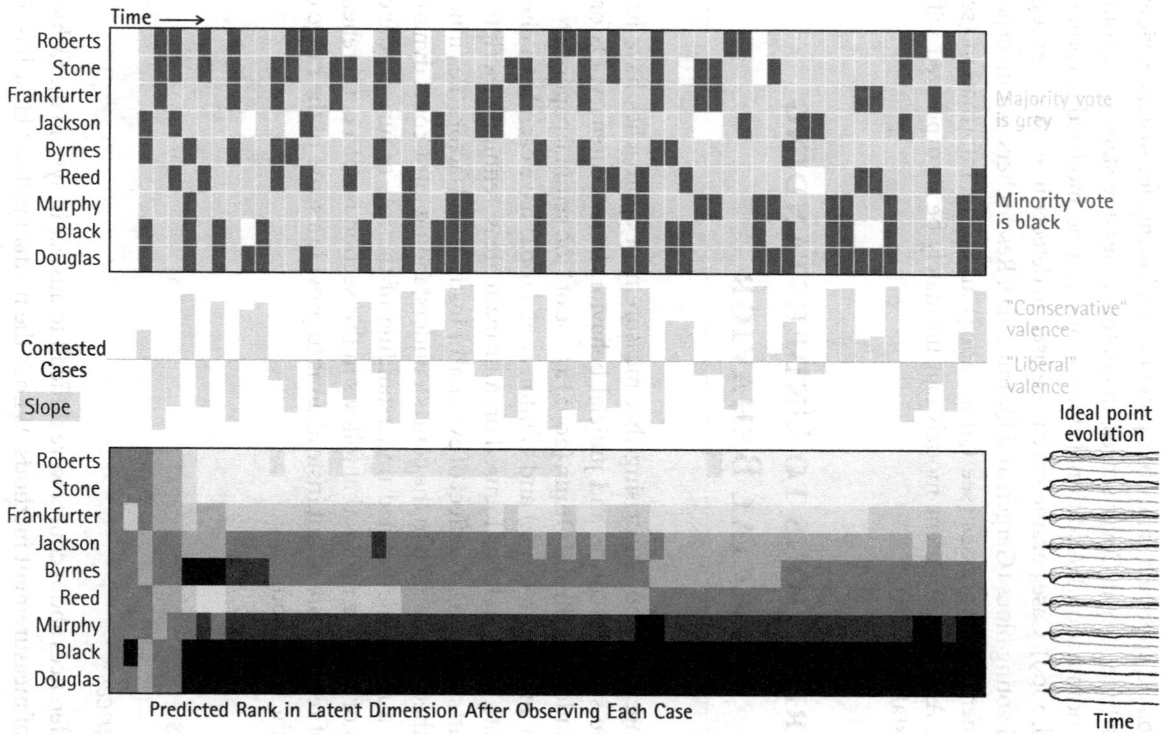

FIGURE 26.3 Illustration of Bayesian updating with judicial votes from the 1941 term

Source: Authors.

Note: The top panel represents cases sorted by date of decision, with boxes indicating judicial votes for the majority (minority) in light grey (dark grey). The middle panel presents the estimated case slopes, estimating the association between the position and a vote for the majority. The bottom panel presents the estimated ranks of the justices in the unidimensional space. To identify the model, Justice Black is assumed to be negative and Justice Frankfurter is assumed to be positive, so lower ranks can be interpreted as more consistent with the "liberal" wing of the Court.

to impose constraints on judges known to be quite dissimilar—for example, assuming Justices Frankfurter to be positive and Justice Black to be negative.

Second, the approach easily provides direct measures of uncertainty in quantities of interest. It is straightforward, for example, to calculate the probability that one justice is more "liberal" than another.[3]

Third, the model-based approach is flexible, potentially allowing, for instance, viewpoints to evolve over time. (Segal-Cover scores, in contrast, measure static views only around the time of nomination.) Additional dimensions can be modeled (Jackman 2001; Dunworth et al. 2009). Case parameters can be used to detect dimensions orthogonal to conventional voting blocs (Gergen and Quinn 2012). Researchers can incorporate diverse data-generating processes (see Quinn 2004) and prior information (see Bafumi et al. 2005). And measurement models can ultimately be incorporated with analysis models (Gustafson 2003).

Contributions to Understanding Judicial Behavior

Given these advantages, it is not surprising that measurement approaches have had broad impact on the study of courts and judicial behavior. In its centenary, Oxford University Press included Martin and Quinn (2002) as one of "100 seminal papers" from 180 journals. Martin and Quinn (2002) and Clinton et al. (2004) have each been cited over 800 times to date.[4] Research has focused on four main areas: refining descriptive inferences about courts; studying the effect of external or institutional factors (i.e., much of positive political theory as applied to the courts); understanding intra-court dynamics; and developing a more fine-grained understanding of the role of jurisprudence across discrete areas of law. The review that follows in this section is not a comprehensive meta-analysis of research areas, but instead aims to provide a sense of the range of rich applications of these methods.

Research Areas

Descriptive Inferences

Many descriptive inferences about courts were difficult to answer in systematic fashion prior to the advent of measurement methods. Who is the median justice? How has the Supreme Court evolved over time?

Martin et al. (2004) show that IRT methods easily allow researchers to determine the (posterior) probability that a justice is the median in any term. Moreover, with straightforward application of the methods, they find that the median justice fluctuates over time, that Justice O'Connor trended to the left from 1994 to 2002, and that the methods help in predicting the impact of vacancies on the Court (see also Epstein and Jacobi 2008).

Epstein et al. (2007a) address the phenomenon of ideological drift, answering comprehensively how frequently the viewpoints of justices change over their tenure. They study voting patterns from 1937 to 2005, applying dynamic IRT, and find that drift occurs quite frequently. These results call into question how easily presidents can deploy the appointment power to entrench preferences in the judiciary.

Lauderdale and Clark (2012) deploy a measurement method similar in spirit and incorporate issue codes from the Supreme Court Judicial Database and case citation proximity to estimate the position of the median justice across cases and time. They find that the identity of the median justice is quite sensitive to the area of law.

Staudt et al. (2007) study whether majority coalition homogeneity is associated with how "consequential" a decision is. They measure homogeneity by the standard deviation of ideal points in the coalition and measure the consequential nature of a case by whether it is reported on the front page of *The New York Times*. They find that homogeneous coalitions result in more consequential decisions.[5] In a related vein, Clark (2009) uses dynamic ideal points to propose a measure of polarization on the Court.

While descriptive inferences based on measurement methods have primarily focused on the U.S. Supreme Court, these methods have applicability to all multimember courts. Alarie and Green (2007), for instance, apply IRT methods to study the Supreme Court of Canada, resolving competing claims about Justice Frank Iacobucci's career.

External and Institutional Factors

Many theories of courts posit that there are influences *external* to the court and/or that inter-institutional interactions structure judicial behavior. While ideal points provide only summaries of inter-judge differences within a court, they nonetheless have found wide applicability in studying external and institutional factors.

Public Opinion

Epstein and Martin (2010) formally test the proposition most recently associated with Friedman (2009) that public opinion influences Supreme Court decisions. If correct, this channel of influence might ease concerns about the countermajoritarian difficulty. Epstein and Martin (2010) model (using logistic regression) whether the Court reached a liberal or conservative decision, using the Stimson's quarterly public mood measure as the primary explanatory variable and ideal points as one of several control variables. They find that public mood is associated with the propensity of decisions, while noting that this correlation does not reflect the *influence* of public opinion per se.

Malhotra and Jessee (2014) deploy IRT methods to place public opinion and the Supreme Court directly in the same common space. They conduct a survey, polling respondents about their views on ten Supreme Court cases, which they jointly scale with the judicial votes over the same time period. They find the Court to be roughly representative of the median citizen.

Separation of Powers

Bailey (2007) and Bailey and Chang (2001) compile a new data set on "bridge" observations, that is, positions taken by presidents and members of Congress on Supreme Court cases. Capitalizing on such an augmented data set to fit an IRT model potentially allows researchers to place different institutions (i.e., the Congress, the presidency, and the judiciary) on a common scale, thereby opening up broad areas of inquiry about the separation of powers and positive political theory. Sala and Spriggs (2004), for example, use Nominate scores (Poole and Rosenthal 1997) and Supreme Court ideal point measures to test whether popular branches constrain judicial decision-making.

Harvey and Friedman (2009) show that discretionary jurisdiction matters for understanding congressional influence on judicial decisions: using ideal points, the Court appears much less likely to grant cert on cases where congressional preferences diverge from those of the Court. Ho and Quinn (2010a) address historical disagreements about the nature of the constitutional revolution of 1937. They show after FDR's landslide election of 1936 and executive threats on the judiciary in the form of the Court-packing plan, Justice Roberts shifted sharply to the left, but trended gradually back to the right once FDR gained control of the Court. This calls into question "internalist" accounts of the New Deal Court, which emphasize gradual and foreseeable jurisprudential development (e.g., Cushman 1998).

Bonica and Woodruff (2015) use campaign finance records to scale state Supreme Court justices on a common dimension and demonstrate the usefulness of these scores for testing separation of powers models. Because the approach does not rely on voting records, it holds great promise as a more exogenous measure of preferences.

Judicial Hierarchy

Epstein et al. (2007b) extend Supreme Court ideal points to provide Judicial Common Space (JCS) scores for all justices and Court of Appeals judges sitting from 1953 to 2000. They combine data from Nominate scores and Giles et al. (2001), and use unconstrained confirmed Supreme Court nominees to transform ideal points onto the Nominate scale. JCS scores thereby allow researchers to address questions about lower court compliance with higher courts. Westerland et al. (2010) use the JCS scores to study how the Courts of Appeals treat Supreme Court precedent and find strong evidence of hierarchical control by the contemporary (but not "enacting") Court.

Intra-Court Dynamics

Ideal points have also been useful for understanding dynamics internal to courts. Black and Boyd (2012) study whether "litigant status" affects the likelihood of cert grants, using ideal points as a control variable. Carrubba et al. (2012) find evidence consistent with the notion that the median justice in the majority coalition—instead of, as often conventionally assumed, the median justice overall or the opinion author—most influences a decision. Lauderdale and Clark (2014) find similar results.

Fischman (2011) develops a closely related measurement method that has the virtue of endogenizing the cost of dissent. Using a sample of immigration asylum cases in the Ninth Circuit, he recovers preferences with respect to asylum relief and finds evidence consistent with consensus voting.

Jurisprudence

One of the most exciting areas of application of measurement methods lies in the intersection of politics, jurisprudence, and judicial doctrine (Lax 2011). Lindquist and Klein (2006) study Supreme Court cases resolving a circuit split from 1985 to 1995 and find that jurisprudential considerations, such as the number of circuits supporting one side, are important, controlling for ideal points.

While automated methods to determine specific doctrinal areas of cases are promising (e.g., Clark and Lauderdale 2010 use citation data to locate cases in "doctrine space"), other work combines ideal points with directly meaningful data about jurisprudence or specific doctrinal areas. Law (2004) collects nearly 2,000 immigration asylum cases in the Ninth Circuit from 1992 to 2001. He documents strategic publication: Republican judges, for instance, appear more likely to grant asylum relief in published cases, but overwhelmingly deny relief in unpublished cases. Epstein and Segal (2006) show that ideological voting in First Amendment cases is muted when other values, such as privacy or equality, are at stake. Sag et al. (2009) use ideal points to examine intellectual property decisions.

Raso and Eskridge (2010) use an exhaustive database on standards of review applied by the Supreme Court in administrative law cases from 1984 to 2006. While they present evidence that the application of deference standards are associated with ideal points, the *announced* deference standard also substantially influences the likelihood to affirm an agency. Ho and Ross (2010) study the history of the standing doctrine to test the counterintuitive proposition that standing was invented by liberal justices to insulate the New Deal from judicial review. Collecting and coding the population of standing disagreements in the Supreme Court from 1921 to 2006, they show there is indeed a distinct historical period around the New Deal where liberal justices systematically vote to deny standing relative to conservative justices (as measured by ideal points), a pattern that reverses post-New Deal.

Gergen and Quinn (2012) collect cases decided by the New York Court of Appeals from 1900 to 1941, applying IRT methods to non-unanimous cases. While there is a dominant dimension that characterizes voting differences, they show that cases also changed substantially over the observation period and that judges appeared to divide along three orthogonal dimensions: moralism, legalism, and pragmatism. By applying fine-grained models to temporal subsets, they discover differences in torts, constitutional, and labor cases. Torts, for instance, did not appear to be ideologically shaped during this historical period.

Methodological Role

While we've discussed the four main areas shaped by measurement methods, this subsection provides a typology to understand what methodological role ideal points play in those studies. Although the typology is not exhaustive and mutually exclusive, roughly four different roles can be gleaned from the literature. First, for many studies, ideal points are themselves the direct quantity of interest. Epstein et al. (2007a), for instance, examine whether Justice Blackmun trended to the left over his tenure. Second, in the vast majority of studies using ideal points, they are deployed as control variables or as measures of ideological influence, typically in a regression analysis. Third, a number of studies calculate transformations of ideal points, such as to measure homogeneity of the majority coalition (Staudt et al. 2007). Fourth, a number of studies augment conventional voting data with other information, typically at the case level, refitting the IRT model to derive new quantities of interest. Table 26.1 places the studies discussed above in the typology. While the frequency in Table 26.1 does not necessarily correspond to the frequency in the published literature, a predominant usage of ideal point models (certainly of Martin Quinn scores) appears to be (2).

Limitations

While much has been learned using measurement methods, there are also considerable limitations with the use and interpretation of the scores.

First, while one virtue of IRT approaches is that they can be motivated by a theory of spatial voting in some contexts, such approaches may not be directly applicable to judicial voting. Conventional assumptions, such as sincere voting, quadratic utility functions over policies located in a unidimensional space, and a discrete choice between the status quo and a proposal, may be less plausible for courts than for legislatures.

Second, if spatial voting does not apply directly, the estimated positions of θ cannot easily be interpreted as *policy* positions (or revealed preferences) per se. θ could just as well capture *jurisprudential* differences. Despite these limitations, θ can still be useful in the study of judicial behavior, by providing a summary of the principal differences of judges based on voting patterns.

Table 26.1 A typology of the role of ideal points in judicial behavior

Role of ideal points	Studies
(1) Direct quantity of interest	Alarie and Green (2007); Bonica and Woodruff (2015); Epstein et al. (2007a); Gergen and Quinn (2012); Ho and Quinn (2010a); Lauderdale and Clark (2012); Law (2004); Martin et al. (2004)
(2) Control variable/"ideological influence"	Black and Boyd (2012); Epstein and Martin (2010); Epstein and Segal (2006); Harvey and Friedman (2009); Lindquist and Klein (2006); Raso and Eskridge (2010); Sag et al. (2009); Sala and Spriggs (2004)
(3) Transformation	Carrubba et al. (2012); Clark (2009); Epstein and Jacobi (2008); Epstein et al. (2007b); Staudt et al. (2007); Westerland et al. (2010)
(4) Baseline augmented with other data	Bailey (2007); Ho and Quinn (2008); Ho and Ross (2010); Malhotra and Jessee (2014)

Notes: (1) "Direct quantity of interest" indicates that the primary goal of the paper is to draw inferences about the position of judges, using ideal points; (2) "Control variable/ 'ideological influence' " indicates that the primary use of ideal points is to model the effect of ideology or control for it; (3) "Transformation" indicates that a transformation of ideal points is used (e.g., to place judges on a common scale with other political actors); (4) "Baseline augmented with other data" indicates that judicial voting data are augmented with other information, typically at the case level, re-estimating ideal points.

Third, because ideal points are identified solely by dispositional votes in non-unanimous cases—typically aggregated over all issue areas—the approach ignores information that may be of greatest interest to scholars of courts, that is, the content of judicial decisions in distinct areas of law. While ideal points succinctly summarize voting differences, they do not directly capture jurisprudentially meaningful dimensions, such as judicial restraint, formalism versus functionalism, textualism versus purposivism, due process, and incorporation. And the latter dimensions are often of greater interest to scholars interested in law and doctrine.

A Way Forward: An Illustration with Justice Jackson and Nuremberg

We posit that one way forward lies in deploying both measurement models and more fine-grained, jurisprudentially meaningful, data collection. To illustrate, we address a long-standing question about Justice Jackson's service on the Court: Did his views shift substantially after he served at Nuremberg? Did it matter by area of law? Understanding Jackson also informs a much broader and fundamental debate about judicial behavior (White 2005): Do *external* experiences affect the internal jurisprudence of the Court?

The "Scholarly Disagreement" subsection discusses the prior literature on the subject, which is characterized by intense disagreement about whether Nuremberg changed Jackson, and, if so, in what parts of his jurisprudence. Most scholars have relied principally on a handful of cases, chiefly *Barnette* and *Terminiello*, with only a few attempts to study voting patterns, none deploying modern measurement methods.

The section "Aggregate Evidence" discusses results for aggregate cases, confirming that Jackson indeed appeared to shift to the right post-Nuremberg. The "Granular Evidence" subsection develops a data collection protocol to study more specific claims about Justice Jackson's First Amendment, civil liberties, and due process jurisprudence.

Scholarly Disagreement

Scholars have opined widely about the impact of Nuremberg on Jackson. One school posits that Jackson became sharply more conservative post-Nuremberg. Upon Jackson's death, Justice Frankfurter wrote that Nuremberg had a "profound influence" on Jackson, teaching him "how ultimately fragile the forces of reason are and how precious the safeguards of law" (Frankfurter 1955). Louis Jaffe wrote that Nuremberg "awakened him to the basic problem of order" (Jaffe 1955: 997). Henry Abraham concluded that "the one liberal judicial activist, who had so often sided with Black, Douglas, Murphy, and Rutledge, had become profoundly cautious, a markedly narrow interpreter of the Bill of Rights. He now more often than not sided with the Frankfurter wing of the Court" (Abraham 1999: 178). Glendon Schubert, tallying conservative and liberal decisions, concluded that Jackson's "behavior changed sharply and significantly" after Nuremberg (Schubert 1965: 963). Many others conjectured similarly (e.g., Rodell (labeling Jackson a "turncoat-to-conservatism") (Rodell 1955: 279)). The "Two Jacksons" hypothesis has become so engrained that scholars have simply divided his jurisprudence into two distinct periods: before and after Nuremberg (see, e.g., Ray 1995).

But the hypothesis remains contested. What we could dub the "continuity school" posits that Jackson remained "fundamentally the same justice" before and after Nuremberg (Hockett 1990: 281). To begin, Hockett argues that Jackson's positions in *Terminiello* and *Barnett* are easily reconciled: both decisions deploy a balancing test, weighing private speech interests against public order. Moreover, Hockett points to a number of pre-Nuremberg cases that similarly rely on a balancing test and reject a strong "preferred freedoms" doctrine (Hockett 1990, 1996). Dennis Hutchinson argues that Jackson is "misestimated to misunderstood" (Hutchinson 1996: 108). "If anything, Nuremberg provided powerful cumulative evidence supporting views Jackson was developing *before* he went overseas" (Hutchinson 1996: 114, emphasis added). The continuity school is not without some empirical support. Domnarski (2006), who discusses some change, calculates Jackson's agreement rate with Justice Frankfurter, and finds that rate is comparable pre- and post-Nuremberg.

Two common challenges are pointed out by the continuity school. Pritchett notes that "the rather erratic nature of [Jackson's] opinions ma[kes] it difficult to catalog him" (Pritchett 1954: 18). In addition, while the European experience appears vividly in Jackson's post-Nuremberg opinions,[6] Nuremberg's impact may have been more on the pen than in the disposition. As Paul Freund notes, "his acquaintance with European experience colored his opinions, if it was not actually decisive in his judgments" (Freund 1955: 17).

Another possibility is that the two schools talk at cross-purposes. Sweeping statements about Jackson's jurisprudence at large may miss distinct and divergent effects of Nuremberg on Jackson's jurisprudence. Louis Jaffe (1955: 967–8, 982), for instance, conjectures that Nuremberg taught Jackson about the importance of public order, affecting distinctly his civil liberties decisions. Schubert, on the other hand, argues that the shift is pronounced in economic cases and not civil liberties.

Indeed, more fine-grained jurisprudential claims feature in the qualitative scholarship about Jackson. First, with *Terminiello* and *Barnette*, many scholars focus particularly on Jackson's First Amendment jurisprudence. By that account, Nuremberg taught Jackson about the failures of the Weimar Republic to tamp down offensive speech. Second, others have argued that Nuremberg caused Jackson to take a more limited view on incorporation of the Bill of Rights against the states (Jaffe 1955: 981). Indeed, Jackson himself attributed his increased deference to local officials to Nuremberg (Jackson 1955: 573). Third, some scholars identify a more general disposition favoring judicial restraint (Hutchinson 1996: 115–16), as Nuremberg may have heightened Jackson's sense of the limitations of judicial process.

While First Amendment, Fourth Amendment, and judicial restraint views would be associated with a conservative shift (at this historical juncture), scholars have also identified areas of law seemingly associated with a liberal shift. Hockett argues that Nuremberg, by highlighting the dangers of government intervention, caused Jackson to become more liberal in procedural due process cases. In addition, Hockett notes that Nuremberg strengthened Jackson's view of the Fourth Amendment as a protection against arbitrary government (Hockett 1990: 294–5).

In short, there is little empirical agreement on whether and how Nuremberg affected Jackson. Aggregated evidence of voting patterns may even mask effects in particular areas of jurisprudence. While some scholars have studied voting patterns (e.g., Schubert, Domnarski), none have deployed modern measurement methods.

Aggregate Evidence

We first investigate the broadest claim about Jackson's change. Figure 26.4 presents static ideal point estimates, allowing for separate ideal points for Jackson pre- and post-Nuremberg, with horizontal lines plotting 95 percent credible intervals. Placements of the justices comport with conventional understandings of the Court. For instance, pre-Nuremberg, the "liberal" coalition of Black, Douglas, Rutledge, and Murphy often squared off against the more "conservative" coalition of Stone, Frankfurter, Reed, and Jackson, with Roberts frequently in solo dissent. The measures, as expected, corroborate

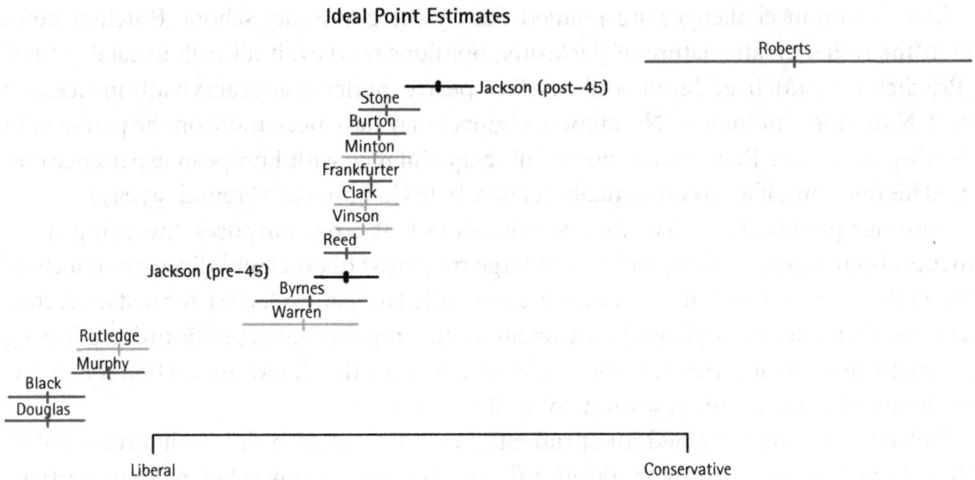

FIGURE 26.4 Static (median) ideal point estimates with 95 percent credible intervals for the 1941–53 terms

Source: Authors.

Note: Justices are sorted from left to right by median ideal point, with separate ideal points for Jackson pre and post-Nuremberg. Justices in dark grey first served on the Stone Court; those in light grey first served under Vinson. To identify the model, the ideal point priors for Justices Black and Frankfurter are assumed to be negative and positive, respectively.

and formalize qualitative understandings of the voting blocs of the Court. Most importantly, the model also confirms the "Two Jacksons" hypothesis: pre-Nuremberg, Jackson is close to the median position on the Court; post-Nuremberg (with Roberts's retirement), he occupies the right-most side of the Court (posterior p-value < 0.001). The shift indeed appears substantial.

To allow for more general shifts in jurisprudence over time (as well as to avoid Type I error that can result from static pre-post comparison), Figure 26.5 plots results from a dynamic ideal point model. Because we are interested primarily in Justice Jackson, we set the smoothness of evolution such that estimates of the justices other than Jackson comport with received wisdom. Again, the model reveals that Justice Jackson shifts substantially to the right post-Nuremberg.

Granular Evidence

Vigorous disagreements about Justice Jackson, however, focus not just on changes over time across all cases, but specifically about the impact of Nuremberg on particular aspects of his jurisprudence. To study this, we collected new data to test the most common conjectures about Jackson's evolution. Our approach does not provide a generalized way to define issue areas; instead, the lynchpin for our case selection was whether the criteria accord with the ones implicit in Jackson scholarship.

Our data collection process worked as follows. First, we collected the superset of all cases cited in the Jackson literature for discrete areas of law. Second, we used a data set of

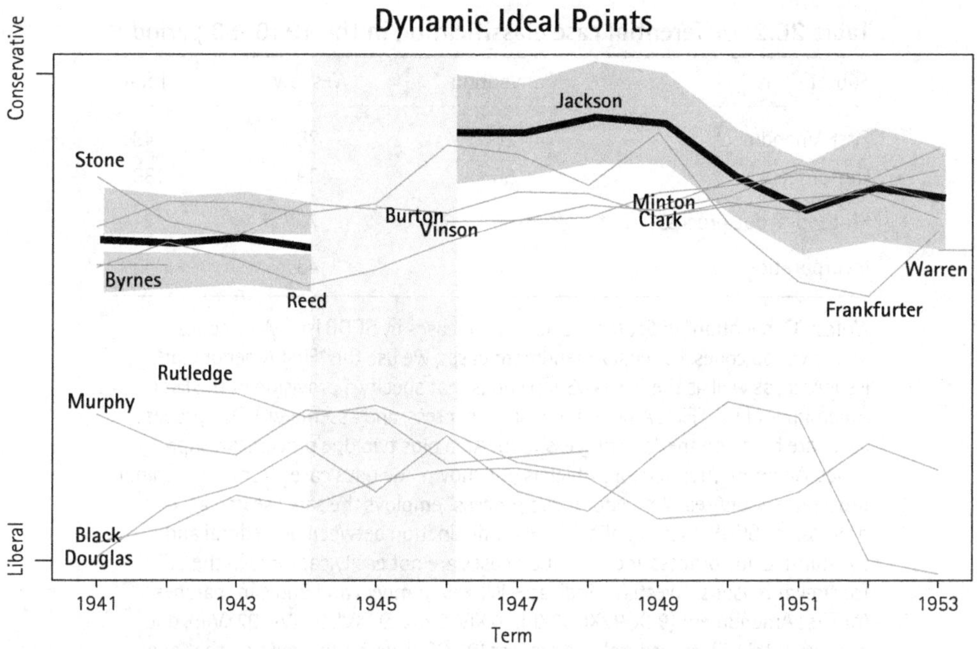

FIGURE 26.5 Median dynamic ideal points for all justices, with separate pre- and post-Nuremberg trends for Jackson

Source: Authors.

Note: The solid lines represent the (pointwise) posterior median ideal points. The grey bands provide pointwise 95 percent credible regions for Justice Jackson. For ease of visibility, Justice Roberts is omitted from this figure (but included in the estimation). The results suggest that Jackson shifted to the right post-Nuremberg.

all Westlaw (WL) Key Numbers for each case, merged with the Supreme Court Judicial Database (SCDB) issue and law codes to determine which key numbers and SCDB codes best predicted the presence of a case discussed in the literature.[7] WL has the particular virtue of employing actual attorneys that key cases. The goal here was to enumerate the population of cases in which specific issues were at stake, overcoming some of the weaknesses of SCDB issue codes, chiefly the fact that only one issue is assigned to a case (when Supreme Court cases often involve multiple issues) and that issue codes are assigned based on the perceived policy issue, not necessarily the jurisprudential issue (Harvey and Woodruff 2011; Ho and Quinn 2010b).

Table 26.2 presents an overview of the cases resulting from this data collection procedure for First Amendment, due process, and incorporation. We present data for the 1946–53 terms because SCDB data is not yet available pre-Nuremberg. The first column indicates the number of cases coded as in these areas by conventional SCDB issue codes. One difficulty associated with the conventional approach lies in distinguishing procedural due process, substantive due process, and incorporation cases, especially as individual cases can raise multiple, interrelated issues.[8] Table 26.2 hence provides distinct rows for capturing different subsets of cases. The second column indicates the number of cases captured by deploying WL searches and key numbers to approximate the issue

Table 26.2 Differential case classification in the 1946–53 period

Subset	Convention	Westlaw	Total
First Amendment	26	28	48
Due process	56	139	139
Procedural due process	56	76	121
Incorporation	0	43	43

Notes: "Convention" indicates the number of cases by SCDB issueArea codes and lawSupp codes. For First Amendment cases, we use the "First Amendment" issueArea, as well as the five lawSupp codes that specify a provision of the First Amendment (e.g., "First Amendment (speech, press, and assembly)"). Due process cases are based on the "due process" issueArea plus two due process lawSupp codes. An alternative version, which is not shown, includes cases from the criminal procedure issueArea. "Procedural due process" employs the same search as "due process," as SCDB does not allow for easy distinction between procedural and substantive due process. Incorporation cases are not easily captured in the SCDB for similar reasons. "Westlaw" indicates WL key numbers and Boolean searches for First Amendment (92X, 92XI, 92XIII, 92XIV, 92XV, 92XVI, 92XVII, 92XVIII), due process (92XXVII), procedural due process (92XXVII, with the condition that one of the following conditions are also met: (i) due process or a similar phrase is proximate to "procedur!" within the headnote or within the body of the text and in the same paragraph, or (ii) the key numbers of Criminal Law (92XXVII(H), (iii) Civil Actions and Proceedings (92XXVII(E)), or (iv) Search, Seizure, and Confiscation (92XXVII(G)23), which are all nested under "due process"), and incorporation (a pure Boolean search centered around the Fourteenth Amendment, with the additional requirement that either certain words appear in close proximity to "incorporat!" or the key number for "Relationship to Other Constitutional Provisions–Incorporation" (92k3848) is used.

area contemplated by Jackson scholars. WL returns a much higher number of cases involving these issues, likely because SCDB reduces each case down to a single issue. For instance, SCDB returns fifty-six cases involving due process, compared to 139 via WL.

Our approach is by no means ideal, but it shows one path forward. It may be over-inclusive, capturing cases that involve a particular issue when the voting disagreement may not have centered on that issue. In reviewing samples of SCDB-identified cases, however, we determined that the conventional approach was under-inclusive relative to the cases discussed in the scholarly literature.[9] Combining these two sources provides an avenue forward by incorporating better measurement (via Westlaw attorneys) of the legal disputes at issue.

One basic trade-off in applying measurement methods to subsets of cases is bias-variance. Smaller subsets of cases will decrease bias of ideal points in particular areas of law, but will increase the variability of estimates. Because of this trade-off, Figure 26.7 plots static results on the subset of First Amendment cases, where the total number of

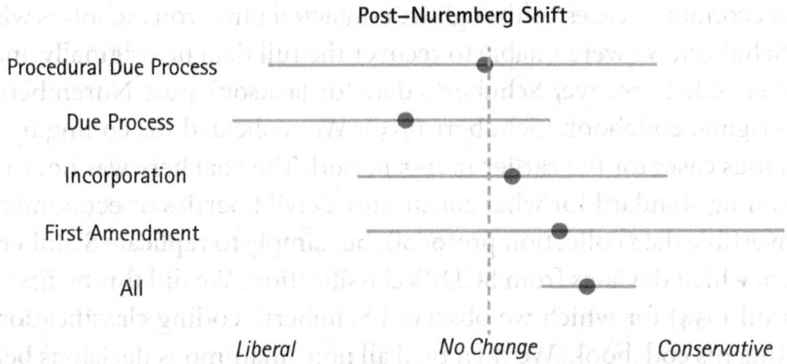

FIGURE 26.6 Median post-Nuremburg shift for subsets of cases and all cases, 1941–53

Source: Authors.

Note: The dotted vertical line tracks the origin. The grey dots are plotted at the median shift mark, representing the median change between Jackson's pre-Nuremberg and post-Nuremberg jurisprudence. The horizontal seems show the confidence interval.

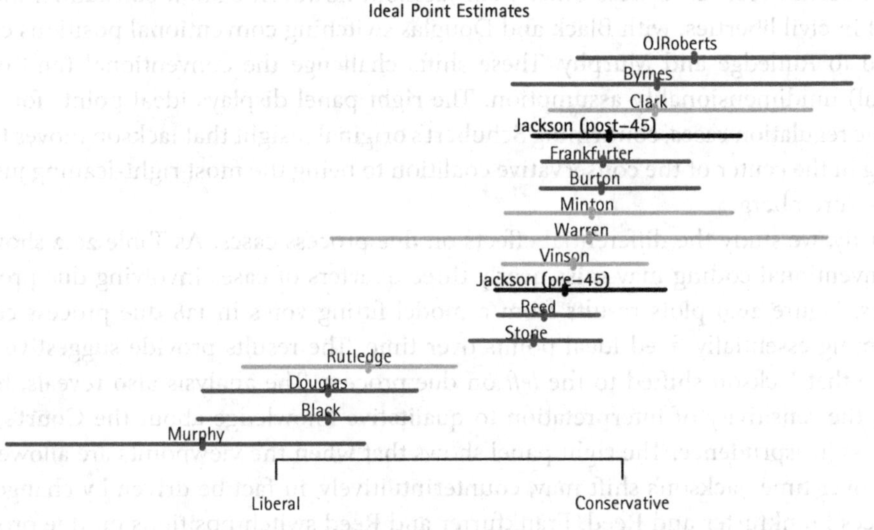

FIGURE 26.7 Static ideal points in First Amendment cases, 1941–53

Source: Authors.

cases is small ($n = 48$). The results reveal little evidence of any broader shift in Jackson's views toward the First Amendment based on the voting record. Figure 26.6 plots the difference in Jackson's ideal point before and after Nuremberg in other areas, revealing much uncertainty.

We now examine the hypothesis that there were distinct patterns in civil liberties cases more broadly. Glendon Schubert was the first to compare decisions in civil liberties and economics cases. Although we contacted numerous scholars who collaborated with Schubert, we were unable to recover the full data he originally analyzed. We were, however, able to recover Schubert's data for Jackson's post-Nuremberg tenure as well as his original codebook (Schubert 1959). We replicated his coding by classifying non-unanimous cases for the earlier 1941–5 period. The goal here was not to determine afresh the coding standard for what constitutes a civil liberties or economics case (not an incontrovertible data collection protocol), but simply to replicate Schubert's original classification, which deviates from SCDB's classification. We did this by first reading all cases (up until 1954) for which we observed Schubert's coding classification and then supplementing his codebook. We then read all non-unanimous decisions between 1941 and 1945 and categorized them as pertaining to civil liberties, economic regulation, or neither.[10] This resulted in a total of 257 civil liberties cases and 323 economics cases during Jackson's time on the Court. Instead of Schubert's manual coding of case votes as liberal or conservative, we use measurement methods to formalize whether there is a statistically distinguishable effect in these subsets.

Figure 26.8 plots results from dynamic estimates. The left panel displays ideal points in civil liberties cases, showing that there is in fact little evidence of a shift in Jackson's civil liberties record. Justices other than Jackson, however, exhibit substantial movement in civil liberties, with Black and Douglas switching conventional positions compared to Rutledge and Murphy. These shifts challenge the conventional (and often useful) unidimensionality assumption. The right panel displays ideal points for economic regulation cases, confirming Schubert's original insight that Jackson moves from being in the center of the conservative coalition to being the most right-leaning justice post-Nuremberg.

Lastly, we study the differential effects on due process cases. As Table 26.2 showed, a conventional coding may miss nearly three quarters of cases involving due process issues. Figure 26.9 plots results from a model fitting votes in 138 due process cases, assuming essentially fixed ideal points over time. The results provide suggestive evidence that Jackson shifted to the *left* on due process. The analysis also reveals, however, the sensitivity of interpretation to qualitative knowledge about the Court's due process jurisprudence. The right panel shows that when the viewpoints are allowed to vary over time, Jackson's shift may, counterintuitively, in fact be driven by changes in Justices Frankfurter and Reed. Frankfurter and Reed switch positions on due process over time, with Reed evolving to the right and Frankfurter seemingly evolving to the left. Assuming Reed to be constant essentially drives a kind of wedge between pre- and post-Nuremberg Jackson in the static model.

Methodologically, this example demonstrates the importance of conducting sensitivity analyses of measurement models. Substantively, which results (and priors) are more credible? This is where deeper understanding of due process jurisprudence and more meaningful understanding of case law, with a particular focus on Frankfurter and Reed, becomes critical. Pre-Nuremberg, Jackson and Roberts, for instance, joined a dissenting opinion written by Justice Frankfurter in *Rice v. Olson*, 324 U.S. 786 (1945), in which the majority found that a petitioner was entitled to a hearing about whether he

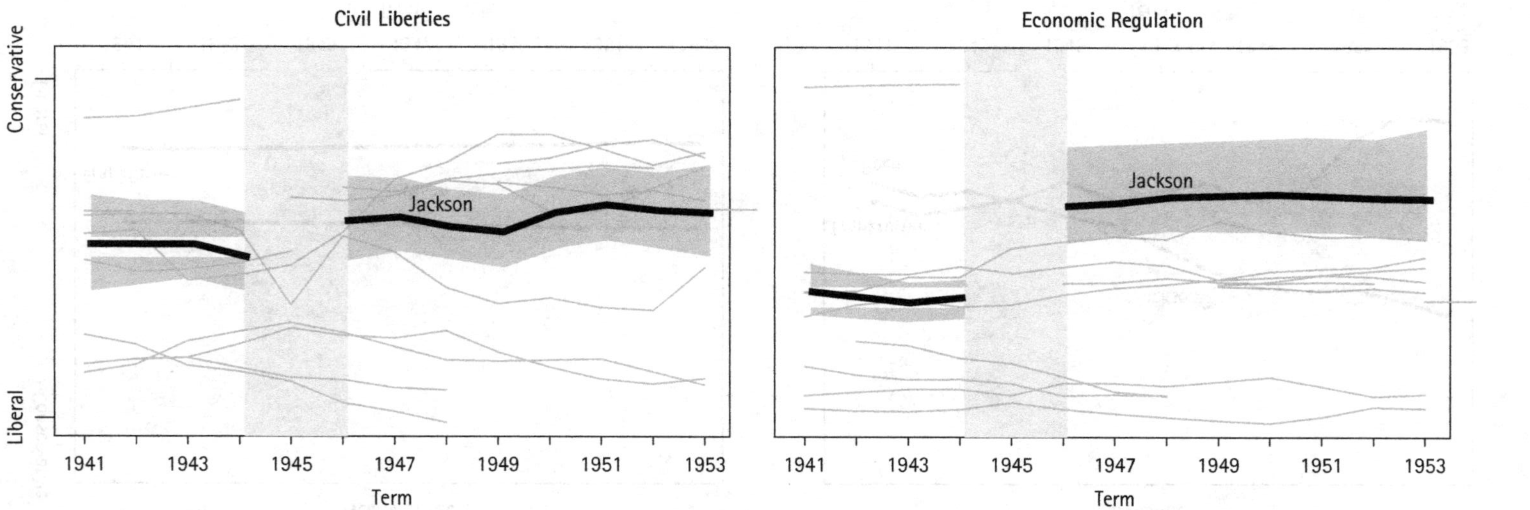

FIGURE 26.8 Ideal point estimates for economic regulation cases and civil liberties cases

Source: Authors.

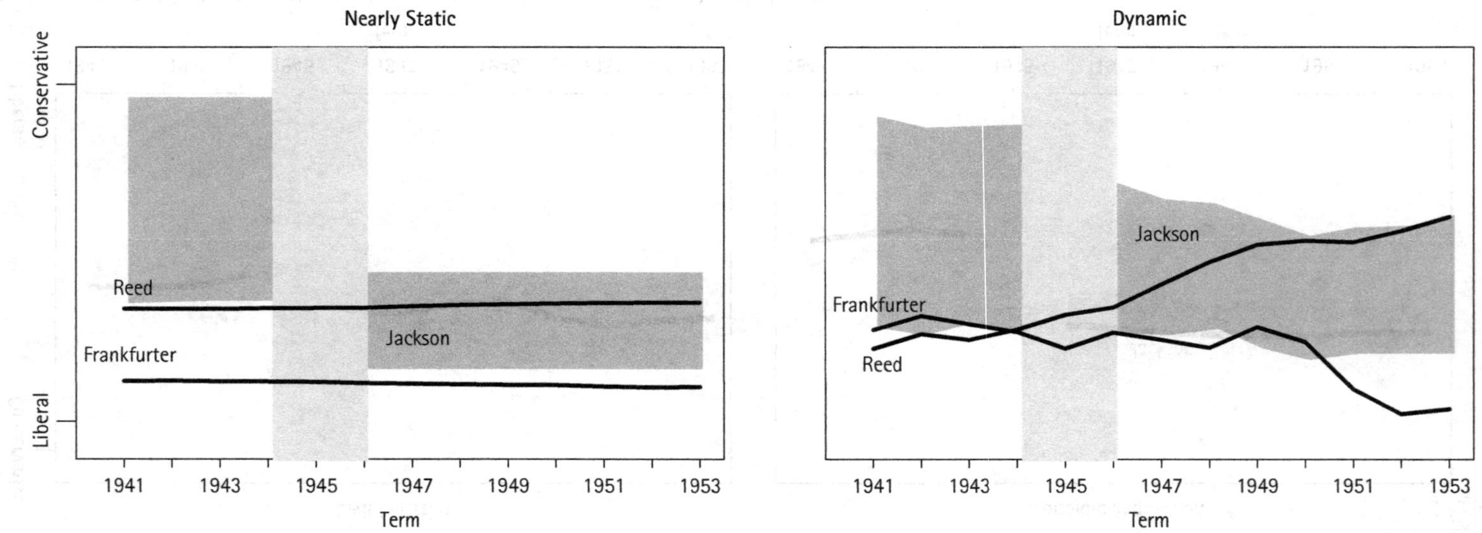

FIGURE 26.9 Divergent inferences about Nuremberg's effect on Jackson's due process views

Source: Authors.

Note: The left panel fits nearly static ideal points, while the right panel allows for ideal point evolution, resulting in divergent inferences about Nuremberg's effect on Jackson's due process views. Only auxiliary information can resolve which inference to believe.

was unconstitutionally deprived of his right to counsel. Yet did Frankfurter shift or stay constant?

Frankfurter's evolution is driven by numerous cases where he is in dissent with Justices Black and Douglas. But the dichotomization by SCDB into majority versus minority positions overlooks critical differences between their positions on several cases. In *Adler v. Board of Educ. of City of New York*, 342 U.S. 485 (1952), for instance, the majority upheld a state law making a member of a subversive organization ineligible for public school employment. To be sure, Frankfurter, Black, and Douglas dissented. But on very different grounds. Frankfurter dissented on the grounds that the case in not justiciable. Black and Douglas, on the other hand, dissented on the merits, finding that the state law violated the First Amendment.

The ideal point evolution of Frankfurter to the left may hence be partly an artifact of failure by SCDB voting data to distinguish distinct jurisprudential decisions, for example, Frankfurter's judicial restraint is mistaken for a merits decision in *Adler* and in two other due process cases, *Burns v. Wilson*, 346 U.S. 137 (1953) and *Garner v. Board of Public Works of City of Los Angeles*, 341 U.S. 716 (1951). The way forward would be to develop a better way to distinguish and classify these types of positions taken by judges. It is perhaps not a surprise that by aggregating and dichotomizing complex decisions, scholars have been limited in capturing other dimensions of decision-making.

On the other hand, in ten of thirteen due process cases, Frankfurter dissented on the merits with Douglas and Black. While this defies one historical view of Frankfurter's increasingly conservative role on the Court (see, e.g., Domnarski 2006: 69; Urofsky 1991: 94–5), there are reasons to believe the dynamic model over the static one. First, Domnarski (2006) notes that "with the new, more conservative Truman appointees of Clark, Minton, Vinson, and Burton, Frankfurter became by contrast more liberal and dissented in a number of important cases" (p. 68), particularly with his rivals Douglas and Black.[11] Second, Justice Jackson also increasingly voted on the merits with Douglas and Black in due process cases, but only starting in the early 1950s (i.e., not immediately after Nuremberg).[12]

While there is hence suggestive evidence that Jackson diverged in due process cases, the inference depends critically on better measurement of due process cases and qualitatively grounding identification assumptions.

Nonetheless, the broad evidence provides support for the view that Jackson's jurisprudence was at its core altered after Nuremberg.

Conclusion

Our study of Jackson has illustrated the virtues and limitations of measurement methods. While such approaches have the virtue of formalizing what other scholars are already engaged in when counting cases, the approach cannot displace more detailed study of case law. For instance, this approach tells us little about the mechanism that could have driven Jackson's change. An alternative hypothesis, for instance, is that Jackson changed not because of Nuremberg, but because he had been passed over for the position of Chief Justice at the same time. Our voting results complement and inform, rather than substitute for, the qualitative historical literature on Jackson.

Although measurement technology has invigorated the study of judicial politics, the next generation of work cannot proceed by technology alone. As Epstein et al. (2007b) described research on the judicial hierarchy, the field remains "theory rich and data poor." The path forward involves jurisprudentially meaningful issue coding, tailored to voting disagreement in a case, coupled with advances in measurement technology.

Put differently by Pritchett: "There is no method by which an IBM machine can be used as a substitute for scholarship" alone (Pritchett 1954: 189 (quoting John P. Frank 1948)).

Technical Appendix

Let J denote the set of judges and K the set of cases, the voting data **Y** is comprised of:

$$y_{jk} = \begin{cases} 0 & \text{if } j \text{ voted in the minority on } k \\ 1 & \text{if } j \text{ voted in the majority on } k \\ \text{missing} & \text{if } j \text{ did not vote on } k \end{cases}$$

The probability of a judicial vote for the majority is conventionally modeled via a probit link:

$$P\left(y_{jk}=1\right)=\Phi\left(-\alpha_k+\beta_K\theta_{jt}\right) \quad j\in J,\ \ k\in K$$

where $\Phi(\cdot)$ is the standard normal CDF and t represents the term in which case k was decided.[13] The probability of a majority vote thereby depends on three latent (unobserved) parameters:

1. $\boldsymbol{\alpha}$, which can be roughly thought of as the dissent parameter (in IRT terms, the "item difficulty" parameter), modeling how much dissensus a case will generate;
2. $\boldsymbol{\beta}$, which can be thought of as the valence parameter (in IRT terms, the "item discrimination" parameter), modeling how much dissent is driven by a common underlying dimension; and
3. $\boldsymbol{\theta}$, which captures the position of the justices in the common dimension (often times referred to as the ideal point), which may, but does not necessarily, vary by term.

The sampling density can then be written as:

$$p(\mathrm{Y} \mid \alpha, \beta, \theta) \propto \prod_{k \in K} \prod_{j \in J} \Phi\,(-\alpha_k + \beta_k \theta_{jt})^{y_{jk}} \left[1 - f\ \left(-\alpha_k + \beta_k \theta_{jt}\right)\right]^{(1-y_{jk})}$$

with $J_k = \{j \in J\colon y_{jk} \neq missing\}$ representing the set of justices participating on case k. The point at which $P(y_{jk} = 1) = 0.5$ is often referred to as the cutpoint, namely the location that divides the majority and the minority in a case (and is a simple function of the dissent and valence parameters: $\frac{\alpha_k}{\beta_k}$).

Measurement methods jointly estimate the parameters ($\boldsymbol{\alpha}$, $\boldsymbol{\beta}$, and $\boldsymbol{\theta}$). To fit the model in a fully Bayesian framework, prior distributions on the parameters are required. The priors for $\boldsymbol{\theta}$ are that:

$$\theta_{j0} \overset{\text{iid}}{\sim} \mathcal{N}(0,1).$$

which reflect prior "ignorance" about the justice locations at the time of appointment, and, in conjunction with priors on $\boldsymbol{\alpha}$ and $\boldsymbol{\beta}$, determine the cardinal scale of the common dimension. To allow for viewpoints to change, θ_{jt} may follow a Gaussian random walk in time:

$$\theta_{jt} \overset{ind}{\sim} \mathcal{N}\left(\theta_{j(t-1)}, \tau_j^2\right)$$

The "smoothness" of the walk is determined by $\boldsymbol{\tau}$, which follows an inverse gamma distribution with parameters c_j and d_j setting the prior mean and variance:

$$\tau_j^2 \overset{ind}{\sim} \mathcal{IG}\left(c_j / 2, d_j / 2\right).$$

The parameters c_j and d_j are determined a priori by the researcher, with lower (higher) values corresponding to less (more) variability over terms. Martin and Quinn (2002) were the first to generalize the model to allow for evolving ideal points, often now dubbed the Martin-Quinn scores.[14] When $\tau_j = 0\, \forall\, j$, the ideal points are "static" for each justice, converging to the model by Clinton et al. (2004). Greater values of τ (as determined by c_j and d_j) allow for more term-by-term variability.

The priors for $\boldsymbol{\alpha}$ and $\boldsymbol{\beta}$ reflect prior "ignorance" about the cases:[15]

$$\alpha_k \overset{iid}{\sim} \mathcal{N}(0,5),\ k \in K$$

$$\beta_k \overset{iid}{\sim} \mathcal{N}(0,5),\ k \in K$$

These classes of models can be fit using Markov Chain Monte Carlo methods, as in the MCMC-pack implementation in the R programming language (Martin and Quinn 2013).

Notes

1. We thank Nick Parrillo for encouraging us to study Justice Jackson, Aubrey Jones for outstanding research assistance, and Rebecca Morris for helpful comments. Many of the ideas (but none of the errors) are drawn from joint work with Ho's long-time collaborator Kevin Quinn.
2. The only study deploying measurement techniques coming close to the question about Jackson is Epstein et al. (2007a), which notes that Jackson's jurisprudence trended to the right over time. Epstein et al., however, did not specifically address the question about Nuremberg's effect on Jackson, presenting aggregate results on ideological drift across all justices serving from 1937–2005.
3. With a sample of $M = 1{,}000$ draws of θ from the posterior distribution, each simulated draw denoted by θ^m, the quantity can be readily calculated by:

$$P\left(\theta_{j1} > \theta_{i1}\right) \approx \frac{1}{M}\sum_{m=1}^{M}\Pi\left(\theta_{j1}^{m} > \theta_{i1}^{m}\right).$$

4. These are based on citation counts in Google Scholar from September 2015.
5. See also Ho and Quinn (2008) (finding that close decisions are far more likely to be covered by newspaper editorials).
6. See, e.g., *Terminiello*, 337 U.S. 1 (1949); *Shaughnessy v. Mezei*, 345 U.S. 206 (1953); *Dennis v. United States*, 341 U.S. 494 (1941); *Kunz v. New York*, 340 U.S. 290 (1951).
7. In the terminology of SCDB, these were the "issueArea" and "lawSupp" codes.
8. Incorporation, for instance, obviously happens via the due process clause. The Jackson scholarship does not define these categories in exhaustive and mutually exclusive ways.
9. More ideal would be a data collection process closer to that of Ho and Ross (2010).
10. We were unable to establish a pattern between Schubert's classification system and other classification systems, such as Westlaw's Key Numbers or the United States Supreme Court Database. This makes sense because Schubert admits that his classification system does not "correspond to those employed by constitutional law scholars" (Schubert 1959: 159).
11. This is potentially an example of bridging sensitivity.
12. Relatively little scholarship exists on Reed. See Note (1949).
13. A logistic link could alternatively also be used.
14. See also Bailey (2007) (developing a parametric approach to modeling moving ideal points).
15. Ho and Quinn (2010a) develop an alternate parameterization, assuming (α_k, β_k) to be independently drawn from a uniform distribution on the region $\left\{\alpha_k, \beta_k : \alpha_k \in [-4,4], \beta_k \in [-2,2], \alpha_k / \beta_k \in [-2,2]\right\}$. This has the convenient interpretation that the prior on the cutpoints dividing the majority and minority in a case are a uniform distribution.

References

Abraham, H. J. 1999. *Justices, Presidents, and Senators: A History of the US Supreme Court Appointments from Washington to Clinton*. Lanham, MD: Rowman & Littlefield.

Alarie, B. R. D., and Green, A. 2007. "The Reasonable Justice: An Empirical Analysis of Frank Iacobucci's Career on the Supreme Court of Canada." *University of Toronto Law Journal* 57(2): 195–226.

Bafumi, J., Gelman, A., Park D. P., and Kaplan, N. 2005. "Practical Issues in Implementing and Understanding Bayesian Ideal Point Estimation." *Political Analysis* 13(2): 171–87.

Bailey, M., and Chang, K. H. 2001. "Comparing Presidents, Senators, and Justices." *Journal of Law, Economics, & Organization* 17: 477–506.

Bailey, M. A. 2007. "Comparable Preference Estimates across Time and Institutions for the Court, Congress, and Presidency." *American Journal of Political Science* 51(3): 433–48.

Black, R. C., and Boyd, C. L. 2012. "US Supreme Court Agenda Setting and the Role of Litigant Status." *Journal of Law, Economics, & Organization* 28(2): 286–312.

Bonica, A., and Woodruff, M. J. 2015. "A Common-Space Measure of State Supreme Court Ideology." *Journal of Law, Economics, & Organization* 31(3): 472–98.

Carrubba, C., Friedman, B., Martin, A. D., and Vanberg, G. 2012. "Who Controls the Content of Supreme Court Opinions?" *American Journal of Political Science* 56(2): 400–12.

Clark, T. S. 2009. "Measuring Ideological Polarization on the United States Supreme Court." *Political Research Quarterly* 62(1): 146–57.

Clark, T. S., and Lauderdale, B. 2010. "Locating Supreme Court Opinions in Doctrine Space." *American Journal of Political Science* 54(4): 871–90.

Clinton, J. D., Jackman, S., and Rivers, D. 2004. "The Statistical Analysis of Roll Call Data." *American Political Science Review* 98: 355–70.

Cushman, B. 1998. *Rethinking the New Deal Court*. New York, NY: Oxford University Press.

Domnarski, W. 2006. *The Great Justices, 1941–54: Black, Douglas, Frankfurter, and Jackson in Chambers*. Ann Arbor, MI: University of Michigan Press.

Dunworth, A., Fischman, J., and Ho, D. E. 2009. "Policy Voting: What Amici Tell Us about Law." *Unpublished Manuscript*.

Epstein, L., and Jacobi, T. 2008. "Super Medians." *Stanford Law Review* 61(1): 37–99.

Epstein, L., and Martin, A. D. 2010. "Does Public Opinion Influence the Supreme Court—Possibly Yes (But We're Not Sure Why)." *University of Pennsylvania Journal of Constitutional Law* 13: 263–81.

Epstein, L., Martin, A. D., Quinn, K. M., and Segal, J. A. 2007a. "Ideological Drift among Supreme Court Justices: Who, When, and How Important." *Northwestern University Law Review* 101: 1483–542.

Epstein, L., Martin, A. D., Segal, J. A., and Westerland, C. 2007b. "The Judicial Common Space." *Journal of Law, Economics, & Organization* 23(2): 303–25.

Epstein, L., and Mershon, C. 1996. "Measuring Political Preferences." *Annual Review of Political Science* 40: 261–94.

Epstein, L., and Segal, J. A. 2006. "Trumping the First Amendment." *Washington University Journal of Law and Policy* 21: 81–121.

Fischman, J. B. 2011. "Estimating Preferences of Circuit Judges: A Model of Consensus Voting." *Journal of Law, Economics, & Organization* 54(4): 781–809.

Frank, J. P. 1950. "The United States Supreme Court: 1949–1950." *University of Chicago Law Review* 18(1): 1–54.

Frankfurter, F. 1955. Foreword. *Columbia Law Review* 55(4): 435–7.

Freund, P. A. 1955. "Individual and Commonwealth in the Thought of Mr. Justice Jackson." *Stanford Law Review* 8: 9–25.

Friedman, B. 2009. *The Will of the People: How Public Opinion Has Influenced the Supreme Court and Shaped the Meaning of the Constitution*. New York, NY: Farrar, Straus and Giroux.

Gergen, M. P., and Quinn, K. M. 2012. "Common Law Judicial Decision Making: The Case of the New York Court of Appeals 1900–1941." *Buffalo Law Review* 60: 897–1002.

Giles, M. W., Hettinger, V. A., and Peppers, T. 2001. "Picking Federal Judges: A Note on Policy and Partisan Selection Agendas." *Political Research Quarterly* 54(3): 623–41.

Gustafson, P. 2003. *Measurement Error and Misclassification in Statistics and Epidemiology: Impact and Bayesian Adjustments*. Boca Raton, FL: CRC.

Harvey, A., and Friedman B. 2009. "Ducking Trouble: Congressionally Induced Selection Bias in the Supreme Court's Agenda." *Journal of Politics* 72(2): 574–92.

Harvey, A., and Woodruff, M. 2013. "Confirmation Bias in the United States Supreme Court Judicial Database." *Journal of Law, Economics, & Organization* 29(2): 414–60.

Heckman, J. J., and Snyder J. M. 1997. "Linear Probability Models of the Demand for Attributes with an Empirical Application to Estimating the Preferences of Legislators." *RAND Journal of Economics* 28: S142–89.

Ho, D. E., and Quinn, K. M. 2008. "Measuring Explicitly Political Positions of Media." *Quarterly Journal of Political Science* 3: 353–77.

Ho, D. E., and Quinn, K. M. 2010a. "Did a Switch in Time Save Nine?" *Journal of Legal Analysis* 2: 1–45.

Ho, D. E., and Quinn, K. M. 2010b. "How Not to Lie with Judicial Votes: Misconceptions, Measurement, and Models." *California Law Review* 98: 813–76.

Ho, D. E., and Ross, E. L. 2010. "Did Liberal Justices Invent the Standing Doctrine? An Empirical Study of the Evolution of Standing, 1921–2006." *Stanford Law Review* 62: 591–668.

Hockett, J. D. 1990. "Justice Robert H. Jackson, the Supreme Court, and the Nuremberg Trial." *Supreme Court Review* 1990: 257–99.

Hockett, J. D. 1996. *New Deal Justice: The Constitutional Jurisprudence of Hugo L. Black, Felix Frankfurter, and Robert H. Jackson*. Lanham, MD: Rowman & Littlefield.

Hutchinson, D. J. 1996. "Justice Jackson and the Nuremberg Trials." *Journal of Supreme Court History* 21(1): 105–16.

Jackman, S. 2001. "Multidimensional Analysis of Roll Call Data via Bayesian Simulation: Identification, Estimation, Inference, and Model Checking." *Political Analysis* 9(3): 227–41.

Jackson, R. H. 1955. "The Reminiscences of Robert H. Jackson." Interviews conducted in 1952 and 1953 by Harlan B. Phillips. Oral History Research Office, Butler Library, Columbia University, NY.

Jaffe, L. L. 1955. "Mr. Justice Jackson." *Harvard Law Review* 68(6): 940–98.

Lauderdale, B. E., and Clark, T. S. 2012. "The Supreme Court's Many Median Justices." *American Political Science Review* 106(4): 847–66.

Lauderdale, B. E., and Clark, T. S. 2014. "Who Controls Opinion Content? Testing Theories of Authorship Using Case-Specific Preference Estimates for the US Supreme Court." Unpublished manuscript.

Law, D. S. 2004. "Strategic Judicial Lawmaking: An Empirical Investigation of Ideology and Publication on the US Court of Appeals for the Ninth Circuit." *University of Cincinnati Law Review* 73: 817–66.

Lax, J. R. 2011. "The New Judicial Politics of Legal Doctrine." *Annual Review of Political Science* 14: 131–57.

Lindquist, S. A., and Klein, D. E. 2006. "The Influence of Jurisprudential Considerations on Supreme Court Decisionmaking: A Study of Conflict Cases." *Law & Society Review* 40(1): 135–62.

Malhotra, N., and Jessee, S. A. 2014. "Ideological Proximity and Support for the Supreme Court." *Political Behavior* 36: 1–30.

Martin, A. D., and Quinn, K. M. 2002. "Dynamic Ideal Point Estimation via Markov Chain Monte Carlo for the U.S. Supreme Court, 1953–1999." *Political Analysis* 10: 134–53.

Martin, A. D., and Quinn, K. M. 2013. *MCMCpack: Markov Chain Monte Carlo (MCMC) Package*. R package version 1.3-4.

Martin, A. D., Quinn, K. M., and Epstein, L. 2004. "The Median Justice on the United States Supreme Court." *North Carolina Law Review* 83: 1275–322.

Note. 1949. "Mr. Justice Reed: Swing Man or Not?" *Stanford Law Review* 1(4): 714–29.

Poole, K. T., and Rosenthal, H. 1985. "A Spatial Model for Legislative Roll Call Analysis." *American Journal of Political Science* 29: 357–84.

Poole, K. T., and Rosenthal, H. 1991. "Patterns of Congressional Voting." *American Journal of Political Science* 35(February): 228–78.

Poole, K. T., and Rosenthal, H. 1997. *Congress: A Political-Economy History of Roll Call Voting*. New York, NY: Oxford University Press.

Pritchett, C. H. 1954. *Civil Liberties and the Vinson Court*. Chicago, IL: University of Chicago Press.

Quinn, K. M. 2004. "Bayesian Factor Analysis for Mixed Ordinal and Continuous Responses." *Political Analysis* 12(4): 338–53.

Raso, C. N., and Eskridge, W. N. 2010. "Chevron as a Canon, Not a Precedent: An Empirical Study of What Motivates Justices in Agency Deference Cases." *Columbia Law Review* 110: 1727–817.

Ray, L. K. 1995. "A Law Clerk and his Justice: What William Rehnquist Did Not Learn from Robert Jackson." *Indiana Law Review* 29: 535–92.

Rodell, F. 1955. *Nine Men: A Political History of the Supreme Court from 1790 to 1955*. New York, NY: Random House.

Sag, M., Jacobi, T., and Sytch, M. 2009. "Ideology and Exceptionalism in Intellectual Property: An Empirical Study." *California Law Review* 97(3): 801–56.

Sala, B. R., and Spriggs, J. F. 2004. "Designing Tests of the Supreme Court and the Separation of Powers." *Political Research Quarterly* 57(2): 197–208.

Schubert, G. 1959. *Quantitative Analysis of Judicial Behavior*. Glencoe, IL: Free Press.

Schubert, G. 1965. "Jackson's Judicial Philosophy: An Exploration in Value Analysis." *American Political Science Review* 59(4): 940–63.

Segal, J. A., and Cover, A. D. 1989. "Ideological Values and the Votes of U.S. Supreme Court Justices." *American Political Science Review* 83: 557–65.

Staudt, N., Friedman, B., and Epstein, L. 2007. "On the Role of Ideological Homogeneity in Generating Consequential Constitutional Decisions." *University of Pennsylvania Journal of Constitutional Law* 10(2): 361–86.

Urofsky, M. 1991. "Conflict among the Brethren: Felix Frankfurter, William O. Douglas, and the Clash of Personalities and Philosophies on the United States Supreme Court." *Duke Law Journal* 1: 71–113.

Westerland, C., Segal, J. A., Cameron, C. M., and Comparato, S. 2010. "Strategic Defiance and Compliance in the US Court of Appeals." *American Journal of Political Science* 54(4): 891–905.
White, G. E. 2005. "Constitutional Change and the New Deal: The Internalist/Externalist Debate." *American Historical Review* 110: 1094–115.

Cases Cited

Adler v. Board of Educ. of City of New York, 342 U.S. 428 (1952).
Burns v. Wilson, 346 U.S. 137 (1953).
Garner v. Board of Public Works of City of Los Angeles, 341 U.S. 716 (1951).
West Virginia State Board of Education v. Barnette, 319 U.S. 624 (1943).

CHAPTER 27

THE USE OF OBSERVATIONAL DATA TO STUDY LAW AND THE JUDICIARY

SARA C. BENESH

THE subfield of political science that focuses on the courts has, for quite some time, been fairly self-conscious about what it ought to be and whether or not the scientific study of courts is either possible or advisable (see, e.g., Louthan 1973; Maveety 2003). In this chapter, I consider the evolution of the field formerly known as public law[1] in order to trace the influence of multi-user databases on the field. After the behavioral revolution, data becomes indispensable. Although many of the pioneers of judicial research started to employ quantitative measures of judicial decisions decades ago, it was only when reliable and publicly available data sets became available that the scientific study of the courts ignited. The continued importance of multi-user, publicly available data sets to both quantitative and more traditional legal scholars confirms the substantial influence of Harold J. Spaeth's database and its progeny. I spend some time focusing on that particular source of data and its critics and its impacts before concluding that the very essence of "public law" as a scientific discipline is due to its reliance on empirical methods to answer important, theoretically driven questions, and the Spaeth database and others like it have been essential to the field's development into a political science of judging. True also, though, that qualitative accounts of judicial behavior have also greatly benefitted from the empirical account of judging made possible by the databases.

A BRIEF HISTORY OF THE DISCIPLINE

Pritchett argues that before 1948, "political scientists were not doing research on the judiciary. They were studying constitutional law. They were reading judicial decisions. They were reconstructing judicial philosophies out of the written opinions of members of the Supreme Court … But a concern with the judiciary as a functioning part of the political system, related to other political institutions and processes, had not been developed" (Pritchett 1969: 27, as quoted in Louthan 1973: 89). More history or legal analysis than political science, this traditional way of studying courts, though very dearly held by many in the discipline (see, e.g., Mendelson 1964), began to strain credulity when the Court started behaving in a much more political manner (see, e.g., Schubert 1966), and many members of the discipline saw that analyses like these were unnecessarily distancing the study of courts from the rest of social science in general and political science in particular (Peltason 1953). Hence, dating as far back as 1953, scholars argued for a more mainstream political science approach to judging, treating judges' decisions similarly to decisions made by other political actors, given that they, like other political actors, are subject to a variety of influences and make decisions that allocate power (Peltason 1953). Peltason argued, "if we turn our attention to the judiciary as a facet in the group struggle and relate the activities of judges to that of other groups, we can begin to develop a political science of public law without trying to 'out-history' the historians, 'out-law' the lawyer, or 'out-psychology' the psychologist" (p. 56). This call for a focus on the scientific study of judging seems ahead of its time, for, while it comes years after Pritchett's masterful analysis of the Roosevelt Court (Pritchett 1948), it would be many years more before Glendon Schubert began to strongly make the argument for empirically studying decisions and their causes (Schubert 1958). Indeed, the reaction to Schubert's argument—the bitter controversy surrounding the seemingly common-sense notion that attitudes matter to decision-making, treating such an argument as akin to blasphemy—demonstrates that Peltason's view from 1953 was not widely held.[2]

Is Public Law Political Science?

Given that political science in the United States in many ways began with a concern over issues of public law,[3] it is odd that, at some point, the study of law and courts became something for the lawyers to do; something outside the mainstream of political science. But public law scholars were late to the shift in focus of the behavioralists from normative and descriptive research to behavioral, scientific methods, and much of their early work was published in law journals rather than political science journals (Schubert 1966). As Bond notes, "the beginning of scientific inquiry is the *fact/value dichotomy*" (2007: 899, his emphasis). Legal realism, the behavioral revolution in social science, and the reality of the behavior of the Supreme Court, moved the field along toward a focus on empiricism rather than normativism. Indeed, as the crises surrounding the New Deal played out, no one could continue to ignore the Supreme Court as an integral part of the political system (Schubert 1966). Once scholars started considering the Court as a political institution staffed with political actors, moving from values to facts in Bond's language, scholars of the Court could use the same methods other political scientists were using to study their subject, hence placing the study of courts squarely within the "social sciences rather than with the humanities" (Schubert 1966: 610). Schubert, in 1958, advocated "the analysis of judicial decision-making as an aspect of political behavior," demonstrating the sorts of questions one could ask about judges using experiments, content analysis, and game theory. In that article, he introduces cumulative scaling, an empirical way to measure the agreement among justices and the ideological positions they take in cases (Schubert 1958: 1007). He elaborates on these themes in his very famous book, *Quantitative Analysis of Judicial Behavior* (1959), and many empirical analyses of judicial behavior followed (see, e.g., Nagel 1961; Ulmer 1969; Kort 1966; Spaeth 1964). Still, though, the continued consideration by those studying courts of the institutional constraints on judicial behavior, focused as they were on courts as being "different" from other institutions, put them a bit at odds with the rest of the political science discipline (Maveety 2003). And the field itself had and continues to have a substantial debate over the utility and desirability of quantitative versus qualitative analysis.

Of course, internal debate over the behavioral approach and its lack of consideration for law may have contributed to the increased distance between those who study courts and other political scientists as it drove some in the courts group to whole-heartedly focus on the content of Court decisions, engaging more in doctrinal analysis and normative legal theory, turning other political scientists away from their now less- relevant work (Maveety 2003). Pritchett argued, in 1968, that the behaviorist scholars, who put the political back into the study of the courts and gave the courts community the language and methodology to speak to the rest of political science as a profession, are to be credited for the increase in prestige of the study of courts, but he also hoped that the empirical, behavioral approach would not end up to be the only one accepted by those working in the field.[4]

Rise of Empiricism and the Need for Data

Regardless of the extent to which it succeeded or the capacity it has to succeed, the integration sought of "public law" into the mainstream of the social science discipline of political science relied on behavioralism and, hence, data (Schubert 1966; Pritchett 1968; Grossman and Tannenhaus 1969). "Science requires both theoretical models from which operationalized hypotheses can be inferred and methods for testing such hypotheses with data derived from empirical observations" (Schubert 1966: 600–1). "Behavioralists advocate a scientific approach with the goal of developing systematic theory out of research that has been carefully designed in advance, that operationalizes the relationships among variables, that employs an articulate methodology, and that relies upon quantification and (so far as possible) statistical measurement" (Schubert 1967a: 120). While both Schubert and Pritchett note that quantitative analyses are not the only fruitful way to study courts (Schubert 1967b; Pritchett 1968; Burbank 2011 agrees), Schubert (and later, Djupe and Epstein 1998, and Spaeth and Segal 2000, and Bond 2007, and many others) argue that, to do *science* (or at least something closely related to it) and in order that the study of law and courts become more mainstream within the discipline of political science, one needs to accept quantification "as an indispensable component of empirical scientific inquiry" (Schubert 1968: 420). Systematizing the observation of relevant empirical facts via reliable and replicable data collection is, then, key (Bond 2007).

But, data contained in a systematized set of observations need not be seen merely as a tool for quantitative research, as empirical information continued in such a collection may also be put to good use by qualitative researchers. The next section focuses on the most prevalent such collection: the *Supreme Court Database*, which is widely used by both quantitative and qualitative scholars of the U.S. Supreme Court.

The Spaeth Database

While there are criticisms of the enterprise of collecting observational data in general as well as arguments over the ways in which Spaeth has done so in particular, it is clear that the most frequently used observational data set on law and courts, the *Supreme Court Database*—the Spaeth data, as it is commonly known—has spawned an enormous amount of scholarship and we have learned an inordinate amount because of its availability. It has also influenced similar efforts worldwide, including databases on other courts (see, e.g., the *Songer Database*, the *Auburn Database*, the *State Supreme Court Database*, the *High Courts Database*, and the *U.S. District Courts Database*)[5] and other institutions (see, e.g., the *Comparative Constitutions Project*).[6]

The *Supreme Court Database* began as a bit of hubris on Spaeth's part, as he acknowledges thinking that much of the relatively new empirical research being done on courts was not as good as it could be with better data and that he was just the person to collect and code it (Benesh 2003). He sought and received National Science Foundation funding in 1983, and with continued NSF support, has been able to create, expand, and maintain the data set that colloquially bears his name. The data includes Supreme Court decisions coded for background, chronological, substantive, outcome, and voting/opinion variables (Spaeth and Segal 2000), including citation information, argument and decision dates, issues and legal provisions considered as well as the votes of each justice in the case. The data also codes the background for each case, the reason the Court grants hearing to the case, the litigants to the case and what "type" they are, the legal authority for the Court's decision, and whether the case was decided liberally or conservatively. The data specify the outcome in the case and whether, in deciding the case, the justices overturn precedent or declare a statute to be contrary to the constitution.[7] Using the data, one can ask a variety of questions dealing with the Court's and the justices' behavior as well as obtain rich descriptive data about the Court's and the justices' caseload and history.

While there are criticisms of the data, as detailed later in the chapter, far more scholars praise the collection than denigrate it. Djupe and Epstein (1998) cite the meticulousness of Spaeth's documentation, leading to ease in reproducibility, as well as the data's known reliability, in endorsing the Spaeth data. They demonstrate, in their cross-validation of less transparent author-collected data sets, that something as seemingly inconsequential as the definition of what constitutes a case involving "criminal justice" can have a huge impact on a study's results. Spaeth pays close attention to making all coding decisions eminently clear and it has always been Spaeth's aim to make the decisions he makes as transparent as possible, thereby enabling the analyst to make different decisions if she deems them advisable, including the controversial determination of whether a given case has been decided in a liberal or a conservative direction, discussed in more detail later (Benesh 2003; Spaeth and Segal 2000; Epstein, Knight, and Martin 2003). Ho and Quinn recognize this, urging legal academics to add to the Spaeth database what they see as missing from it.[8] The general availability of the data is of huge service to those seeking to study courts empirically given that they no longer need to spend hours and hours amassing the data to do so, thereby contributing to the movement of public law into a social science of judicial behavior (Epstein, Knight, and Martin 2003). Epstein, Knight, and Martin sought to encourage those in the legal academy to turn to it more frequently as well (2003), and it seems they have been successful.[9] Table 27.1 demonstrates that many citations to the database come in law review articles.[10] Legal academics themselves tout its worth, arguing that the "availability of germane data resides at the heart of empirical legal scholarship," which is seemingly becoming more and more prevalent in law schools (Heise 2003: 826). Data are "the backbone of our knowledge base" (Heise 2003: 829), and "empirical methodologies are well positioned to enhance and complement traditional legal scholarship" (Heise 2003: 849). Shapiro also notes that the availability of the Spaeth data vastly reduces the costs of engaging in that ever-more-important empirical research (2008). But, qualitative researchers may also find much of interest here, and many have, even beyond the legal academy. Only some of the articles cited in Table 27.1 are quantitative analyses of the Supreme Court; quite a few use the database to obtain relevant empirical data used in a qualitative analysis.

Hwong (2004) laments the lack of a similar datasource for other countries, suggesting that more knowledge about his country of interest, Canada, can only be obtained via empirical research, which requires data. Of course, his concern is ameliorated with the release of the aforementioned *High Courts Database*, one of the Spaeth database's progeny.

Be it the legal academy or within political science, in the United States or abroad, this "greatest single resource of data on the Court" (Epstein 2000: 225) has had a huge impact on the field and beyond.

The Impact of the Databases

Epstein (2000: 131) claims that "studies of Supreme Court decision-making nearly always rely on the Spaeth databases for their empirical work," and the front page of the new home of the Database asserts: "In short, the U.S. Supreme Court Database has not

Table 27.1 Citations to the Spaeth database

Books published by:
Cambridge University Press
Lexington Books
Lynne Rienner Publishing
MIT Press
Oxford University Press
Peter Lang
Princeton University Press
Psychology Press
Routledge Press
Springer
State University of New York Press
Susquehanna University Press
Temple University Press
University of Virginia Press
Articles in the following journals:
Law
California Law Review
DePaul Law Review
Duke Law Journal
Hastings Law Journal
Journal of Empirical Legal Studies
Journal of Legal Studies
Saint Louis University Law Review
Stanford Law Review
Supreme Court Economic Review
University of Colorado Law Review
University of Pennsylvania Law Review
Political science
General
American Journal of Political Science
American Political Science Review

(*Continued*)

Table 27.1 Continued

Books published by:
American Politics Research
Annual Review of Political Science
Journal of Political Science
Journal of Politics
Perspectives on Politics
Political Research Quarterly
PS: Political Science & Politics
Southeastern Political Review
Subfield Journals
Journal of Law, Economics, & Organization
Journal of Legal Studies
Judicature
Justice System Journal
Law & Courts
Law & Policy
Law & Social Inquiry
Law & Society Review
Legislative Studies Quarterly
Policy Studies Journal
Political Analysis
Political Communication
Politics & Policy
Publius
Social Networks
Psychology
Journal of Applied Social Psychology
Journal of Business and Psychology
Personality and Social Psychology
Economics
American Economic Review

(*Continued*)

Table 27.1 Continued

Books published by:
Business
Employee Responsibilities and Rights Journal
Criminal justice
American Journal of Criminal Justice
Journal of Contemporary Criminal Justice
Communication
Negotiation and Conflict Management Research
Interdisciplinary
Poetics
Social Science History
Social Science Journal
Public administration
Journal of Public Administration
International
Berghahn Books
European Political Science Review
IEEE International Conference on Acoustics, Speech and Signal Processing
Philippine Political Science Journal
Politikon: South African Journal of Political Studies
Papers presented at the following conferences:
Annual Conference of the American Politics Group
APSA
MPSA
Political Methodology Summer Conference
Public Choice
SPSA
Washington University Ideal Point Estimation Conference
Workshop on Correlated Data
WPSA

Source: Google Scholar search, May 2, 2014 and June 8, 2014

just helped fill gaps in our knowledge. It is one of those rare creatures in the law and social science world: an *invention* that has substantially advanced a large area of study, inspiring research by scholars hailing from no fewer than three and as many as seven disciplines" (Spaeth et al. 2015, emphasis theirs). Benesh (2003) corroborates these assertions via her study of publications from 1991 to 2000 in the top two journals in political science (the *American Political Science Review*, and the *American Journal of Political Science*). Of those articles about law and courts that used some sort of data, Benesh shows that around 80 percent used the Spaeth data. That figure underestimates usage, though, given that the list of articles she cites include studies of public opinion and state supreme courts for which the Spaeth data were obviously irrelevant. She also notes fifty-nine citations to the database in the *Social Science Citation* index as of 2000 (Benesh 2003: 117).

A Google Scholar search similarly demonstrates the pervasiveness of the database, perhaps to an even greater degree: at least 352 studies cite to the database, nearly always because they rely on it for their data (though it is certainly possible that they cite to it to note that it would not be useful or will not be used).[11] However, not all studies that employ the Spaeth data cite it in a way that will get it "counted" by Google Scholar, so that number is also likely an undercount. Indeed, there has not been, until now,[12] any single, clear method to cite to the databases, and many works do so quite casually given how well known the data are. Merely attempting to generate a list of citations demonstrates the wide range in citation formats used by those who wish to attribute something to the database. Add to that problem the fact that there exists more than one database[13] and that the databases have been housed in several different places,[14] and one must consider many different formats in amassing a list of citations. I certainly may have missed some. In my Google Scholar search, I found more than forty-eight independent citation-types that all clearly cite to one of the Spaeth databases. Amassing those citations into a list and then deleting duplicates, I find 352 citations including books, book chapters, peer-reviewed articles, law review articles, conference papers, working papers, and speeches that reference the database, likely because they relied on it for data. This constitutes, in itself, a substantial impact.

However, also evident in that listing of citations is the breadth of influence the database has had. Table 27.1 lists the book publishers and journals that published work citing to the Spaeth data and two things are clear: the best research (research published by the best presses and journals) rely on the data; and, the data has a far reach, well beyond political science and the law, making it quite likely that researchers even far afield are aware of it and have, perhaps, used it. The data have been used in studies in psychology, in analyses of public administration, in criminal justice, economics, business and international research, and studies using the data have been presented at conferences in several different fields. The media has also employed the data to good effect (see, e.g., Liptak 2010). It is surely true that the Spaeth data brought the study of courts into the mainstream of political science—"few law and courts scholars would doubt the valuable insights gained" by data sets like it (Tolley 2013: 7)—but it did so much more than that (and continues to do so), in so many fields.

Criticisms of the Spaeth Database

It is clear, no matter what metric is used, that the Spaeth database has had a far-reaching impact on the scientific study of the Supreme Court.[15] However, no single source of data will be without error nor will any systematic coding scheme be universally applauded, regardless of how carefully it was designed and how meticulously it defines its choices.

One such choice in the Spaeth database is that over the essence of the case: the coding of the "issue" as the Spaeth database labels it. In his codebook, Spaeth advances the explicit expectation that cases are usually, at bottom, about one thing, and so a single issue code is generally preferred, with some exceptions (Spaeth et al. 2015). The issue, according to Spaeth, refers to the subject matter of the controversy, not its legal basis (which is coded as its "legal provision" instead), and the most important issue of the case is the one on which Spaeth focuses (Spaeth et al. 2015). These two decisions—to code the *most important* issue and to focus on the *public policy* rather than the legal basis—are arguably controversial. Ho and Quinn, for example, think the preference for a single issue is overly reductionist and may have resulted in an artifact that we take to be a real finding—that the justices see the cases in a unidimensional space that ideology can fairly readily explain (Ho and Quinn 2010: 852). This is a problem because "the issues less central from a public policy standpoint may precisely present the complex doctrines that defy 'liberal' or 'conservative' classification" (Ho and Quinn 2010: 852).

Shapiro also questions this preference for a single issue code in each case (Shapiro 2008). She argues that the Spaeth coding results in underinclusiveness on issues (especially those she considers to be "legal issues") as well as on legal provisions (the legal basis for the Court's decision) (Shapiro 2008: 490). Because of this underinclusiveness, she argues, the extant findings regarding the prevalence of ideology over legal considerations should be considered with skepticism, especially given that the determination over which issue to code is not as transparent as it could be. While it is likely true that one could add issues to cases in the database, it is not nearly as self-evident that doing so would be a useful addition. And, while Shapiro makes a good point that the determination of the most important issue is, in some ways, "invisible and … based on unarticulated criteria," that determination is likely not very difficult to make in nearly all cases (Shapiro 2008: 511). Most students of the Court have written case briefs in some undergraduate or law course and in so doing have followed a similar process to the one Spaeth follows in identifying the major issue in the case. Shapiro overestimates, I think, the extent to which these decisions are controversial, and underestimates the benefit of having coded the heart of the matter to which the case reaches in order that scholars might use those decisions to understand decision-making, seems substantial. And, it is unclear that Shapiro's implicit assumption in coding more issues—that they are all equally important to understanding of the case outcome—is defensible either. True, a scholar interested in legal doctrine will not get much from the database. However, should a reliable and valid means exist to code legal doctrine (as, e.g., Segal and Howard

2002 attempt do with originalism), scholars may certainly do so, adding those variables to their copy of the database.

Additional criticism, as mentioned earlier, centers on the most-used variables in the database: the outcome variables, which include a liberal/conservative direction variable. Young, for example, argues that coding a decision as liberal or conservative is "put forward as intuitive and non-controversial," while he sees them as problematic and non-obvious and "crude," making a philosophical argument over the definition of liberalism and conservativism and their complexity (Young 2002: 1189). Ho and Quinn assert, "The U.S. Supreme Court Database is a landmark data collection effort, single-handedly responsible for major findings in the study of judicial behavior, yet its directional codings—credible in many instances—can be questionable" (Ho and Quinn 2010: 837). They also advocate a more straightforward outcome variable that just measures, in standing cases for example, whether the Court favors or opposes issuing standing. Stearns further argues that requiring each case outcome to be coded as liberal or conservative may, in fact, be a "self-fulfilling prophecy" given that "the databases were constructed in reference to, and in large part with confidence in, the attitudinal model" (Stearns 2000: 238). It is likely that Harvey and Woodruff would agree, and they go even further, arguing that the coding in the database suffers from confirmation bias given that the choice of which issue to code sometimes drives the ideological direction of the coding (2011). The seriousness of their claim makes a bit more attention to their argument justified.

Comparing the Spaeth directional variable to what they call an "objectively coded outcome variable" (created via the DW-NOMINATE scores of the legislators passing the federal statute at issue in cases involving statutory interpretation, and then categorizing the directionality as the same or different depending on whether the Court overturns or upholds the statute), the authors show that, for the 1980–93 terms, the database codes cases as conservative far more frequently than the statute-based measure does. This is evidence, they argue, that "a coder's expectations about how the justices' preferences affect case outcomes may be biasing that coder's issue coding decisions" which, in turn, affects the directionality coded for the case. In other words, Harvey and Woodruff charge that the coders (in all of the instances they consider, Spaeth himself) choose an issue that comports with the ideological direction he expects a given Court to rule in rather than the equally acceptable issue code he could have used that would have produced the opposite outcome (Harvey and Woodruff 2011). Again, this is a hefty charge, and it strains credulity given the systematic coding process described in the documentation used by Spaeth at this time. In addition, it is unclear why an ideology measure that is, when a statute is overturned, merely the opposite of the Congressional ideology of those voting in favor of a bill is somehow better or value-free. While I agree with them over the *FTC* v. *SCTLA* (493 U.S. 411) case they cite (e.g., that it is more of an antitrust than a free speech case, which would, in fact, reverse the direction from conservative to liberal), one error does not an argument make. Indeed, in considering the list of cases the authors use in making their argument, I find that in nearly every instance, the Spaeth coding was eminently reasonable and the outcome measure used by the authors—the extent to which Democrats voted in favor of the statute at issue and the Court's action on the statute—severely wanting. While I address their claims more specifically elsewhere,[16] for now, a few examples suffice to demonstrate the problems with their argument.

In *Hannah v. Larche* (363 U.S. 420), the procedures of the Federal Commission on Civil Rights are in question, given that it does not allow for confrontation of witnesses. The database codes this as a due process case and codes the outcome as conservative, as the Court finds that confrontation is not necessary to due process in hearings conducted by this particular body. Harvey and Woodruff assert that this ought to have been coded as a liberal outcome given that the law at issue is a liberal one and the Court does not overturn it (2011). True, the creation of the Commission was the result of Democratic legislation, but that it does not protect some rights of those who come before the commission is not a typically "liberal" position.

Similarly, a classically liberal law, the Social Security Act (SSA), is at issue in *Flemming v. Nestor* (363 U.S. 603), where the Court upholds the termination of old-age benefits to the plaintiff, deported due to membership in the Communist Party. Harvey and Woodruff would consider this decision, which upholds the constitutionality of the SSA, to be a liberal one. It is surely true that more Democrats than Republicans voted for the SSA, but the inclusion of these anti-communist measures was possibly a compromise or possibly a product of the times, and a decision upholding the exclusion of benefits due to Communist Party members is surely not a liberal decision, even if the statute itself was favored by Democrats. Passage of a statute and its application are two very different things, and Spaeth rightly considers the application of the statute to a given situation, as does the Court. In addition, considering an entire statute--every single provision—to have the same ideological direction as the statute as a whole (as measured by yea votes on the full measure), may be too much. When Spaeth codes case outcomes as liberal or conservative, as discussed earlier, many argue his measure is too blunt. However, court cases have a clear winner and a clear loser. When Harvey and Woodruff rely on the votes of legislators on a piece of legislation as a whole and the Court's treatment of that legislation in its entirety, it is far grosser, ignoring as it does the many facets of any given piece of legislation and the many reasons for their inclusion. In addition, it counts the Court's decision as opposite only when the Court takes the relatively extraordinary step of overturning it (Keith 2007). I do not see this as an improvement over the Spaeth model. (There are many more examples of this sort of problem among the cases they consider to be wrongly coded by Spaeth.)

Even when a particular law is arguably correctly labeled, as a whole, as liberal or conservative, the Court's decision overturning a portion of it, referencing as it does a particular application of the statute, is not necessarily its ideological opposite. Consider *U.S. v. Freed* (401 U.S. 601). The National Firearms Act is probably correctly considered to be a liberal piece of legislation. But, in this case, the Court upheld it, but made a conservative decision—that the registration requirements it imposed on transfers did not constitute self-incrimination. A decision against an accused is rightly considered to be conservative, and that case is coded as such by Spaeth. The application of the law, in this case, limits the rights of those accused of a particular crime. There are many examples like this in the Harvey and Woodruff list as well. But it should not be surprising when a prior, liberal Congress passes legislation that is later limited in its application by a conservative Supreme Court. This is not unlike what happened after *Miranda v. Arizona* (384 U.S. 436). I doubt we would code a case like *Rhode Island v. Innis* (446 U.S. 291), which came after *Miranda* and was decided considering the precedent in *Miranda* as a liberally decided case merely because it didn't overturn *Miranda*. Why should we do so when it comes to statutes enacted by Democrats (or Republicans facing a liberal Court)?

There are instances as well where Harvey and Woodruff ascribe directionality to a statute that likely doesn't have one (the statute creating the Postal Service, in *USPS v. Council of Greenburgh*, 453 U.S. 114, for example) or ascribe a directionality to a nearly unanimously approved statute (the Victims of Crime Act, at issue in *U.S. v. Munoz-Florez*, 495 U.S. 385). Indeed, in *Munoz-Florez*, the claim of confirmation bias is particularly difficult to sustain given that Spaeth might have coded this case, in which a judge sentences a defendant to make a contribution to the Crime Victims Fund because he committed a federal misdemeanor (aiding illegal alien entry), as a criminal case (either involving financial statutory interpretation or sentencing), but instead chose the arguably better federal taxation code, given that the question was whether this forced contribution amounted to a tax and was hence unconstitutional under the Origination Clause, leading him to a liberal rather than conservative outcome for the conservative Rehnquist Court.

Indeed, the argument that many of the issue codes are equally viable for a given case is inconsistent with the database's focus, however amenable to criticism, on the *most important* issue. Surely one could not argue that the number of issues that could *plausibly* be considered to be the *most important* at issue in a given case is very large. Consider *FTC v. Superior Court*, 493 US. 411, concerning a lawyer boycott due to low compensation for court-appointed counsel. The FTC charged the lawyers with price-fixing and violating the Sherman Act, while the lawyers argued that they ought to be exempted from such a charge given the expressive content of their boycott. The Court found that the actions by the lawyers violated the Sherman Act as it was aimed more at economic benefits than at free expression. One could plausibly code this case as involving attorney compensation or antitrust, but isn't the crux of the issue really whether or not the Court saw the boycott as expressive? That expression, and not the Sherman Act, is what Spaeth codes as the most important issue, making the case one decided in a conservative direction.

Given the above, I see the confirmation bias claim as unsubstantiated. As a side note, given the new format of the database and the interface used to code cases, wherein separate coders focus on the issue/direction and the voting coalitions (such that the issue/direction coders do not consider the opinion author in any conscious, systematic way), a claim of confirmation bias will become even more incredible.

Even after all of these criticisms, though, there is still an easy fix for any who quibble with the coding Spaeth employed: change it. Those who deem certain coding rules to be problematic can recode those variables. Those who deem the database to exclude important information can add it. As noted earlier, Spaeth has always been very vocal about the database's customizability. The decision rules are clear. If one dislikes them, one can alter them. The coding in the Database is but a foundation for others to build upon and modify, with fullest blessings from its creator. Indeed, its transparency and adaptability is part of its beauty.

Studying Courts Using Data

The study of courts has been tremendously advanced via the availability of data, key to an empirical, scientific analysis of the decision-making of the political actors that make up the judiciary. Data availability has also enabled a rich and complete description of its work. While no database containing observational data will ever be perfect, the substantial contributions made to the knowledge base on judicial behavior of the Spaeth data cannot be ignored, nor can the contributions of the Spaeth database's progeny (including the *Songer Database*,[17] the Brace and Hall *State Supreme Court Database*,[18] the *National High Courts Database*,[19] and the *U.S. District Court Database*)[20] be overstated.[21] The *Songer Database*, for example, has revolutionized the study of the intermediate appellate courts in the federal system, providing the opportunity for scholars to learn about and test hypotheses about circuit judge behavior in a way that was impossible before it existed (Hurtwitz and Kuersten 2012). And again, not only is it the case that quantitative research has flourished as a result, but we also know more factual information about the Courts of Appeals than ever before, driving further research and analysis (see, Songer, Sheehan, and Haire 2000).[22] And without the systematic use of observational data in empirical scholarship, the *science* in political science would be suspect. Certainly, one can study courts in a variety of ways and historical, institutional, biographical, and doctrinal work should be supported and continued (and, indeed, can and does also benefit from the contents of these databases). But if we want to study courts as another political institution in the way of a political scientist, even if we wish to treat it as somehow special, we need observational data.[23] Lucky for us, the Spaeth data are available, current, valid, reliable, inclusive, and easier to use than ever before, and its progeny continue to grow.[24] Indeed, the Spaeth database itself is expanding, being backdated so that we have reliable data going back to the earliest Courts, enabling us to learn even more than we have already. Continuing on this path of expanding the data is an important goal, and, like Epstein, Knight, and Martin (2003), Ho and Quinn (2010), and Stearns (2000), I am hopeful that ever more aspects of judicial decision-making will be coded and made available for analysis[25] so that we can learn more, in a rigorous and systematic way, about the myriad influences on judicial decision-making.

Notes

1. I say formerly because, generally speaking, those studying courts in political science departments today label their field "judicial behavior" or "judicial politics" or "law and courts." As Maveety notes, there was much hand-wringing surrounding the movement away from the public law label, which referred to the distinction between private lawsuits and those between an individual and the government, though many position descriptions still use it (Maveety 2003: 3).

2. See Benesh (2003) for a discussion of a particularly heated exchange at a conference in 1960, as told through letters between Harold Spaeth and Glendon Schubert.
3. As Schubert (1966) and Maveety (2003) discuss, many of the first "political science" departments had their genesis in public law. For example, Columbia created the first School of Political Science in 1880 when Theodore Dwight and John Burgess could not agree over whether or not public law ought to be taught in a law school. Most of the early courses in the school were offered by professors with joint appointments with the law school and centered around law. (Students in the department also took courses from history and economics.) The scholars affiliated with this School and those affiliated with the department of politics at Princeton, another early program, envisioned a descriptive, yet empirical, but also normative study of politics and government based on the German model (Maveety 2003). Scholars coming later were more interested in a "behavioral, functionalist, and 'scientific' approach" (Maveety 2003: 2).
4. He ends his 1968 article with a quote many considering the history and development of the field of law and courts have used: "Let a hundred flowers bloom" (p. 509). Just before that, Pritchett says, "Hopefully the field of public law ... will remain catholic enough to accommodate those political scientists who continue to find interest in the data of constitutional history, judicial biography, jurisprudence, the philosophies of judges, and commentaries on Supreme Court decisions. There are both traditionalists and behaviorists who think that the gate is strait and the way narrow into the public law kingdom, but a more sensible text for all to contemplate is the old Chinese saying, 'Let a hundred flowers bloom'" (Pritchett 1968: 509).
5. The *U.S. District Court Database* will be made available very soon at the Inter-University Consortium for Political and Social Research at the University of Michigan.
6. Formal citations for all of these databases are in the references.
7. See Spaeth and Segal 2000 for more detail, or visit the database's new home at supremecourtdatabase.org.
8. Ho and Quinn (2010) argue that "clear conceptions of legal doctrine" (2010: 852) are missing from the database, and, while it is mostly true that Spaeth does not code various legal arguments, Ho and Quinn do seemingly miss the contributions of the individual-level databases, when they suggest that legal academics might also add more "jurisprudentially meaningful data" on the reasons for, for example, disagreement among the justices (2010: 853). By focusing on the individual justices and their opinions, the individual-level database would indeed demonstrate, for example, whether dissents were over the same issues or whether, instead, one justice focused on jurisdiction while another focused on the actual substantive issue in the case. See Benesh and Spaeth (2007) for an analysis of a similar question.
9. Epstein and King, in their discussion of replication standards and good empirical work, also point to the database as a way to improve the empirical research of legal academics (Epstein and King 2002).
10. Of course, this citation count may be a substantial undercount given both the tendency for casual citation to the Spaeth databases (discussed below) as well as due to incomplete coverage of law reviews in Google Scholar, at least according to HeinOnline (see http://heinonline.blogspot.com/2009/11/heinonline-or-google-scholar-why-you.html).
11. The search used was "Spaeth Database" and the search was conducted on May 2, 2014 and rechecked via the search "Unites States Supreme Court Database" on June 8, 2014. The numbers reported consider 100 pages of results for each search.

12. The new home for the database, supremecourtdatabase.org, suggests the following citation: Harold J. Spaeth, Lee Epstein, Andrew D. Martin, Jeffrey A. Segal, Theodore J. Ruger, and Sara C. Benesh. 2015. *Supreme Court Database*, Version 2015 Release 01. URL: http://supremecourtdatabase.org. I discuss the new home and all that it adds later in this chapter.
13. There is the big, original database, composed only of decisions on the merits (which used to be called *allcourt*), the one covering only the Vinson and Warren Courts and including conference vote data along with merit voting data (the old *vinwar* data set), the expanded Burger Court database, which adds conference vote data for that Court (*burger*), and the justice-centered databases (called *rehnflpd, burgflpd,* and *warflpd*).
14. First, the data were available via ICPSR at the University of Michigan. Then, the Program for Law and Judicial Politics at Michigan State University housed them. They subsequently moved to the University of Kentucky's Judicial Research Initiative, which itself moved to the University of South Carolina. There is now a link from the Judicial Research Initiative's website to the database's new and permanent home at Washington University in St. Louis, at supremecourtdatabase.org.
15. Some criticize that impact, however, and the degree to which it has limited study of more legally oriented variables, as discussed above. Benesh (2003), for example, considers whether the database may have moved the field into a more single-minded pursuit of quantitative studies, or whether it may have stymied theory-building by making data so readily available.
16. See Benesh, n.d.
17. The *U.S. Appeals Court Database* available online at the Judicial Research Initiative, http://artsandsciences.sc.edu/poli/juri/appct.htm.
18. The *State Supreme Court Data Project* is available online at http://www.ruf.rice.edu/~pbrace/statecourt/.
19. The *National High Courts Database* is also available via the Judicial Research Initiative at the University of South Carolina: http://artsandsciences.sc.edu/poli/juri/highcts.htm.
20. The *U.S. District Courts Database* will soon be housed at the Inter-University Consortium for Political and Social Research at the University of Michigan, https://www.icpsr.umich.edu/icpsrweb/landing.jsp.
21. Many other publicly available data sets exist as well. For one catalogue of them, see Tolley (2013).
22. A series of Google Scholar searches for citations to the "Songer Database" or the "U.S. Courts of Appeals Database" (considering the first ten pages of results) suggests that at least forty-six papers used the data to answers questions about the circuit courts since its inception in the late 1990s. This is most assuredly an undercount given that many known books on the circuit courts that employ the data are not among the search results. It is likely the *Songer Database* suffers from the same lack of agreed-upon citation format as the Spaeth database did.
23. Of course, many would take umbrage at my classification of more qualitative work as something other than science. See Thomas (2006) for a solid argument against mine.
24. Earlier critiques of the database complained about how complicated its structure was, making it far less useful to those less familiar with data analysis and statistical programs (see, e.g., Benesh 2003, Stearns 2000), and Benesh (2006) was written explicitly to help people successfully navigate the choices one needed to make to run analyses that made sense. The new version of the Spaeth database, however, makes all of those issues moot,

as it incorporates better, more user-friendly technology to allow users to explore and run simple analyses on the data online, without downloading it into a statistical package. A given case can be explored without consulting the codebook for what a specific numeric issue code means because the information produced is in words rather than numbers. And records in the Database are linked to the full opinion in the case so checking on coding or exploring particular arguments is extremely easy. Finally, the new homepage offers measures of salience and ideology that are state-of-the-art and easily importable into the Database.

25. Already, legalistic variables have been coded and analyzed in individual research projects. For example, Segal and Howard (2002) code for the use of "originalism" in one paper, and legislative deference in another (2004). Spaeth and Segal attempt to measure the influence of precedent (1999). Richards and Kritzer consider "jurisprudential regimes" (2002) and Bartels (2009) considers levels of scrutiny. Benesh and Spaeth consider case framing as a legal constraint (2007). And, Corley, Howard, and Nixon (2005) consider use of the *Federalist* papers.

References

Bartels, B. 2009. "The Constraining Capacity of Legal Doctrine on the United States Supreme Court." *American Political Science Review* 103(3): 474–95.

Benesh, S. C. 2003. "Harold J. Spaeth: The Supreme Court Computer." In *The Pioneers of Judicial Behavior*, edited by N. Maveety. Ann Arbor, MI: University of Michigan Press.

Benesh, S. C. 2006. "Becoming an Intelligent User of the Spaeth Databases." *Law & Courts* 16(1): 15–21.

Benesh, S. C. n.d. "A Response to Harvey and Woodruff." Manuscript.

Benesh, S. C., and Spaeth, H. J. 2007. "The Constraint of Law: A Study of Supreme Court Dissensus." *American Politics Research* 35: 755–68.

Bond, J. R. 2007. "The Scientification of the Study of Politics: Some Observations on the Behavior Evolution in Political Science." *Journal of Politics* 69(4): 897–907.

Brace, P., and Hall, M. G. 2005. *State Supreme Court Data Project*. Available at: http://www.ruf.rice.edu/~pbrace/statecourt/.

Burbank, S. B. 2011. "On the Study of Judicial Behaviors: Of Law, Politics, Science, and Humanity." In *What's Law Got to Do With It? What Judges Do, Why They Do It, and What's at Stake*, edited by C. G. Geyh. Stanford, CA: Stanford University Press, 41–70.

Corley, P. C., Howard, R. M., and Nixon, D. C. 2005. "The Supreme Court and Opinion Content: The Use of the Federalist Papers." *Political Research Quarterly* 58(2): 329–40.

Djupe, P. A., and Epstein, L. 1998. "From Schubert's *The Judicial Mind* to Spaeth's *U.S. Supreme Court Judicial Data Base*: A Crossvalidation." *American Journal of Political Science* 42(3): 1012–19.

Epstein, L. 2000. "Introduction: Social Science, the Courts, and the Law." *Judicature* 83(5): 224–7.

Epstein, L., and King, G. 2002. "The Rules of Inference." *University of Chicago Law Review* 69: 1–100.

Epstein, L., Knight, J., and Martin, A. D. 2003. "The Political (Science) Context of Judging." *Saint Louis University Law Journal* 47: 783–817.

Grossman, J. B., and Tanenhaus, J. 1969. "Toward a Renascence of Public Law." In *Frontiers of Judicial Research*, edited by J. B. Grossman and J. Tanenhaus. New York, NY: John Wiley and Sons, 3–25.

Harvey, A., and Woodruff, M. J. 2011. "Confirmation Bias in the United States Supreme Court Judicial Database." *Journal of Law, Economics, & Organization* 29(2): 414–60.

Heise, M. 2003. "The Past, Present, and Future of Empirical Legal Scholarship: Judicial Decision Making and the New Empiricism." *University of Illinois Law Review* 2002(4): 819–50.

Ho, D. E., and Quinn, K. M. 2010. "How Not to Lie with Judicial Votes: Misconceptions, Measurement, and Models." *California Law Review* 98: 813–76.

Hurwitz, M. S., and Kuersten, A. 2012. "Changes in the Circuits: Exploring the Courts of Appeals Databases and the Federal Appellate Courts." *Judicature* 96(1): 23–34.

Hwong, T. 2004. "A Review of Quantitative Studies of Decision Making in the Supreme Court of Canada." *Manitoba Law Journal* 30: 353–82.

Keith, L. C. 2007. "The United States Supreme Court and Judicial Review of Congress, 1803–2001." *Judicature* 90(4): 166–76.

Kort, F. 1966. "Quantitative Analysis of Fact-Patterns and Cases and their Impact on Judicial Decisions." *Harvard Law Review* 79(8): 1595–603.

Liptak, A. 2010. "Court under Roberts Is Most Conservative in Decades." *The New York Times*, July 24. Available at: http://www.nytimes.com/2010/07/25/us/25roberts.html?_r=0.

Louthan, W. C. 1973. "Public Law and Political Science: Subfield or Subterfuge?" *Journal of Legal Education* 26: 87–97.

Maveety, N. 2003. "The Study of Judicial Behavior and the Discipline of Political Science." In *The Pioneers of Judicial Behavior*, edited by N. Maveety. Ann Arbor, MI: University of Michigan Press, 1–51.

Mendelson, W. 1964. "The Untroubled World of Jurimetrics." *Journal of Politics* 26(4): 914–22.

Nagel, S. S. 1961. "Political Party Affiliations and Judges' Decisions." *American Political Science Review* 55(4): 843–50.

Peltason, J. W. 1953. " A Political Science of Public Law." *Southwestern Social Science Quarterly* 34(3): 51–6.

Pritchett, C. H. 1948. *The Roosevelt Court: A Study in Judicial Politics and Values 1937–1947.* New York, NY: The Macmillan Company.

Pritchett, C. H. 1968. "Public Law and Judicial Behavior." *Journal of Politics* 30(2): 480–509.

Pritchett, C. H. 1969. "The Development of Judicial Research." In *Frontiers of Judicial Research*, edited by J. B. Grossman and J. Tanenhaus. New York, NY: John Wiley and Sons, 27–42.

Richards, M. J., and Kritzer, H. M. 2002. "Jurisprudential Regimes in Supreme Court Decision Making." *American Political Science Review* 96(2): 305–20.

Schubert, G. A. 1958. "The Study of Judicial Decision-Making as an Aspect of Political Behavior." *American Political Science Review* 52(4): 1007–25.

Schubert, G. A. 1959. *Quantitative Analysis of Judicial Behavior.* Glencoe, IL: The Free Press.

Schubert, G. A. 1966. "The Future of Public Law." *George Washington Law Review* 34(4): 593–614.

Schubert, G. A. 1967a. "Academic Ideology and the Study of Adjudication." *American Political Science Review* 61(1): 106–29.

Schubert, G. A. 1967b. "Ideologies and Attitudes, Academic and Judicial." *Journal of Politics* 29(1): 3–40.

Schubert, G. A. 1968. "Behavioral Jurisprudence." *Law & Society Review* 2(3): 407–28.

Segal, J. A., and Howard, R. 2002. "An Original Look at Originalism." *Law & Society Review* 1(1): 113–38.

Segal, J. A., and Howard, R. 2004. "A Preference for Deference? The Supreme Court and Judicial Review." *Political Research Quarterly* 3(1): 131–43.

Shapiro, C. 2008. "Coding Complexity: Bringing Law to the Empirical Analysis of the Supreme Court." *Hastings Law Journal* 60: 477–539.

Songer, D. 2010. The United States Courts of Appeals Database. Available at: http://artsandsciences.sc.edu/poli/juri/appct.htm.

Songer, D., Sheehan, R. S., and Haire, S. B. 2000. *Continuity and Change on the United States Courts of Appeals*. Ann Arbor, MI: University of Michigan Press.

Spaeth, H. J. 1964. "The Judicial Restraint of Mr. Justice Frankfurter—Myth or Reality" *Midwest Journal of Political Science* 8(1): 22–38.

Spaeth, H. J., Epstein, L., Martin, A. D., Segal, J. A., Ruger, T., and Benesh, S. C. 2015. *Supreme Court Database*, Version 2015 Release 01. Available at: http://scdb.wustl.edu.

Spaeth, H. J., and Segal, J. A. 1999. *Majority Rule or Minority Will: Adherence to Precedent on the U.S. Supreme Court*. New York, NY: Cambridge University Press.

Spaeth, H. J., and Segal, J. A. 2000. "The U.S. Supreme Court Judicial Data Base: Providing New Insights into the Court." *Judicature* 83(5): 228–35.

Stearns, M. L. 2000. "Why Should Lawyers Care about Institutional Data on Courts?" *Judicature* 83(5): 236–76.

Thomas, G. 2006. "What Dataset? The Qualitative Foundations of Law and Courts Scholarship." *Law & Courts* 16(1): 5–12.

Tolley, M. C. 2013. "Data Sets in the Field of Law and Courts: Advancing Empirical Judicial Research." *Law & Courts* 23(1): 7–18.

Ulmer, S. S. 1969. "The Dimensionality of Judicial Voting Behavior." *Midwest Journal of Political Science* 13(3): 471–83.

Young, E. A. 2002. "Judicial Activism and Conservative Politics." *University of Colorado Law Review* 73: 1139–216.

Other Readings

Carp, R. A., and Manning, K. L. 2015. *U.S. District Court Database*. Available at the Inter-University Consortium for Social Research, University of Michigan.

Elkins, Z., Melton, J., and Ginsburg, T. 2015. *The Comparative Constitutions Project*. Available at http://www.constitute.org.

Haynie, S. L., Sheehan, R. S., Songer, D. R., and Tate, C. N. 2007. *High Courts Judicial Database*. Available at the University of South Carolina Judicial Research Initiative, http://www.cas.sc.edu/poli/juri.

Zuk, G., Barrow, D. J., and Gryski, G. S. 2009. *A Multi-User Data Base on the Attributes of U.S. Appeals Court Judges*. Available at: http://artsandsciences.sc.edu/poli/juri/appct.htm.

Index

Printed in the USA/Agawam, MA
July 12, 2023

812899.007